FLOOR DE GOEDE

DANCING ON THE VOLCANO

ONI PRESS

AN ONI PRESS PUBLICATION

BY FLOOR DE GOEDE

Translated by **LAURA WATKINSON**
All interior photos by **FLOOR DE GOEDE**
Oni Press edition designed by **CAREY HALL** | Original edition designed by **BORINKA**
Edited by **CHRIS CERASI**

Published by Oni-Lion Forge Publishing Group, LLC.
1319 SE Martin Luther King Jr. Blvd. Suite 240 Portland, OR 97214

JAMES LUCAS JONES, president & publisher
CHARLIE CHU, e.v.p. of creative & business dev.
STEVE ELLIS, s.v.p. of games & operations
ALEX SEGURA, s.v.p. of marketing & sales
MICHELLE NGUYEN, associate publisher
BRAD ROOKS, director of operations
KATIE SAINZ, director of marketing
TARA LEHMANN, publicity director
HENRY BARAJAS, sales manager
HOLLY AITCHISON, consumer marketing manager
LYDIA NGUYEN, marketing intern
TROY LOOK, director of design & production
ANGIE KNOWLES, production manager
CAREY HALL, graphic designer
SARAH ROCKWELL, graphic designer

HILARY THOMPSON, graphic designer
VINCENT KUKUA, digital prepress technician
CHRIS CERASI, managing editor
JASMINE AMIRI, senior editor
AMANDA MEADOWS, senior editor
BESS PALLARES, editor
DESIREE RODRIGUEZ, editor
GRACE SCHEIPETER, editor
ZACK SOTO, editor
GABRIEL GRANILLO, editorial assistant
BEN EISNER, game developer
SARA HARDING, entertainment executive assistant
JUNG LEE, logistics coordinator
KUIAN KELLUM, warehouse assistant
JOE NOZEMACK, publisher emeritus

onipress.com facebook.com/onipress twitter.com/onipress instagram.com/onipress

doyouknowflo.com @Flodego @Flodego

FIRST EDITION OCTOBER 2022 | **ISBN** 978-1-63715-088-7
EISBN 978-1-63715-108-2 | **PRINTED IN** CHINA
LIBRARY OF CONGRESS CONTROL NUMBER 2022932178
1 2 3 4 5 6 7 8 9 10

This is a work of nonfiction. Except where permission has been given, all names have been changed.

FLOOR DE GOEDE

DANCING ON THE VOLCANO

Translated by
LAURA WATKINSON

INTRODUCTION

Ever since I discovered I could draw, I have drawn about myself. It was the perfect way for me to express my emotions and convey my thoughts to the world around me.

In 2004, I started the site doyouknowflo.nl with the main goal of making a daily comic. Short autobiographical stories about my life, my relationship with my then-boyfriend, Bas, and the issues of the day. In a relatively quick period of time, I had a small, loyal following who really got to know Flo and Bas and their daily struggles. The first few years' worth of the comics were collected in seven booklets, and the comic was published in several newspapers and magazines. But after years of turning the little moments of our lives into a comic strip, I wanted to do and tell more. I wanted more time and space to tell a bigger story. If the daily comic was *Flo: The TV Show*, this would be *Flo: The Movie*!

And so, in 2012, my first graphic novel, *Dancing on the Volcano*, arrived in the Netherlands. It got great reviews and was available for a couple of years...until it wasn't anymore.

Now, ten years later, I'm so excited that my story is getting a second life. Or should I say, our story. *Dancing on the Volcano* was made when the world was not as evolved as it is now, but it reflects my experiences nonetheless. Bas and I said we would always stay in each other's lives, one way or the other. And we have, although in a different way than in the story you're about to read. Years passed, times changed, but we will always be home to each other.

—Floor de Goede,
April 2022

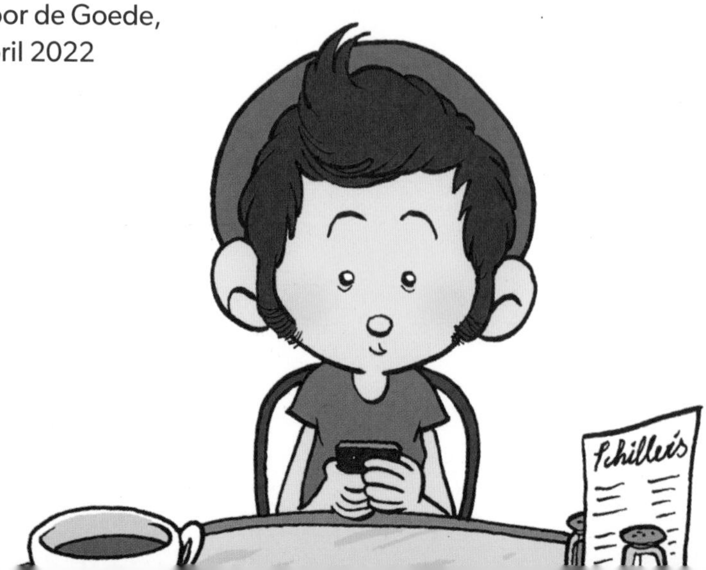
Schiller's

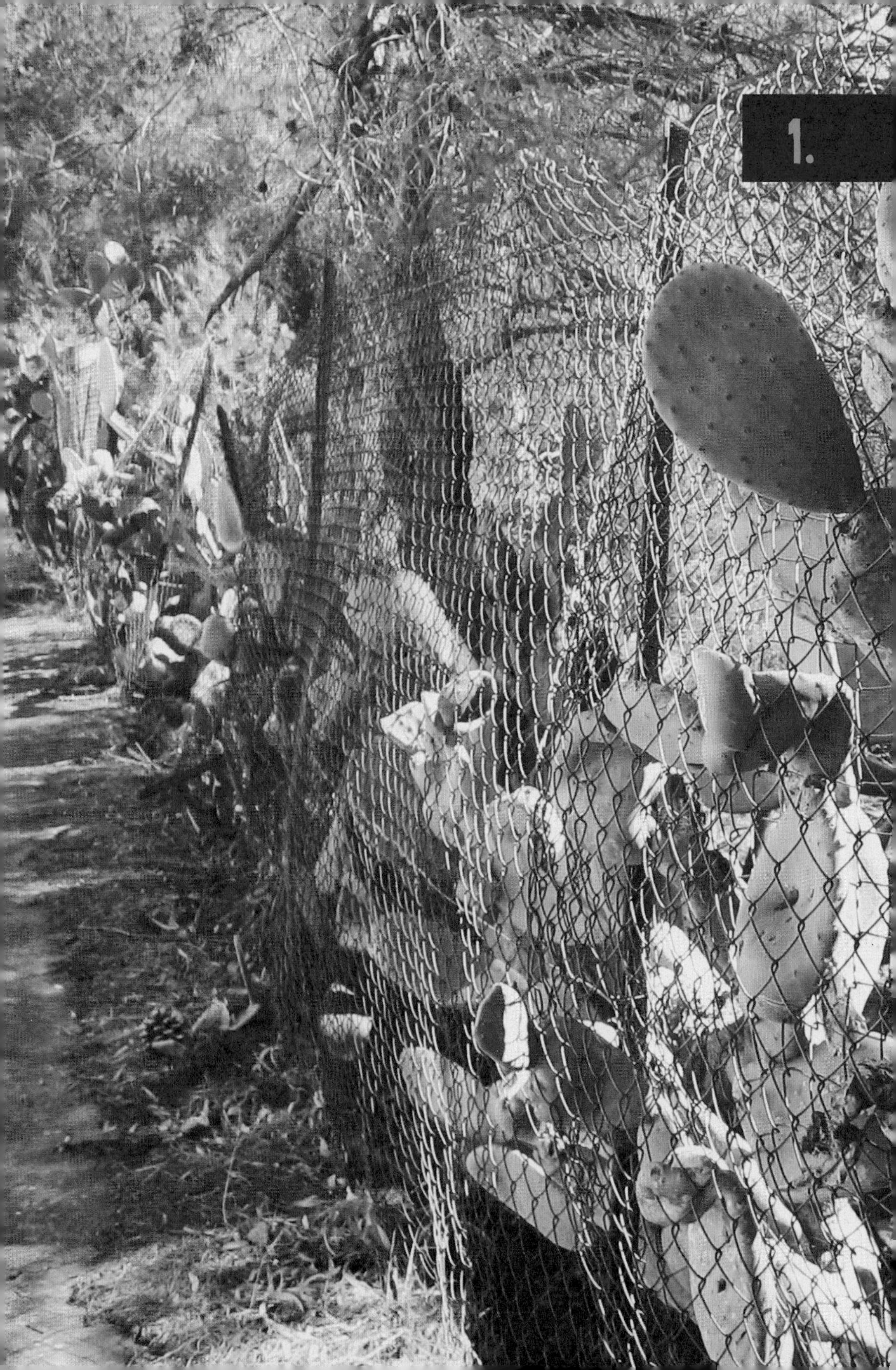
1.

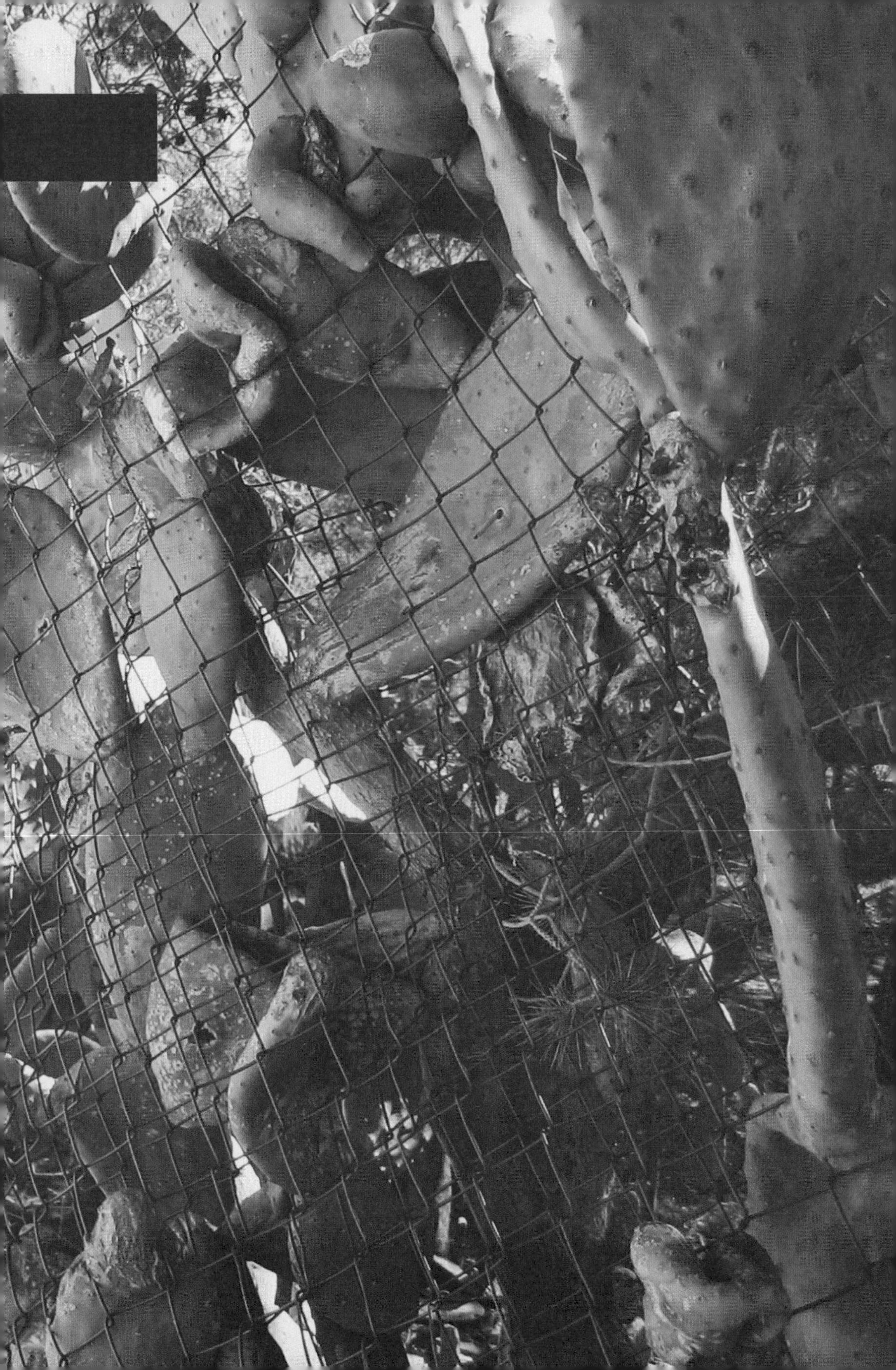

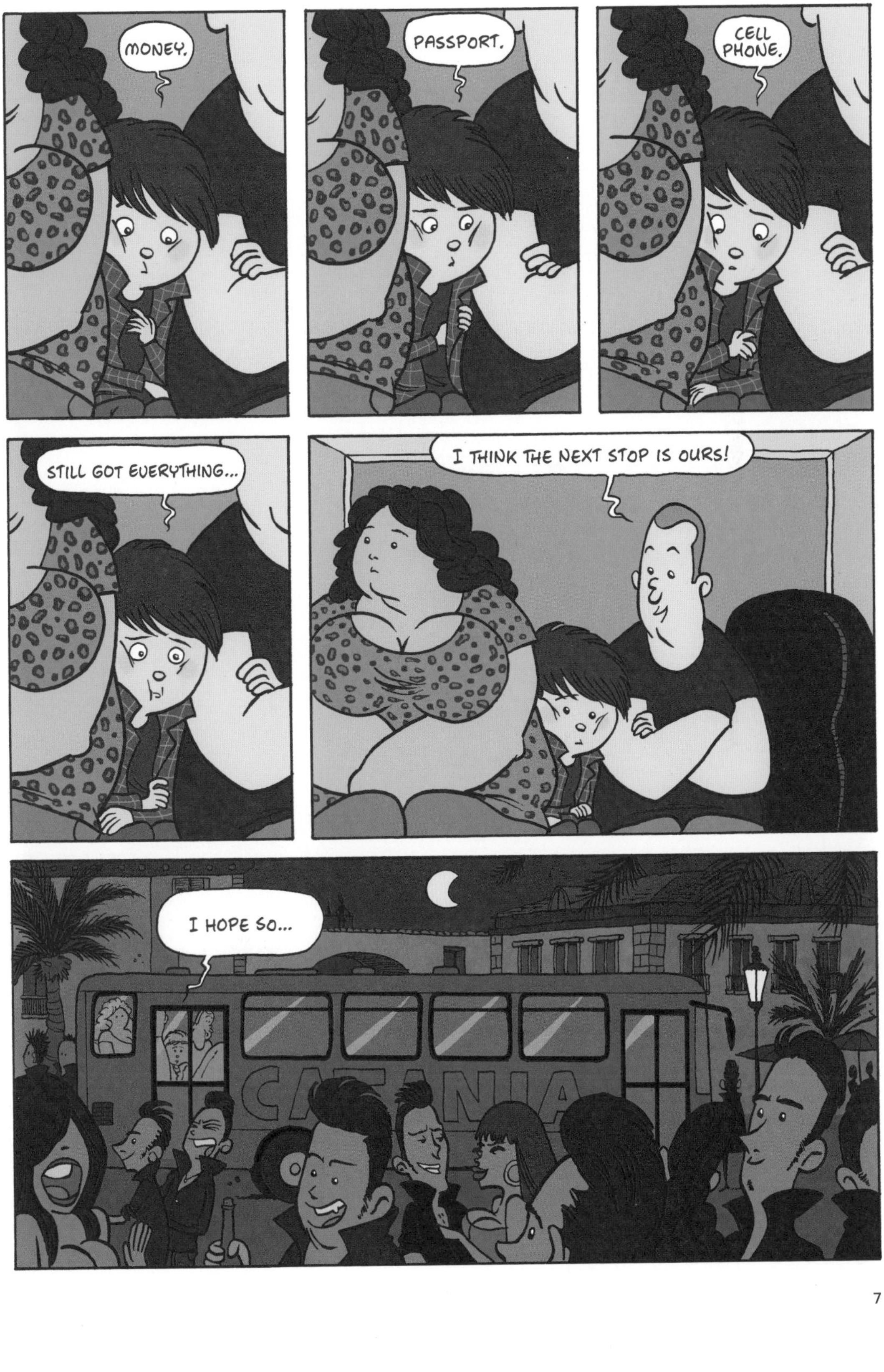
MONEY.
PASSPORT.
CELL PHONE.
STILL GOT EVERYTHING...
I THINK THE NEXT STOP IS OURS!
I HOPE SO...
CATANIA

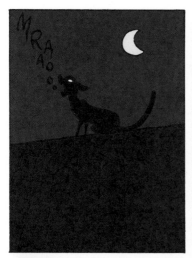

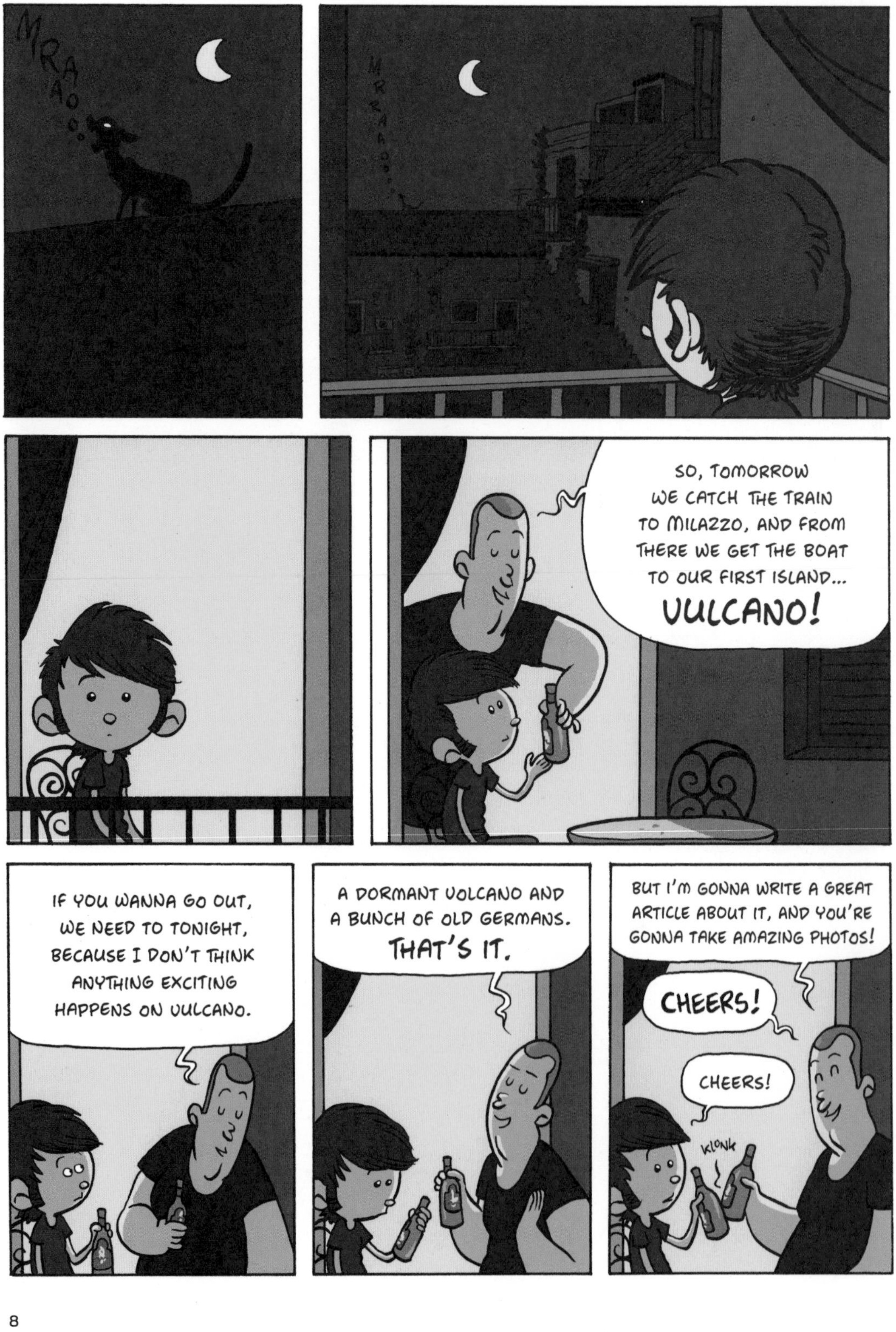
MRAO
MRAAO
SO, TOMORROW WE CATCH THE TRAIN TO MILAZZO, AND FROM THERE WE GET THE BOAT TO OUR FIRST ISLAND... VULCANO!
IF YOU WANNA GO OUT, WE NEED TO TONIGHT, BECAUSE I DON'T THINK ANYTHING EXCITING HAPPENS ON VULCANO.
A DORMANT VOLCANO AND A BUNCH OF OLD GERMANS. THAT'S IT.
BUT I'M GONNA WRITE A GREAT ARTICLE ABOUT IT, AND YOU'RE GONNA TAKE AMAZING PHOTOS!
CHEERS!
CHEERS!
KLONK

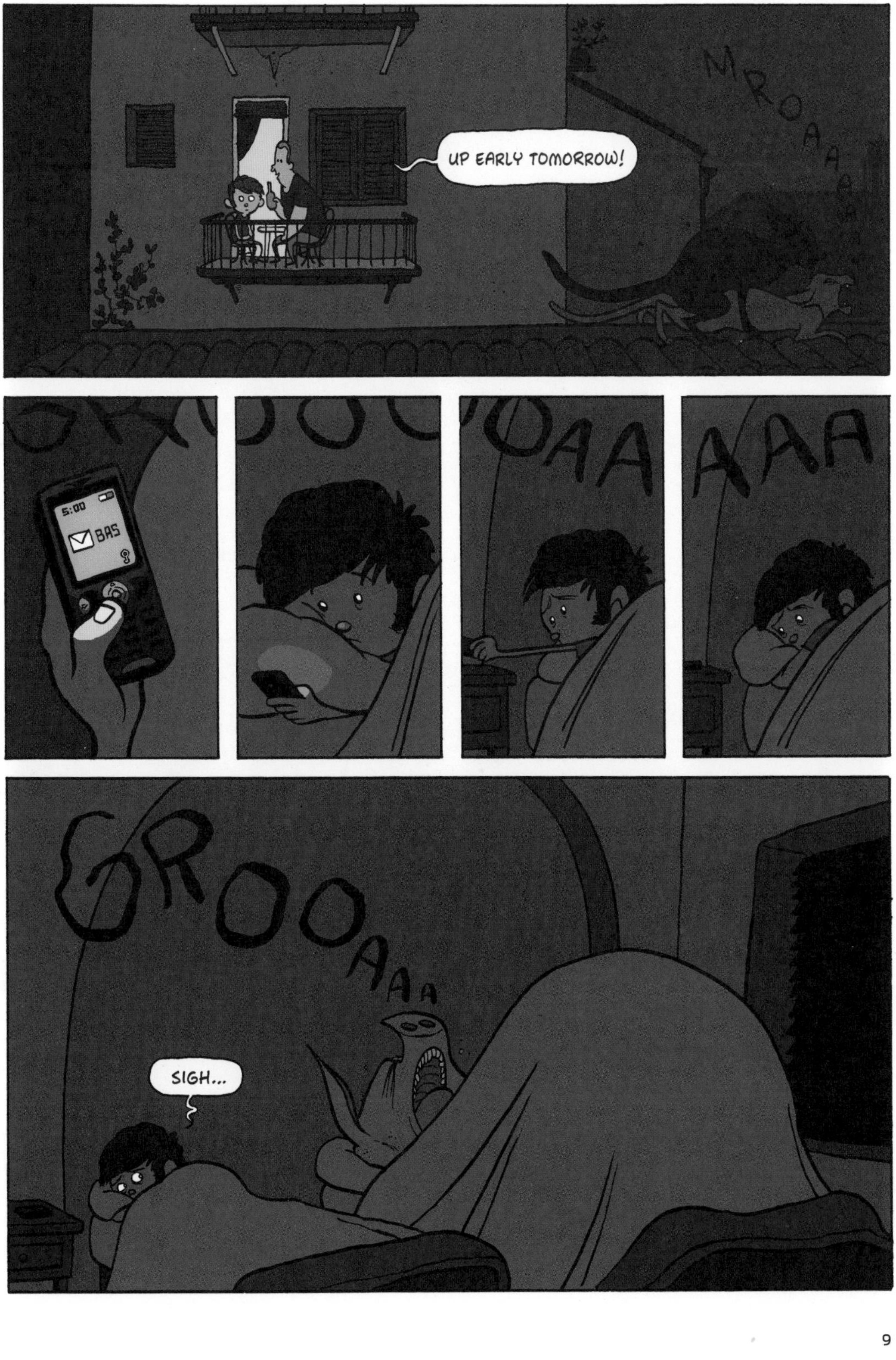
UP EARLY TOMORROW!
MROAAAA
5:00
BAS
OOOOOAAAAAA
GROOOAAA
SIGH...

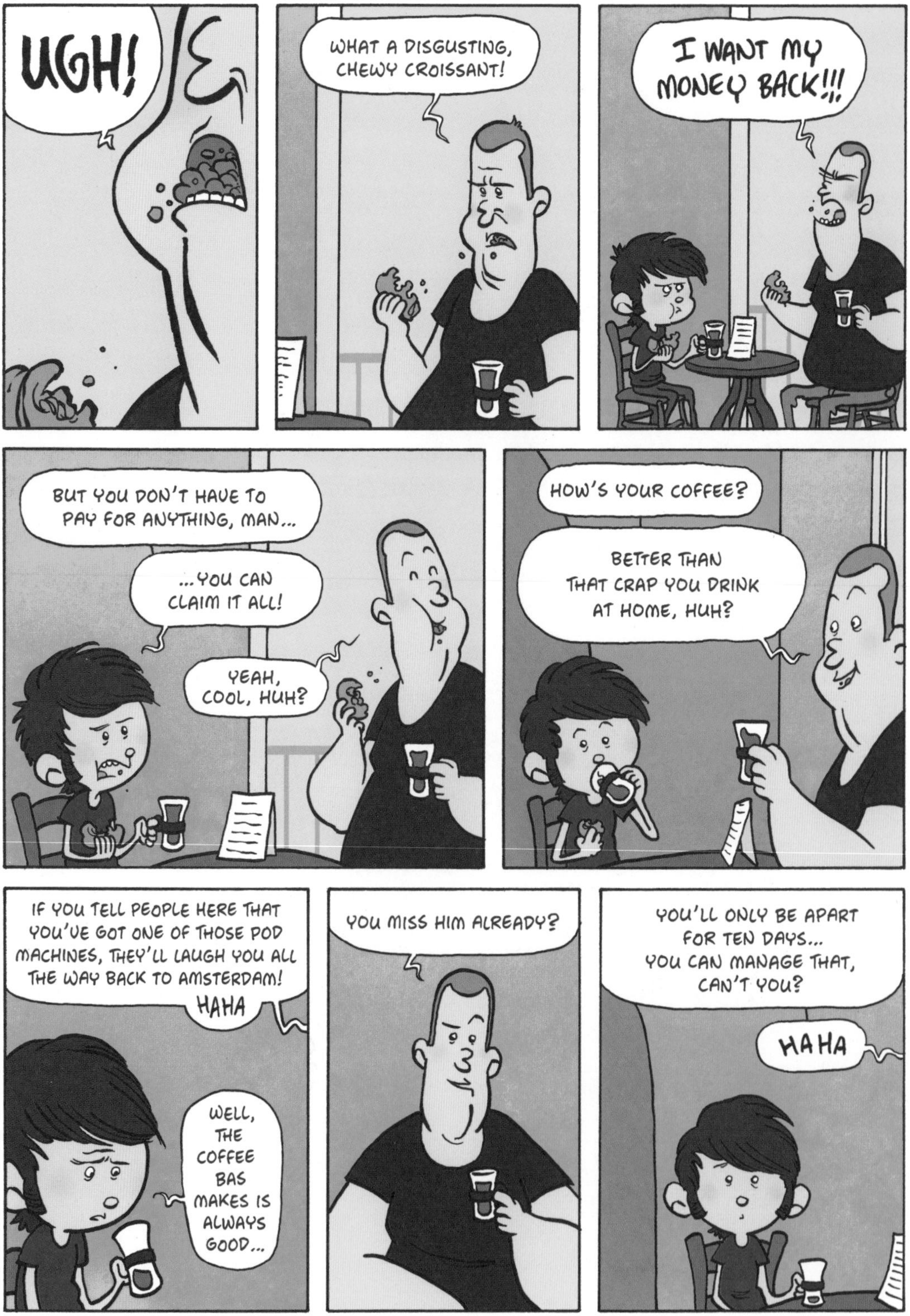
UGH!
WHAT A DISGUSTING, CHEWY CROISSANT!
I WANT MY MONEY BACK!!!
BUT YOU DON'T HAVE TO PAY FOR ANYTHING, MAN...
...YOU CAN CLAIM IT ALL!
YEAH, COOL, HUH?
HOW'S YOUR COFFEE?
BETTER THAN THAT CRAP YOU DRINK AT HOME, HUH?
IF YOU TELL PEOPLE HERE THAT YOU'VE GOT ONE OF THOSE POD MACHINES, THEY'LL LAUGH YOU ALL THE WAY BACK TO AMSTERDAM!
HAHA
WELL, THE COFFEE BAS MAKES IS ALWAYS GOOD...
YOU MISS HIM ALREADY?
YOU'LL ONLY BE APART FOR TEN DAYS... YOU CAN MANAGE THAT, CAN'T YOU?
HAHA

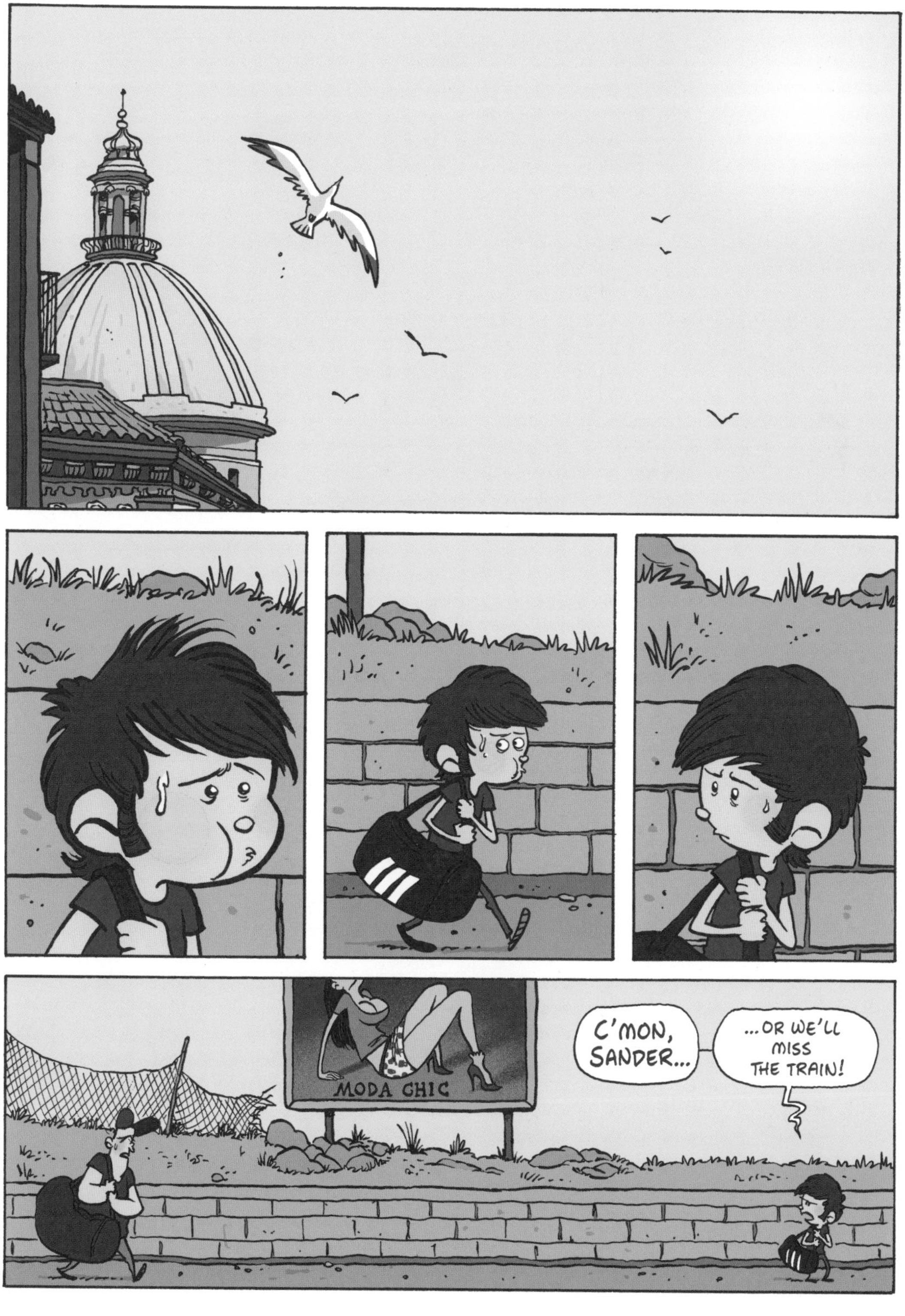
MODA CHIC
C'MON, SANDER...
...OR WE'LL MISS THE TRAIN!

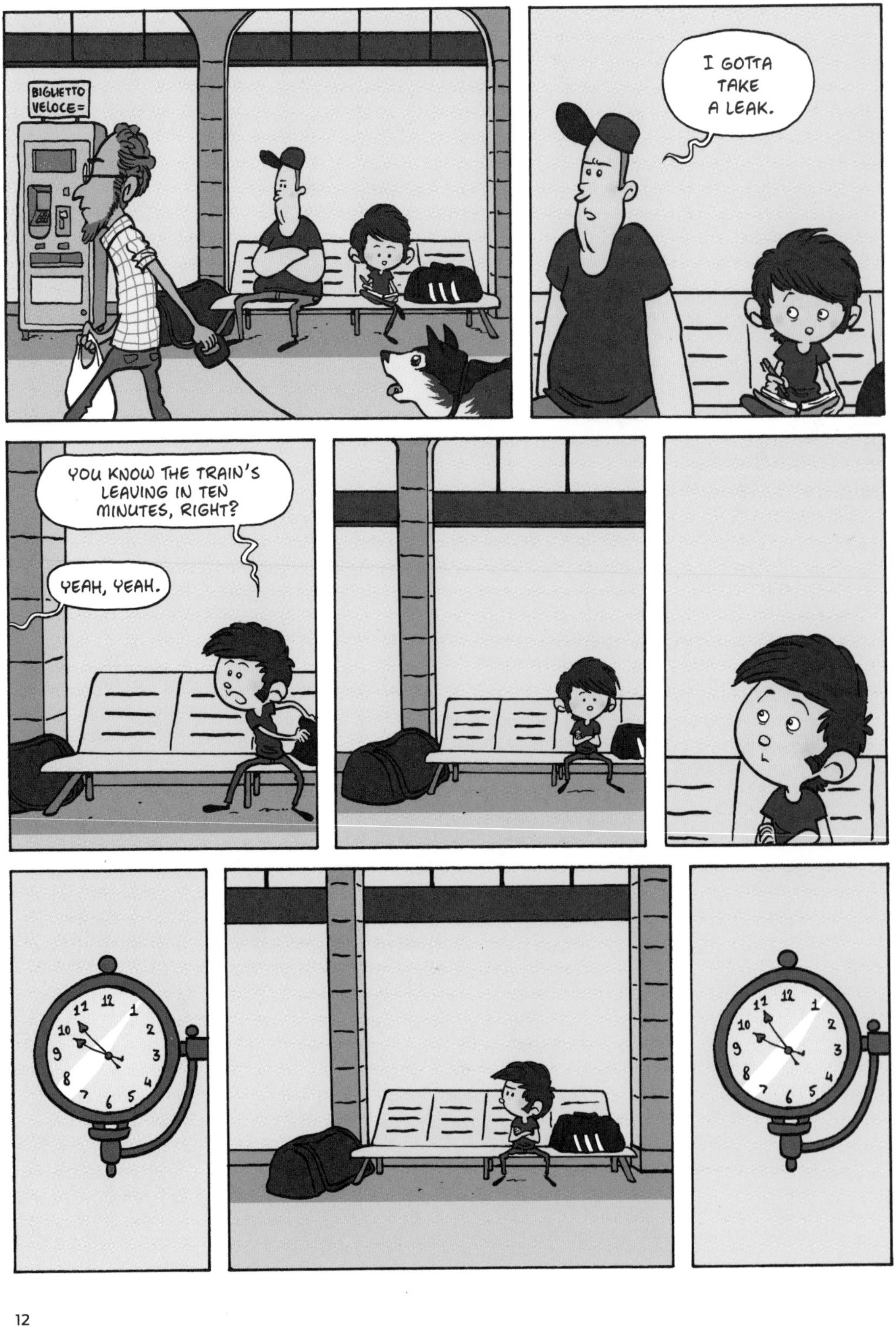
BIGLIETTO VELOCE=
I GOTTA TAKE A LEAK.
YOU KNOW THE TRAIN'S LEAVING IN TEN MINUTES, RIGHT?
YEAH, YEAH.

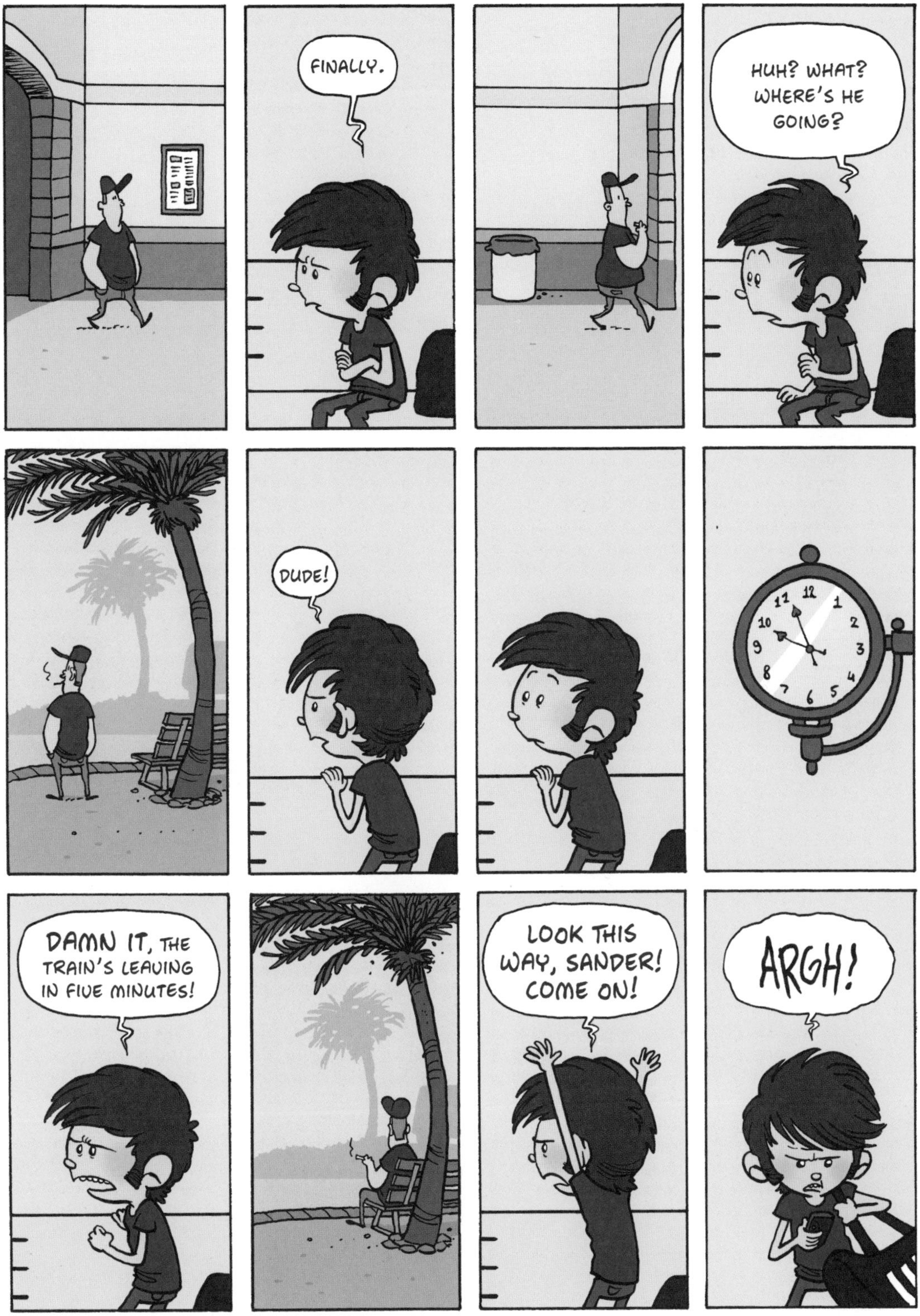
FINALLY.
HUH? WHAT? WHERE'S HE GOING?
DUDE!
DAMN IT, THE TRAIN'S LEAVING IN FIVE MINUTES!
LOOK THIS WAY, SANDER! COME ON!
ARGH!

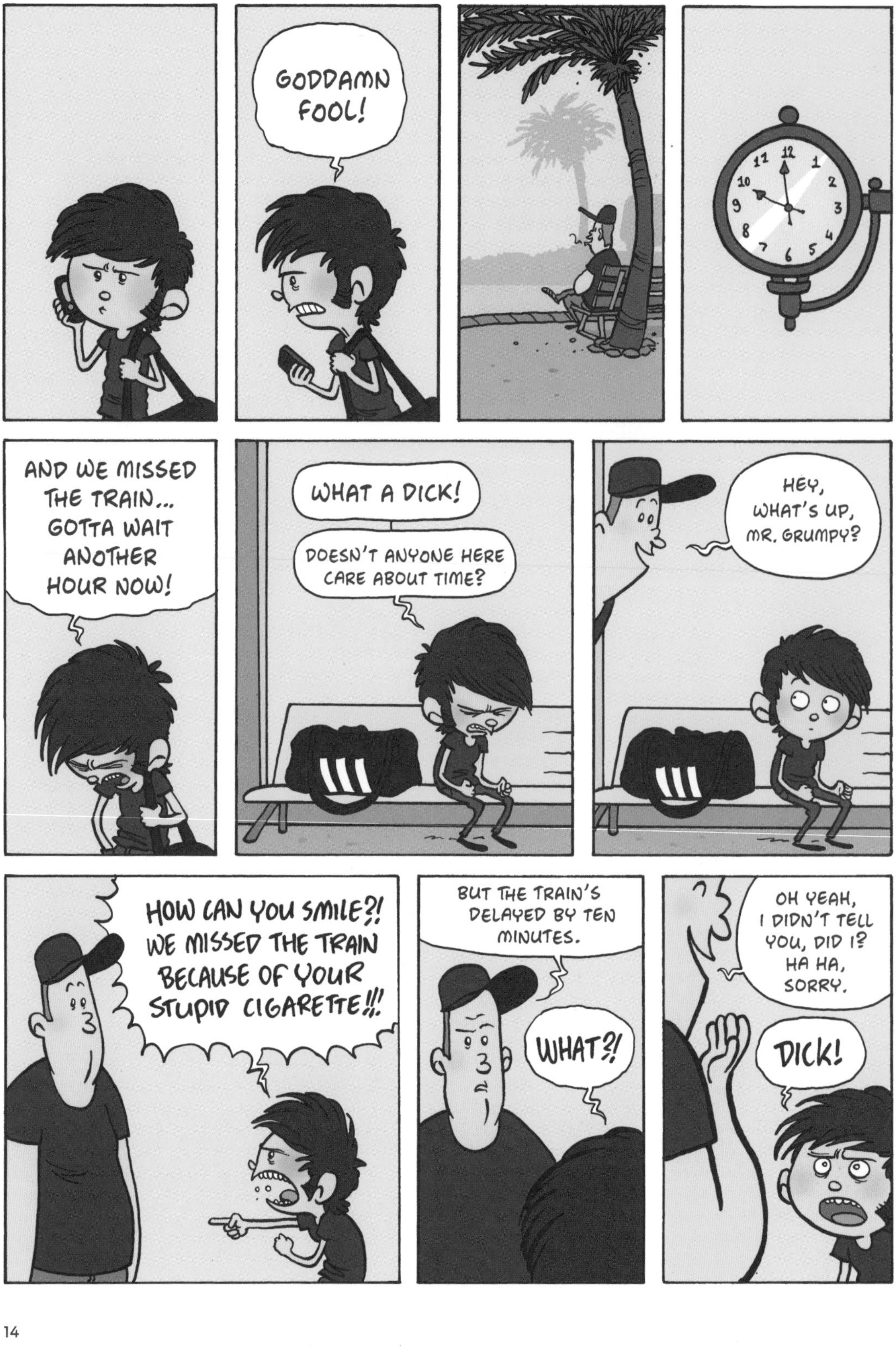
GODDAMN FOOL!
AND WE MISSED THE TRAIN... GOTTA WAIT ANOTHER HOUR NOW!
WHAT A DICK!
DOESN'T ANYONE HERE CARE ABOUT TIME?
HEY, WHAT'S UP, MR. GRUMPY?
HOW CAN YOU SMILE?! WE MISSED THE TRAIN BECAUSE OF YOUR STUPID CIGARETTE!!!
BUT THE TRAIN'S DELAYED BY TEN MINUTES.
WHAT?!
OH YEAH, I DIDN'T TELL YOU, DID I? HA HA, SORRY.
DICK!

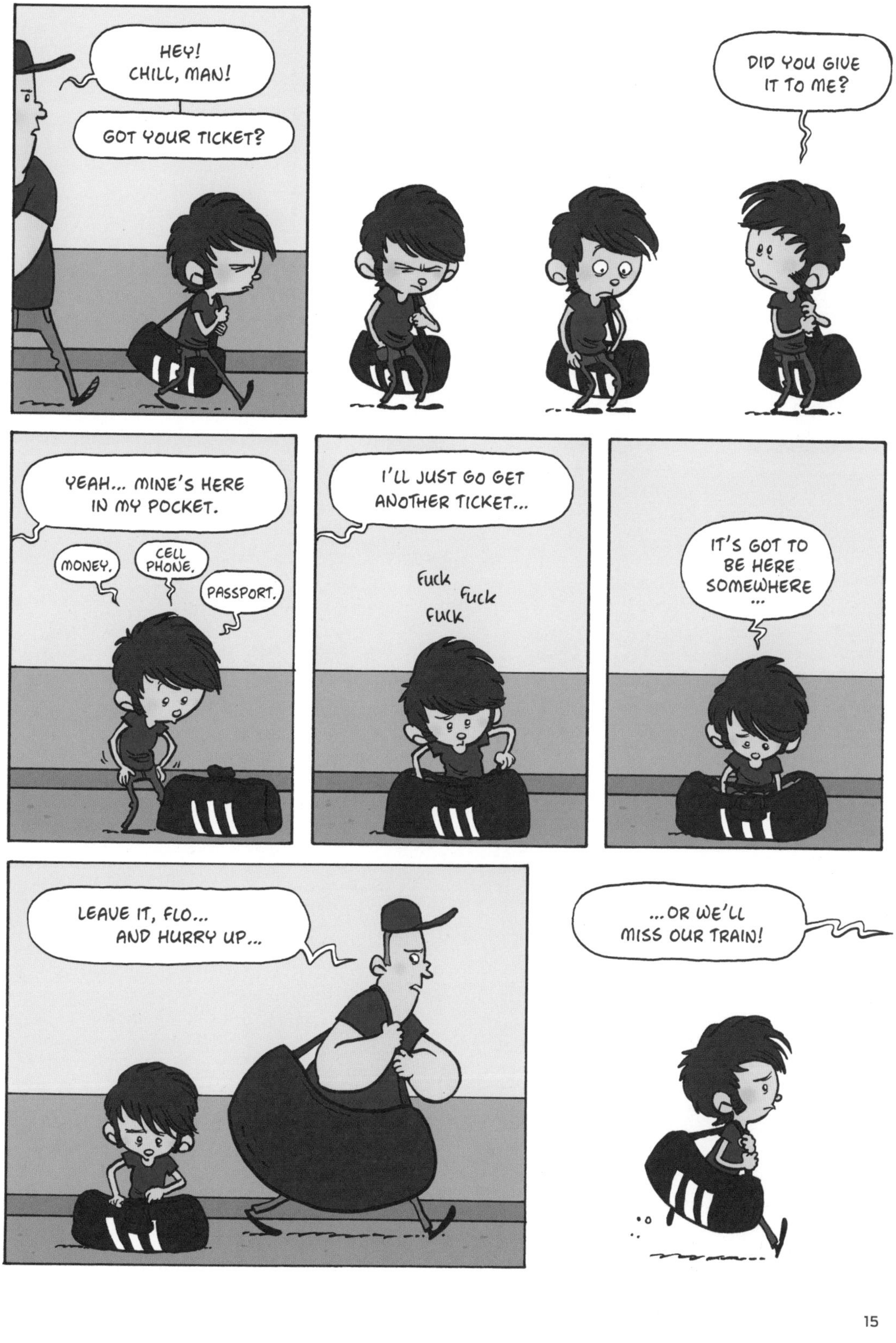

HEY!
CHILL, MAN!
GOT YOUR TICKET?
DID YOU GIVE IT TO ME?
YEAH... MINE'S HERE IN MY POCKET.
MONEY.
CELL PHONE.
PASSPORT.
I'LL JUST GO GET ANOTHER TICKET...
Fuck Fuck Fuck
IT'S GOT TO BE HERE SOMEWHERE ...
LEAVE IT, FLO... AND HURRY UP...
...OR WE'LL MISS OUR TRAIN!

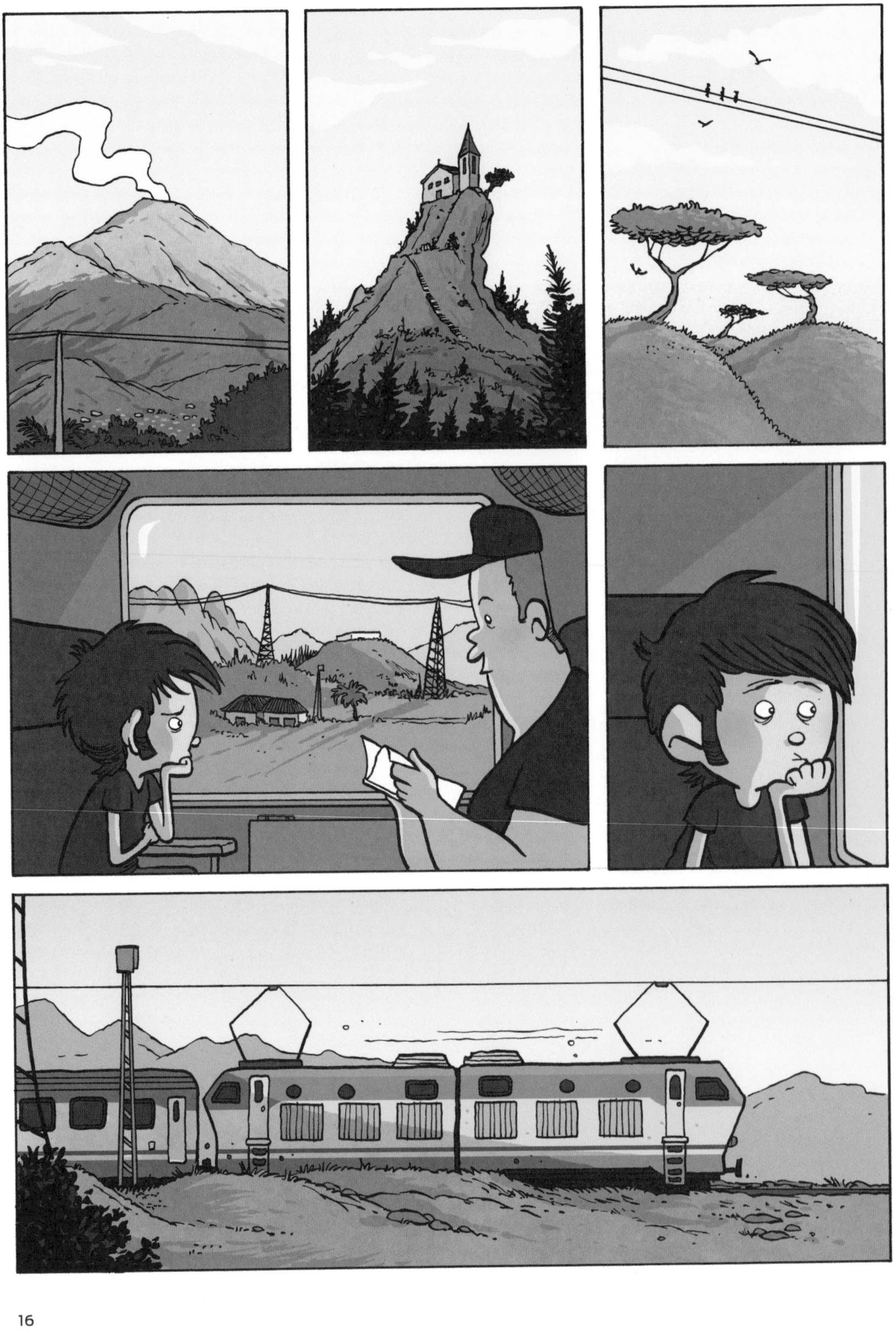

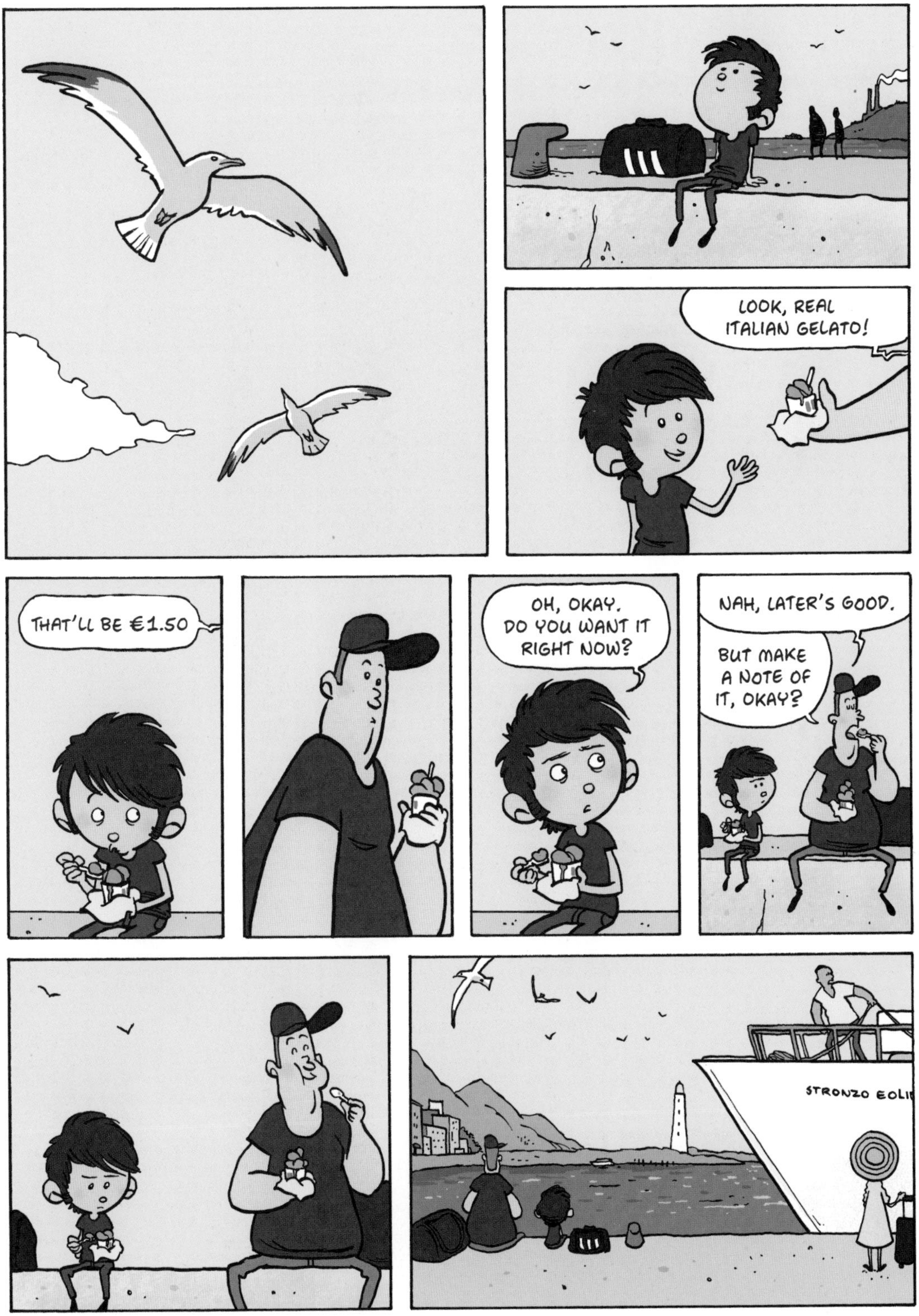
LOOK, REAL ITALIAN GELATO!
THAT'LL BE €1.50
OH, OKAY. DO YOU WANT IT RIGHT NOW?
NAH, LATER'S GOOD.
BUT MAKE A NOTE OF IT, OKAY?
STRONZO EOLI

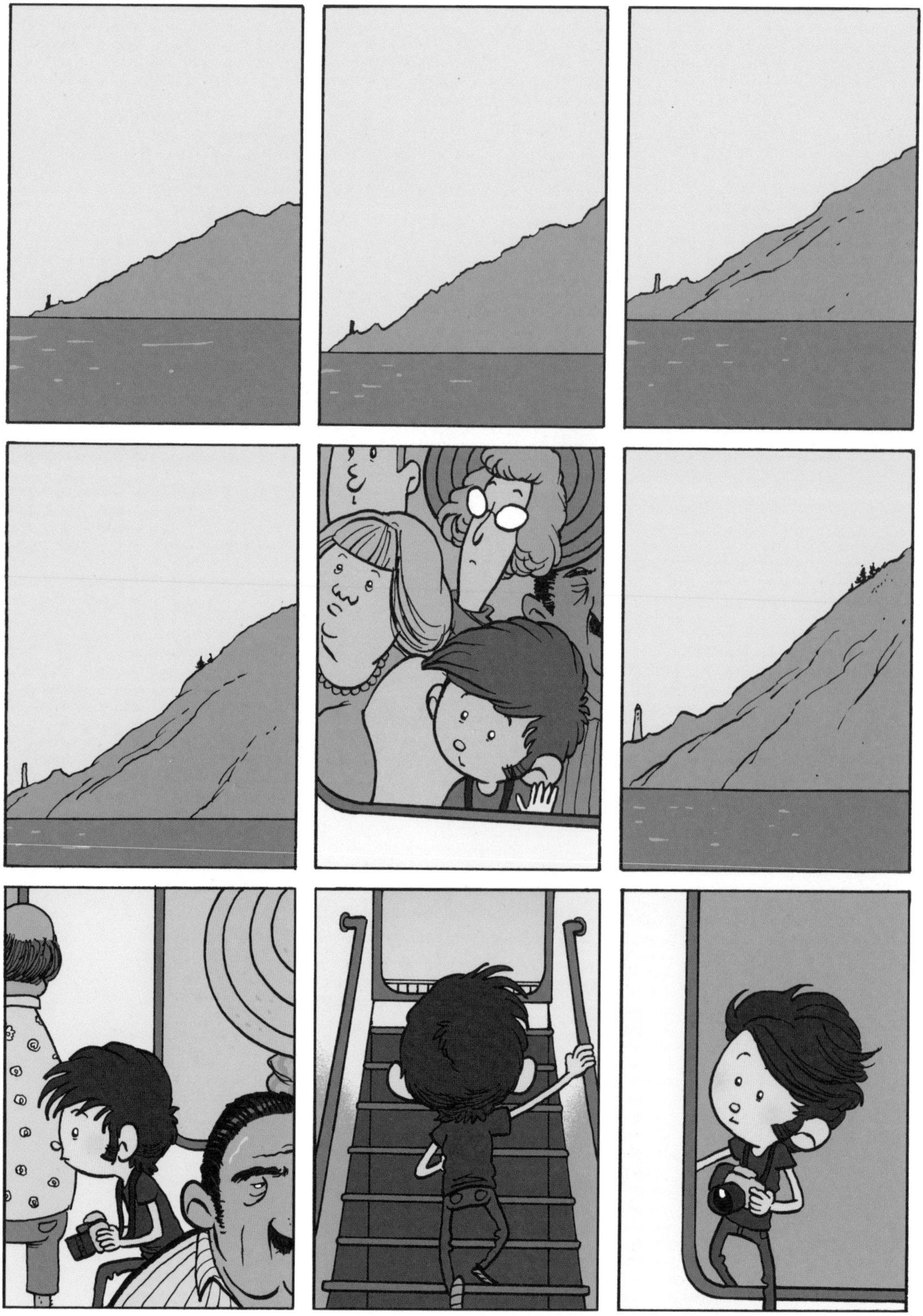

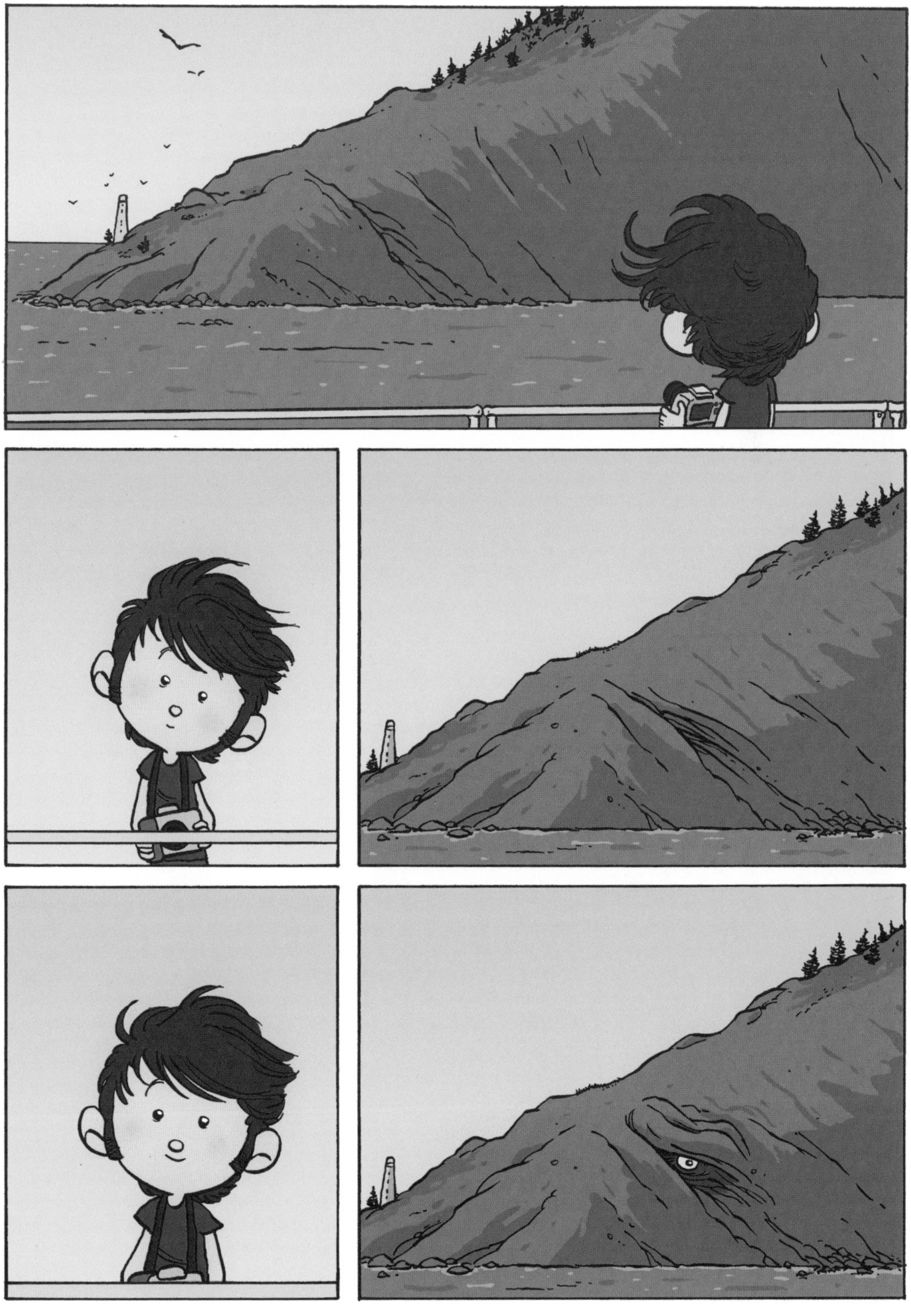

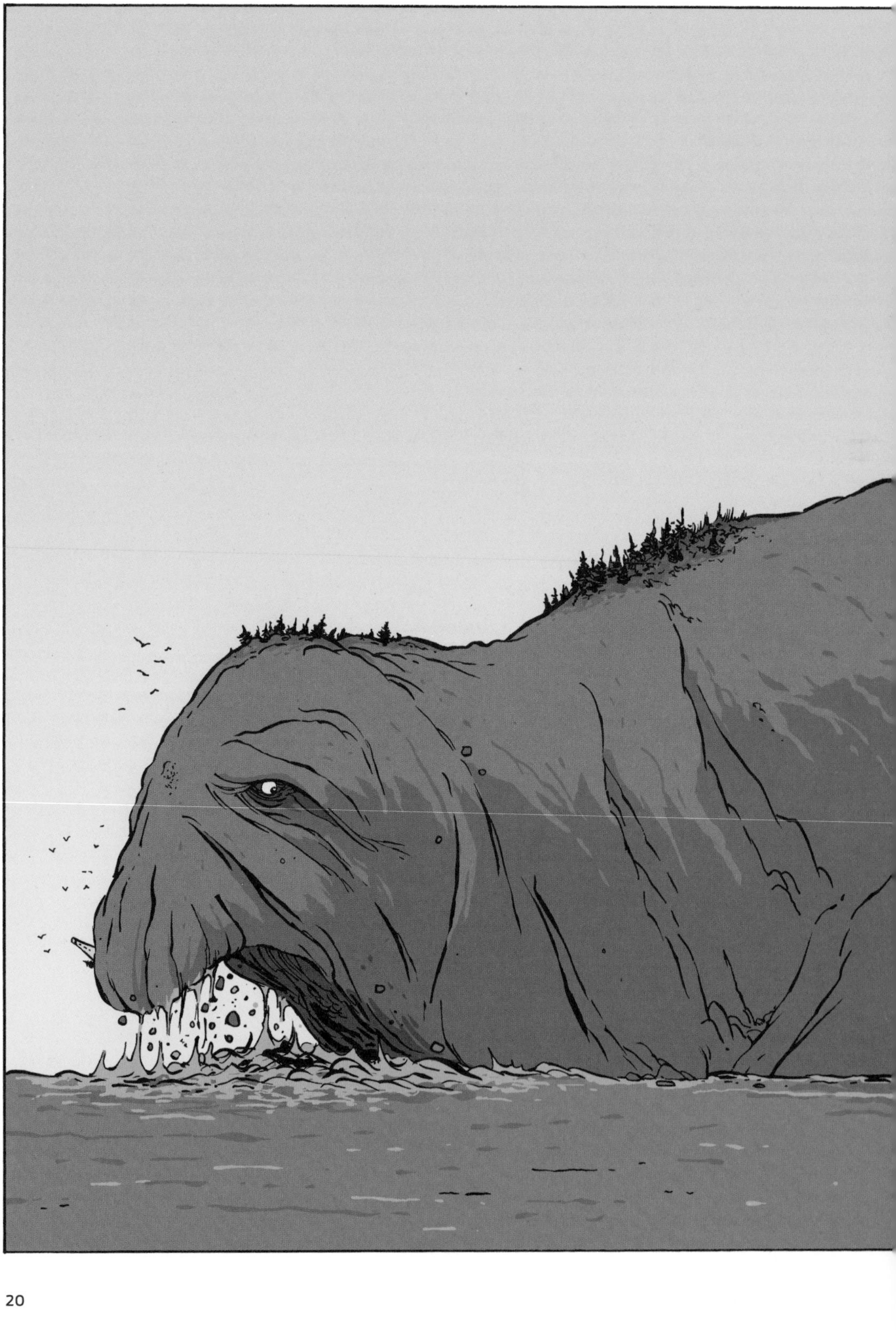

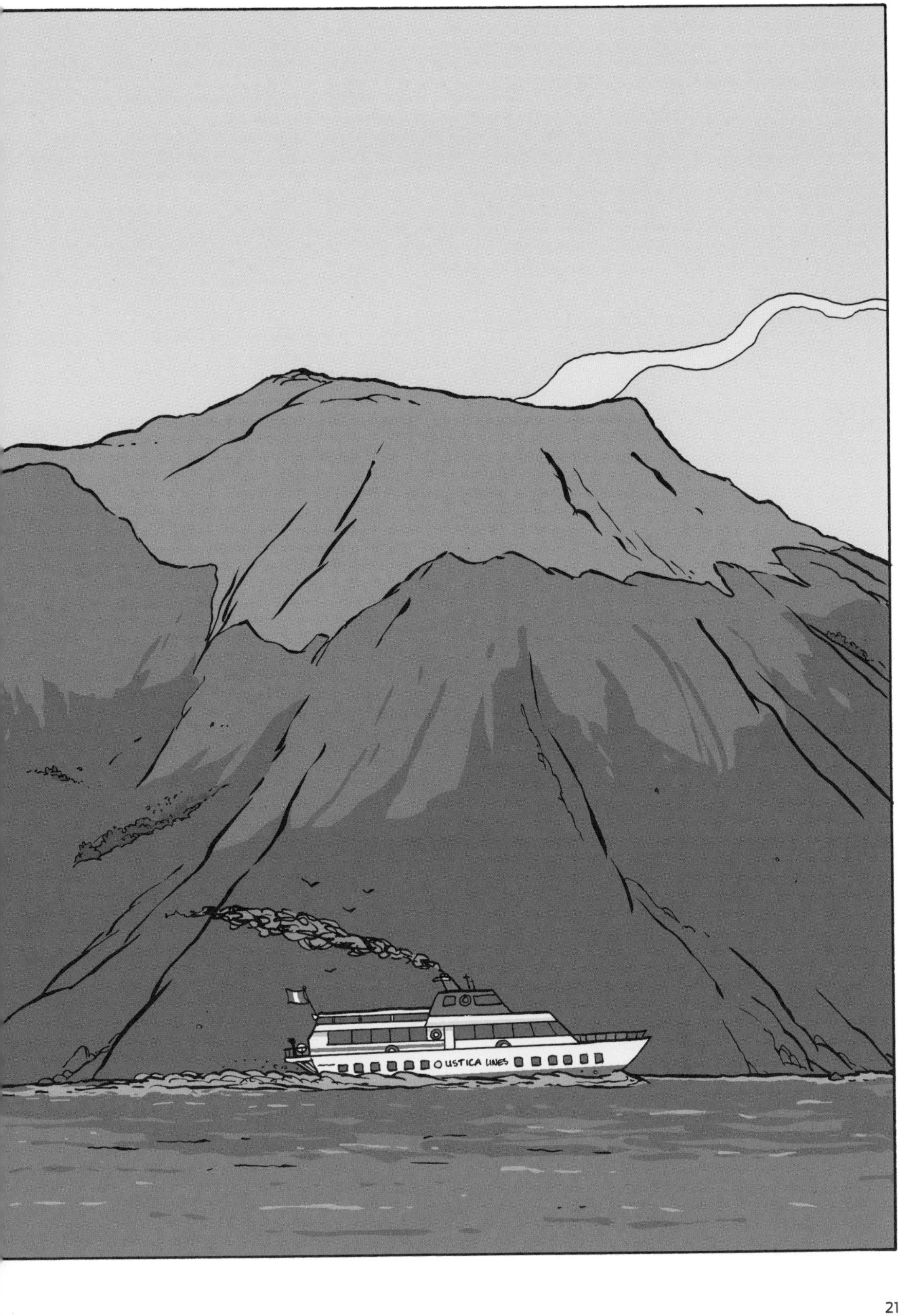
USTICA LINES

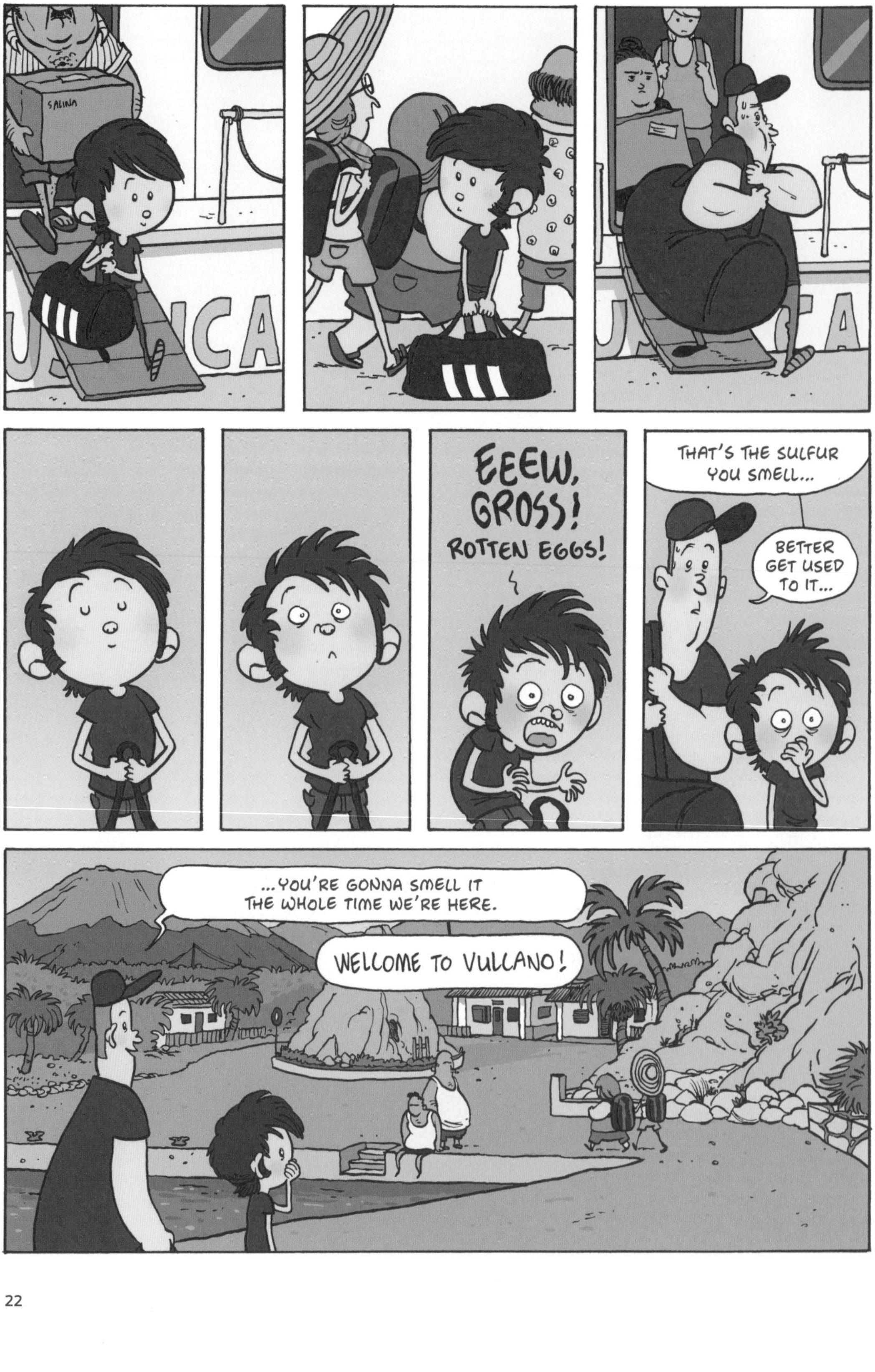
SALINA
EEEW, GROSS!
ROTTEN EGGS!
THAT'S THE SULFUR YOU SMELL...
BETTER GET USED TO IT...
...YOU'RE GONNA SMELL IT THE WHOLE TIME WE'RE HERE.
WELCOME TO VULCANO!

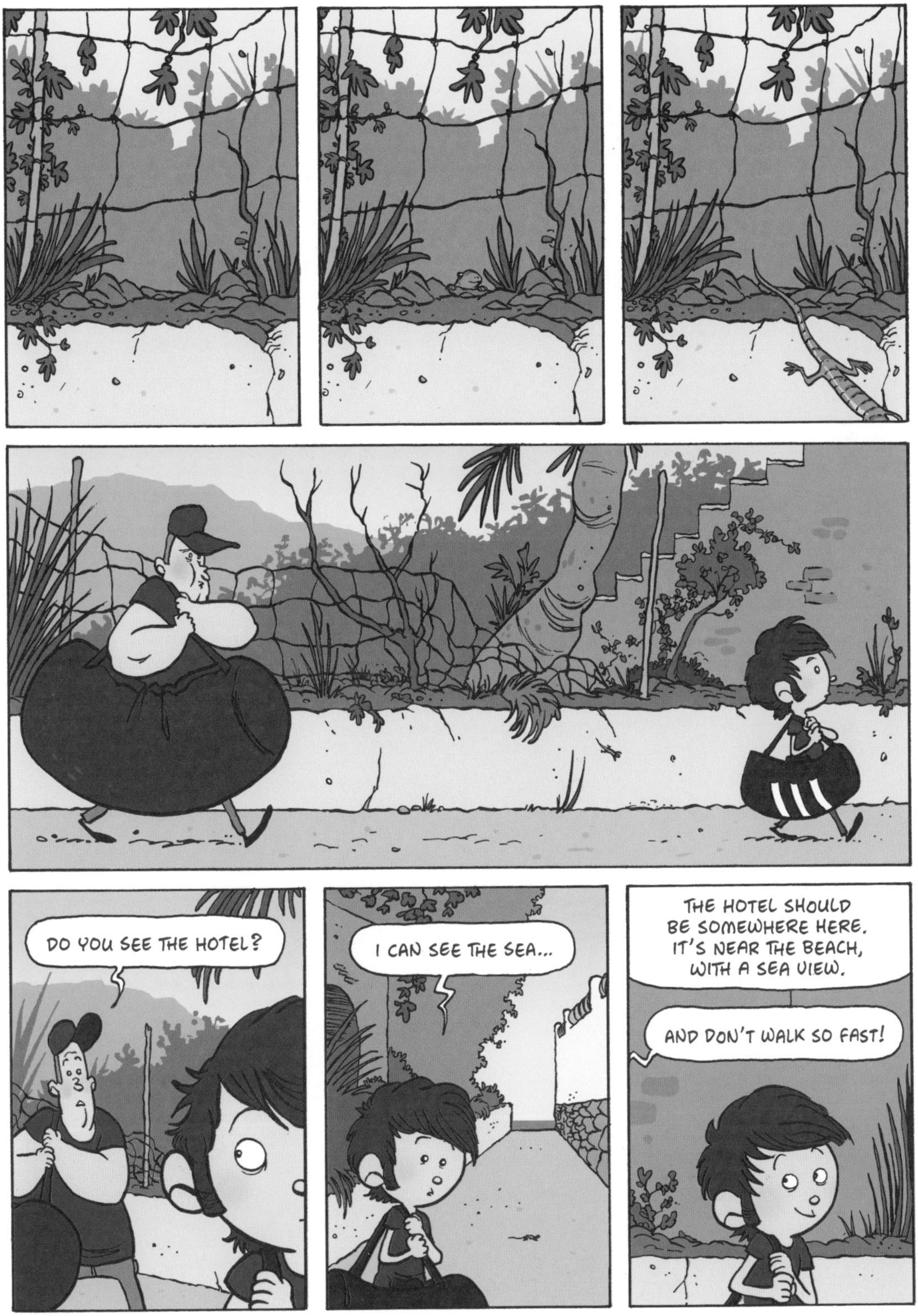
DO YOU SEE THE HOTEL?
I CAN SEE THE SEA...
THE HOTEL SHOULD BE SOMEWHERE HERE. IT'S NEAR THE BEACH, WITH A SEA VIEW.
AND DON'T WALK SO FAST!

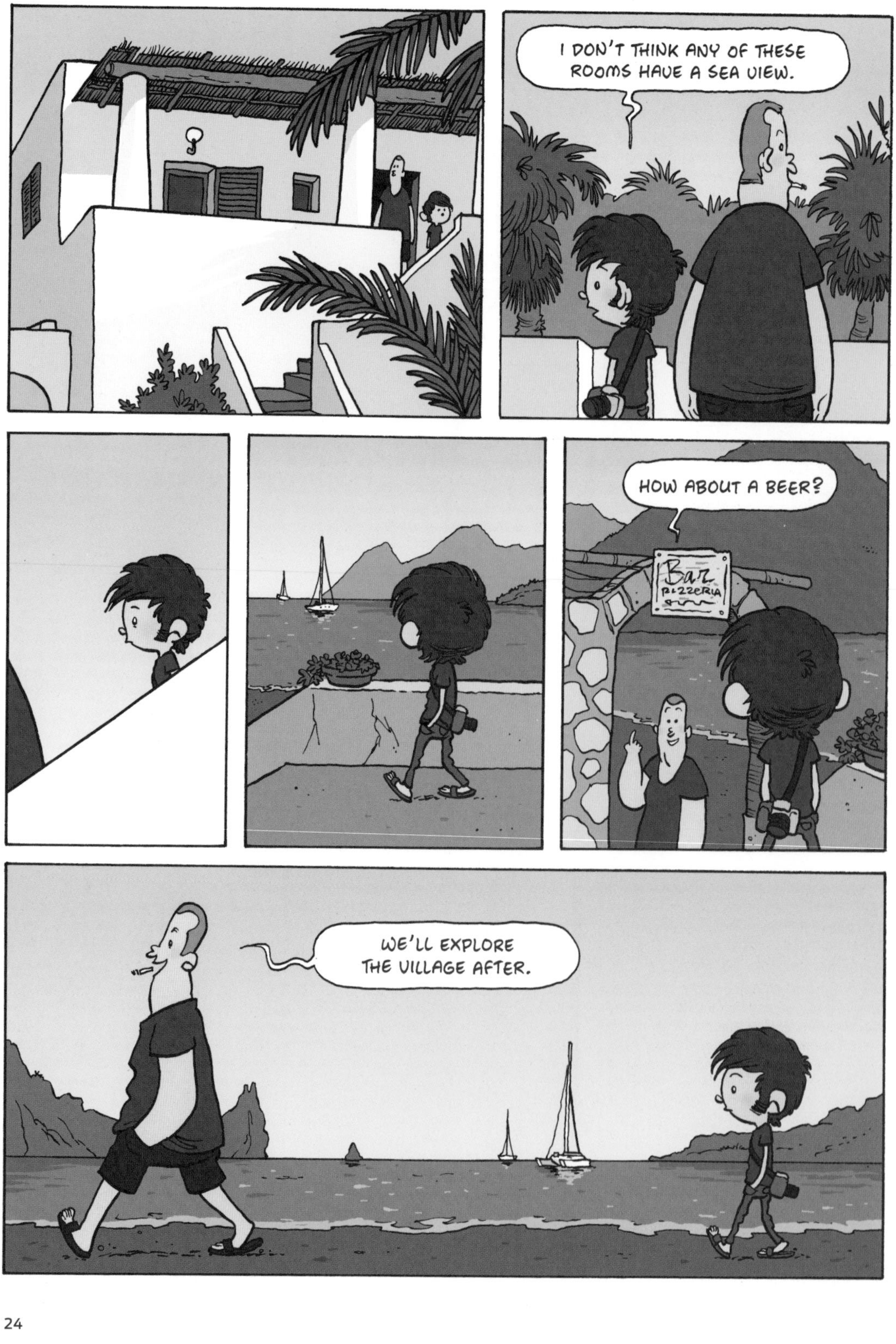
I DON'T THINK ANY OF THESE ROOMS HAVE A SEA VIEW.
HOW ABOUT A BEER?
Bar
PIZZERIA
WE'LL EXPLORE THE VILLAGE AFTER.

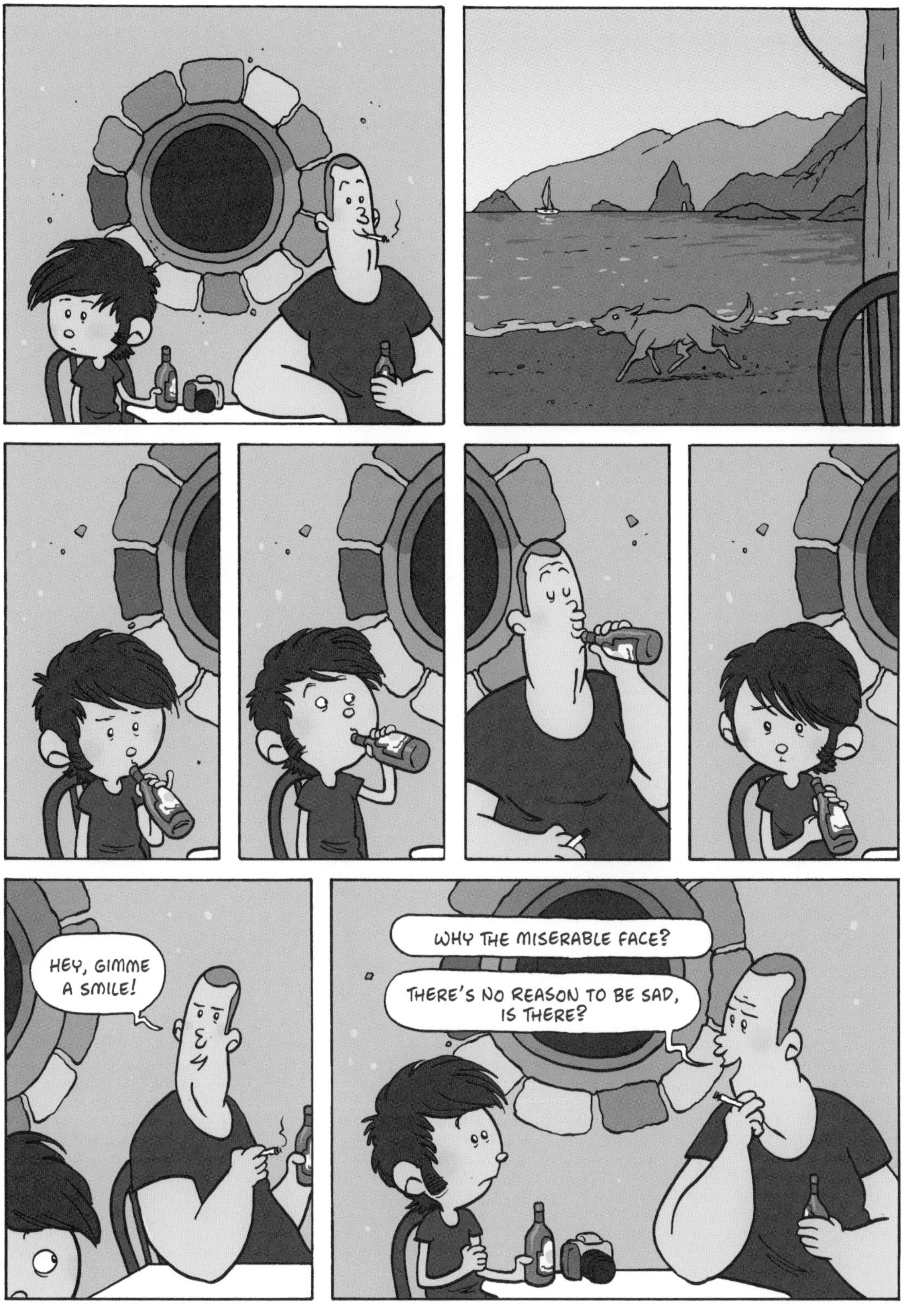
HEY, GIMME A SMILE!
WHY THE MISERABLE FACE?
THERE'S NO REASON TO BE SAD, IS THERE?

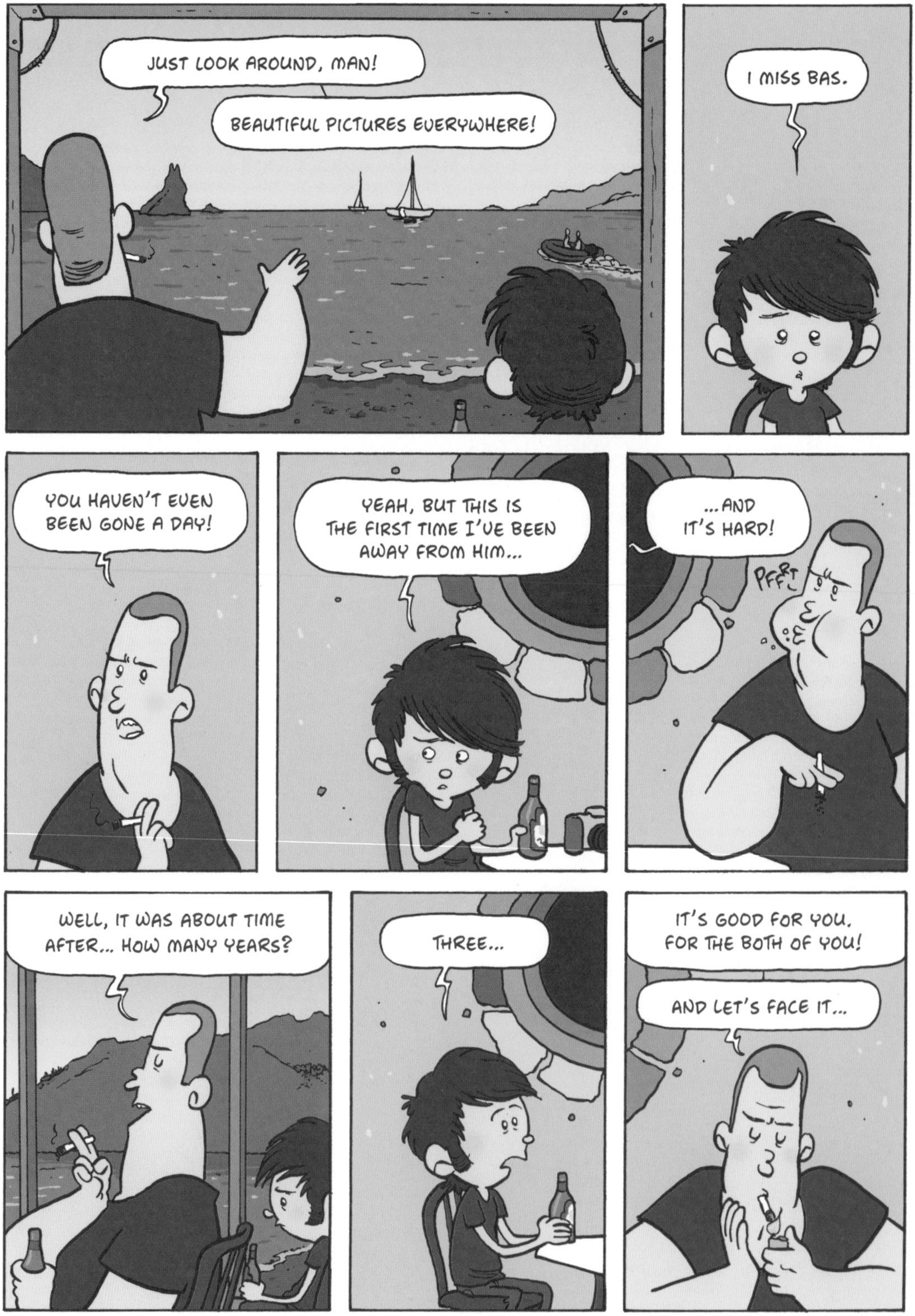
JUST LOOK AROUND, MAN!
BEAUTIFUL PICTURES EVERYWHERE!
I MISS BAS.
YOU HAVEN'T EVEN BEEN GONE A DAY!
YEAH, BUT THIS IS THE FIRST TIME I'VE BEEN AWAY FROM HIM...
...AND IT'S HARD!
PFFRT
WELL, IT WAS ABOUT TIME AFTER... HOW MANY YEARS?
THREE...
IT'S GOOD FOR YOU. FOR THE BOTH OF YOU!
AND LET'S FACE IT...

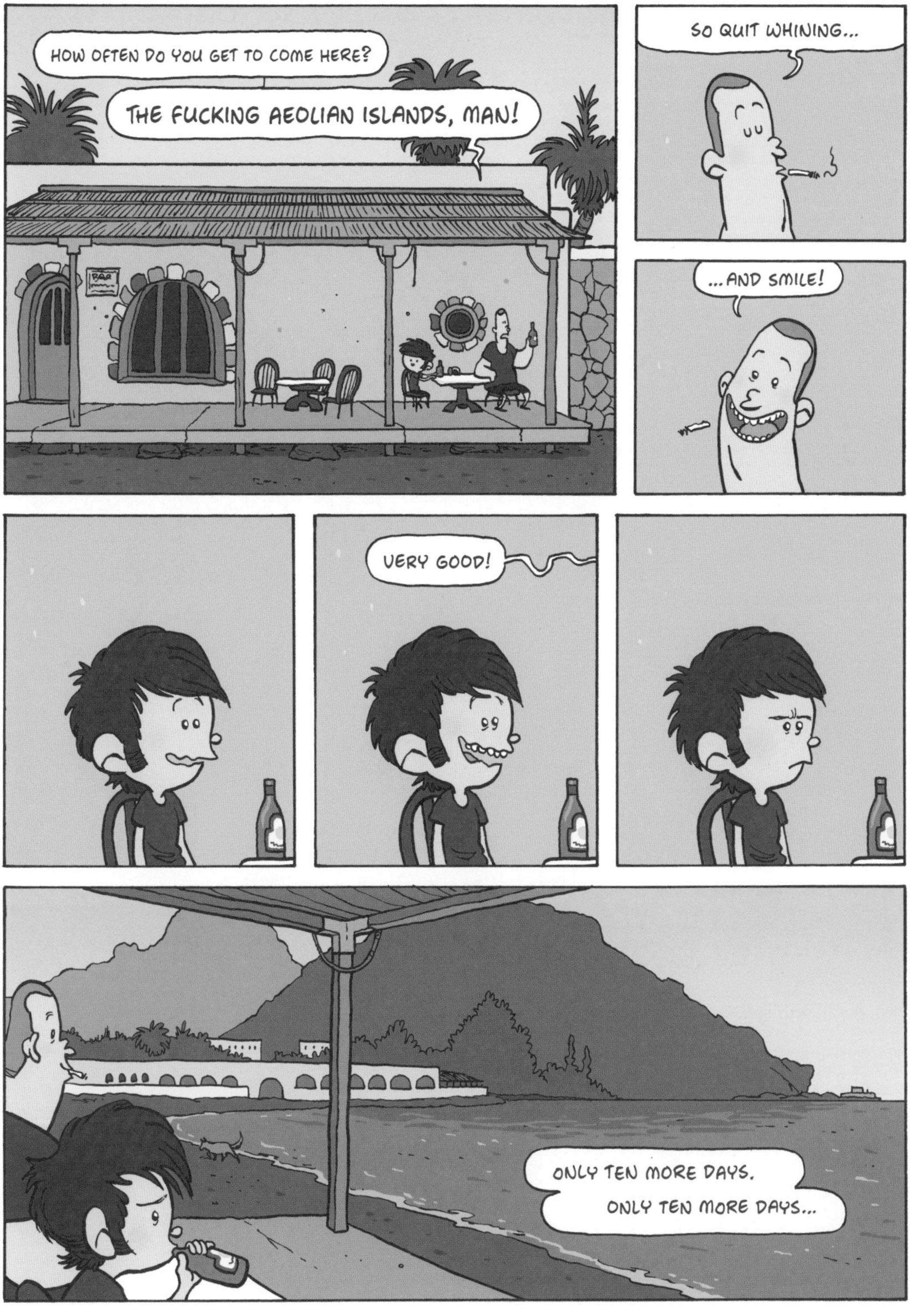
HOW OFTEN DO YOU GET TO COME HERE?
THE FUCKING AEOLIAN ISLANDS, MAN!
BAR
SO QUIT WHINING...
...AND SMILE!
VERY GOOD!
ONLY TEN MORE DAYS.
ONLY TEN MORE DAYS...

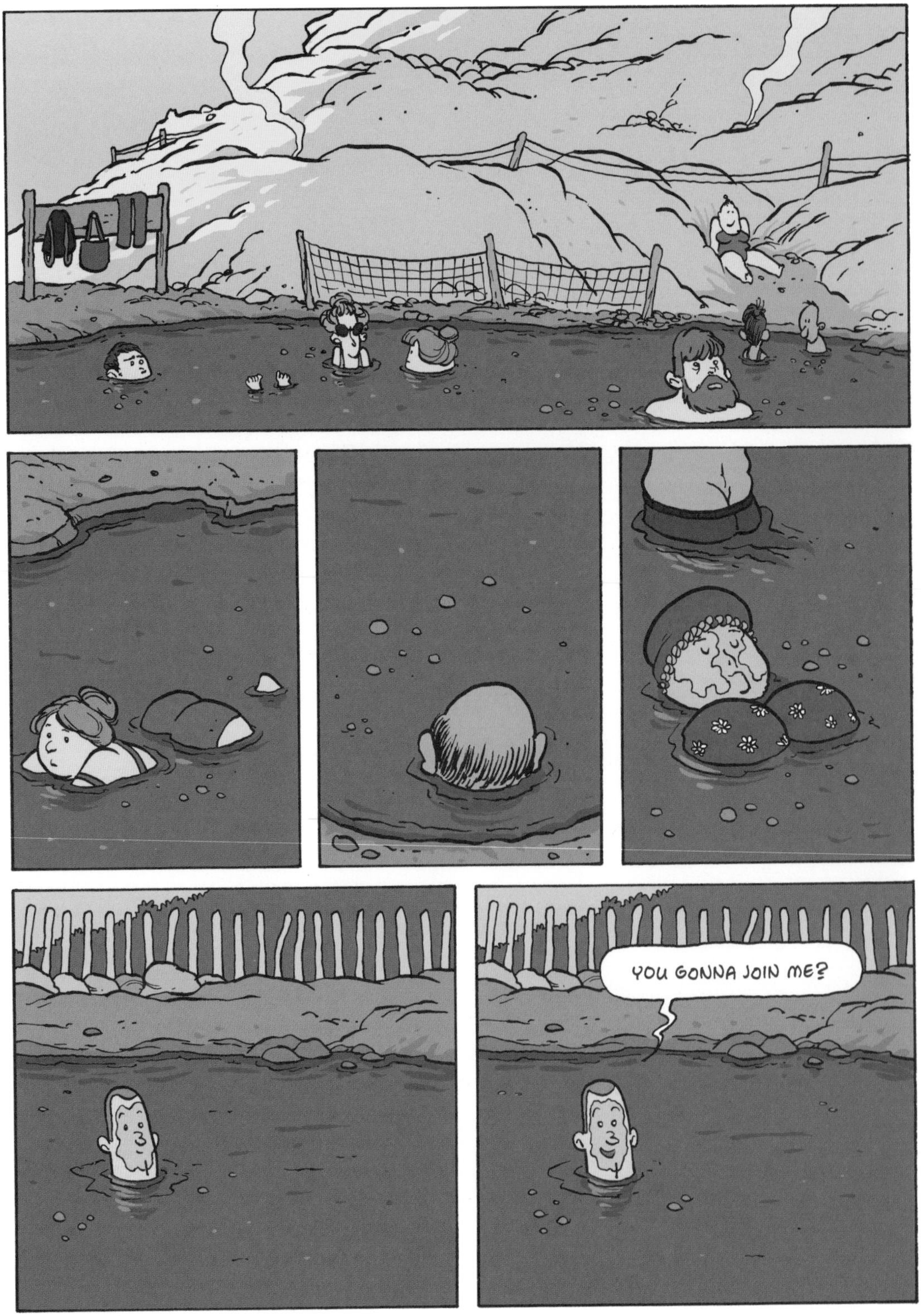
YOU GONNA JOIN ME?

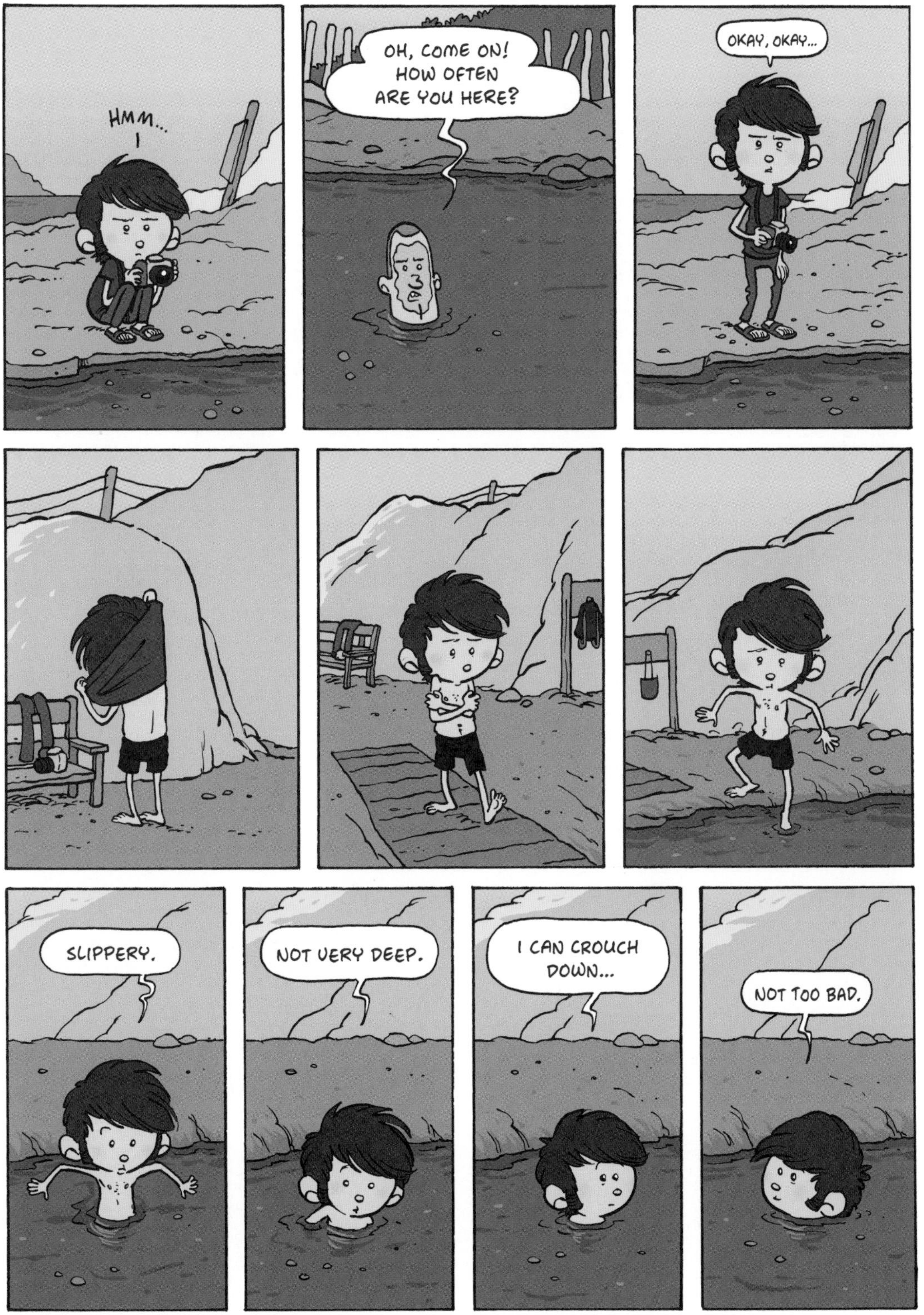
HMM...
OH, COME ON! HOW OFTEN ARE YOU HERE?
OKAY, OKAY...
SLIPPERY.
NOT VERY DEEP.
I CAN CROUCH DOWN...
NOT TOO BAD.

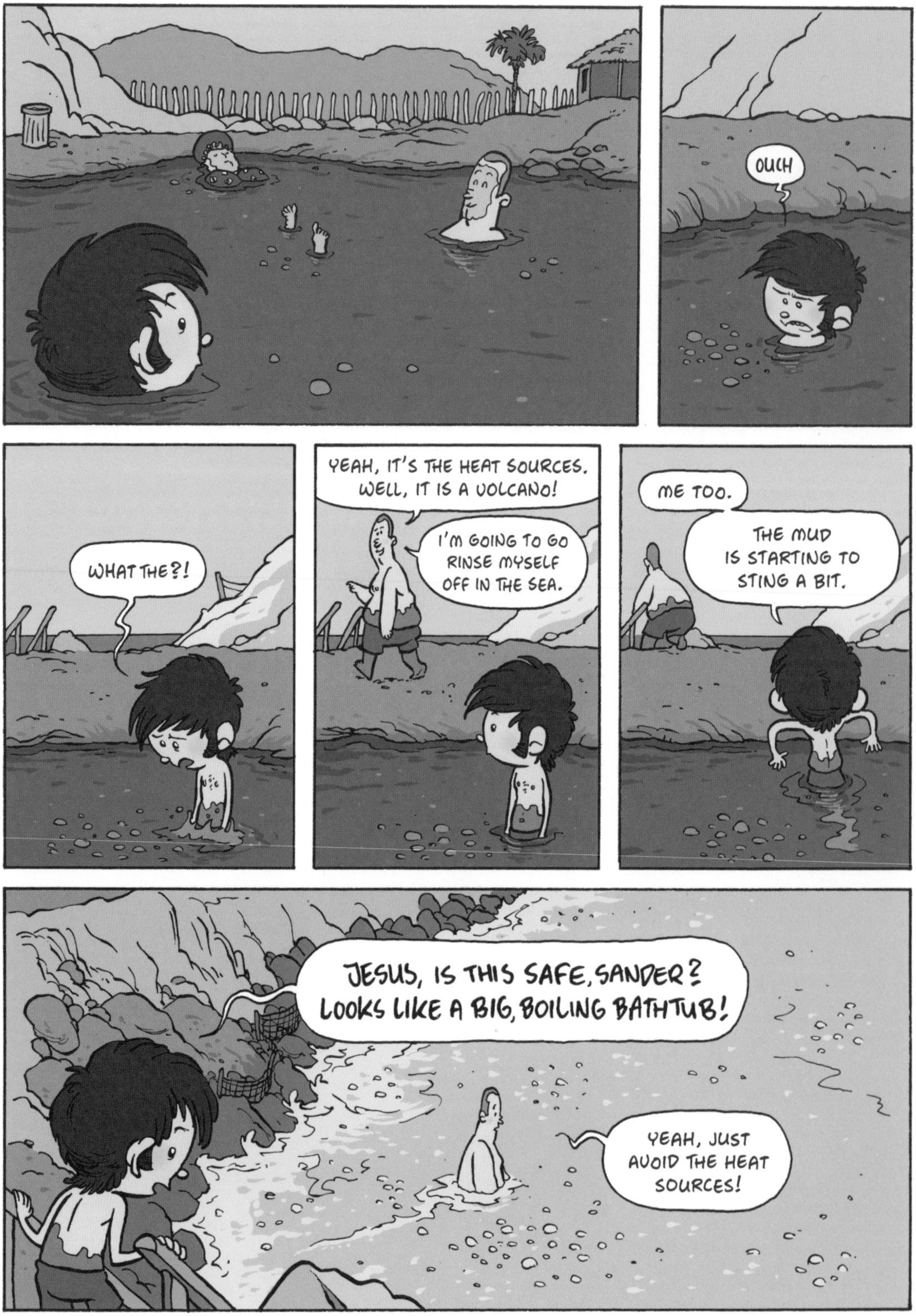
OUCH
WHAT THE?!
YEAH, IT'S THE HEAT SOURCES. WELL, IT IS A VOLCANO!
I'M GOING TO GO RINSE MYSELF OFF IN THE SEA.
ME TOO.
THE MUD IS STARTING TO STING A BIT.
JESUS, IS THIS SAFE, SANDER? LOOKS LIKE A BIG, BOILING BATHTUB!
YEAH, JUST AVOID THE HEAT SOURCES!

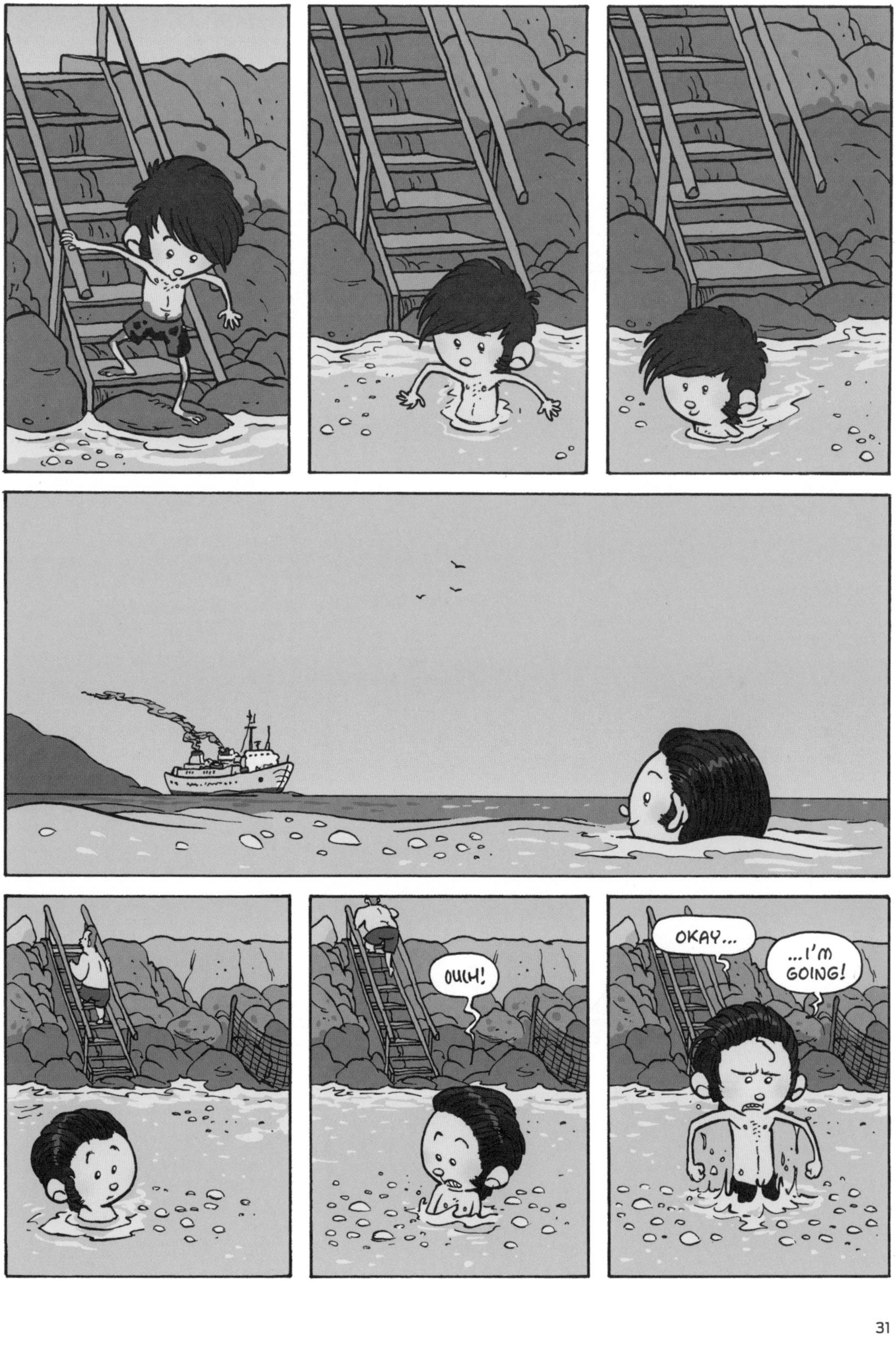
OUCH!
OKAY...
...I'M GOING!

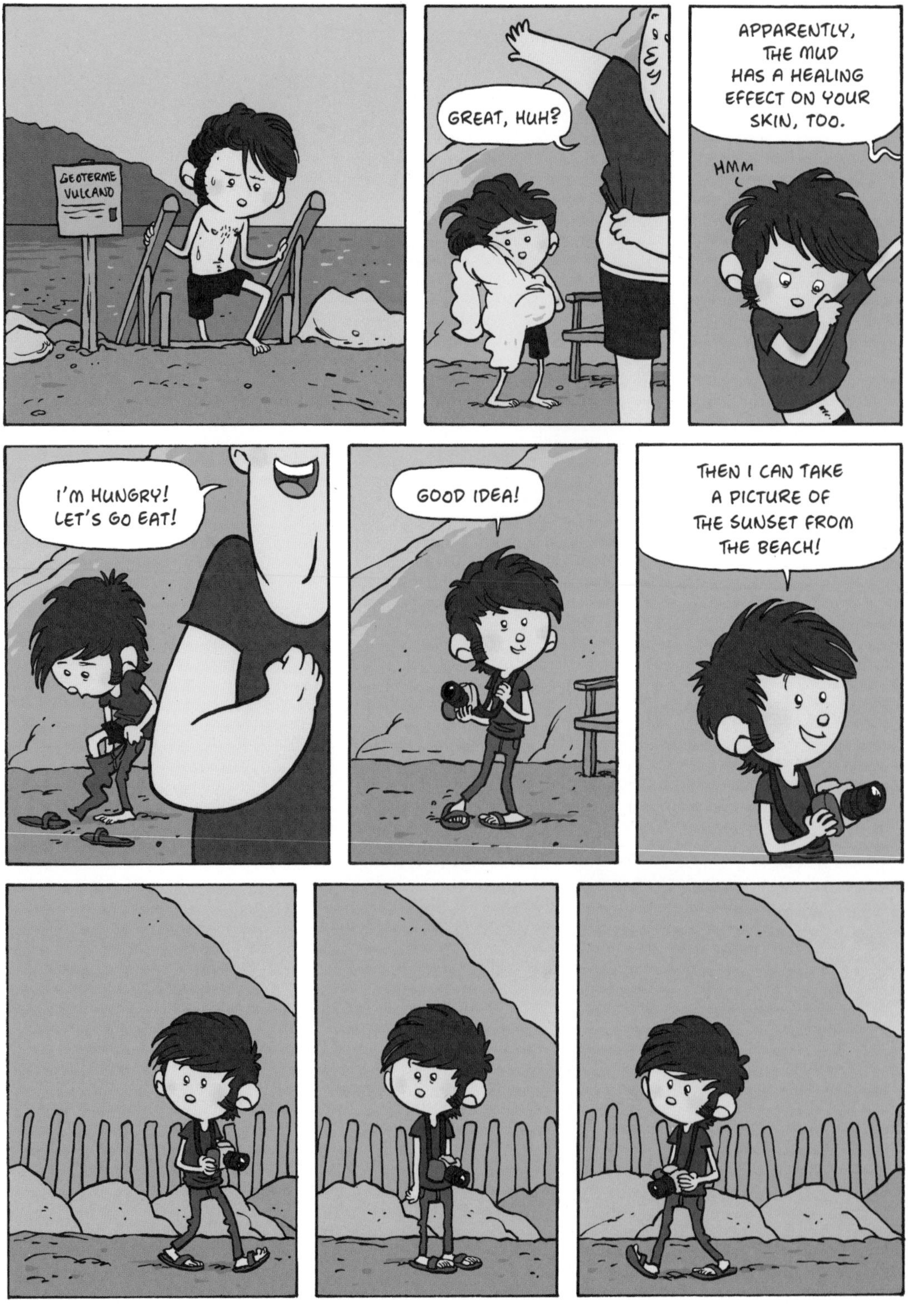
GEOTERME VULCANO
GREAT, HUH?
APPARENTLY, THE MUD HAS A HEALING EFFECT ON YOUR SKIN, TOO.
HMM
I'M HUNGRY! LET'S GO EAT!
GOOD IDEA!
THEN I CAN TAKE A PICTURE OF THE SUNSET FROM THE BEACH!

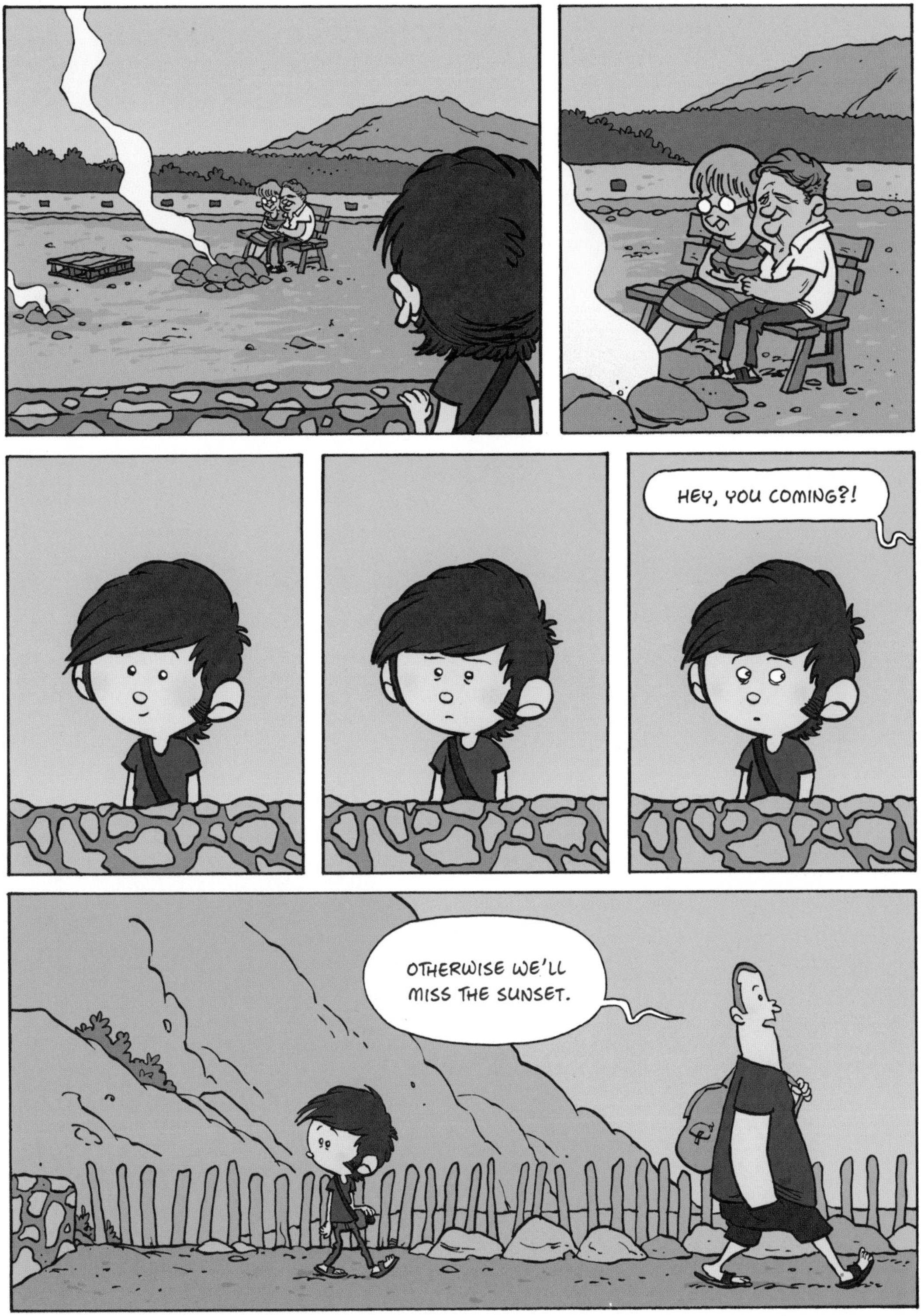
HEY, YOU COMING?!
OTHERWISE WE'LL MISS THE SUNSET.

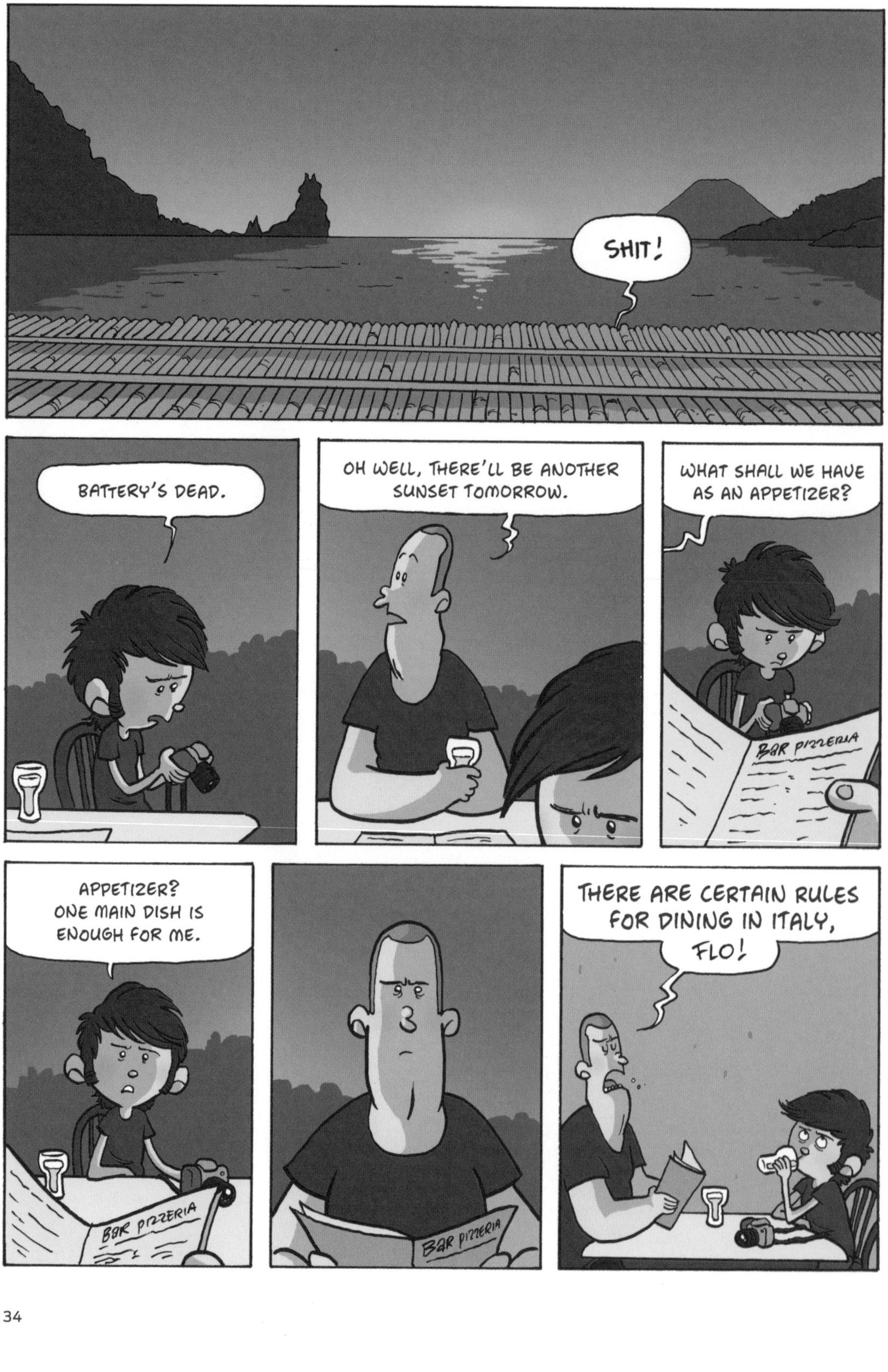
SHIT!
BATTERY'S DEAD.
OH WELL, THERE'LL BE ANOTHER SUNSET TOMORROW.
WHAT SHALL WE HAVE AS AN APPETIZER?
BAR PIZZERIA
APPETIZER? ONE MAIN DISH IS ENOUGH FOR ME.
BAR PIZZERIA
BAR PIZZERIA
THERE ARE CERTAIN RULES FOR DINING IN ITALY, FLO!

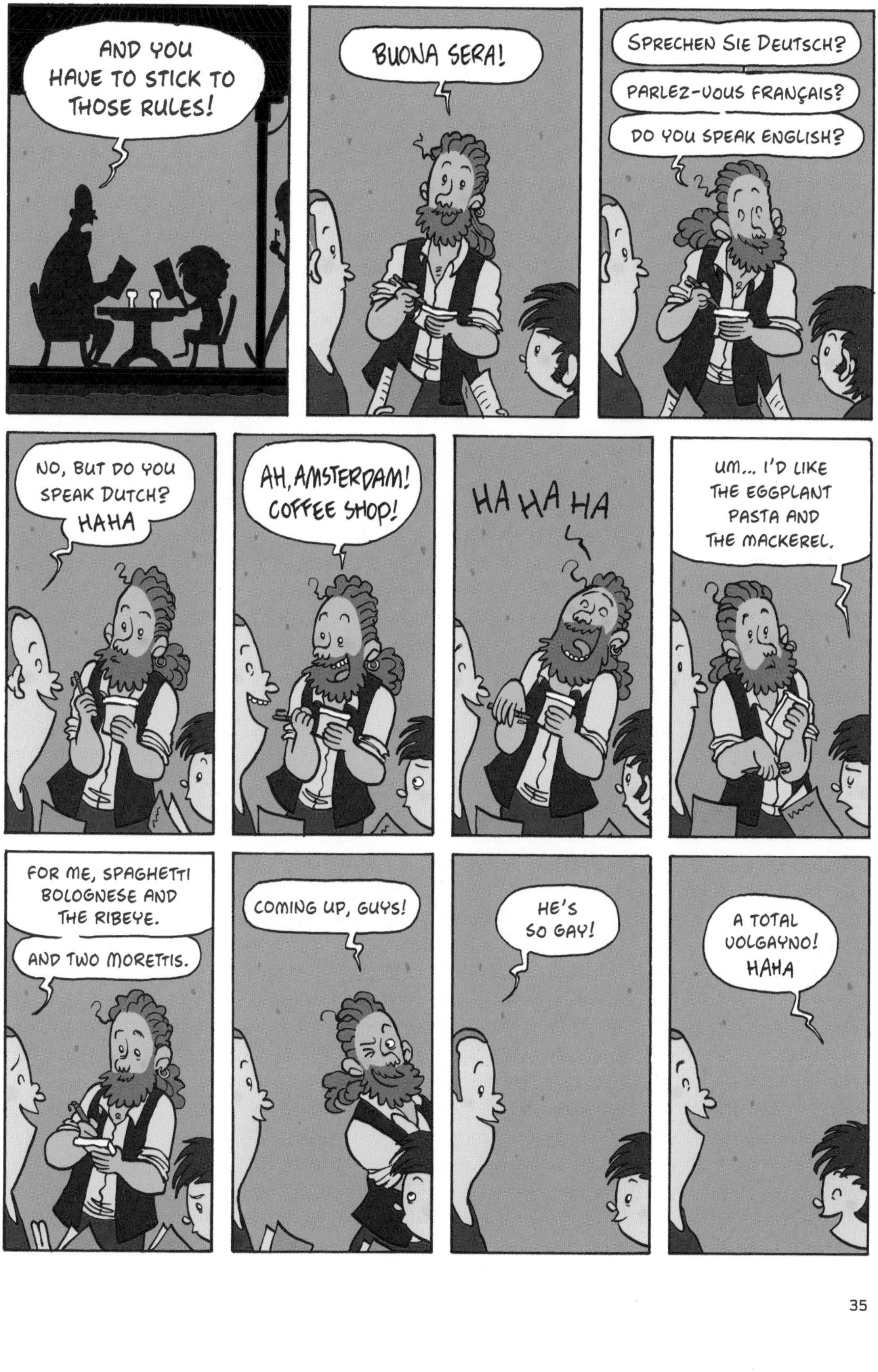
AND YOU HAVE TO STICK TO THOSE RULES!
BUONA SERA!
SPRECHEN SIE DEUTSCH?
PARLEZ-VOUS FRANÇAIS?
DO YOU SPEAK ENGLISH?
NO, BUT DO YOU SPEAK DUTCH? HAHA
AH, AMSTERDAM! COFFEE SHOP!
HA HA HA
UM... I'D LIKE THE EGGPLANT PASTA AND THE MACKEREL.
FOR ME, SPAGHETTI BOLOGNESE AND THE RIBEYE.
AND TWO MORETTIS.
COMING UP, GUYS!
HE'S SO GAY!
A TOTAL VOLGAYNO! HAHA

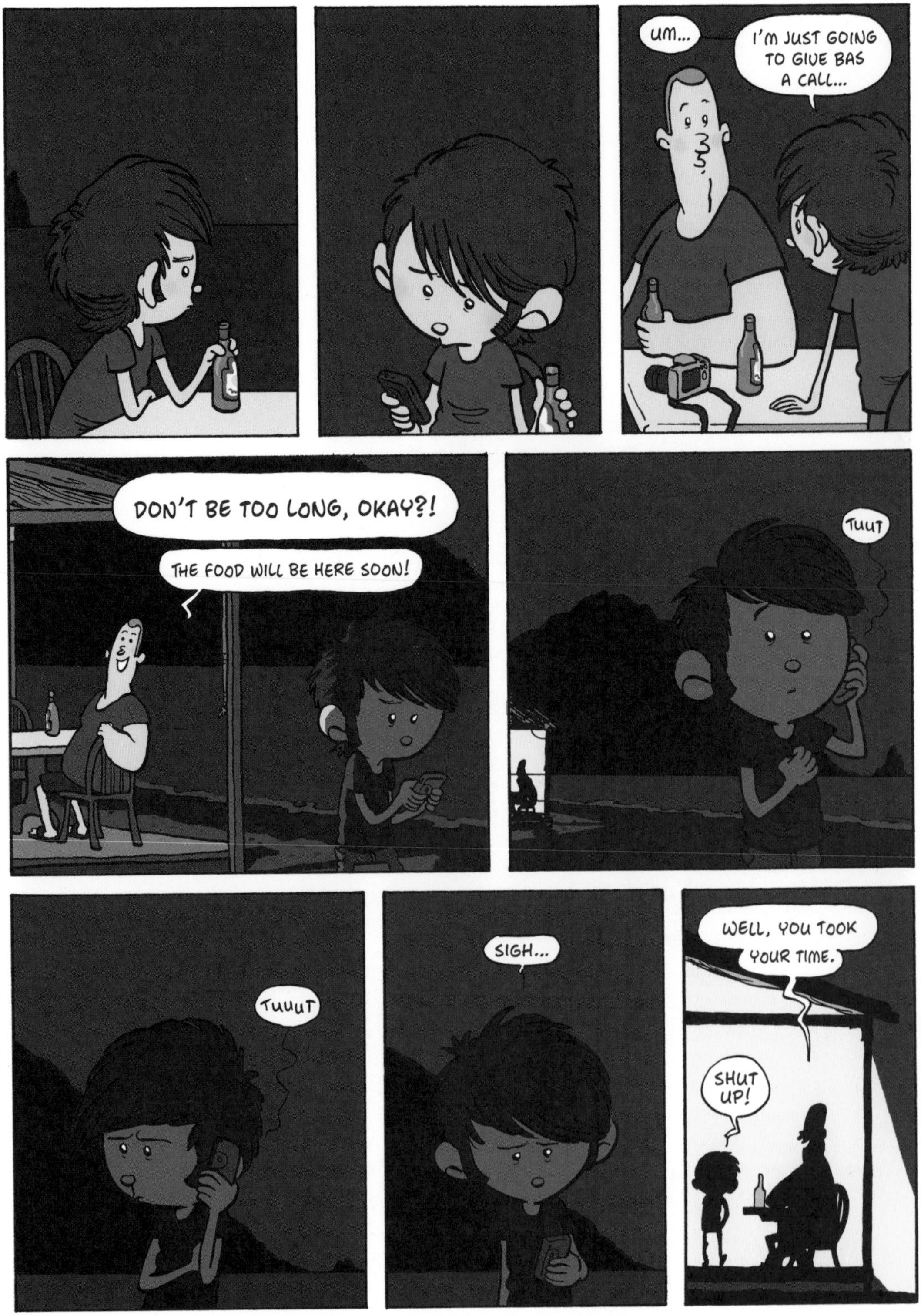
UM...
I'M JUST GOING TO GIVE BAS A CALL...
DON'T BE TOO LONG, OKAY?!
THE FOOD WILL BE HERE SOON!
TUUT
TUUUT
SIGH...
WELL, YOU TOOK YOUR TIME.
SHUT UP!

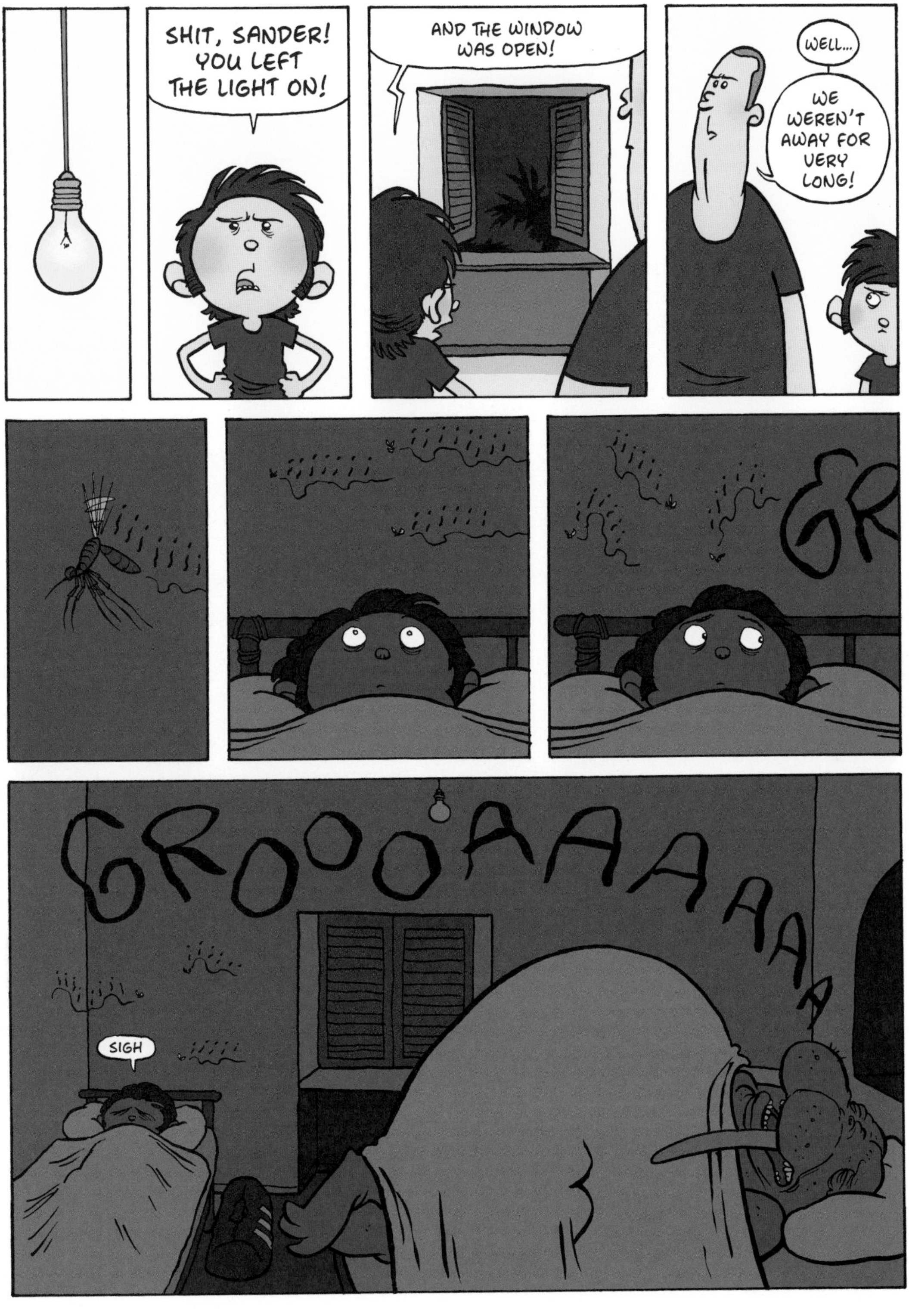
SHIT, SANDER! YOU LEFT THE LIGHT ON!
AND THE WINDOW WAS OPEN!
WELL...
WE WEREN'T AWAY FOR VERY LONG!
GR
GROOOAAAAAAA
SIGH

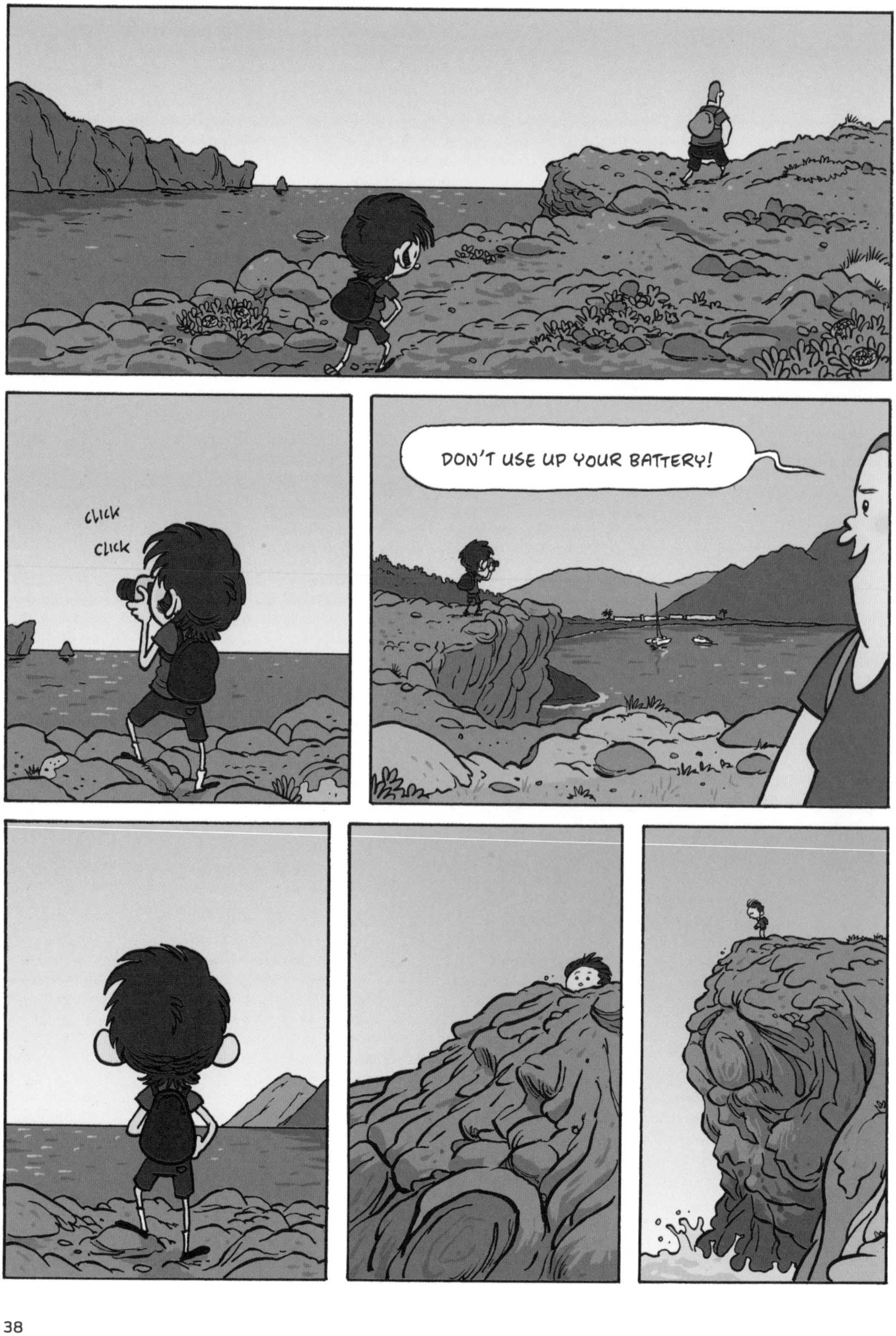
CLICK
CLICK
DON'T USE UP YOUR BATTERY!

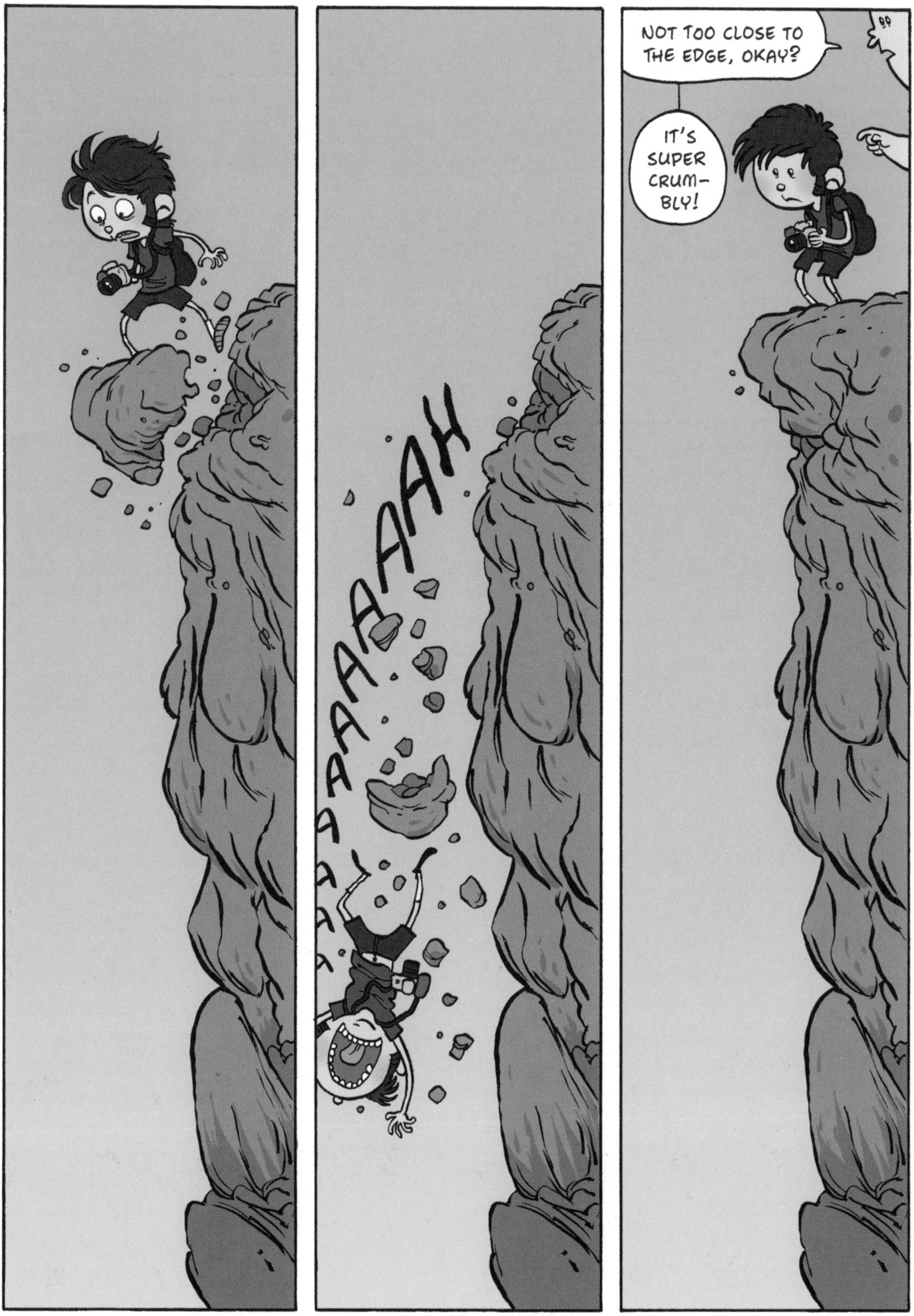
AAAAAAAAAAAH
NOT TOO CLOSE TO THE EDGE, OKAY?
IT'S SUPER CRUM-BLY!

THAT'S THE HOTEL WHERE I ACTUALLY WANTED TO STAY...

...BUT THEY DIDN'T WANT ME.

OH

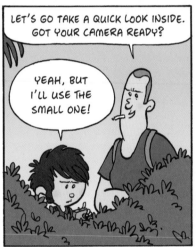

LET'S GO TAKE A QUICK LOOK INSIDE. GOT YOUR CAMERA READY?

YEAH, BUT I'LL USE THE SMALL ONE!

THE BATTERY IN THE BIG ONE'S NEARLY DEAD.

LOSER! LIKE THAT TINY CAMERA LOOKS SO PROFESSIONAL!

JUST USE THE BIG ONE AND FAKE IT.

BUT I'M NOT A PROFESSIONAL PHOTOGRAPHER...

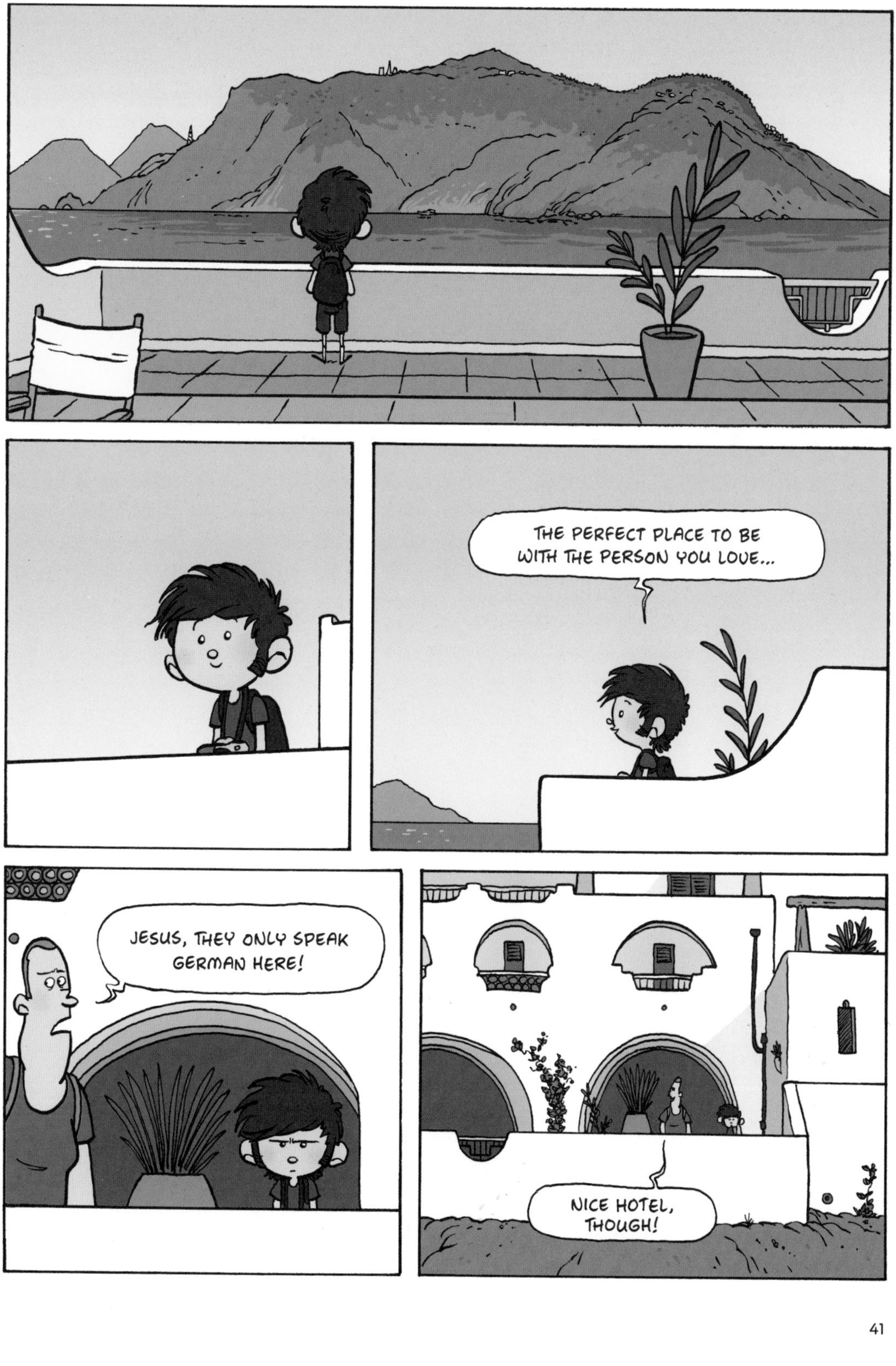
THE PERFECT PLACE TO BE WITH THE PERSON YOU LOVE...
JESUS, THEY ONLY SPEAK GERMAN HERE!
NICE HOTEL, THOUGH!

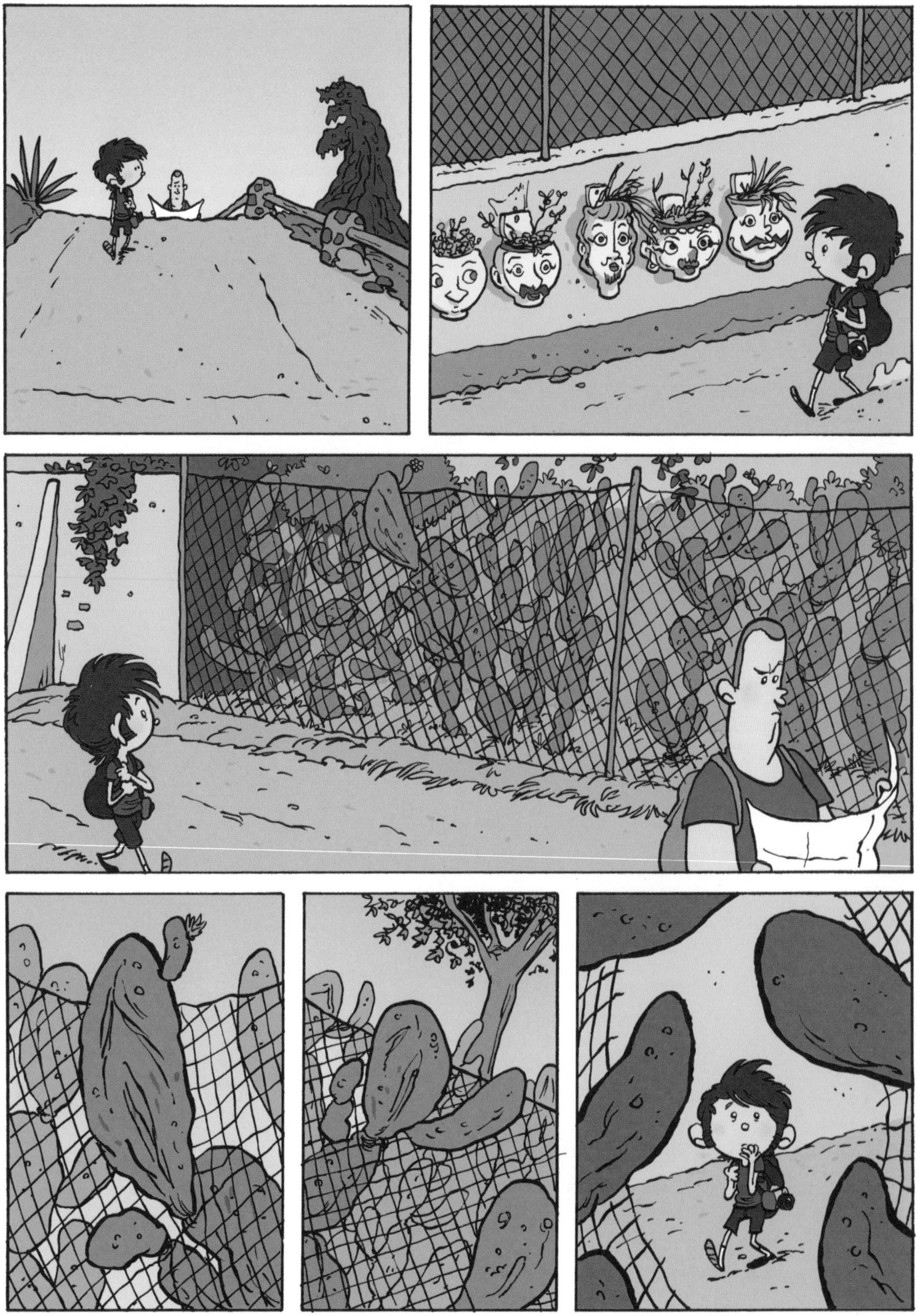

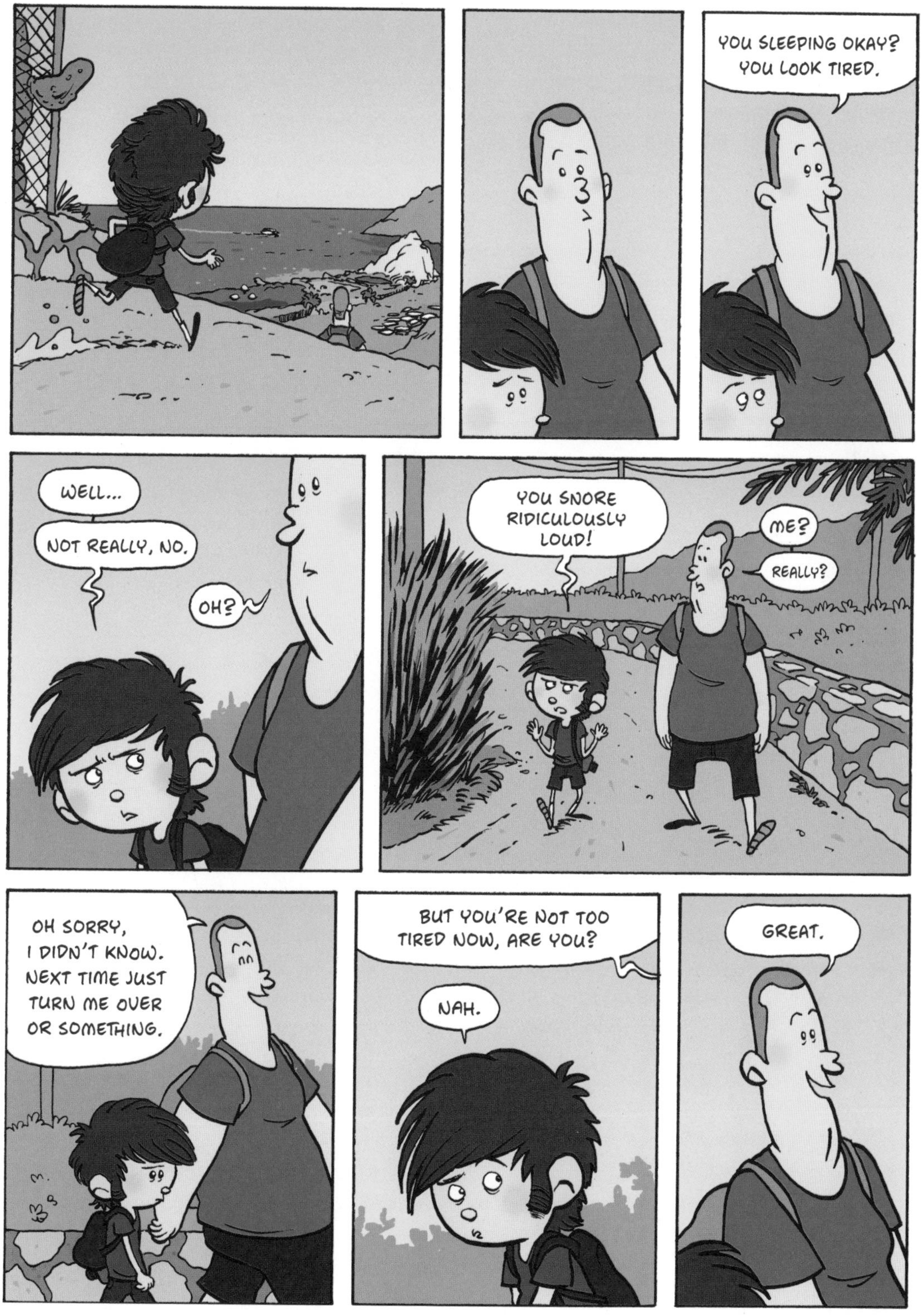
YOU SLEEPING OKAY? YOU LOOK TIRED.
WELL...
NOT REALLY, NO.
OH?
YOU SNORE RIDICULOUSLY LOUD!
ME?
REALLY?
OH SORRY, I DIDN'T KNOW. NEXT TIME JUST TURN ME OVER OR SOMETHING.
BUT YOU'RE NOT TOO TIRED NOW, ARE YOU?
NAH.
GREAT.

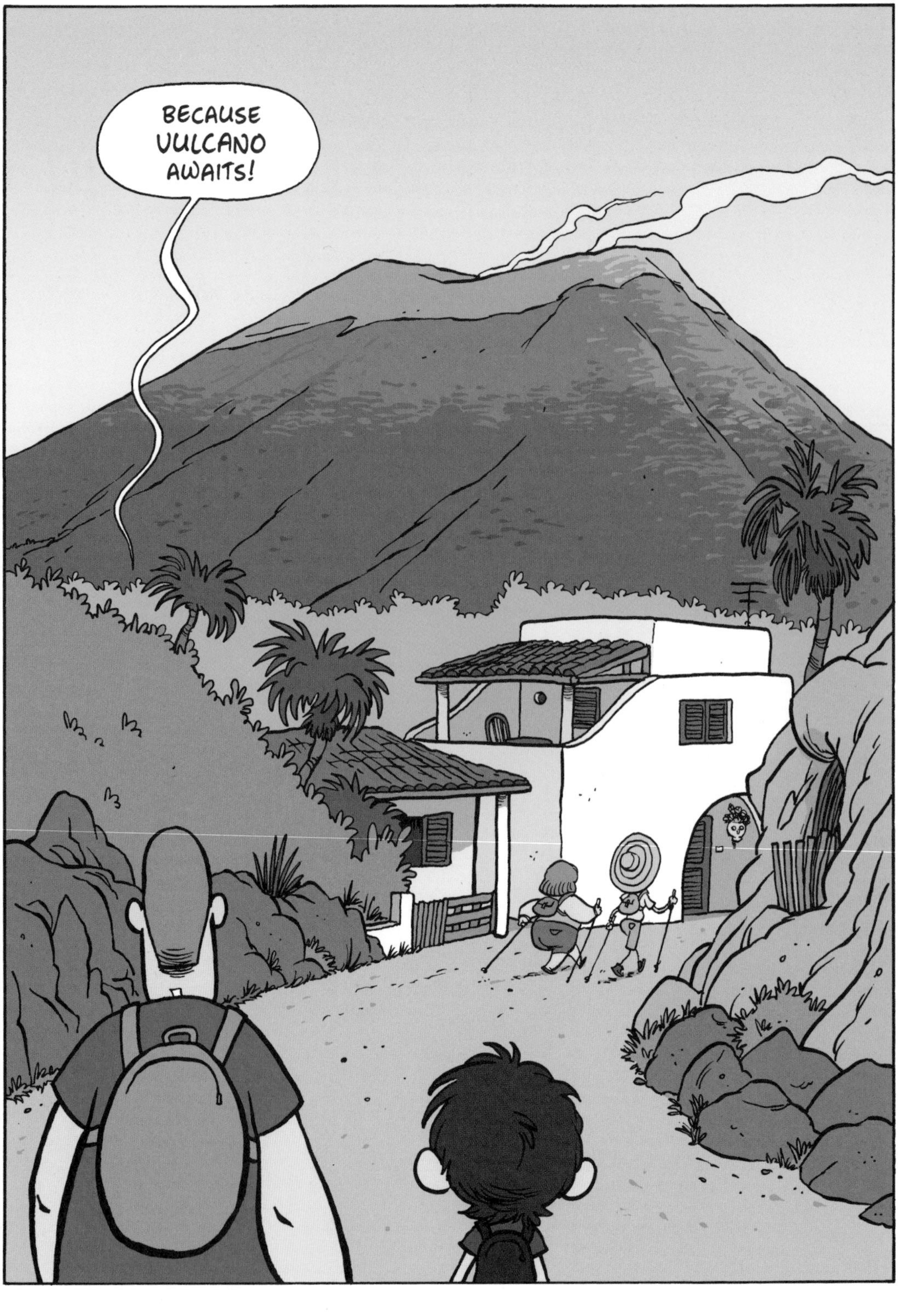
BECAUSE VULCANO AWAITS!

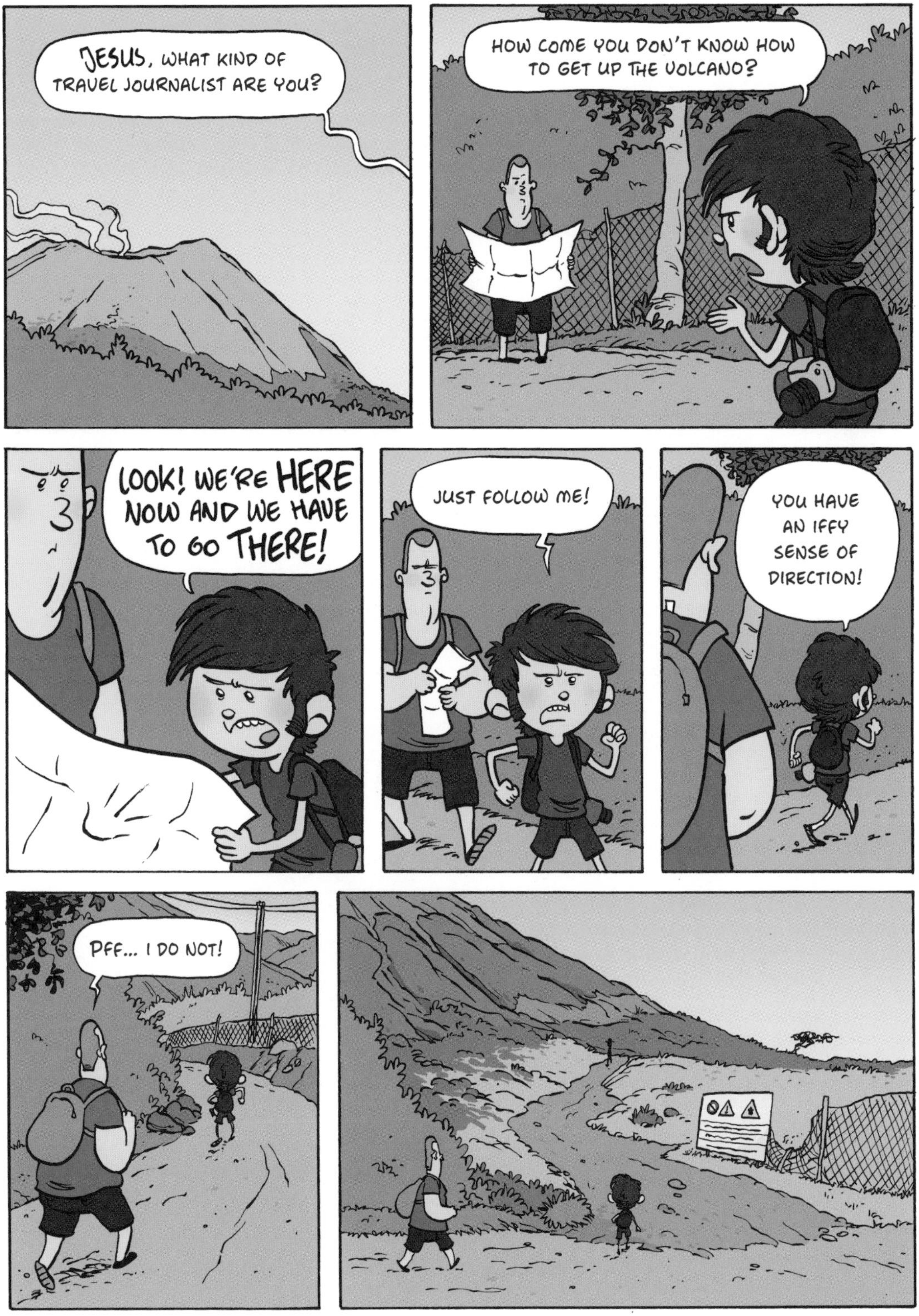
JESUS, WHAT KIND OF TRAVEL JOURNALIST ARE YOU?
HOW COME YOU DON'T KNOW HOW TO GET UP THE VOLCANO?
LOOK! WE'RE HERE NOW AND WE HAVE TO GO THERE!
JUST FOLLOW ME!
YOU HAVE AN IFFY SENSE OF DIRECTION!
PFF... I DO NOT!

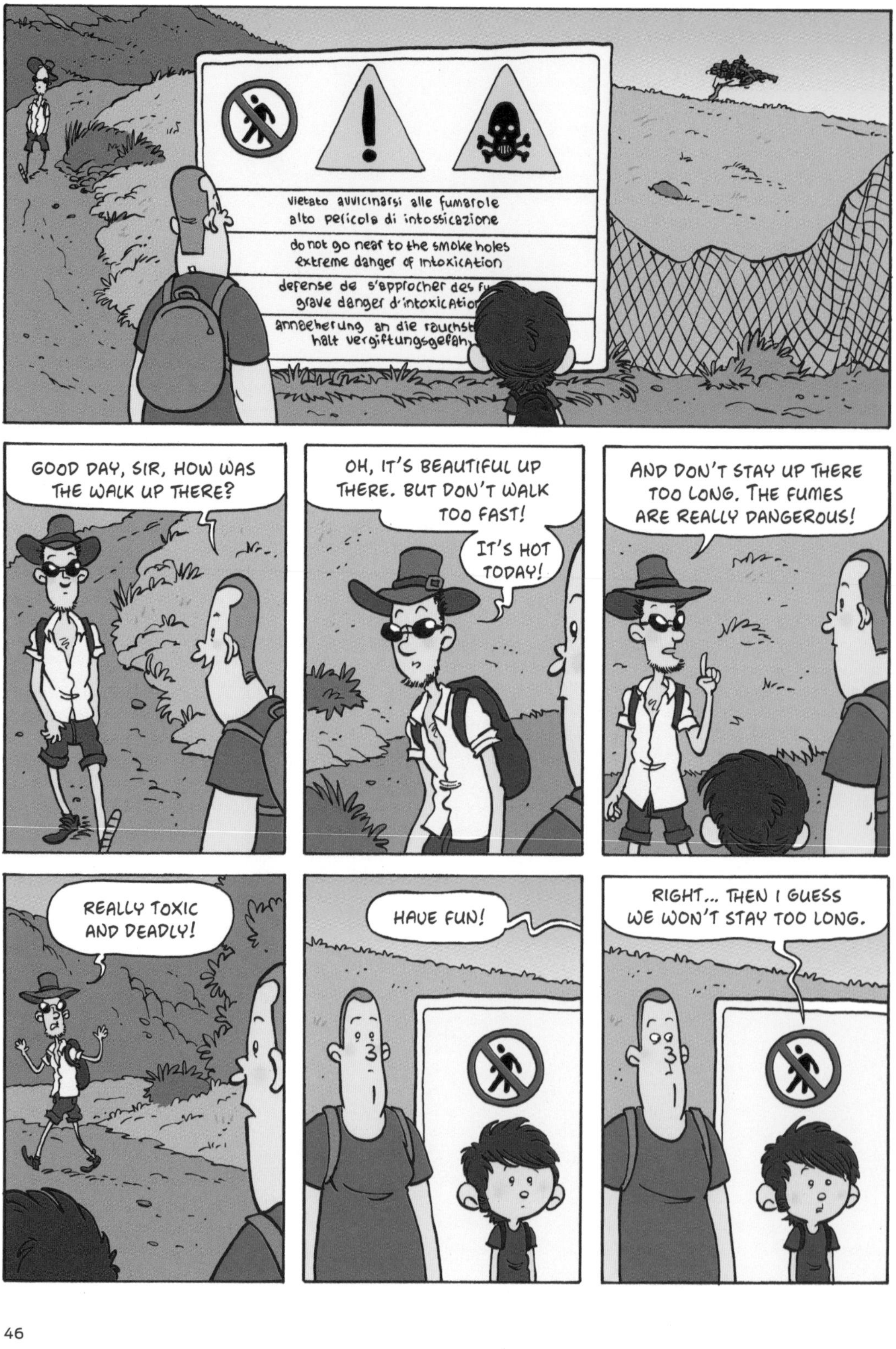
vietato avvicinarsi alle fumarole
alto pericolo di intossicazione
do not go near to the smoke holes
extreme danger of intoxication
defense de s'approcher des f
grave danger d'intoxicatio
annaeherung an die rauchst
halt vergiftungsgefah
GOOD DAY, SIR, HOW WAS THE WALK UP THERE?
OH, IT'S BEAUTIFUL UP THERE. BUT DON'T WALK TOO FAST!
IT'S HOT TODAY!
AND DON'T STAY UP THERE TOO LONG. THE FUMES ARE REALLY DANGEROUS!
REALLY TOXIC AND DEADLY!
HAVE FUN!
RIGHT... THEN I GUESS WE WON'T STAY TOO LONG.

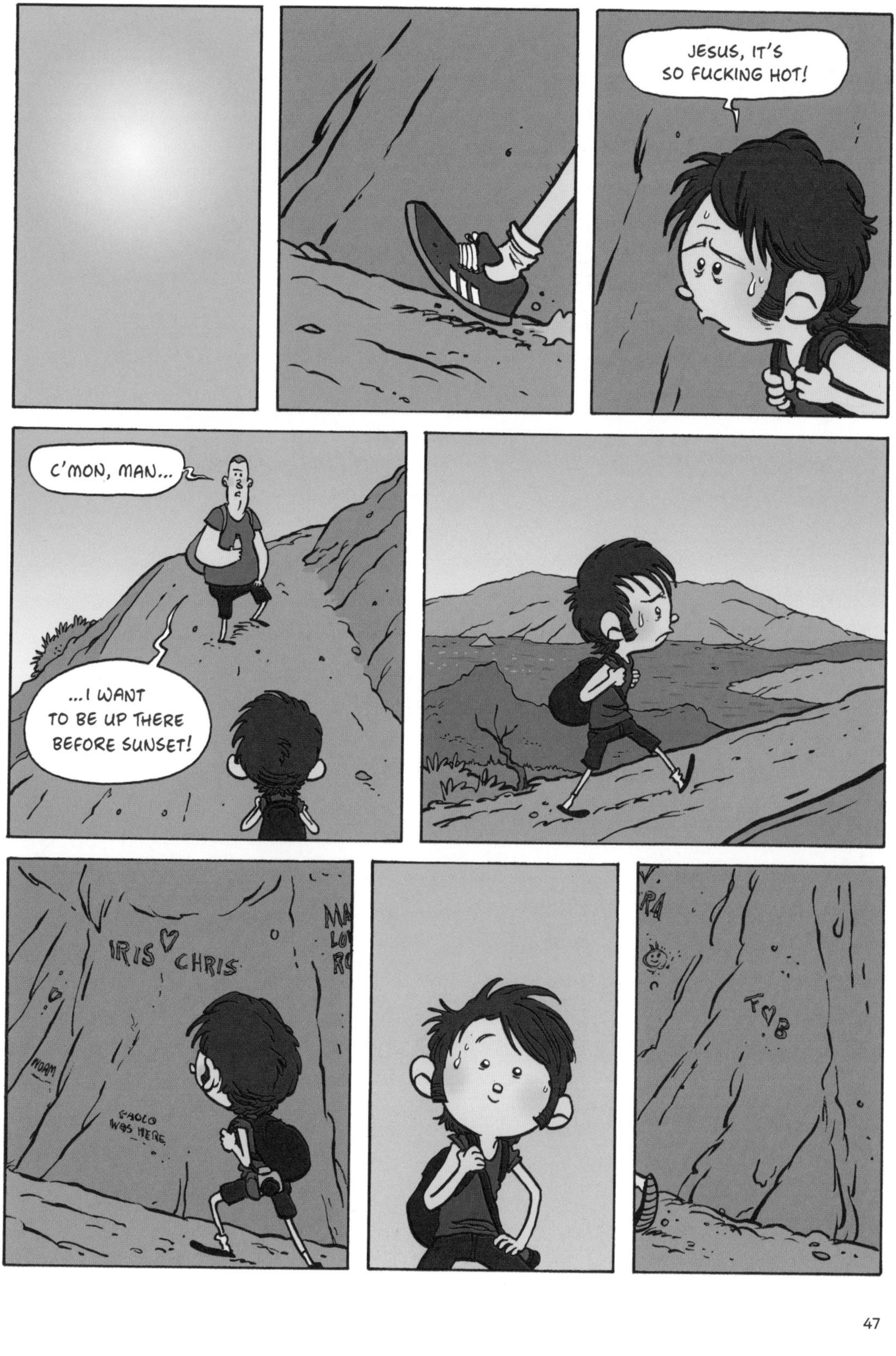
JESUS, IT'S SO FUCKING HOT!
C'MON, MAN...
...I WANT TO BE UP THERE BEFORE SUNSET!
IRIS ♡ CHRIS
NOAM
PAOLO WAS HERE
T♡B

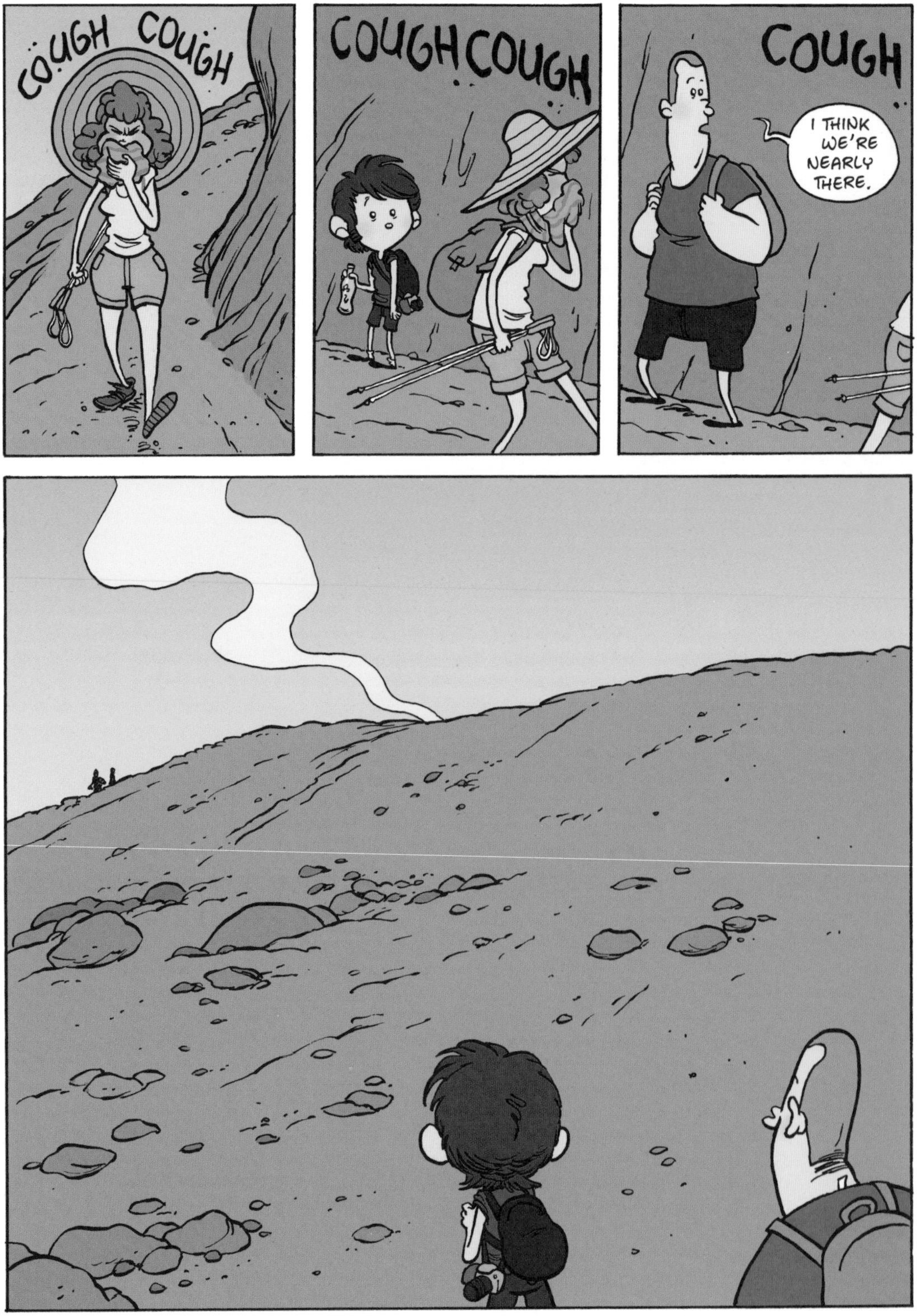
COUGH COUGH
COUGH COUGH
COUGH
I THINK WE'RE NEARLY THERE.

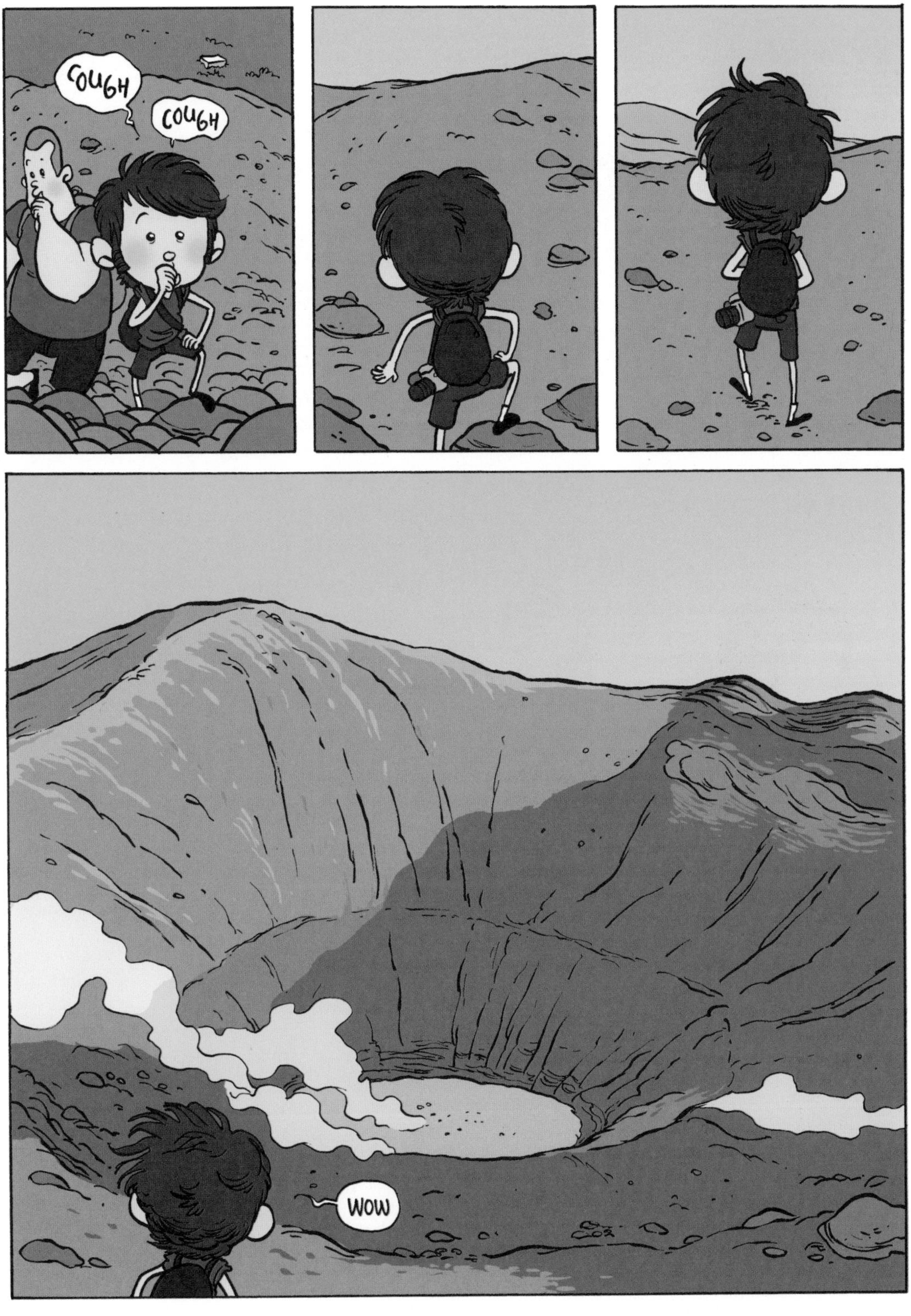
COUGH
COUGH
WOW

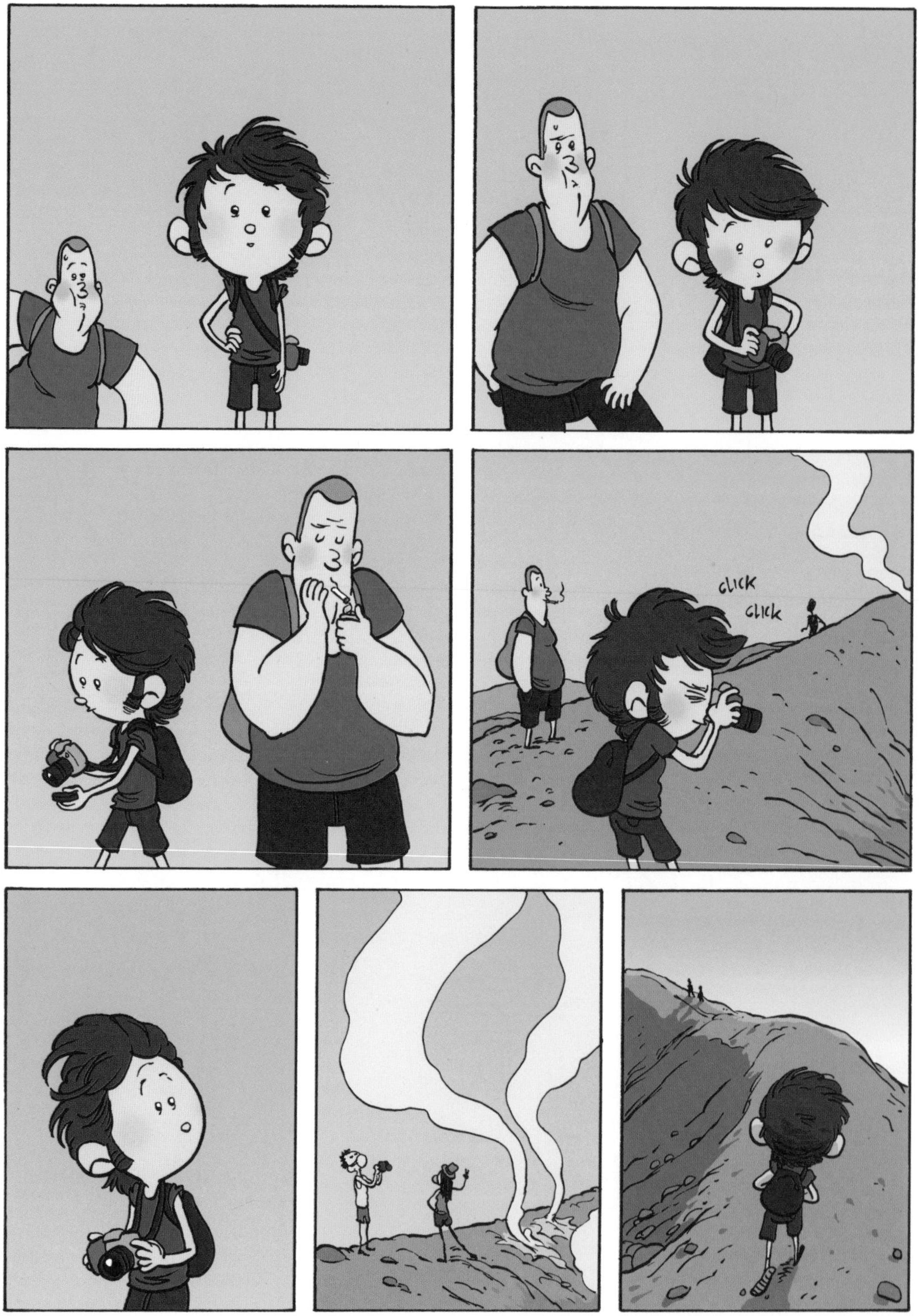
CLICK
CLICK

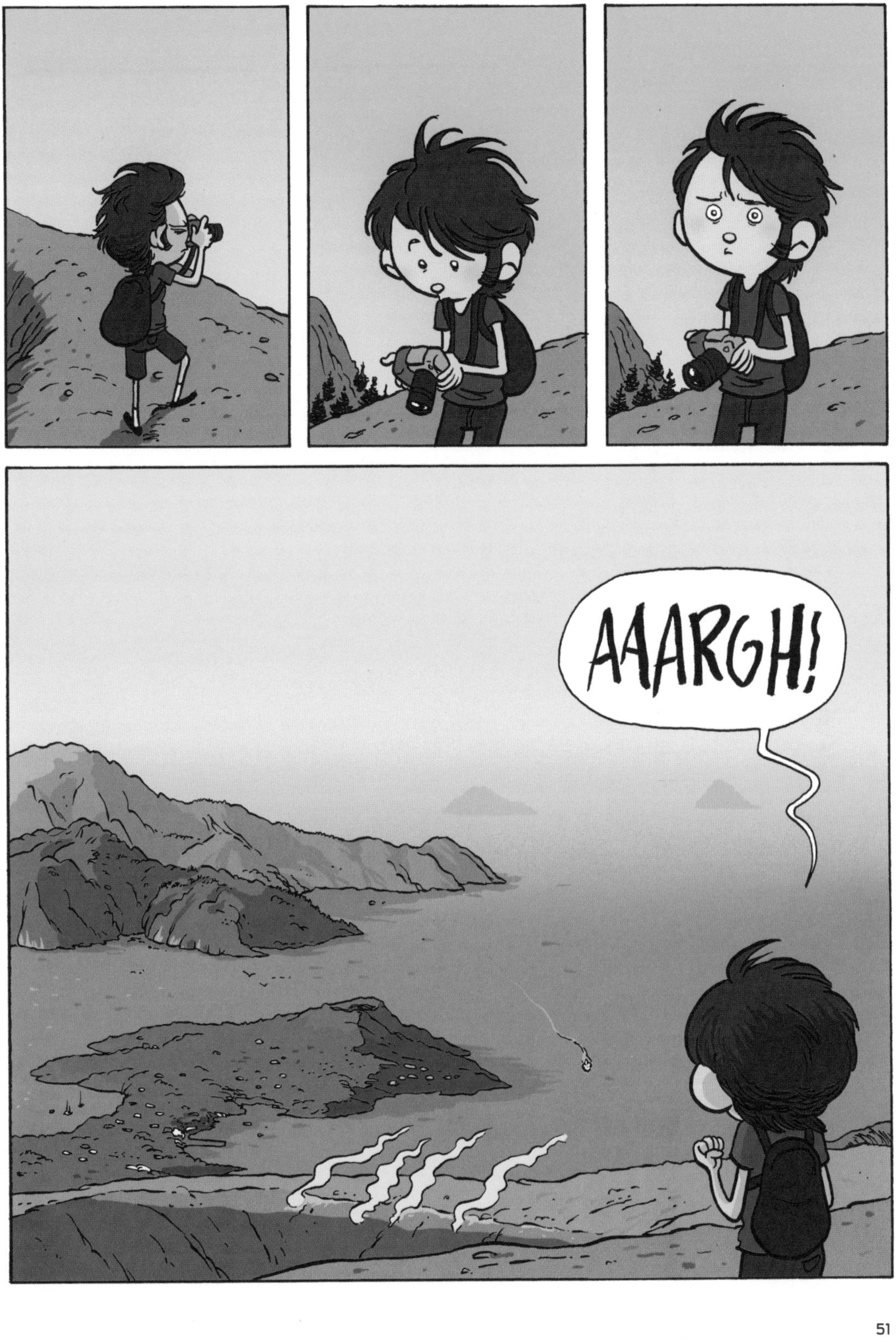
AAARGH!

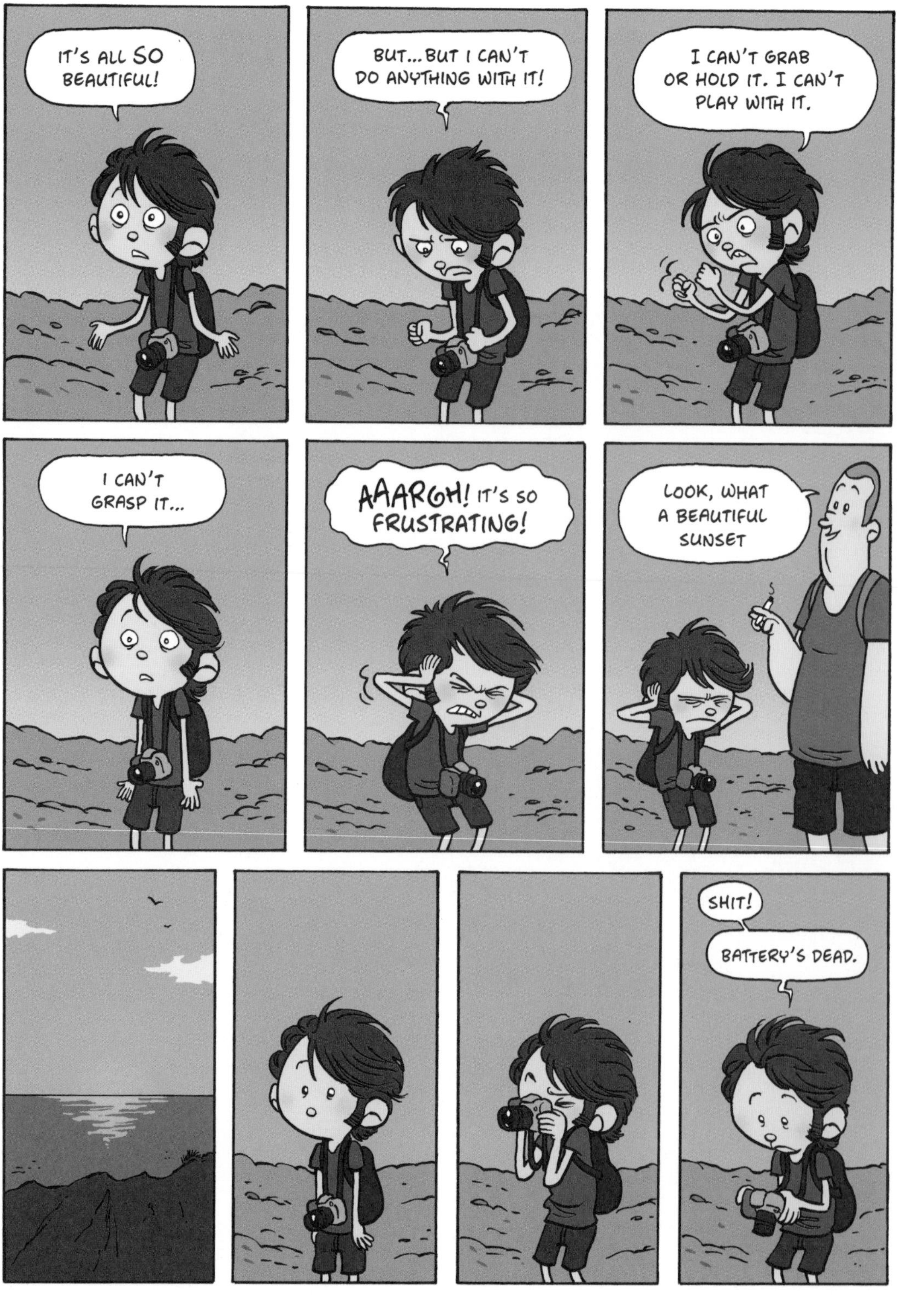
IT'S ALL SO BEAUTIFUL!
BUT... BUT I CAN'T DO ANYTHING WITH IT!
I CAN'T GRAB OR HOLD IT. I CAN'T PLAY WITH IT.
I CAN'T GRASP IT...
AAARGH! IT'S SO FRUSTRATING!
LOOK, WHAT A BEAUTIFUL SUNSET
SHIT!
BATTERY'S DEAD.

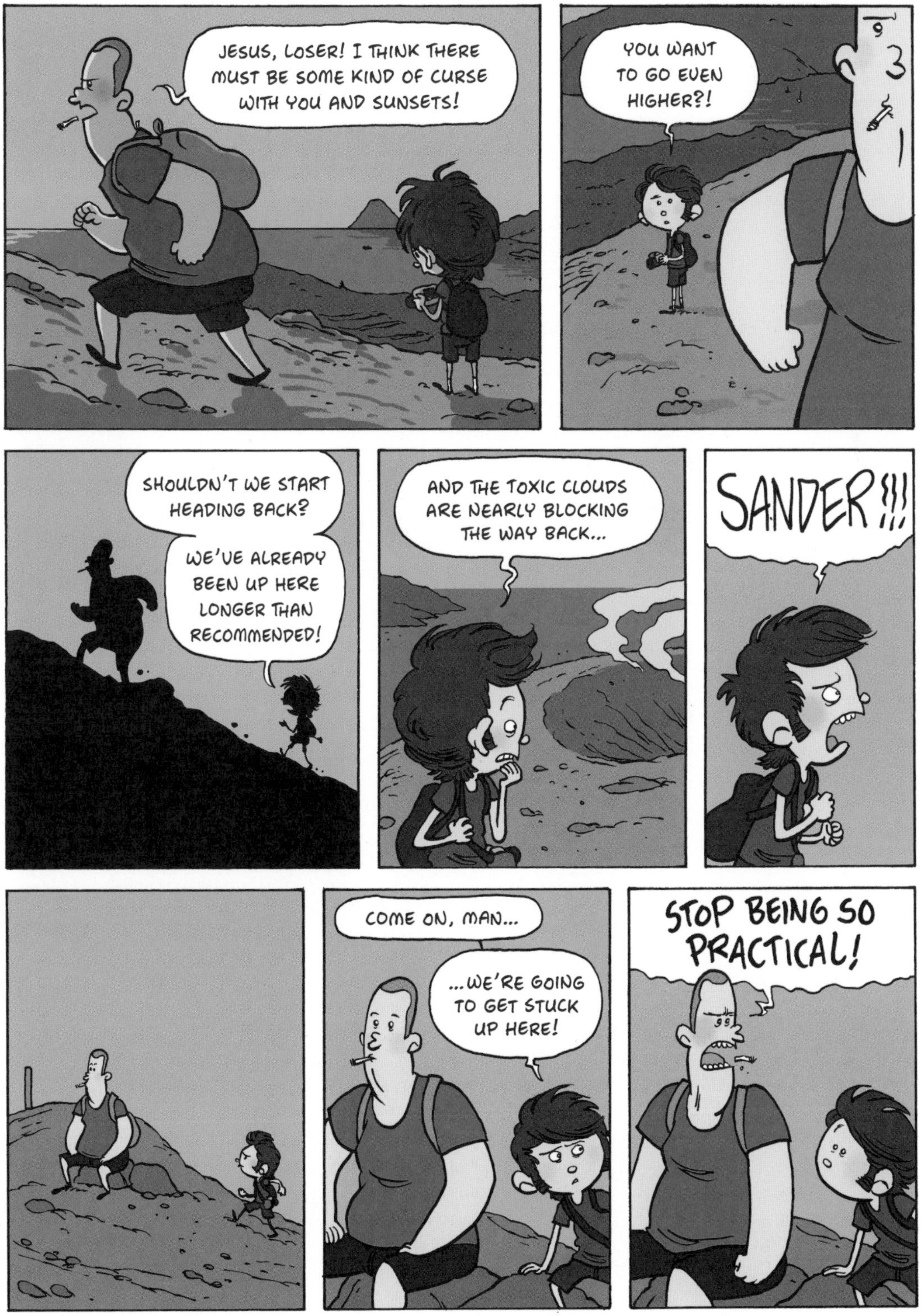
JESUS, LOSER! I THINK THERE MUST BE SOME KIND OF CURSE WITH YOU AND SUNSETS!
YOU WANT TO GO EVEN HIGHER?!
SHOULDN'T WE START HEADING BACK?
WE'VE ALREADY BEEN UP HERE LONGER THAN RECOMMENDED!
AND THE TOXIC CLOUDS ARE NEARLY BLOCKING THE WAY BACK...
SANDER!!!
COME ON, MAN...
...WE'RE GOING TO GET STUCK UP HERE!
STOP BEING SO PRACTICAL!

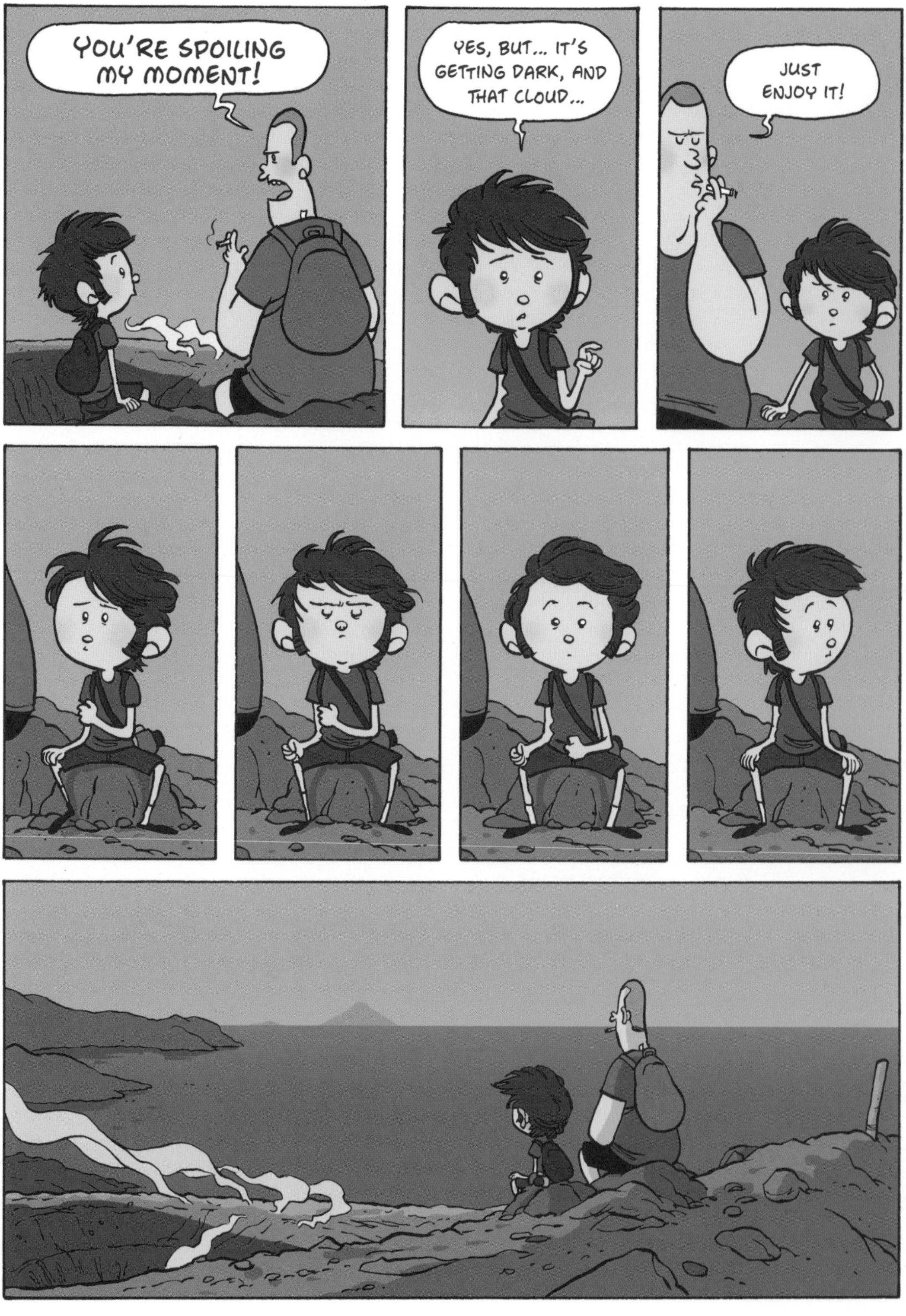
YOU'RE SPOILING MY MOMENT!
YES, BUT... IT'S GETTING DARK, AND THAT CLOUD...
JUST ENJOY IT!

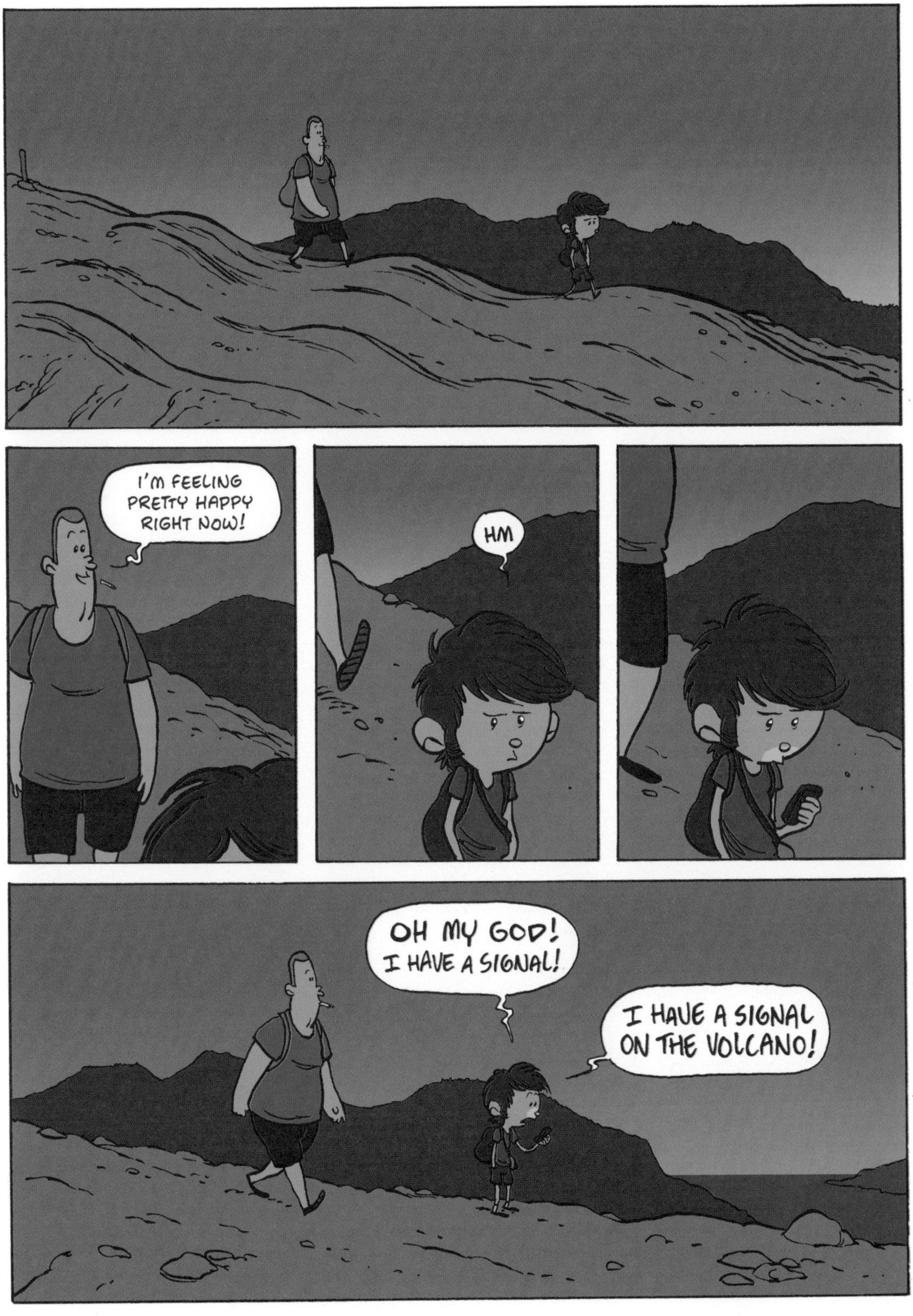
I'M FEELING PRETTY HAPPY RIGHT NOW!
HM
OH MY GOD! I HAVE A SIGNAL!
I HAVE A SIGNAL ON THE VOLCANO!

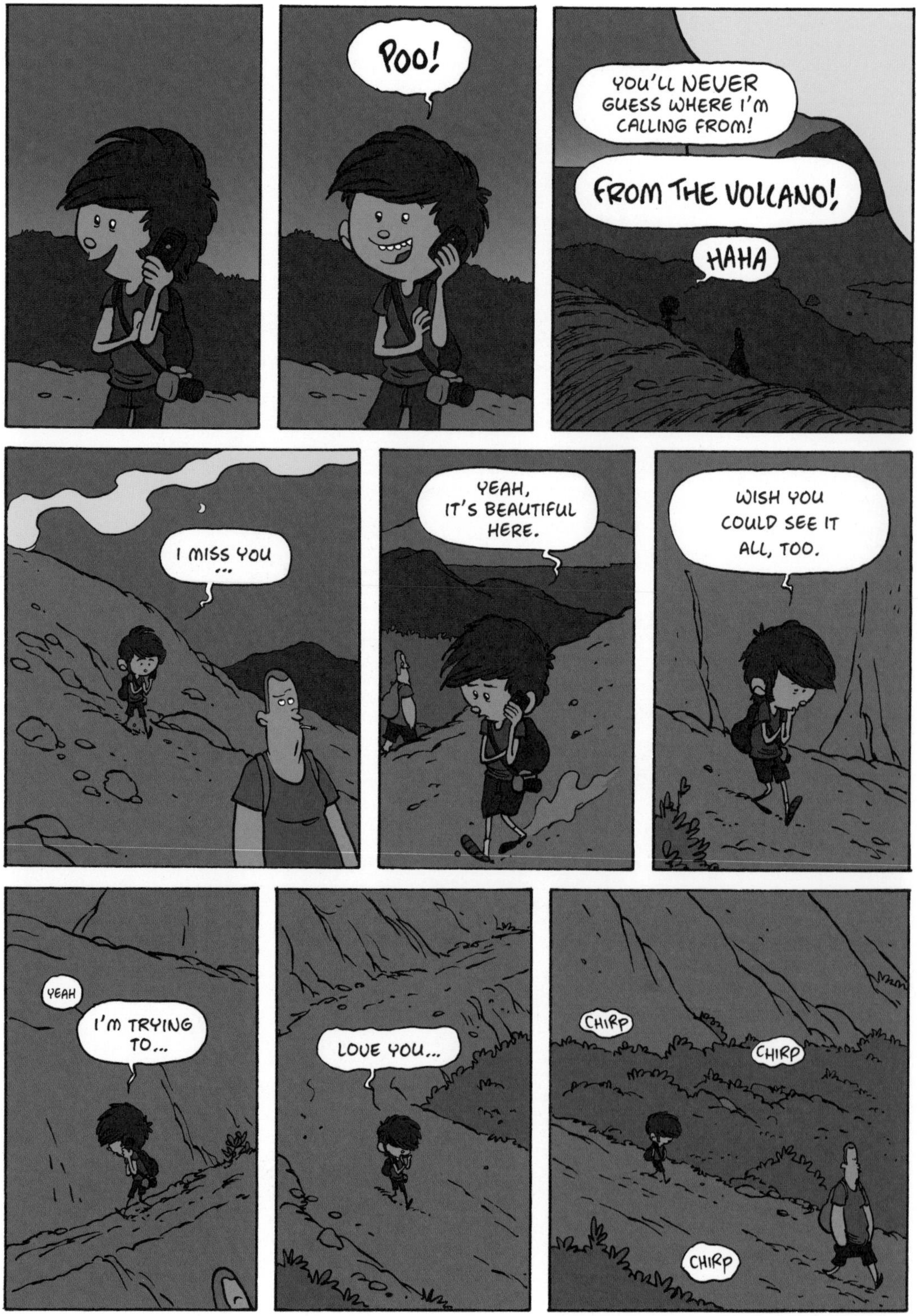
POO!
YOU'LL NEVER GUESS WHERE I'M CALLING FROM!
FROM THE VOLCANO!
HAHA
I MISS YOU ...
YEAH, IT'S BEAUTIFUL HERE.
WISH YOU COULD SEE IT ALL, TOO.
YEAH
I'M TRYING TO...
LOVE YOU...
CHIRP
CHIRP
CHIRP

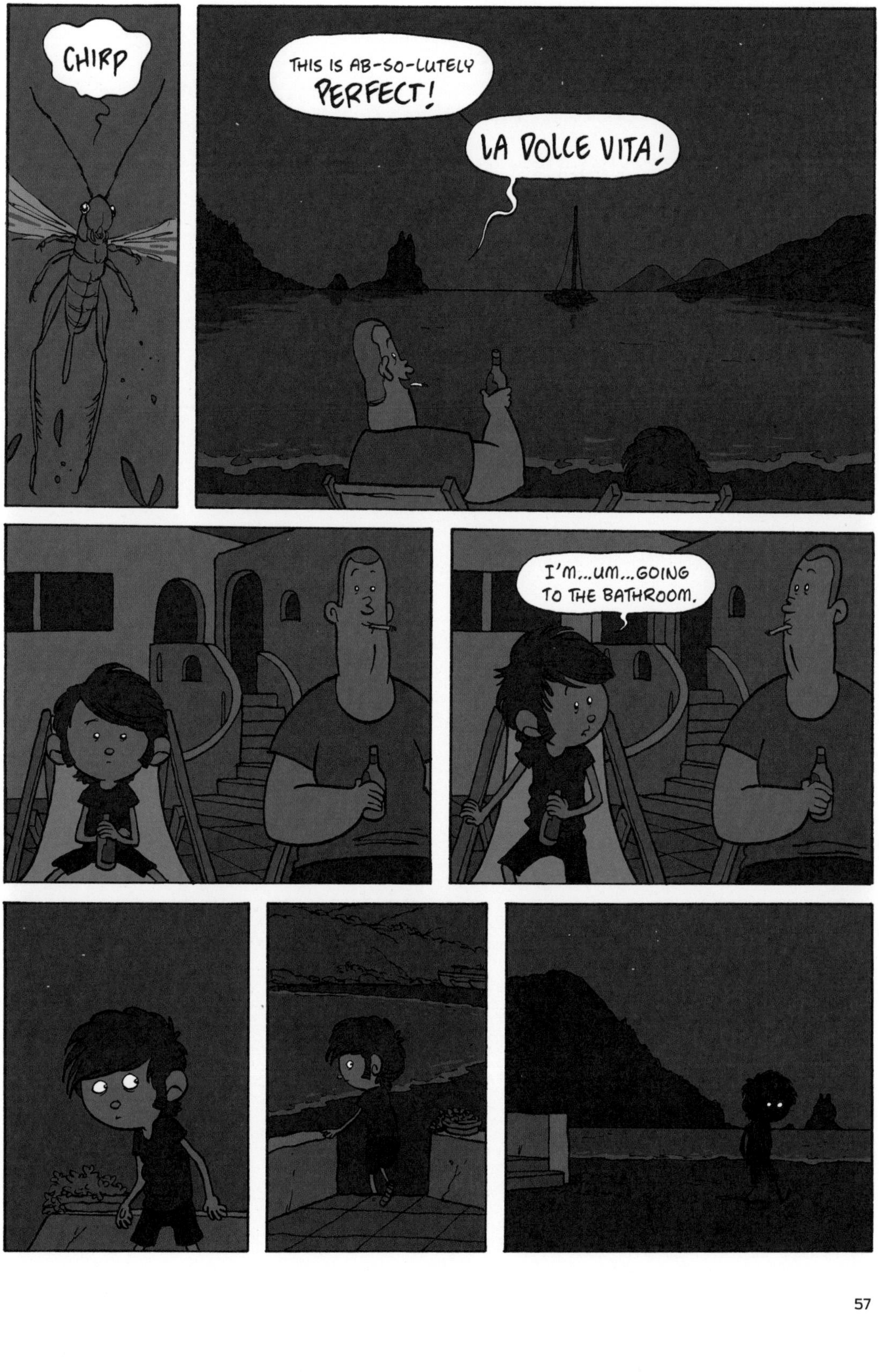
CHIRP
THIS IS AB-SO-LUTELY PERFECT!
LA DOLCE VITA!
I'M...UM...GOING TO THE BATHROOM.

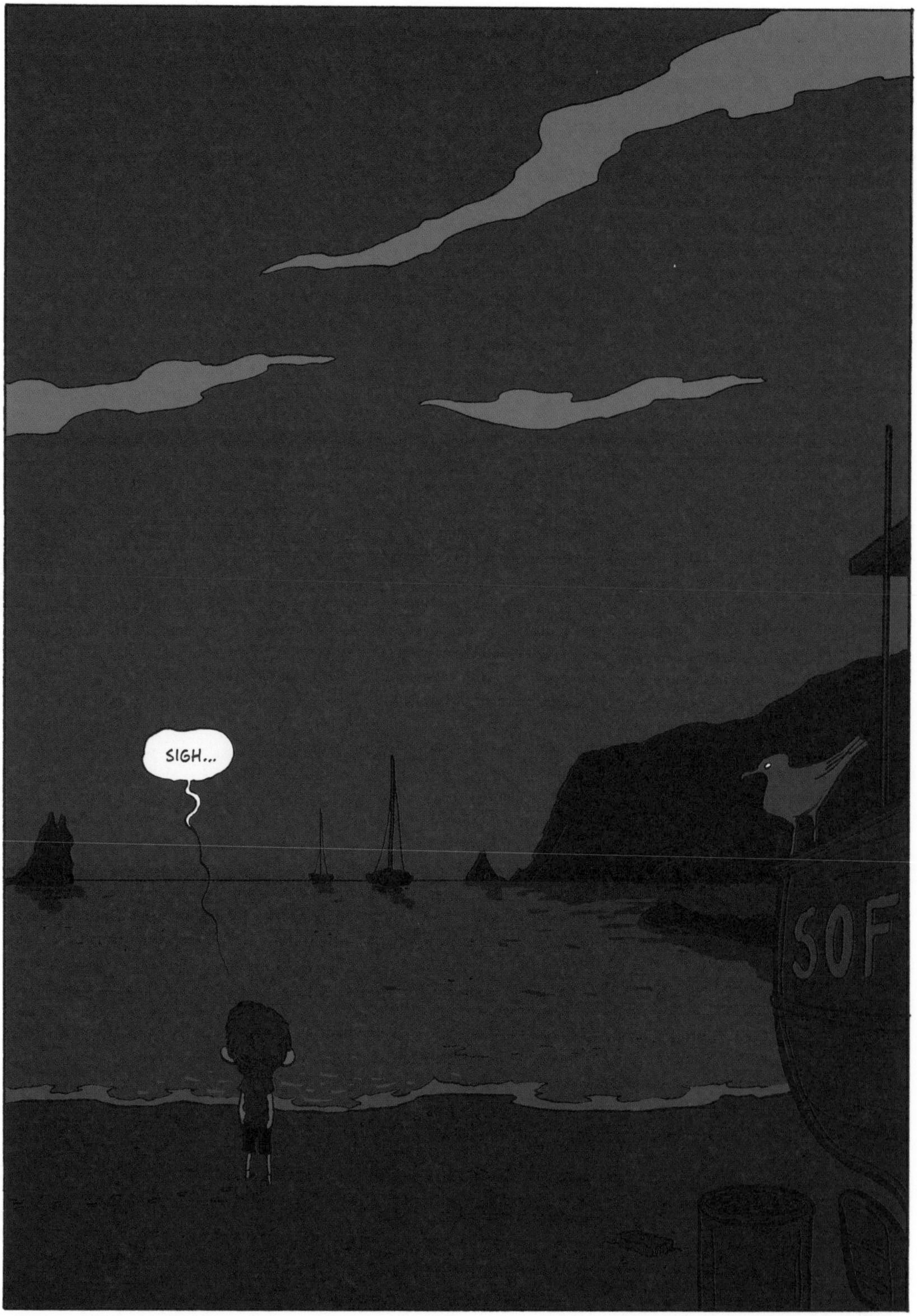
SIGH...
SOF

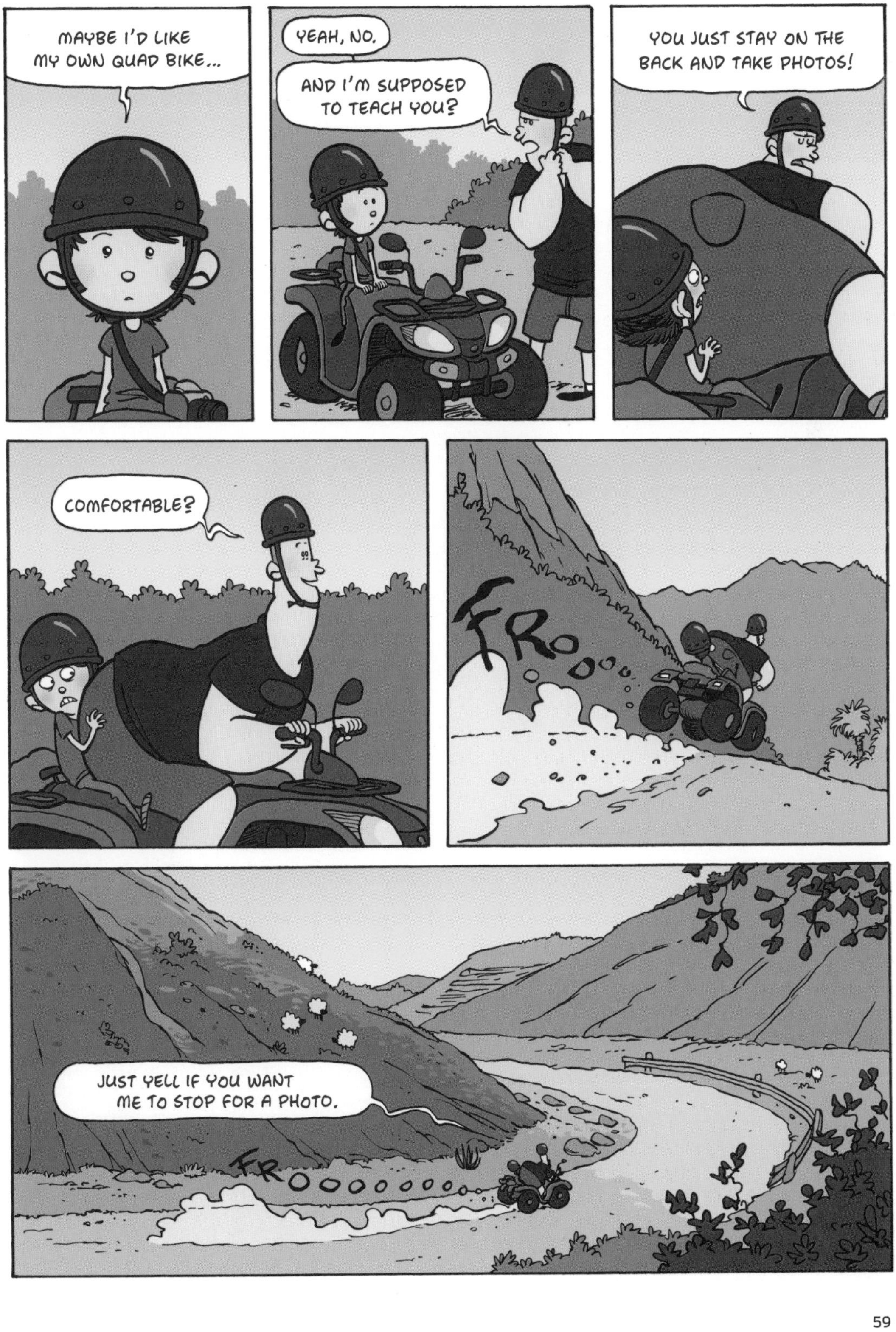
MAYBE I'D LIKE MY OWN QUAD BIKE...
YEAH, NO.
AND I'M SUPPOSED TO TEACH YOU?
YOU JUST STAY ON THE BACK AND TAKE PHOTOS!
COMFORTABLE?
FROOO...
JUST YELL IF YOU WANT ME TO STOP FOR A PHOTO.
FROOOOOOOOO...

PRETTY BIG... FOR A COW.

click

click

I DON'T THINK IT'S A COW.

IT'S TIED UP, ISN'T IT?

YEAH, I GUESS.

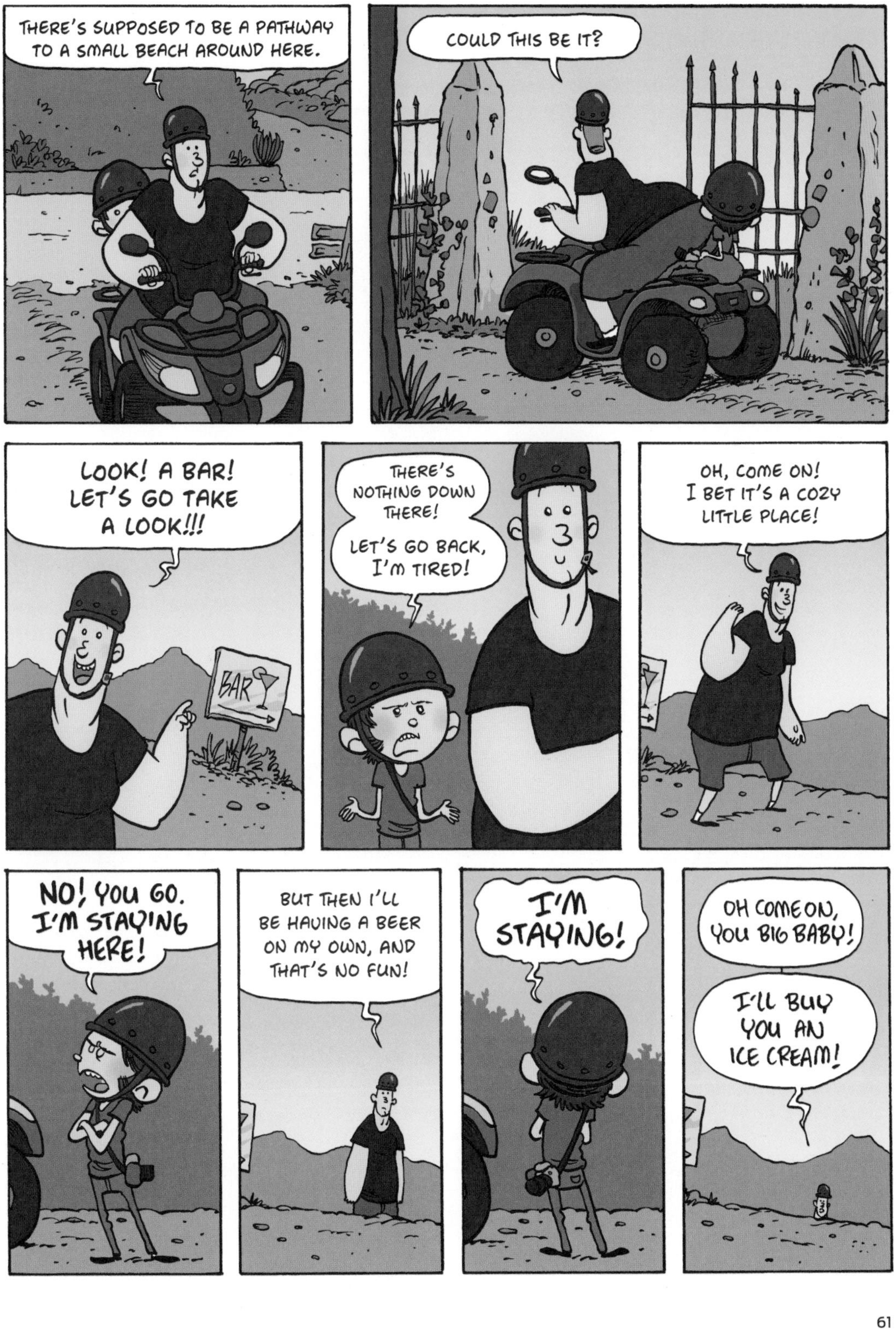
THERE'S SUPPOSED TO BE A PATHWAY TO A SMALL BEACH AROUND HERE.
COULD THIS BE IT?
LOOK! A BAR! LET'S GO TAKE A LOOK!!!
BAR
THERE'S NOTHING DOWN THERE!
LET'S GO BACK, I'M TIRED!
OH, COME ON! I BET IT'S A COZY LITTLE PLACE!
NO! YOU GO. I'M STAYING HERE!
BUT THEN I'LL BE HAVING A BEER ON MY OWN, AND THAT'S NO FUN!
I'M STAYING!
OH COME ON, YOU BIG BABY!
I'LL BUY YOU AN ICE CREAM!

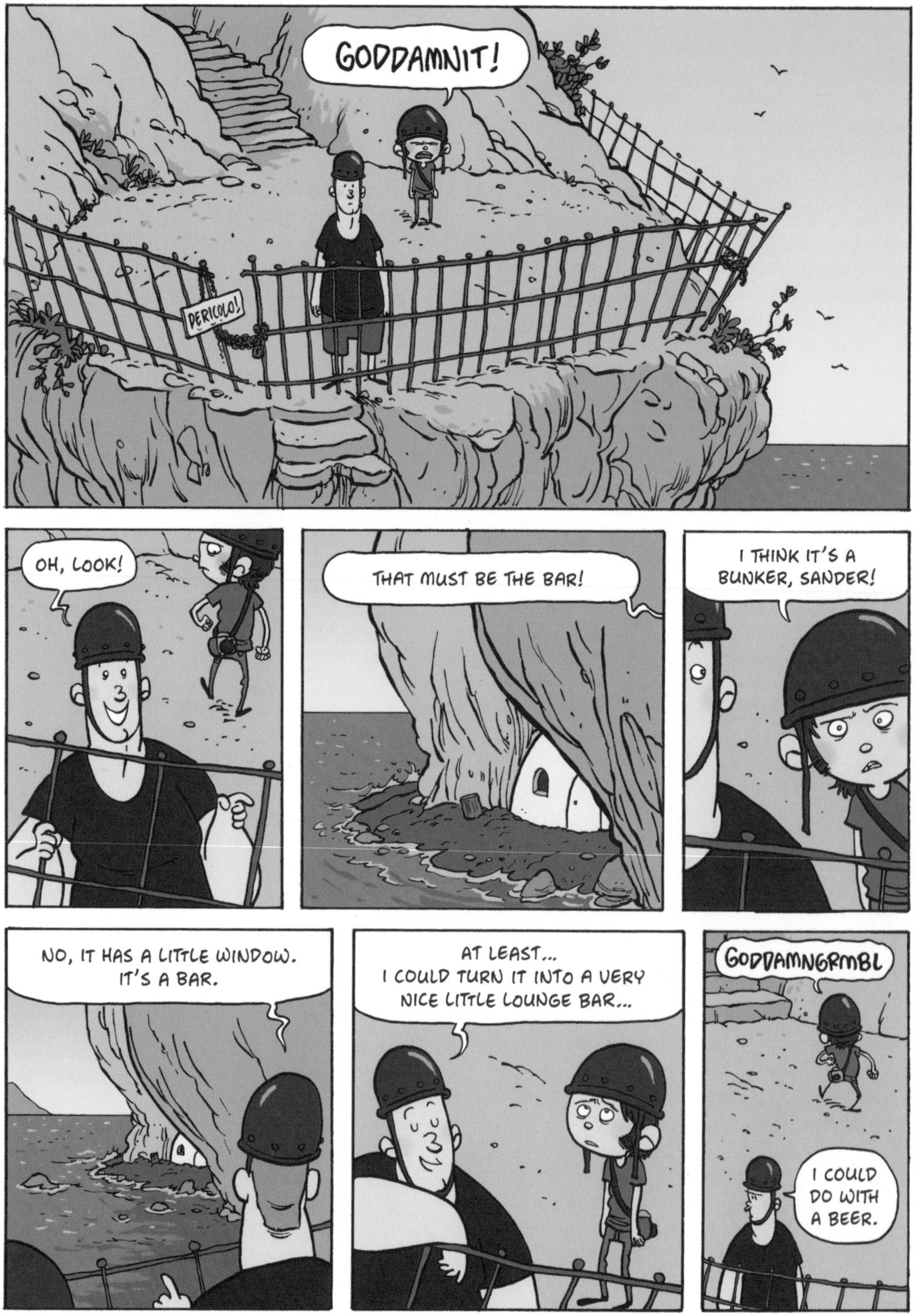
GODDAMNIT!
PERICOLO!
OH, LOOK!
THAT MUST BE THE BAR!
I THINK IT'S A BUNKER, SANDER!
NO, IT HAS A LITTLE WINDOW. IT'S A BAR.
AT LEAST... I COULD TURN IT INTO A VERY NICE LITTLE LOUNGE BAR...
GODDAMNGRMBL
I COULD DO WITH A BEER.

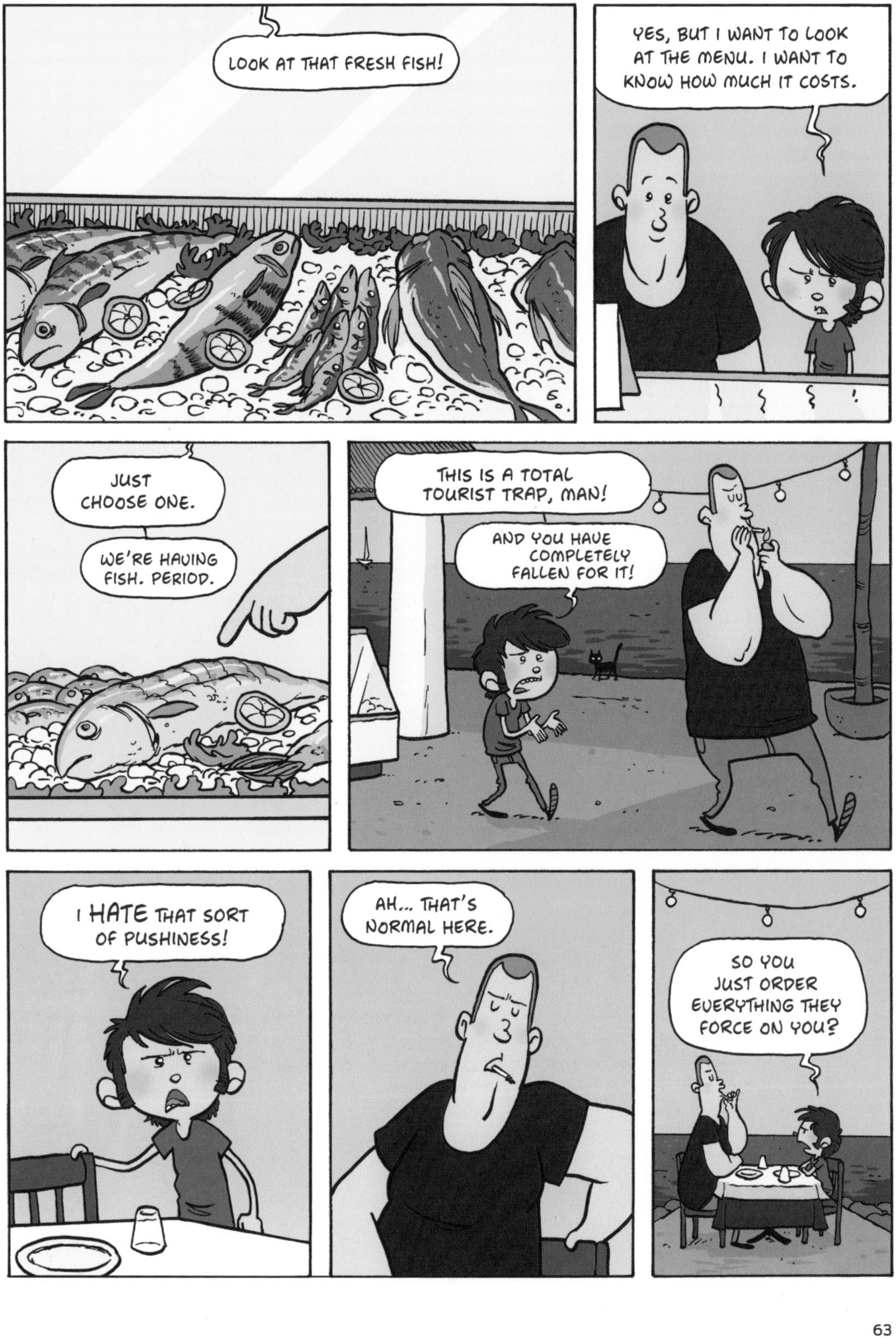
LOOK AT THAT FRESH FISH!
YES, BUT I WANT TO LOOK AT THE MENU. I WANT TO KNOW HOW MUCH IT COSTS.
JUST CHOOSE ONE.
WE'RE HAVING FISH. PERIOD.
THIS IS A TOTAL TOURIST TRAP, MAN!
AND YOU HAVE COMPLETELY FALLEN FOR IT!
I HATE THAT SORT OF PUSHINESS!
AH... THAT'S NORMAL HERE.
SO YOU JUST ORDER EVERYTHING THEY FORCE ON YOU?

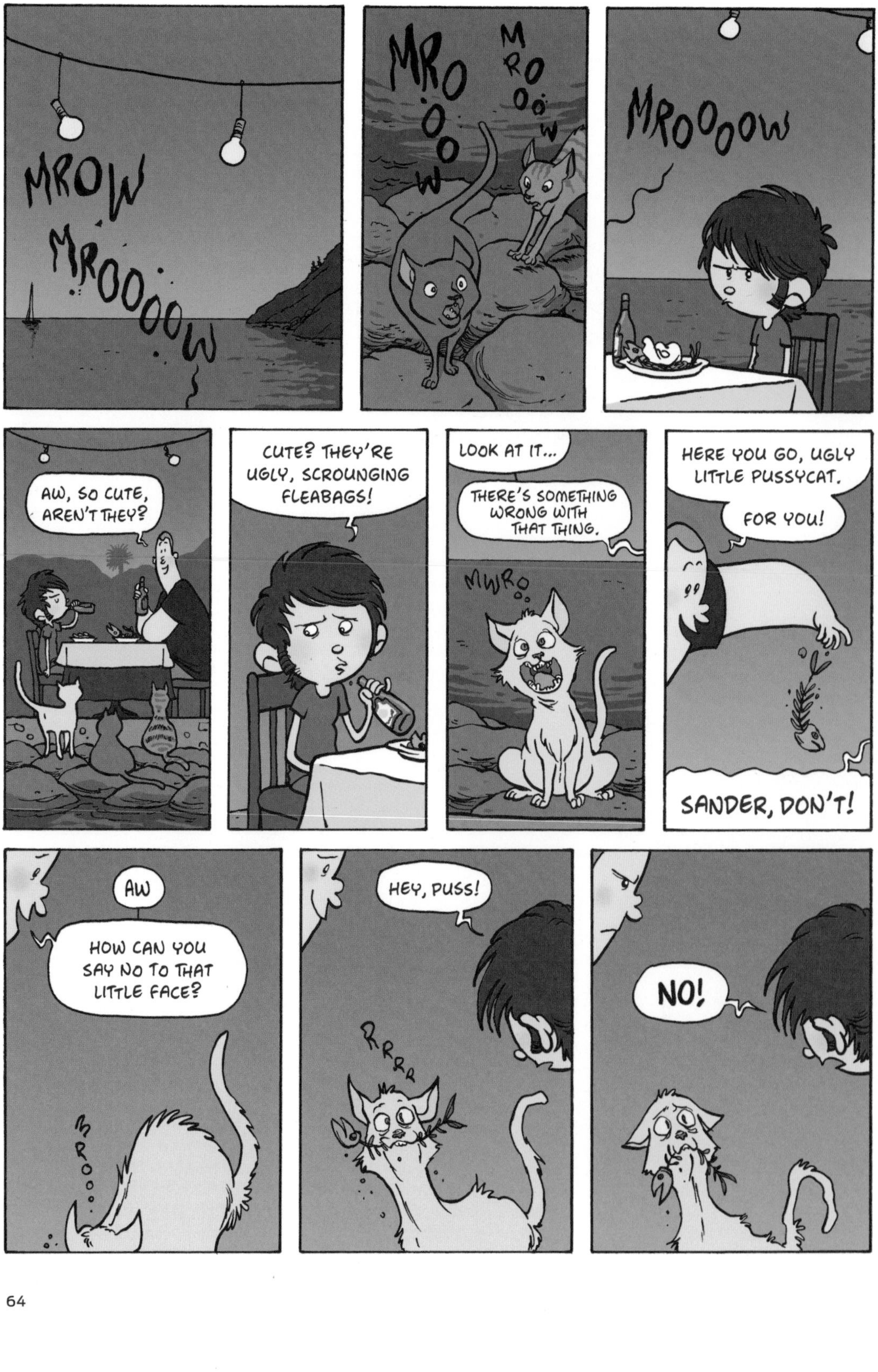
MROW
MROOOOW
MRO
OOW
MROOOW
MROOOOW
AW, SO CUTE, AREN'T THEY?
CUTE? THEY'RE UGLY, SCROUNGING FLEABAGS!
LOOK AT IT...
THERE'S SOMETHING WRONG WITH THAT THING.
MWRO
HERE YOU GO, UGLY LITTLE PUSSYCAT.
FOR YOU!
SANDER, DON'T!
AW
HOW CAN YOU SAY NO TO THAT LITTLE FACE?
MROOO
HEY, PUSS!
RRRR
NO!

BWOooo
BWOA
DAMN FISH.
SNGG
COUGH
COUGH
SNIFF
COUGH
TOOEE
GRROOOOOOEEEE

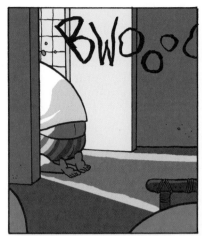

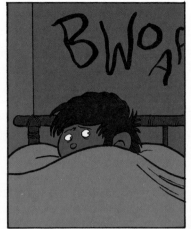

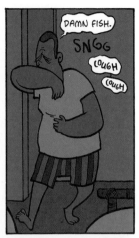

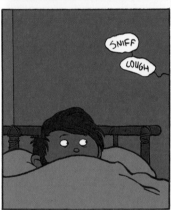

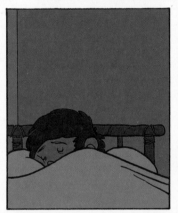

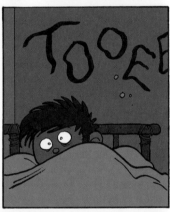

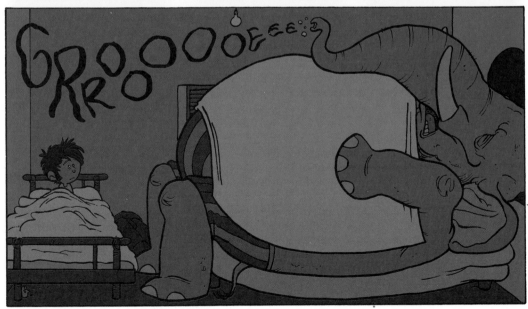

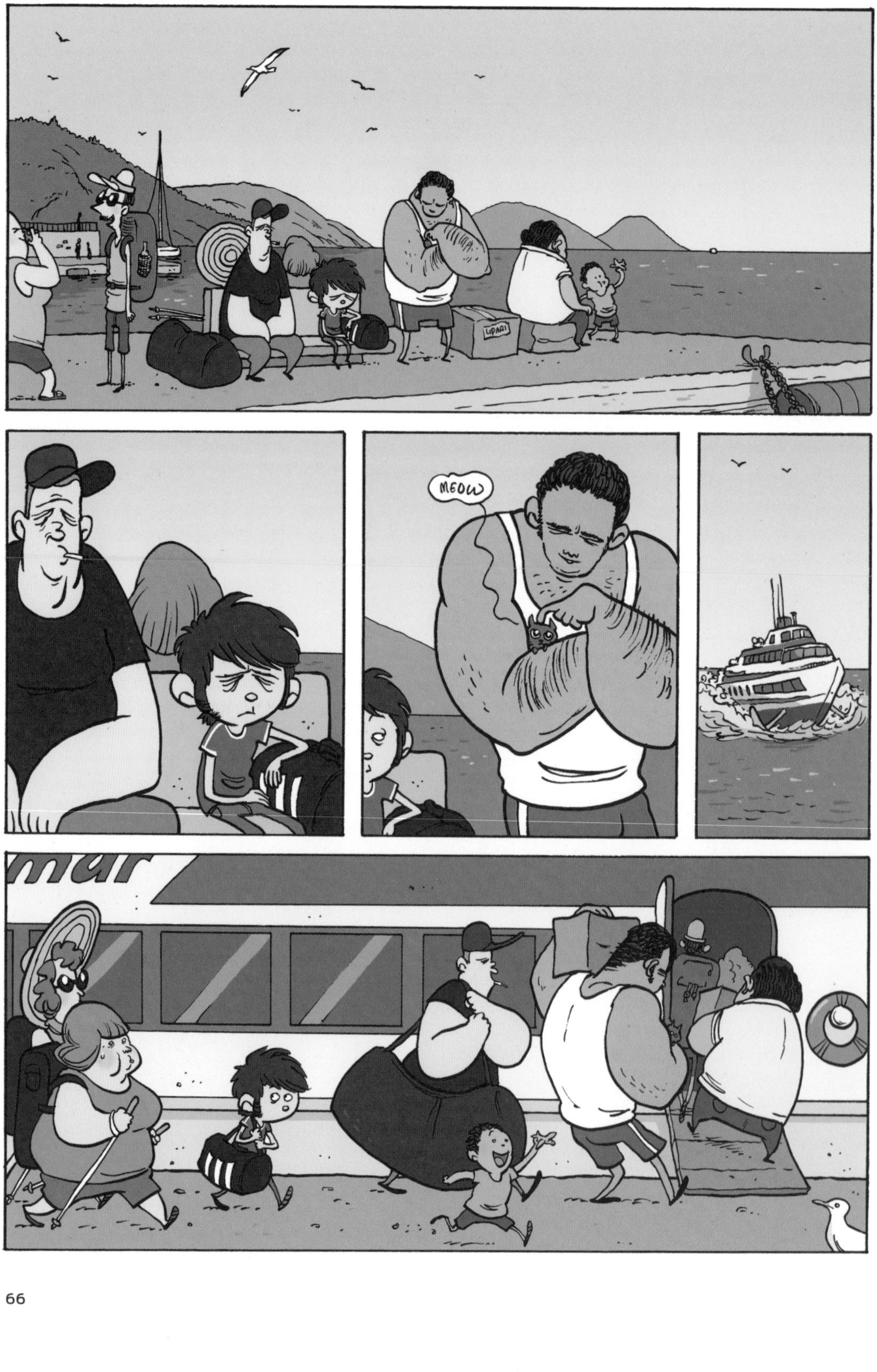
LIPARI
MEOW

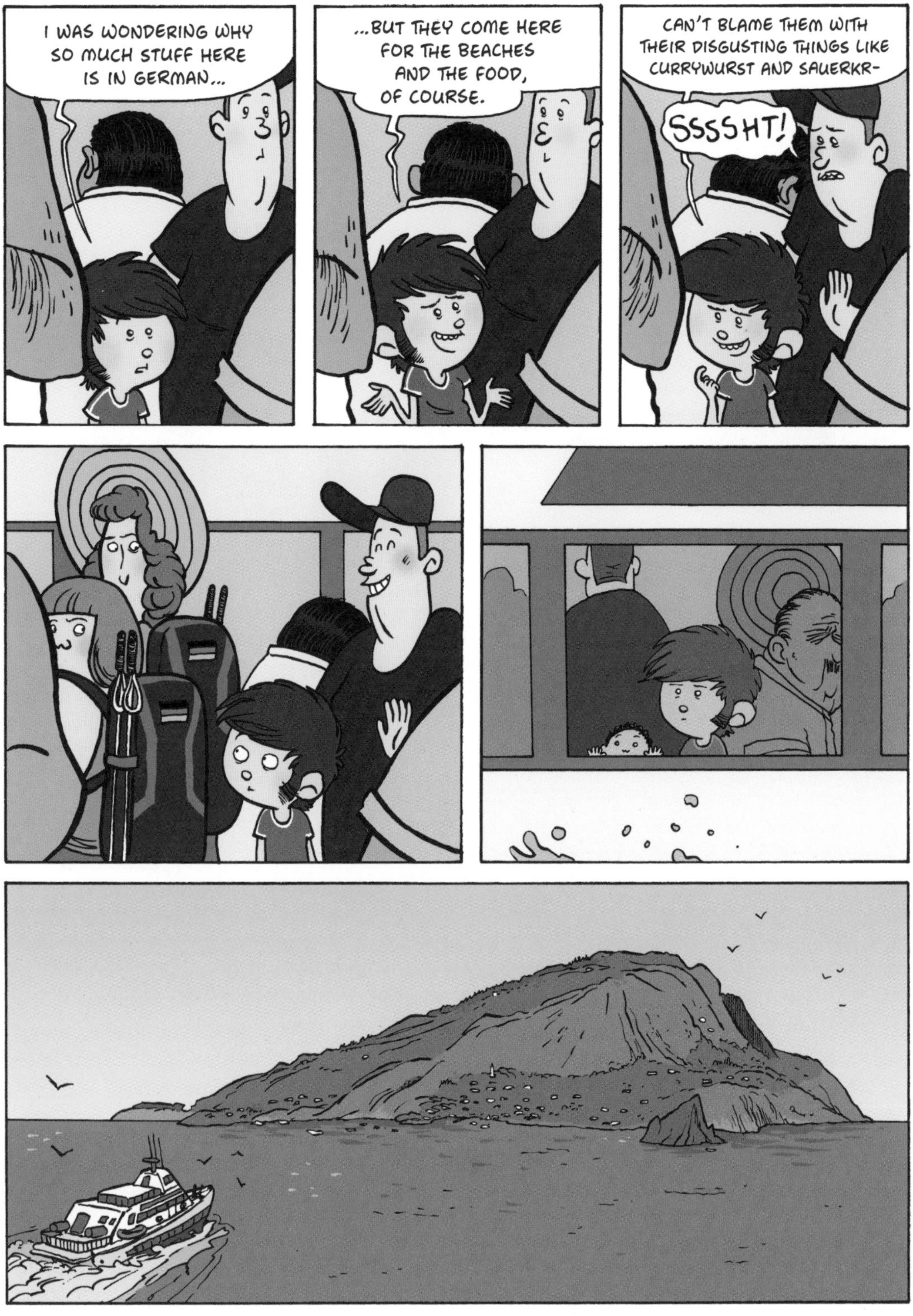

I WAS WONDERING WHY SO MUCH STUFF HERE IS IN GERMAN...
...BUT THEY COME HERE FOR THE BEACHES AND THE FOOD, OF COURSE.
CAN'T BLAME THEM WITH THEIR DISGUSTING THINGS LIKE CURRYWURST AND SAUERKR-
SSSSHT!

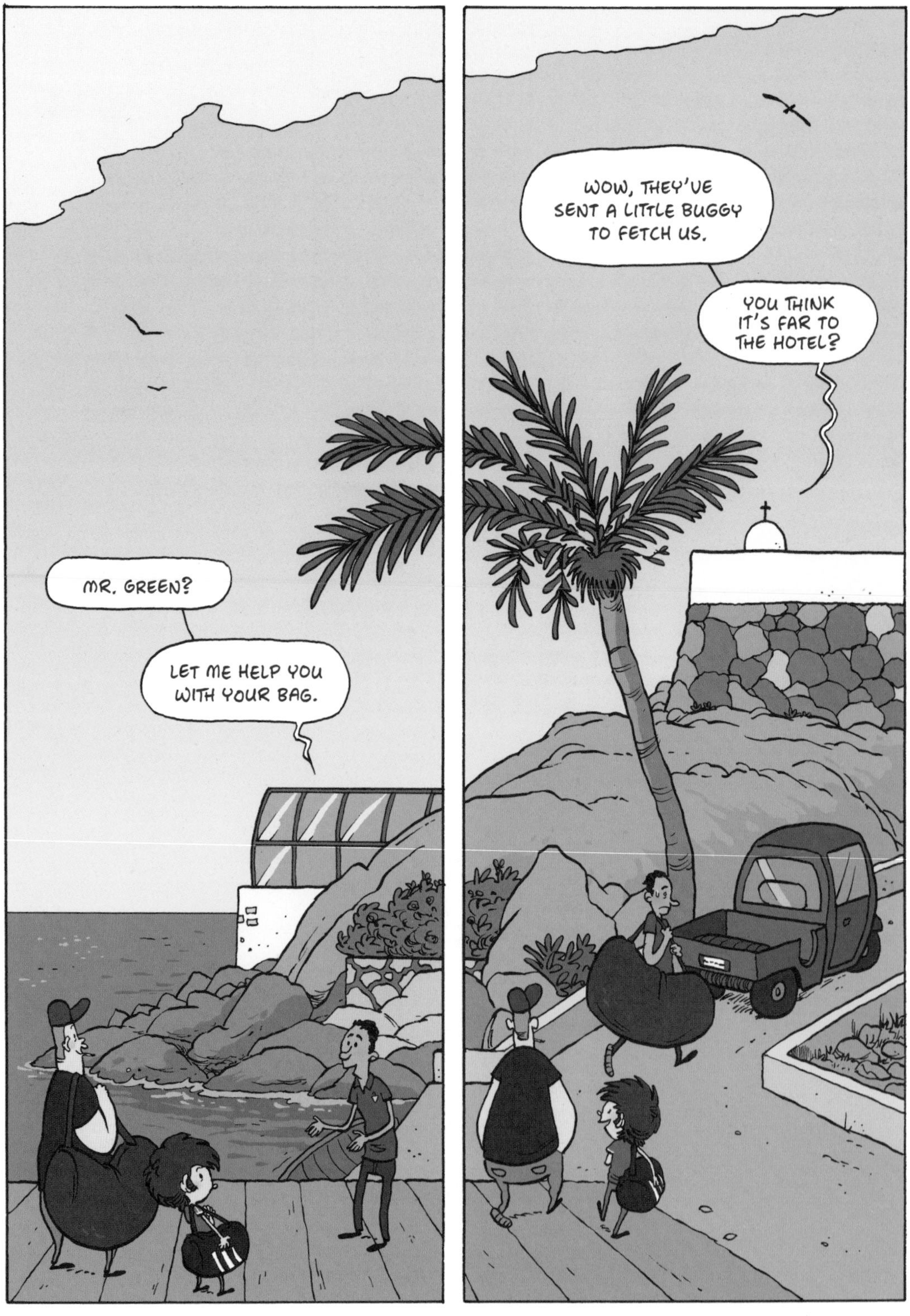
MR. GREEN?
LET ME HELP YOU WITH YOUR BAG.
WOW, THEY'VE SENT A LITTLE BUGGY TO FETCH US.
YOU THINK IT'S FAR TO THE HOTEL?

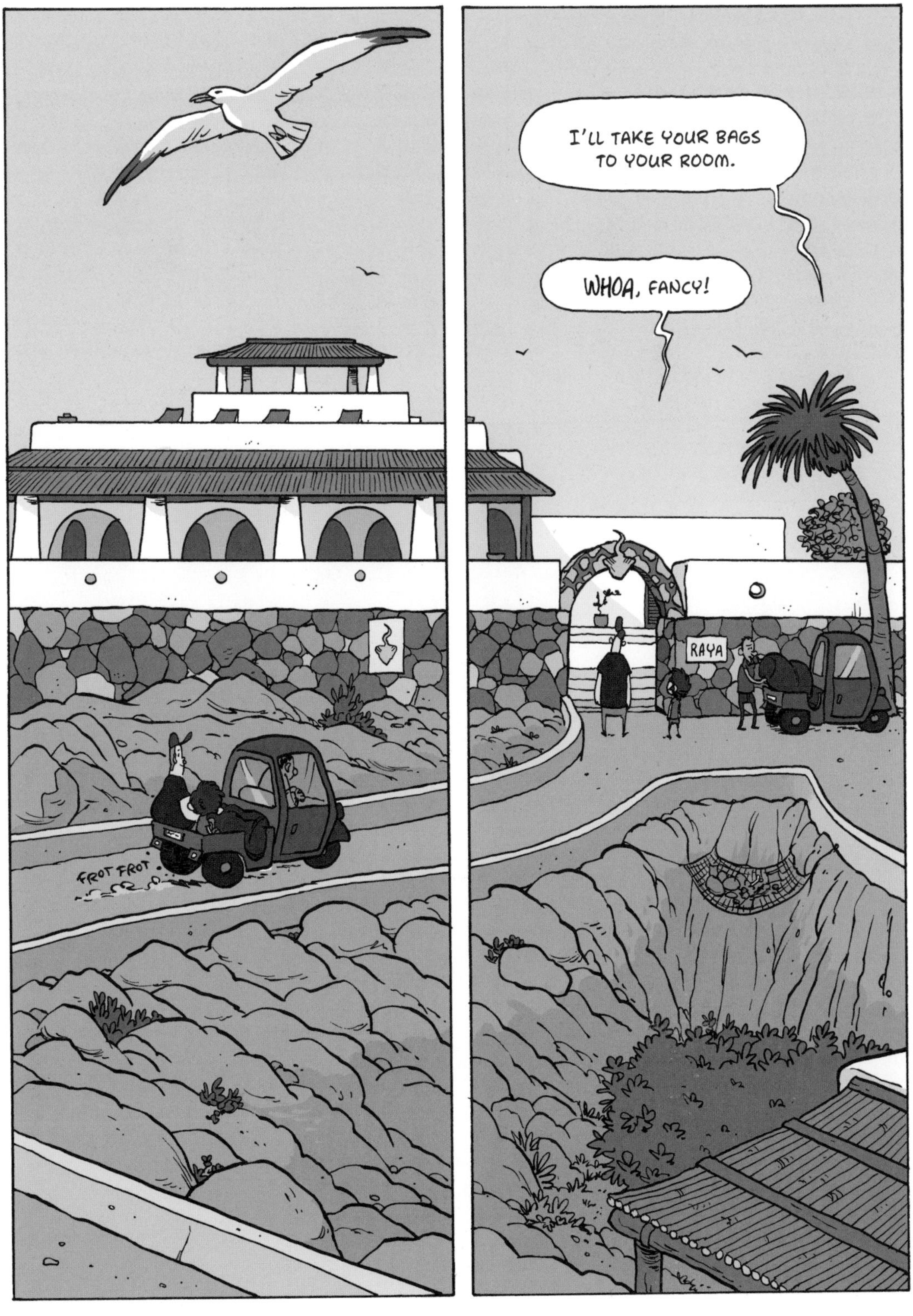
RAYA
FROT FROT
I'LL TAKE YOUR BAGS TO YOUR ROOM.
WHOA, FANCY!

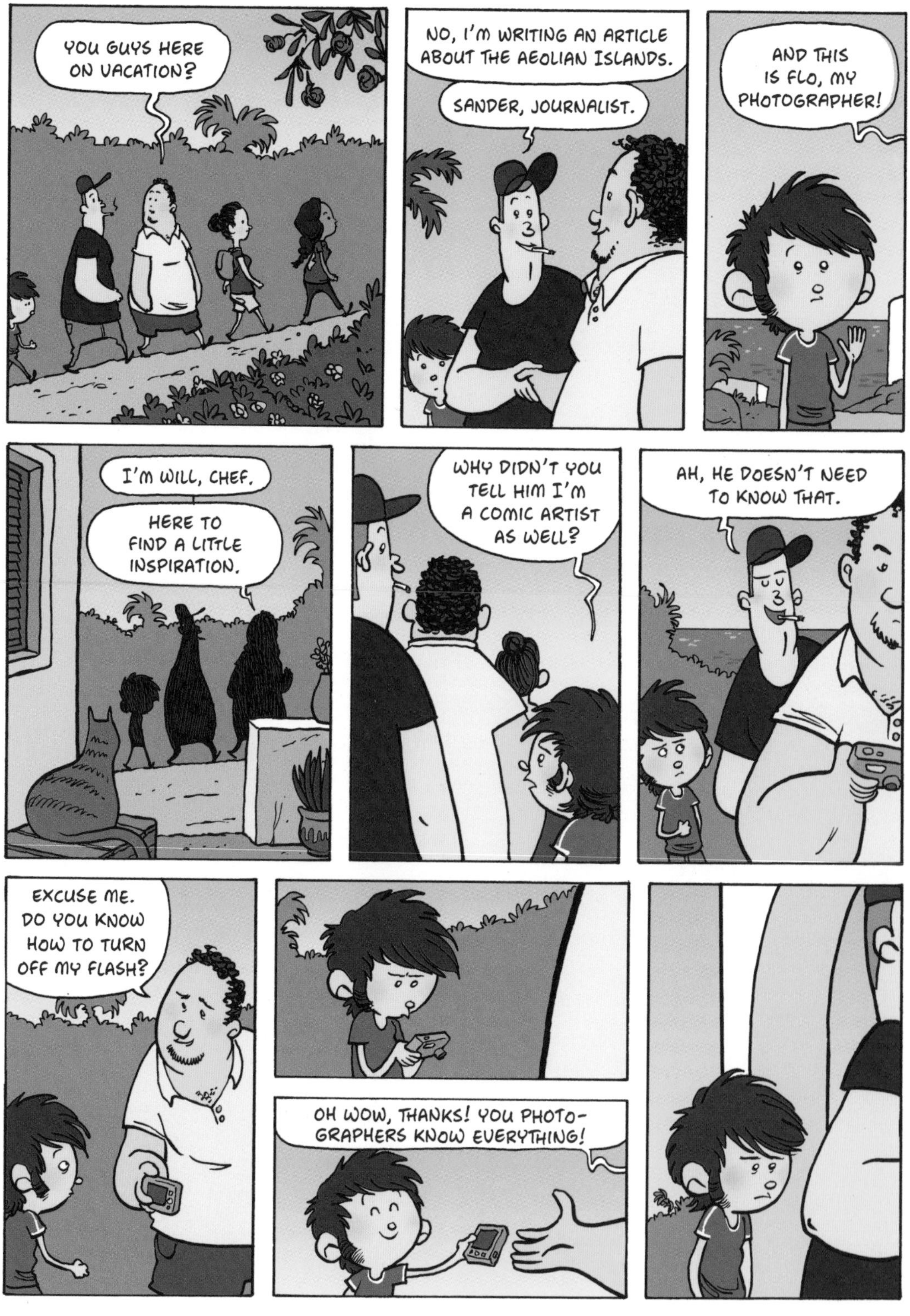
YOU GUYS HERE ON VACATION?
NO, I'M WRITING AN ARTICLE ABOUT THE AEOLIAN ISLANDS.
SANDER, JOURNALIST.
AND THIS IS FLO, MY PHOTOGRAPHER!
I'M WILL, CHEF.
HERE TO FIND A LITTLE INSPIRATION.
WHY DIDN'T YOU TELL HIM I'M A COMIC ARTIST AS WELL?
AH, HE DOESN'T NEED TO KNOW THAT.
EXCUSE ME. DO YOU KNOW HOW TO TURN OFF MY FLASH?
OH WOW, THANKS! YOU PHOTOGRAPHERS KNOW EVERYTHING!

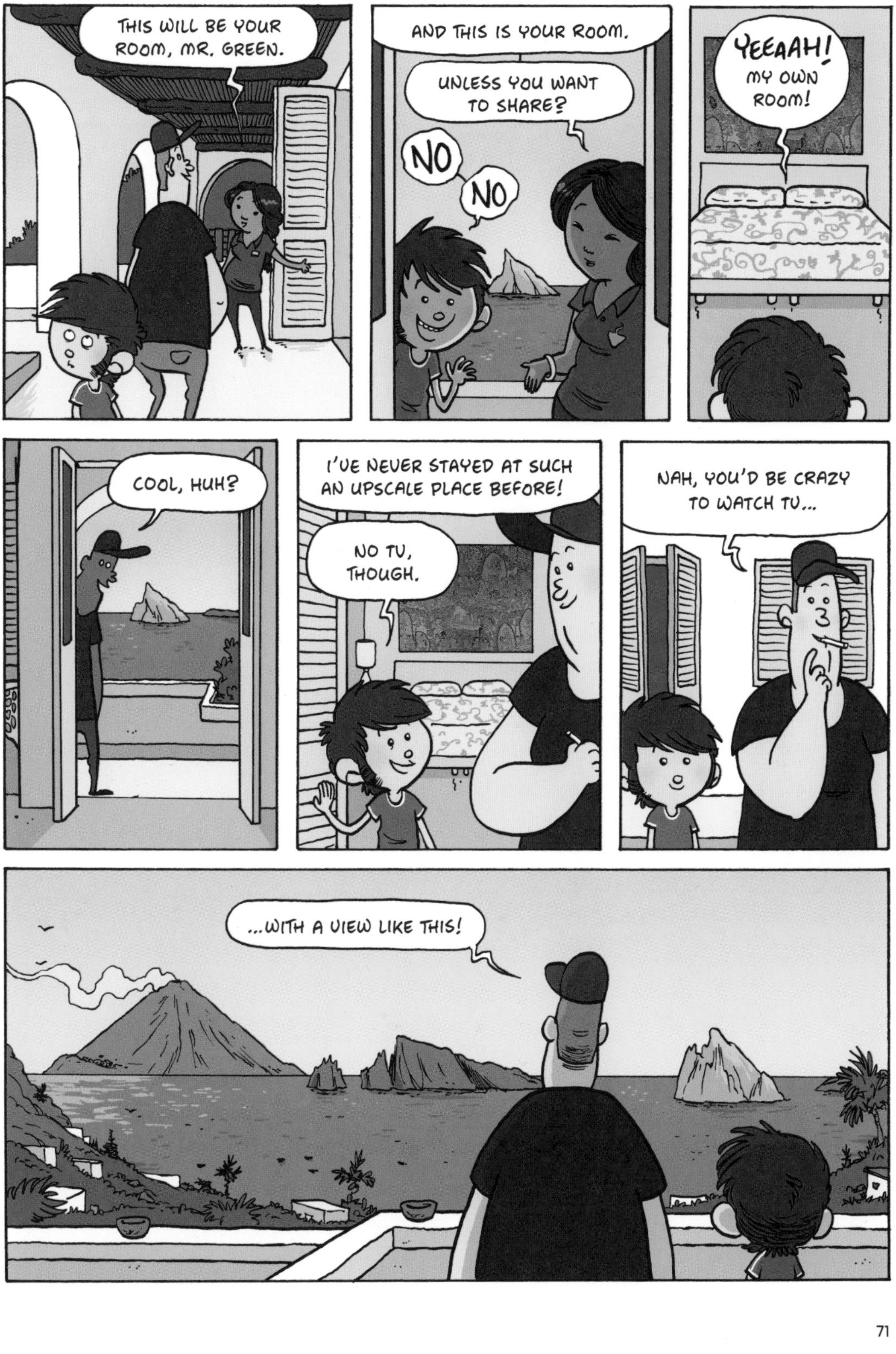
THIS WILL BE YOUR ROOM, MR. GREEN.
AND THIS IS YOUR ROOM.
UNLESS YOU WANT TO SHARE?
NO
NO
YEEAAH! MY OWN ROOM!
COOL, HUH?
I'VE NEVER STAYED AT SUCH AN UPSCALE PLACE BEFORE!
NO TV, THOUGH.
NAH, YOU'D BE CRAZY TO WATCH TV...
...WITH A VIEW LIKE THIS!

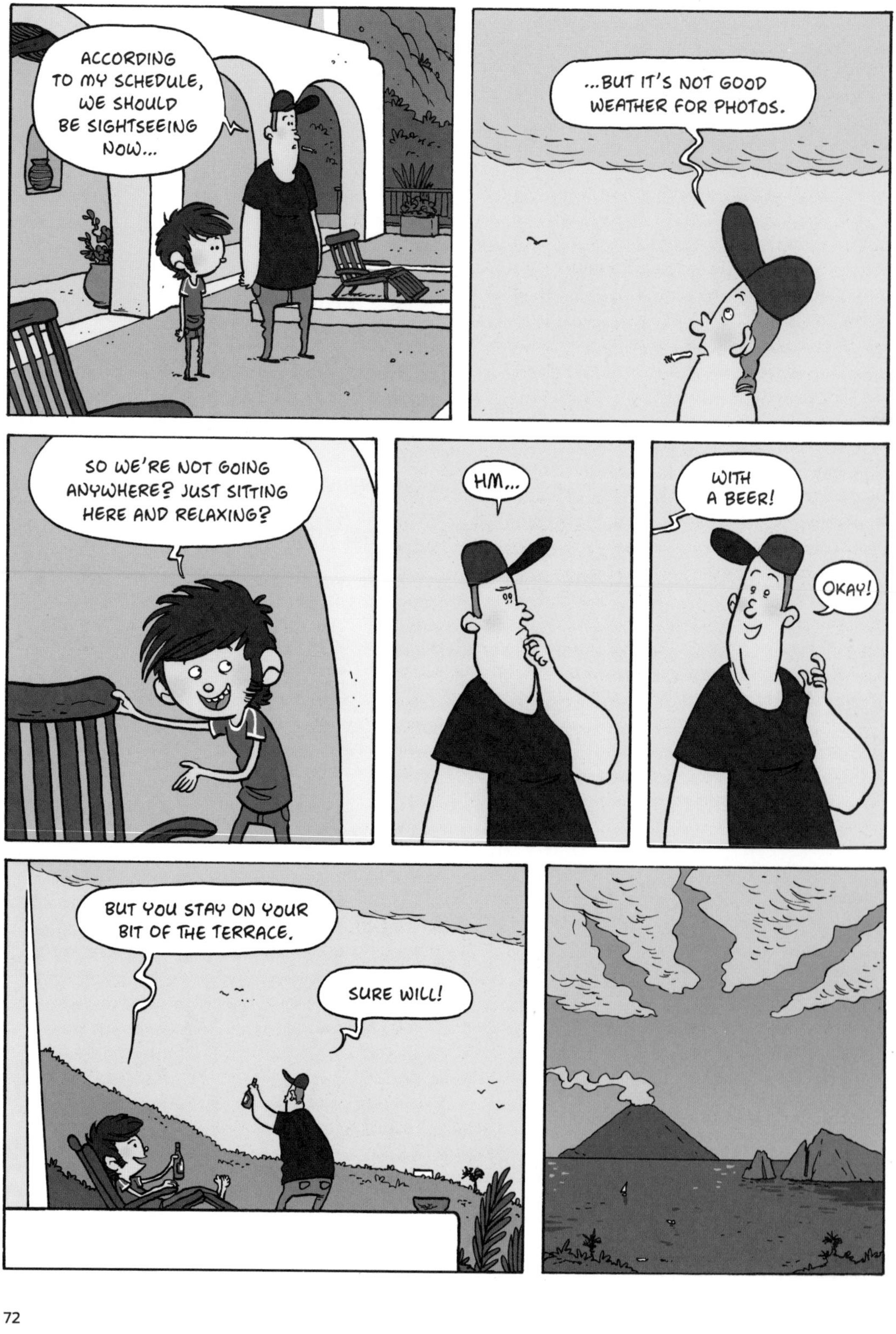
ACCORDING TO MY SCHEDULE, WE SHOULD BE SIGHTSEEING NOW...
...BUT IT'S NOT GOOD WEATHER FOR PHOTOS.
SO WE'RE NOT GOING ANYWHERE? JUST SITTING HERE AND RELAXING?
HM...
WITH A BEER!
OKAY!
BUT YOU STAY ON YOUR BIT OF THE TERRACE.
SURE WILL!

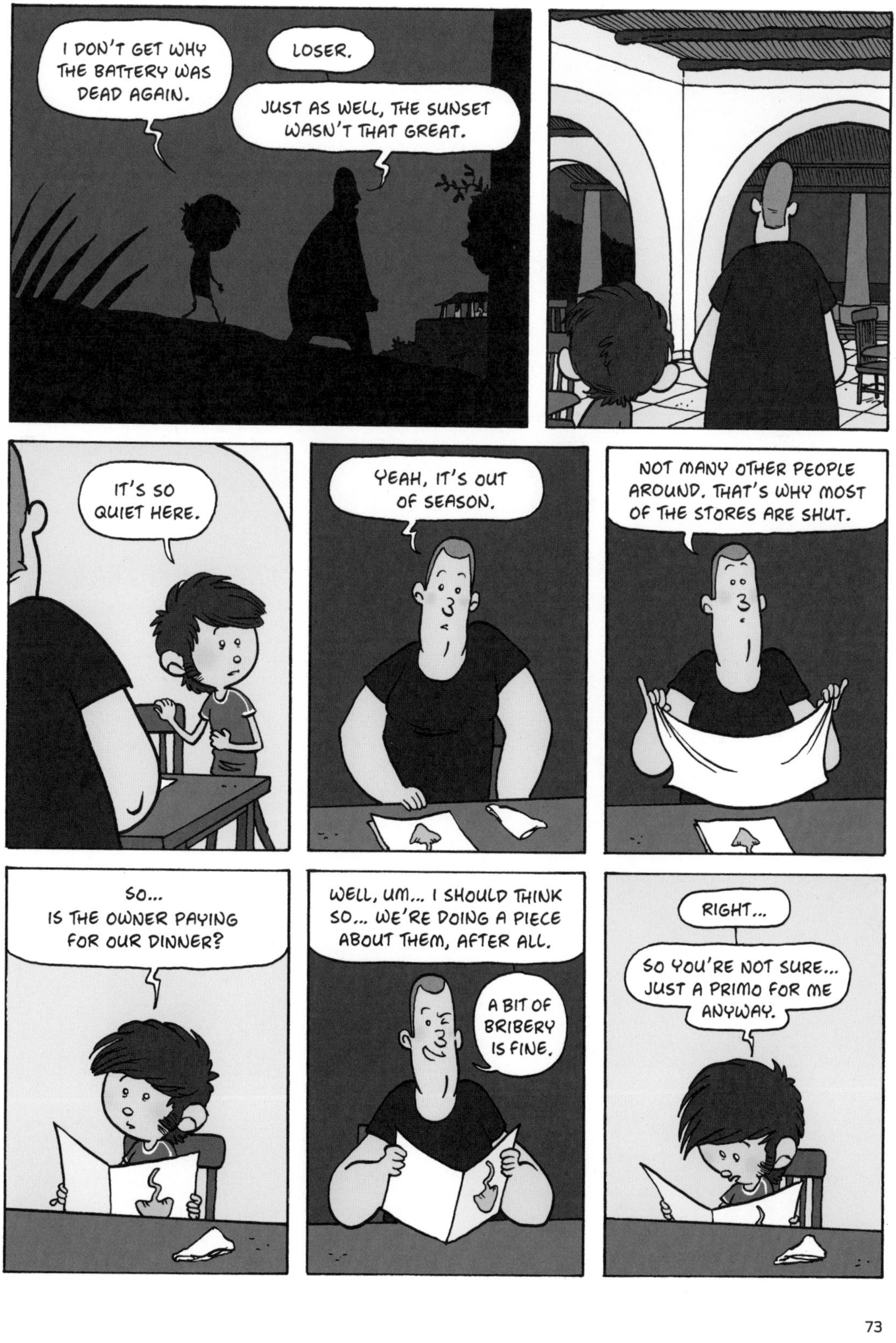
I DON'T GET WHY THE BATTERY WAS DEAD AGAIN.
LOSER.
JUST AS WELL, THE SUNSET WASN'T THAT GREAT.
IT'S SO QUIET HERE.
YEAH, IT'S OUT OF SEASON.
NOT MANY OTHER PEOPLE AROUND. THAT'S WHY MOST OF THE STORES ARE SHUT.
SO... IS THE OWNER PAYING FOR OUR DINNER?
WELL, UM... I SHOULD THINK SO... WE'RE DOING A PIECE ABOUT THEM, AFTER ALL.
A BIT OF BRIBERY IS FINE.
RIGHT...
SO YOU'RE NOT SURE... JUST A PRIMO FOR ME ANYWAY.

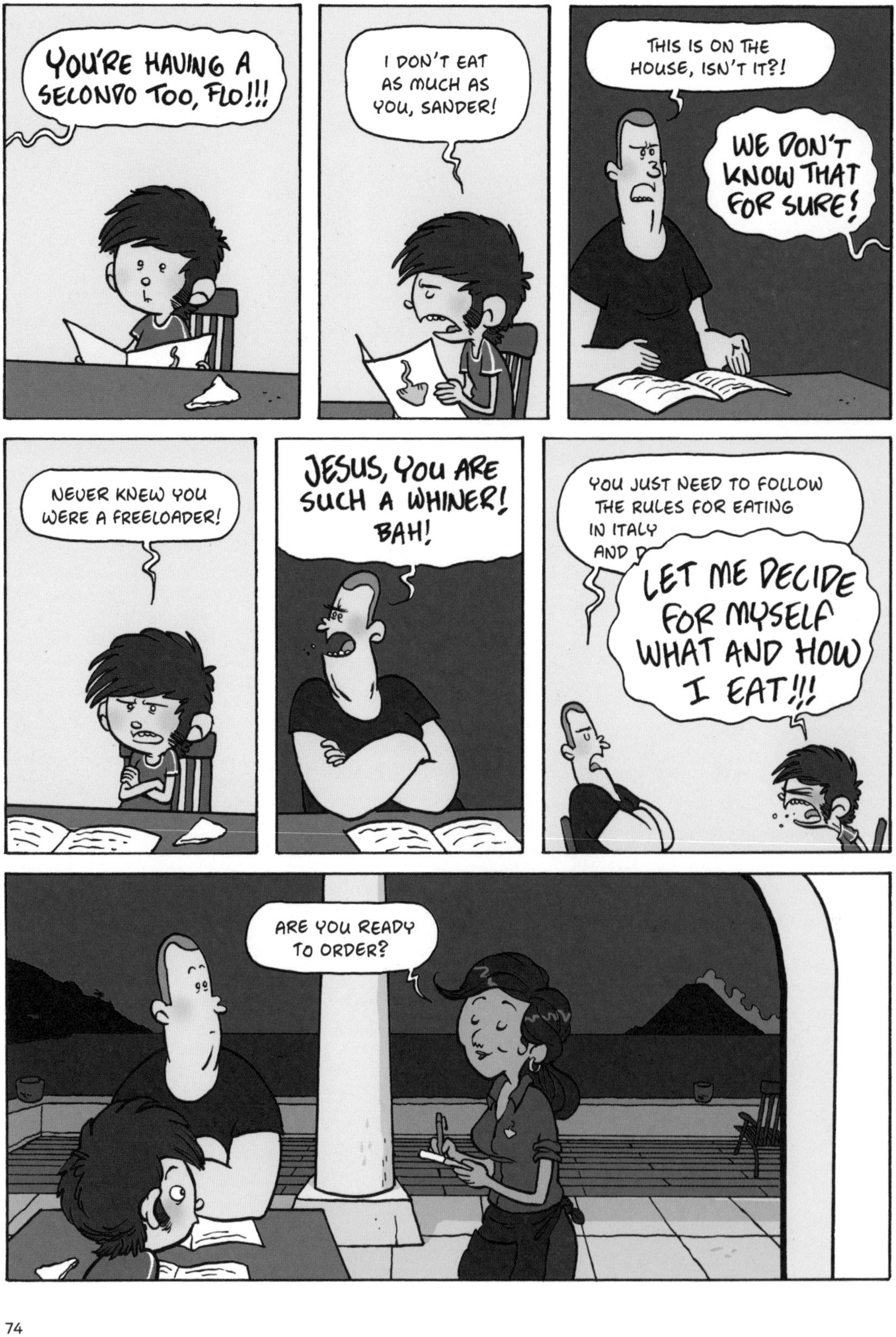
YOU'RE HAVING A SECONDO TOO, FLO!!!
I DON'T EAT AS MUCH AS YOU, SANDER!
THIS IS ON THE HOUSE, ISN'T IT?!
WE DON'T KNOW THAT FOR SURE!
NEVER KNEW YOU WERE A FREELOADER!
JESUS, YOU ARE SUCH A WHINER! BAH!
YOU JUST NEED TO FOLLOW THE RULES FOR EATING IN ITALY AND D
LET ME DECIDE FOR MYSELF WHAT AND HOW I EAT!!!
ARE YOU READY TO ORDER?

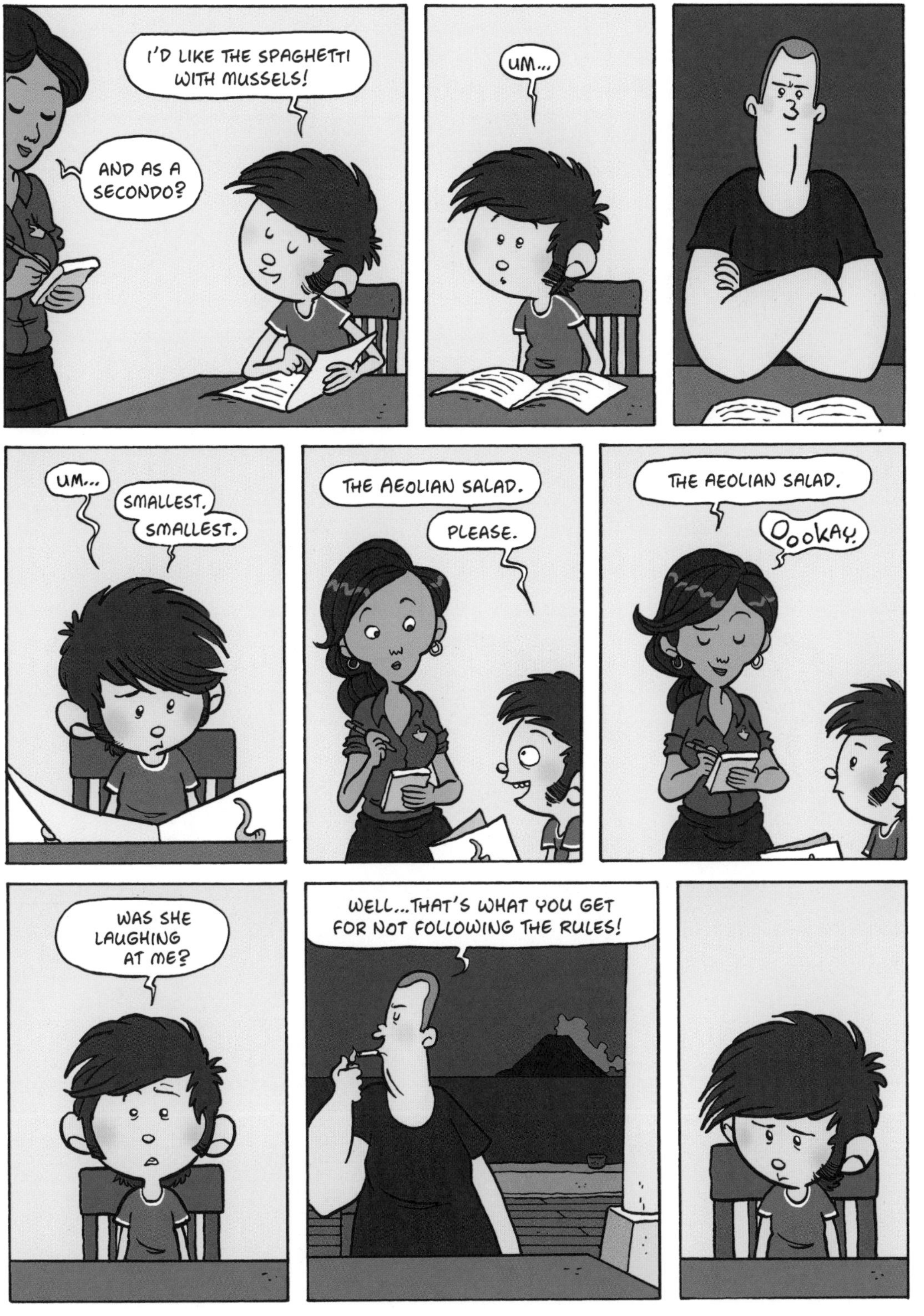
I'D LIKE THE SPAGHETTI WITH MUSSELS!
AND AS A SECONDO?
UM...
UM...
SMALLEST. SMALLEST.
THE AEOLIAN SALAD.
PLEASE.
THE AEOLIAN SALAD.
OooKAY.
WAS SHE LAUGHING AT ME?
WELL...THAT'S WHAT YOU GET FOR NOT FOLLOWING THE RULES!

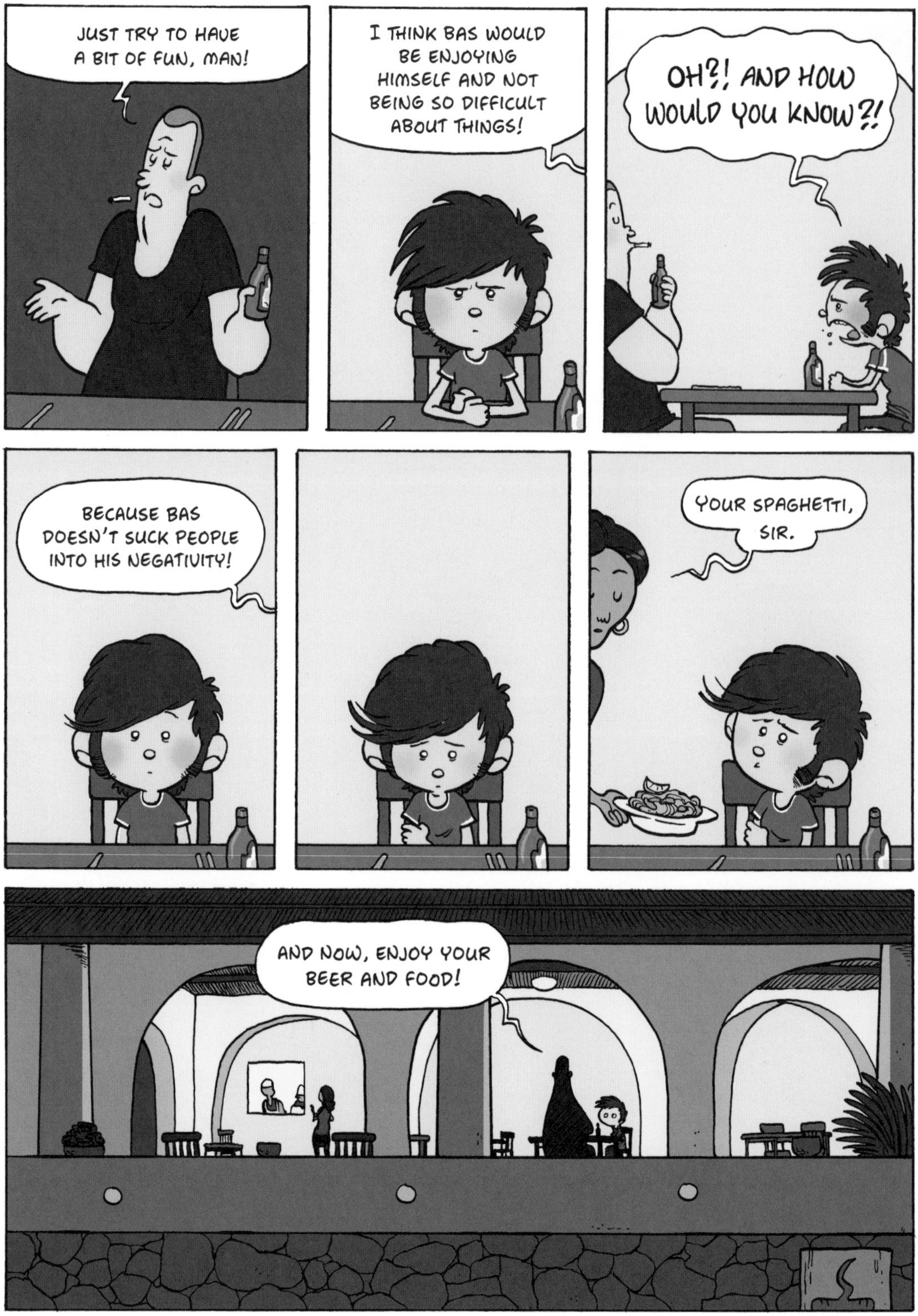
JUST TRY TO HAVE A BIT OF FUN, MAN!
I THINK BAS WOULD BE ENJOYING HIMSELF AND NOT BEING SO DIFFICULT ABOUT THINGS!
OH?! AND HOW WOULD YOU KNOW?!
BECAUSE BAS DOESN'T SUCK PEOPLE INTO HIS NEGATIVITY!
YOUR SPAGHETTI, SIR.
AND NOW, ENJOY YOUR BEER AND FOOD!

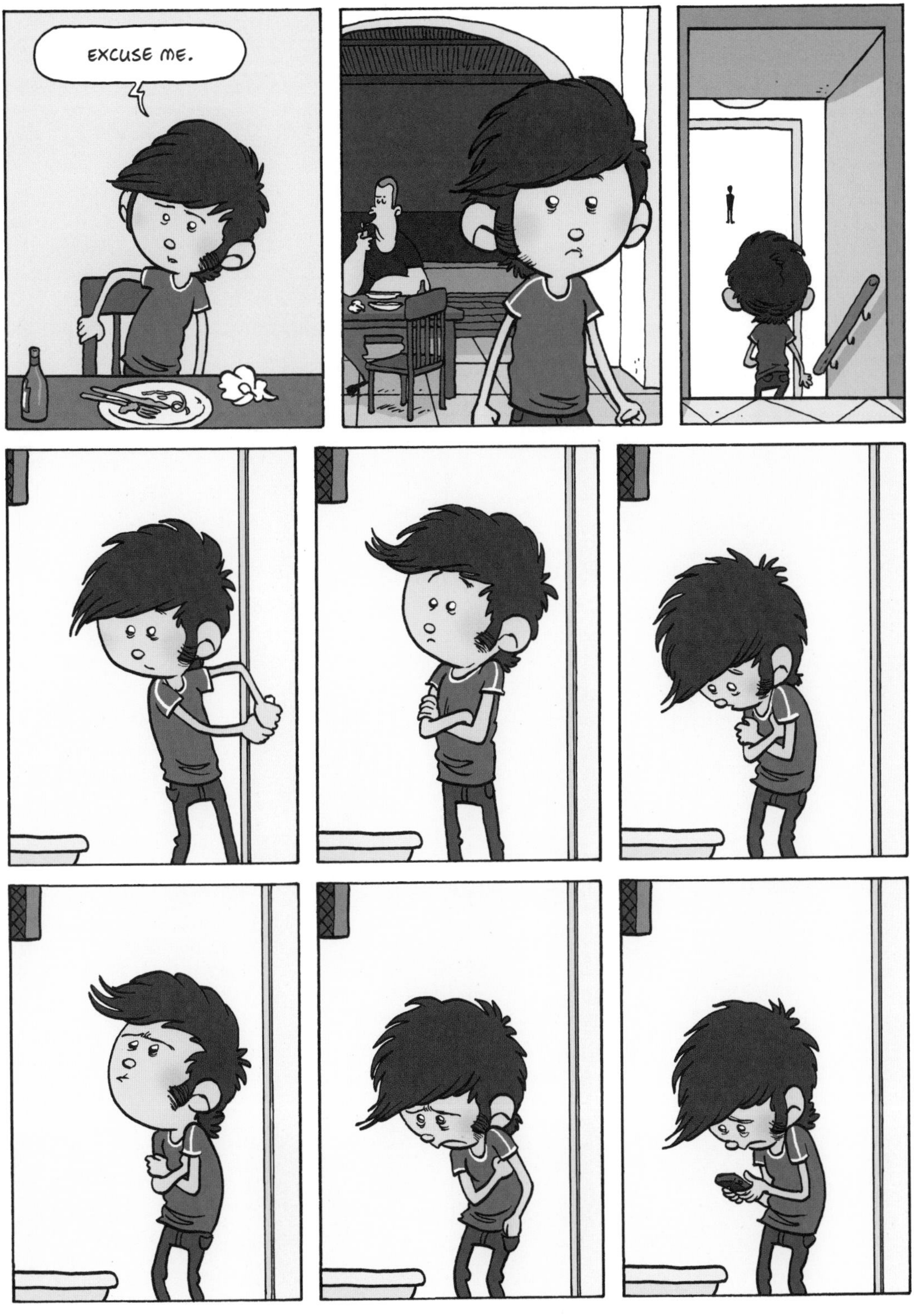
EXCUSE ME.

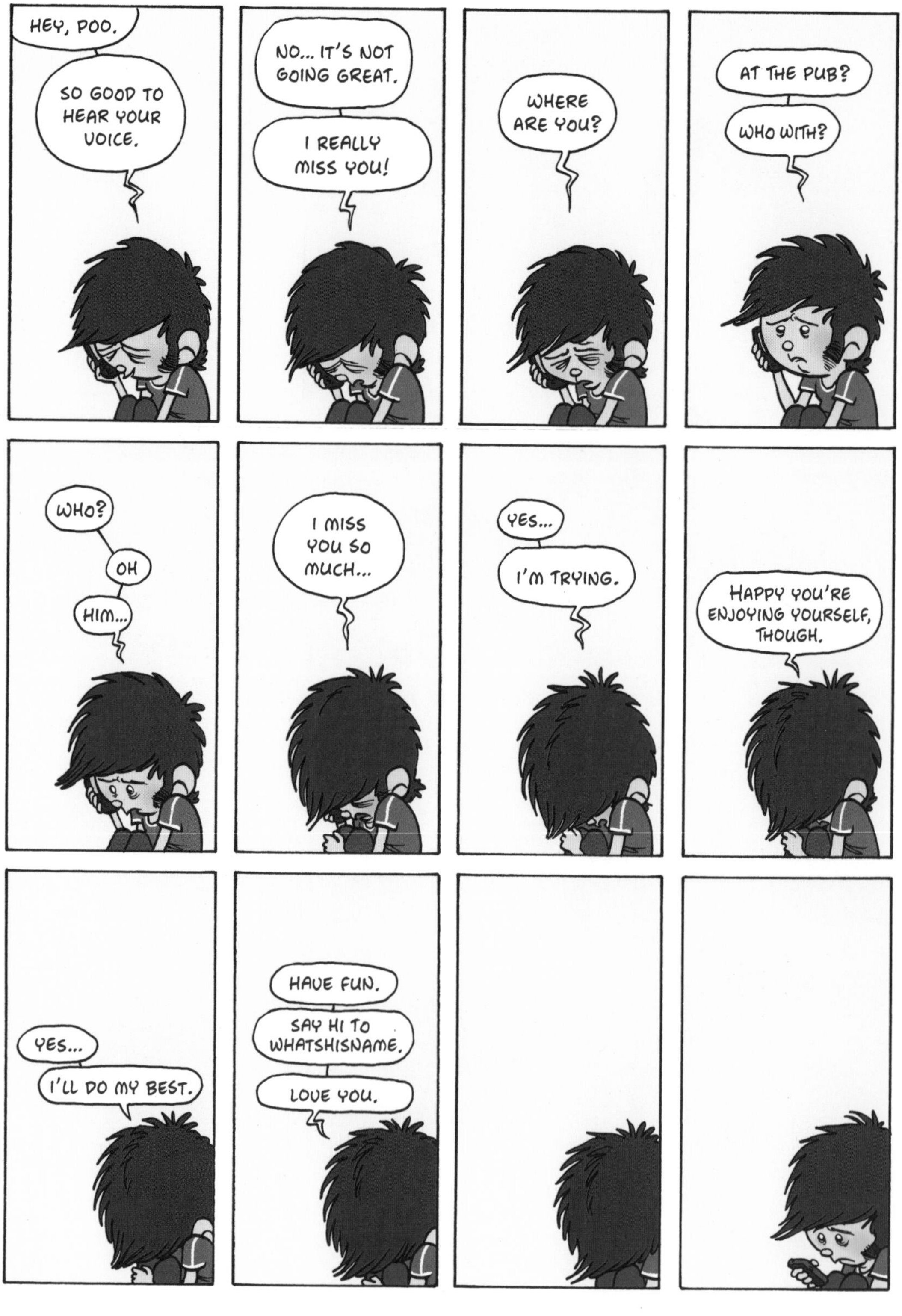
HEY, POO.
SO GOOD TO HEAR YOUR VOICE.
NO... IT'S NOT GOING GREAT.
I REALLY MISS YOU!
WHERE ARE YOU?
AT THE PUB?
WHO WITH?
WHO?
OH
HIM...
I MISS YOU SO MUCH...
YES...
I'M TRYING.
HAPPY YOU'RE ENJOYING YOURSELF, THOUGH.
YES...
I'LL DO MY BEST.
HAVE FUN.
SAY HI TO WHATSHISNAME.
LOVE YOU.

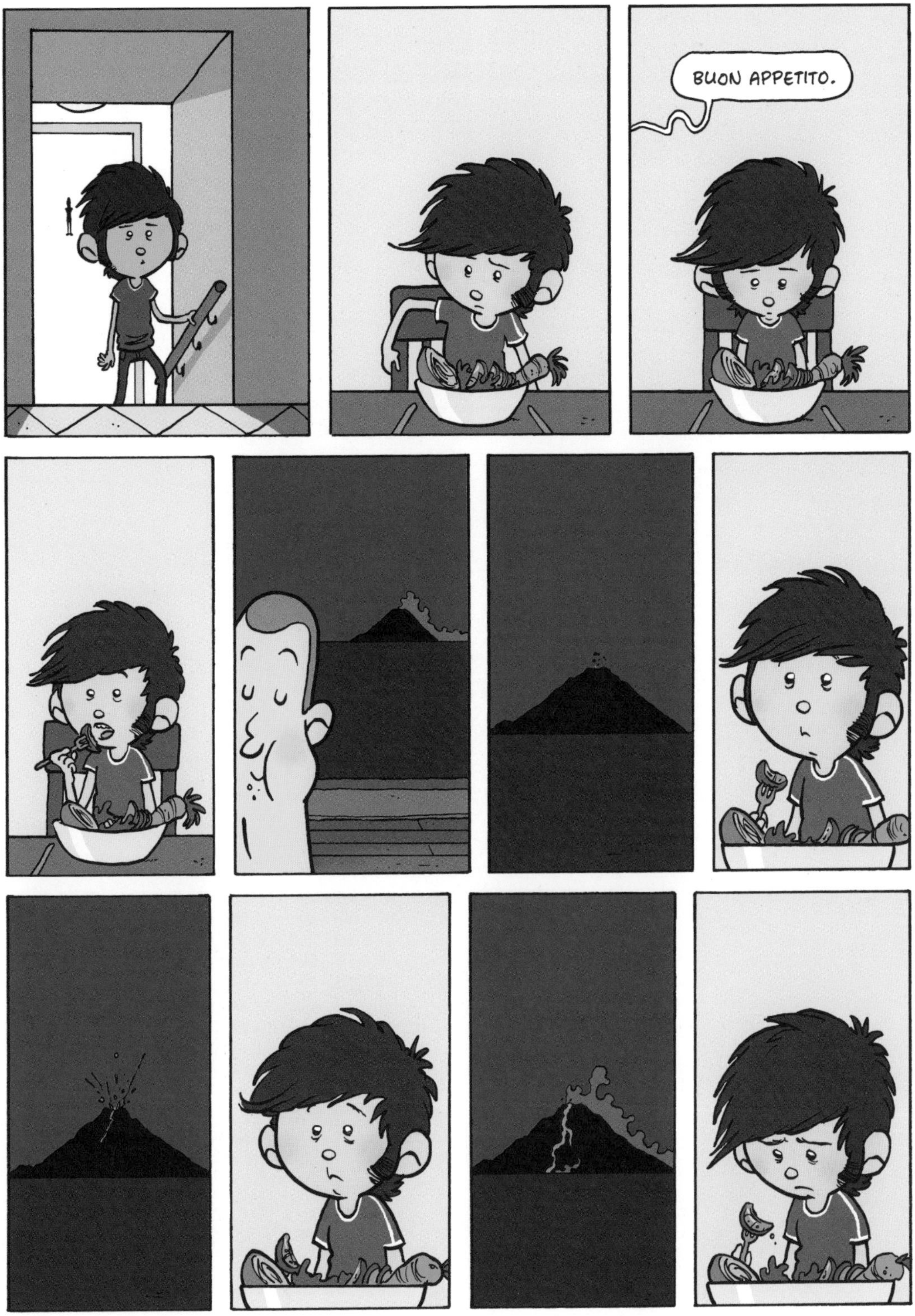
BUON APPETITO.

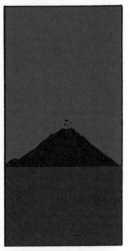

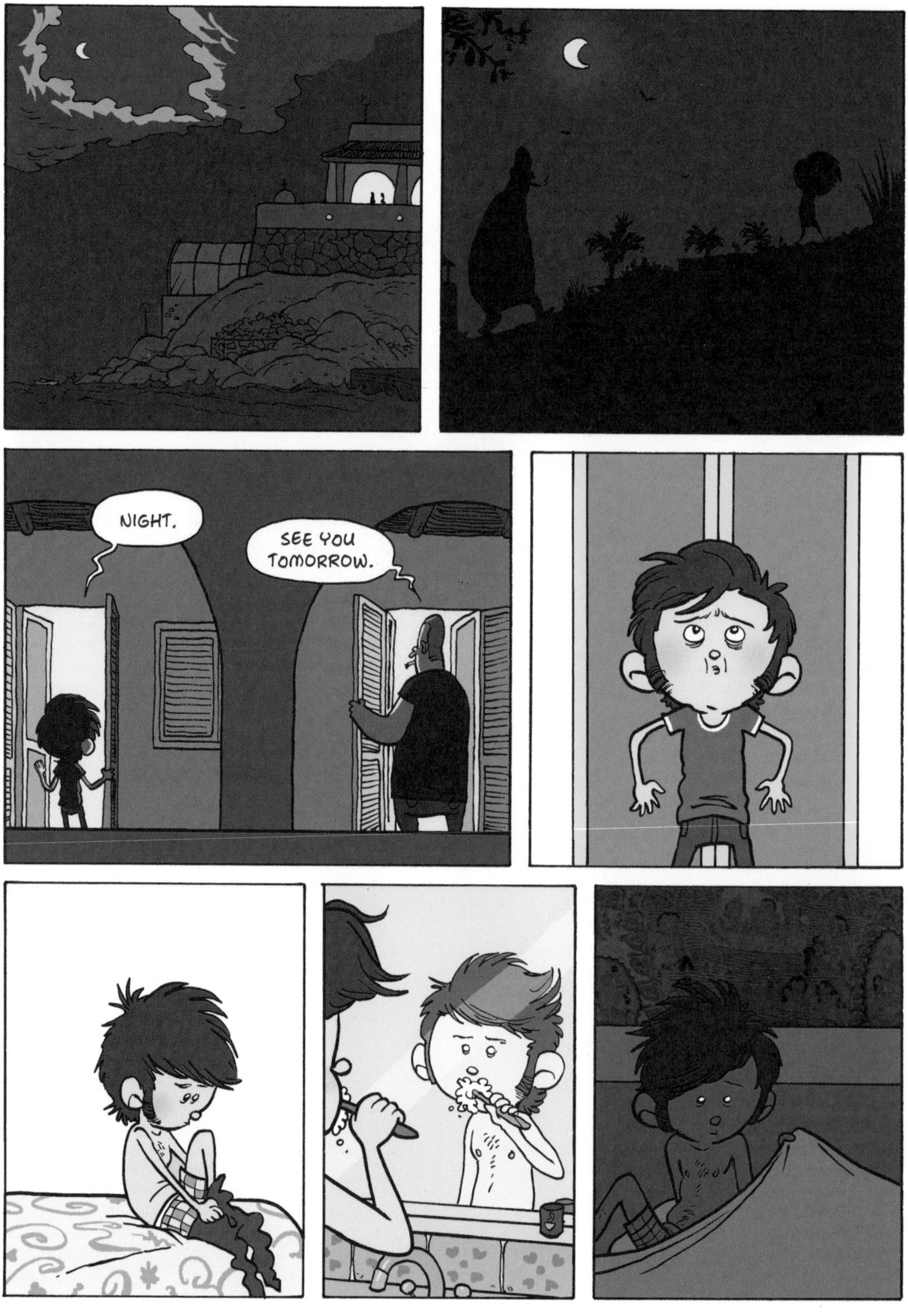
NIGHT.
SEE YOU TOMORROW.

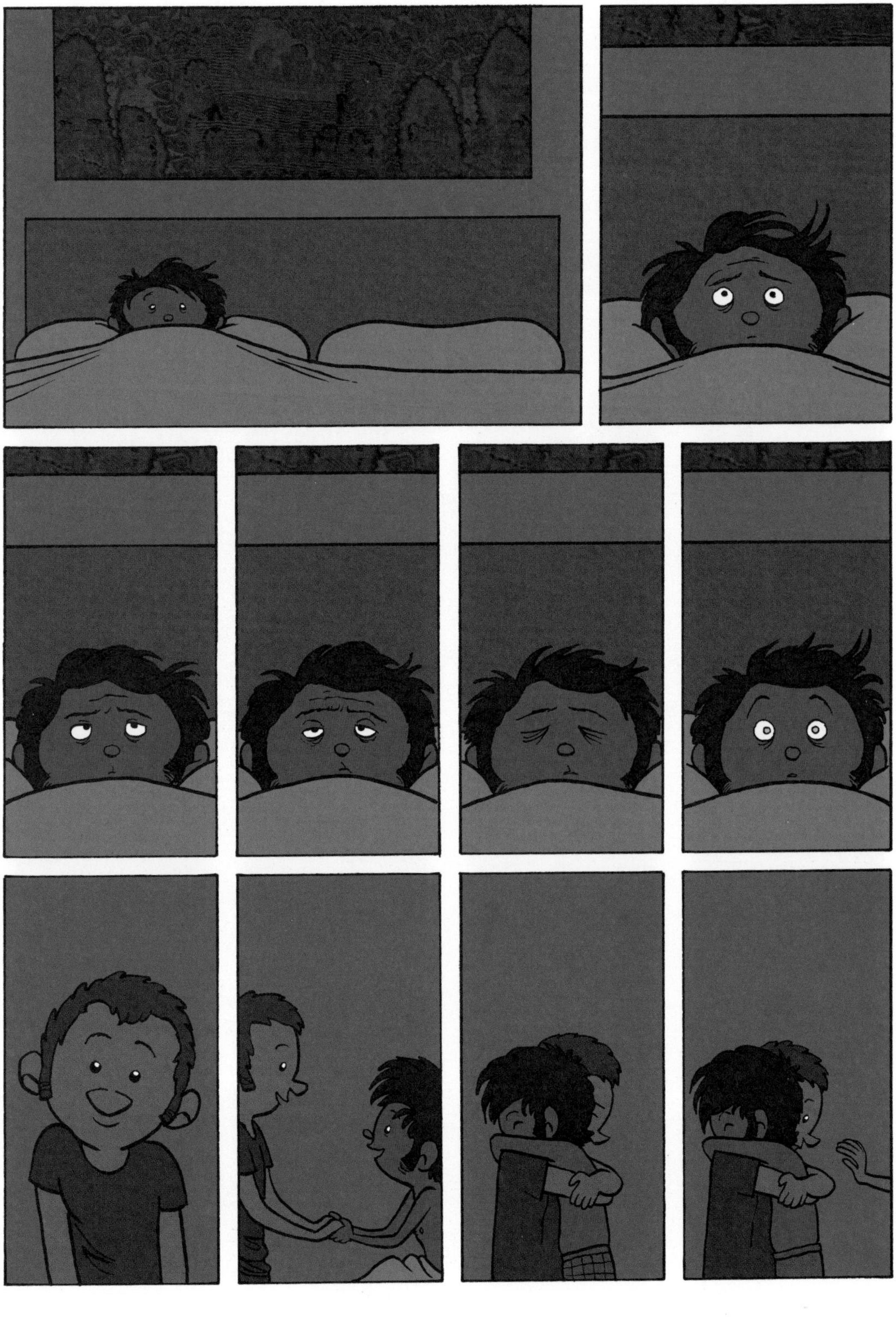

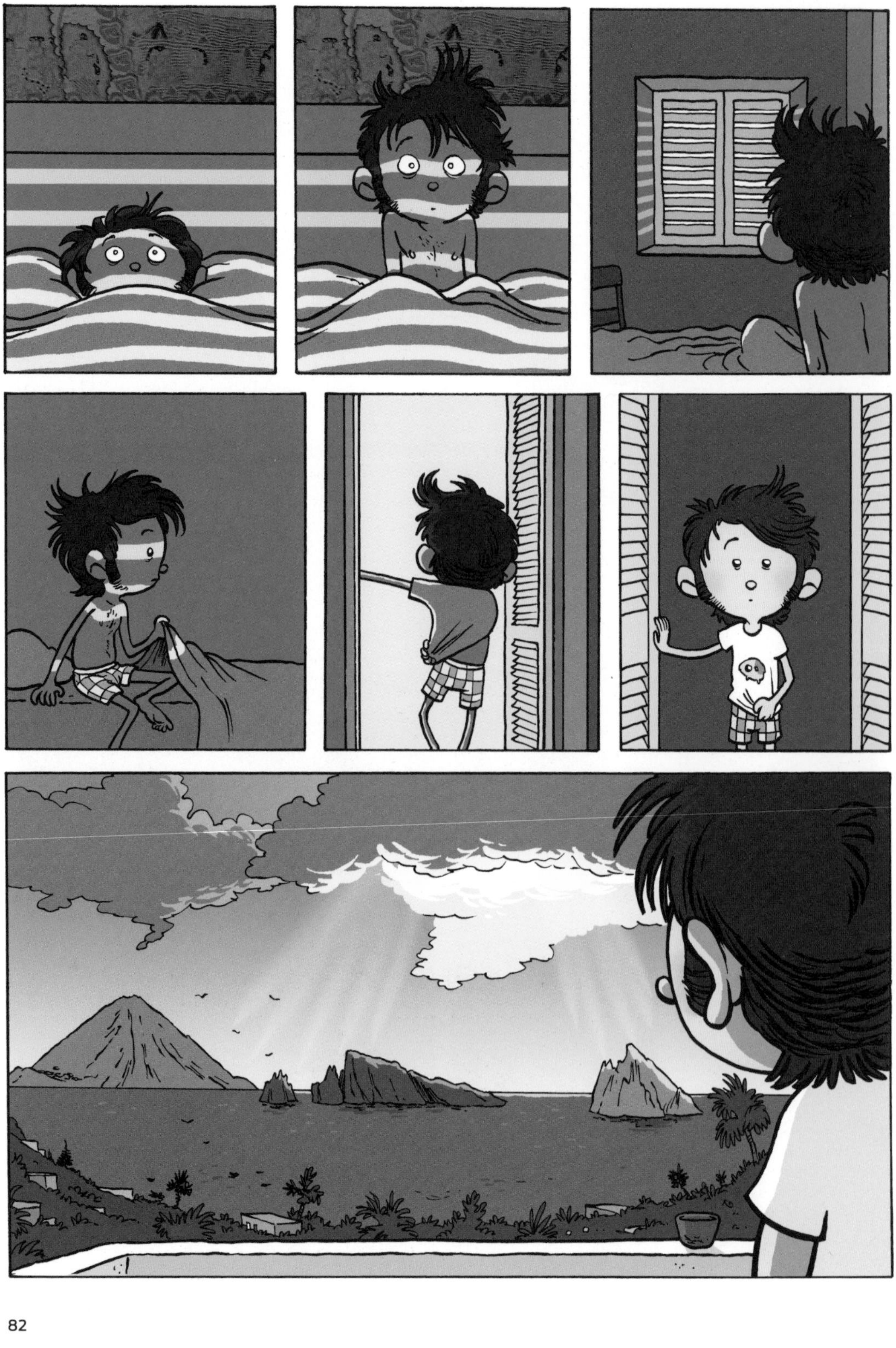

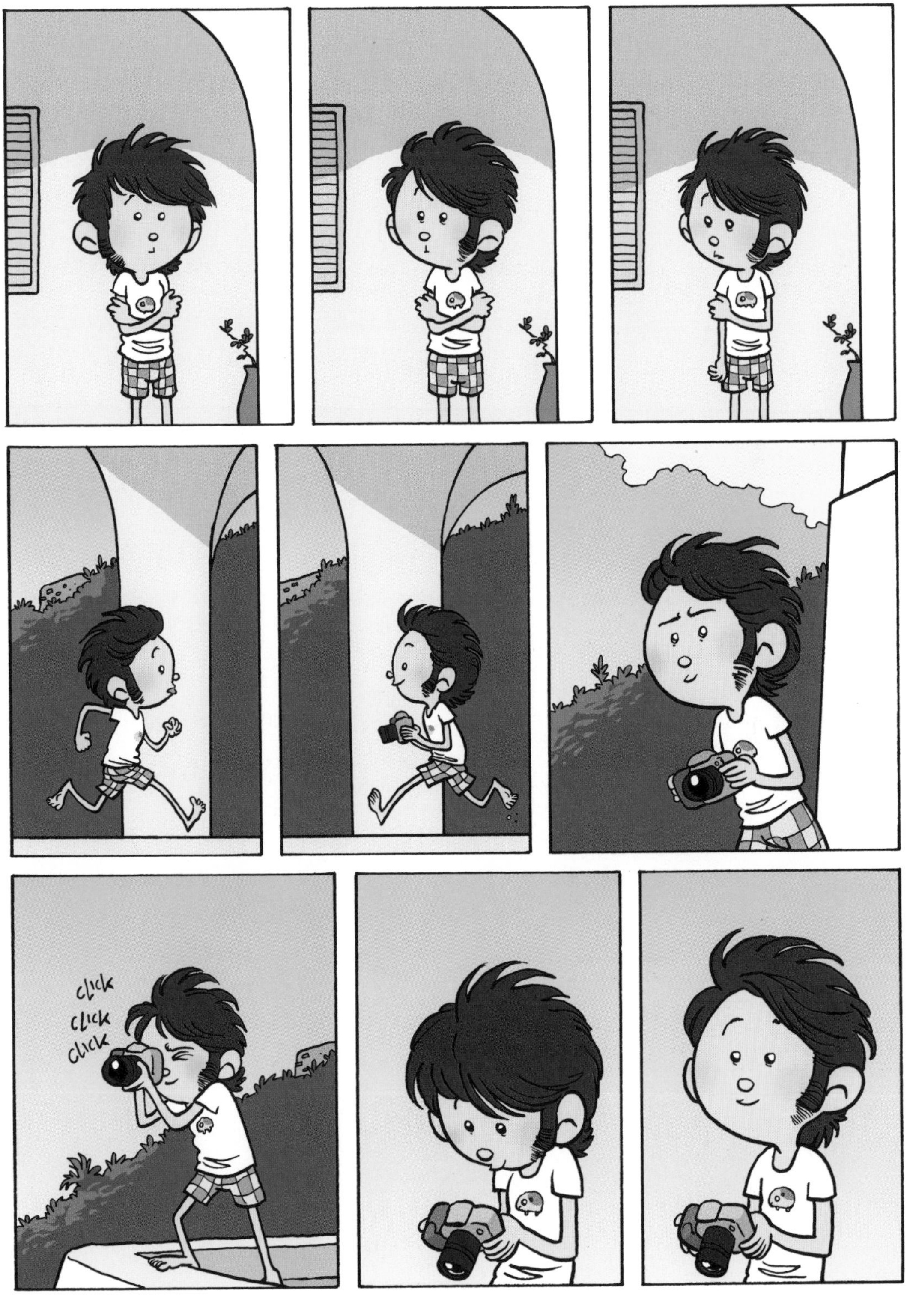
CLICK
CLICK
CLICK

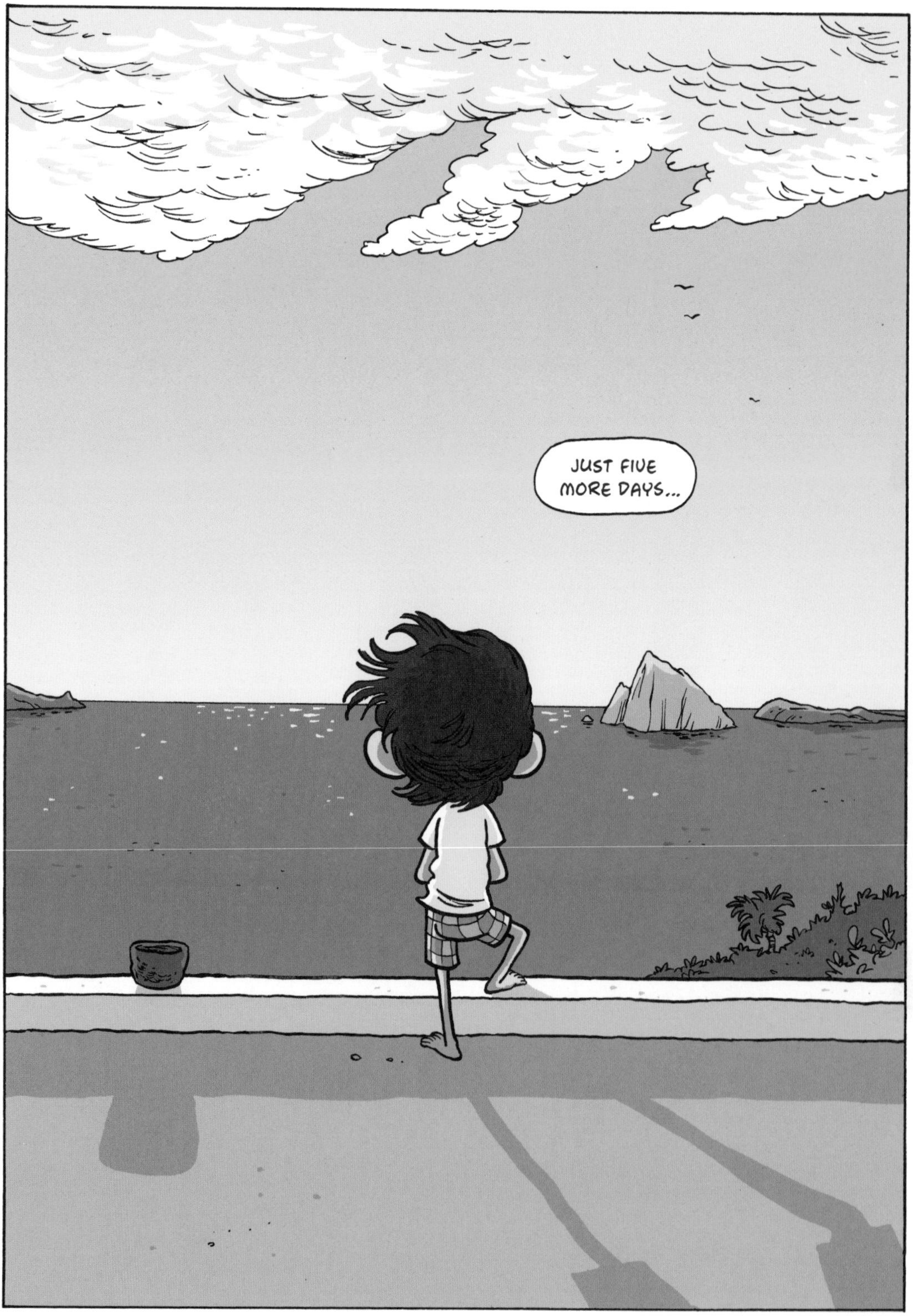
JUST FIVE MORE DAYS...

2.

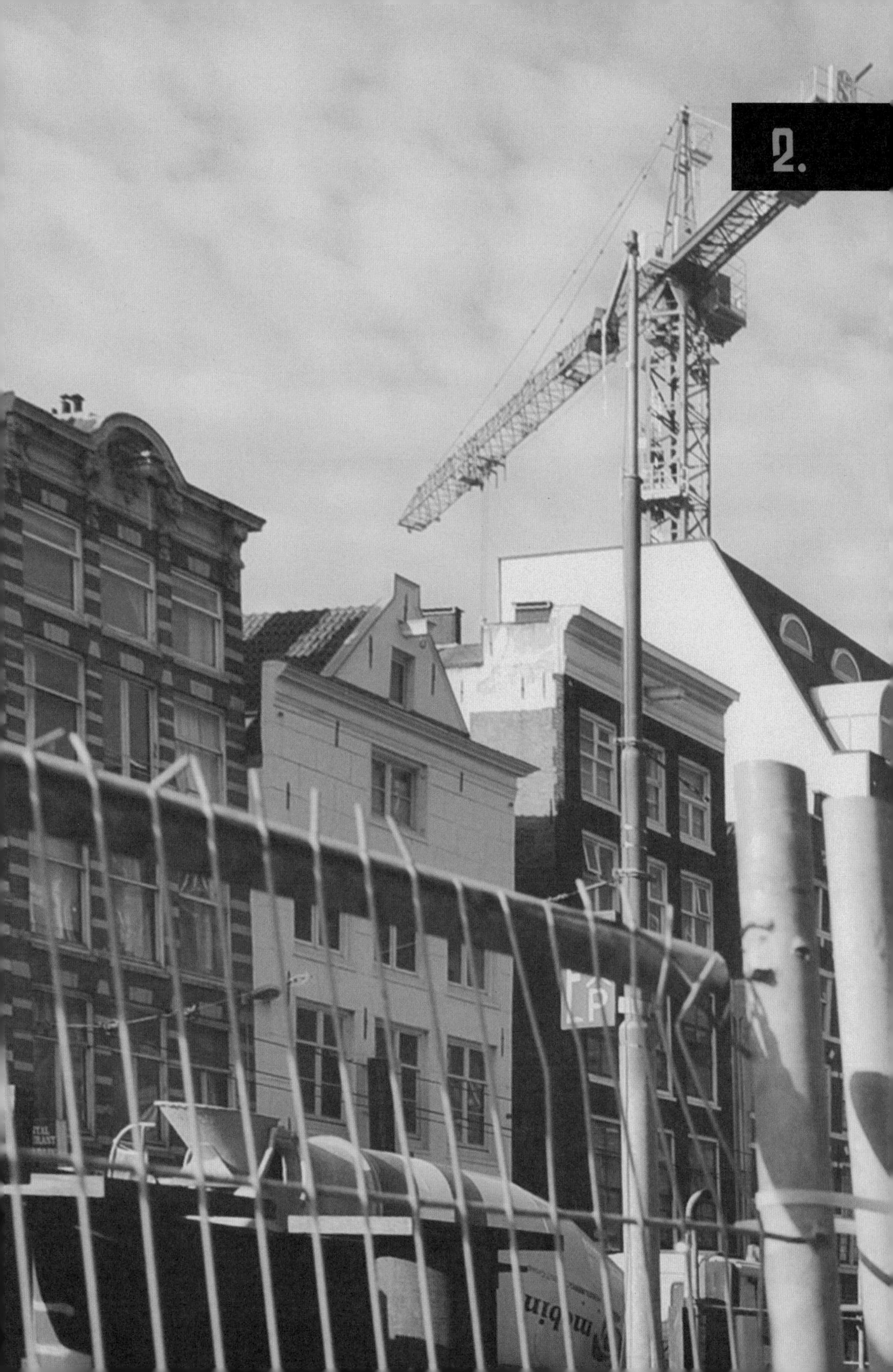

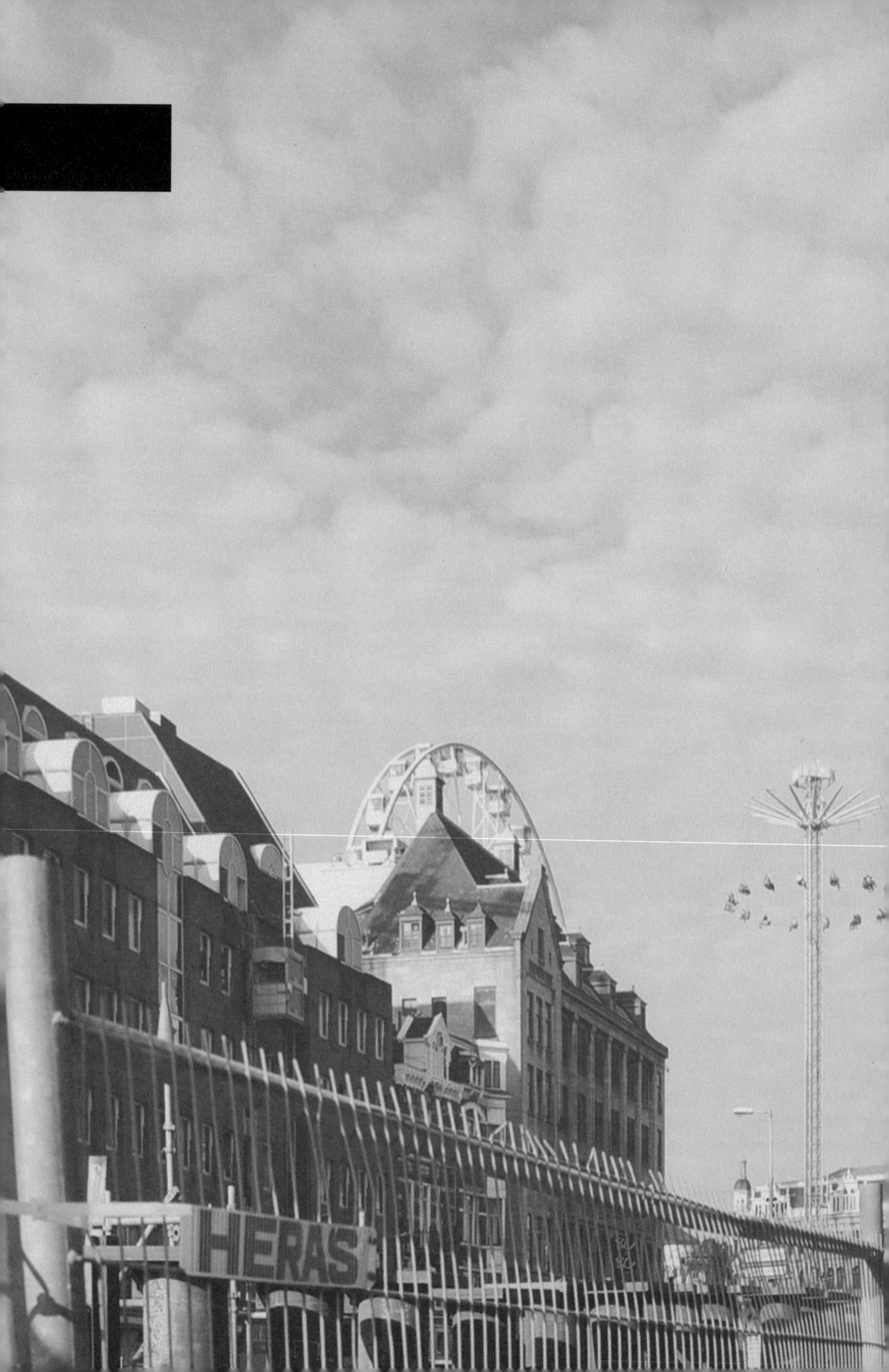
HERAS

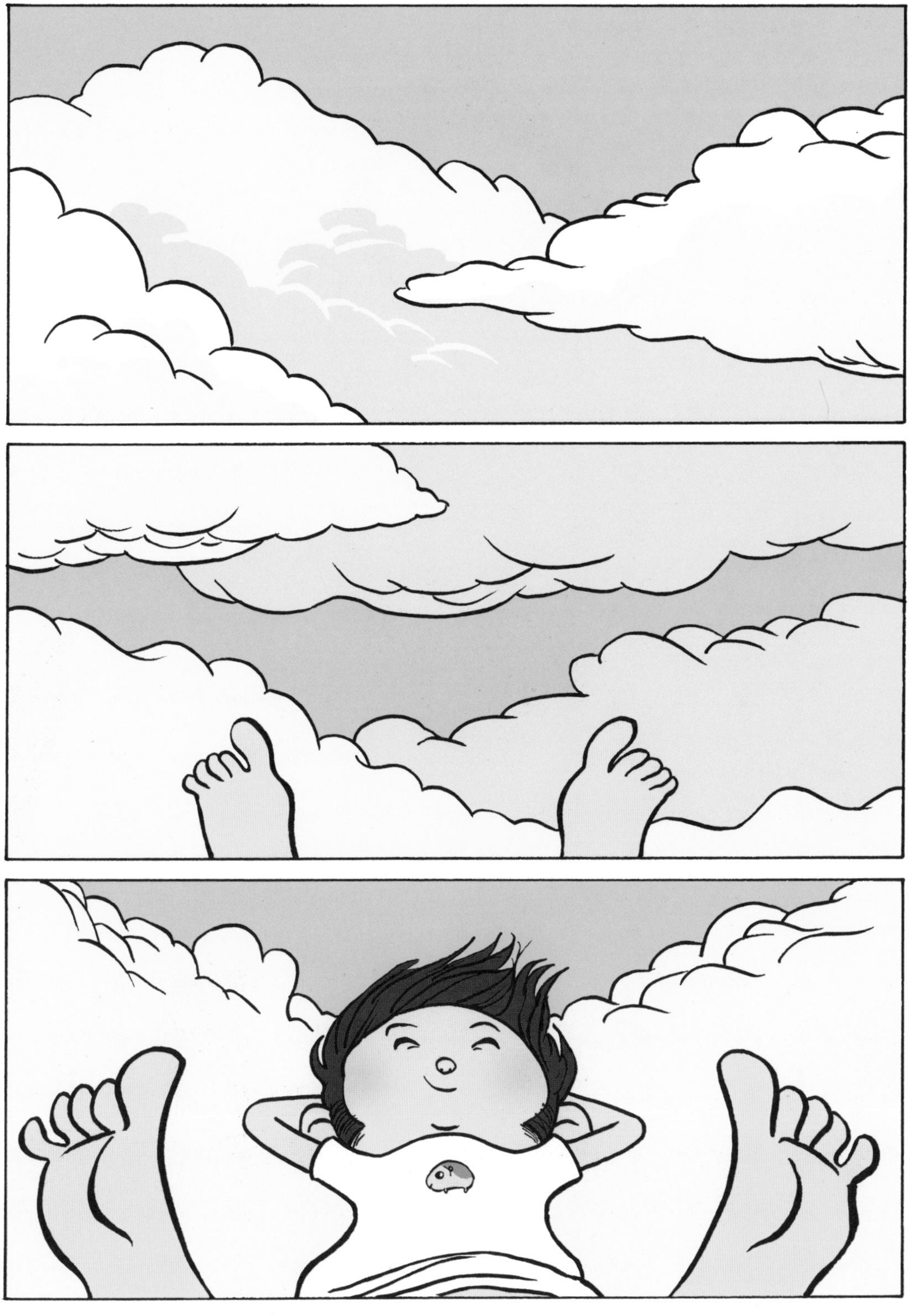

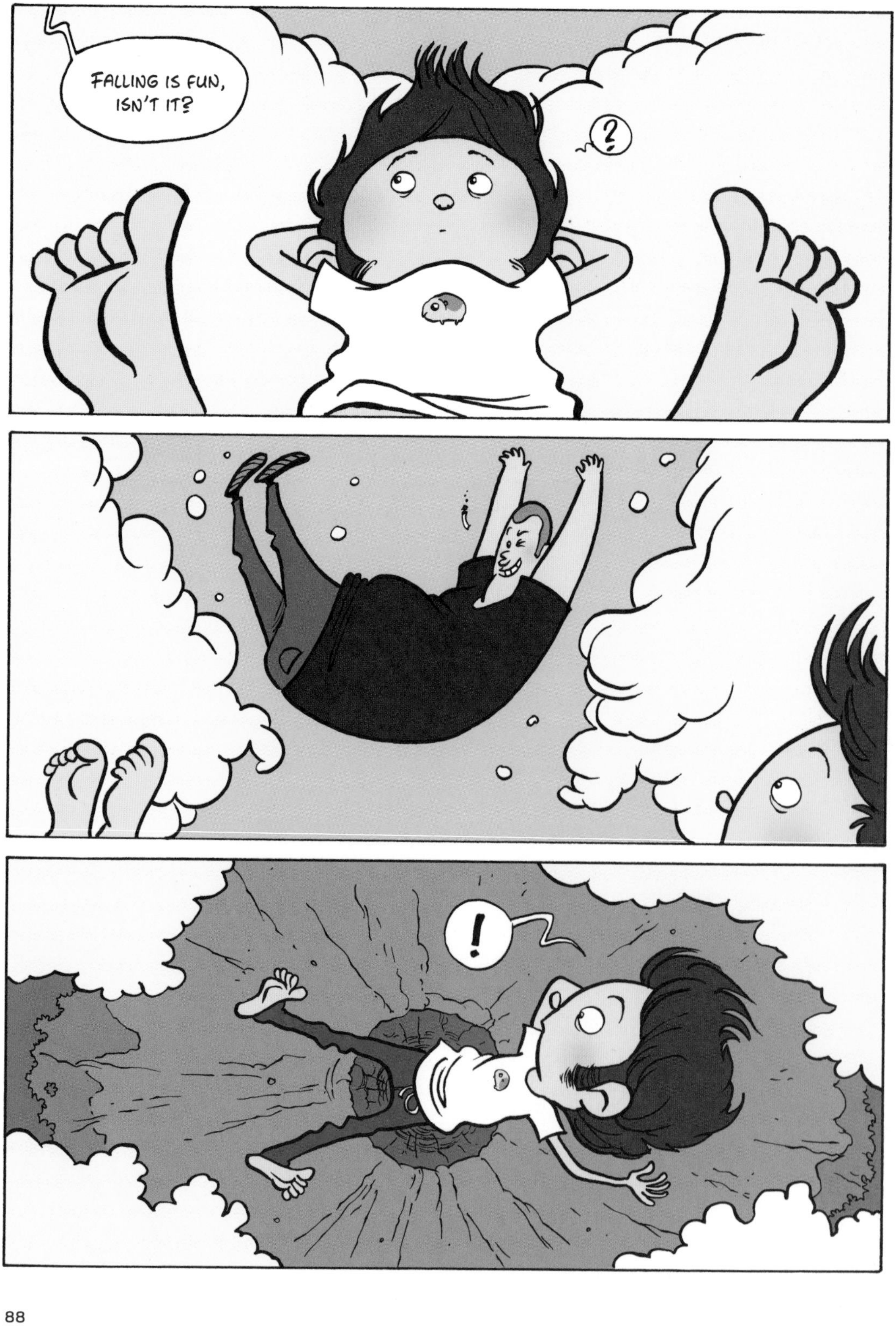
FALLING IS FUN,
ISN'T IT?
?
!

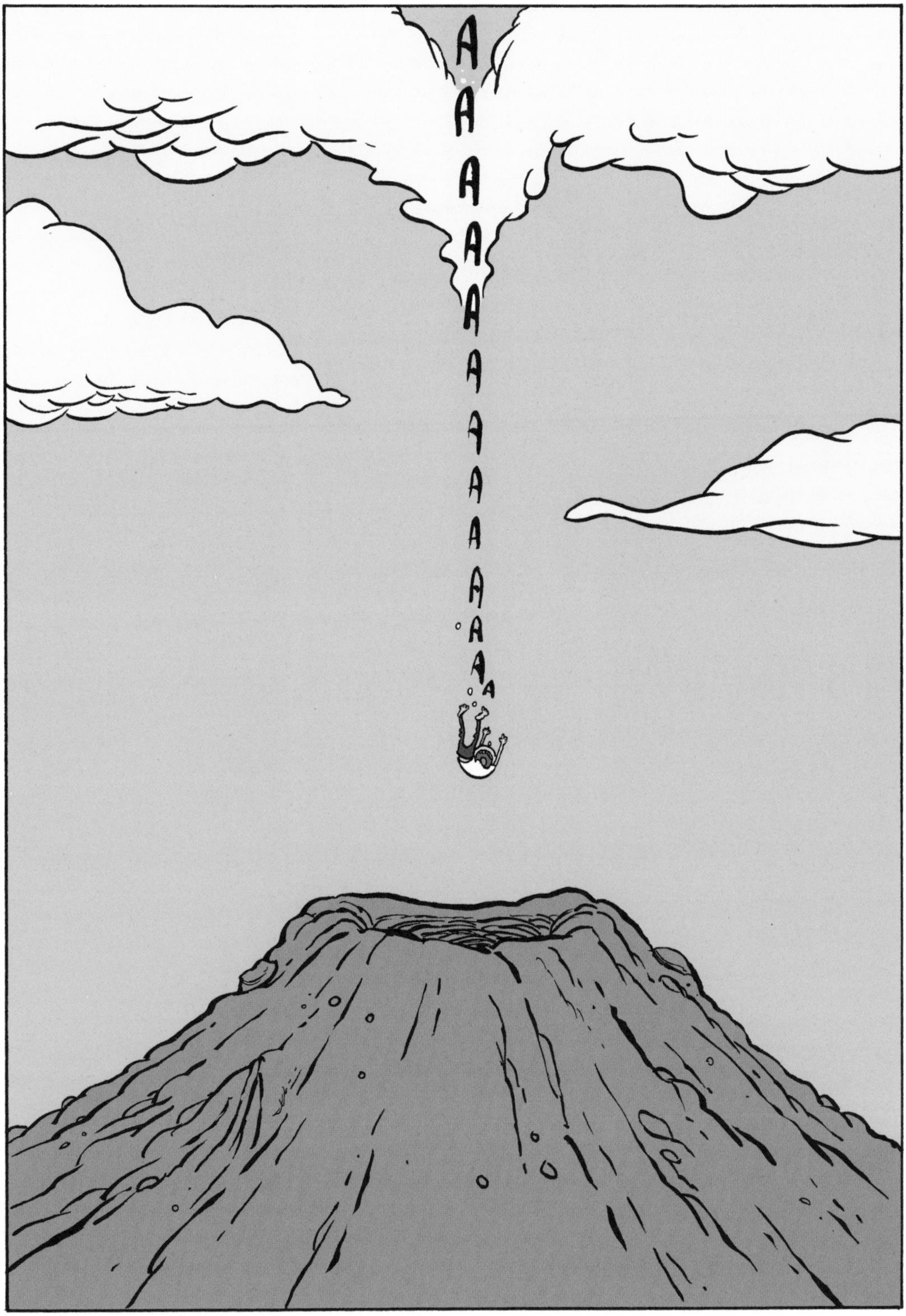
AAAAAAAAAAAAA

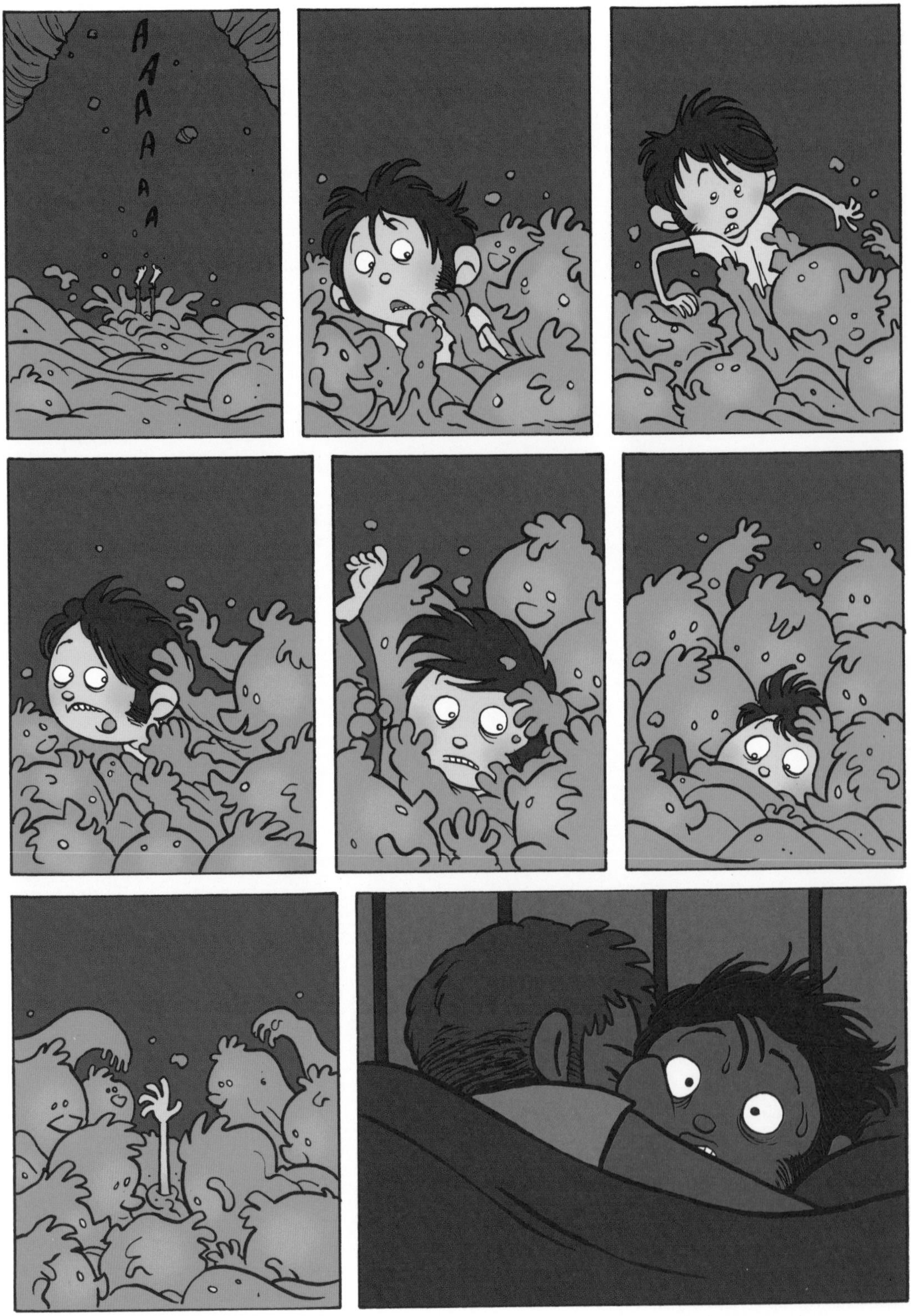
AAAAAAA

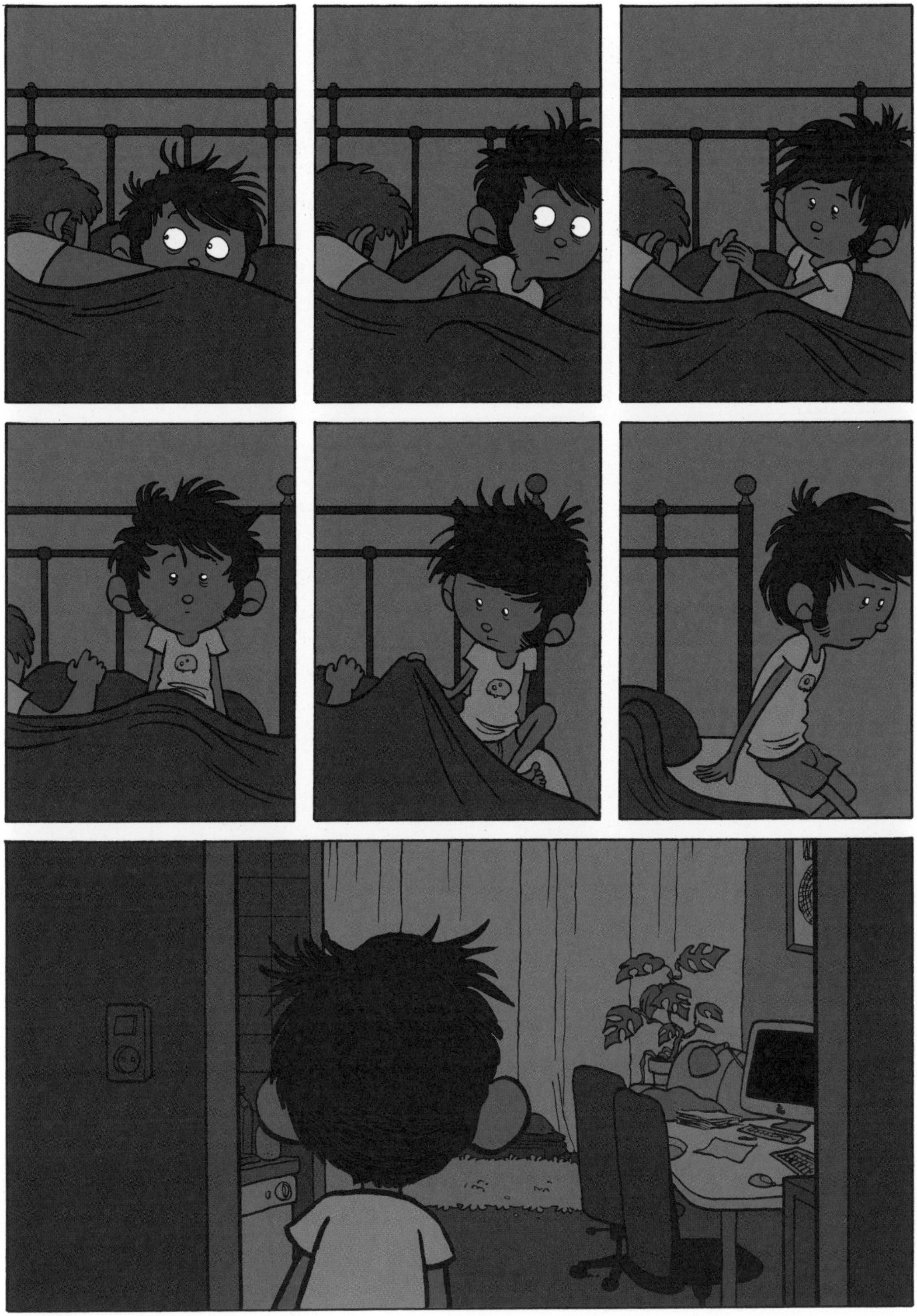

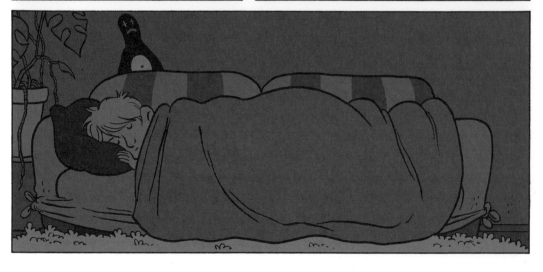

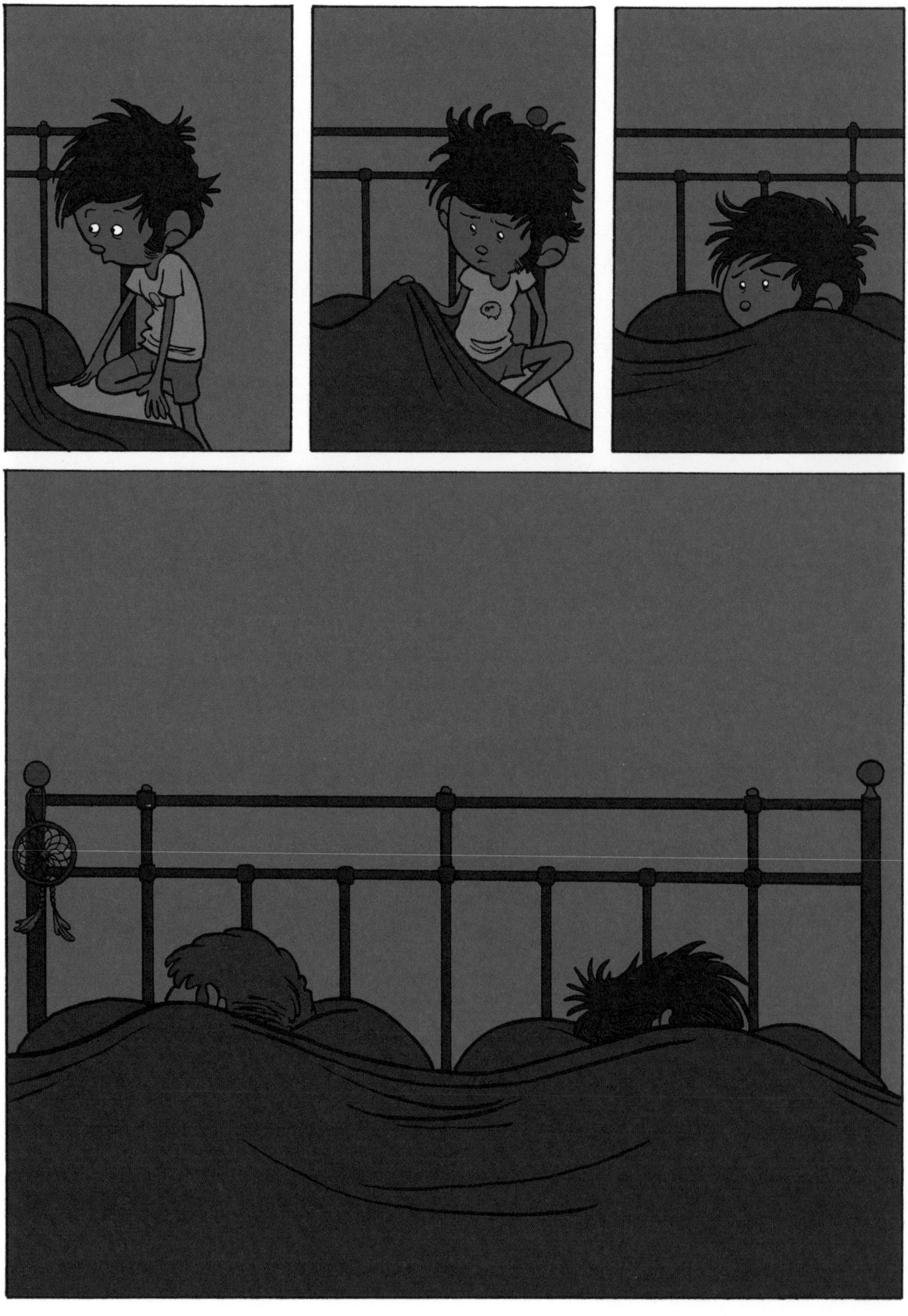

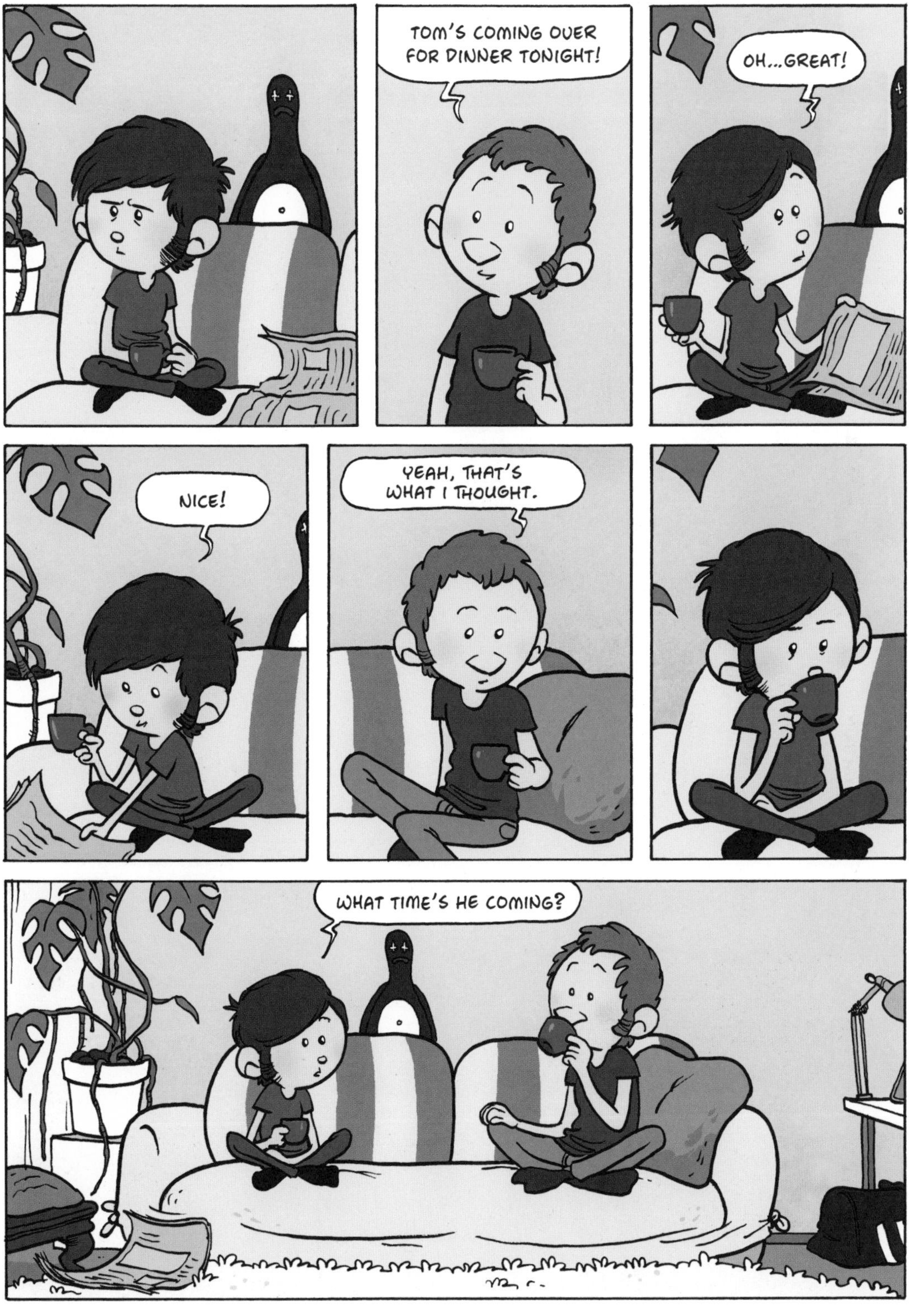
TOM'S COMING OVER FOR DINNER TONIGHT!
OH...GREAT!
NICE!
YEAH, THAT'S WHAT I THOUGHT.
WHAT TIME'S HE COMING?

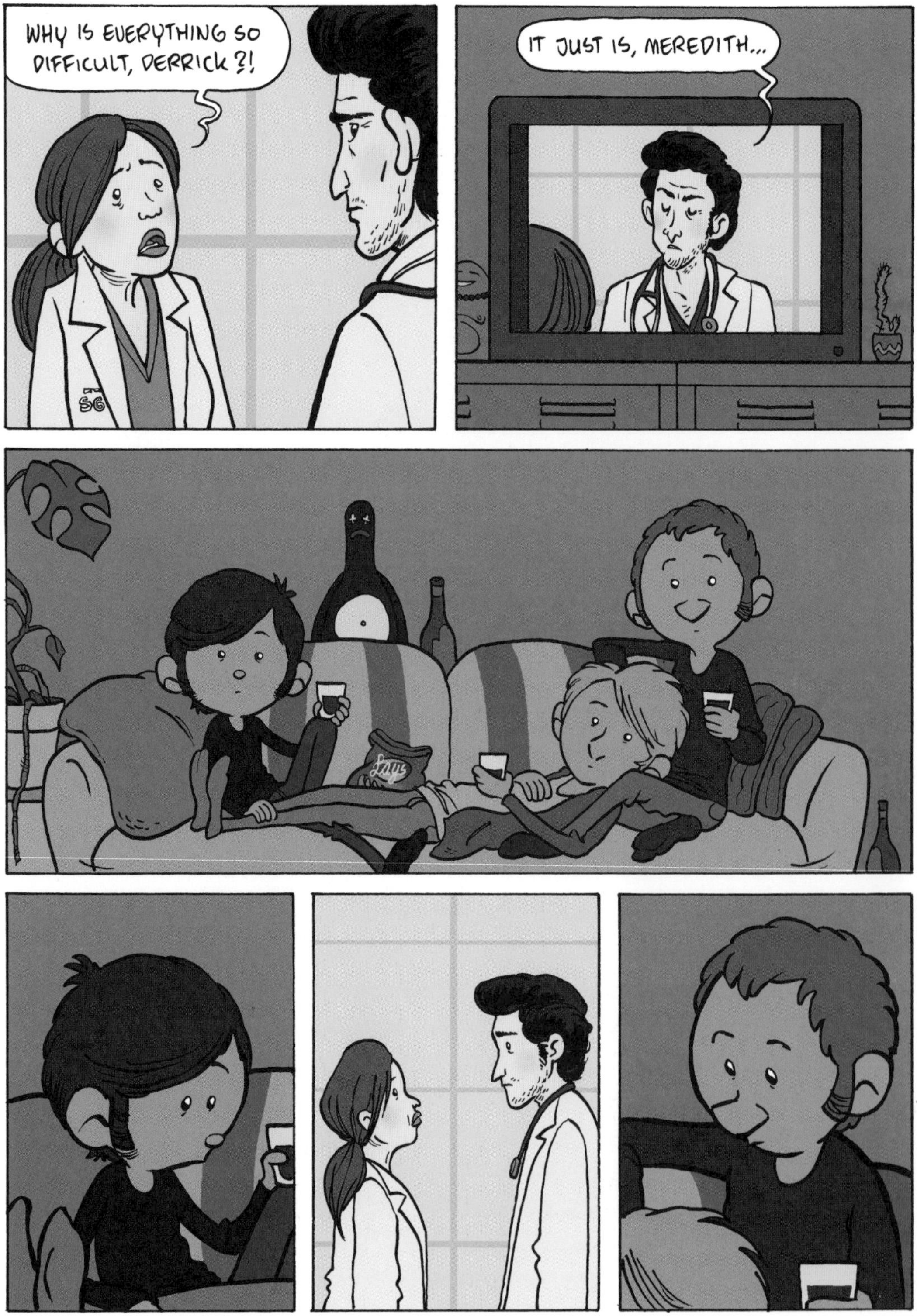
WHY IS EVERYTHING SO DIFFICULT, DERRICK?!
IT JUST IS, MEREDITH...
Lays

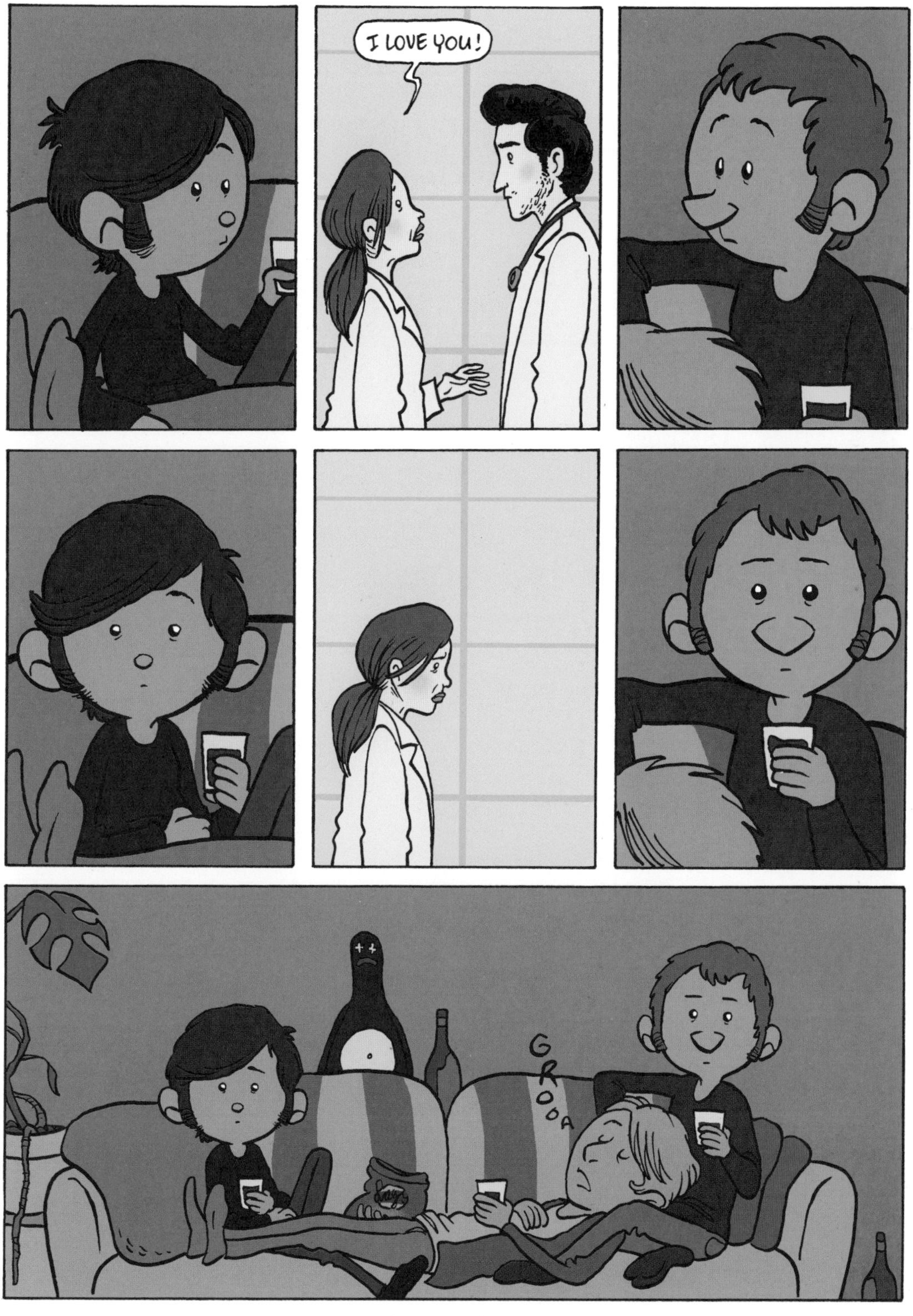
I LOVE YOU!
GROOA

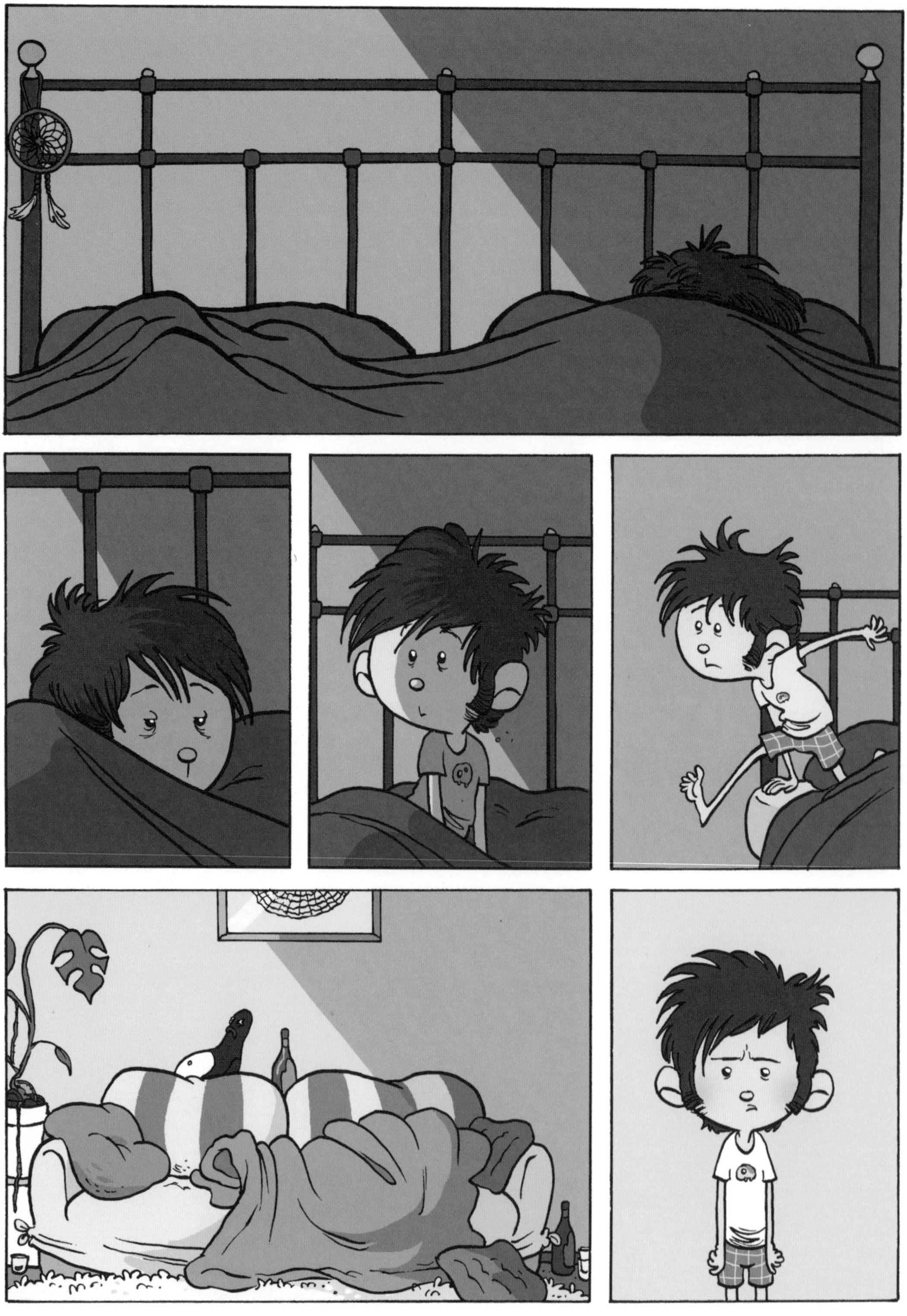

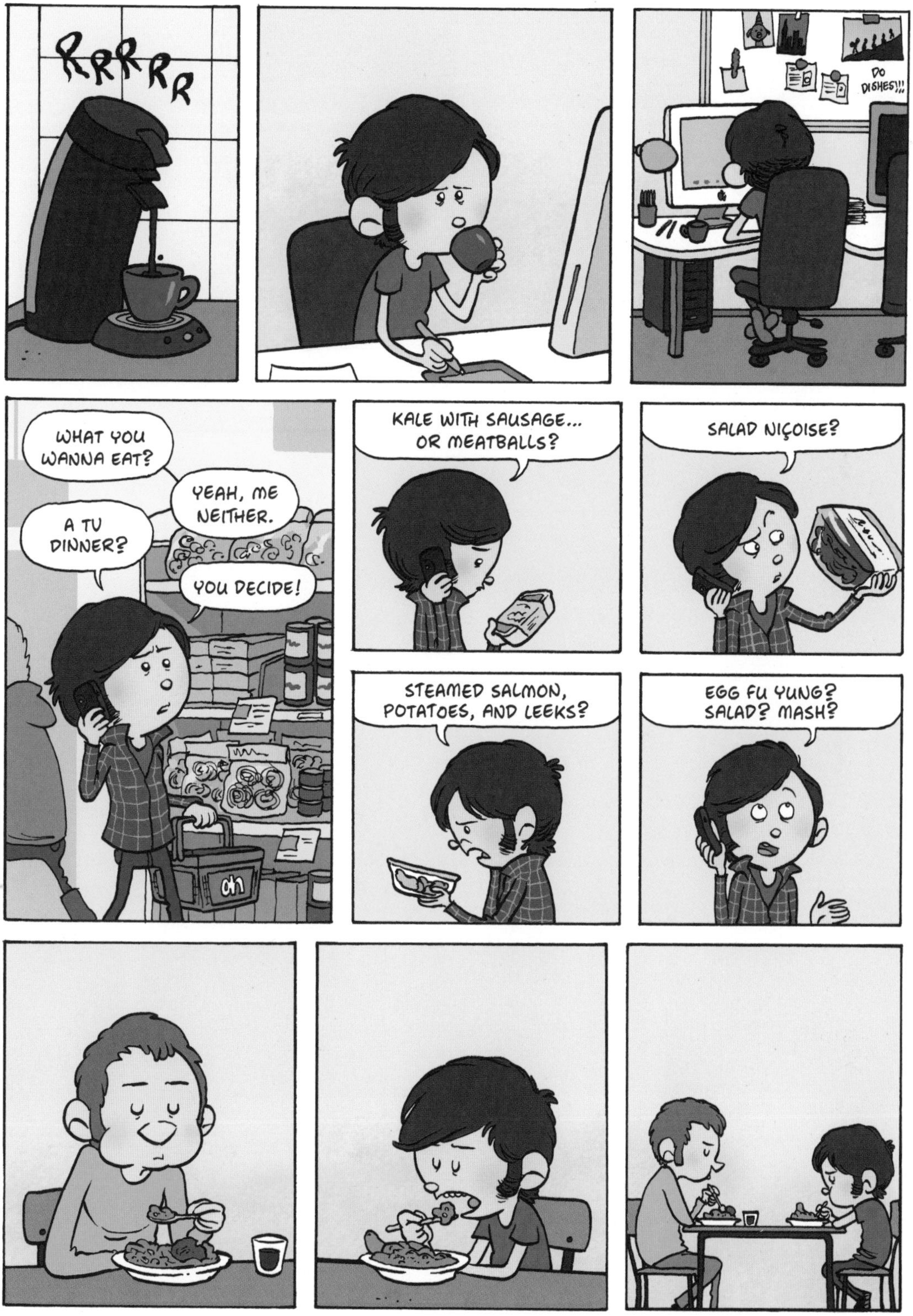
RRRRRR
DO DISHES!!!
WHAT YOU WANNA EAT?
A TV DINNER?
YEAH, ME NEITHER.
YOU DECIDE!
KALE WITH SAUSAGE... OR MEATBALLS?
SALAD NIÇOISE?
STEAMED SALMON, POTATOES, AND LEEKS?
EGG FU YUNG? SALAD? MASH?

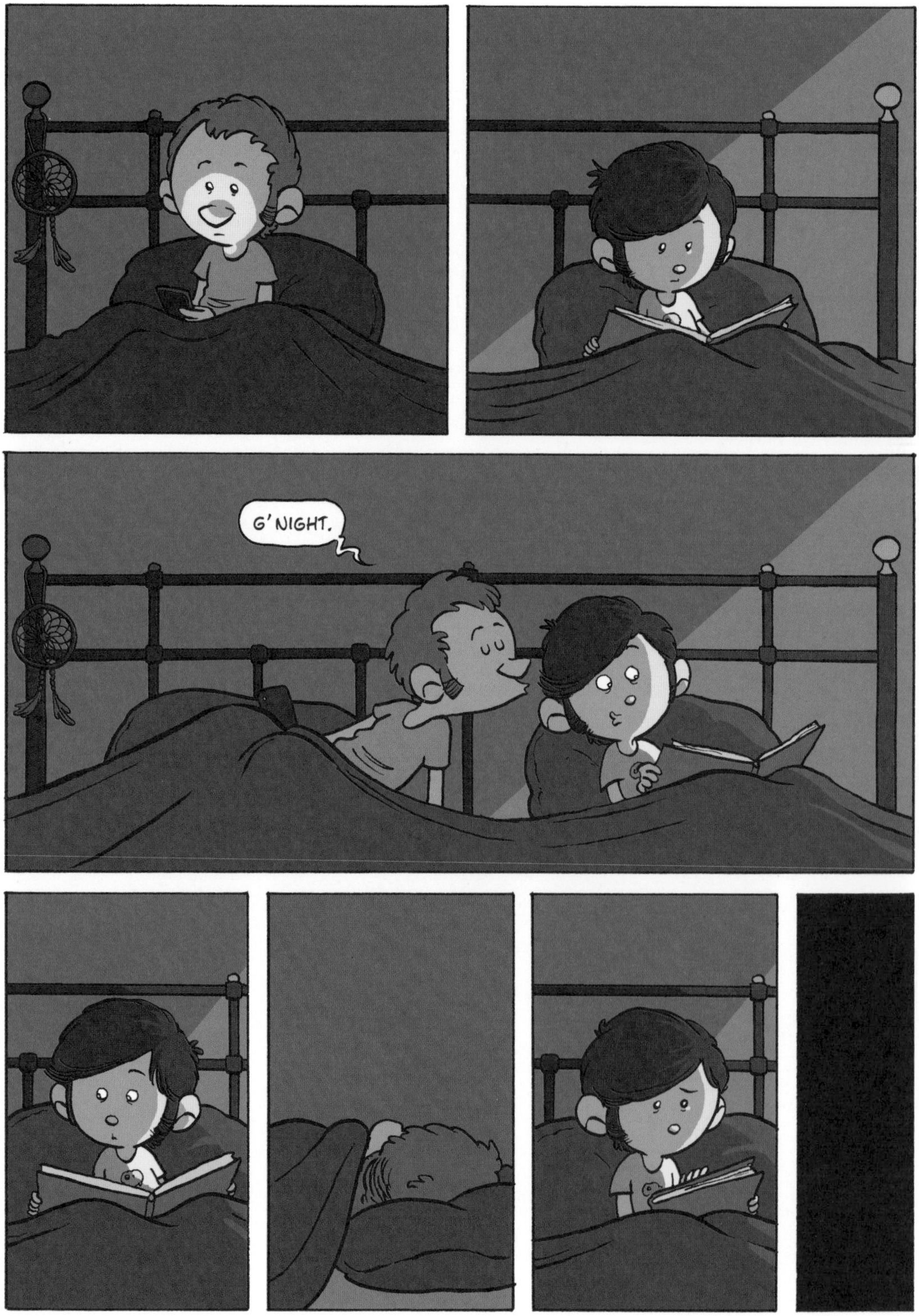
G' NIGHT.

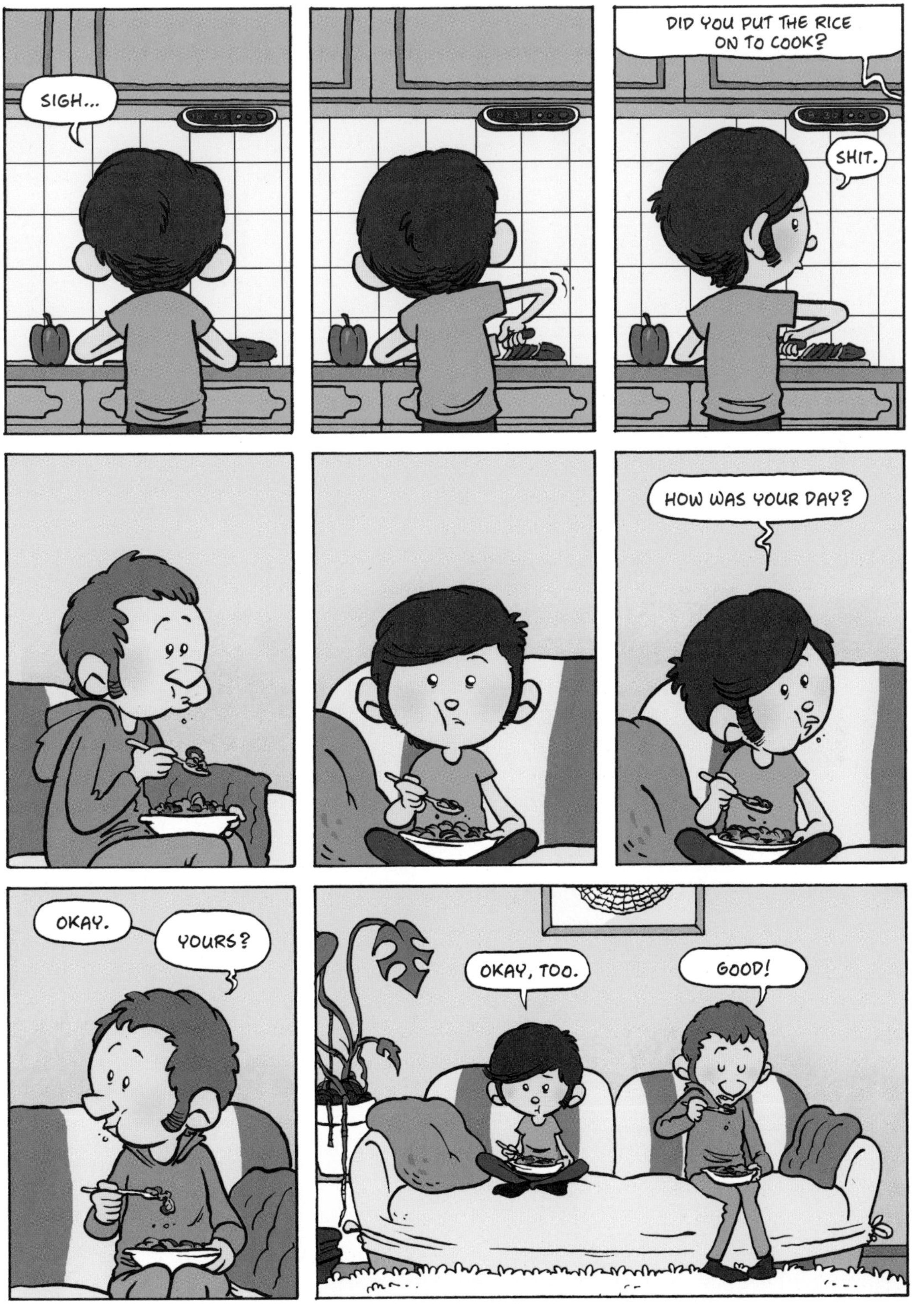
SIGH...
DID YOU PUT THE RICE ON TO COOK?
SHIT.
HOW WAS YOUR DAY?
OKAY.
YOURS?
OKAY, TOO.
GOOD!

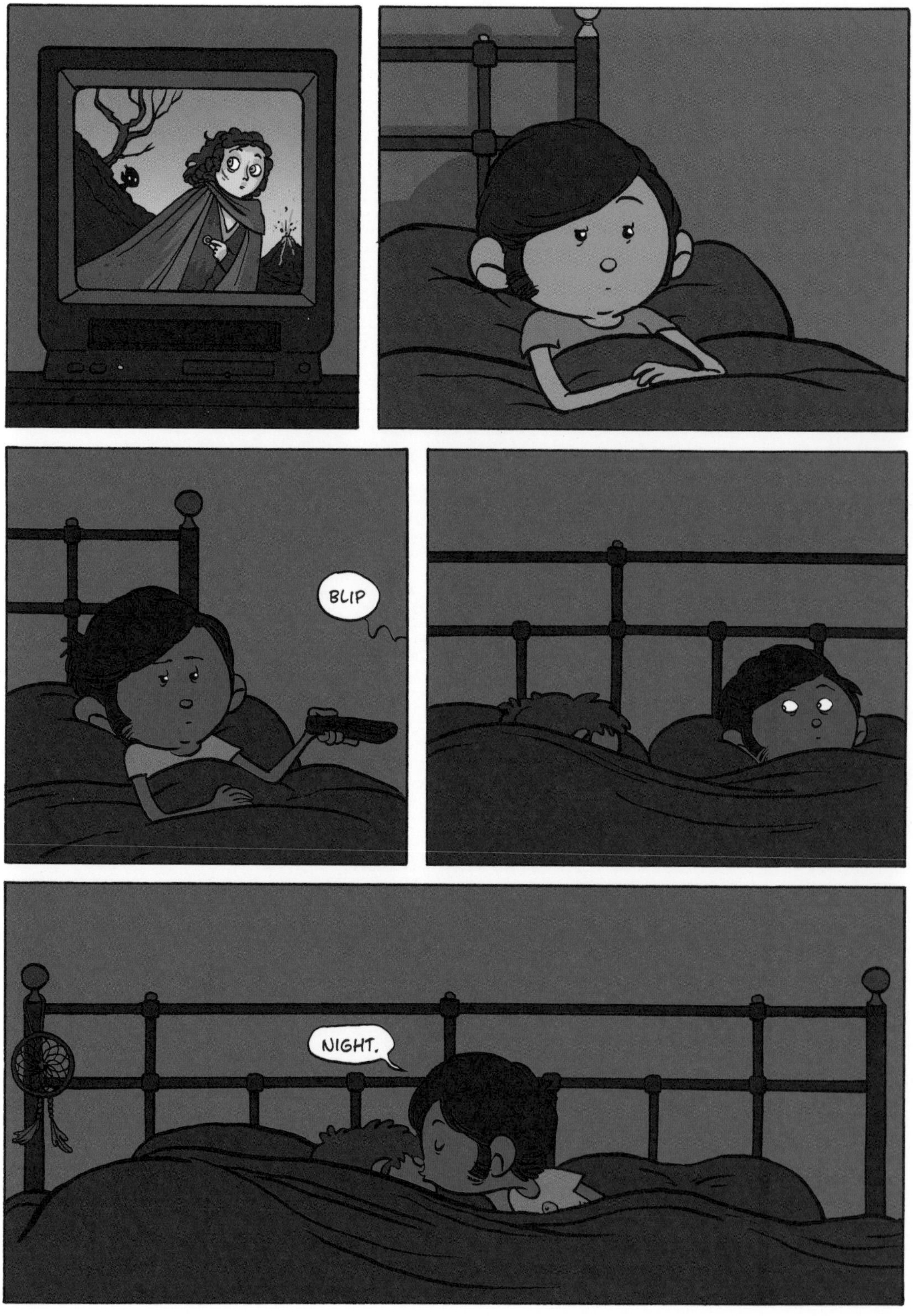
BLIP
NIGHT.

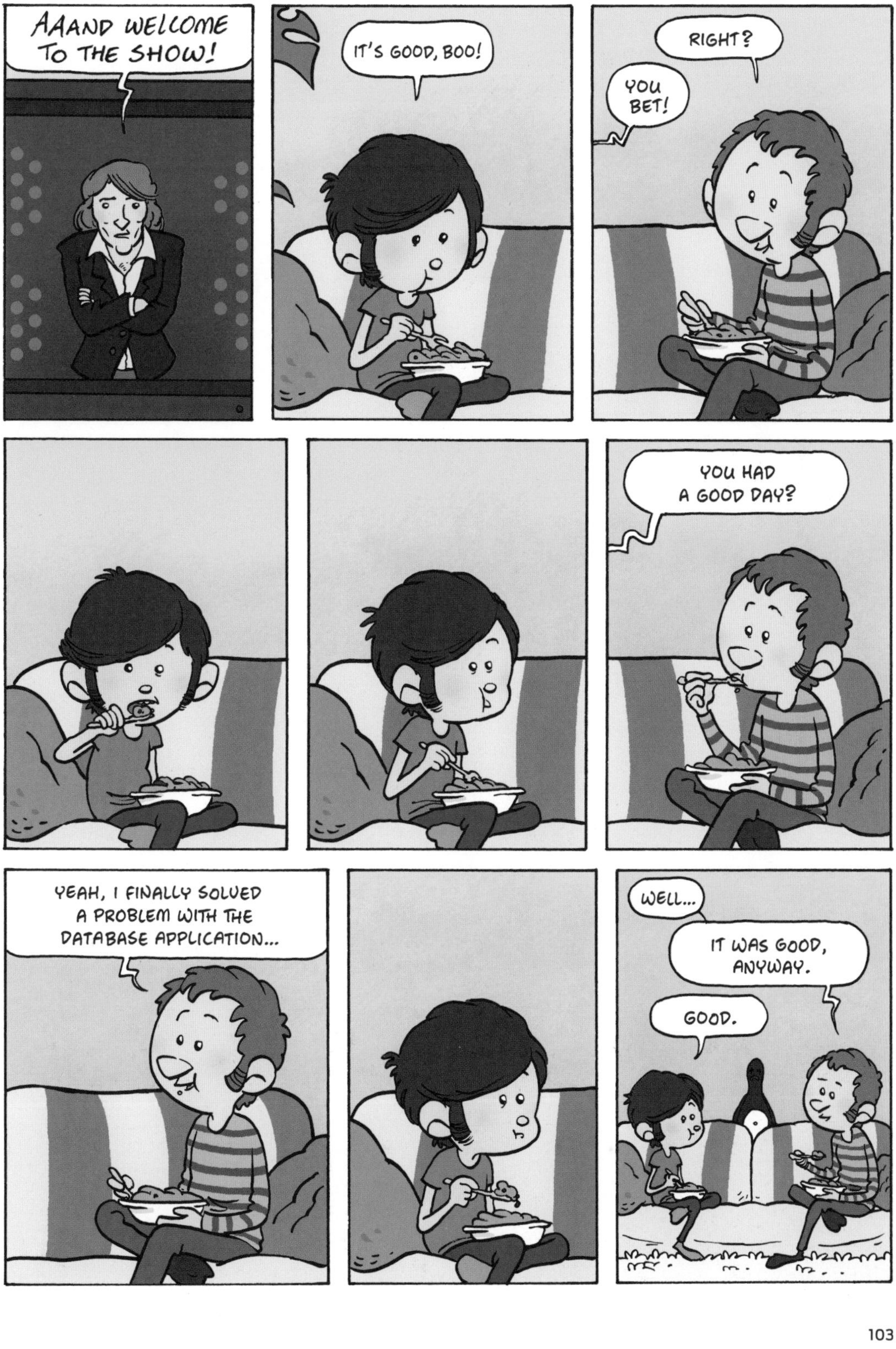
AAAND WELCOME TO THE SHOW!
IT'S GOOD, BOO!
RIGHT?
YOU BET!
YOU HAD A GOOD DAY?
YEAH, I FINALLY SOLVED A PROBLEM WITH THE DATABASE APPLICATION...
WELL...
IT WAS GOOD, ANYWAY.
GOOD.

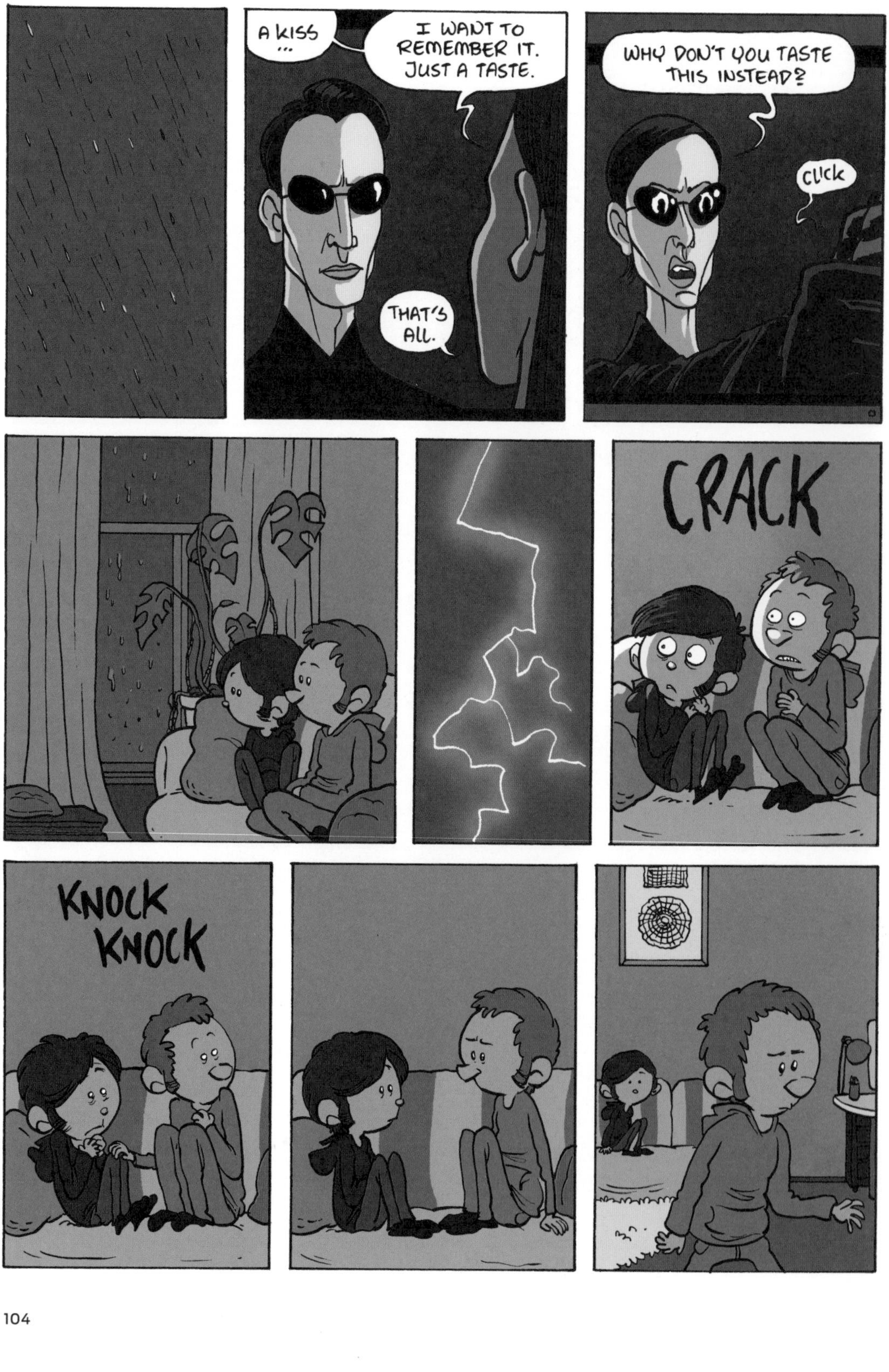
A KISS ...
I WANT TO REMEMBER IT. JUST A TASTE.
THAT'S ALL.
WHY DON'T YOU TASTE THIS INSTEAD?
CLICK
CRACK
KNOCK KNOCK

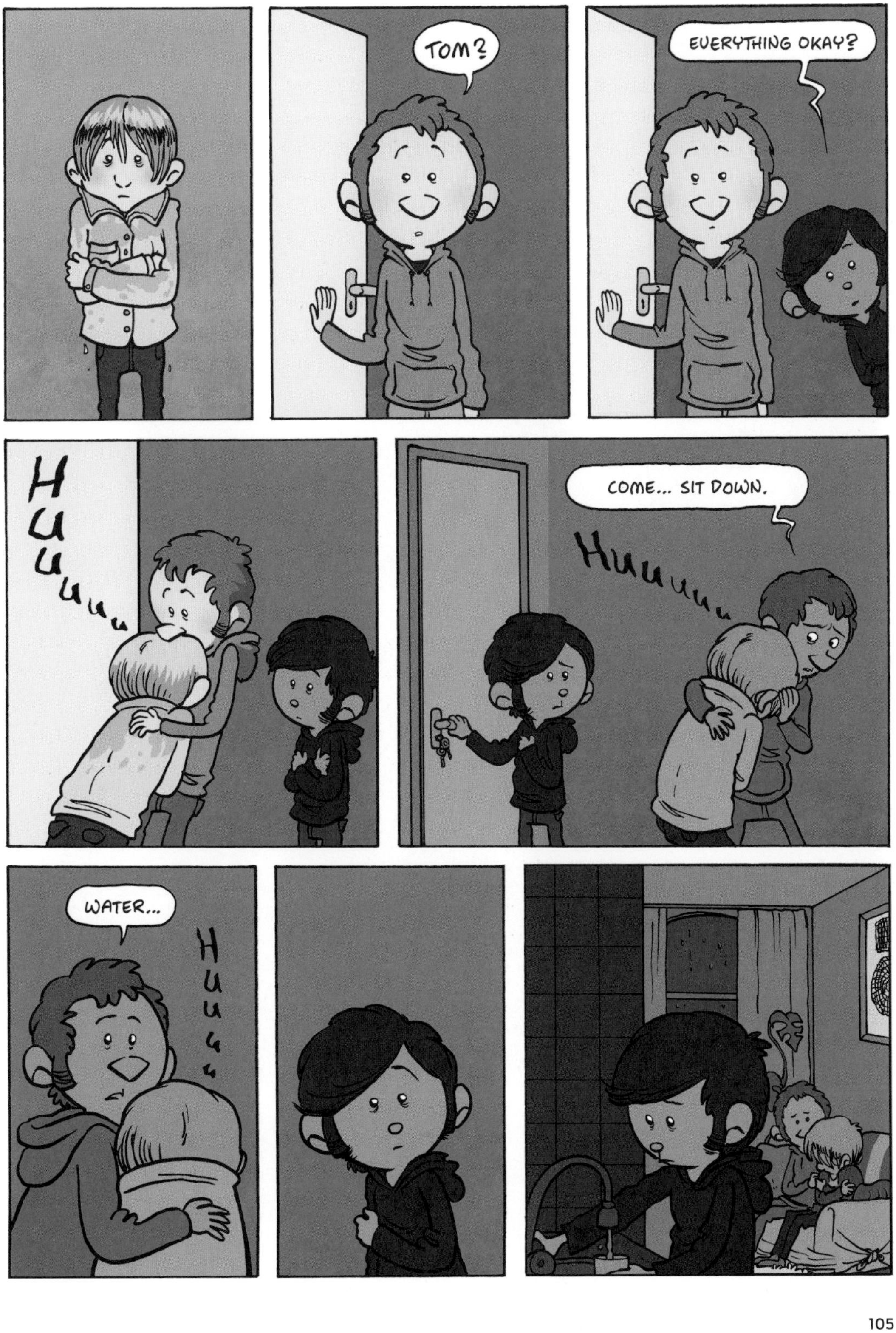
TOM?
EVERYTHING OKAY?
HUUUUU
COME... SIT DOWN.
HUUUUUU
WATER...
HUUUU

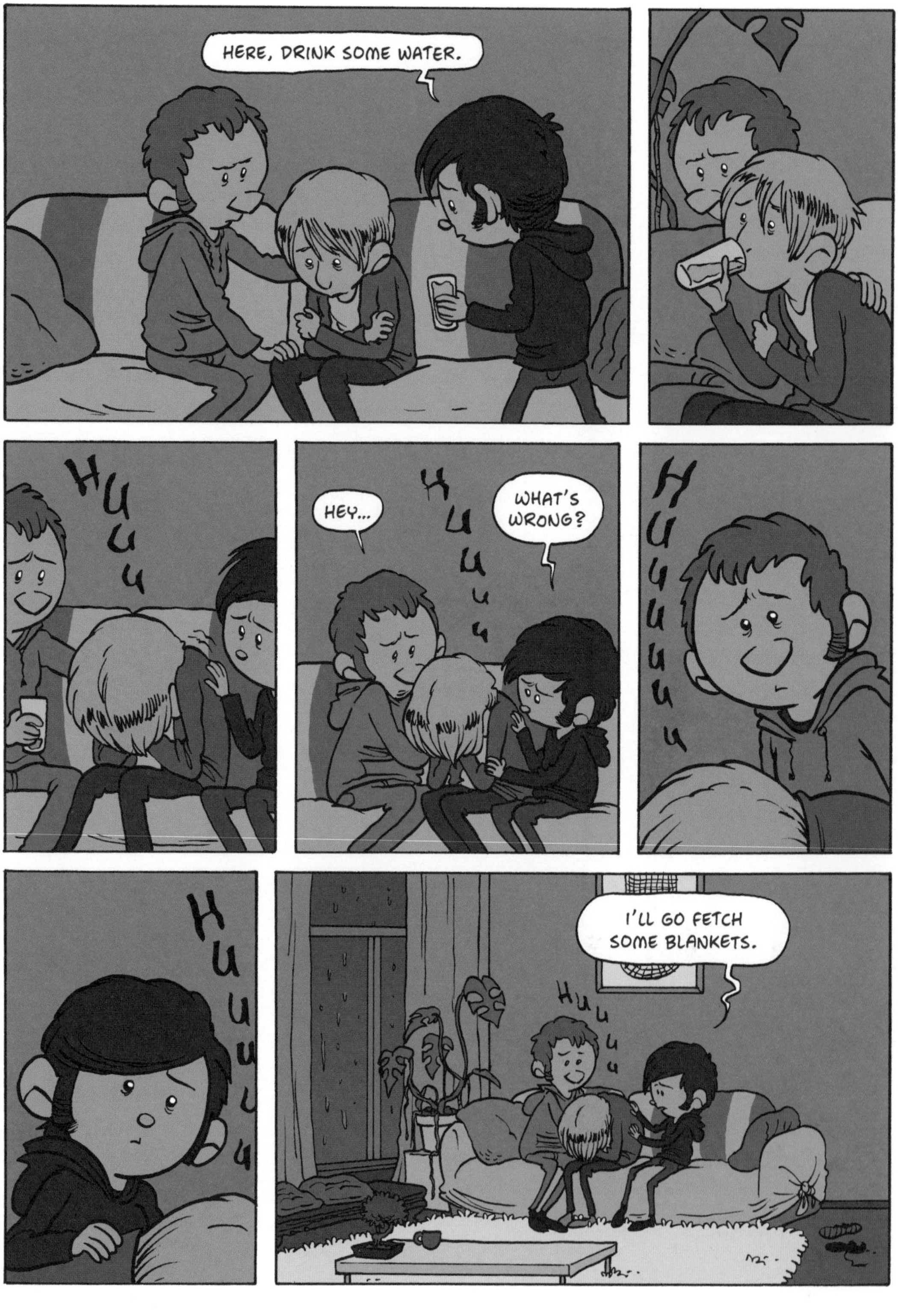
HERE, DRINK SOME WATER.
HUUUU
HEY...
HUUUUU
WHAT'S WRONG?
HUUUUUUUUU
HUUUUUU
I'LL GO FETCH SOME BLANKETS.
HUUUU

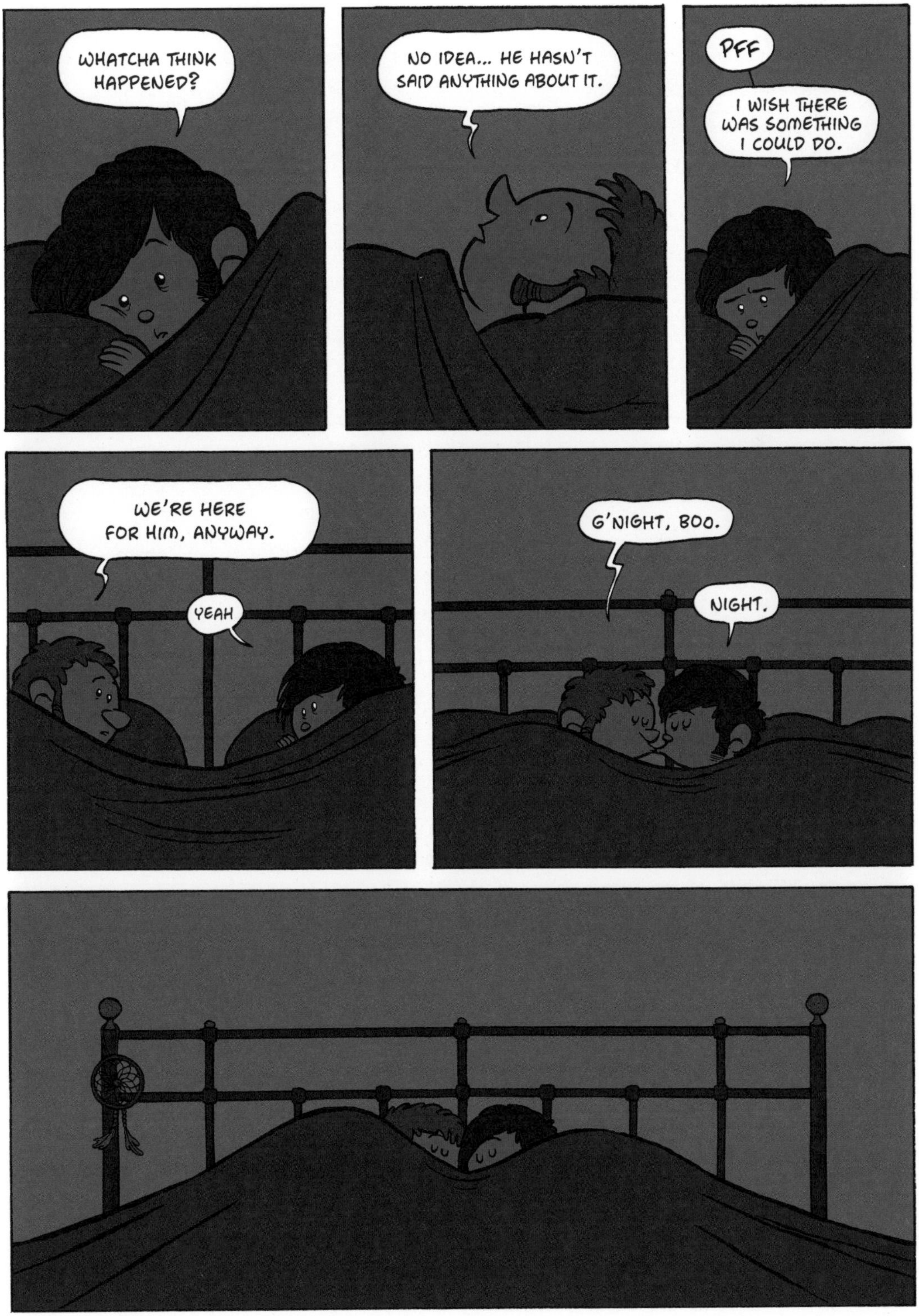
WHATCHA THINK HAPPENED?
NO IDEA... HE HASN'T SAID ANYTHING ABOUT IT.
PFF
I WISH THERE WAS SOMETHING I COULD DO.
WE'RE HERE FOR HIM, ANYWAY.
YEAH
G'NIGHT, BOO.
NIGHT.

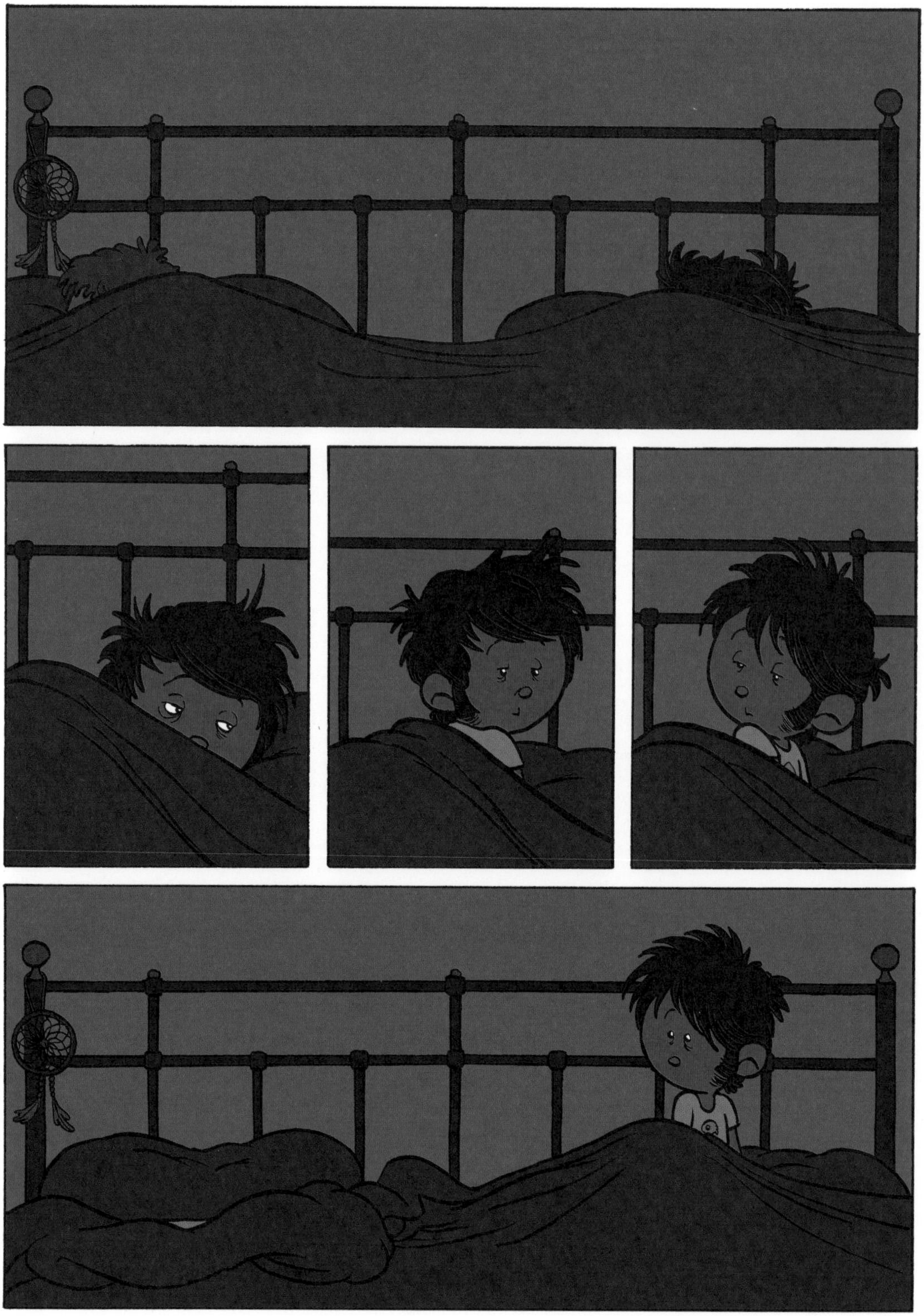

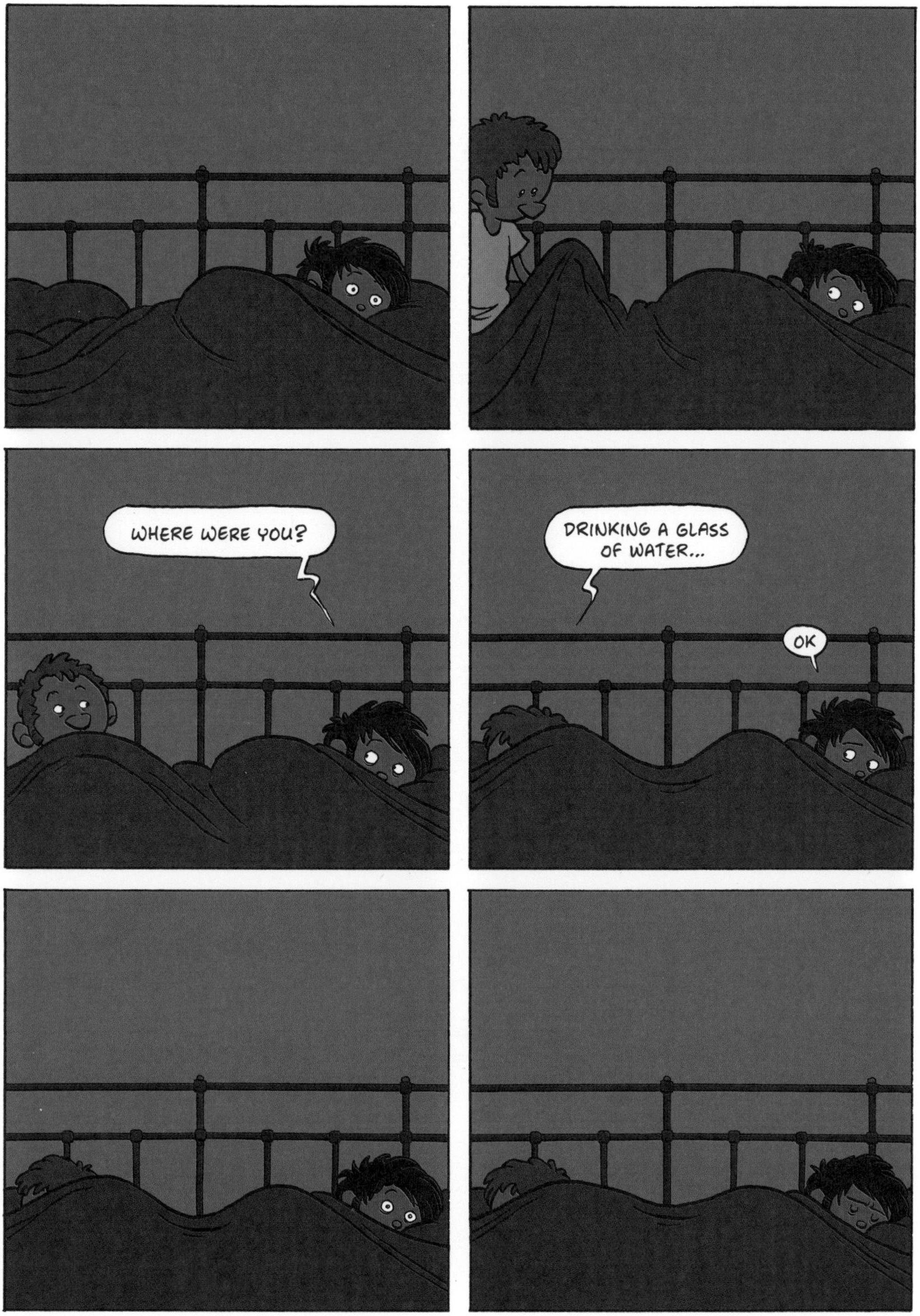
WHERE WERE YOU?
DRINKING A GLASS OF WATER...
OK

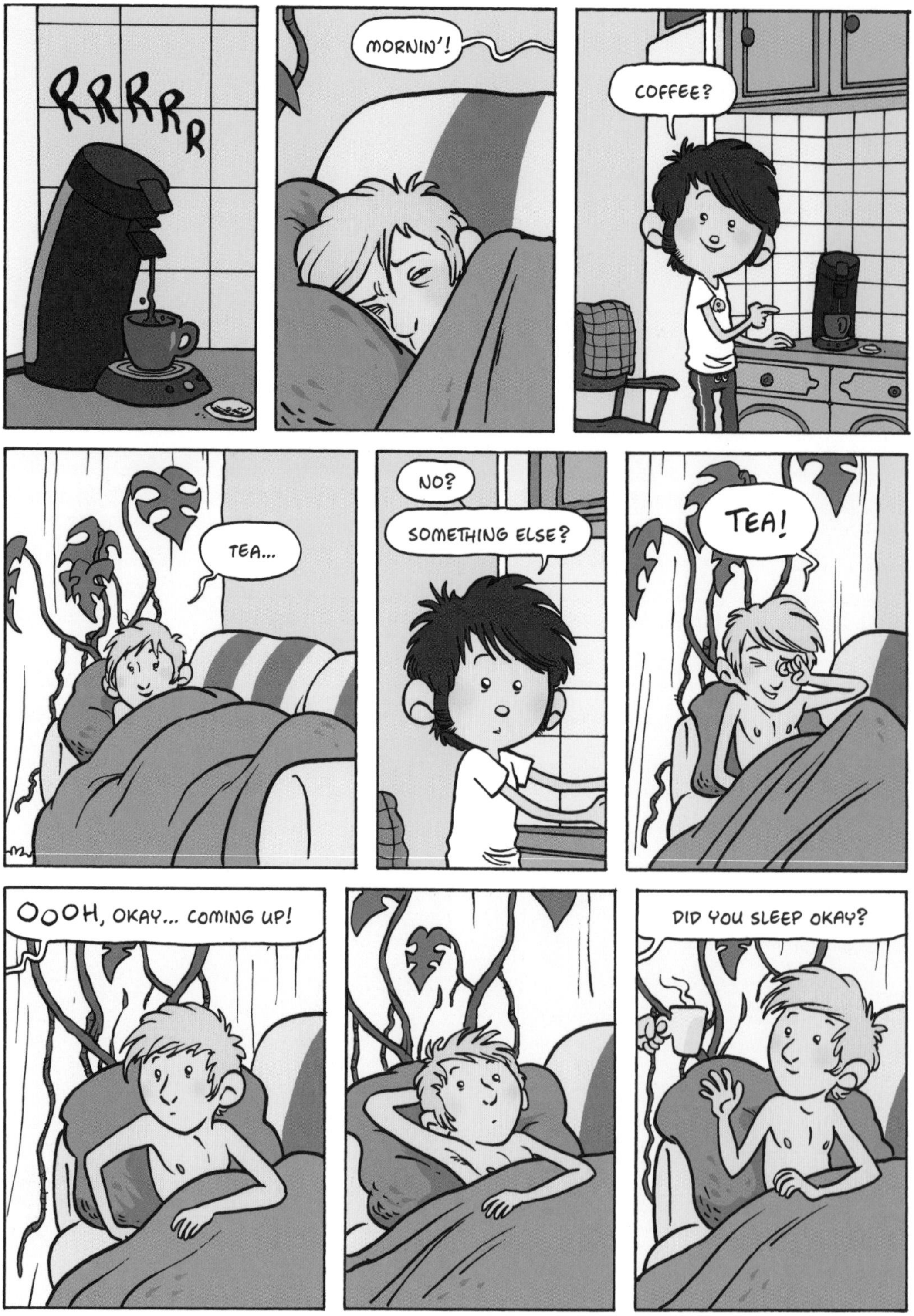
RRRRRR
MORNIN'!
COFFEE?
TEA...
NO?
SOMETHING ELSE?
TEA!
OOOH, OKAY... COMING UP!
DID YOU SLEEP OKAY?

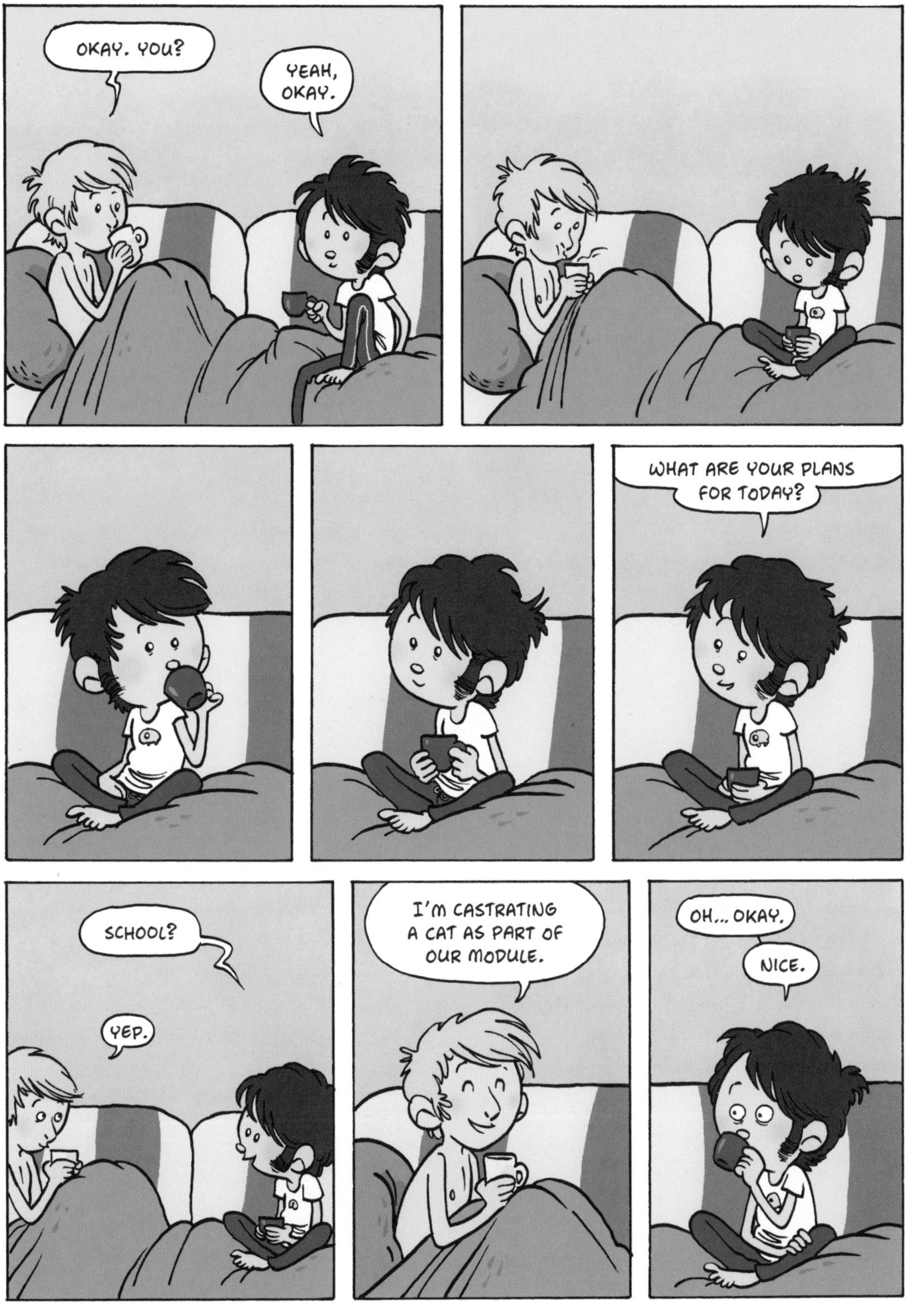
OKAY. YOU?
YEAH, OKAY.
WHAT ARE YOUR PLANS FOR TODAY?
SCHOOL?
YEP.
I'M CASTRATING A CAT AS PART OF OUR MODULE.
OH... OKAY.
NICE.

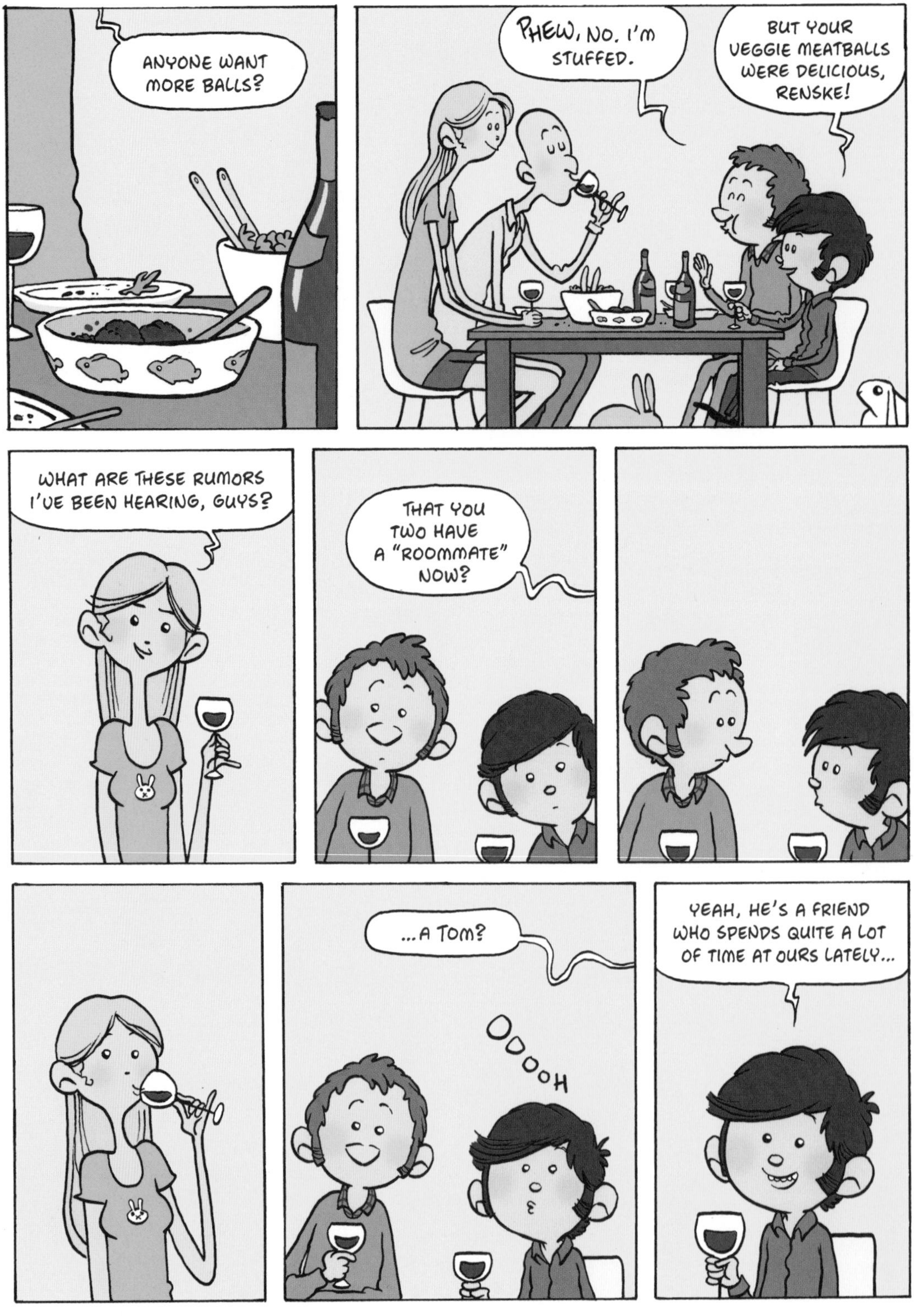

ANYONE WANT MORE BALLS?
PHEW, NO. I'M STUFFED.
BUT YOUR VEGGIE MEATBALLS WERE DELICIOUS, RENSKE!
WHAT ARE THESE RUMORS I'VE BEEN HEARING, GUYS?
THAT YOU TWO HAVE A "ROOMMATE" NOW?
...A TOM?
OOOOH
YEAH, HE'S A FRIEND WHO SPENDS QUITE A LOT OF TIME AT OURS LATELY...

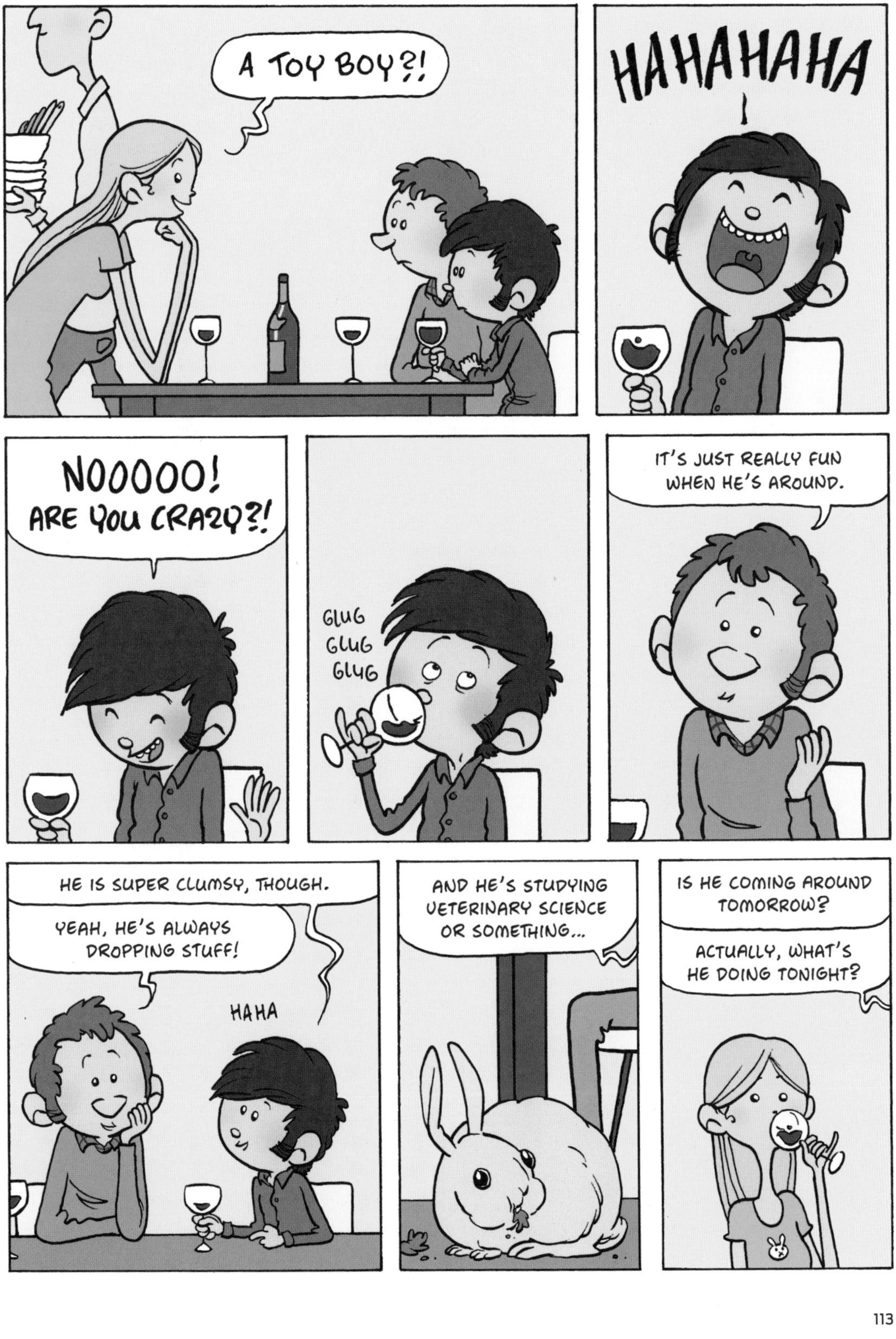
A TOY BOY?!
HAHAHAHA
NOOOOO! ARE YOU CRAZY?!
GLUG GLUG GLUG
IT'S JUST REALLY FUN WHEN HE'S AROUND.
HE IS SUPER CLUMSY, THOUGH.
YEAH, HE'S ALWAYS DROPPING STUFF!
HAHA
AND HE'S STUDYING VETERINARY SCIENCE OR SOMETHING...
IS HE COMING AROUND TOMORROW?
ACTUALLY, WHAT'S HE DOING TONIGHT?

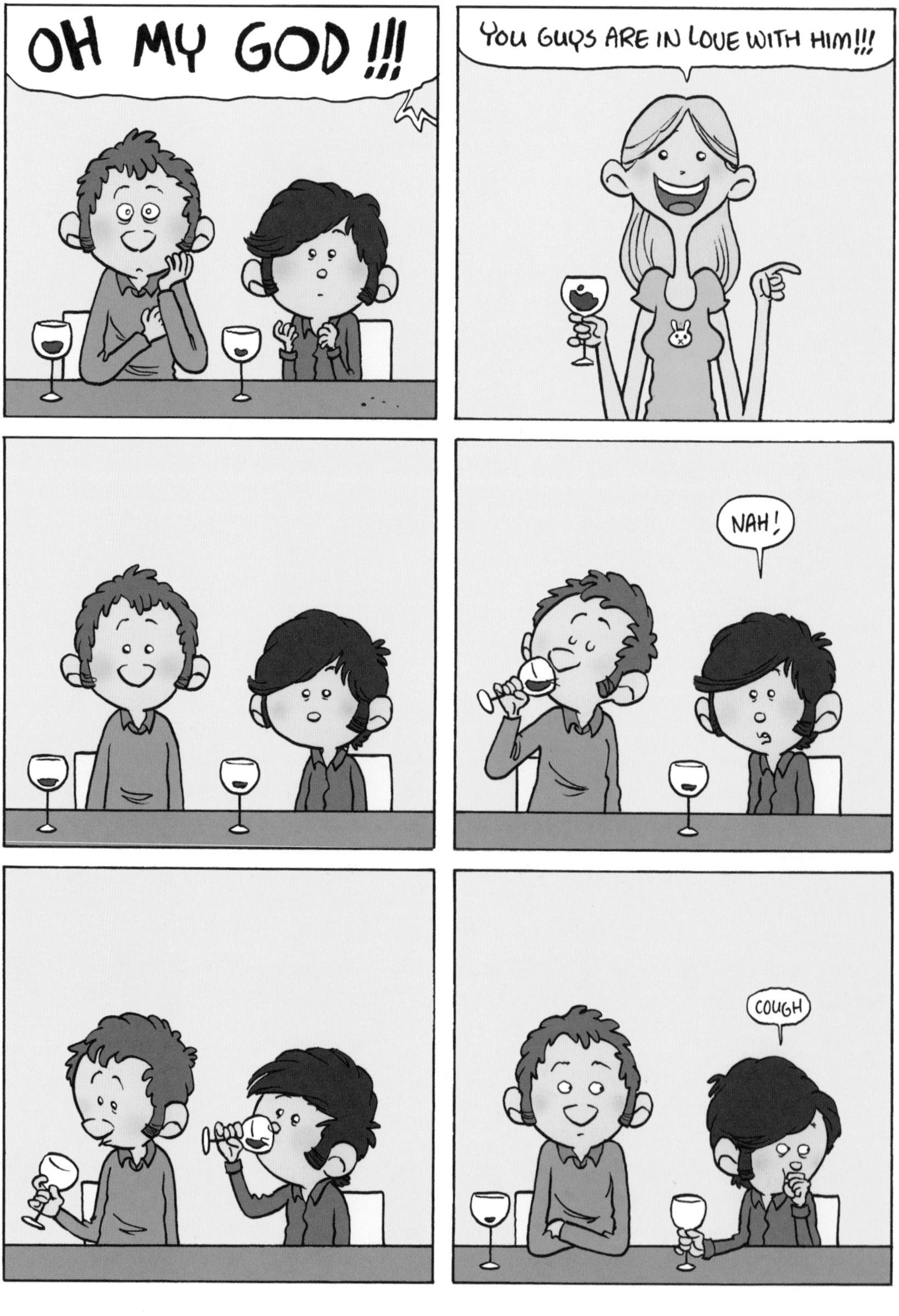
OH MY GOD!!!
YOU GUYS ARE IN LOVE WITH HIM!!!
NAH!
COUGH

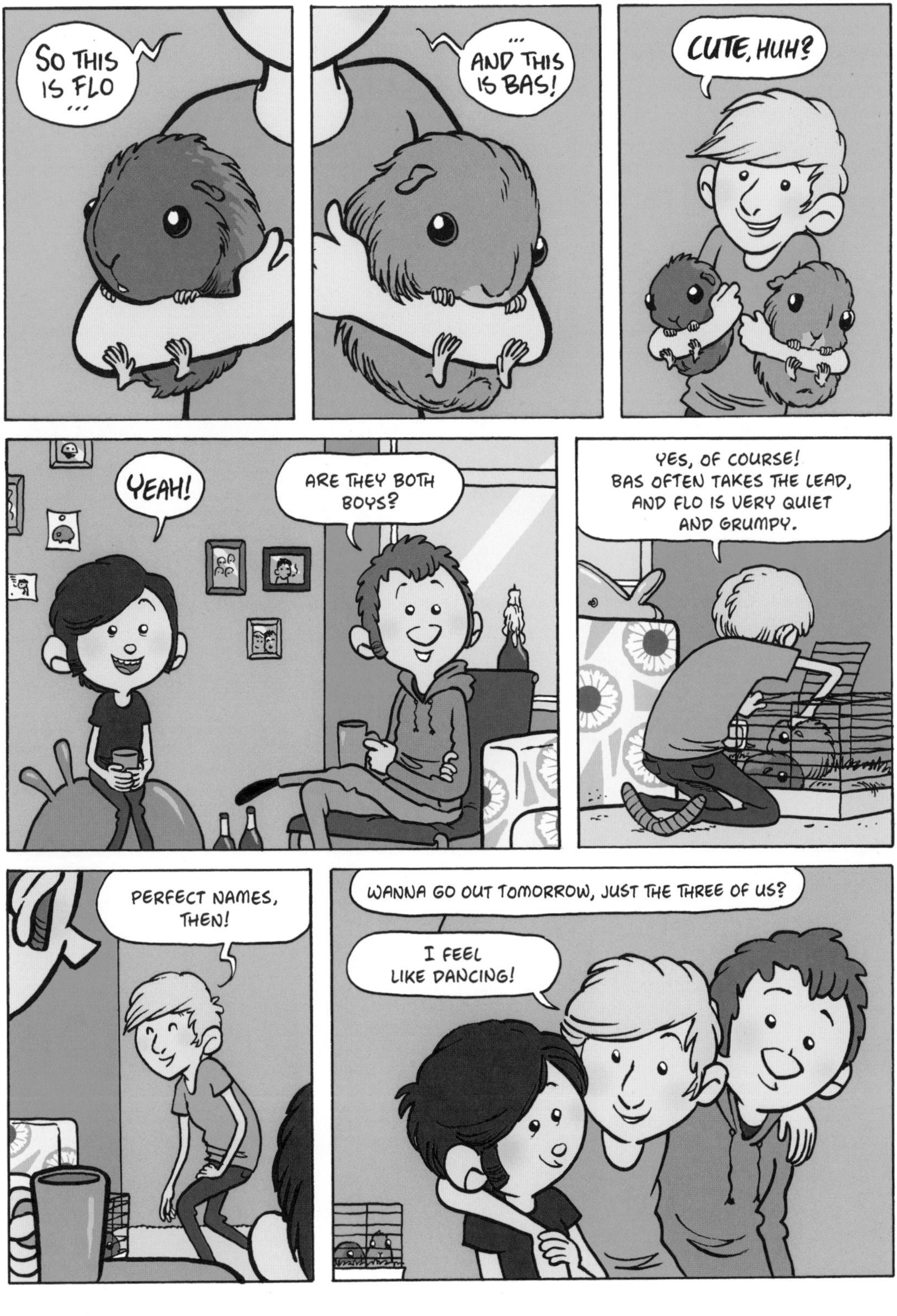
SO THIS IS FLO ...
... AND THIS IS BAS!
CUTE, HUH?
YEAH!
ARE THEY BOTH BOYS?
YES, OF COURSE! BAS OFTEN TAKES THE LEAD, AND FLO IS VERY QUIET AND GRUMPY.
PERFECT NAMES, THEN!
WANNA GO OUT TOMORROW, JUST THE THREE OF US?
I FEEL LIKE DANCING!

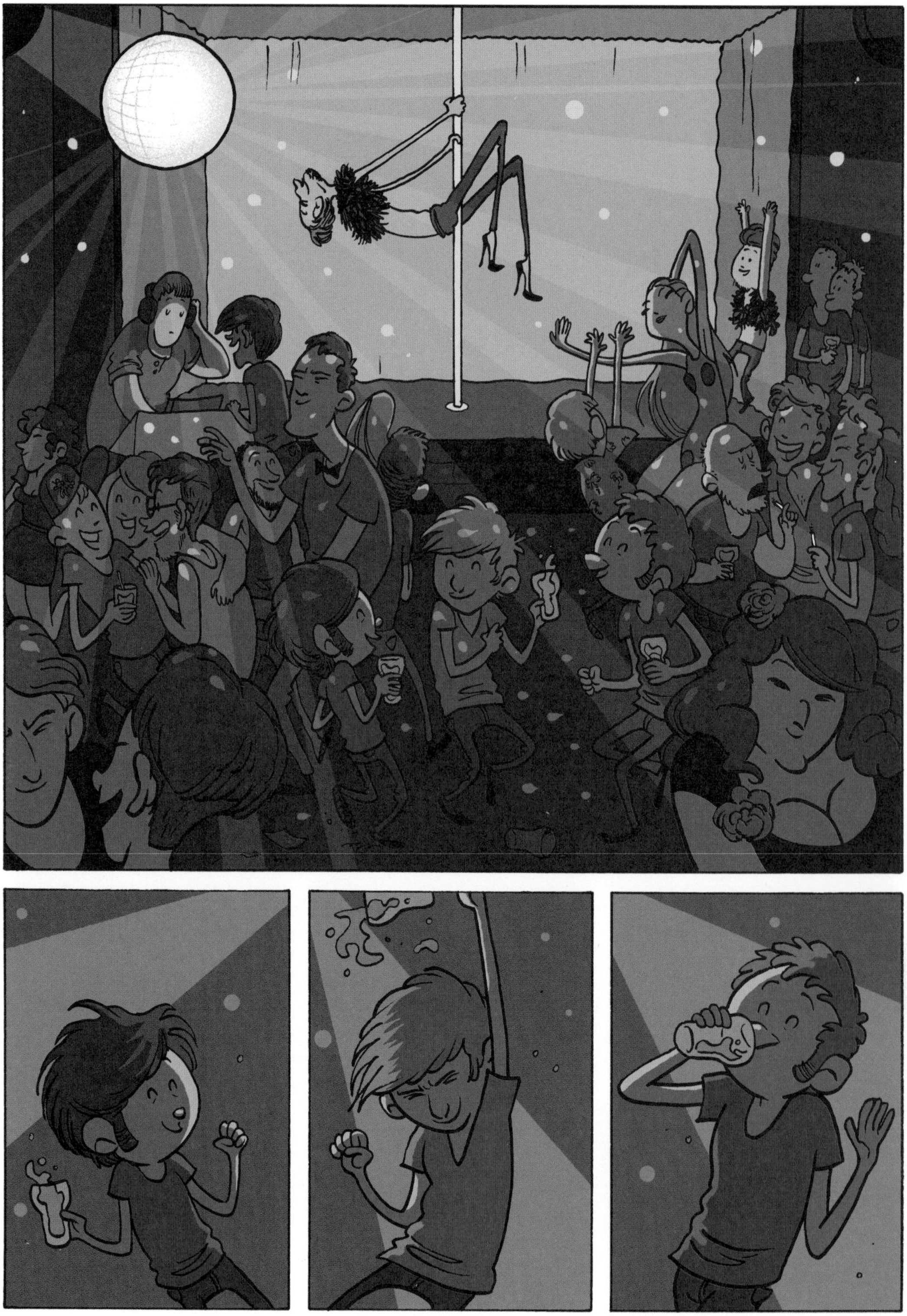

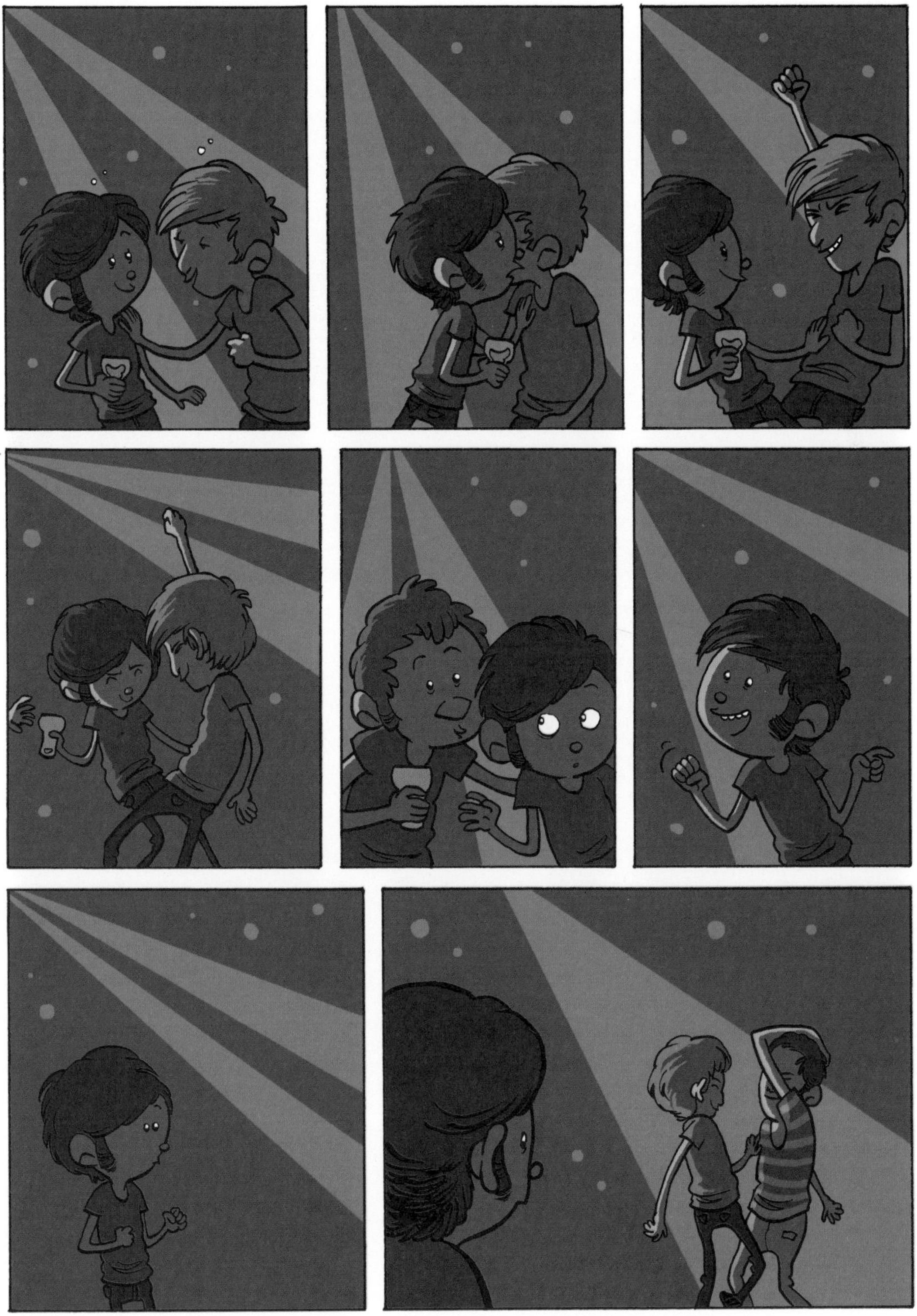

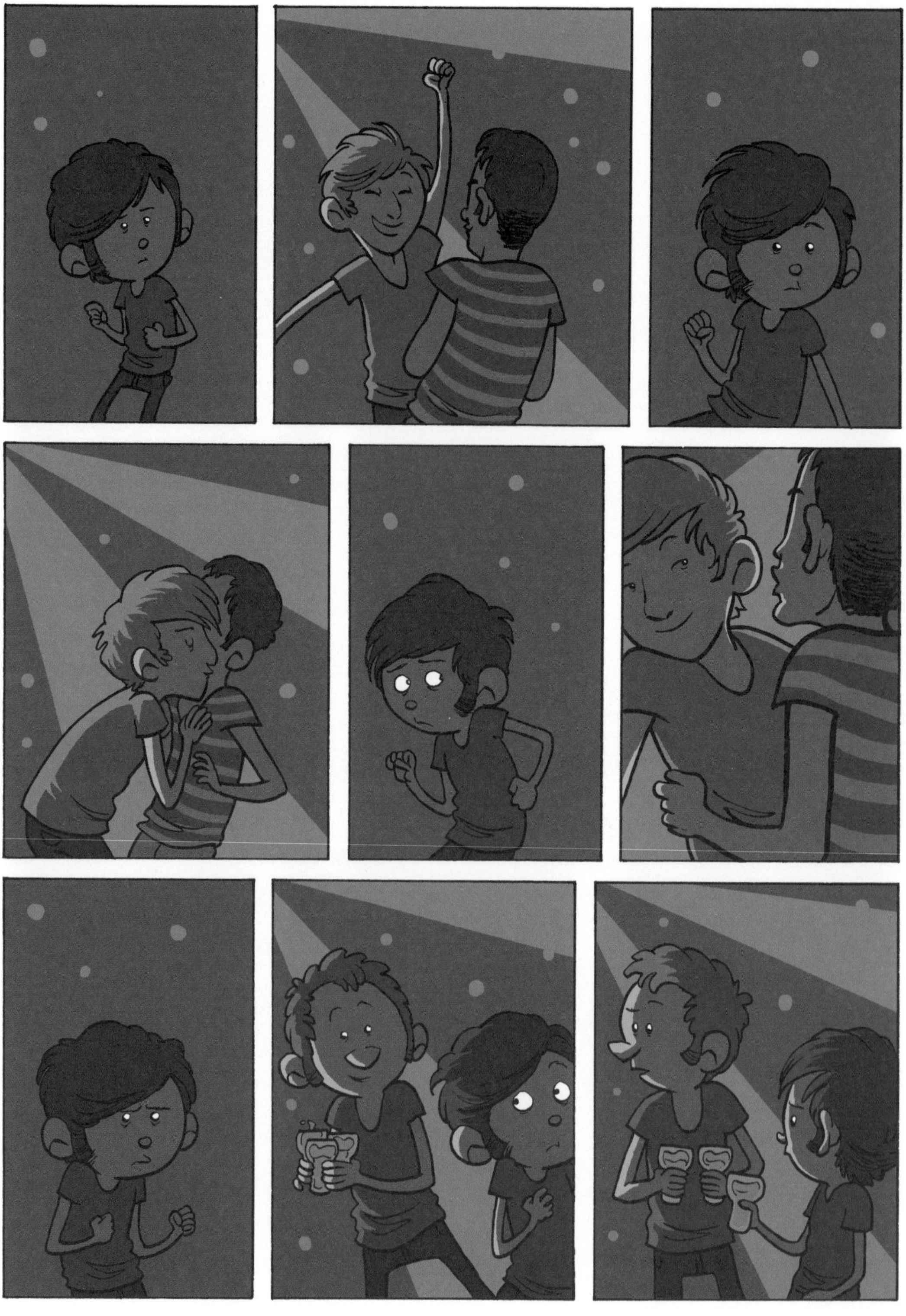

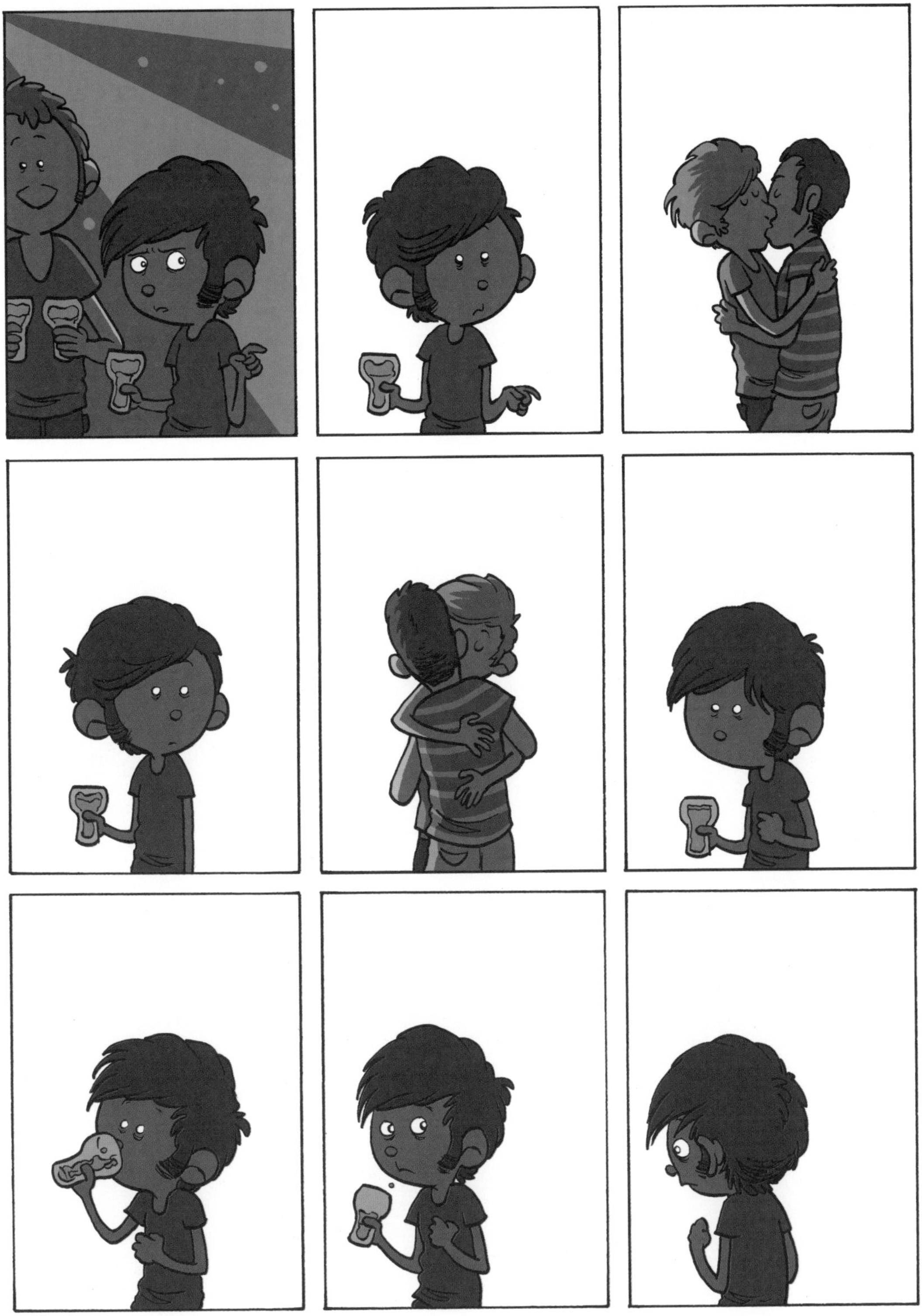

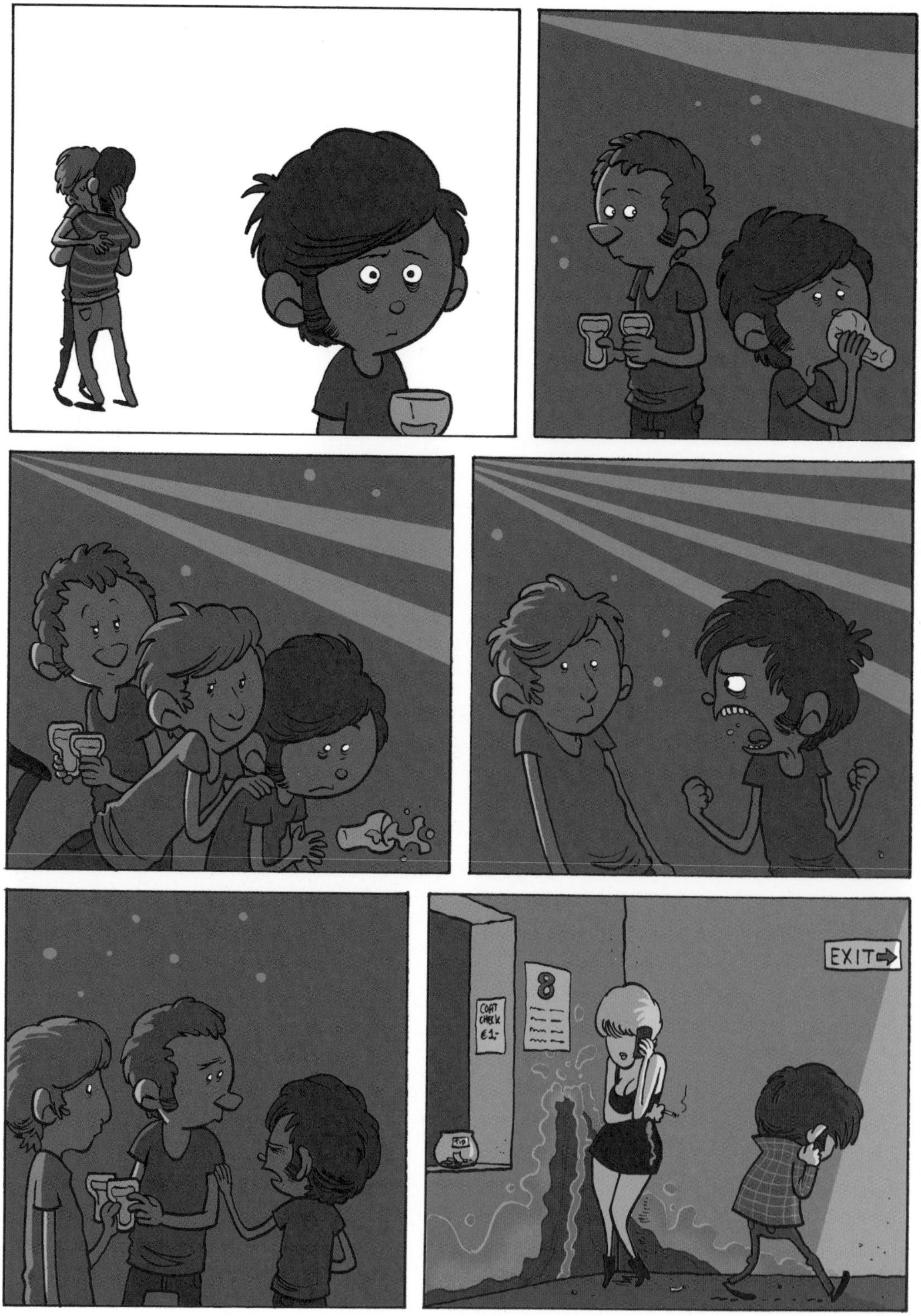
COAT CHECK €1-
EXIT

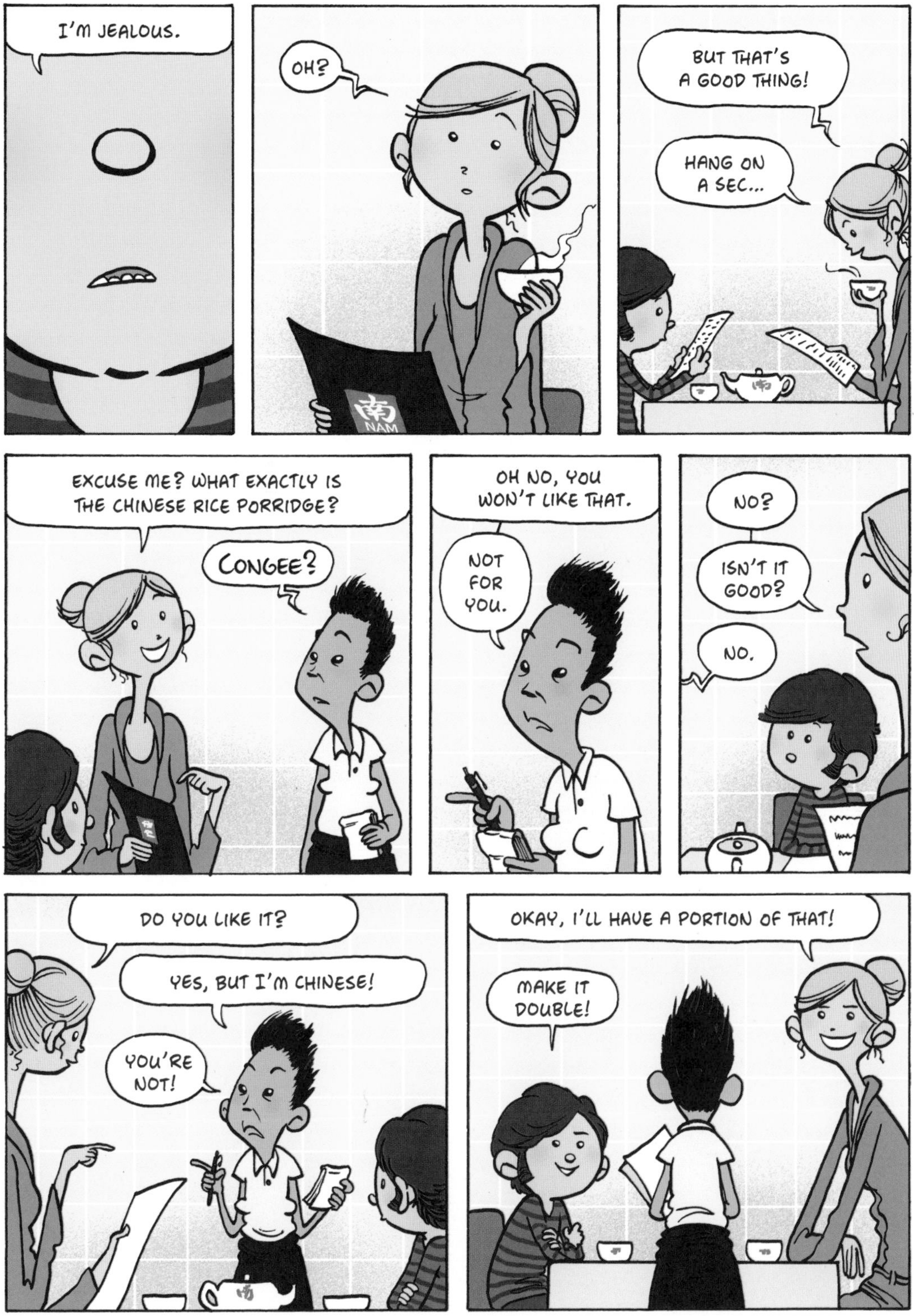
I'M JEALOUS.
OH?
BUT THAT'S A GOOD THING!
HANG ON A SEC...
EXCUSE ME? WHAT EXACTLY IS THE CHINESE RICE PORRIDGE?
CONGEE?
OH NO, YOU WON'T LIKE THAT.
NOT FOR YOU.
NO?
ISN'T IT GOOD?
NO.
DO YOU LIKE IT?
YES, BUT I'M CHINESE!
YOU'RE NOT!
OKAY, I'LL HAVE A PORTION OF THAT!
MAKE IT DOUBLE!

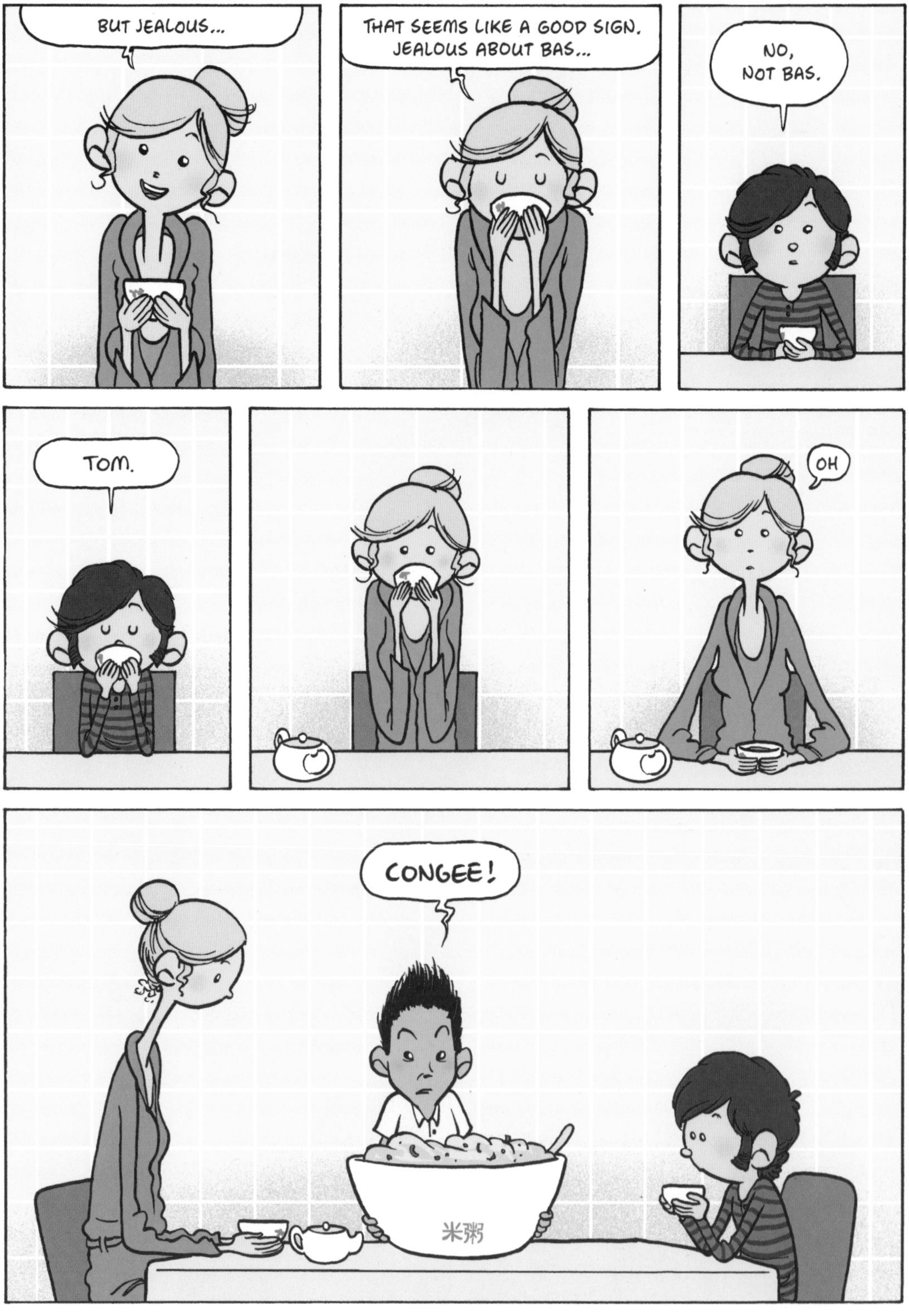
BUT JEALOUS...
THAT SEEMS LIKE A GOOD SIGN. JEALOUS ABOUT BAS...
NO, NOT BAS.
TOM.
OH
CONGEE!
米粥

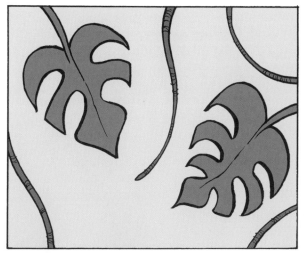

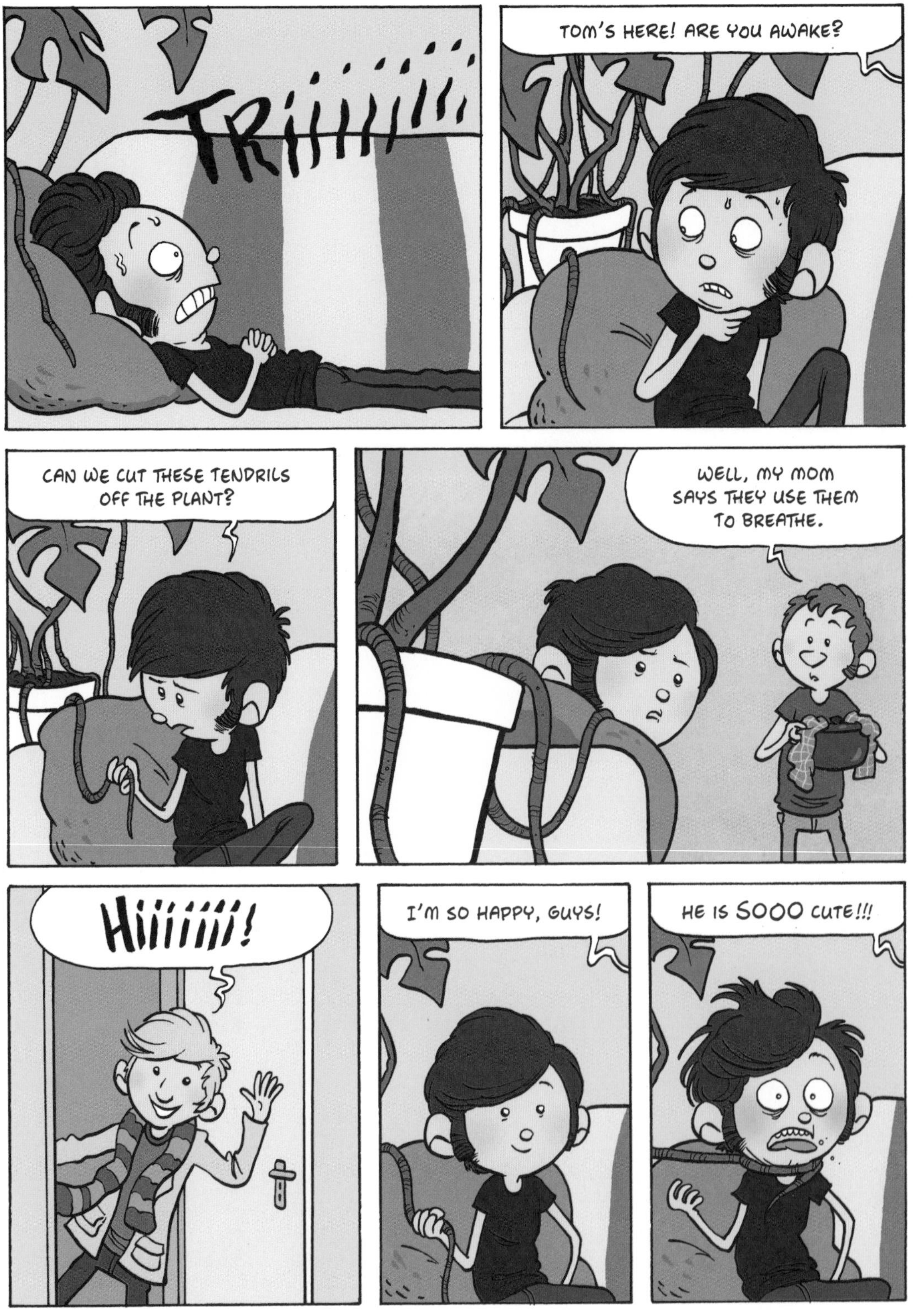
TRiiiiiii
TOM'S HERE! ARE YOU AWAKE?
CAN WE CUT THESE TENDRILS OFF THE PLANT?
WELL, MY MOM SAYS THEY USE THEM TO BREATHE.
Hiiiiiii!
I'M SO HAPPY, GUYS!
HE IS SOOO CUTE!!!

SUPER TASTY, GUYS!

DIDN'T YOU LIKE IT, BOO?

YEAH... BUT JUST NOT THAT HUNGRY.

SO TELL US MORE ABOUT THIS GUY!

I MET HIM WHEN I WAS OUT ONE NIGHT...

AND WE KISSED...

UM, I NEED TO GO PEE.

AND TONIGHT, WE'RE GOING ON A DATE...

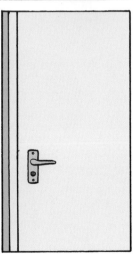

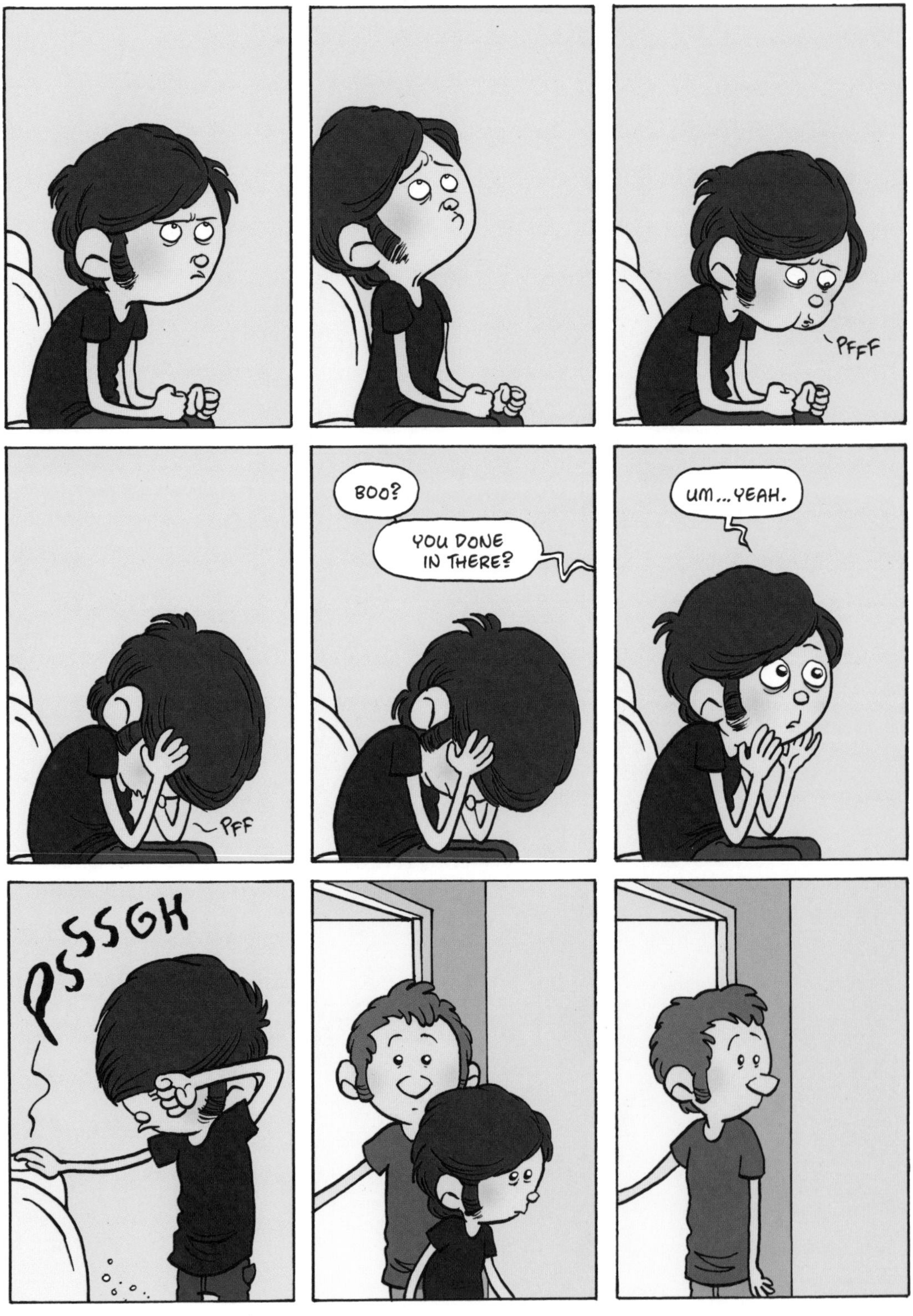
PFFF
PFF
BOO?
YOU DONE IN THERE?
UM... YEAH.
PSSSGH

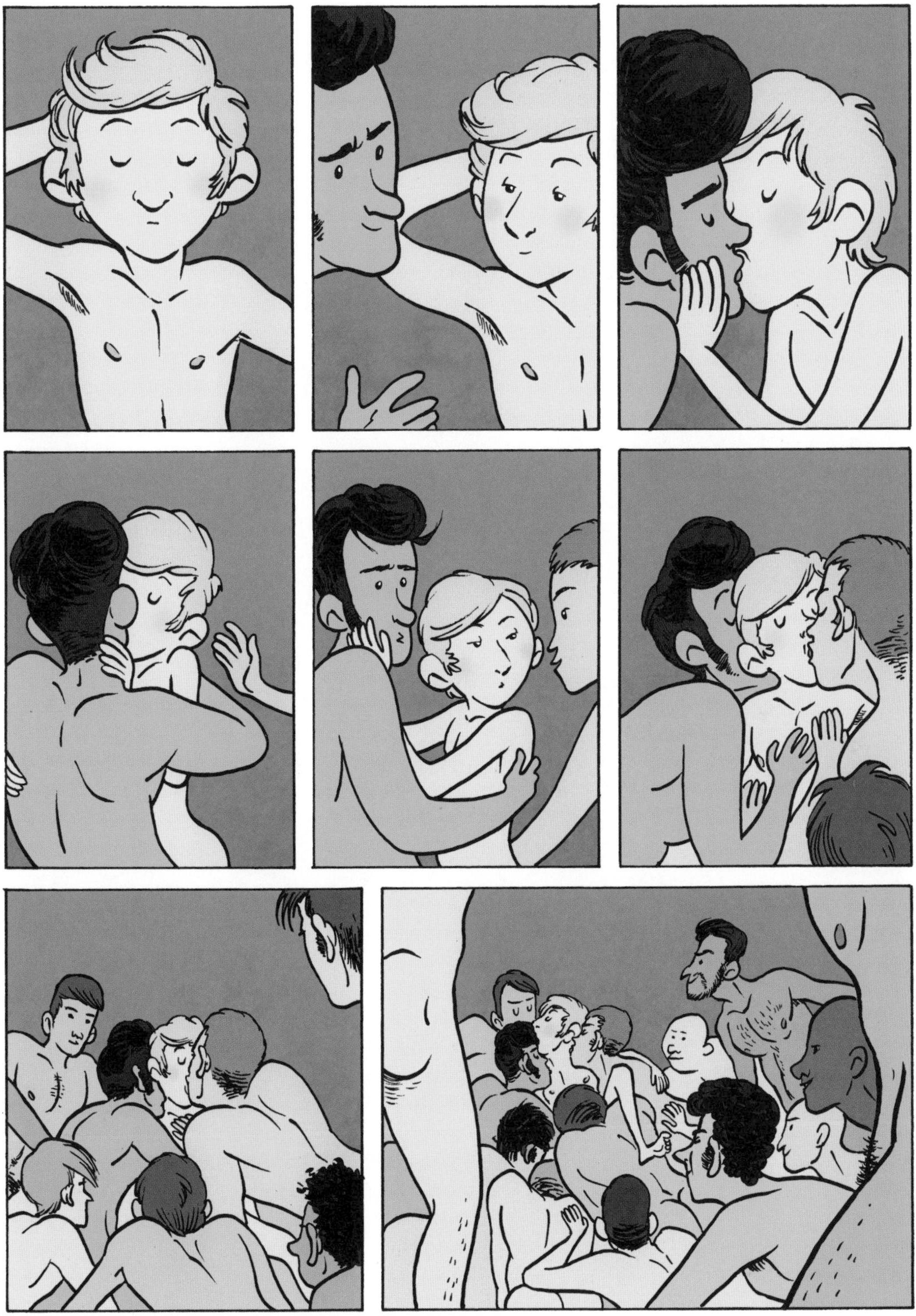

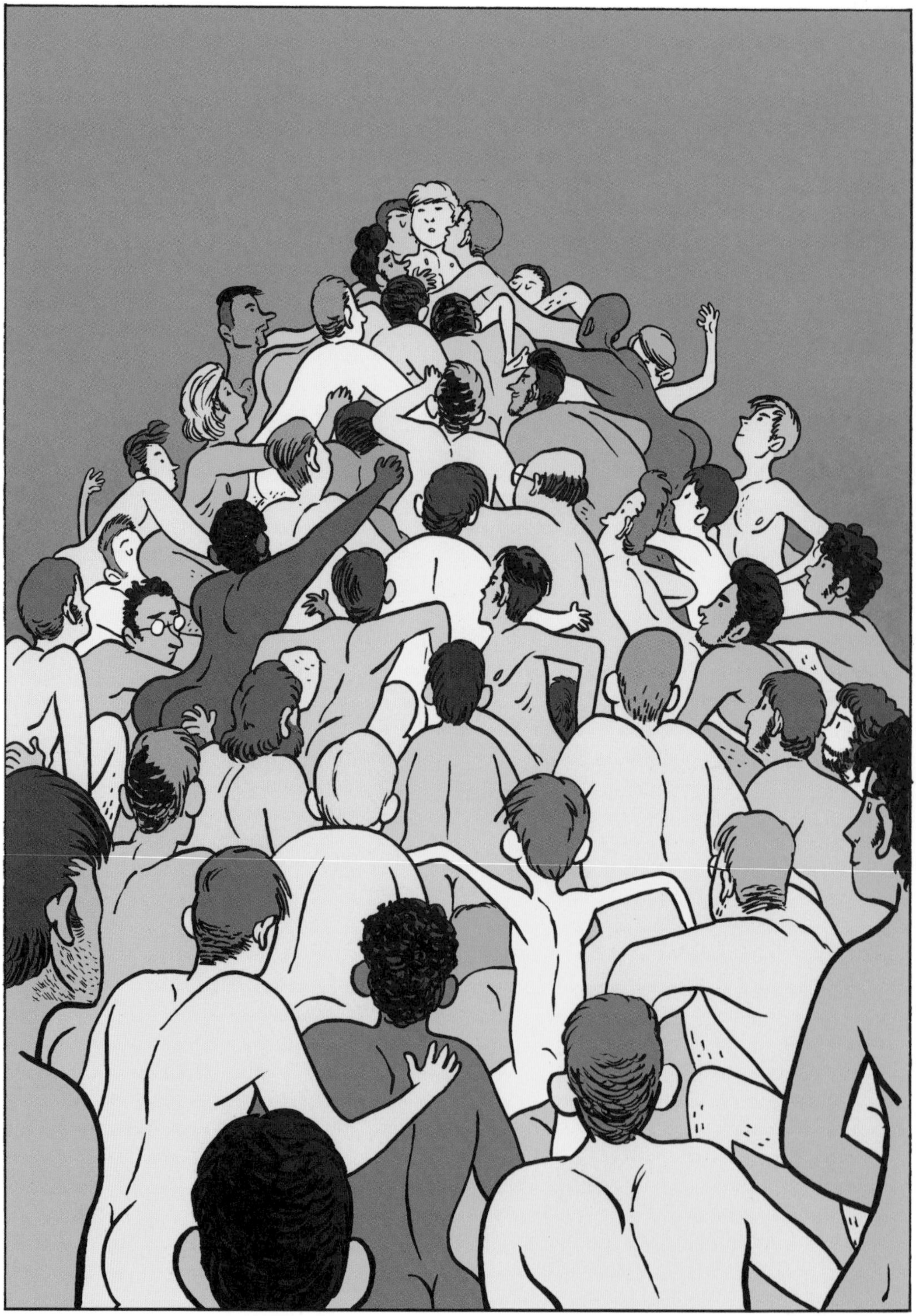

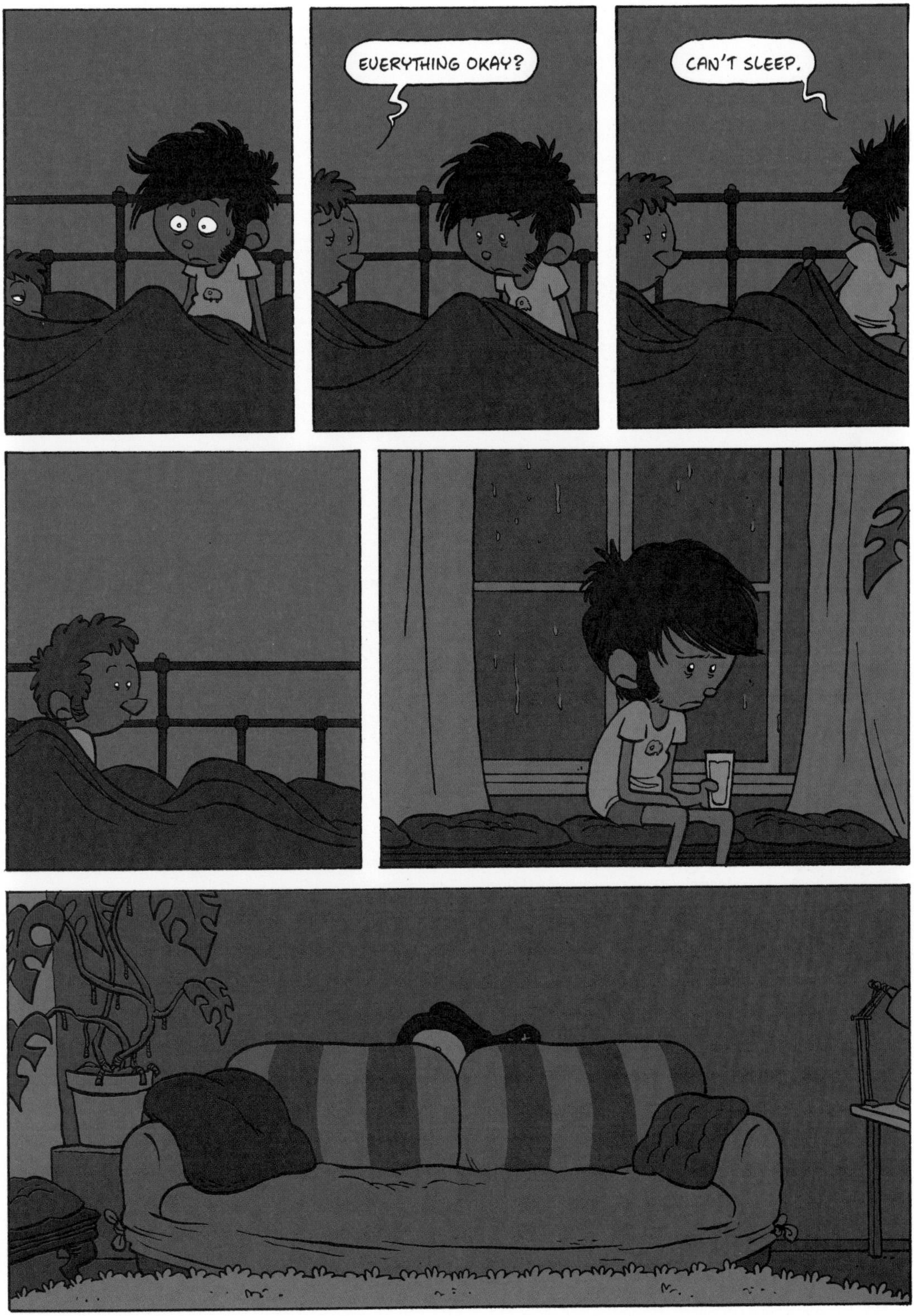
EVERYTHING OKAY?
CAN'T SLEEP.

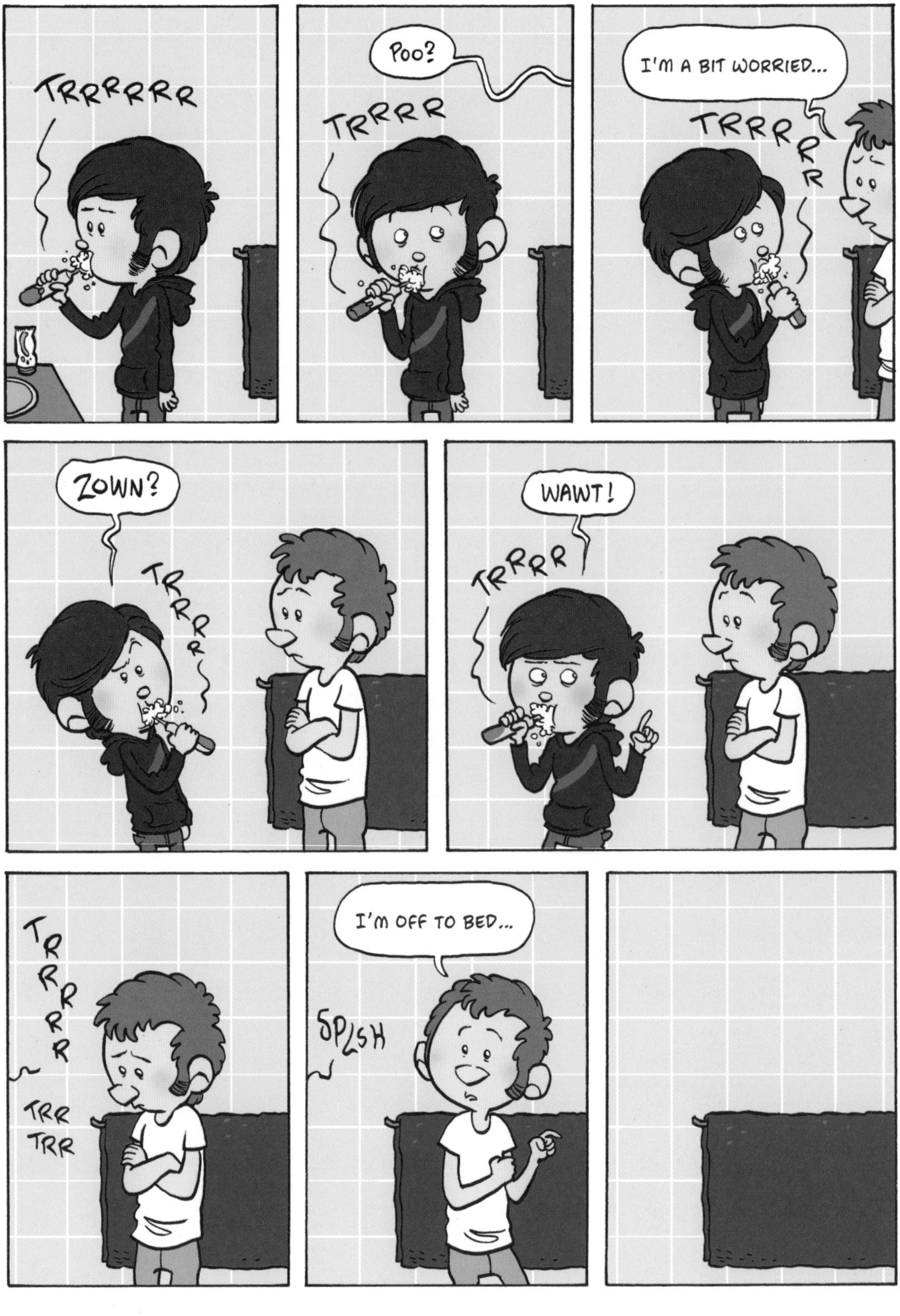
TRRRRRR
POO?
TRRRR
I'M A BIT WORRIED...
TRRRRRR
ZOWN?
TRRRR
WAWT!
TRRRR
TRRRRR
TRR
TRR
I'M OFF TO BED...
SPLSH

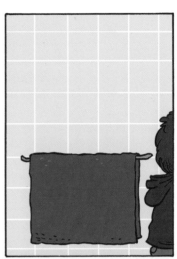

HOW DO YOU FEEL?

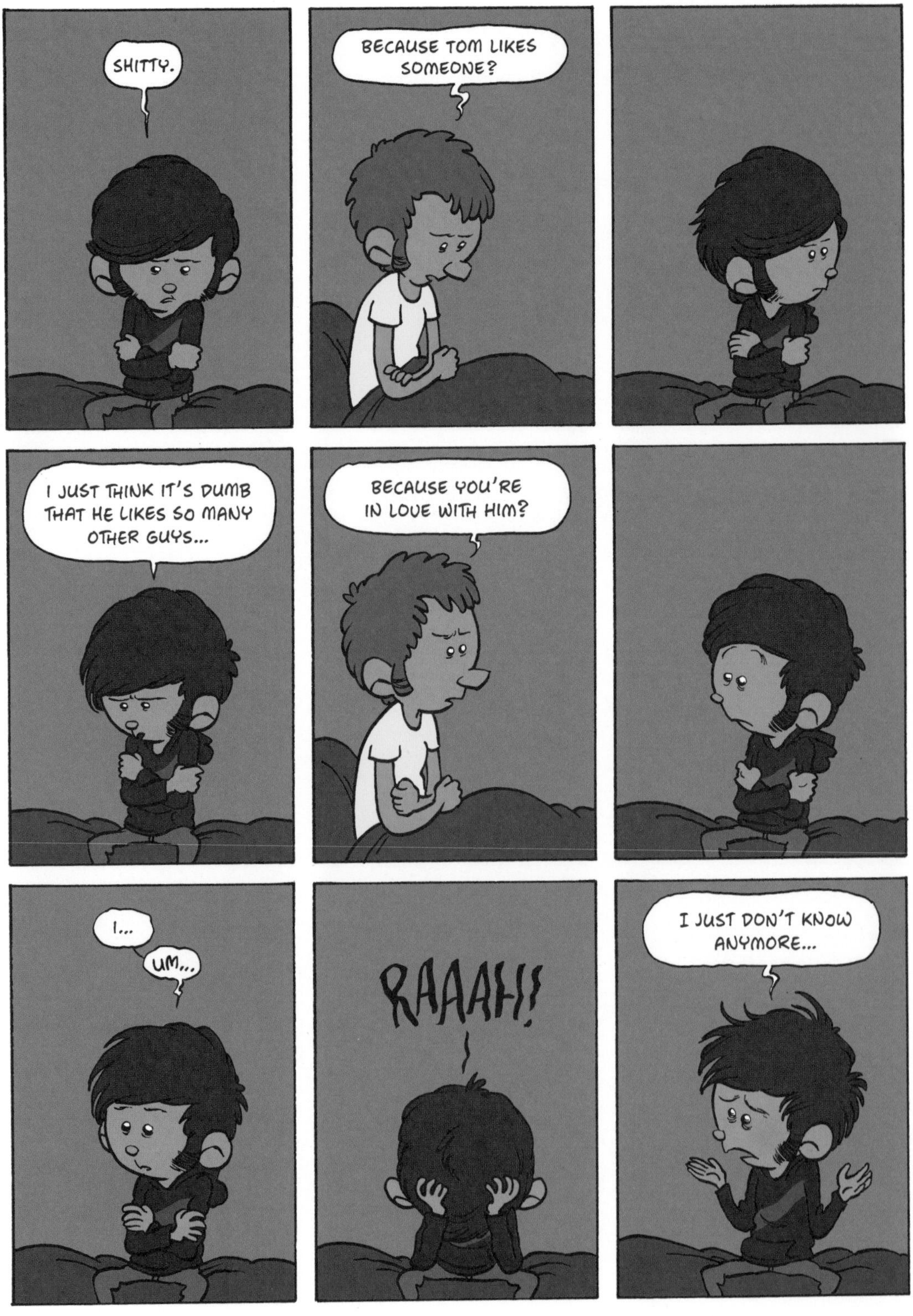
SHITTY.
BECAUSE TOM LIKES SOMEONE?
I JUST THINK IT'S DUMB THAT HE LIKES SO MANY OTHER GUYS...
BECAUSE YOU'RE IN LOVE WITH HIM?
I...
UM...
RAAAH!
I JUST DON'T KNOW ANYMORE...

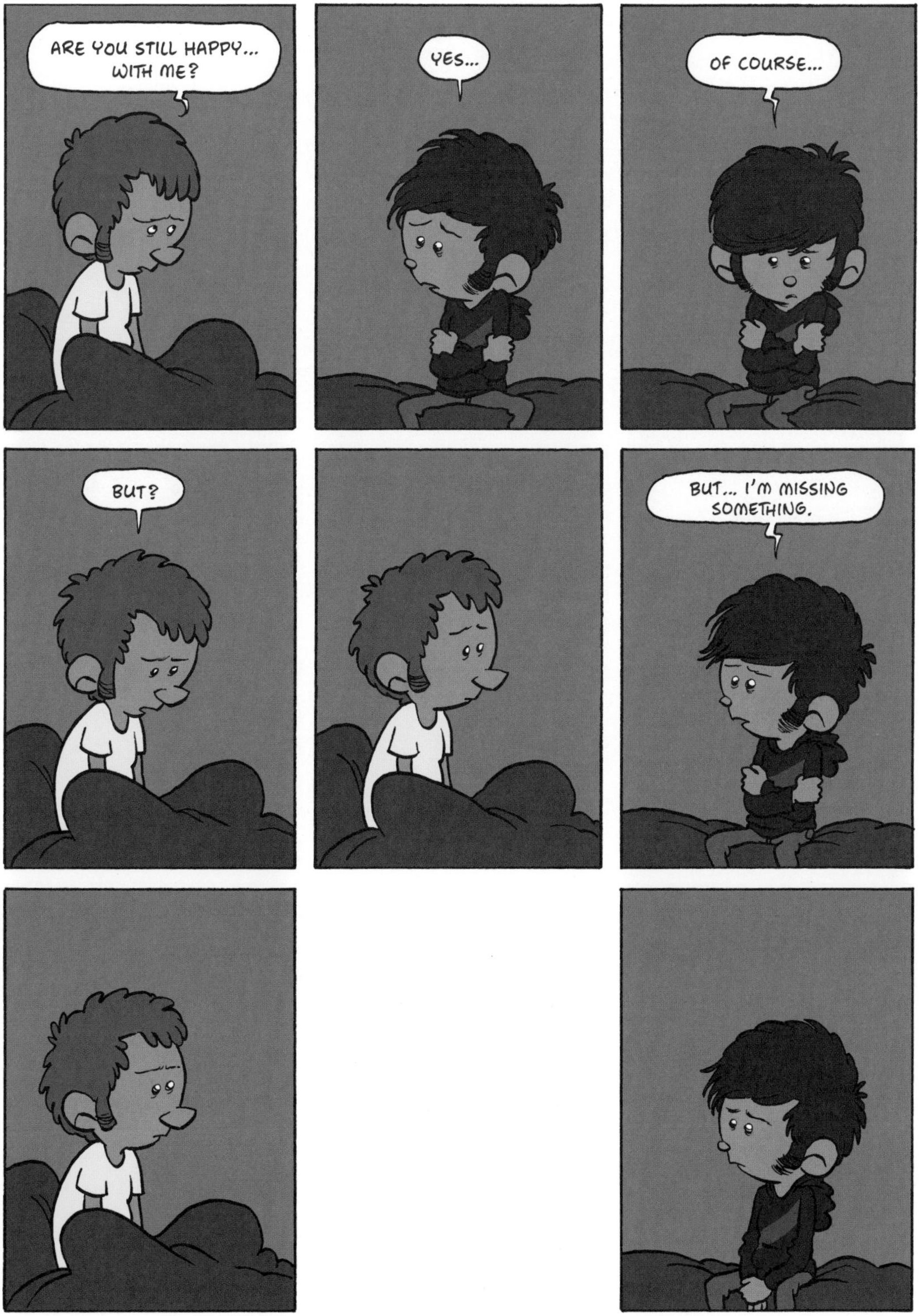
ARE YOU STILL HAPPY... WITH ME?
YES...
OF COURSE...
BUT?
BUT... I'M MISSING SOMETHING.

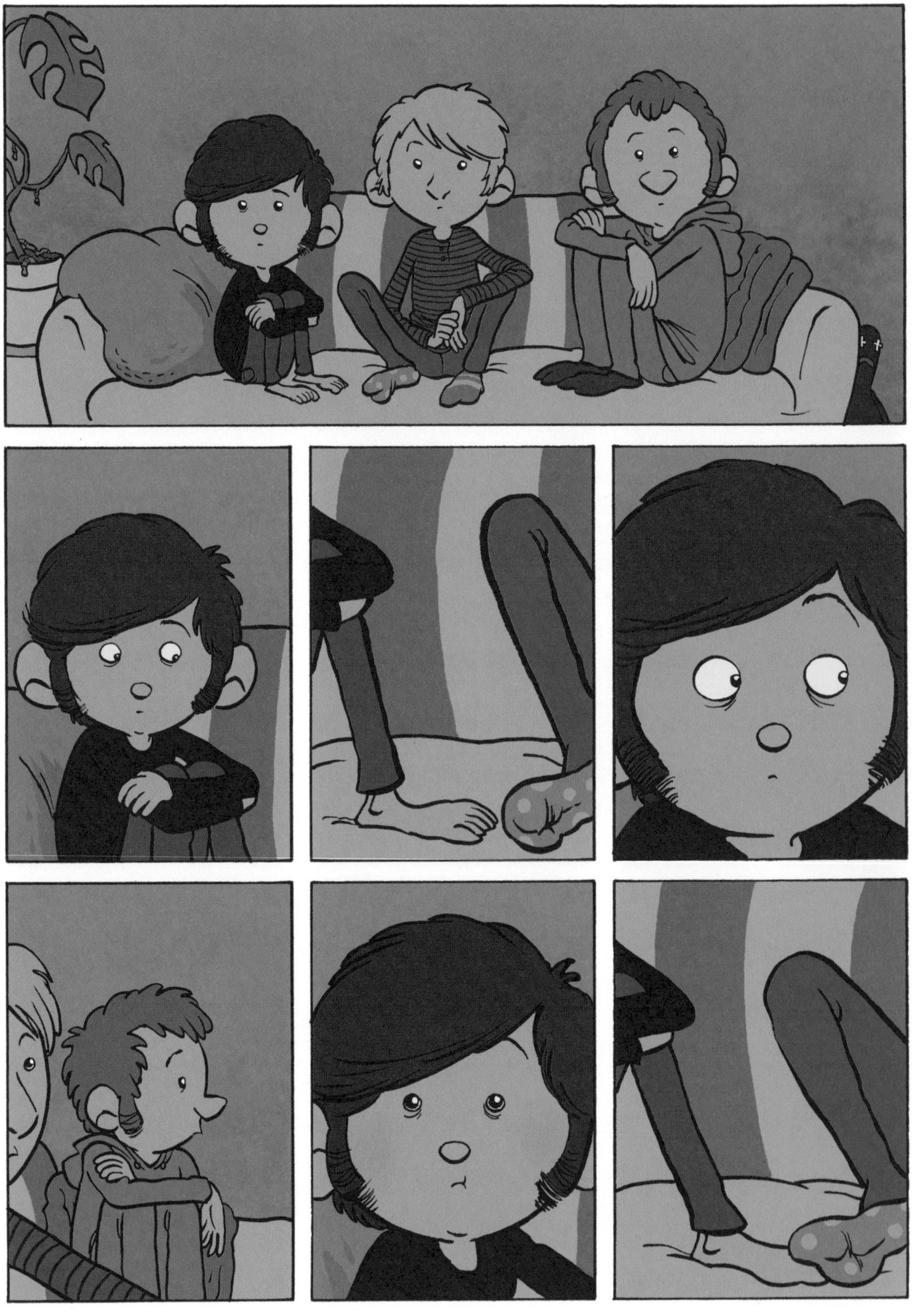

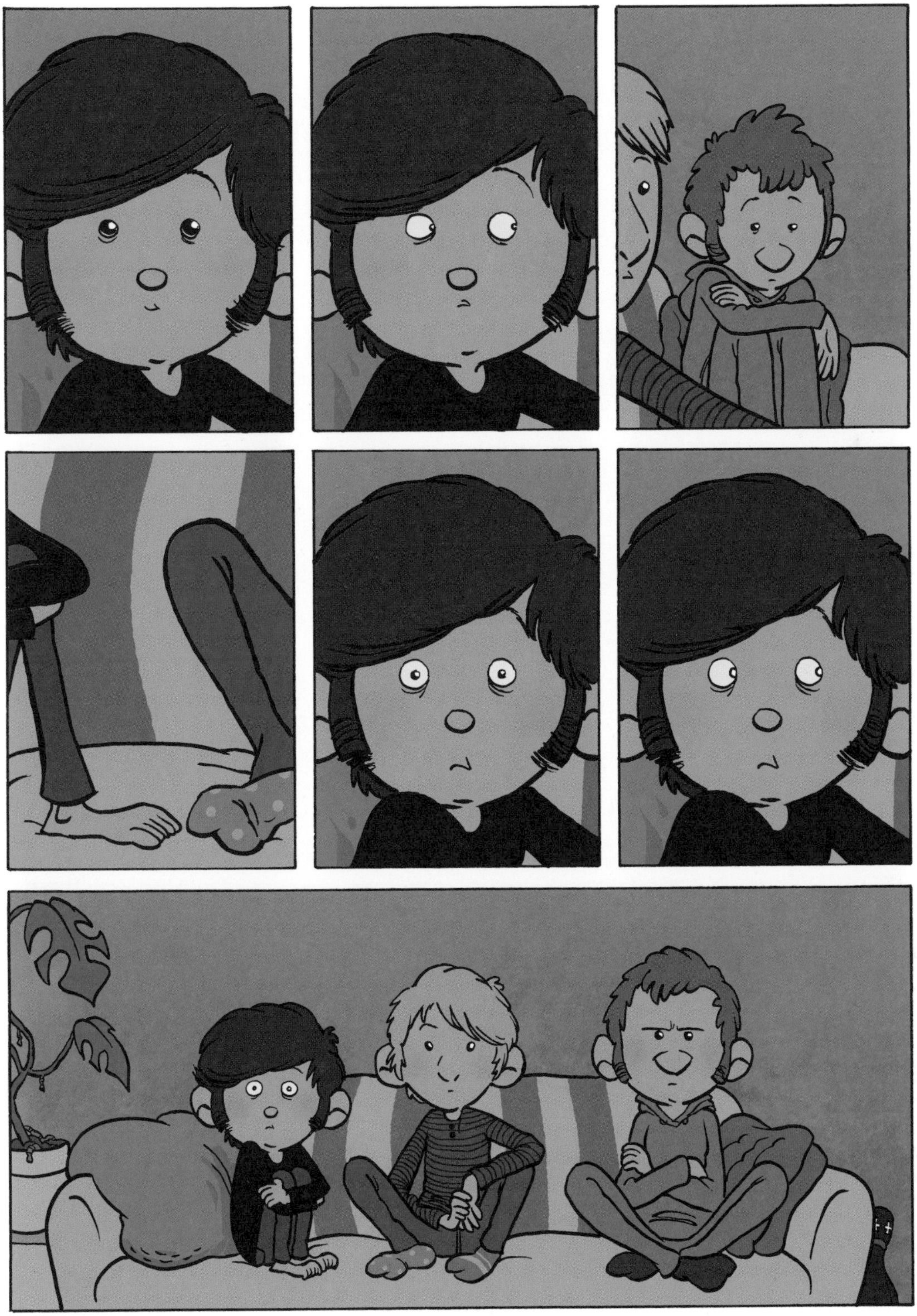

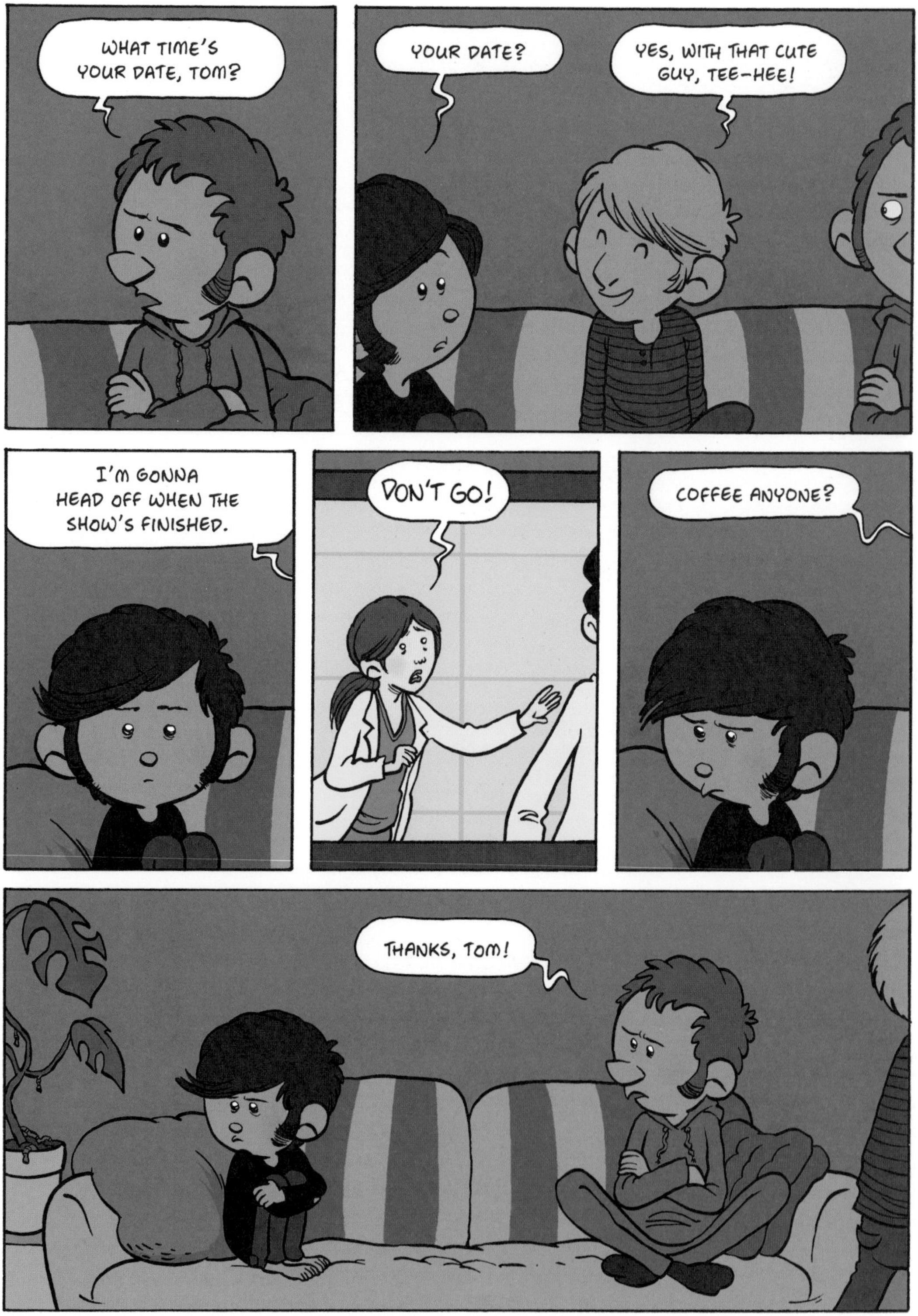
WHAT TIME'S YOUR DATE, TOM?
YOUR DATE?
YES, WITH THAT CUTE GUY, TEE-HEE!
I'M GONNA HEAD OFF WHEN THE SHOW'S FINISHED.
DON'T GO!
COFFEE ANYONE?
THANKS, TOM!

CAN I JUST USE THE RED CUPS?

SURE.

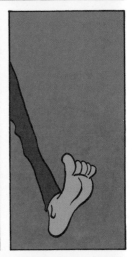

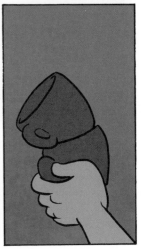

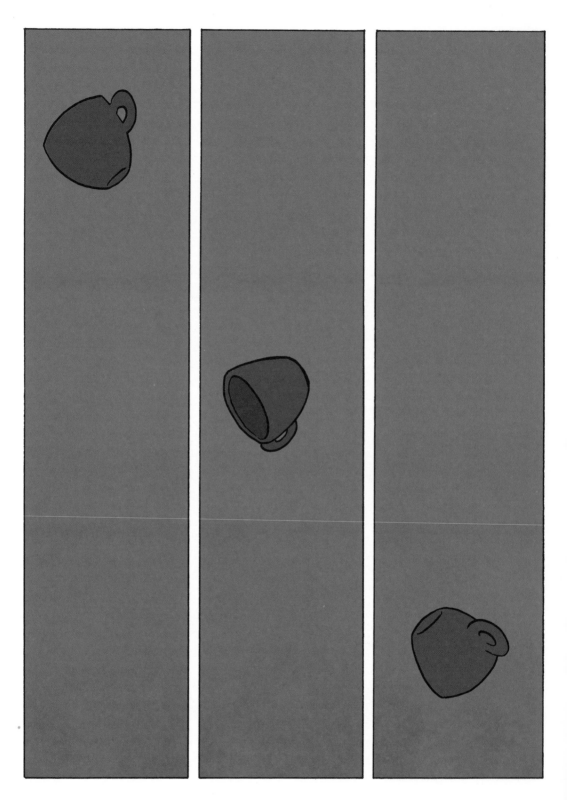

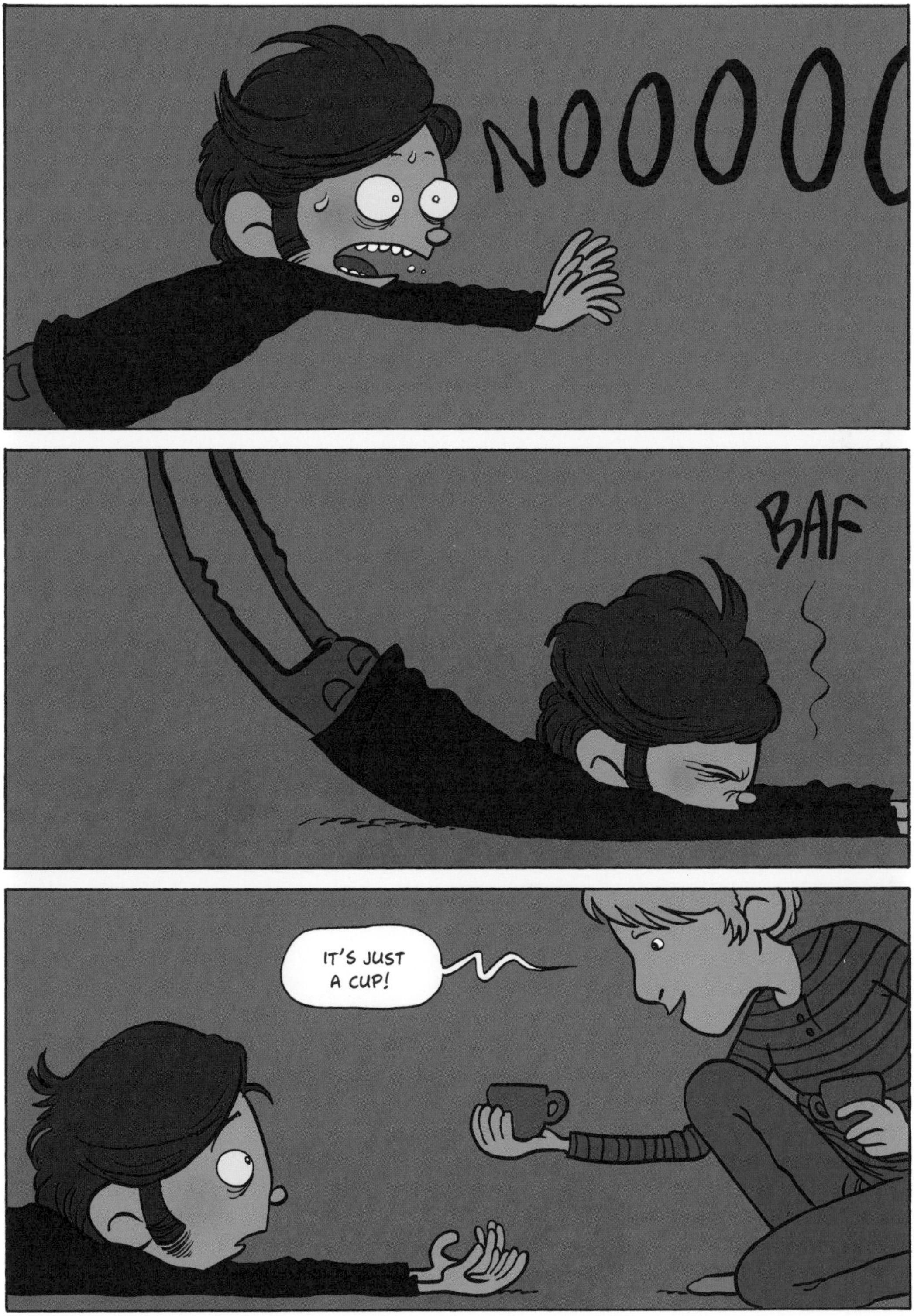
NOOOOO
BAF
IT'S JUST A CUP!

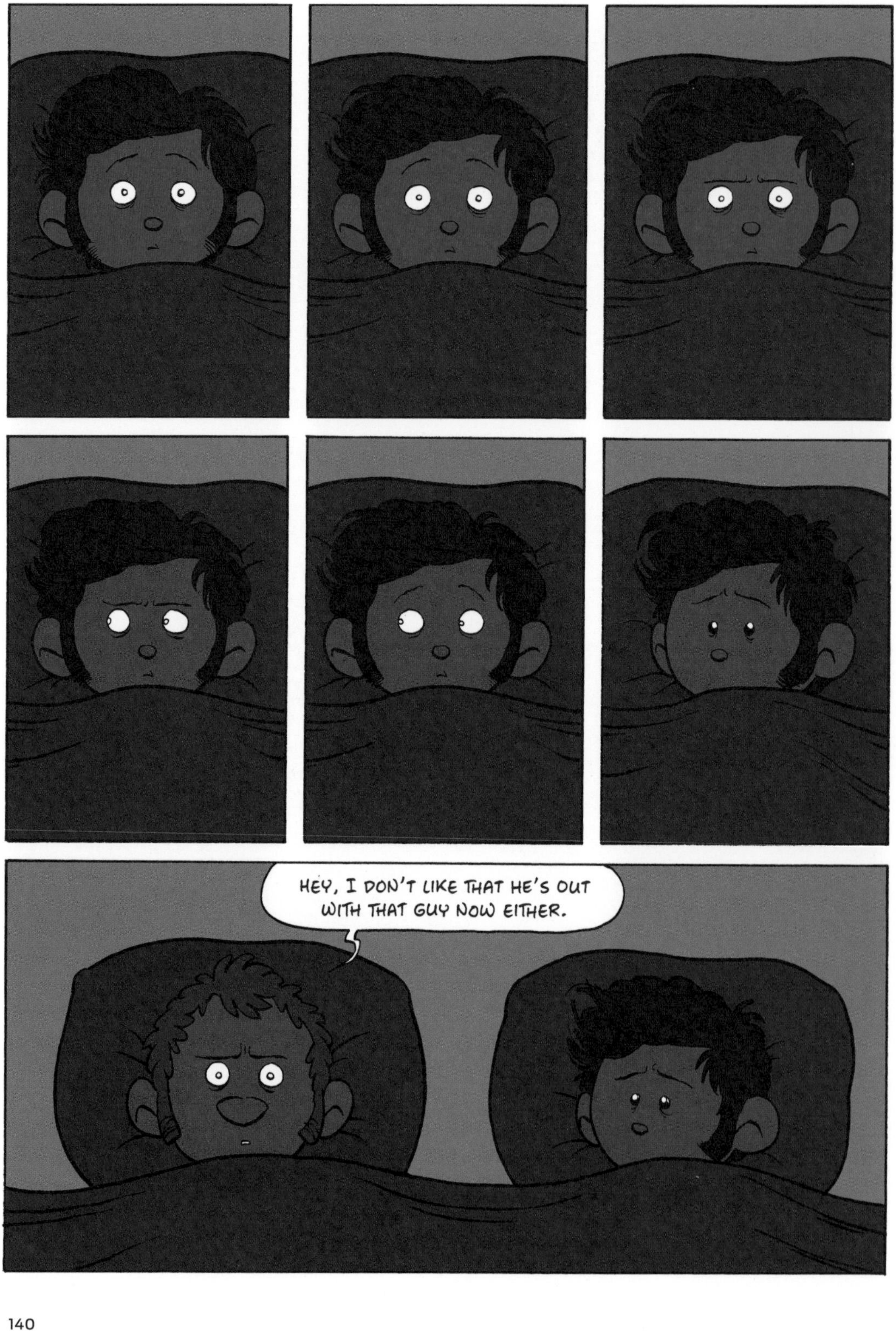
HEY, I DON'T LIKE THAT HE'S OUT WITH THAT GUY NOW EITHER.

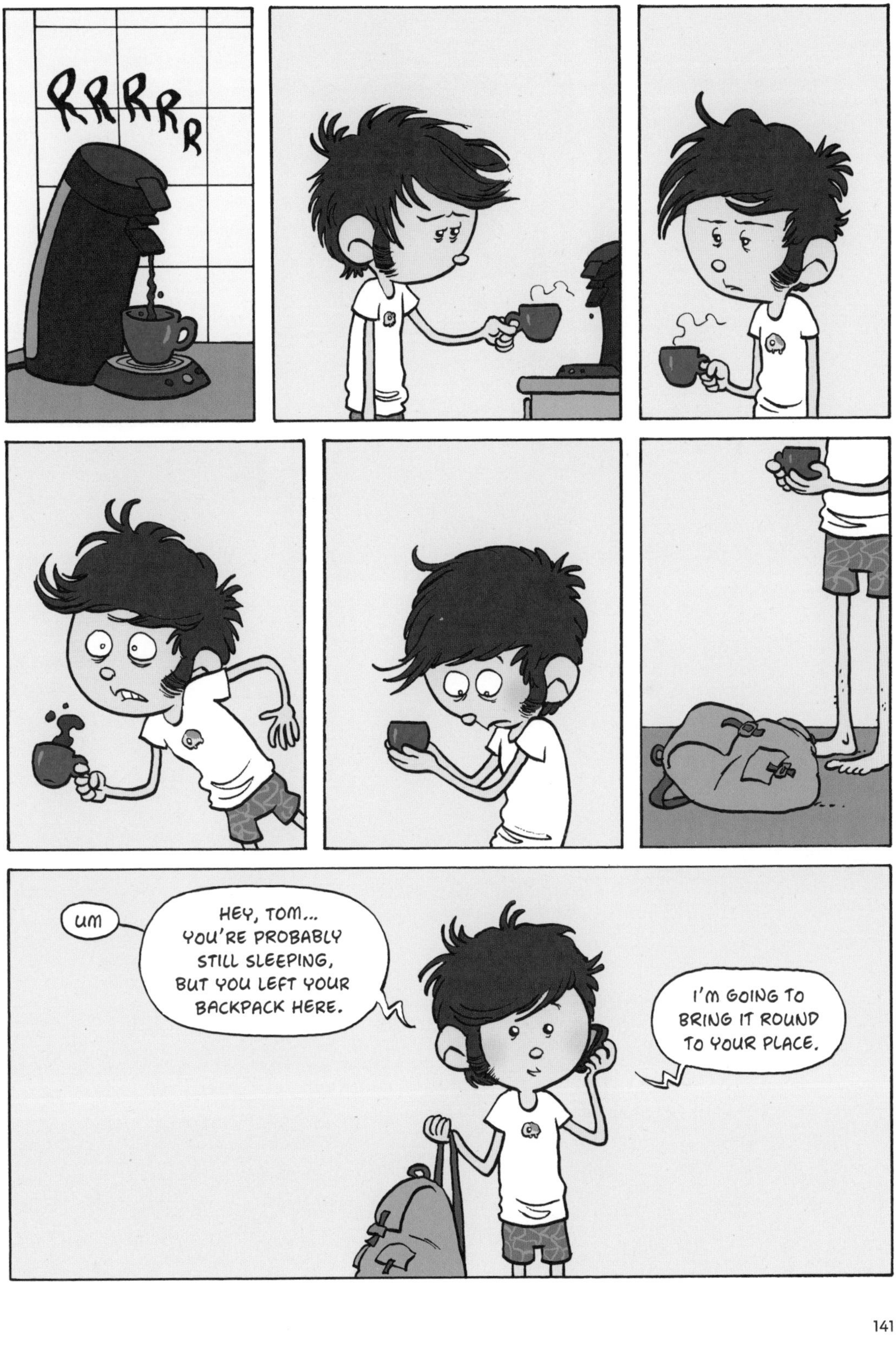
RRRRR
UM
HEY, TOM...
YOU'RE PROBABLY
STILL SLEEPING,
BUT YOU LEFT YOUR
BACKPACK HERE.
I'M GOING TO
BRING IT ROUND
TO YOUR PLACE.

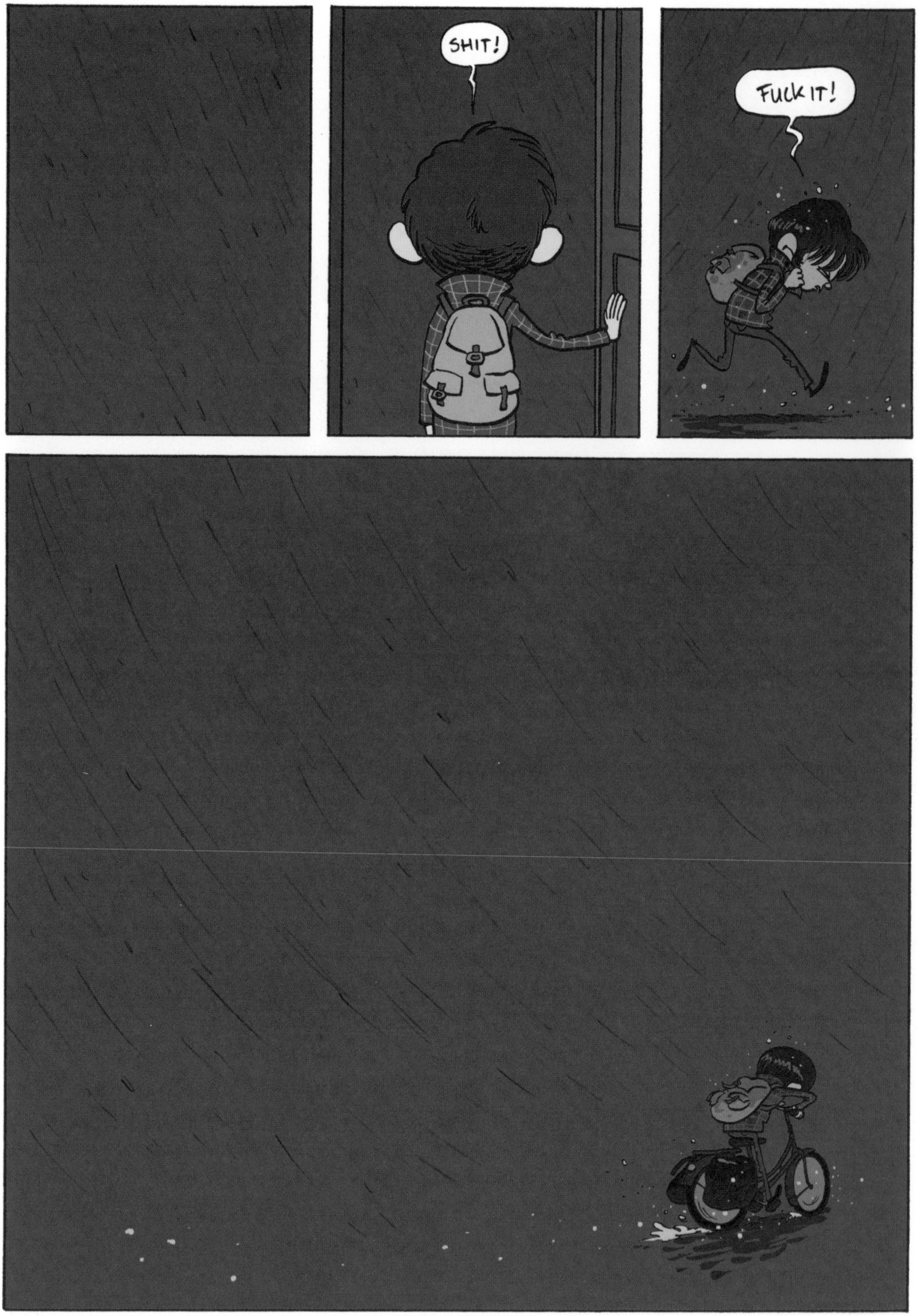
SHIT!
FUCK IT!

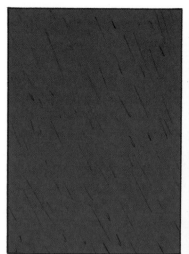

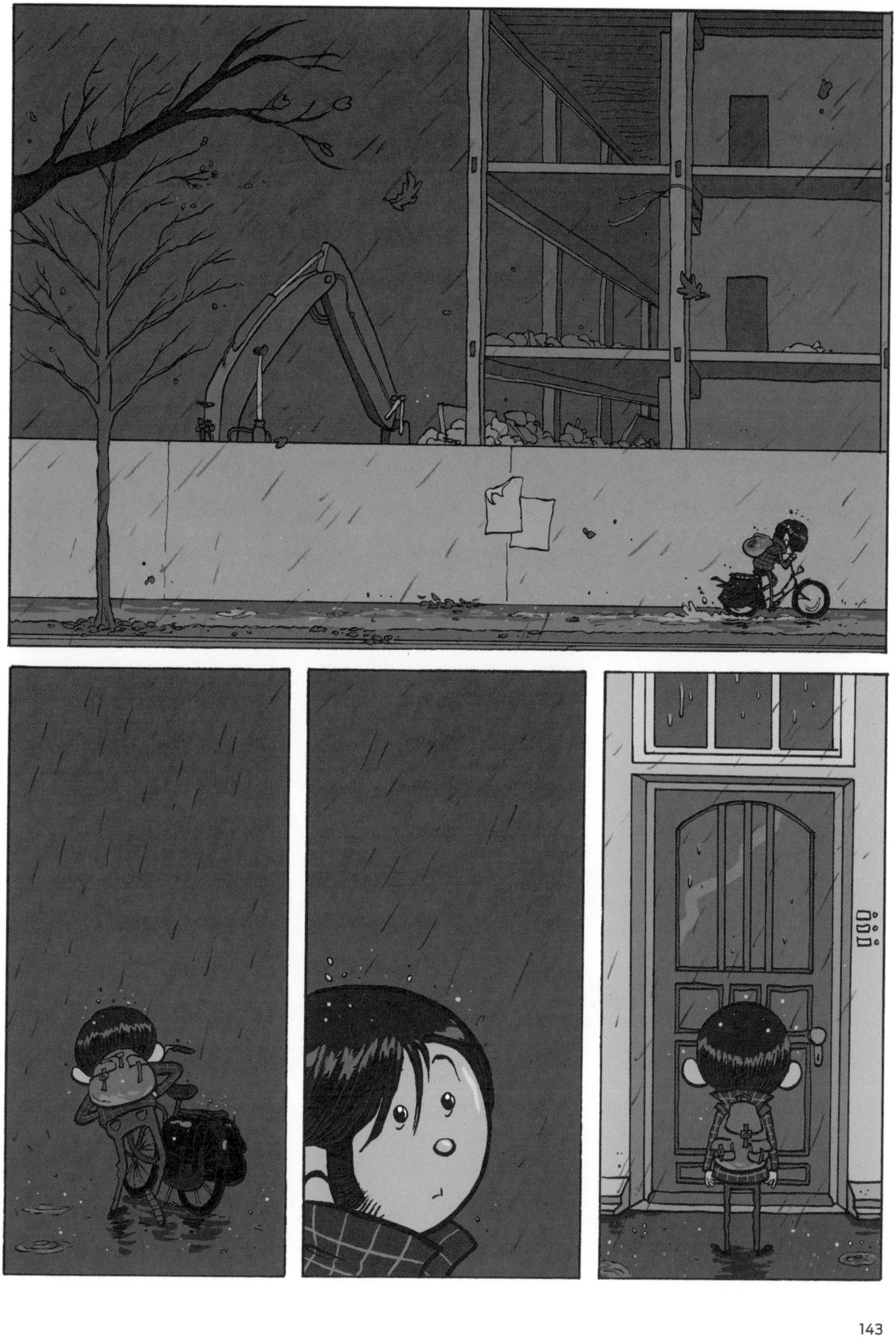

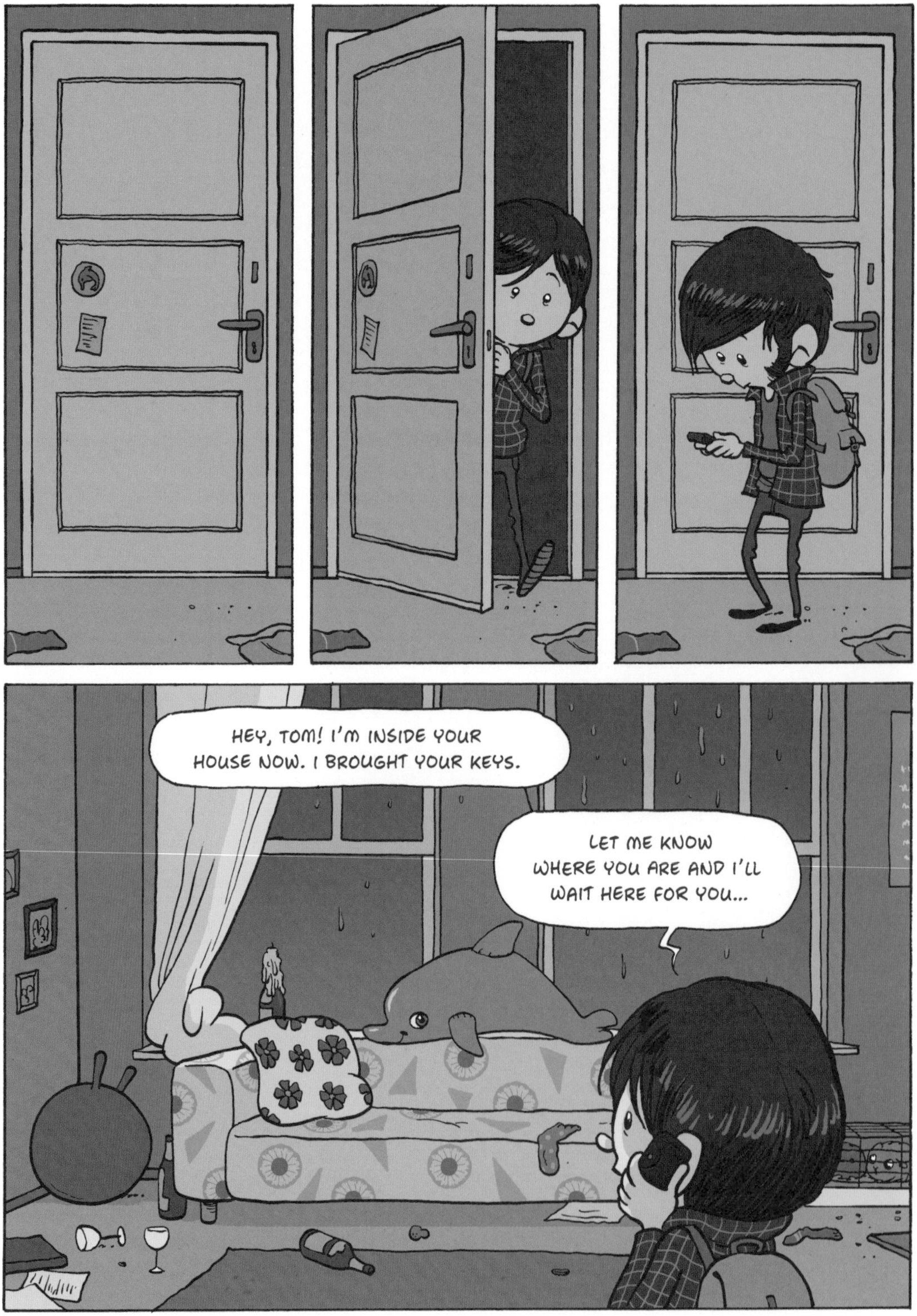
HEY, TOM! I'M INSIDE YOUR HOUSE NOW. I BROUGHT YOUR KEYS.
LET ME KNOW WHERE YOU ARE AND I'LL WAIT HERE FOR YOU...

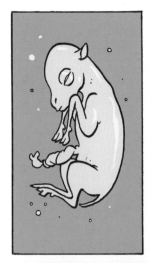

PFF

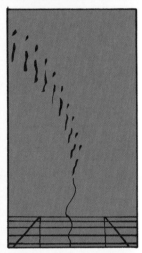

HEEEY!

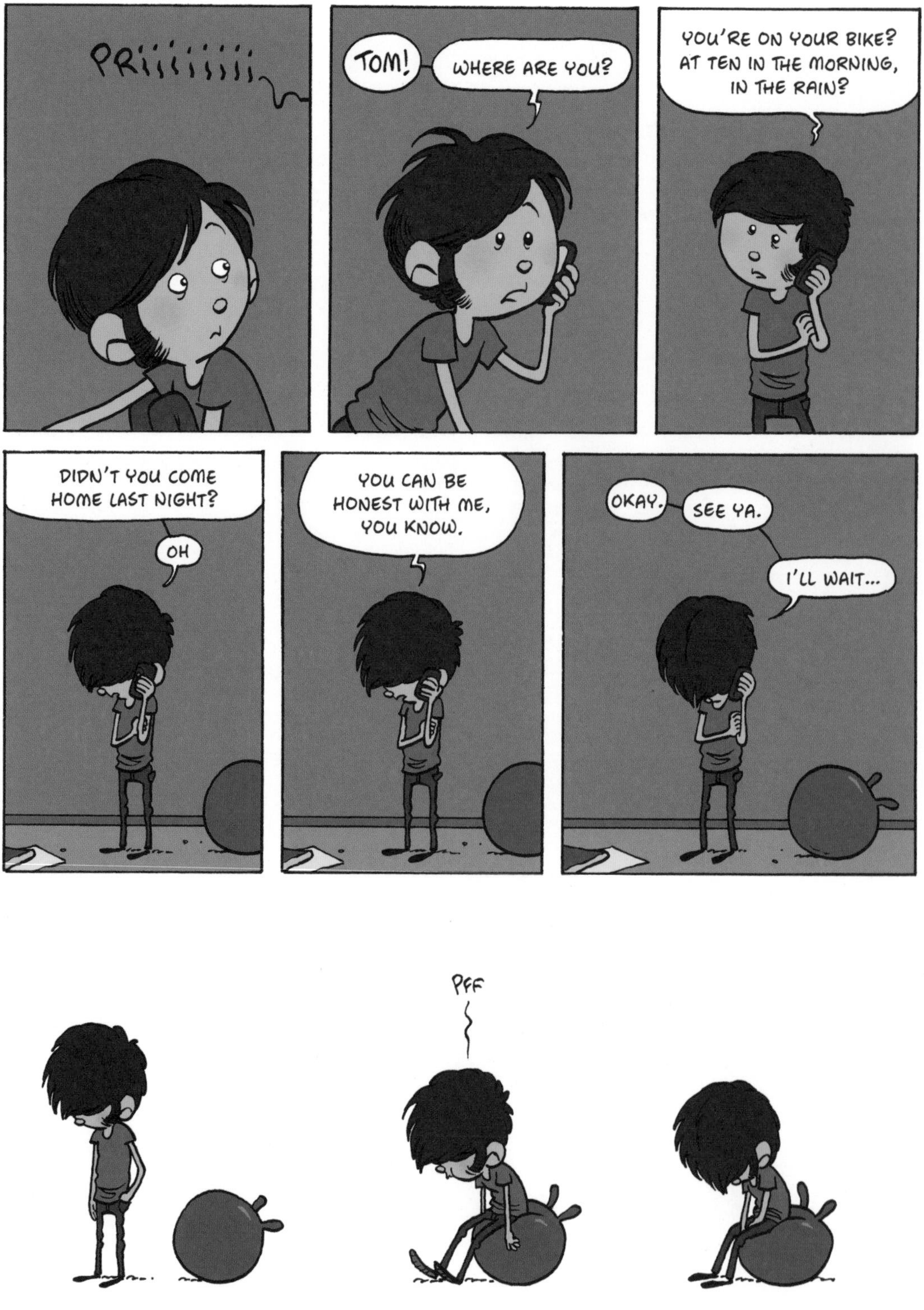
PRiiiiiiiii
TOM!
WHERE ARE YOU?
YOU'RE ON YOUR BIKE? AT TEN IN THE MORNING, IN THE RAIN?
DIDN'T YOU COME HOME LAST NIGHT?
OH
YOU CAN BE HONEST WITH ME, YOU KNOW.
OKAY.
SEE YA.
I'LL WAIT...
PFF

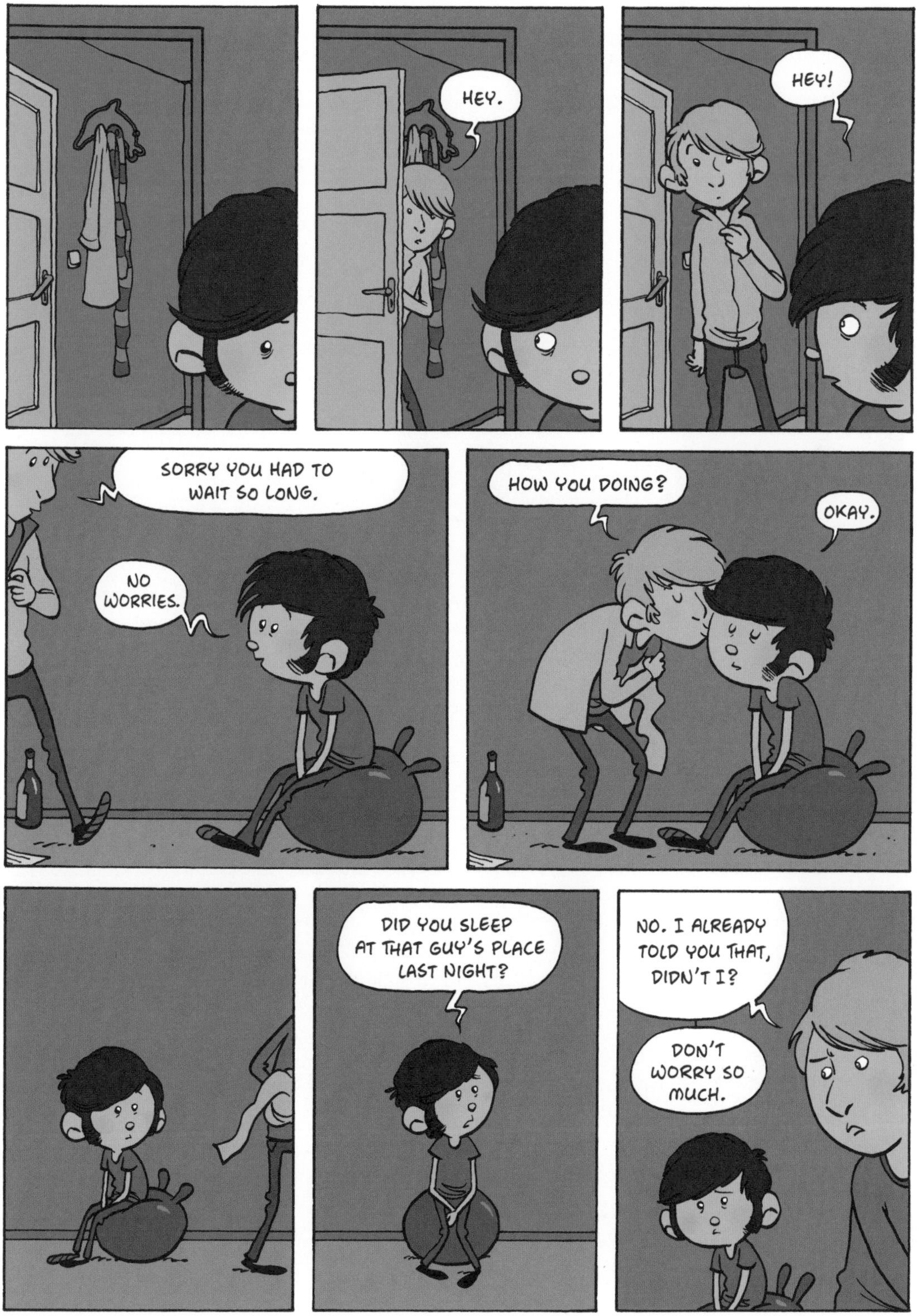
HEY.
HEY!
SORRY YOU HAD TO WAIT SO LONG.
NO WORRIES.
HOW YOU DOING?
OKAY.
DID YOU SLEEP AT THAT GUY'S PLACE LAST NIGHT?
NO. I ALREADY TOLD YOU THAT, DIDN'T I?
DON'T WORRY SO MUCH.

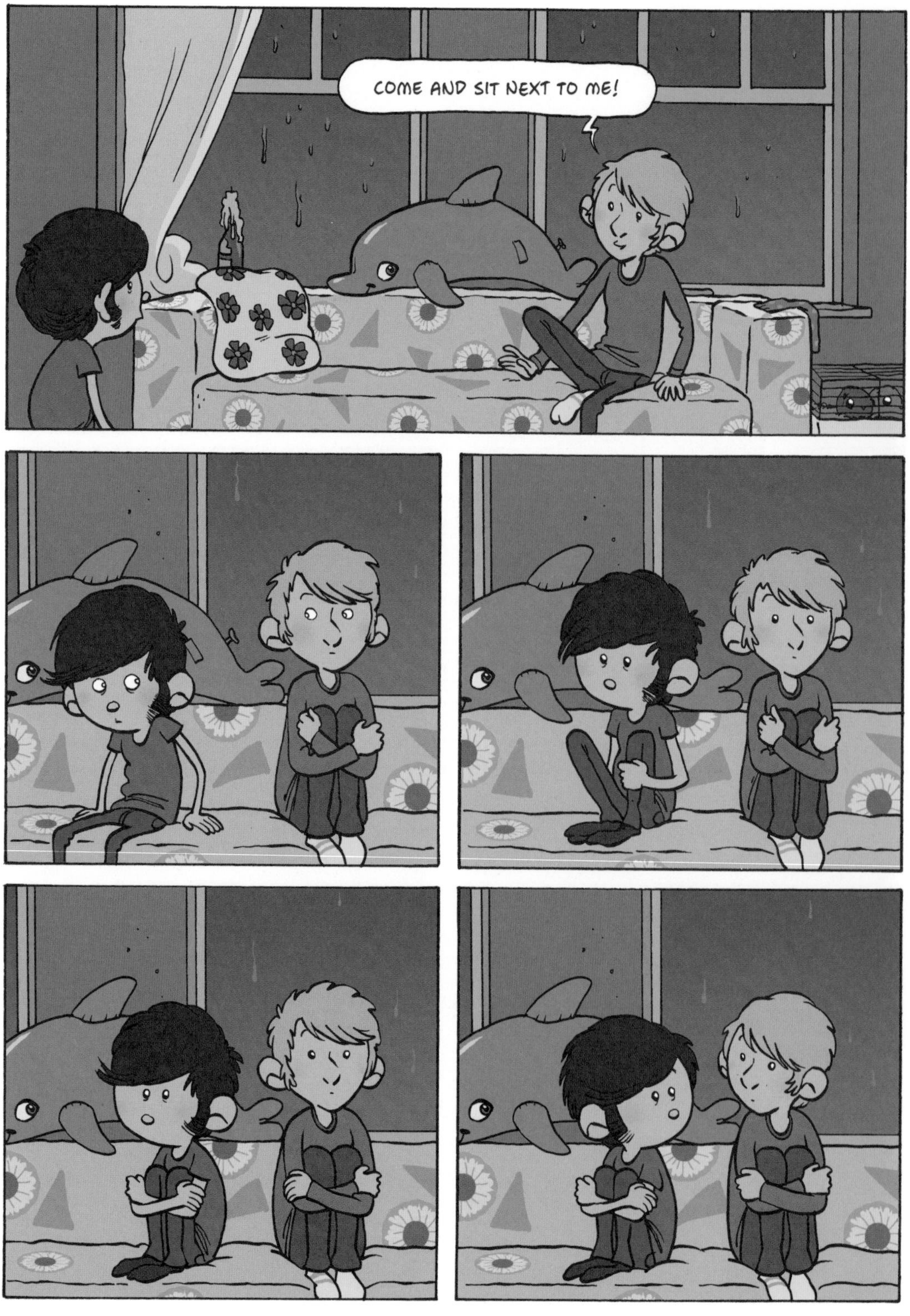
COME AND SIT NEXT TO ME!

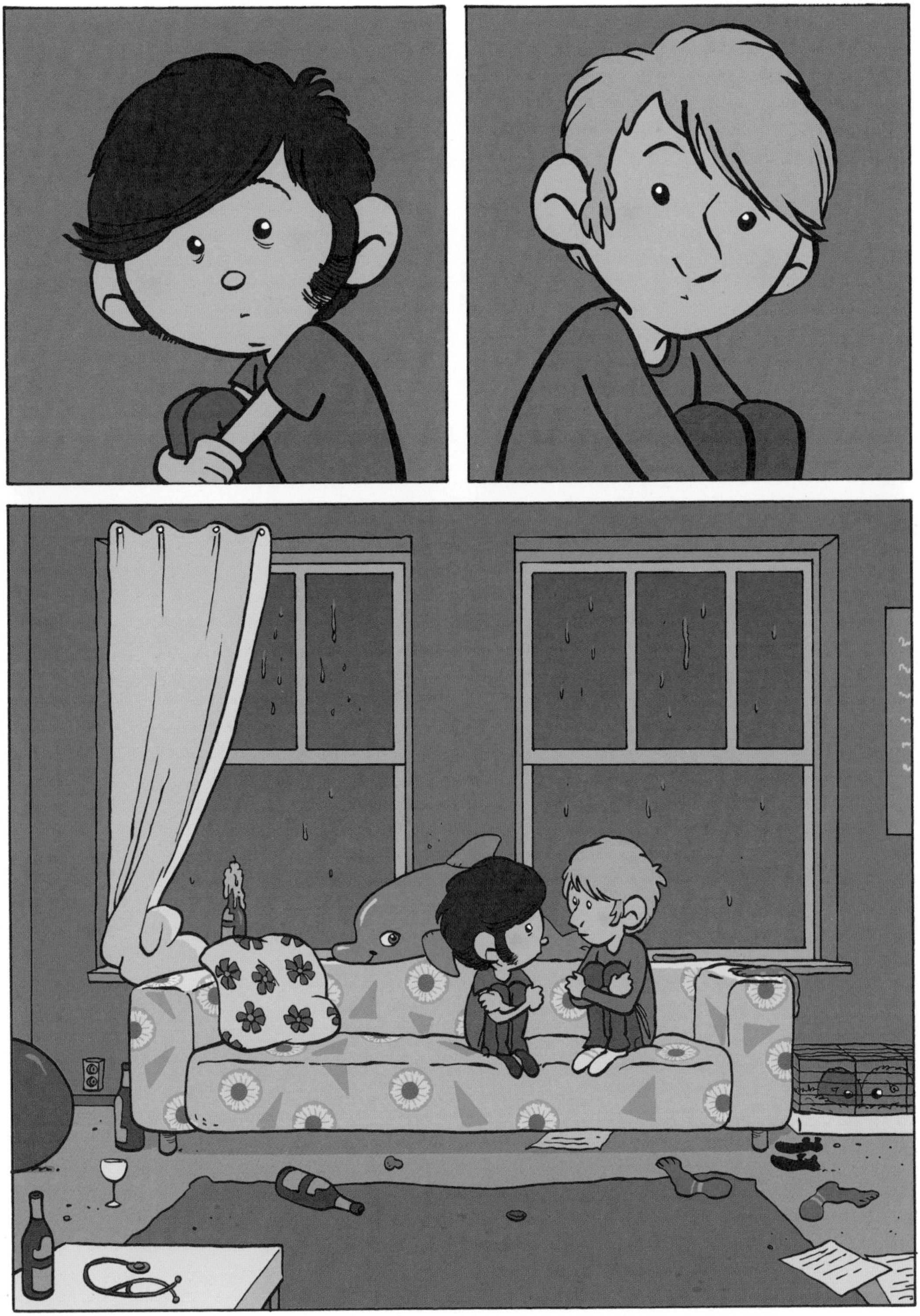

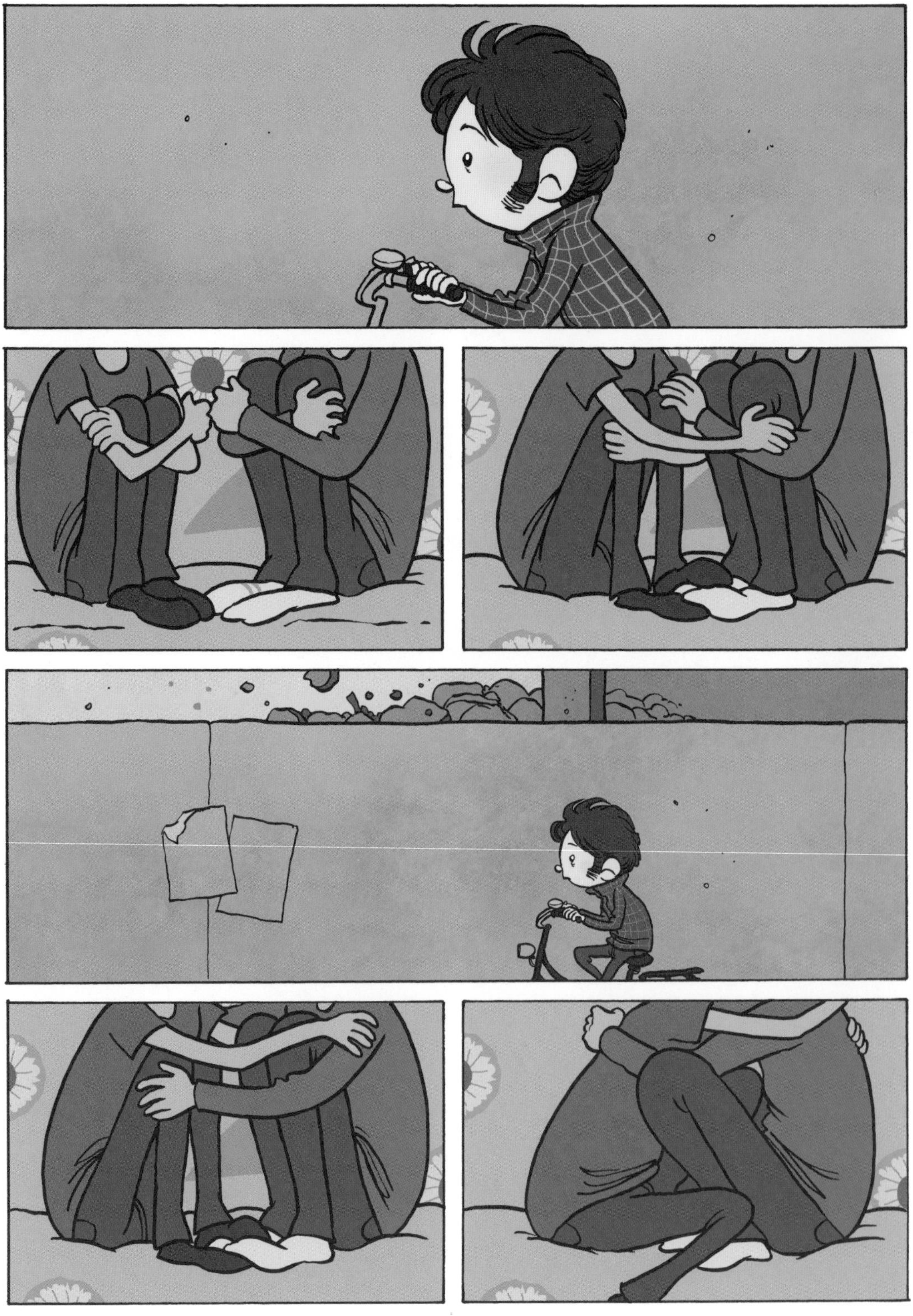

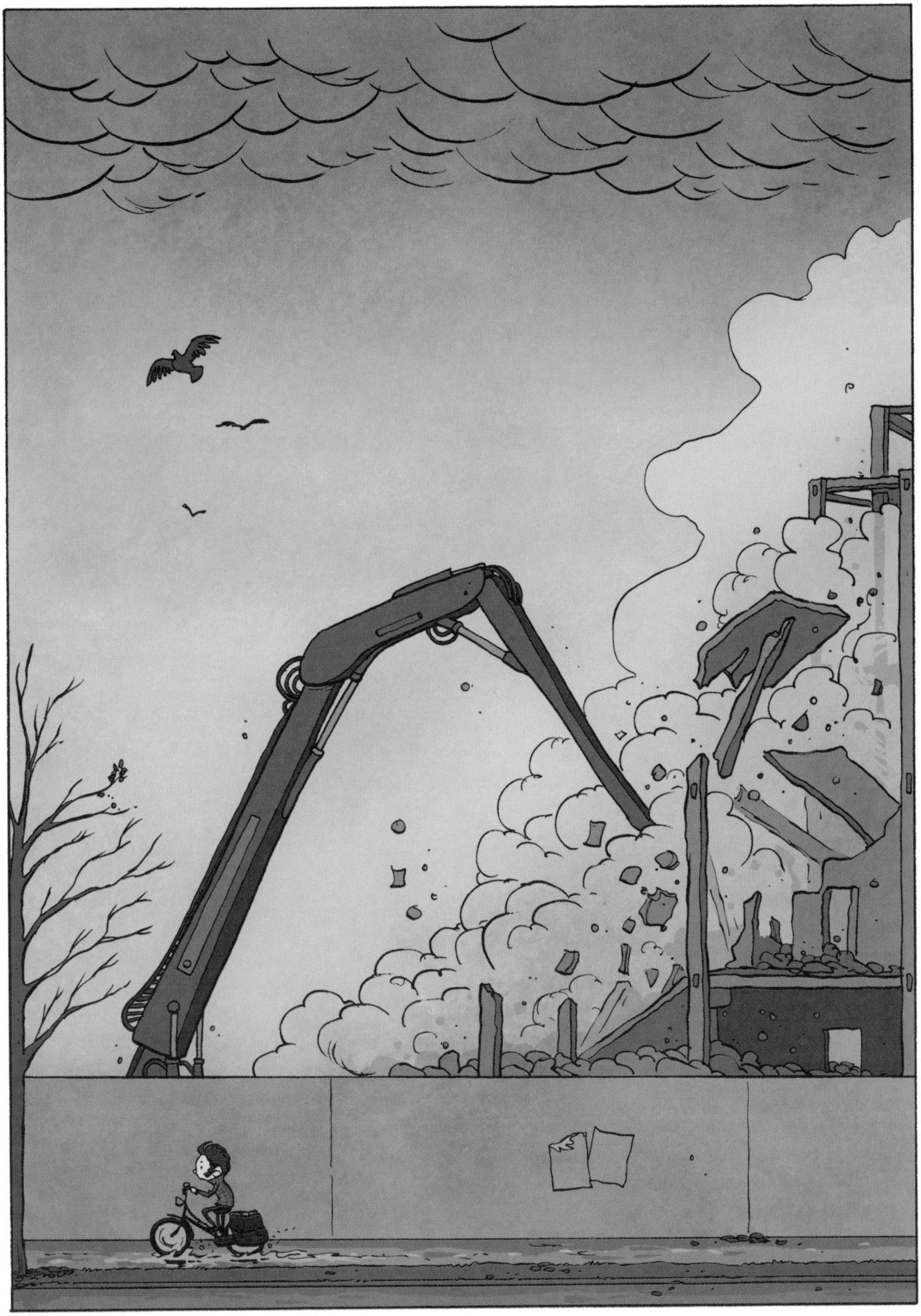

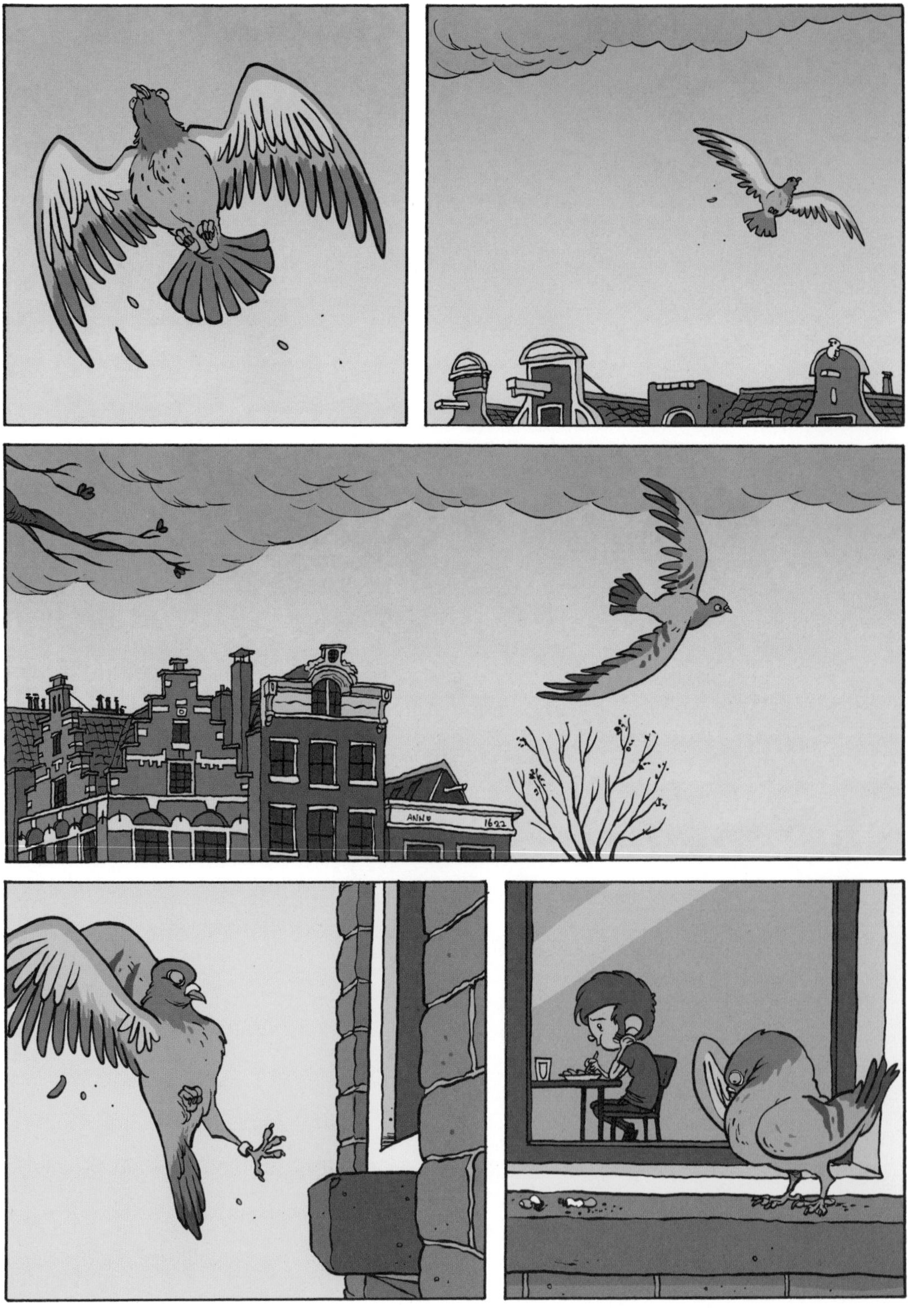
ANNO
1622

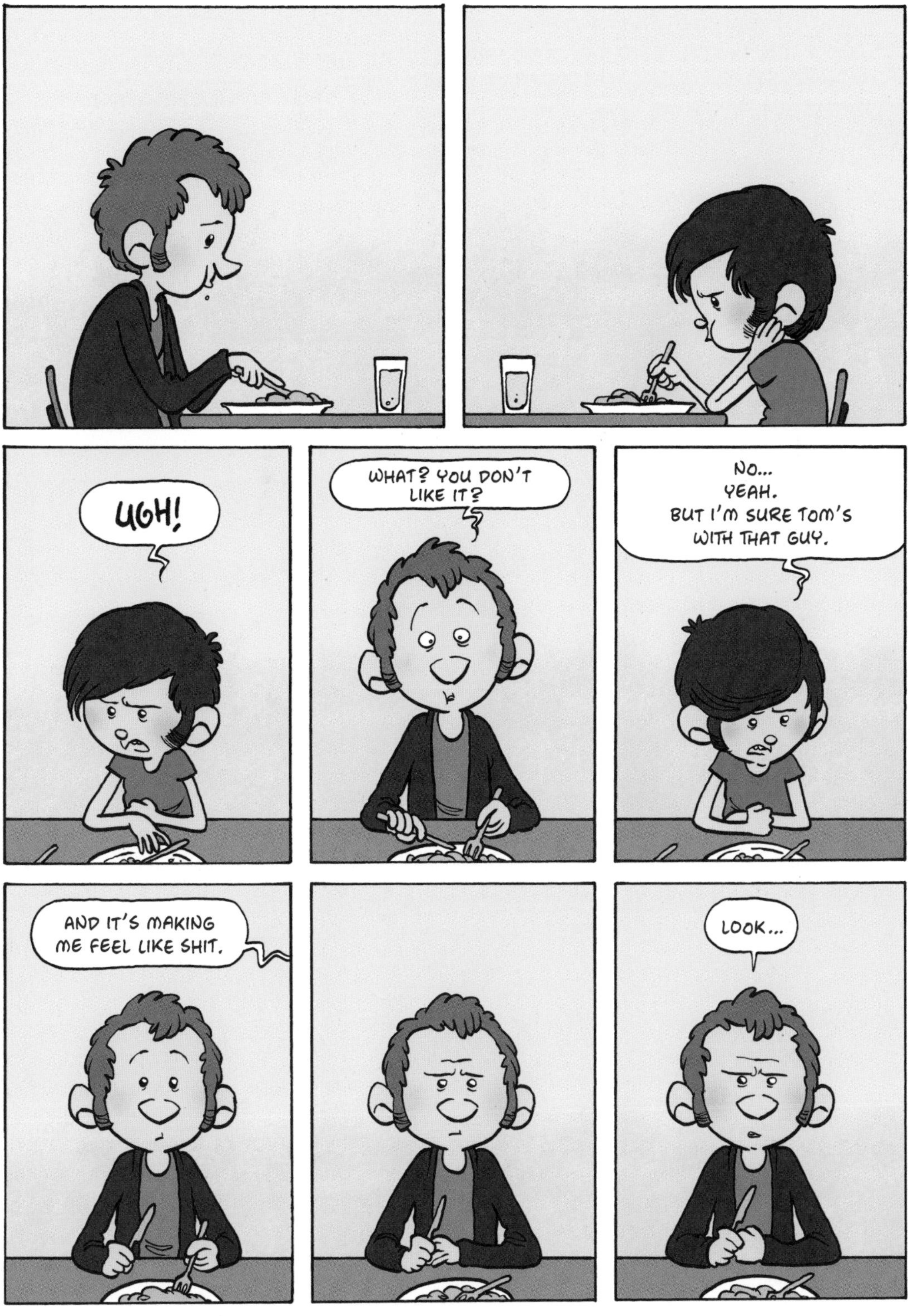
UGH!
WHAT? YOU DON'T LIKE IT?
NO... YEAH. BUT I'M SURE TOM'S WITH THAT GUY.
AND IT'S MAKING ME FEEL LIKE SHIT.
LOOK...

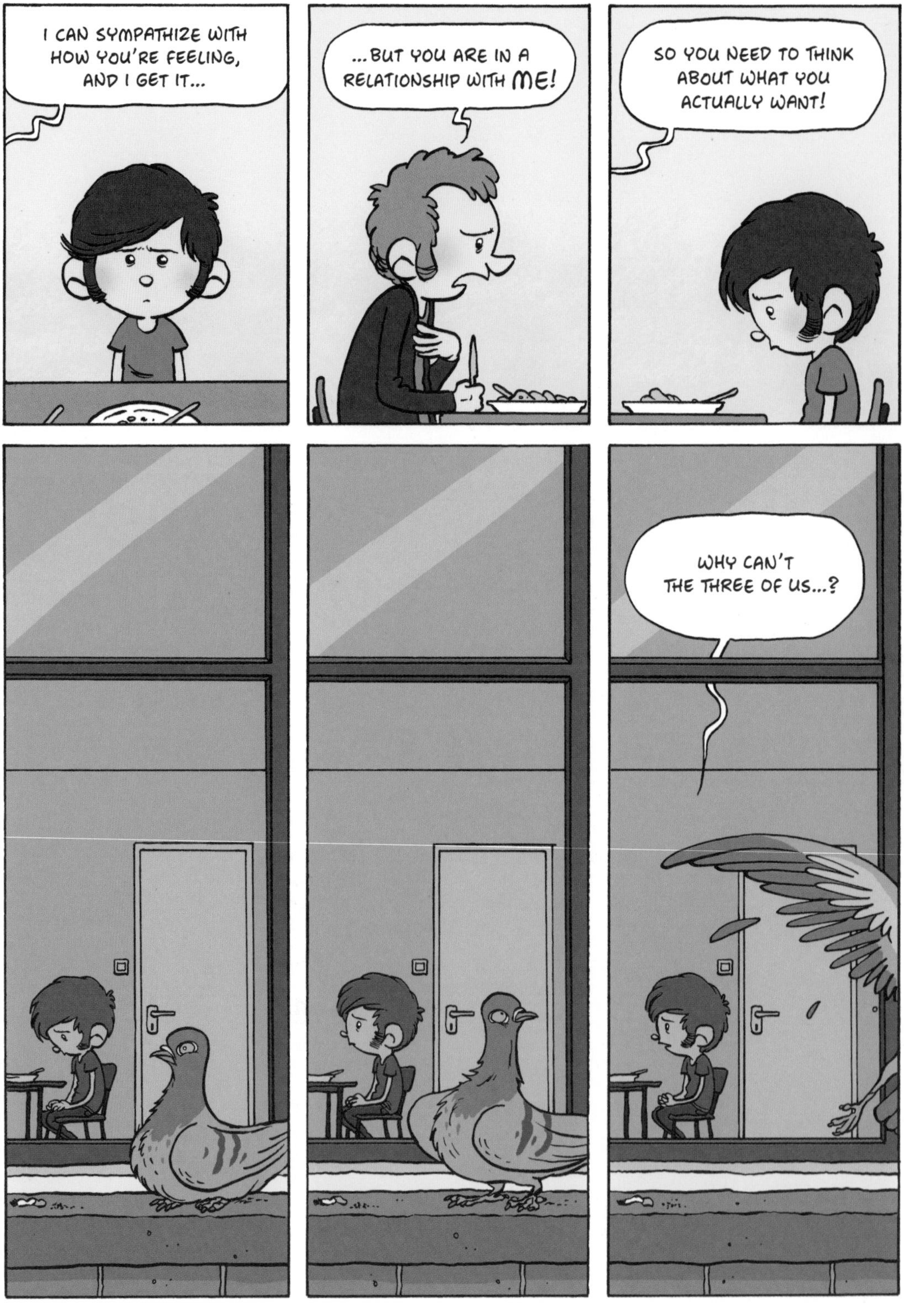
I CAN SYMPATHIZE WITH HOW YOU'RE FEELING, AND I GET IT...
...BUT YOU ARE IN A RELATIONSHIP WITH ME!
SO YOU NEED TO THINK ABOUT WHAT YOU ACTUALLY WANT!
WHY CAN'T THE THREE OF US...?

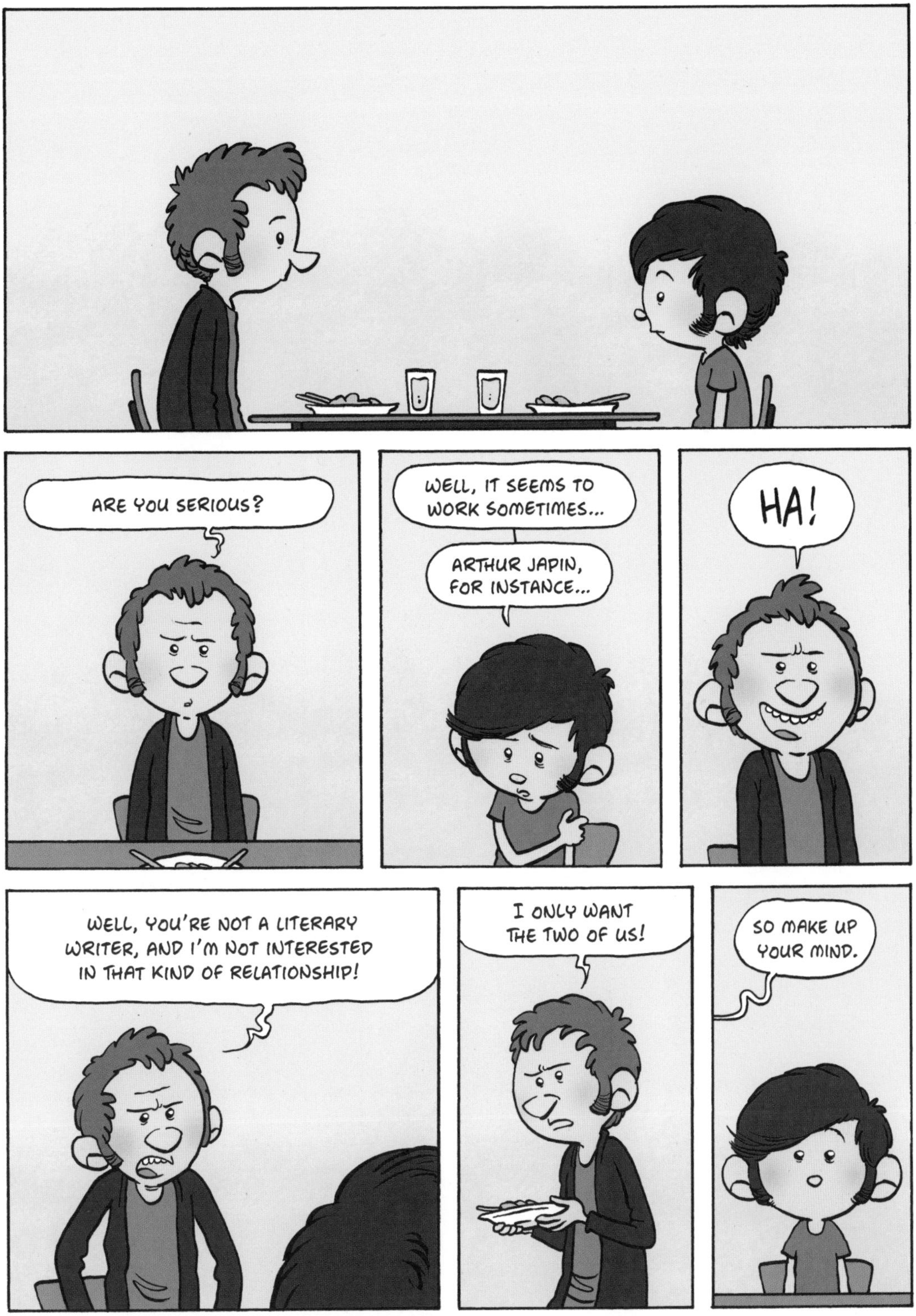
ARE YOU SERIOUS?
WELL, IT SEEMS TO WORK SOMETIMES...
ARTHUR JAPIN, FOR INSTANCE...
HA!
WELL, YOU'RE NOT A LITERARY WRITER, AND I'M NOT INTERESTED IN THAT KIND OF RELATIONSHIP!
I ONLY WANT THE TWO OF US!
SO MAKE UP YOUR MIND.

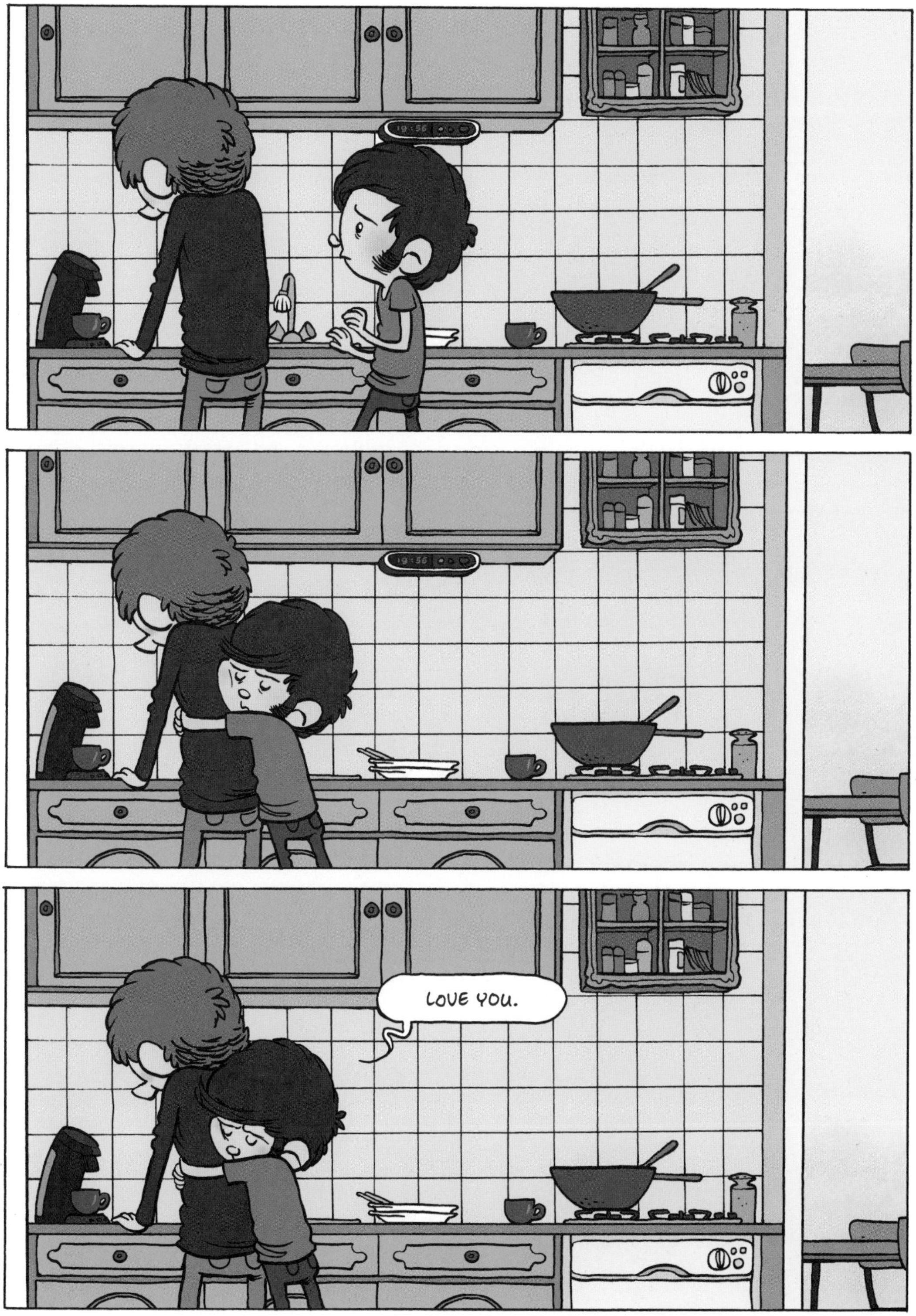
LOVE YOU.

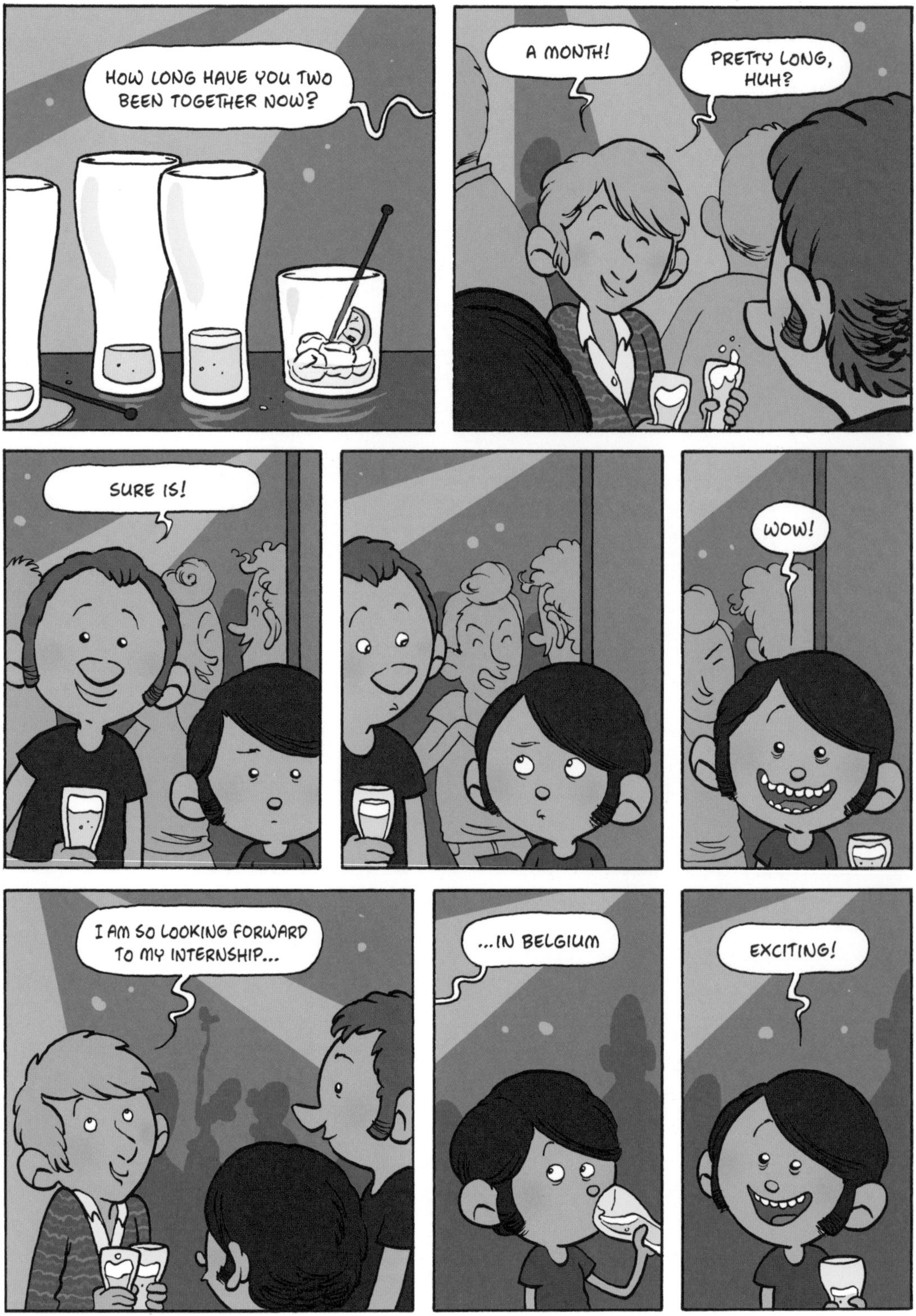
HOW LONG HAVE YOU TWO BEEN TOGETHER NOW?
A MONTH!
PRETTY LONG, HUH?
SURE IS!
WOW!
I AM SO LOOKING FORWARD TO MY INTERNSHIP...
...IN BELGIUM
EXCITING!

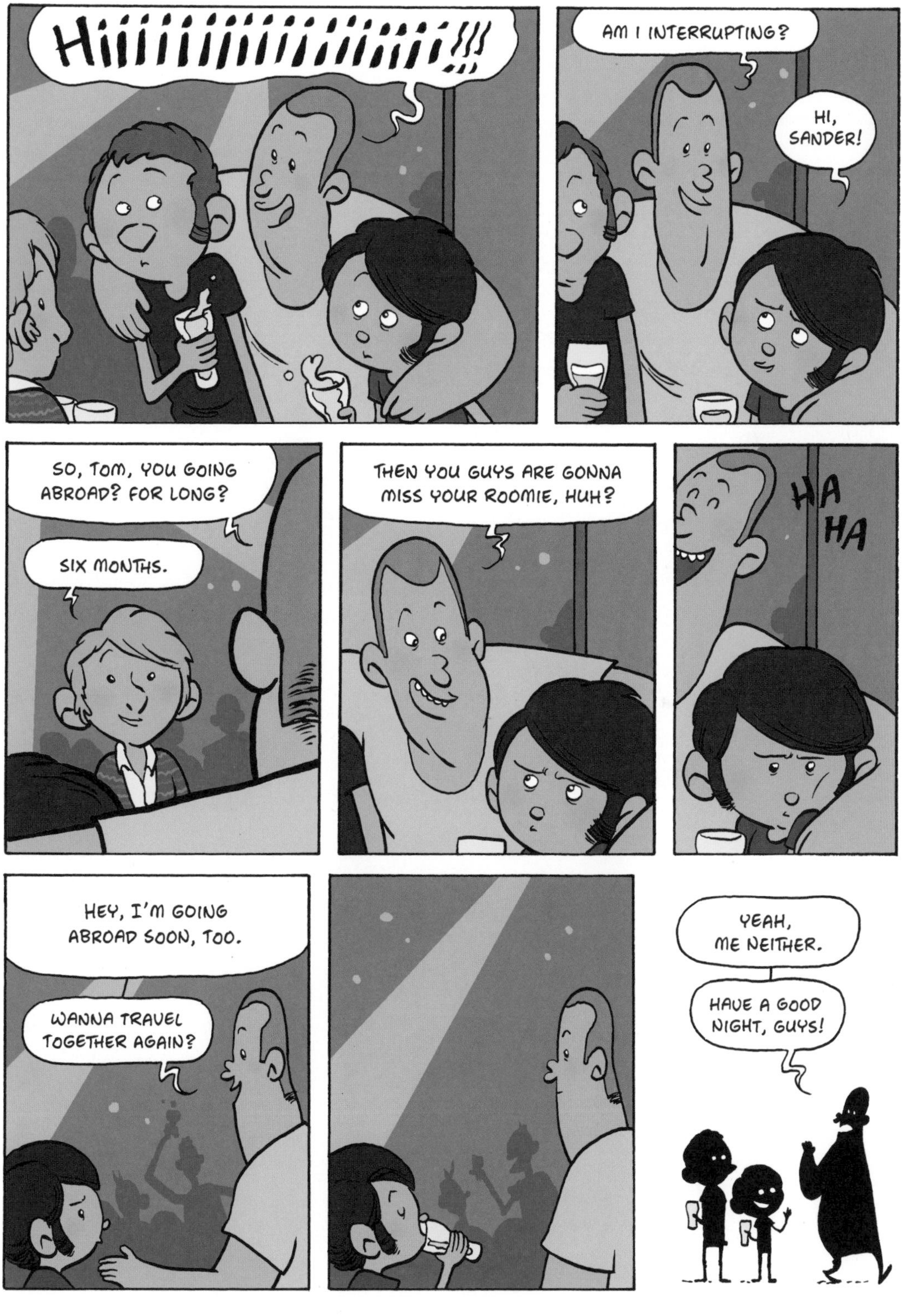
Hiiiiiiiiiiiiiiii!!!
AM I INTERRUPTING?
HI, SANDER!
SO, TOM, YOU GOING ABROAD? FOR LONG?
SIX MONTHS.
THEN YOU GUYS ARE GONNA MISS YOUR ROOMIE, HUH?
HA HA
HEY, I'M GOING ABROAD SOON, TOO.
WANNA TRAVEL TOGETHER AGAIN?
YEAH, ME NEITHER.
HAVE A GOOD NIGHT, GUYS!

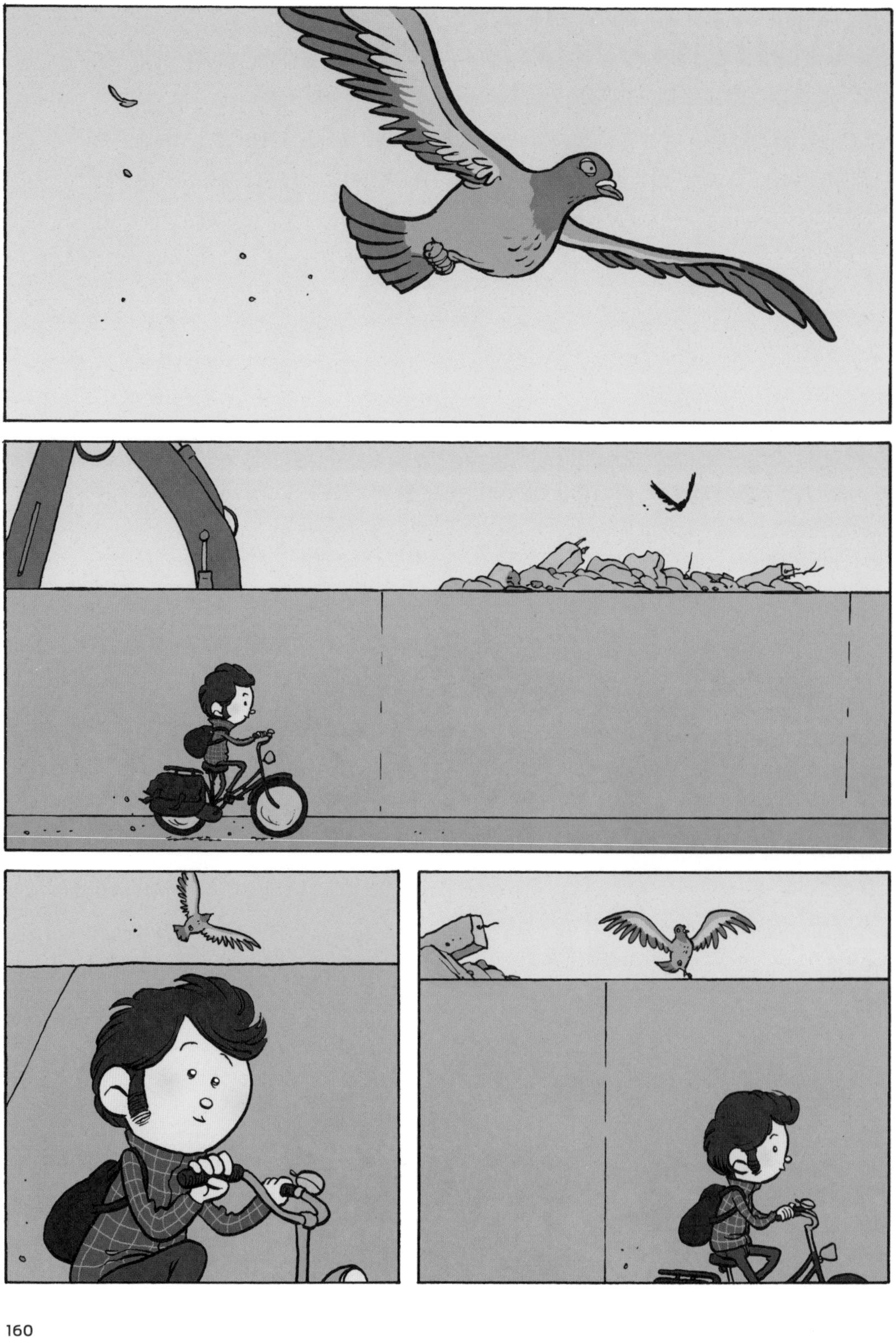

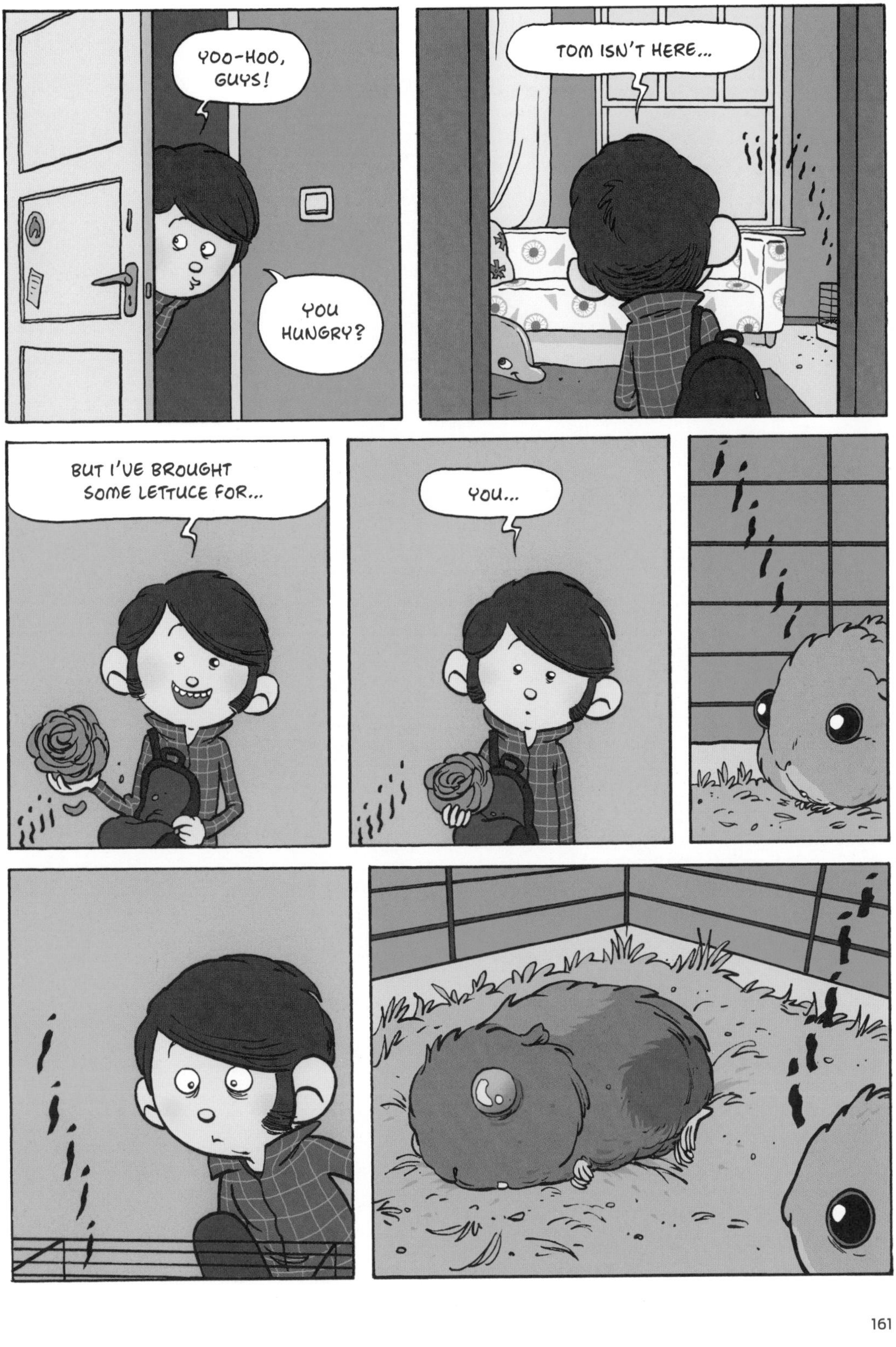
YOO-HOO, GUYS!
YOU HUNGRY?
TOM ISN'T HERE...
BUT I'VE BROUGHT SOME LETTUCE FOR...
YOU...

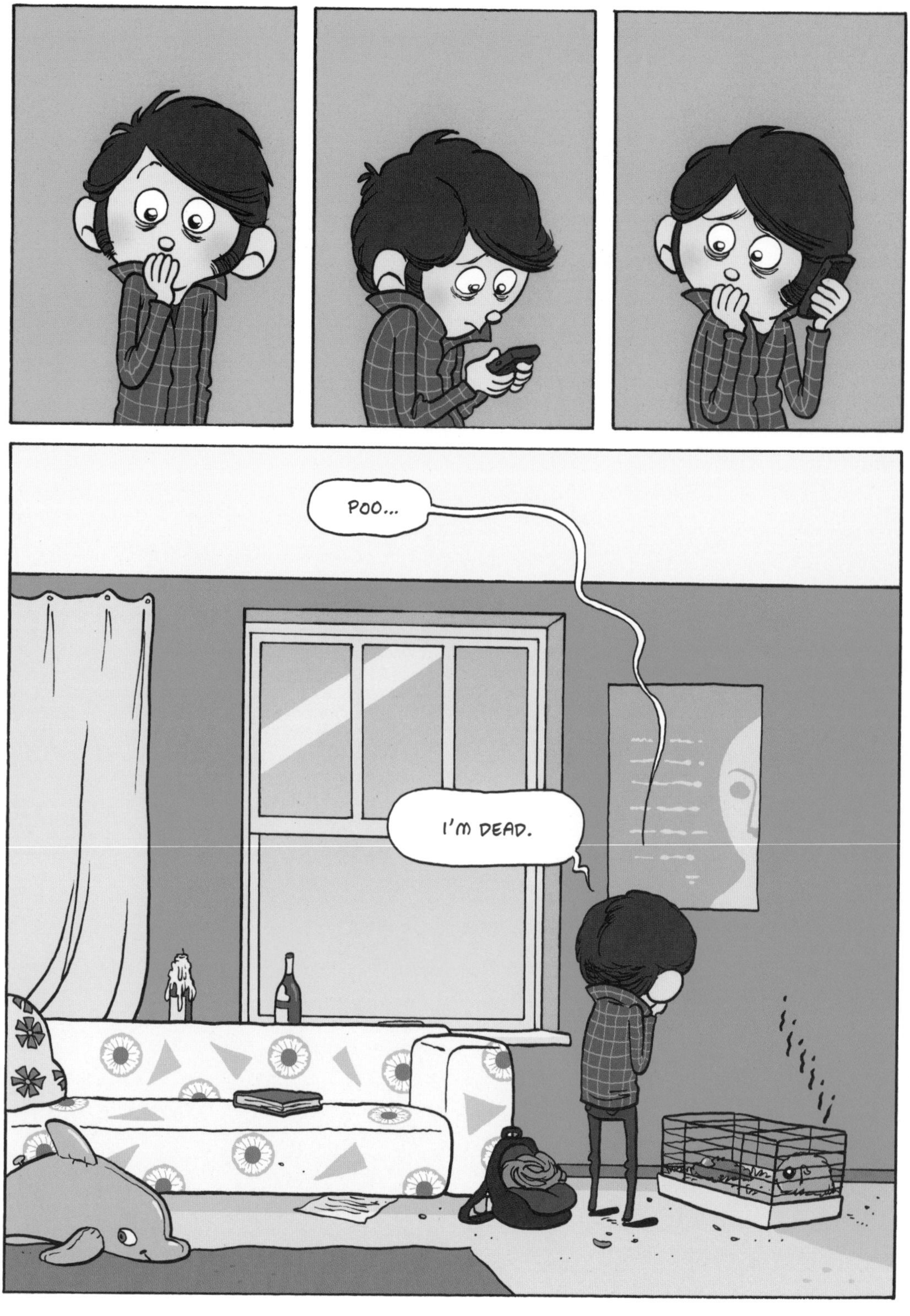
POO...
I'M DEAD.

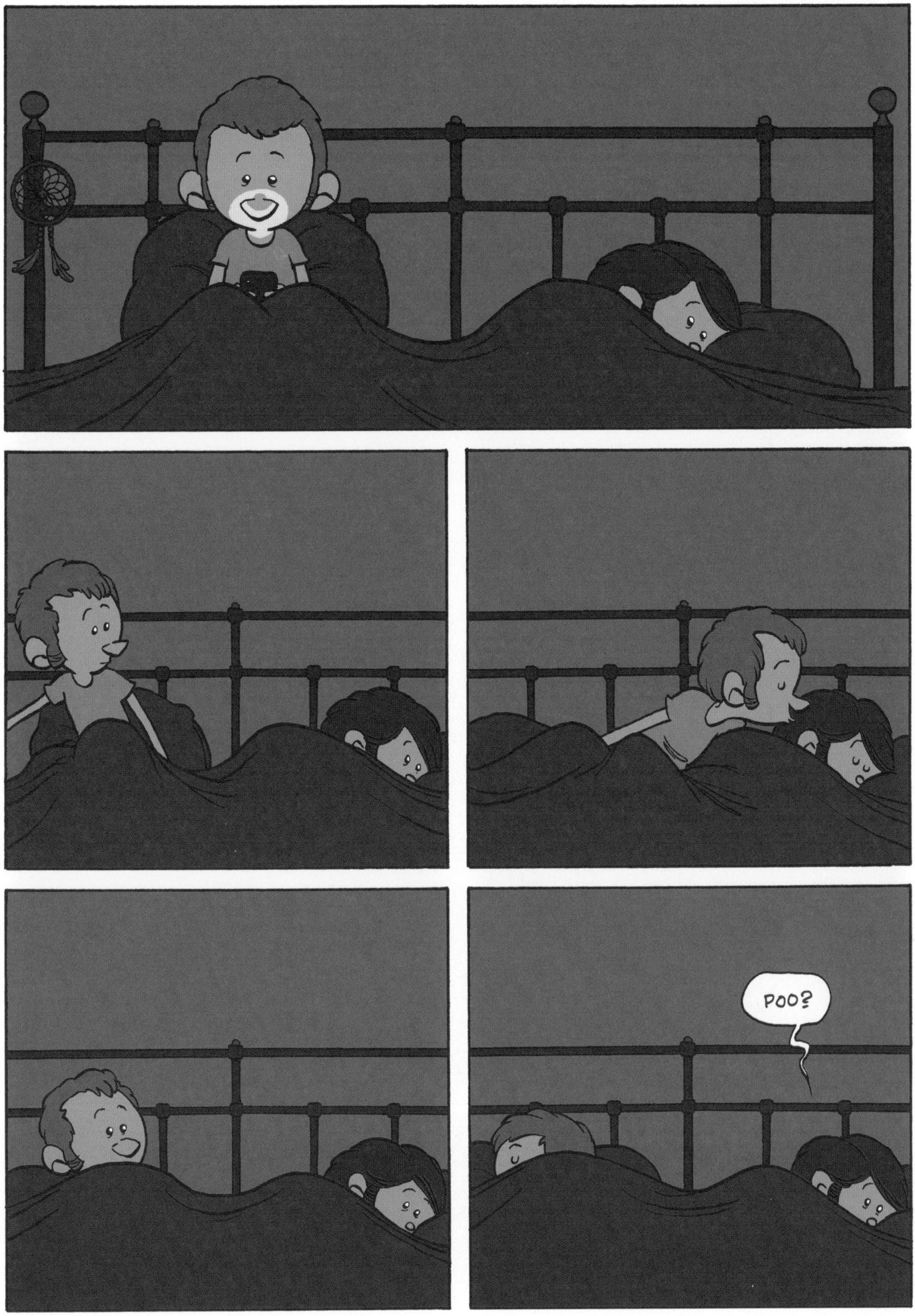
POO?

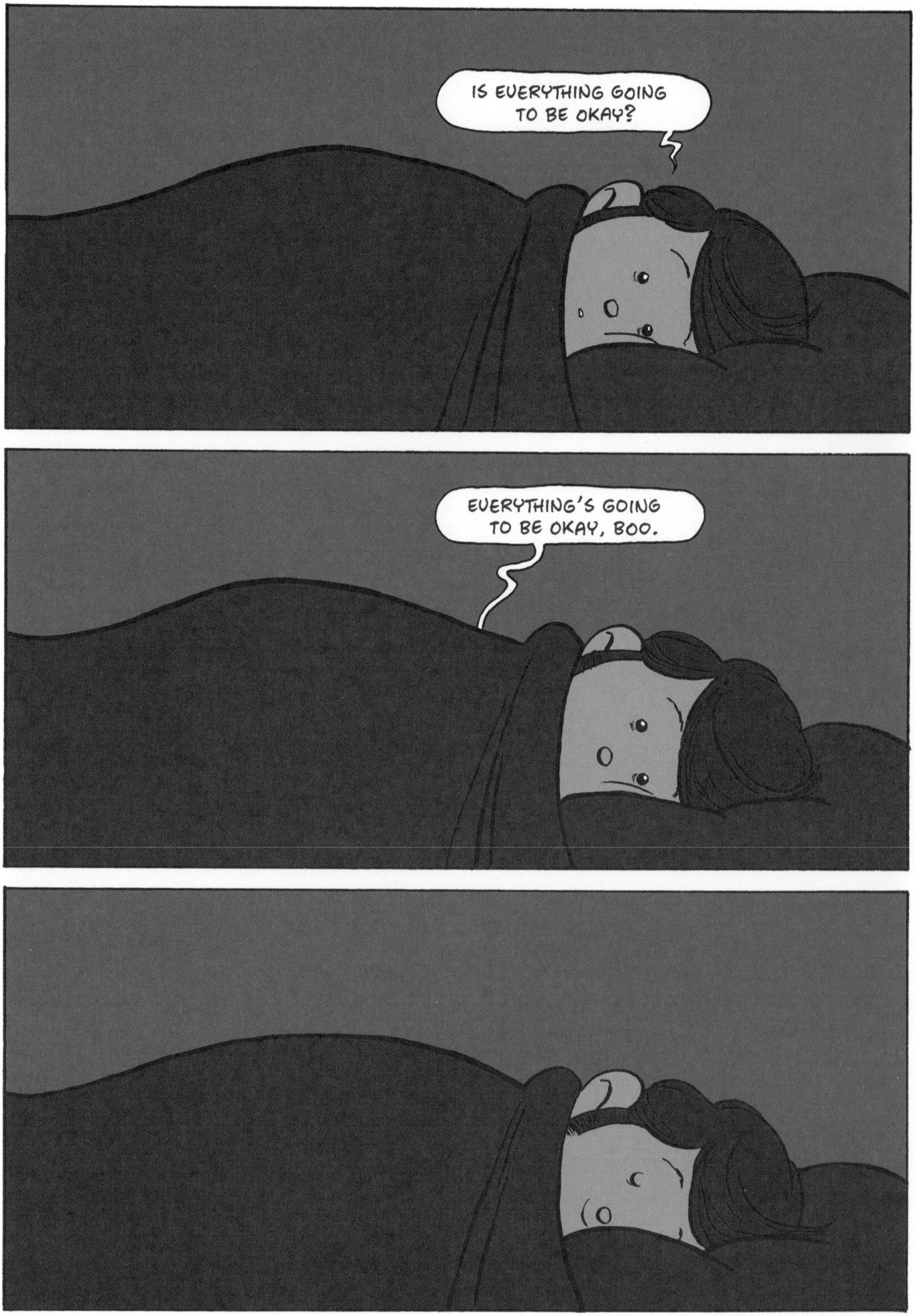
IS EVERYTHING GOING TO BE OKAY?
EVERYTHING'S GOING TO BE OKAY, BOO.

3.

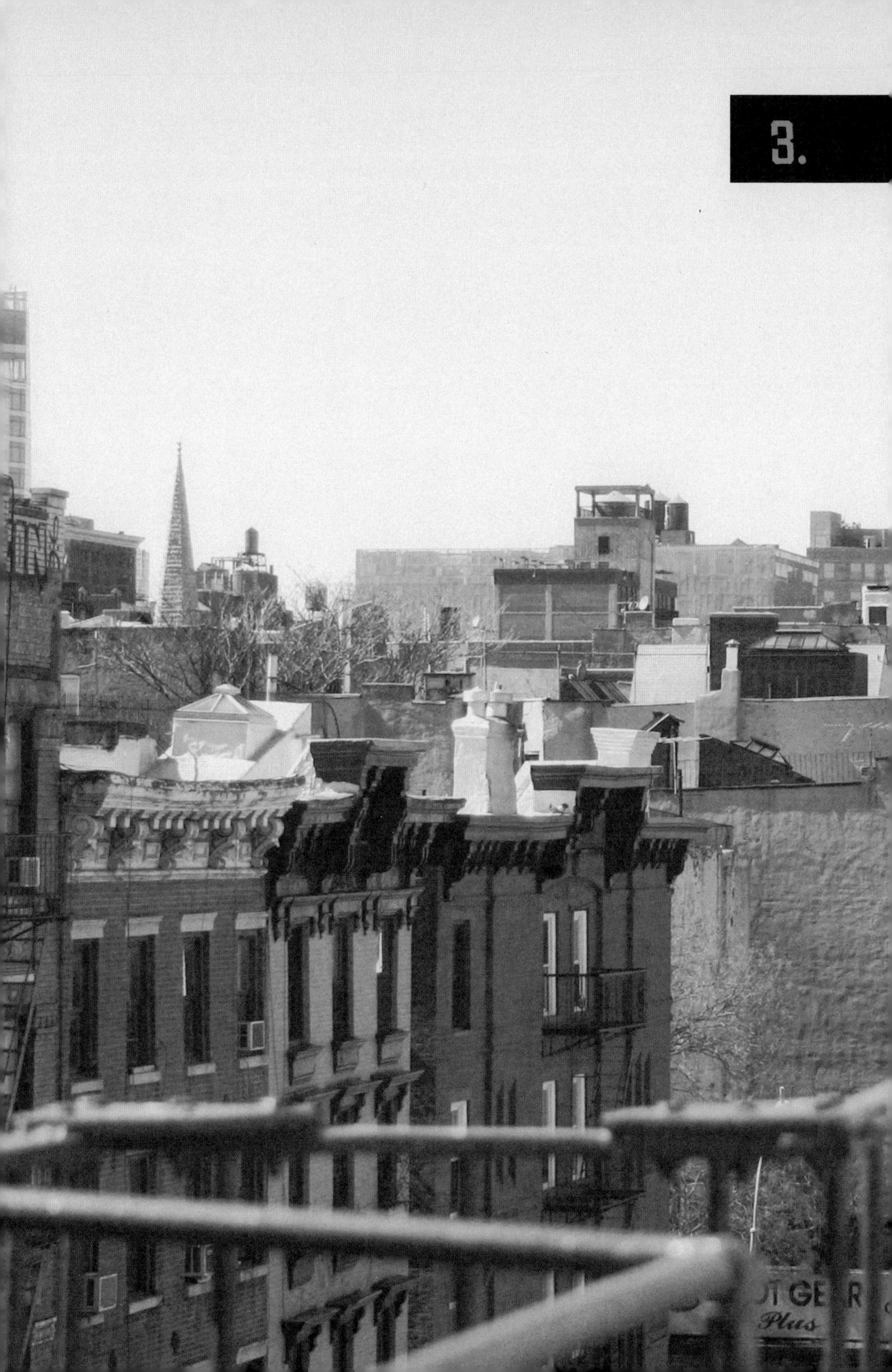
Plus

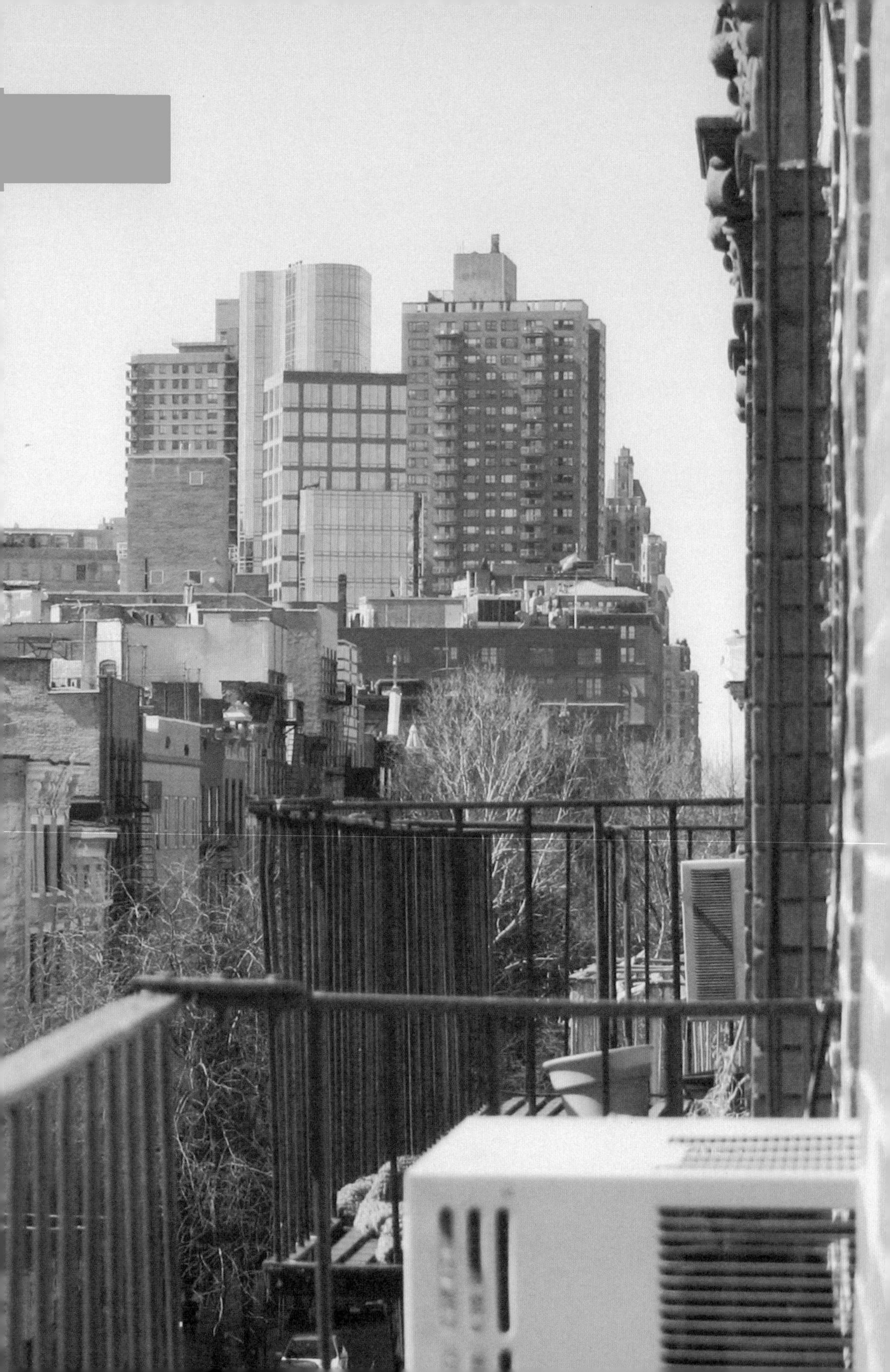

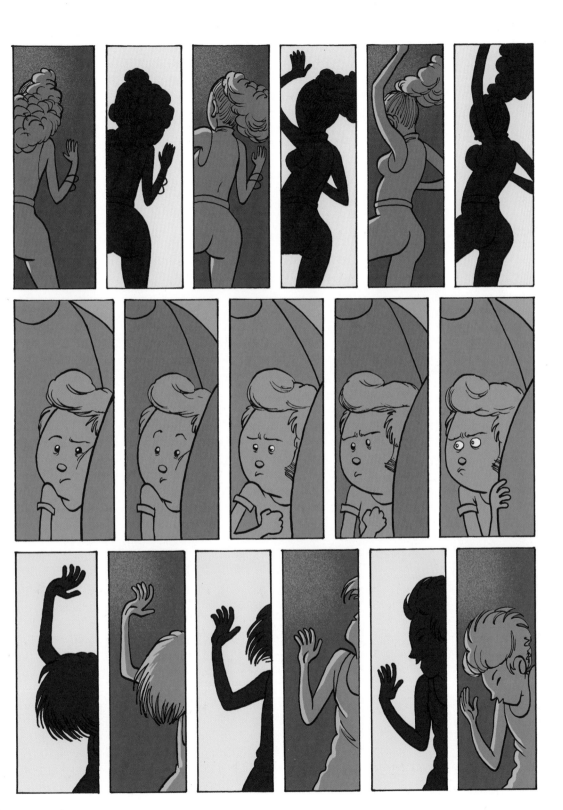

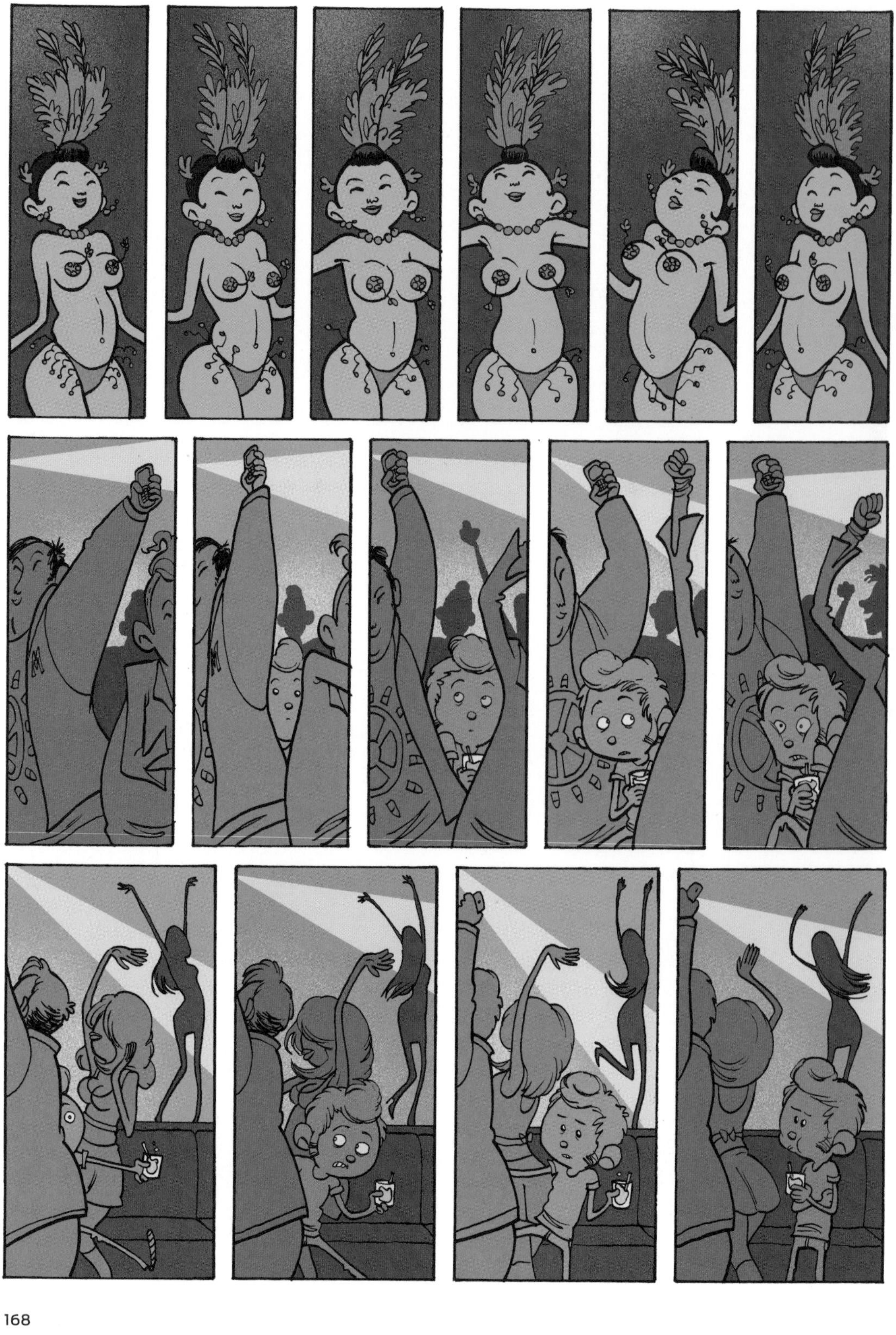

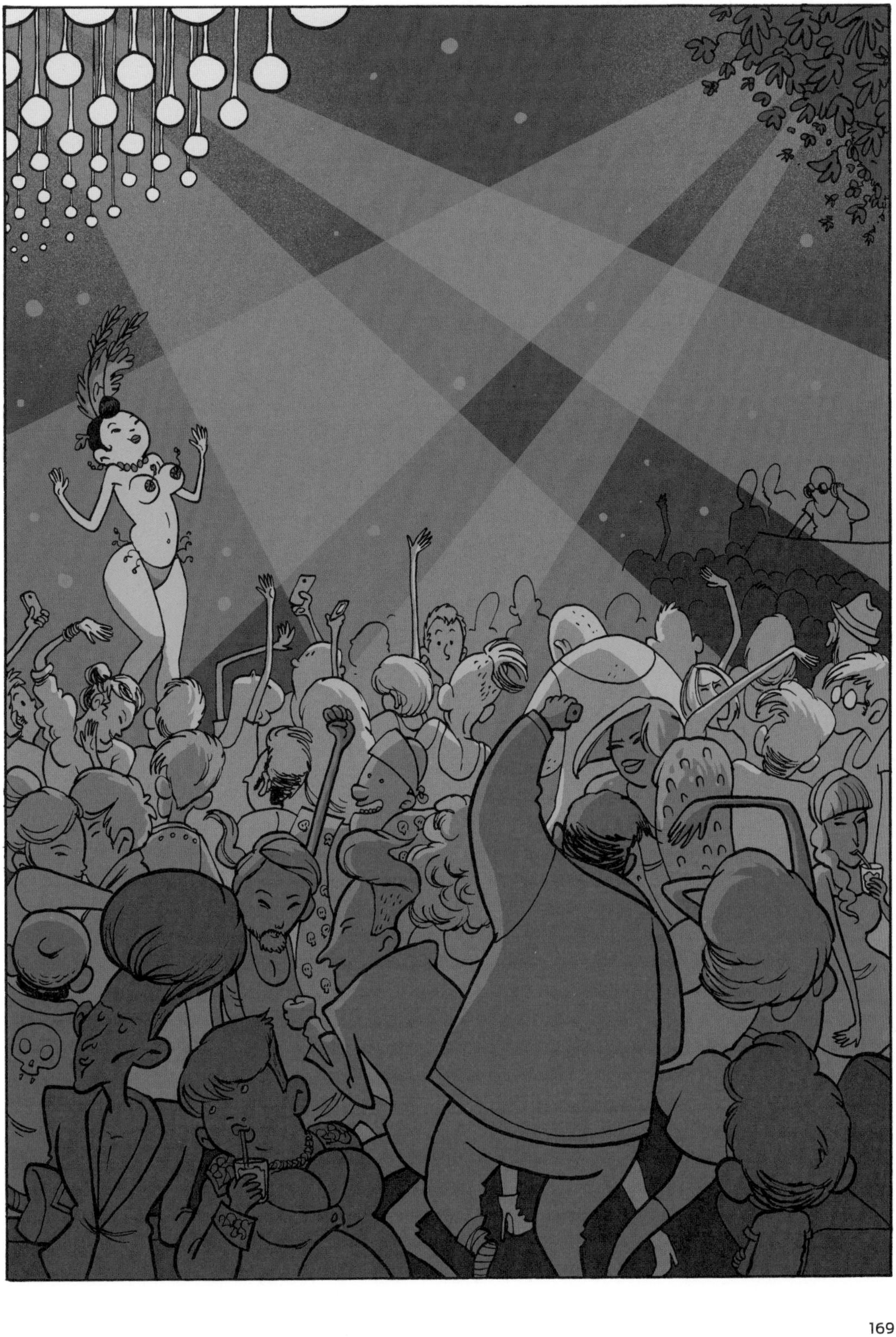

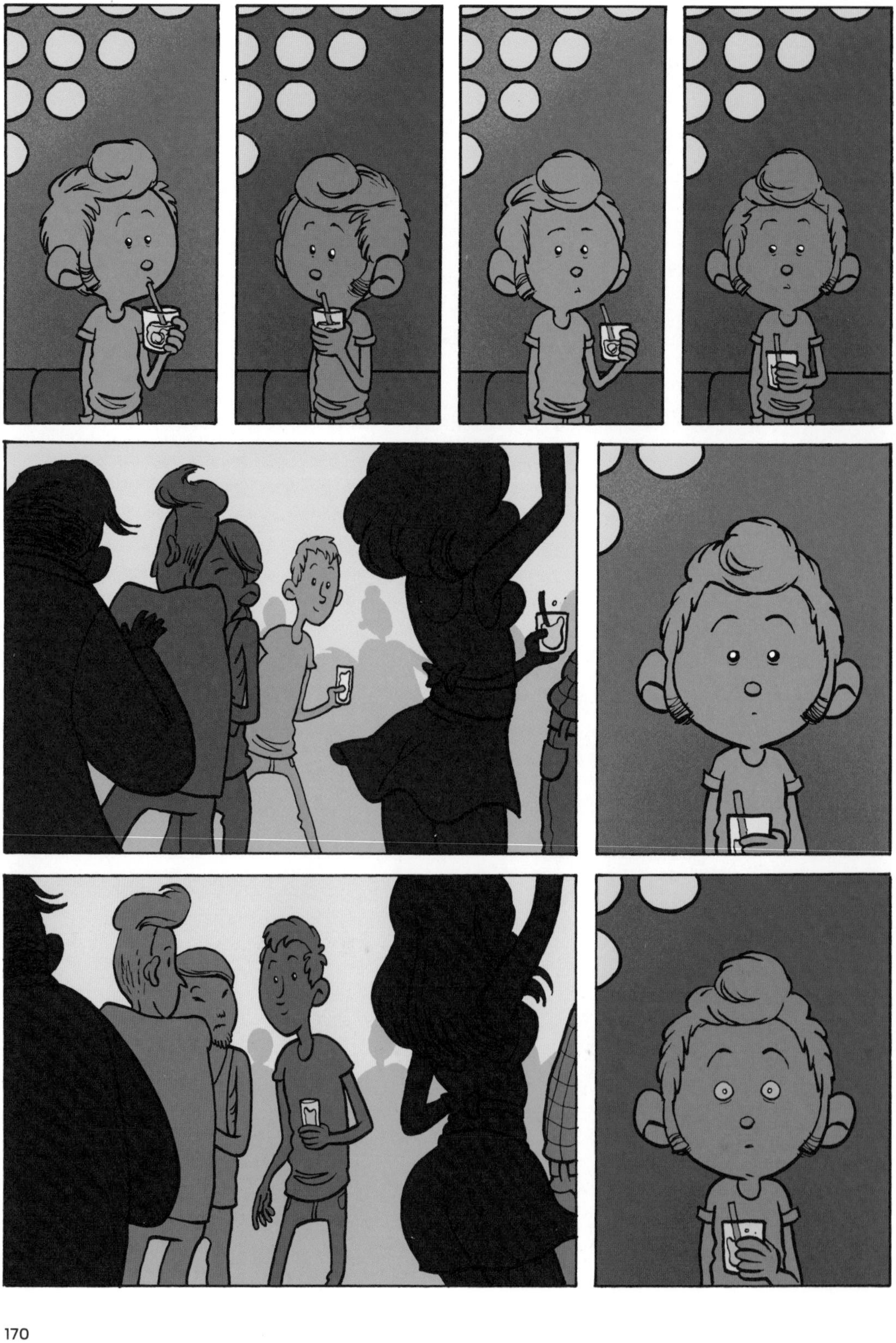

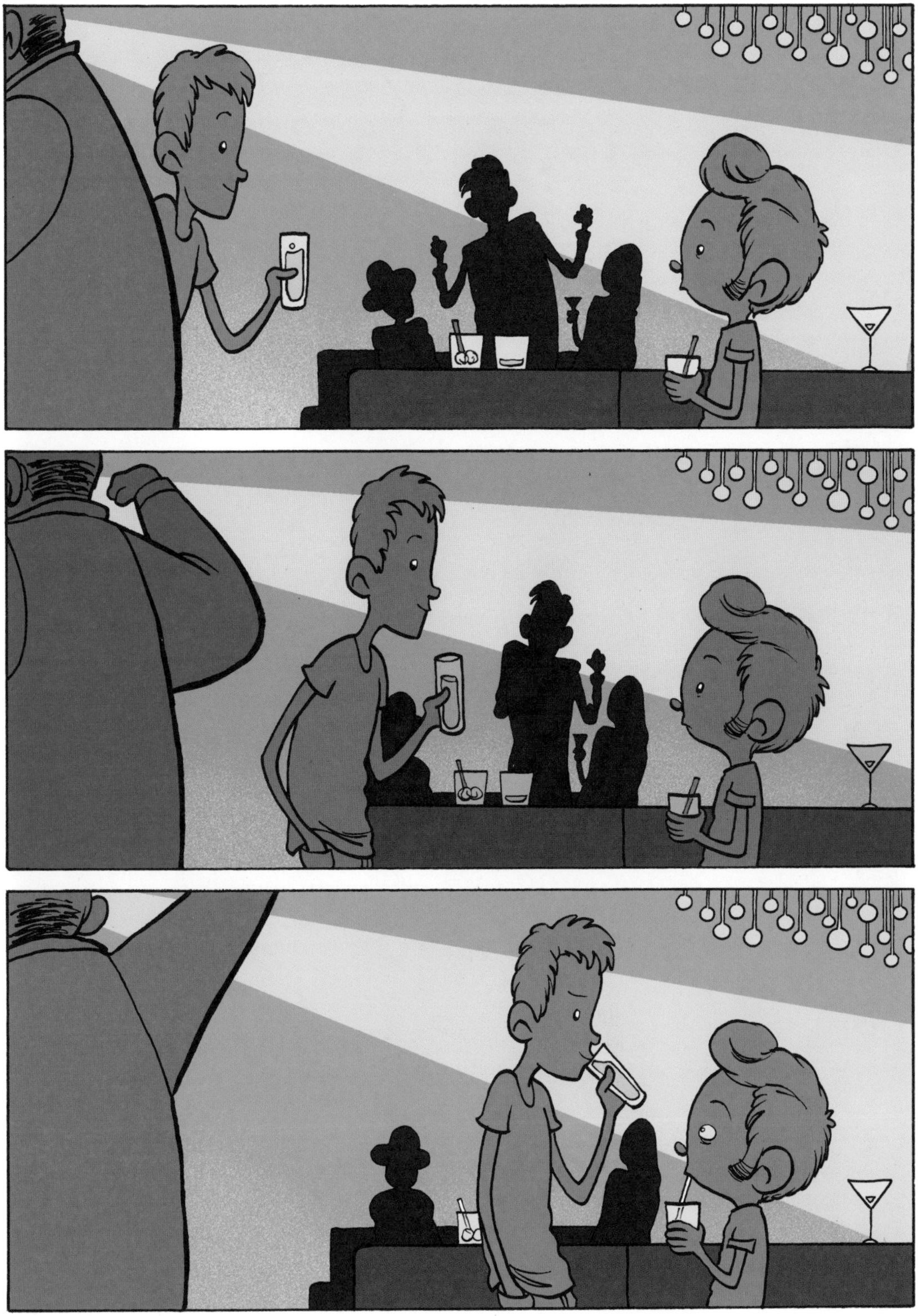

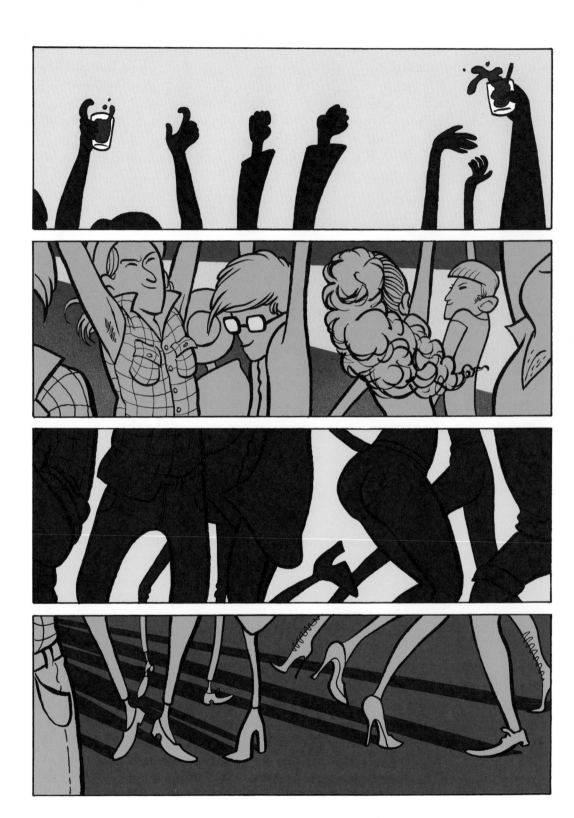

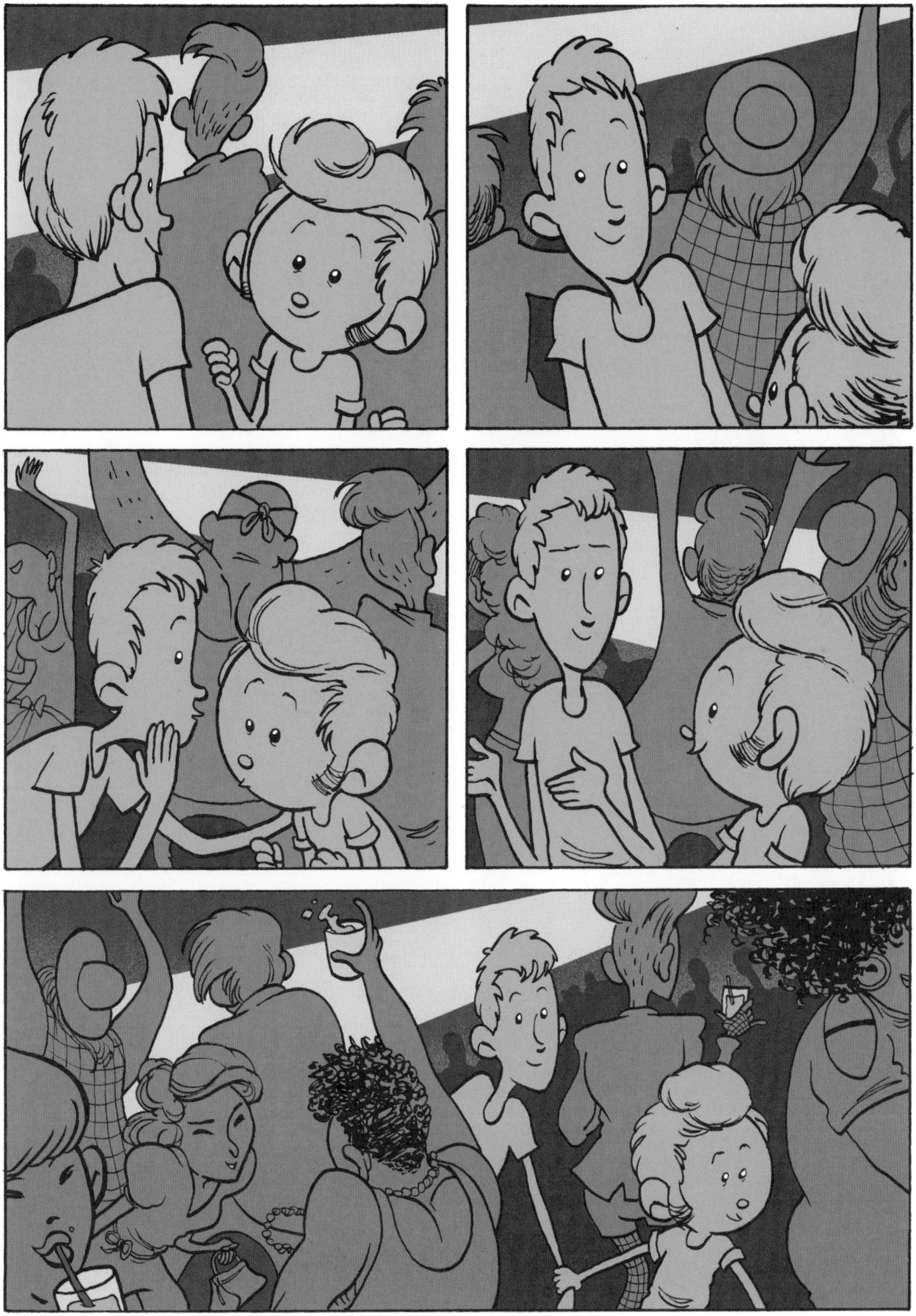

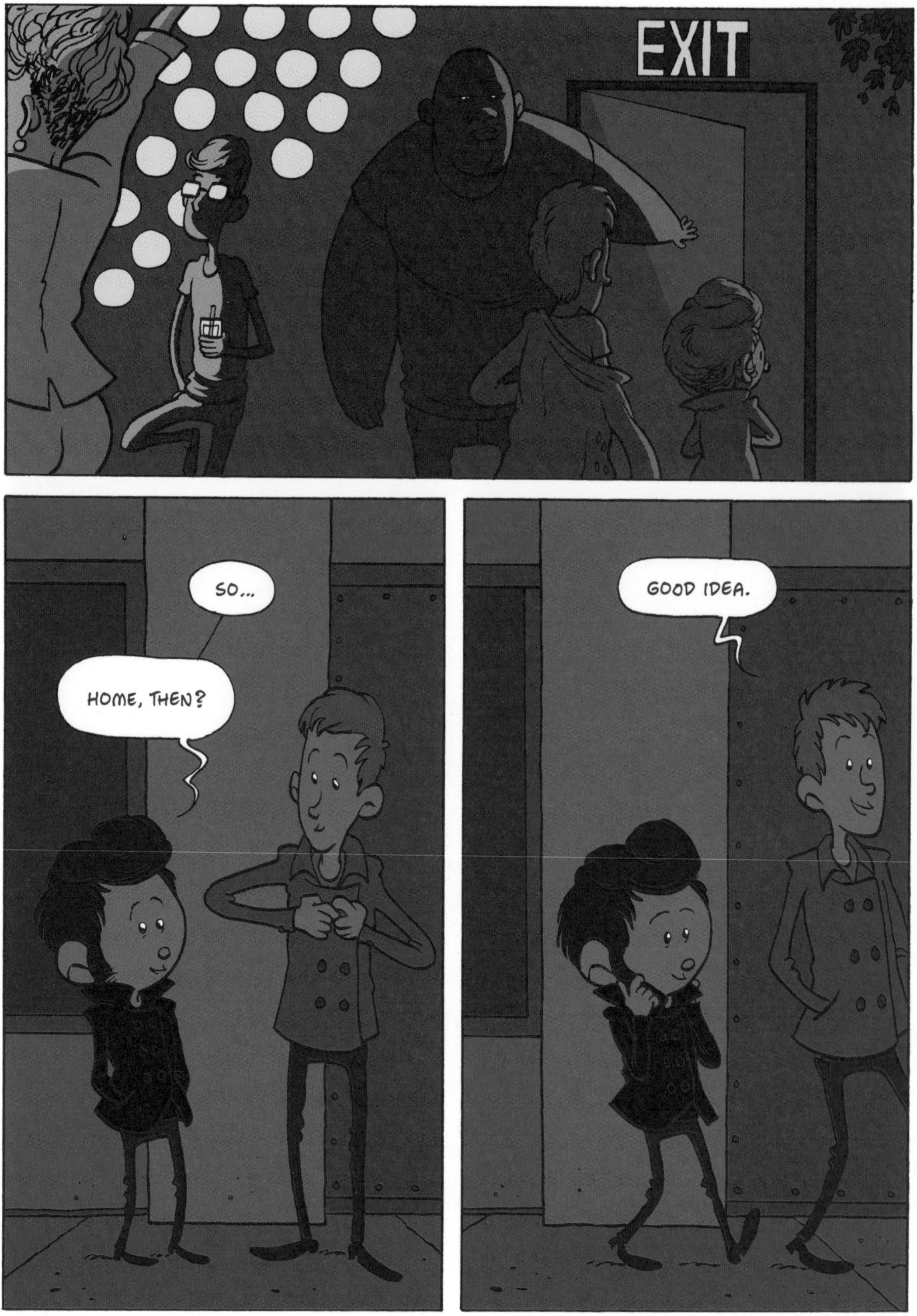
EXIT
SO...
HOME, THEN?
GOOD IDEA.

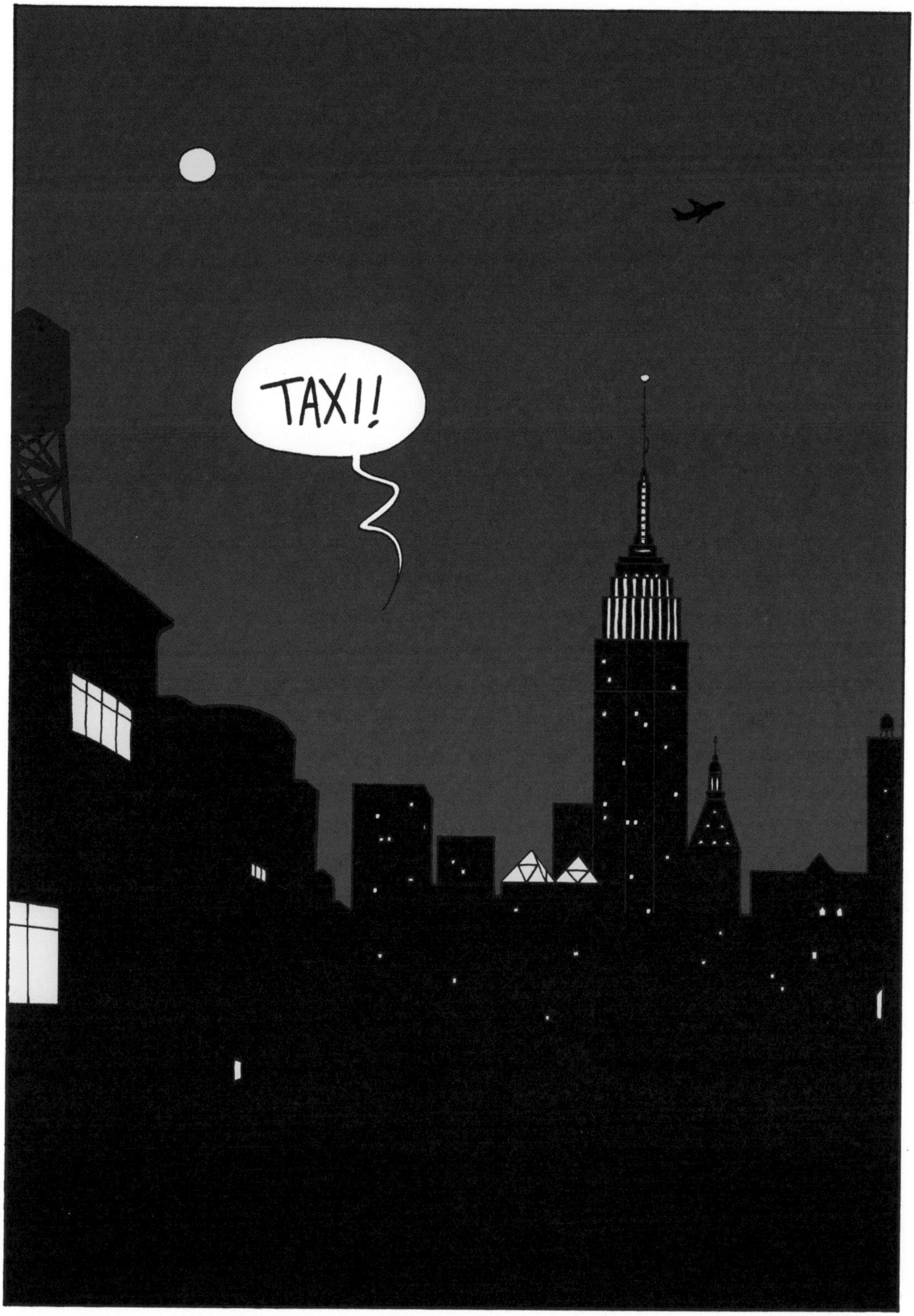
TAXI!

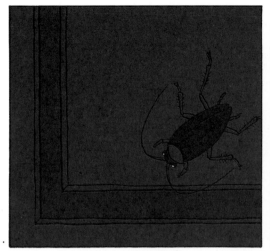

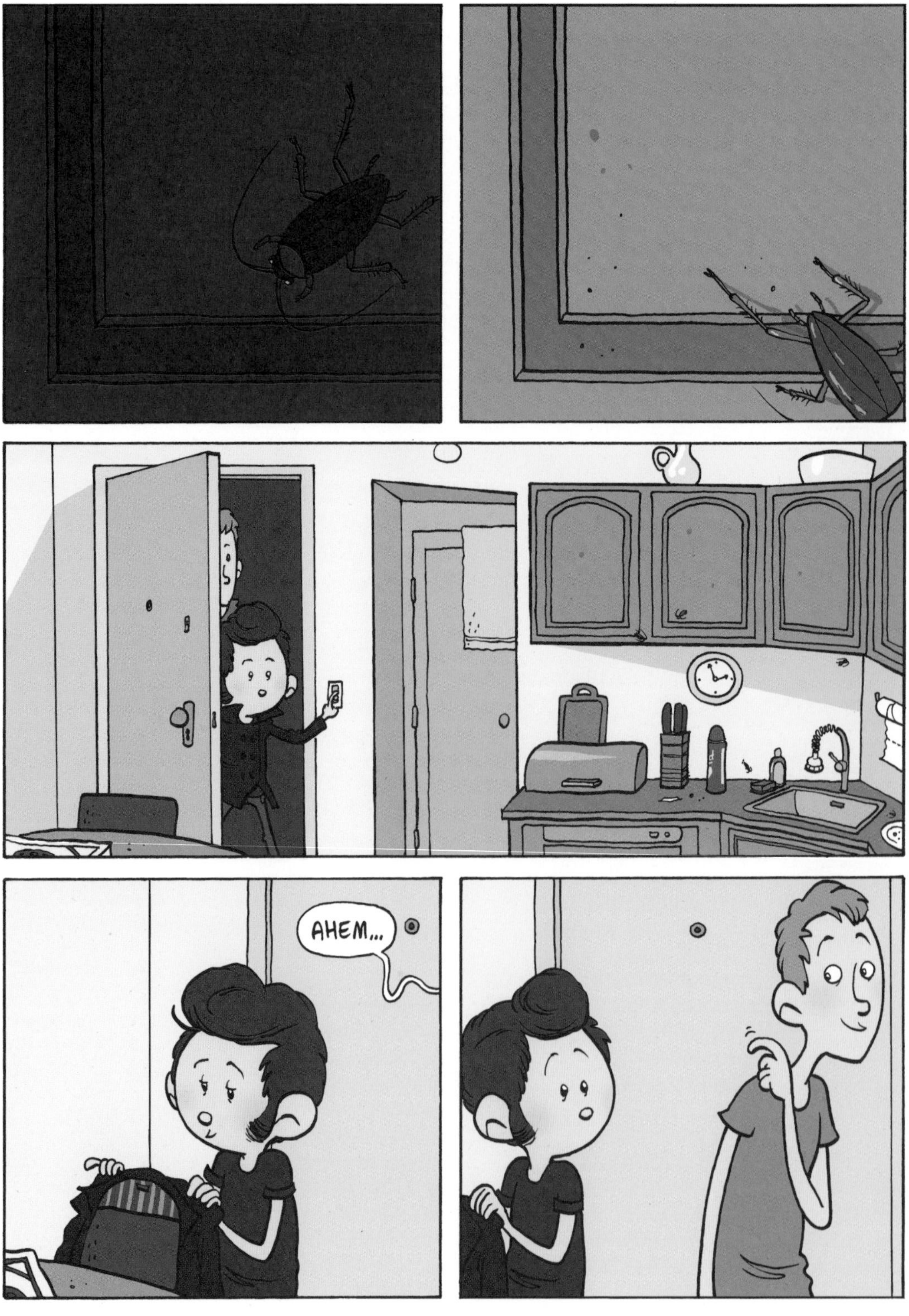
AHEM...

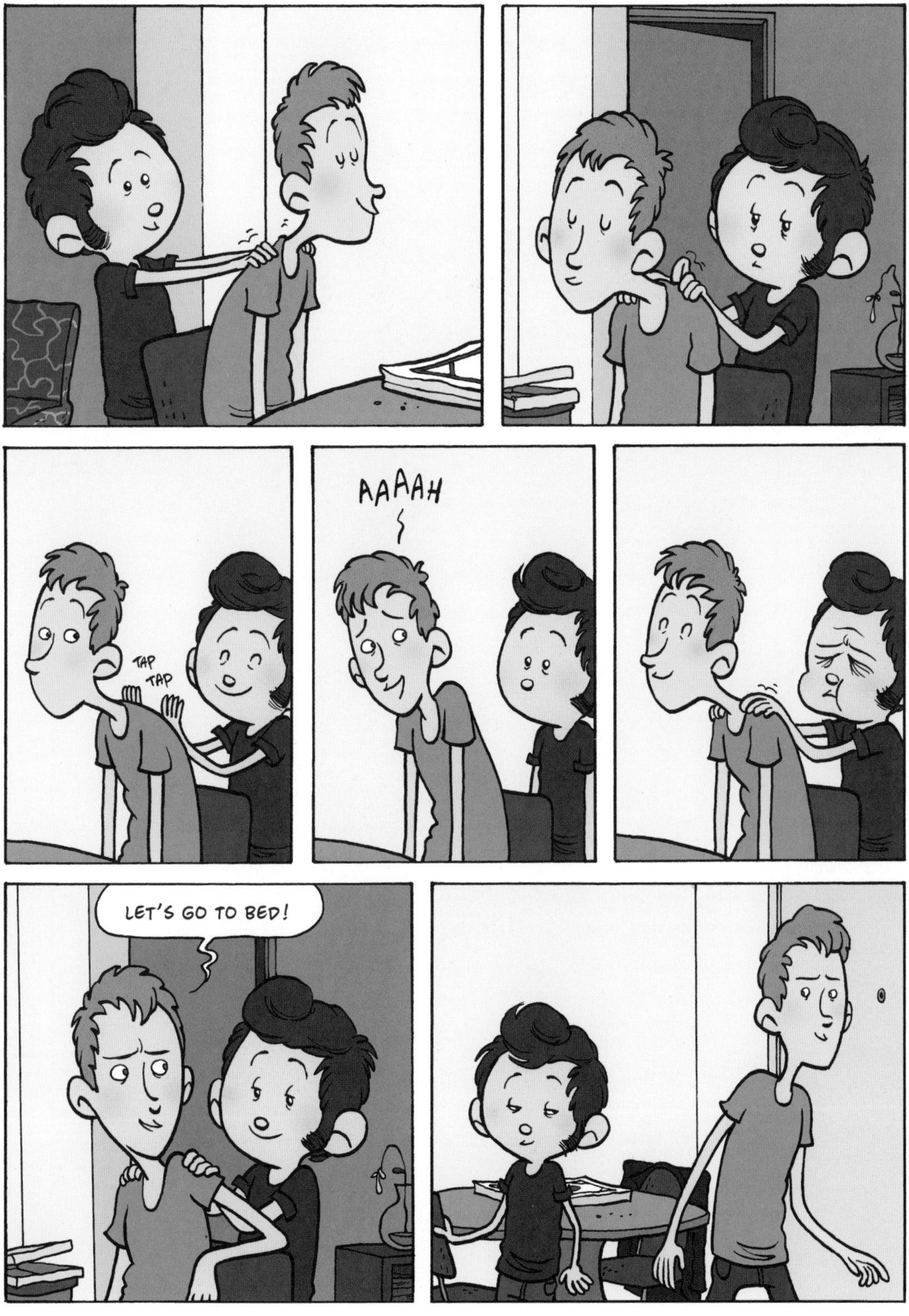
TAP
TAP
AAAAH
LET'S GO TO BED!

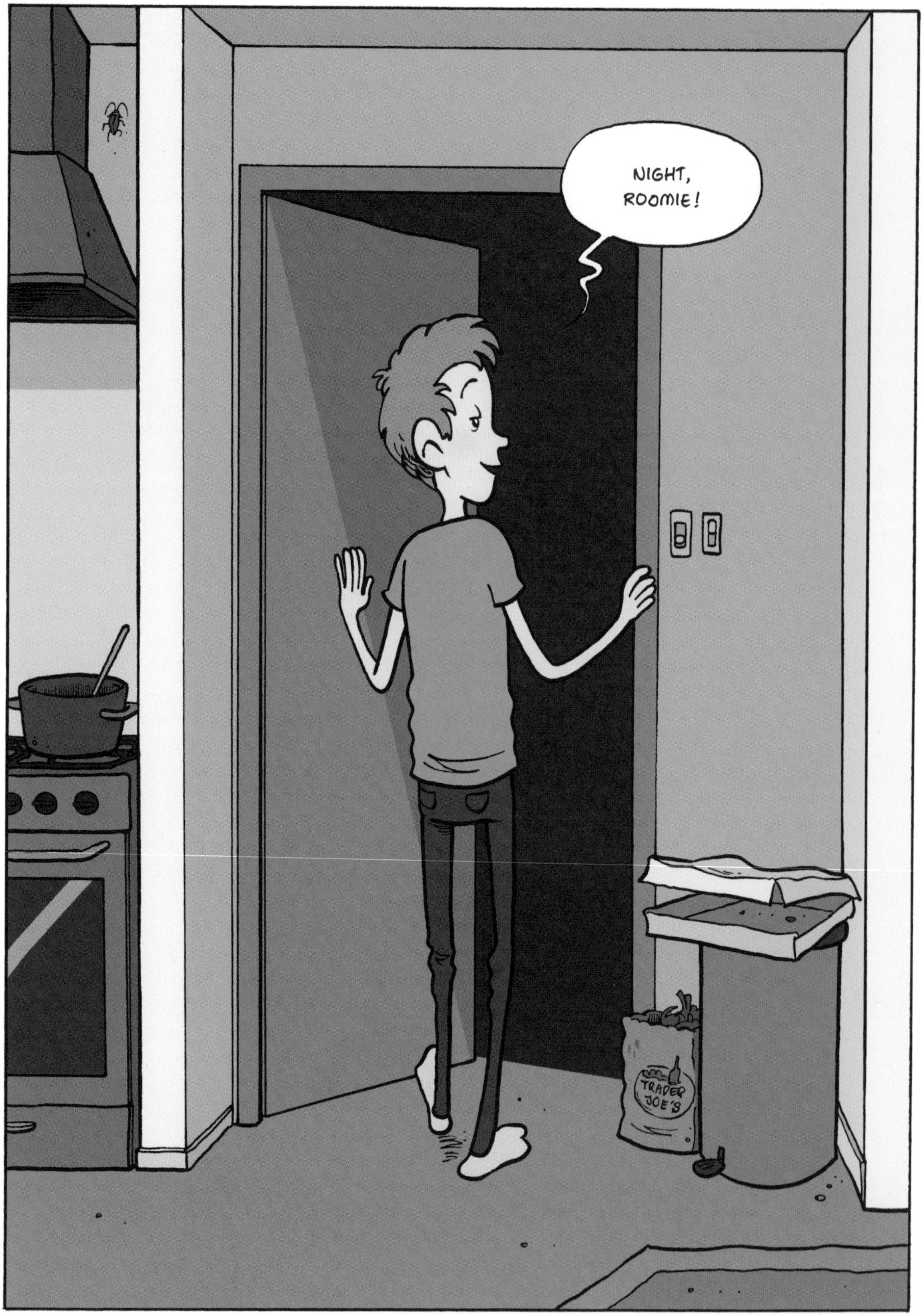
NIGHT,
ROOMIE!
TRADER
JOE'S

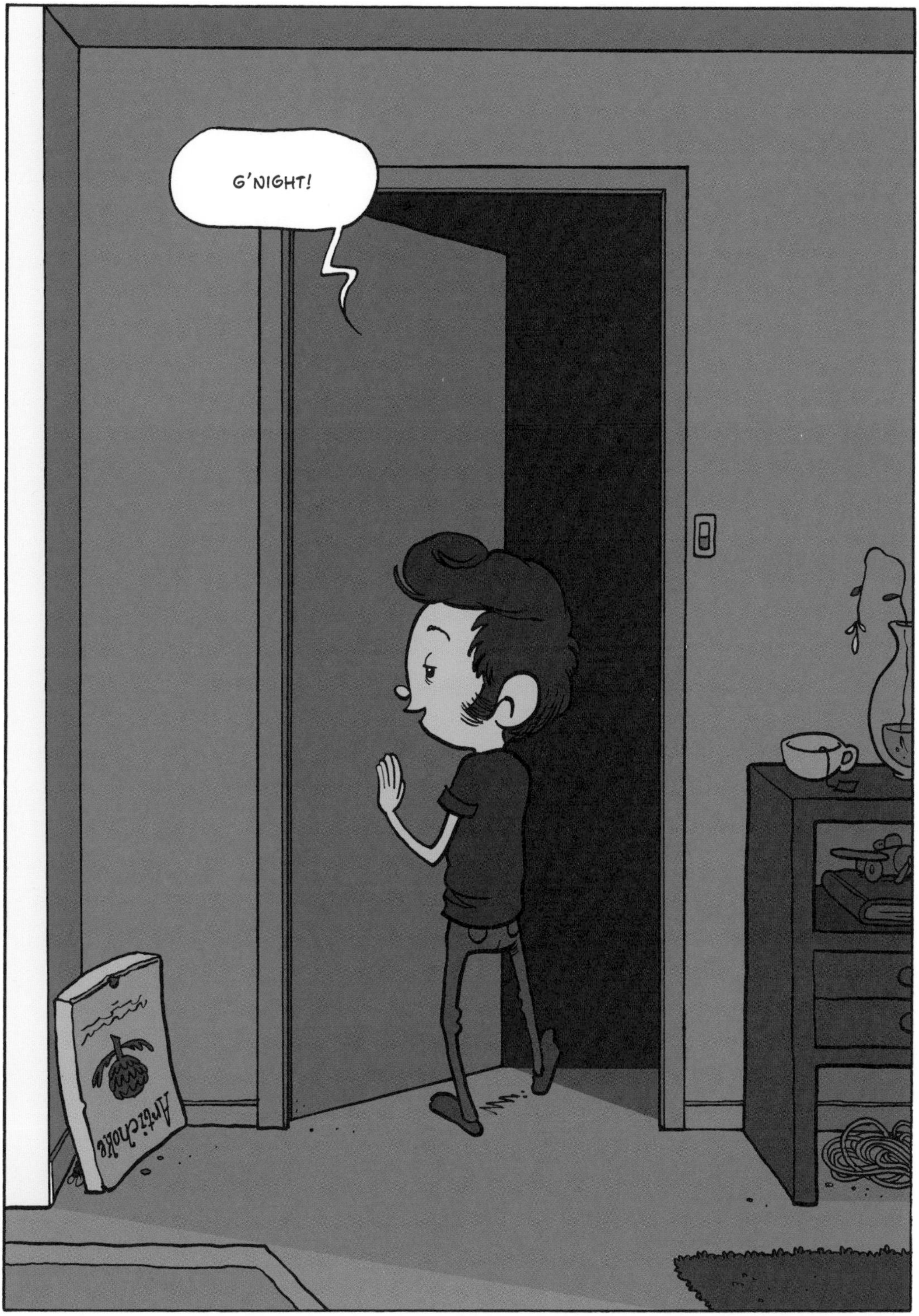
G'NIGHT!
Artichoke

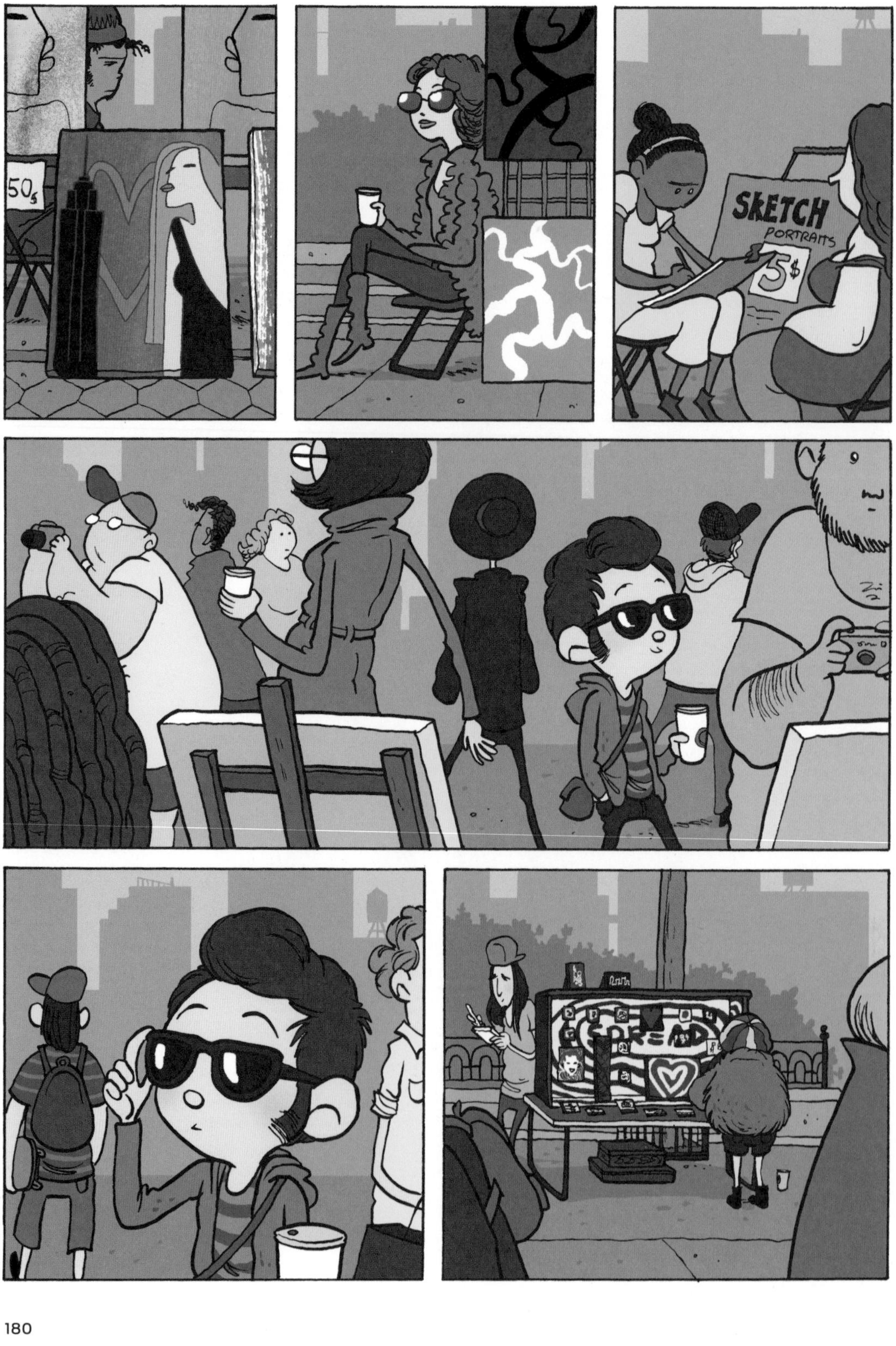
50$
SKETCH
PORTRAITS
5$

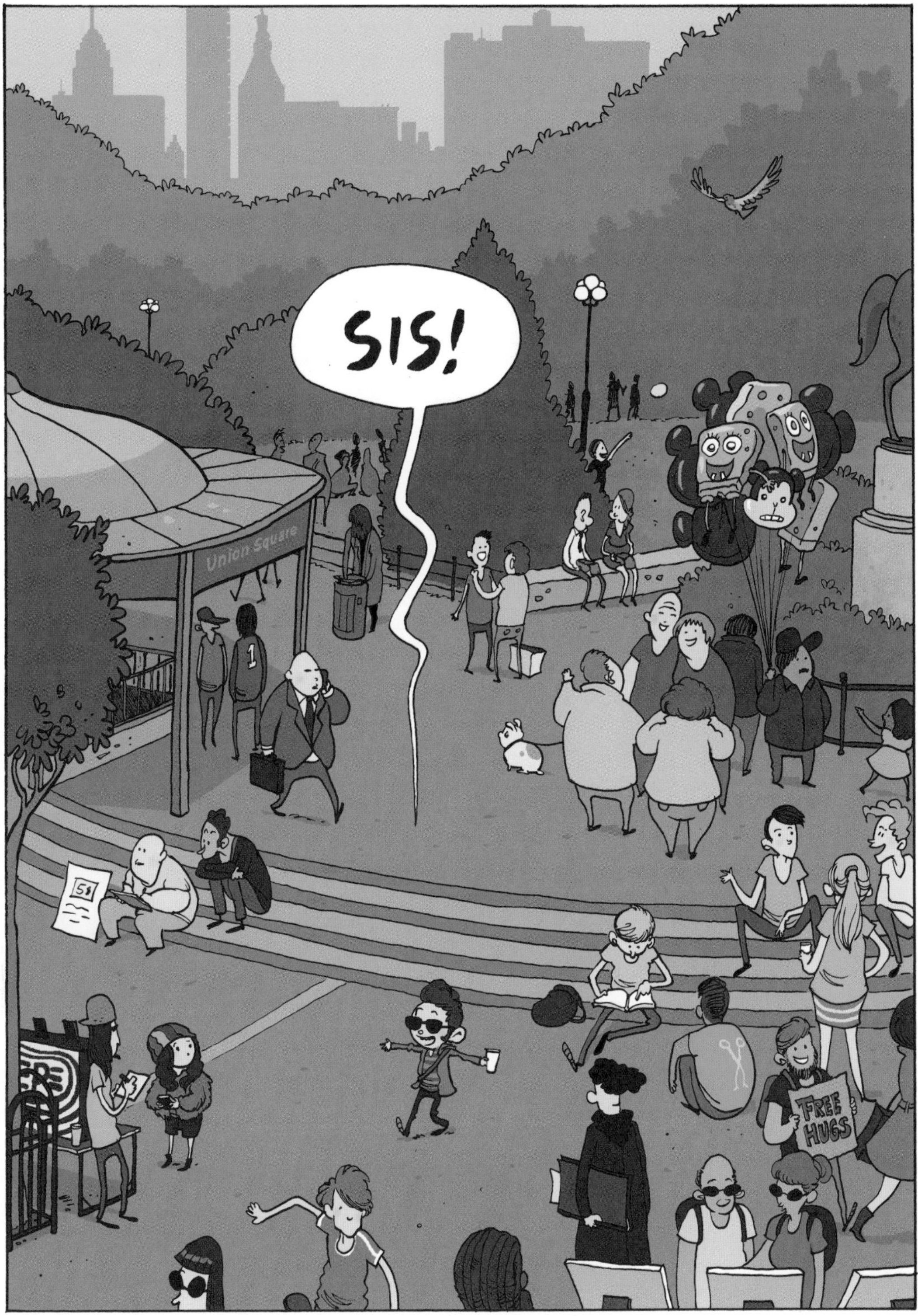
SIS!
Union Square
FREE HUGS

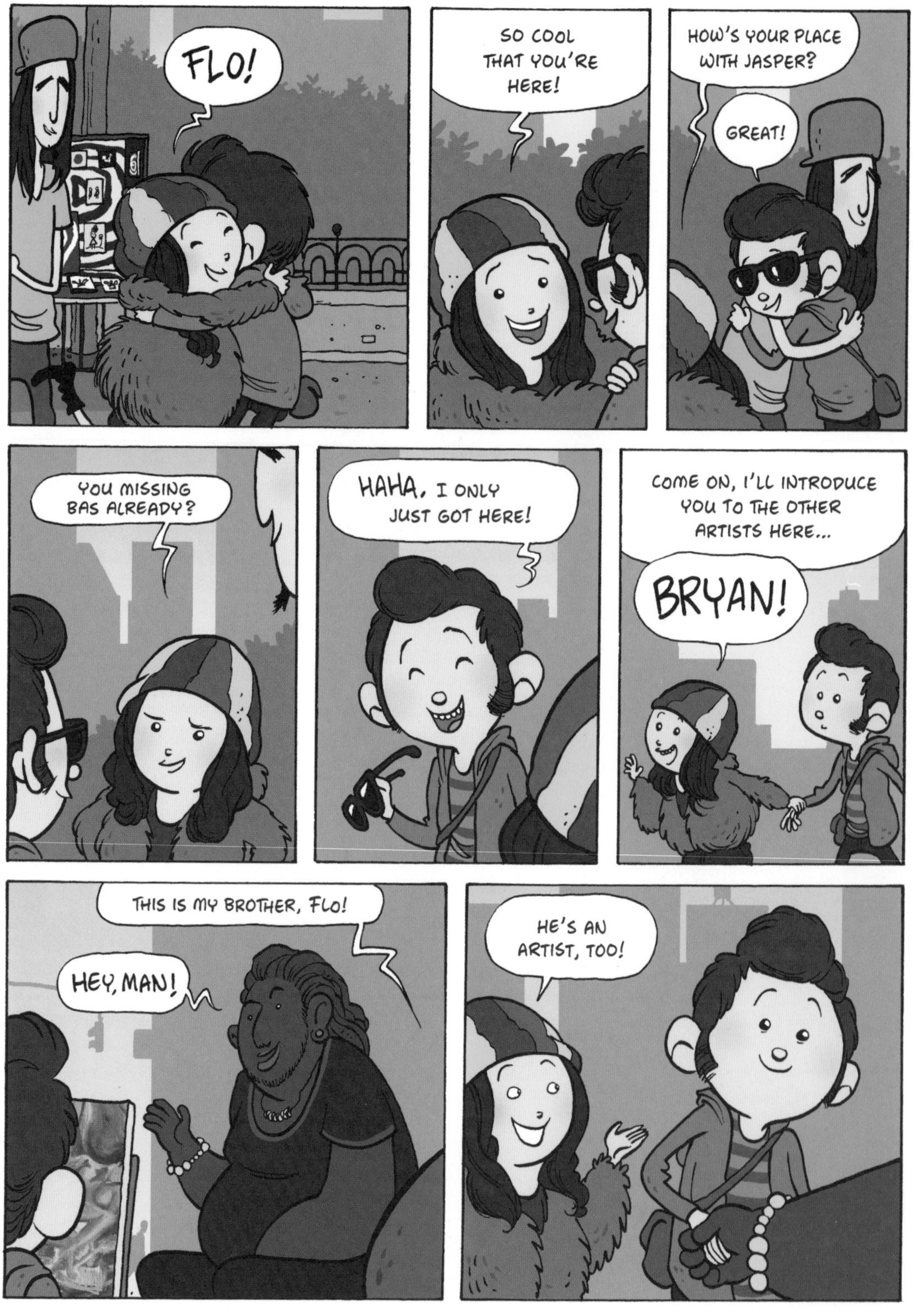
FLO!
SO COOL THAT YOU'RE HERE!
HOW'S YOUR PLACE WITH JASPER?
GREAT!
YOU MISSING BAS ALREADY?
HAHA, I ONLY JUST GOT HERE!
COME ON, I'LL INTRODUCE YOU TO THE OTHER ARTISTS HERE...
BRYAN!
THIS IS MY BROTHER, FLO!
HEY, MAN!
HE'S AN ARTIST, TOO!

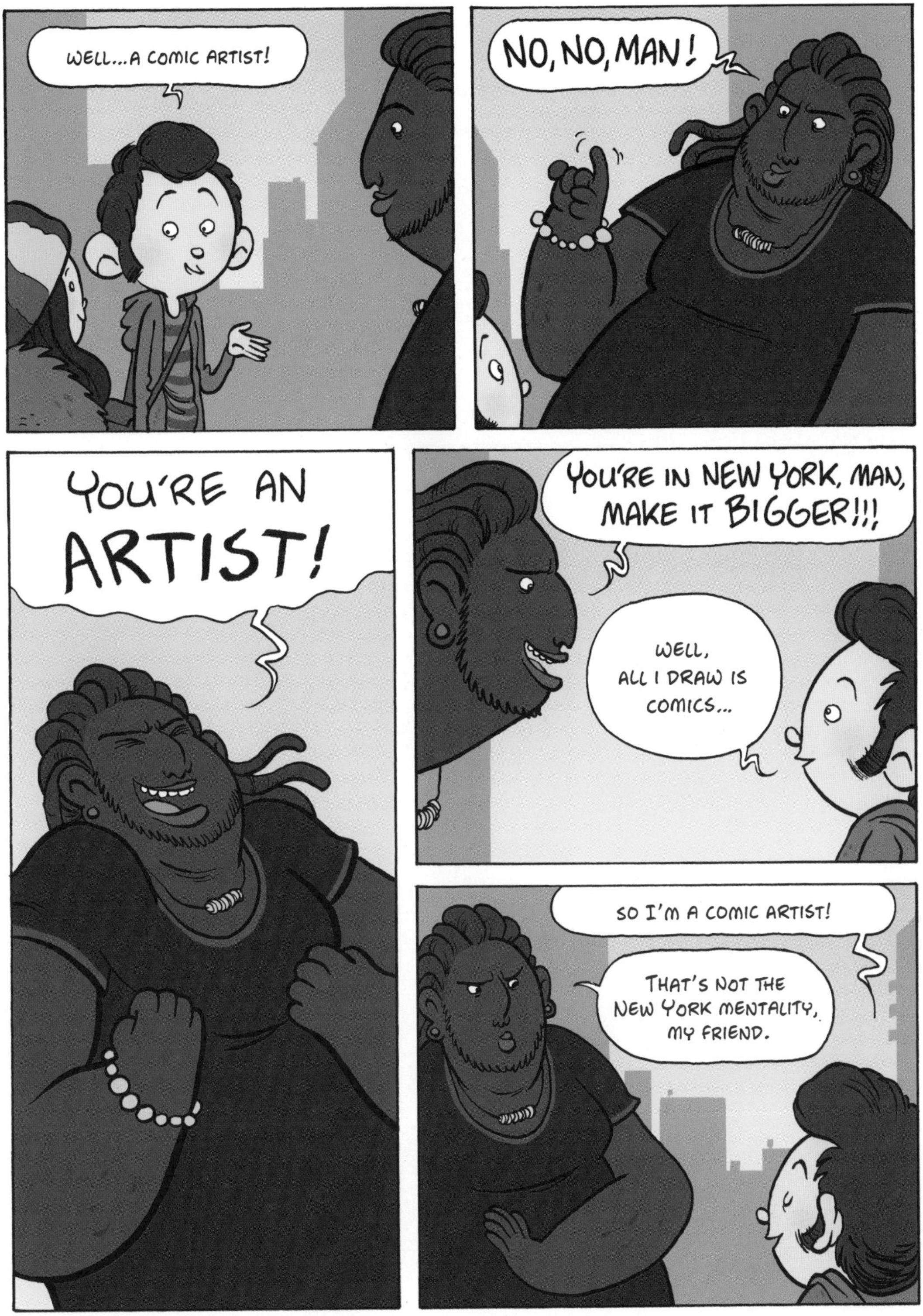
WELL...A COMIC ARTIST!
NO, NO, MAN!
YOU'RE AN ARTIST!
YOU'RE IN NEW YORK, MAN, MAKE IT BIGGER!!!
WELL, ALL I DRAW IS COMICS...
SO I'M A COMIC ARTIST!
THAT'S NOT THE NEW YORK MENTALITY, MY FRIEND.

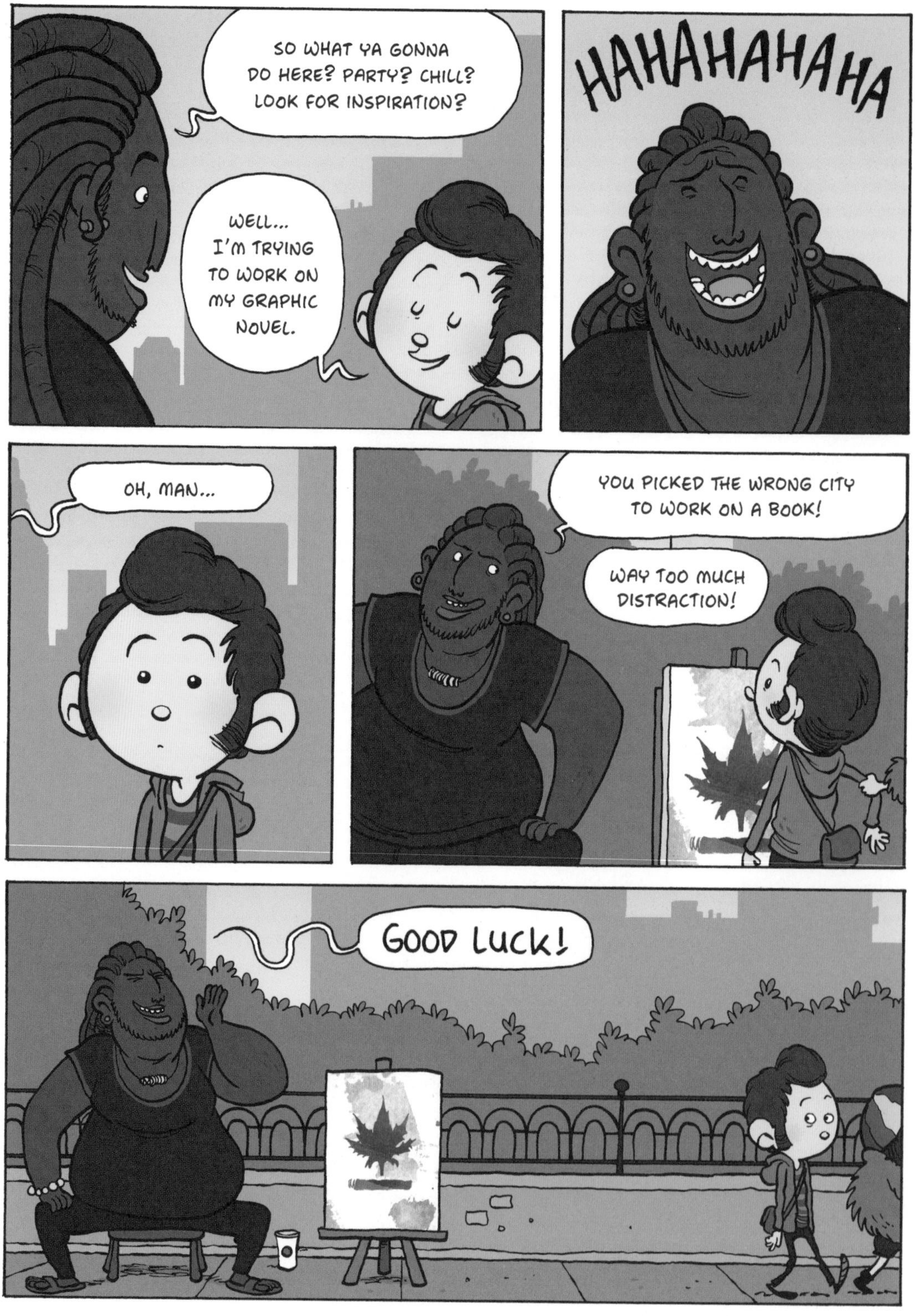
SO WHAT YA GONNA DO HERE? PARTY? CHILL? LOOK FOR INSPIRATION?
WELL... I'M TRYING TO WORK ON MY GRAPHIC NOVEL.
HAHAHAHAHA
OH, MAN...
YOU PICKED THE WRONG CITY TO WORK ON A BOOK!
WAY TOO MUCH DISTRACTION!
GOOD LUCK!

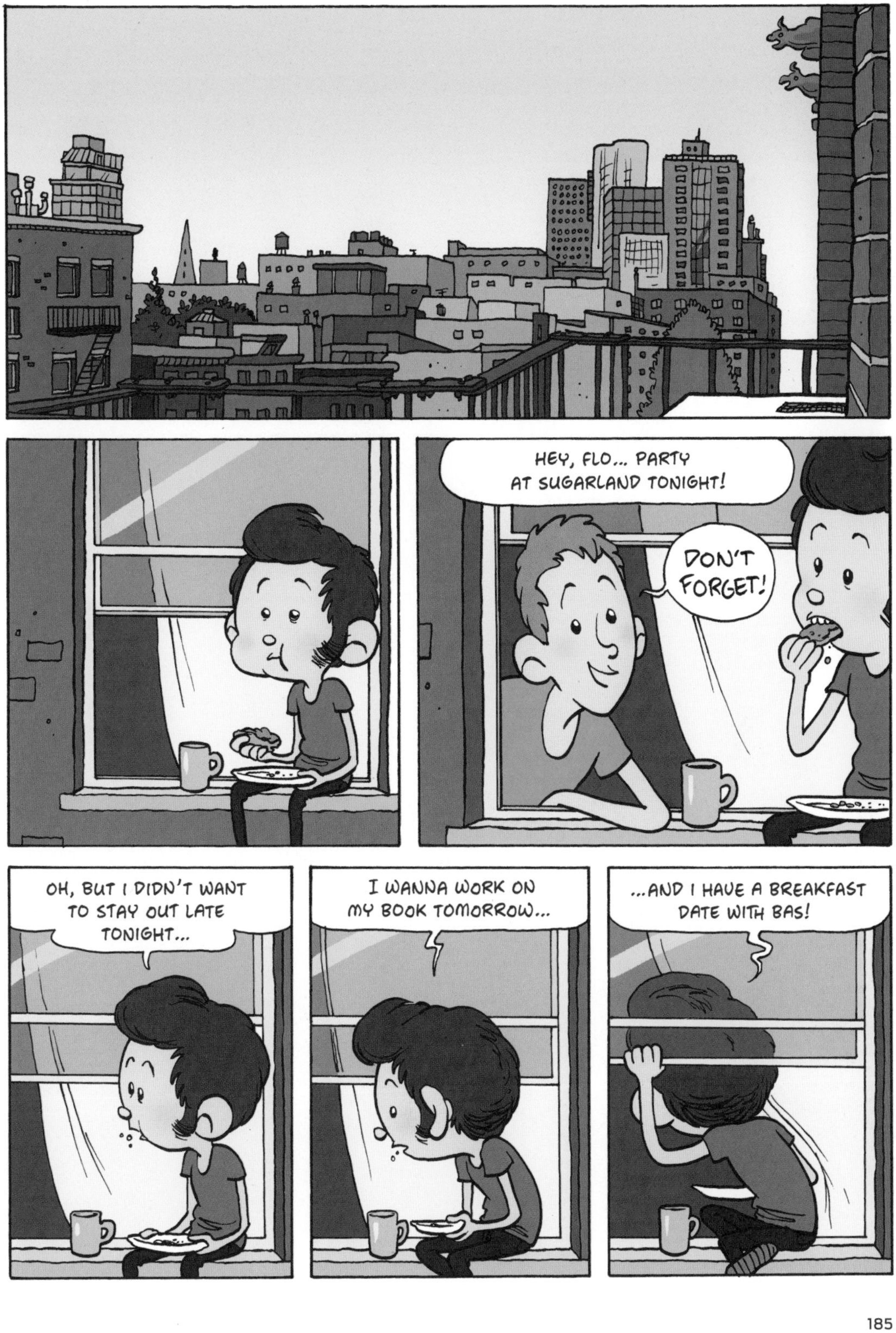
HEY, FLO... PARTY AT SUGARLAND TONIGHT!
DON'T FORGET!
OH, BUT I DIDN'T WANT TO STAY OUT LATE TONIGHT...
I WANNA WORK ON MY BOOK TOMORROW...
...AND I HAVE A BREAKFAST DATE WITH BAS!

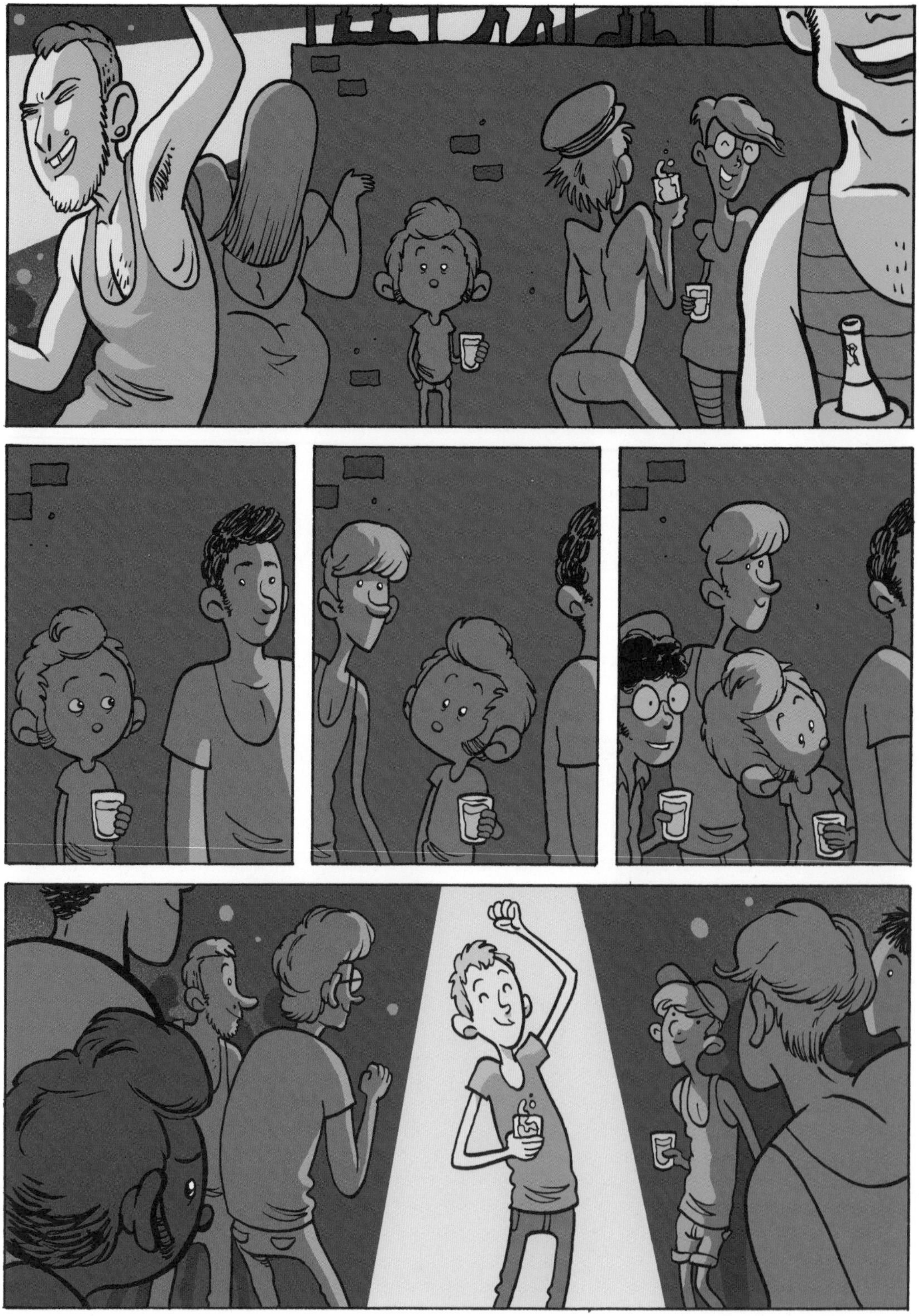

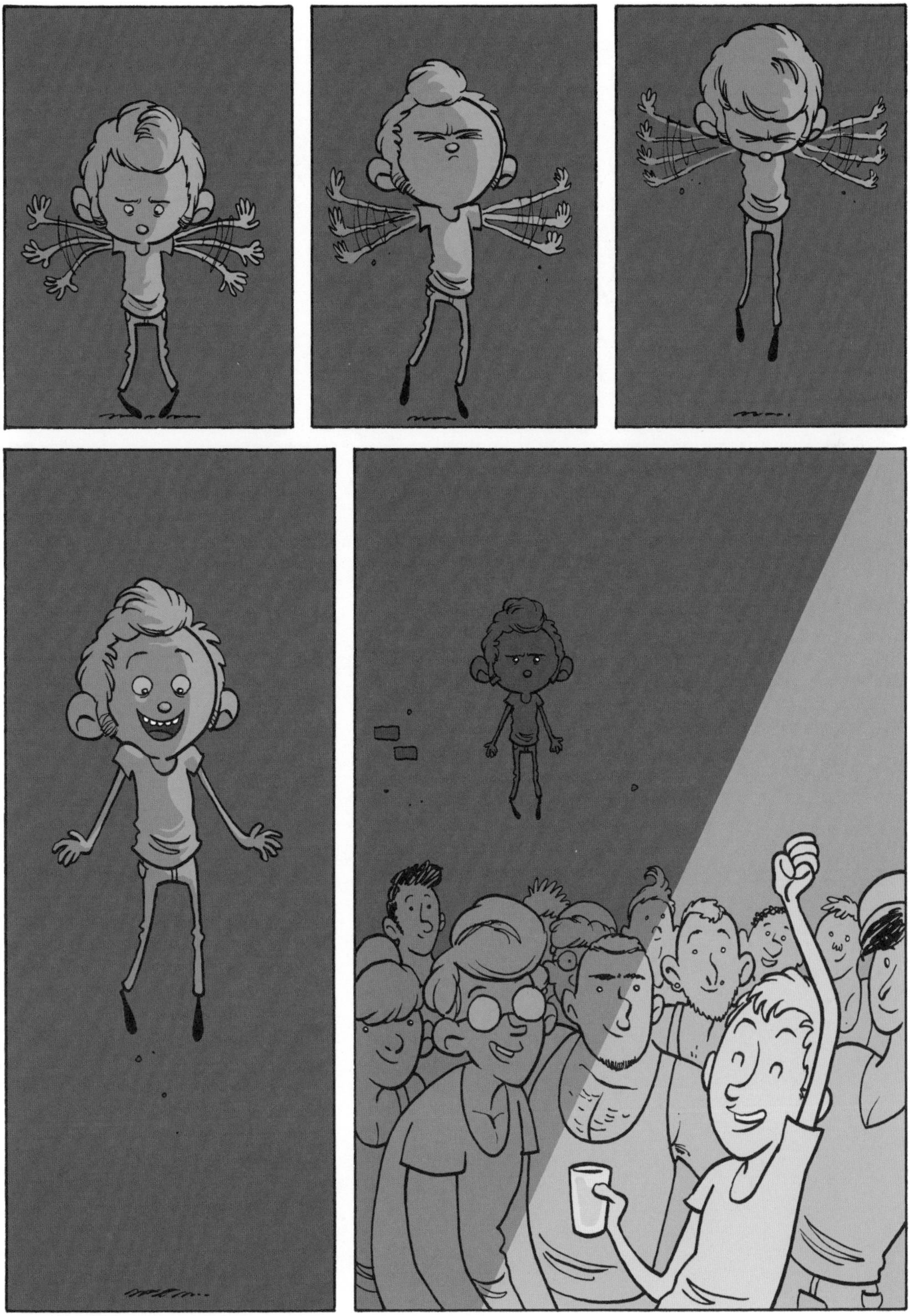

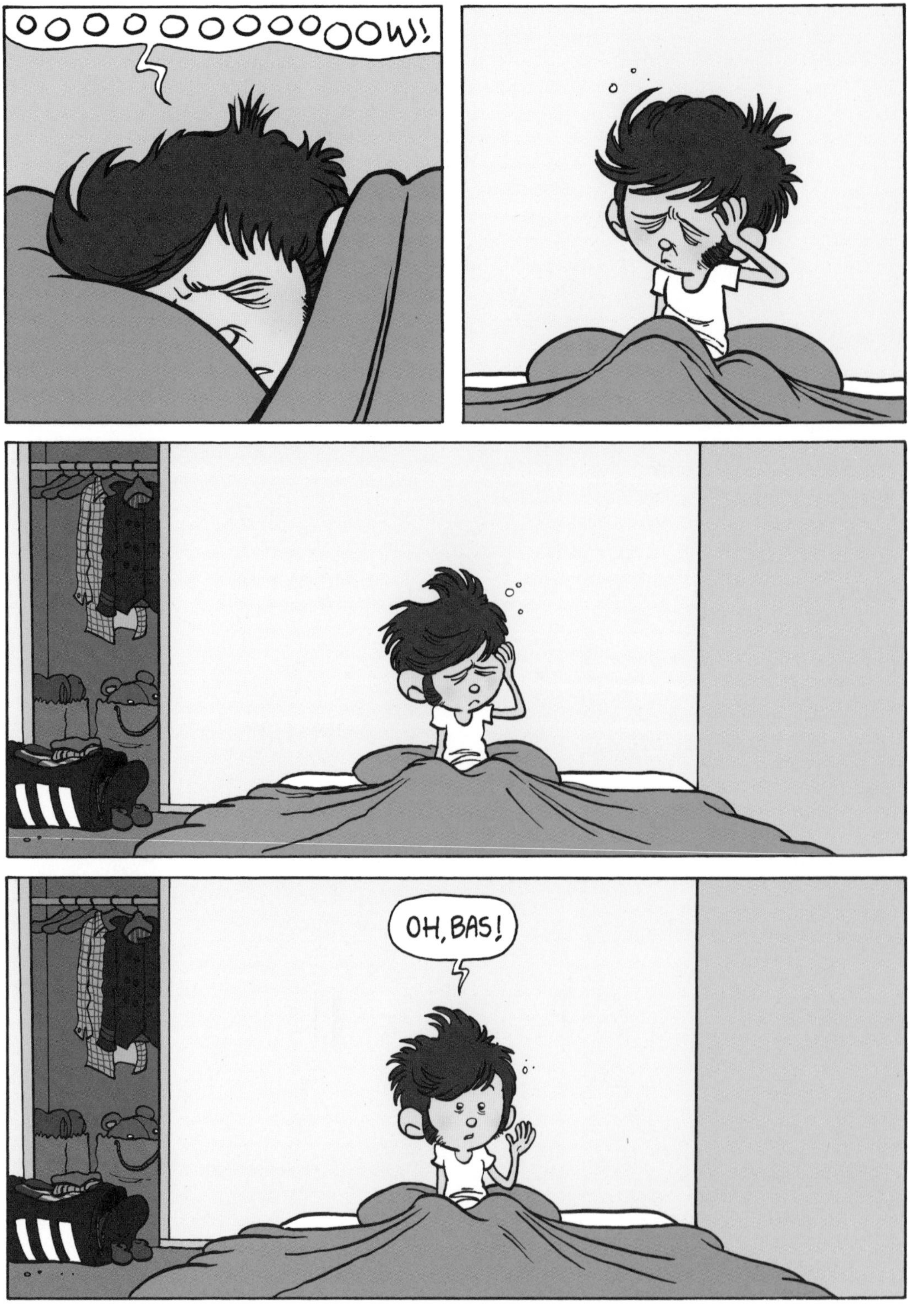
OOOOOOOOOOOOW!
OH, BAS!

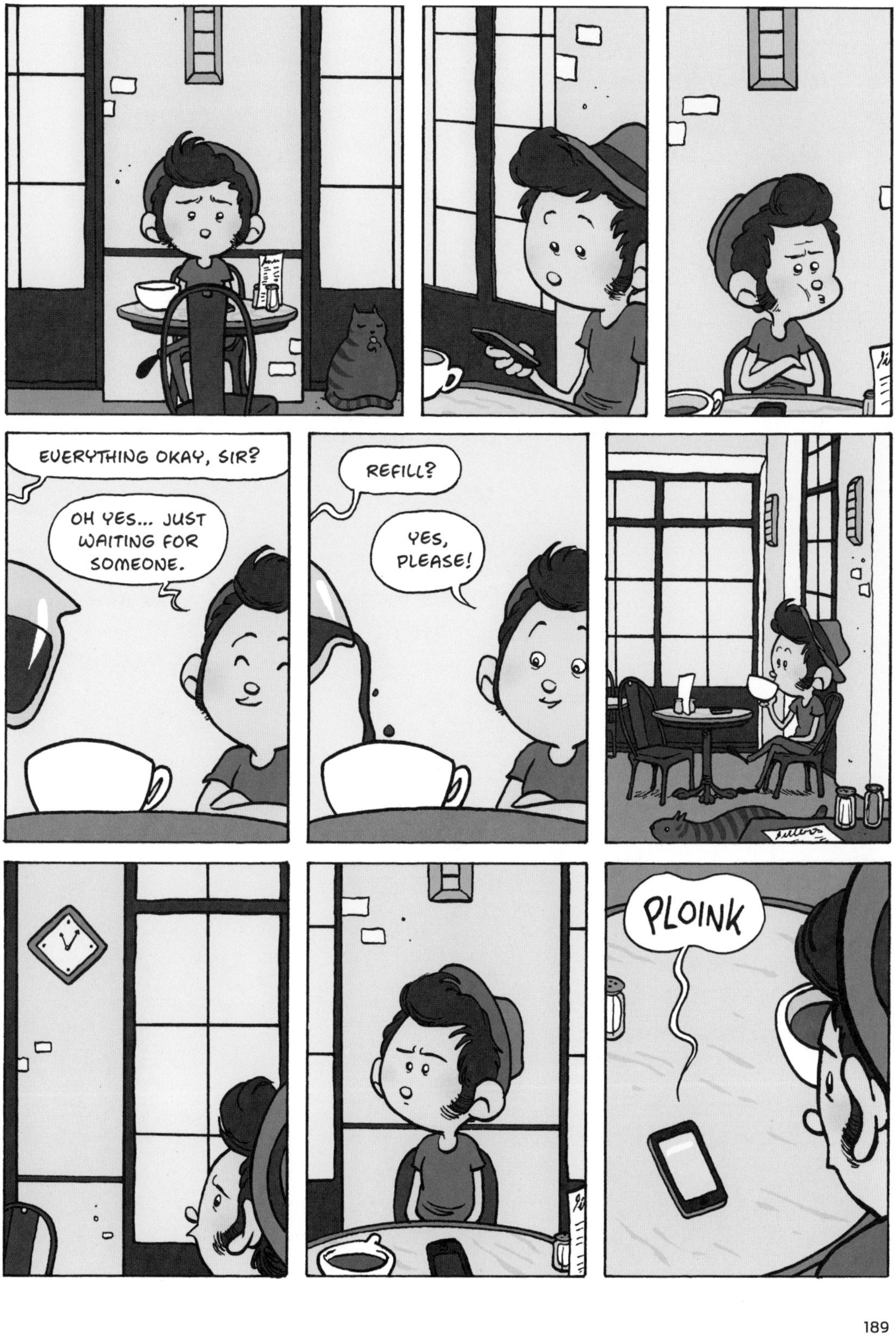
EVERYTHING OKAY, SIR?
OH YES... JUST WAITING FOR SOMEONE.
REFILL?
YES, PLEASE!
PLOINK

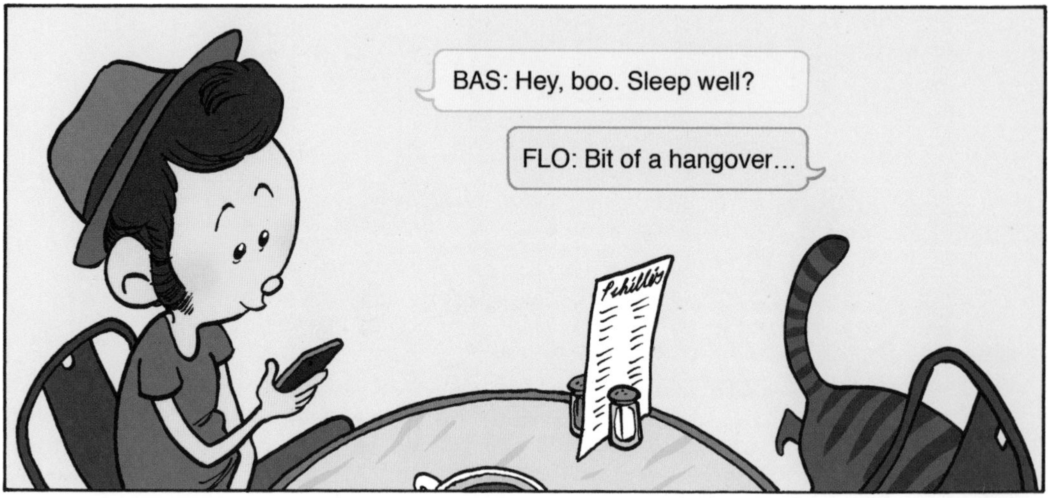
BAS: Hey, boo. Sleep well?
FLO: Bit of a hangover...
Schiller's

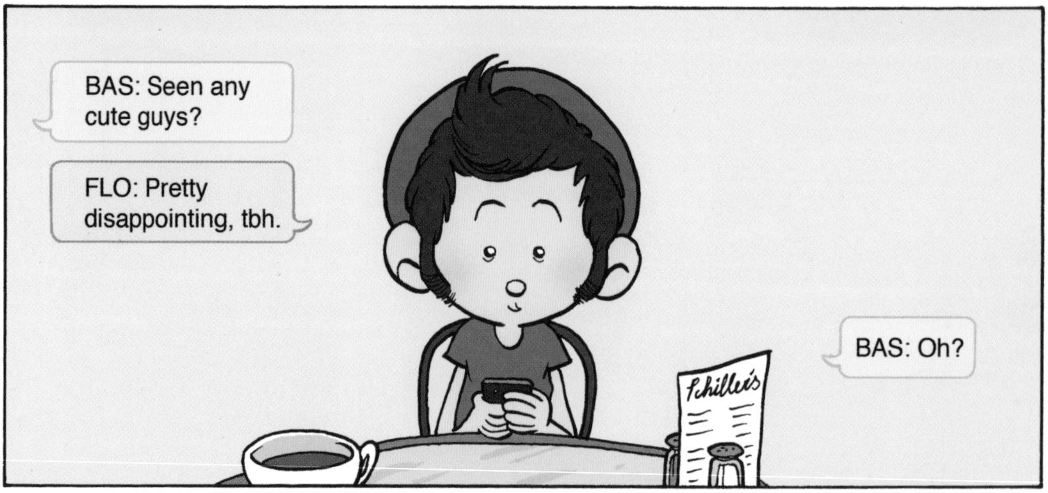
BAS: Seen any cute guys?
FLO: Pretty disappointing, tbh.
BAS: Oh?
Schiller's

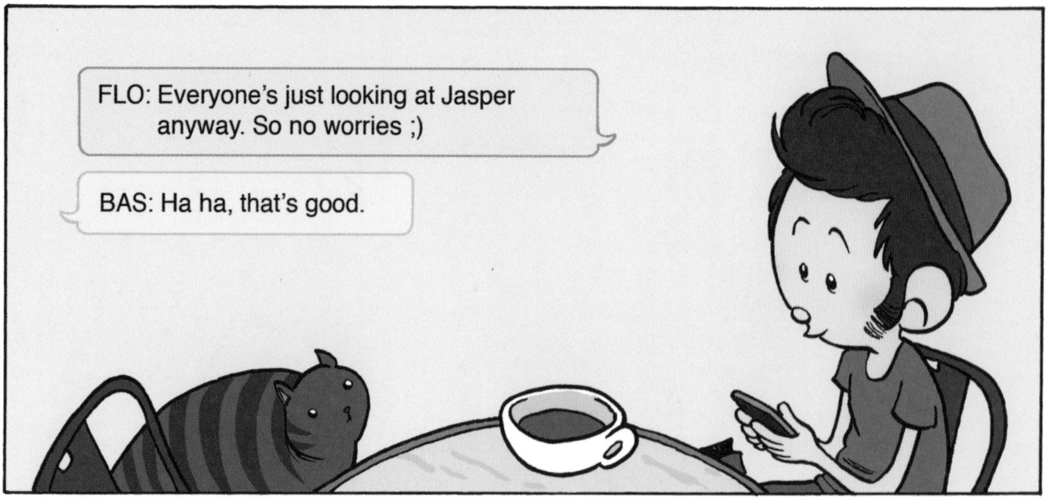
FLO: Everyone's just looking at Jasper anyway. So no worries ;)
BAS: Ha ha, that's good.

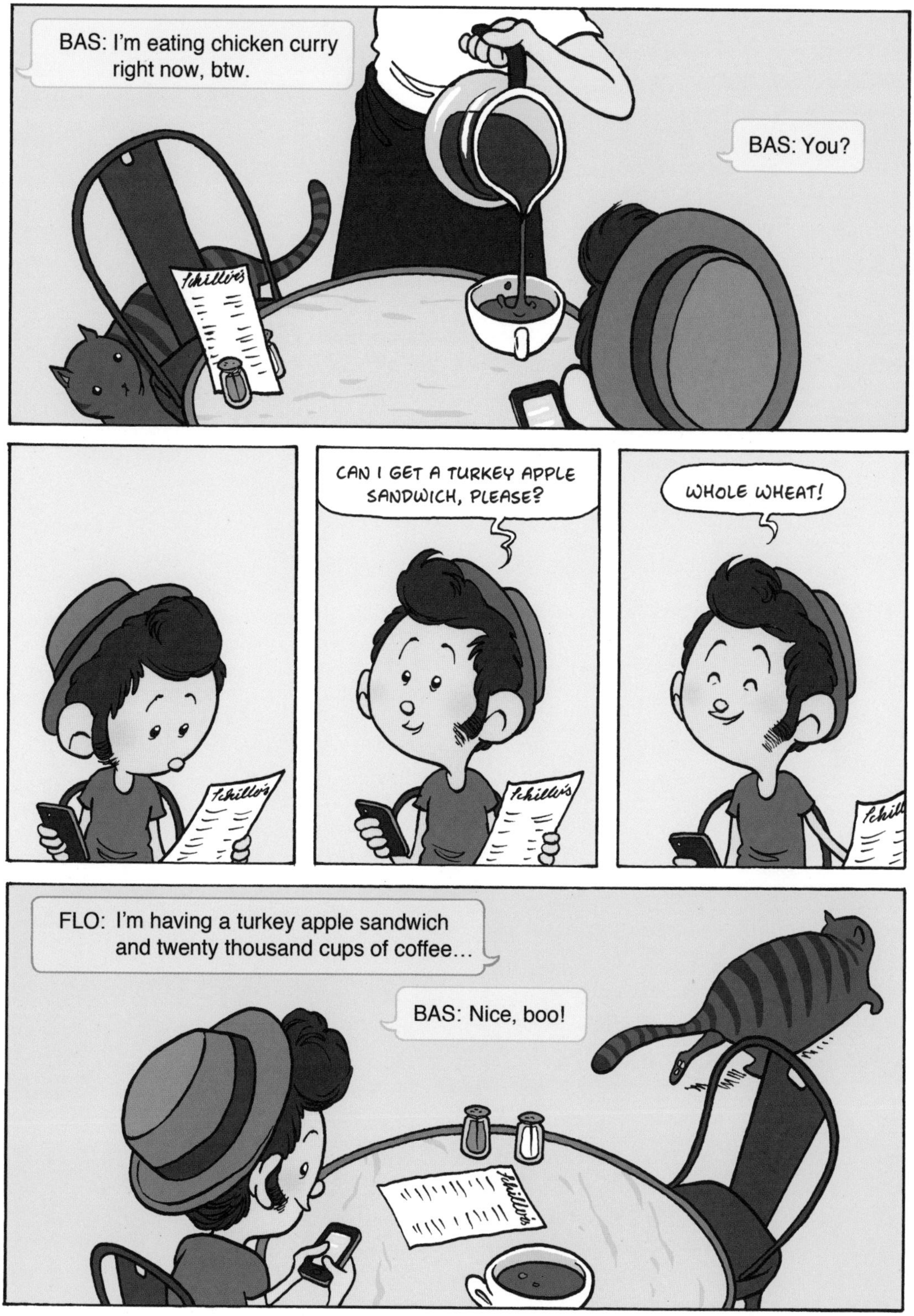
BAS: I'm eating chicken curry right now, btw.
BAS: You?
CAN I GET A TURKEY APPLE SANDWICH, PLEASE?
WHOLE WHEAT!
FLO: I'm having a turkey apple sandwich and twenty thousand cups of coffee…
BAS: Nice, boo!

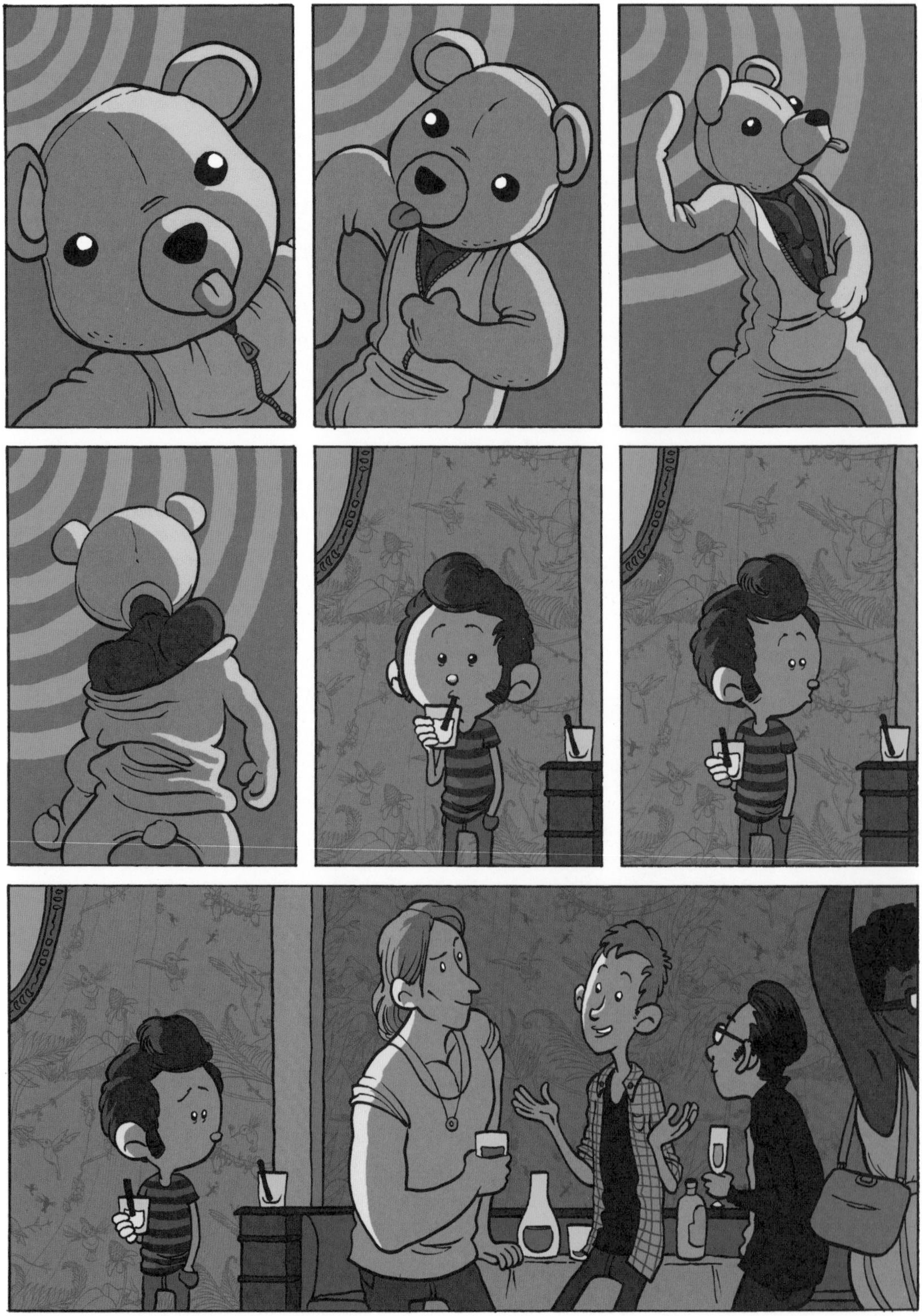

OH, HEY! GUYS, THIS IS MY FRIEND FLO!

HI!!

SO, YOU WANT ANOTHER DRINK, JASPER?

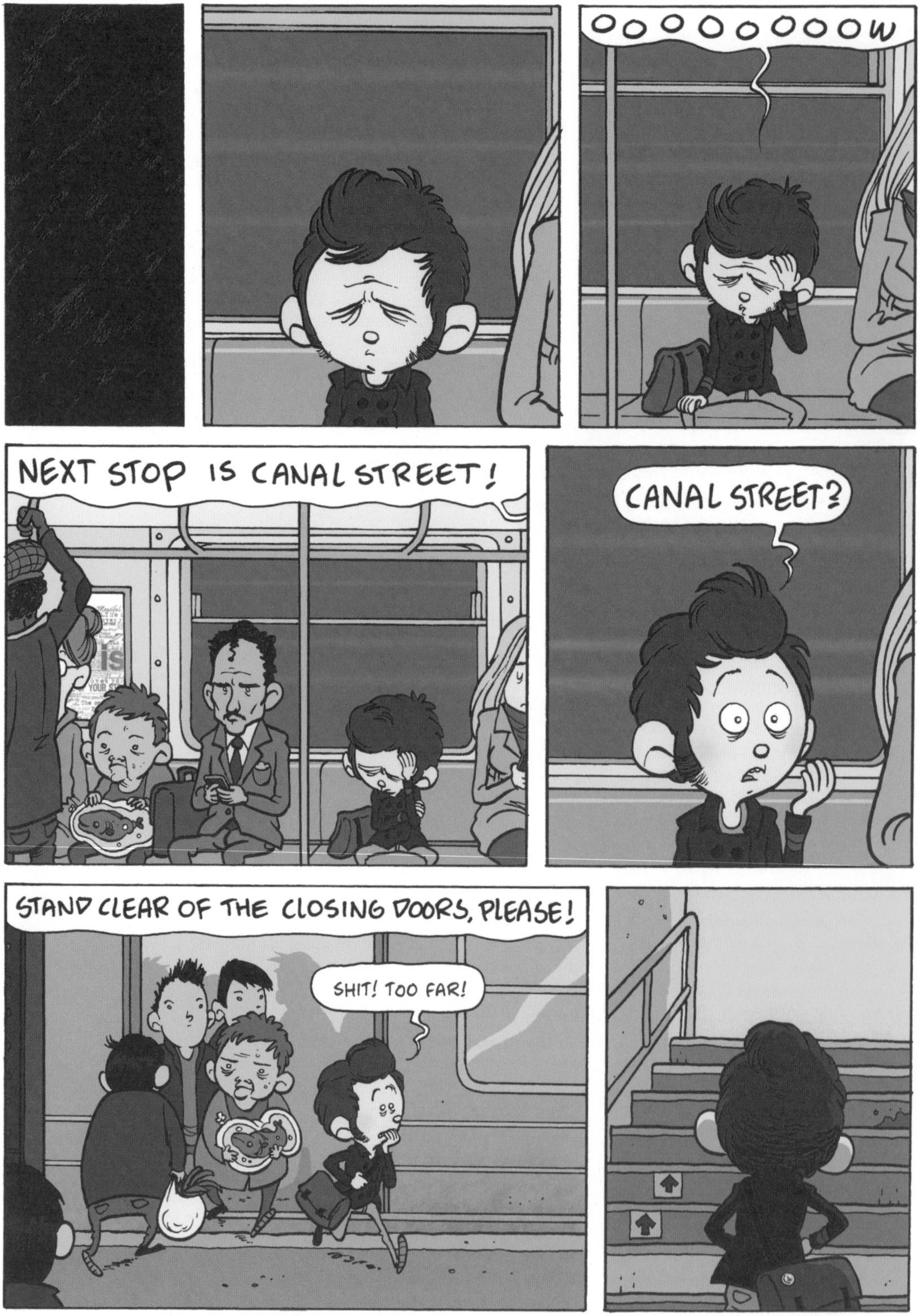
OOOOOOOOOW
NEXT STOP IS CANAL STREET!
CANAL STREET?
STAND CLEAR OF THE CLOSING DOORS, PLEASE!
SHIT! TOO FAR!

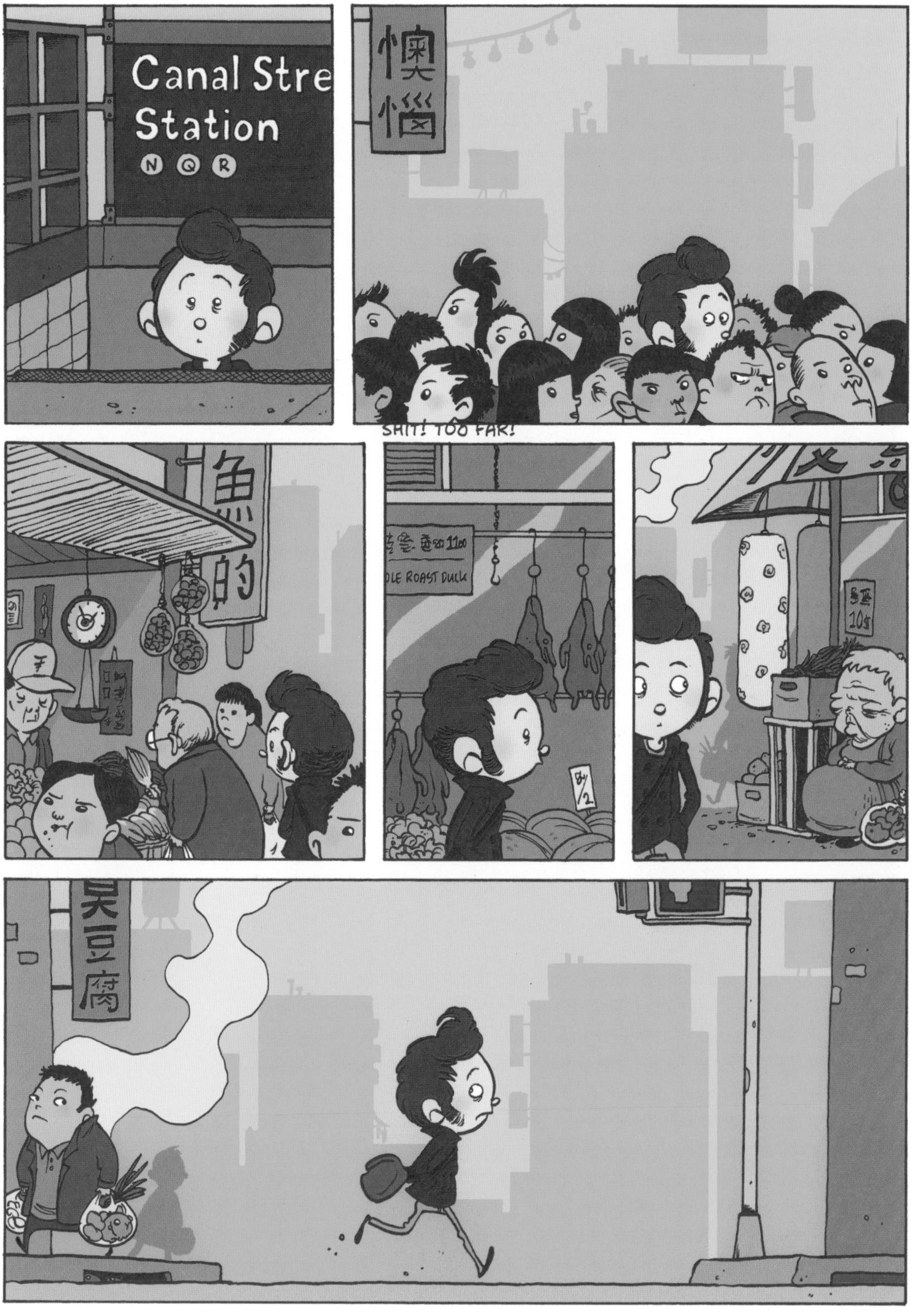
Canal Stre
Station
N Q R
懊惱
SHIT! TOO FAR!
臭豆腐

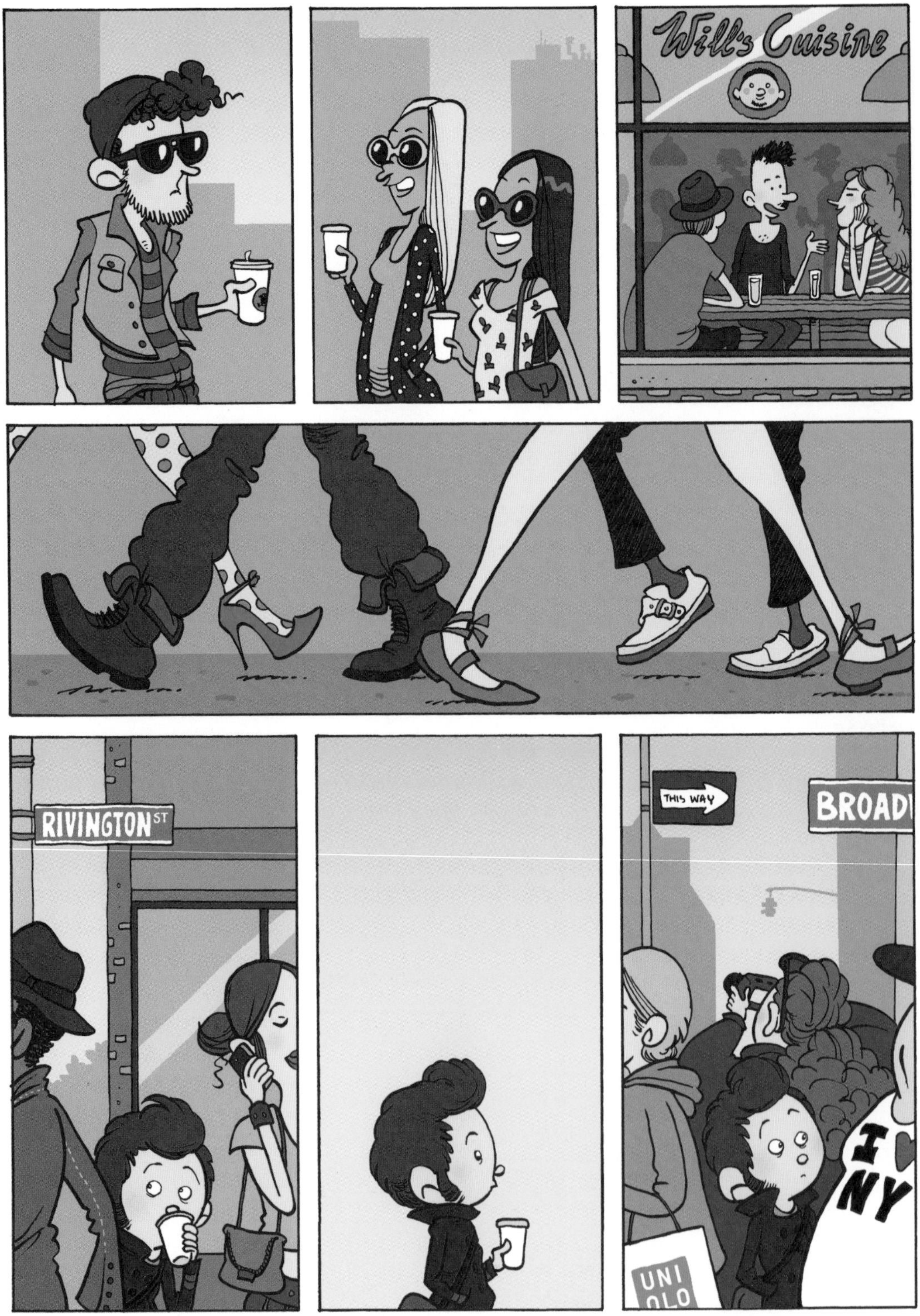
Will's Cuisine
RIVINGTON ST
THIS WAY
BROAD
I NY
UNI
QLO

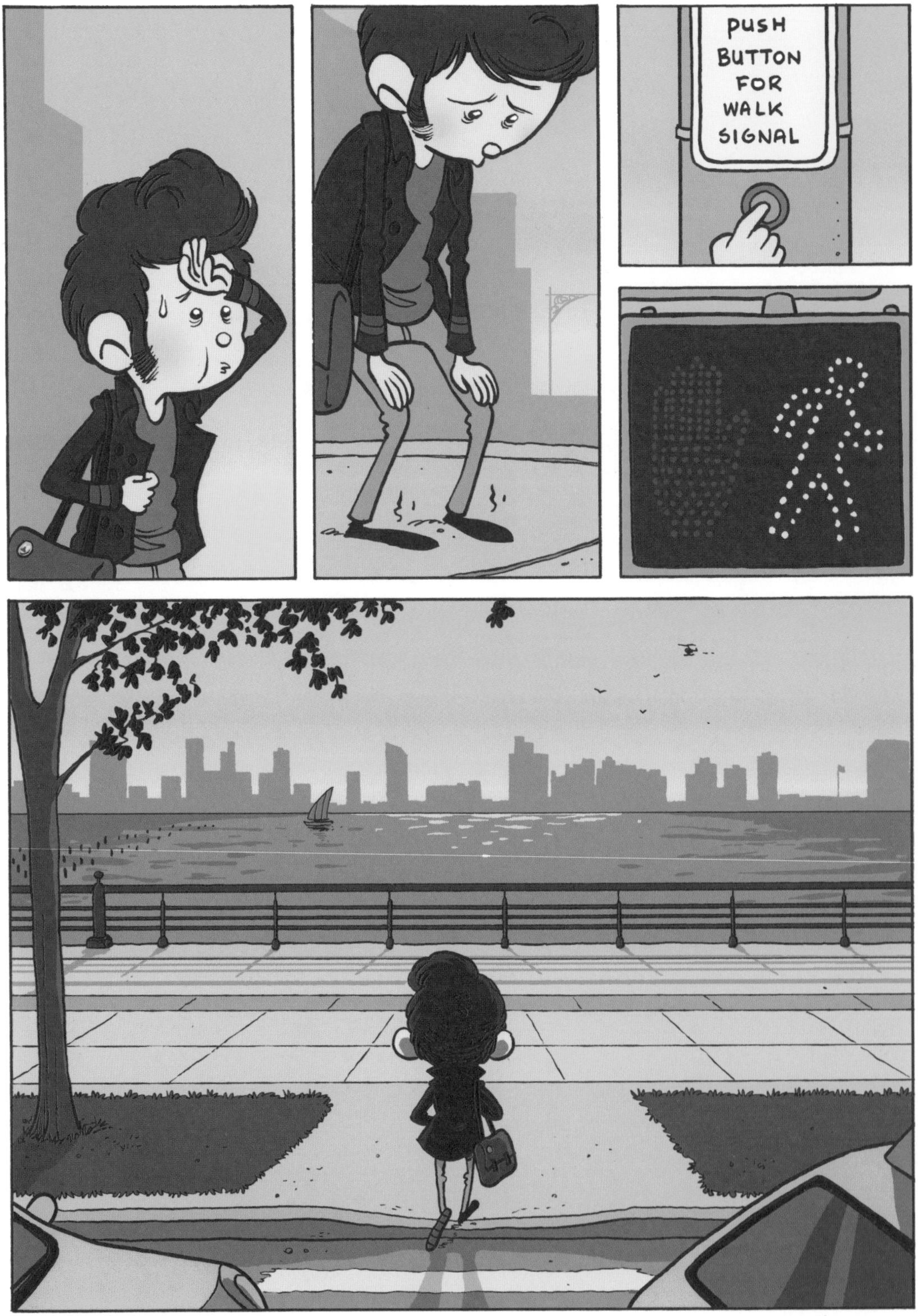
PUSH
BUTTON
FOR
WALK
SIGNAL

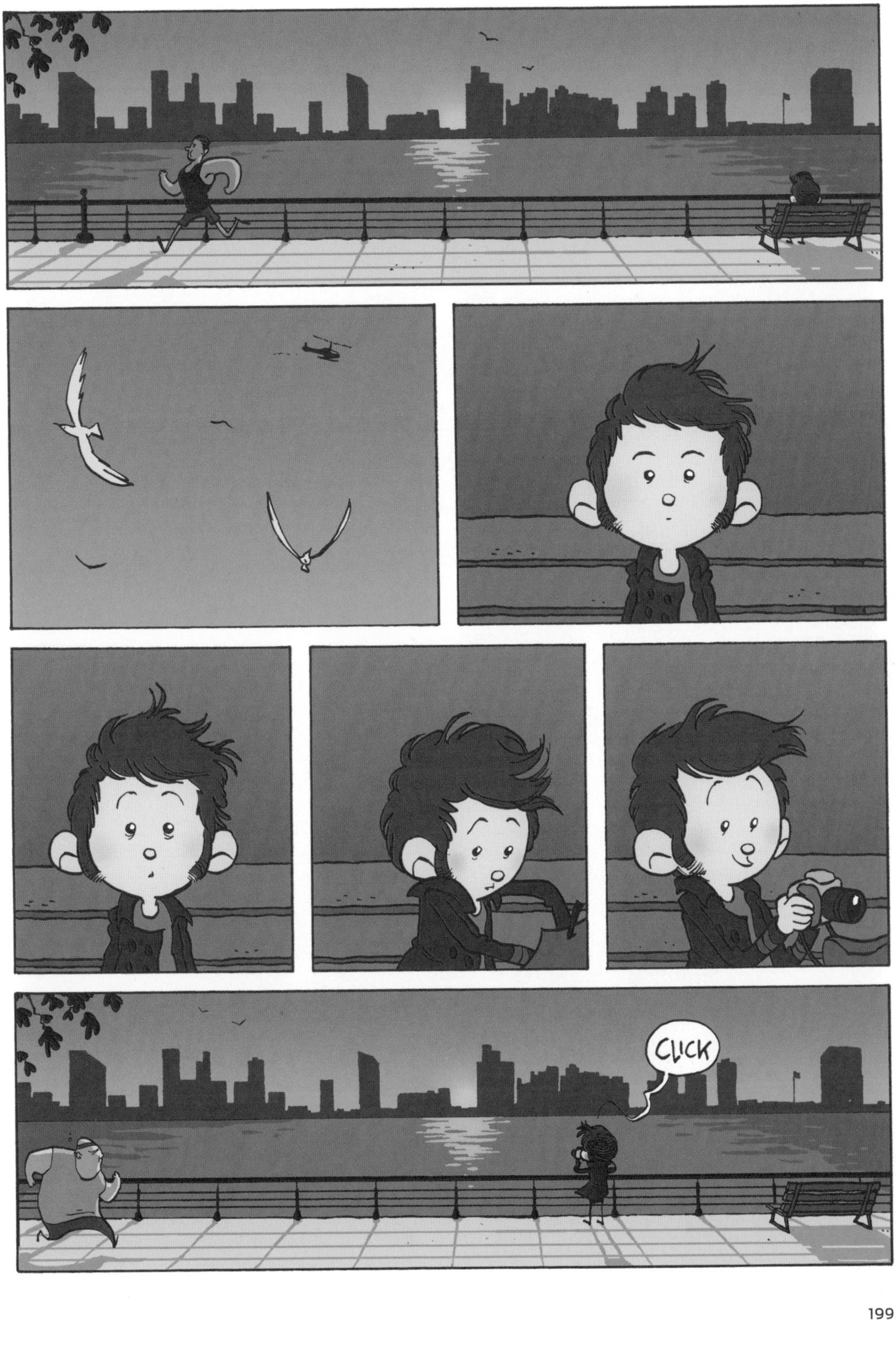
CLICK

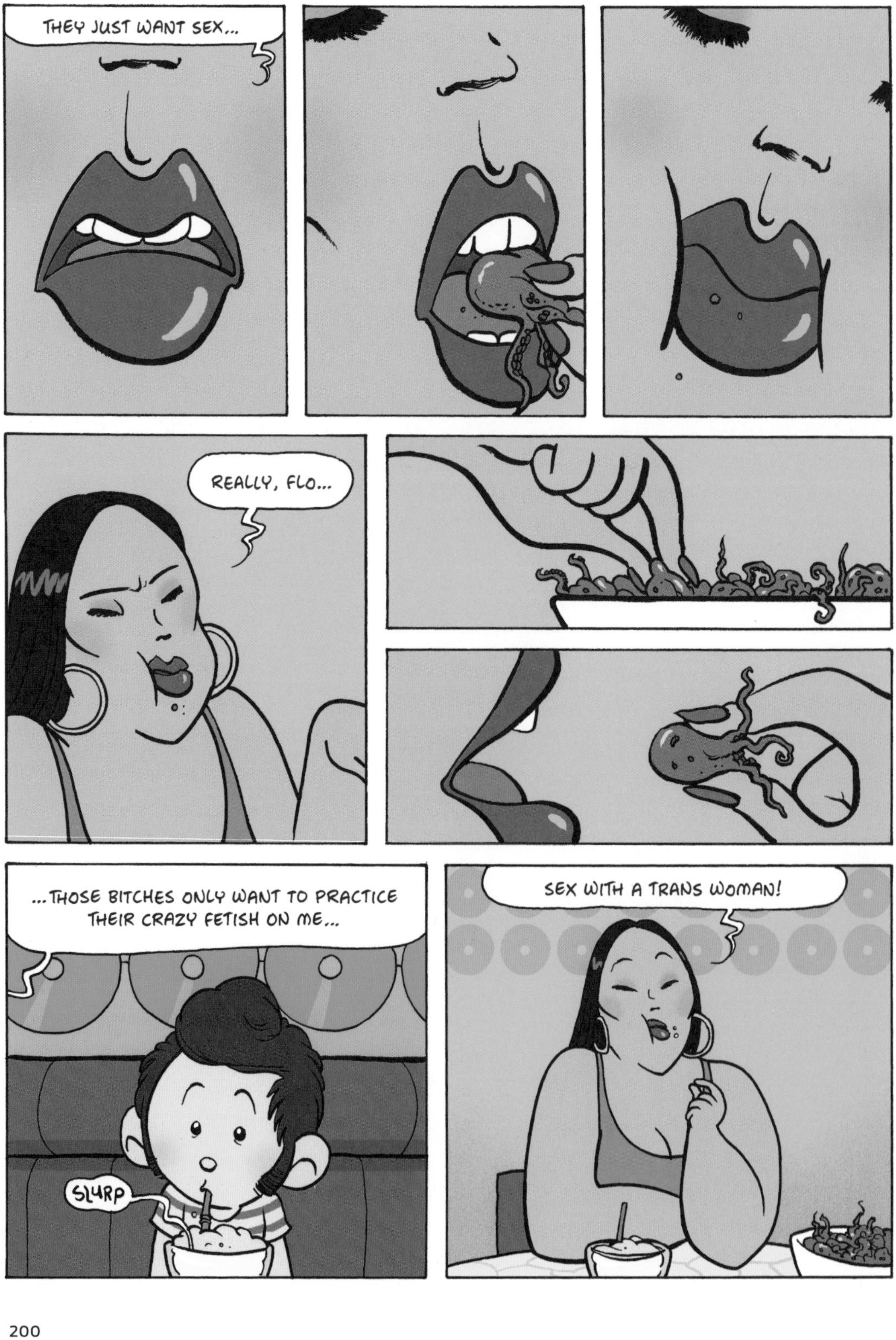
THEY JUST WANT SEX...
REALLY, FLO...
...THOSE BITCHES ONLY WANT TO PRACTICE THEIR CRAZY FETISH ON ME...
SLURP
SEX WITH A TRANS WOMAN!

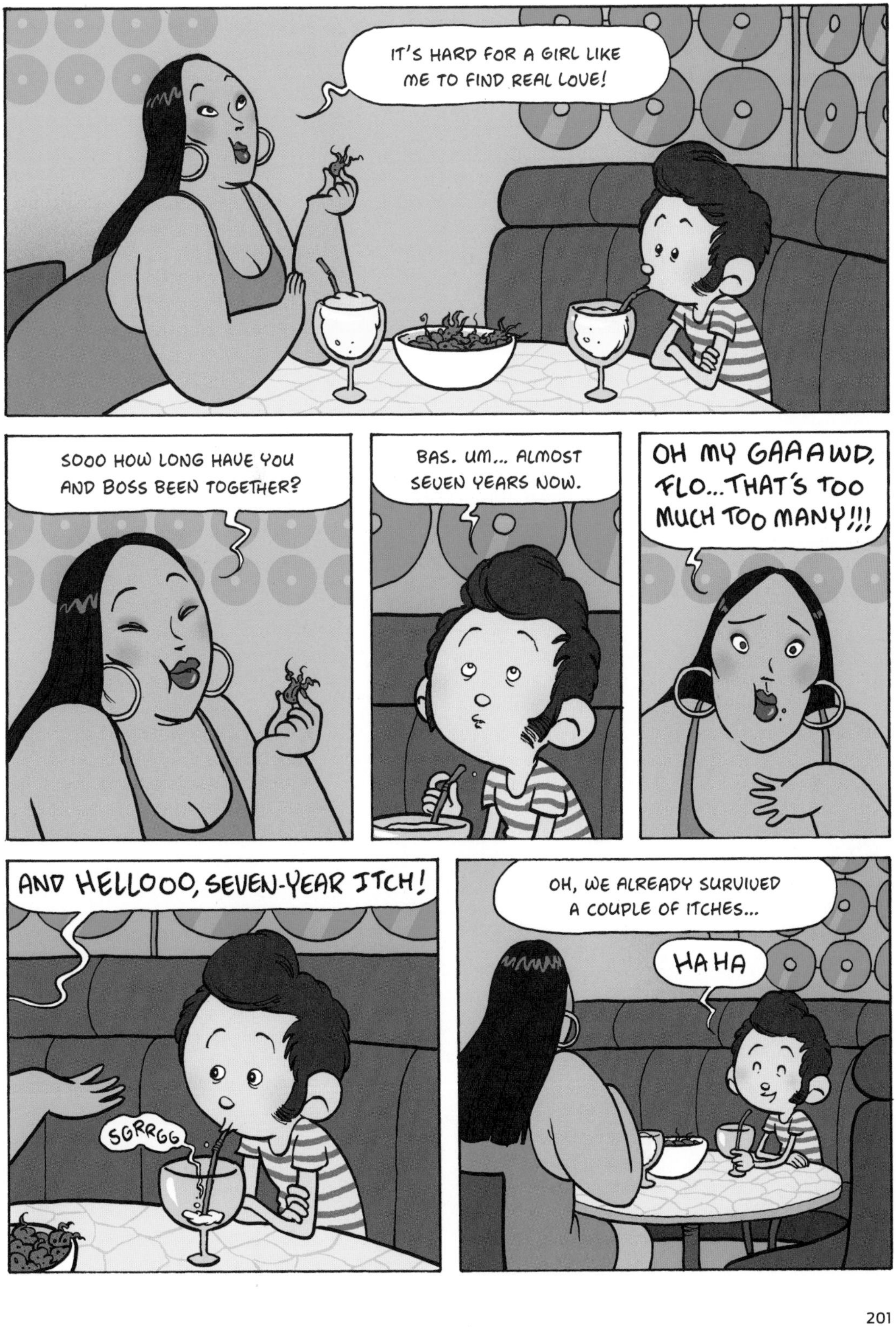
IT'S HARD FOR A GIRL LIKE ME TO FIND REAL LOVE!
SOOO HOW LONG HAVE YOU AND BOSS BEEN TOGETHER?
BAS. UM... ALMOST SEVEN YEARS NOW.
OH MY GAAAWD, FLO...THAT'S TOO MUCH TOO MANY!!!
AND HELLOOO, SEVEN-YEAR ITCH!
SGRRGG
OH, WE ALREADY SURVIVED A COUPLE OF ITCHES...
HAHA

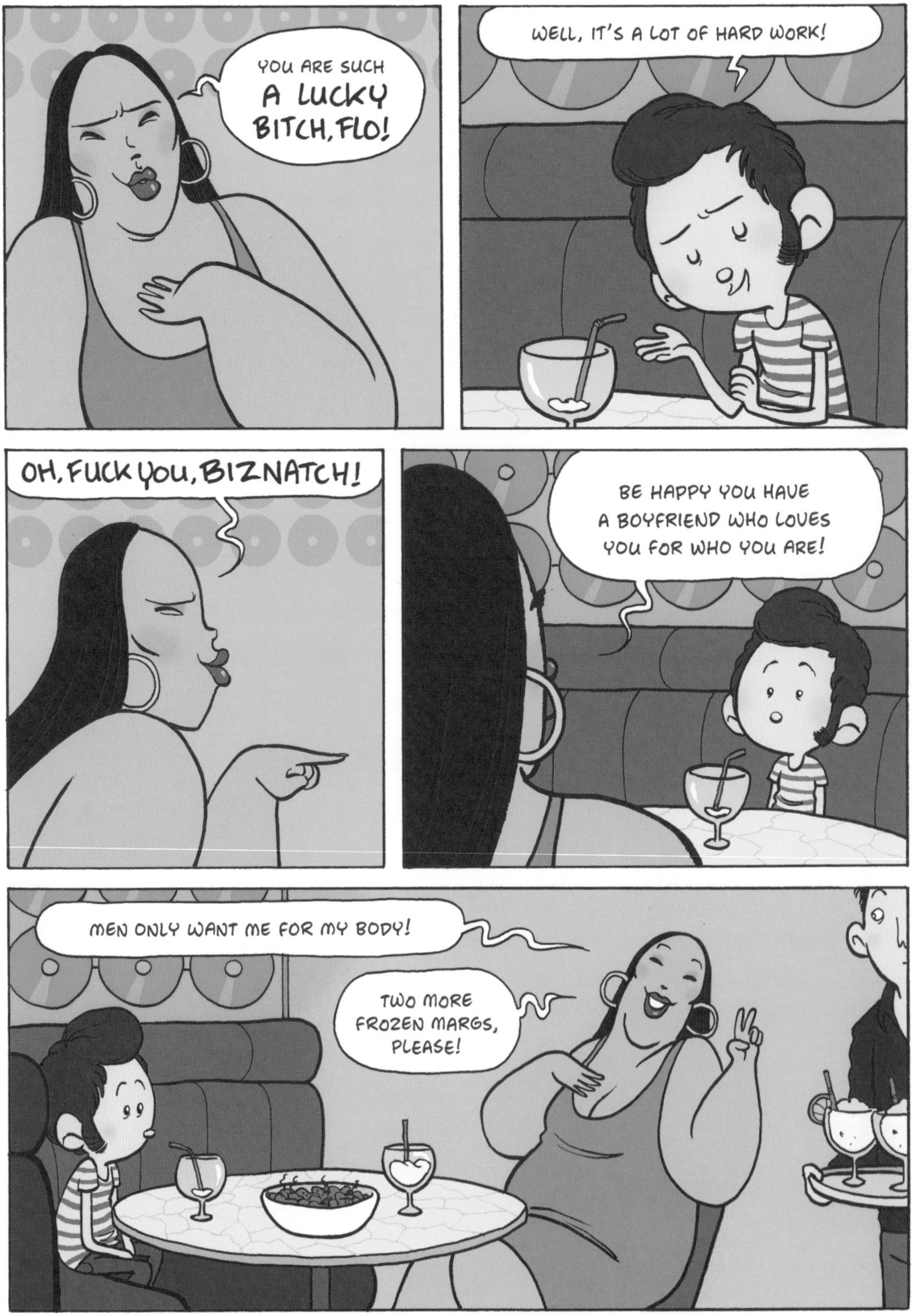
YOU ARE SUCH A LUCKY BITCH, FLO!
WELL, IT'S A LOT OF HARD WORK!
OH, FUCK YOU, BIZNATCH!
BE HAPPY YOU HAVE A BOYFRIEND WHO LOVES YOU FOR WHO YOU ARE!
MEN ONLY WANT ME FOR MY BODY!
TWO MORE FROZEN MARGS, PLEASE!

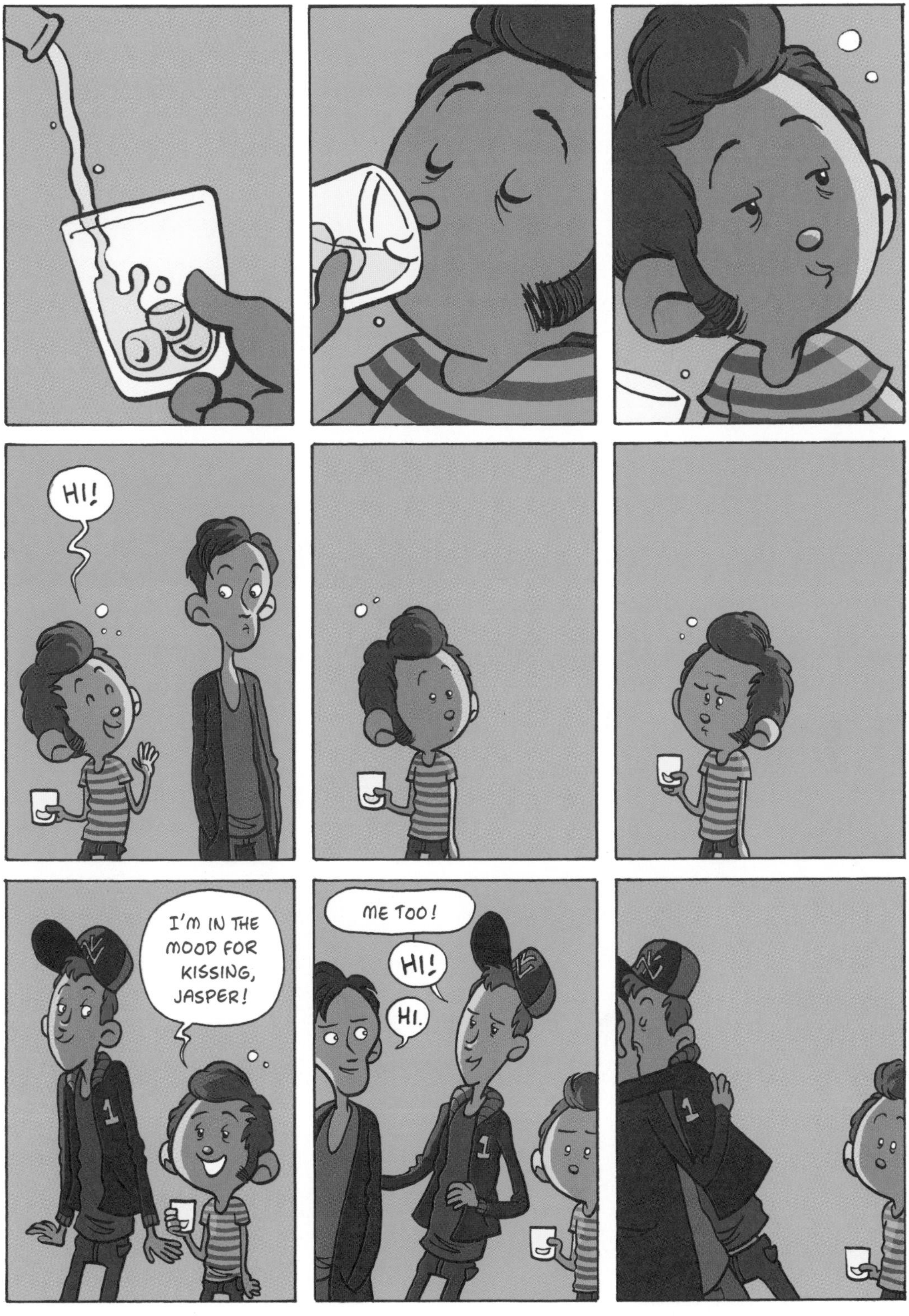
HI!
I'M IN THE MOOD FOR KISSING, JASPER!
ME TOO!
HI!
HI.

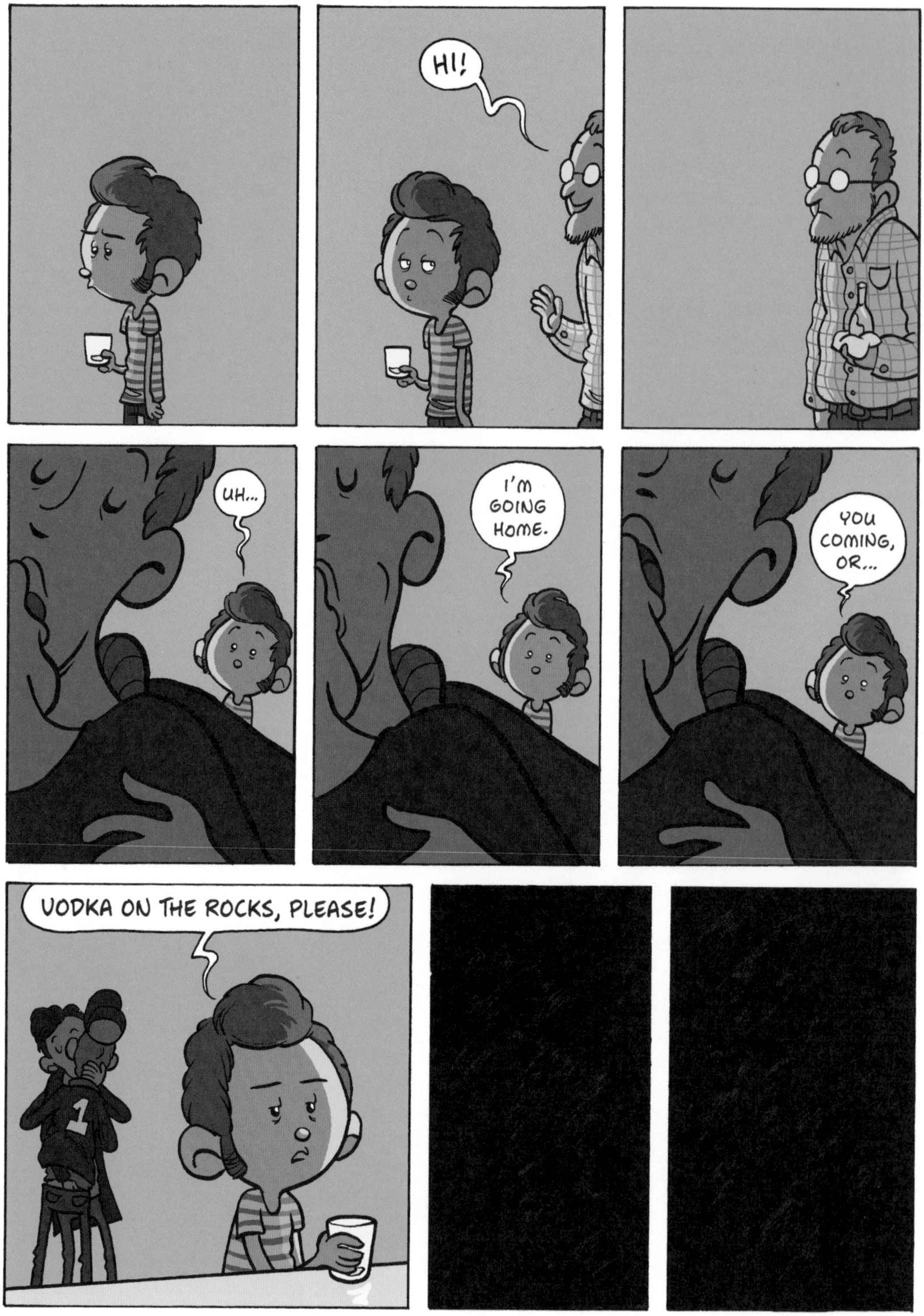
HI!
UH...
I'M GOING HOME.
YOU COMING, OR...
VODKA ON THE ROCKS, PLEASE!

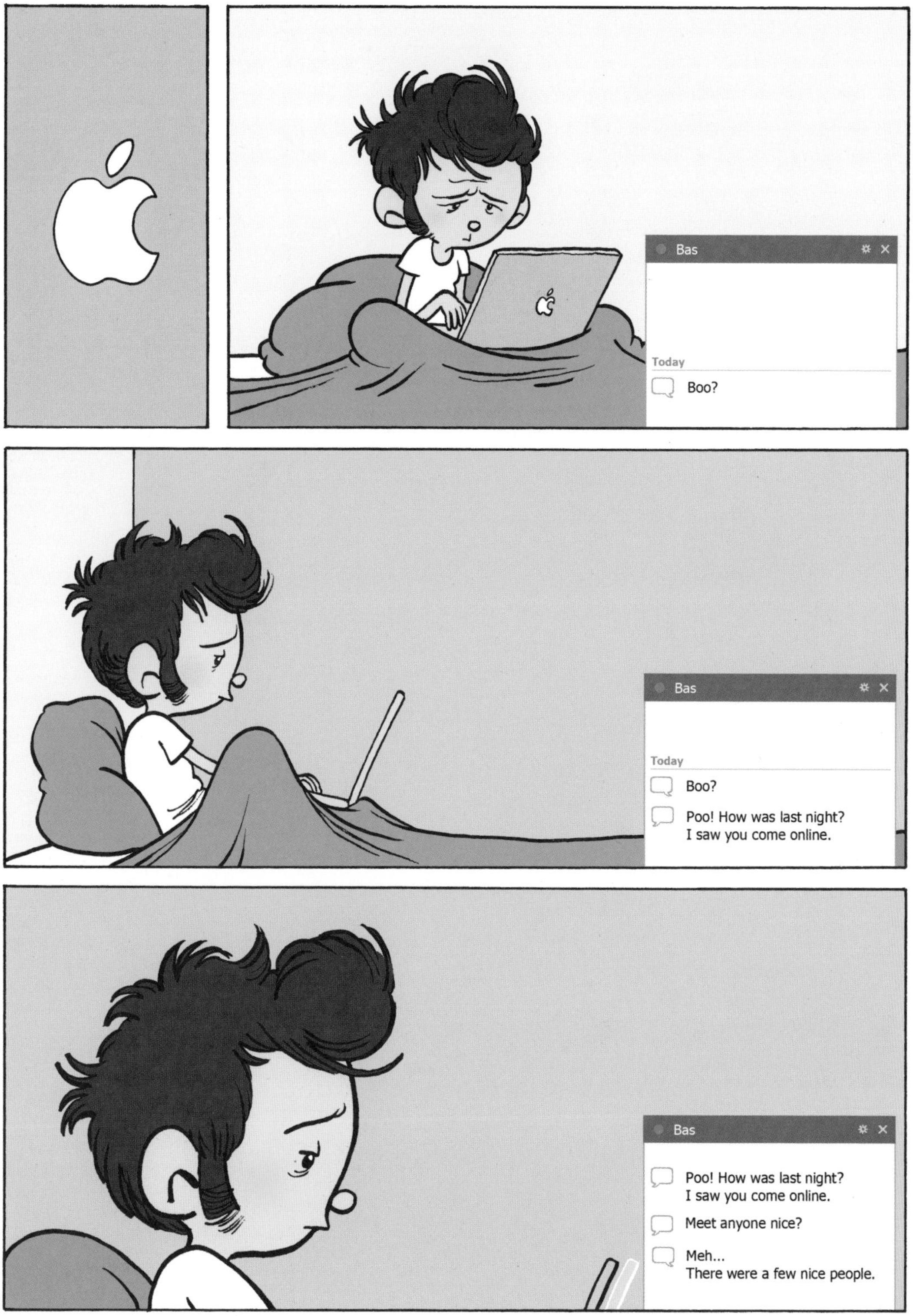
Bas
Today
Boo?
Bas
Today
Boo?
Poo! How was last night?
I saw you come online.
Bas
Poo! How was last night?
I saw you come online.
Meet anyone nice?
Meh...
There were a few nice people.

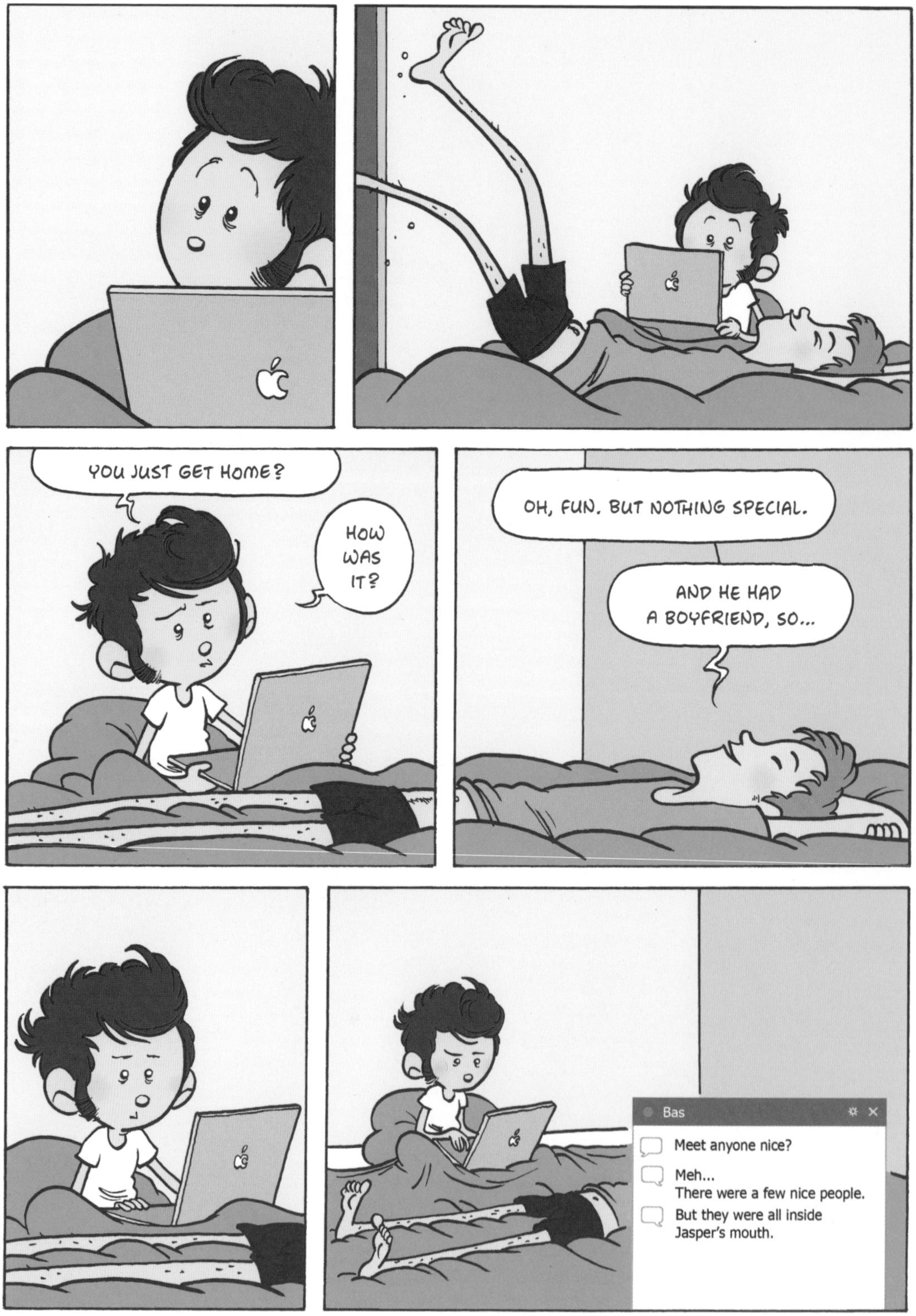
YOU JUST GET HOME?
HOW WAS IT?
OH, FUN. BUT NOTHING SPECIAL.
AND HE HAD A BOYFRIEND, SO...
Bas
Meet anyone nice?
Meh...
There were a few nice people.
But they were all inside
Jasper's mouth.

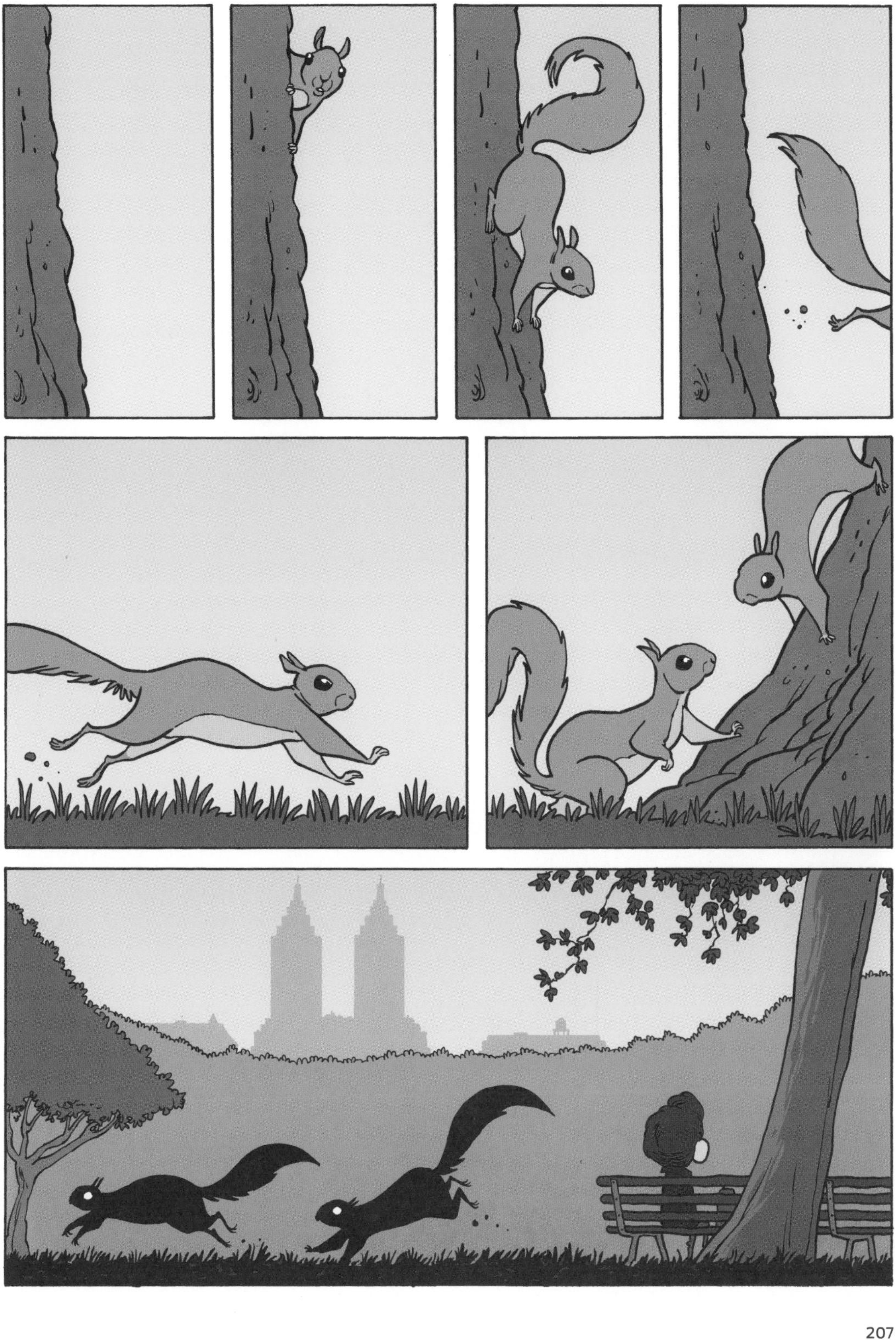

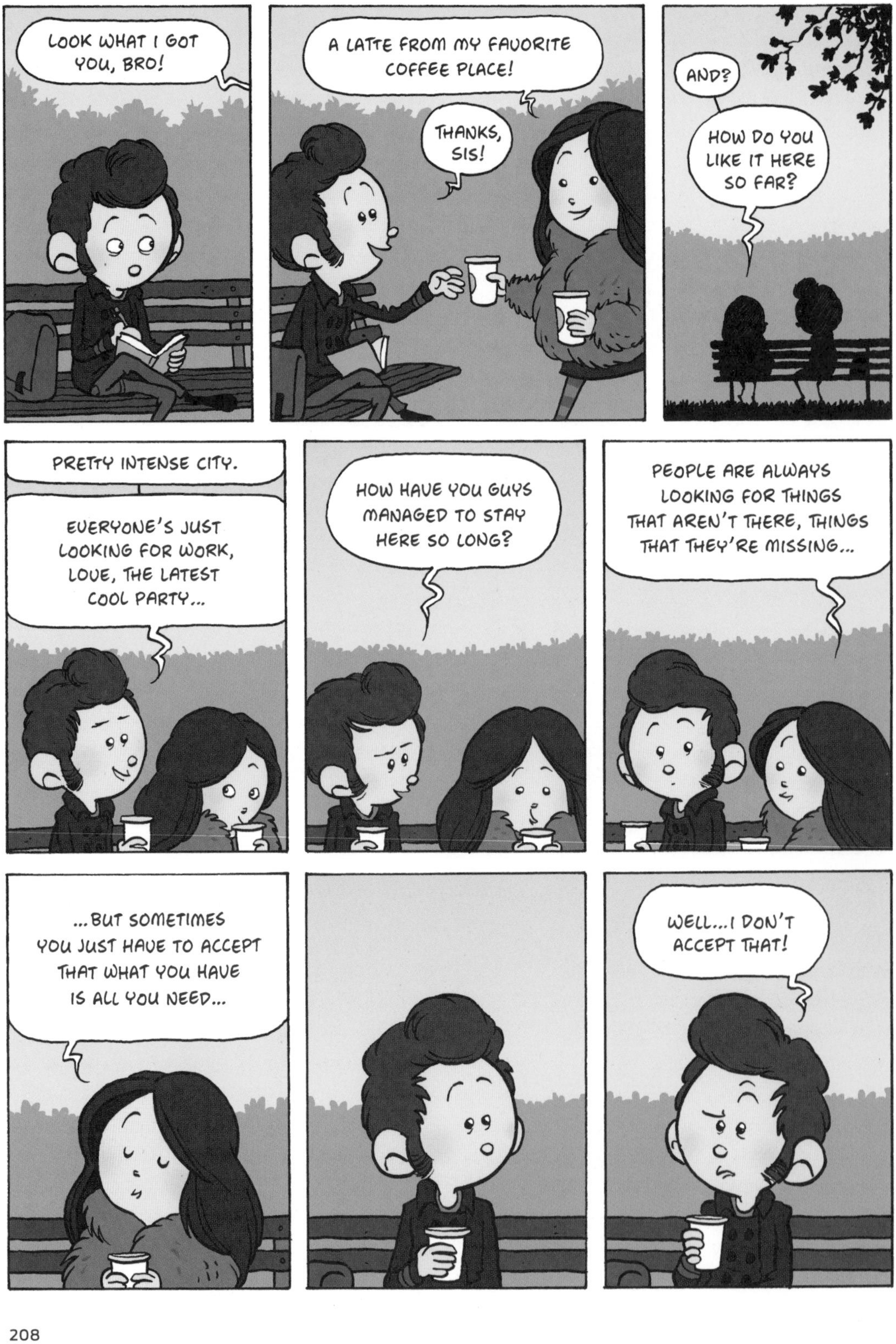
LOOK WHAT I GOT YOU, BRO!
A LATTE FROM MY FAVORITE COFFEE PLACE!
THANKS, SIS!
AND?
HOW DO YOU LIKE IT HERE SO FAR?
PRETTY INTENSE CITY.
EVERYONE'S JUST LOOKING FOR WORK, LOVE, THE LATEST COOL PARTY...
HOW HAVE YOU GUYS MANAGED TO STAY HERE SO LONG?
PEOPLE ARE ALWAYS LOOKING FOR THINGS THAT AREN'T THERE, THINGS THAT THEY'RE MISSING...
...BUT SOMETIMES YOU JUST HAVE TO ACCEPT THAT WHAT YOU HAVE IS ALL YOU NEED...
WELL...I DON'T ACCEPT THAT!

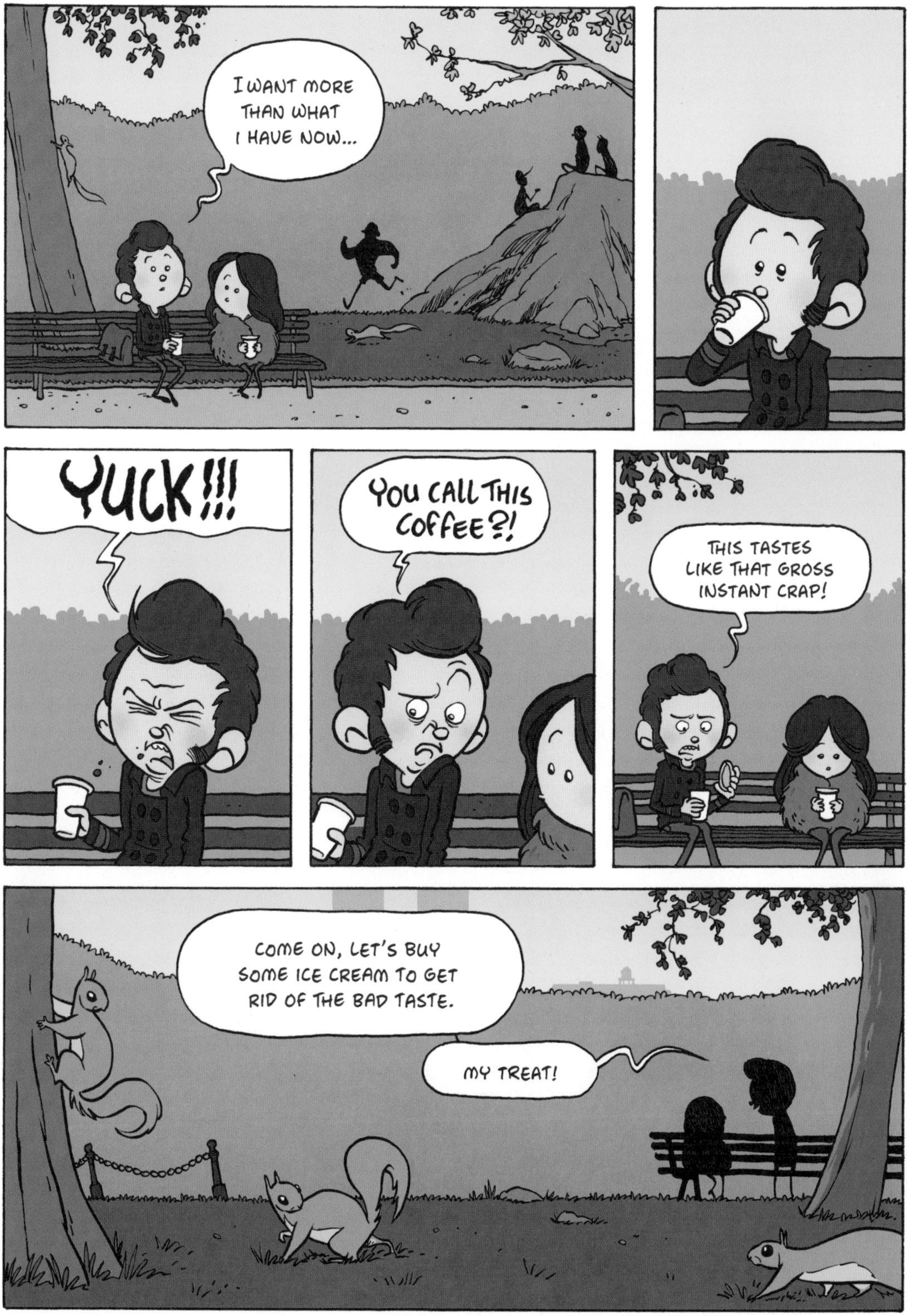
I WANT MORE THAN WHAT I HAVE NOW...
YUCK!!!
YOU CALL THIS COFFEE?!
THIS TASTES LIKE THAT GROSS INSTANT CRAP!
COME ON, LET'S BUY SOME ICE CREAM TO GET RID OF THE BAD TASTE.
MY TREAT!

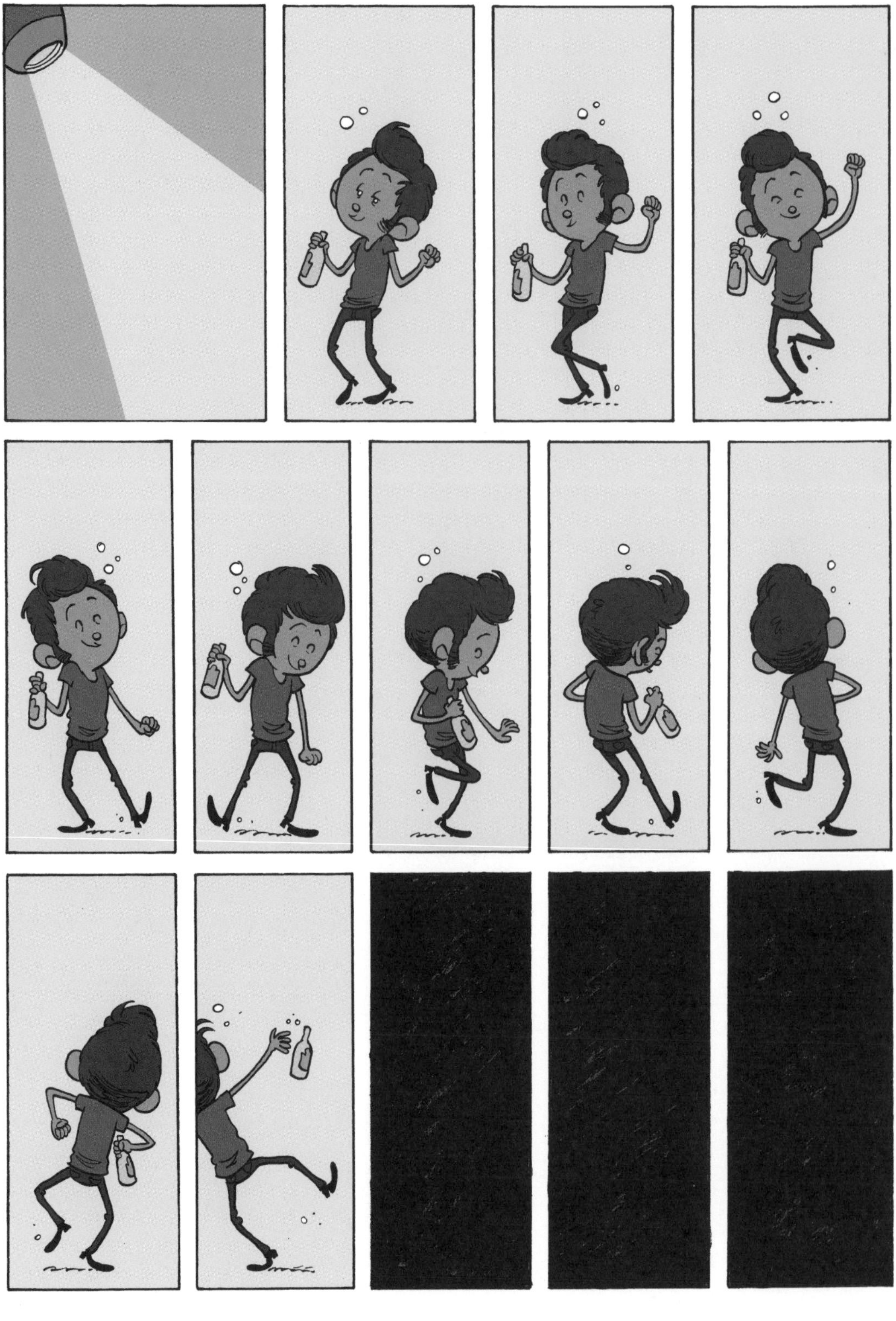

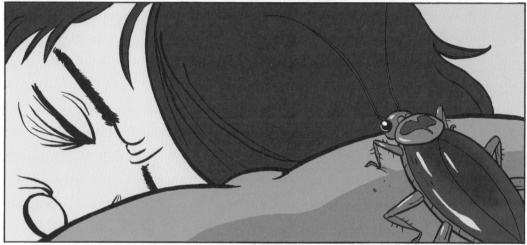

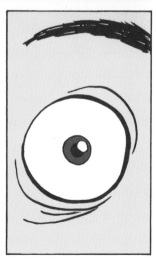

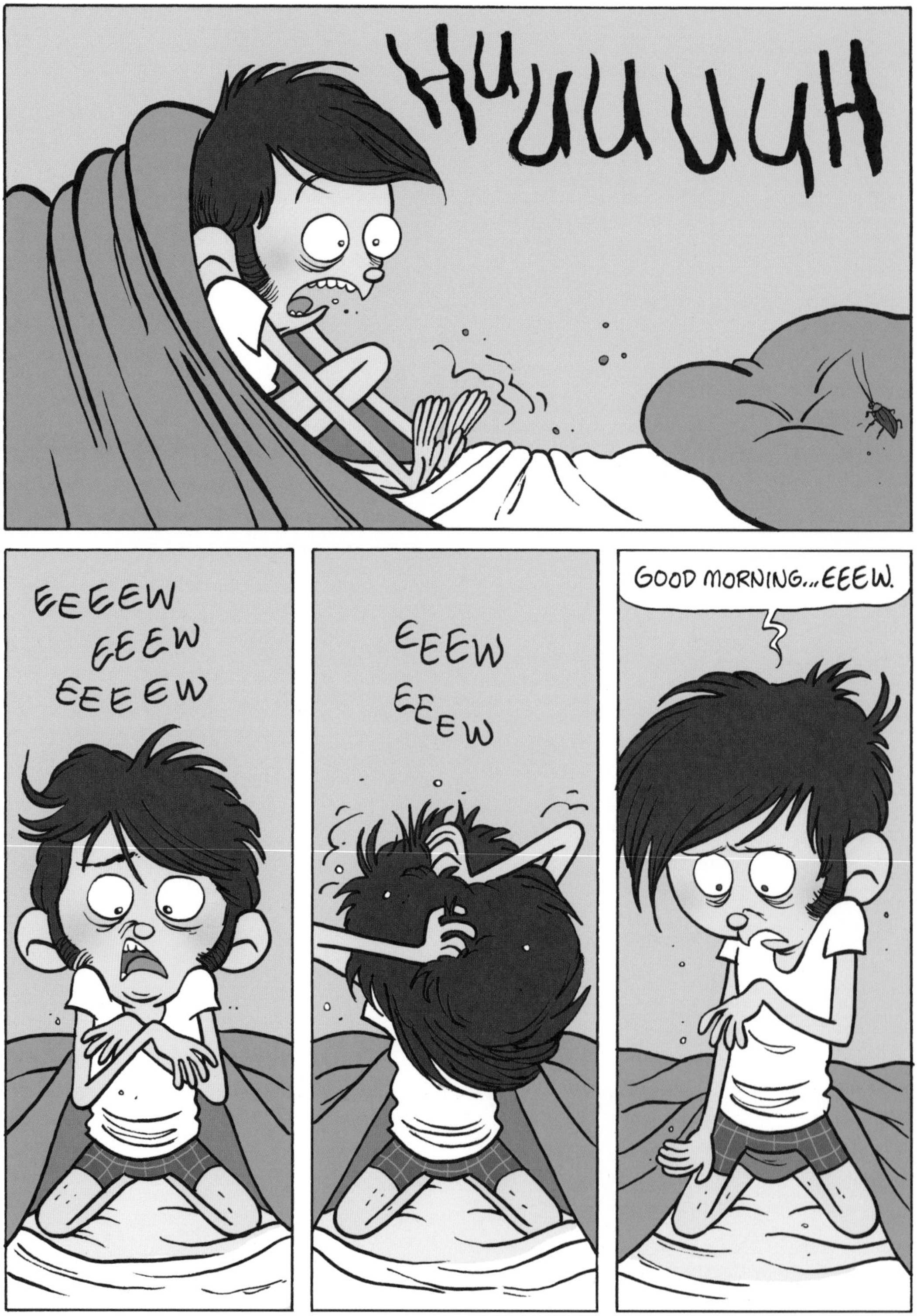
HUUUUUYH
EEEEW
EEEW
EEEEW
EEEW
EEEW
GOOD MORNING... EEEW.

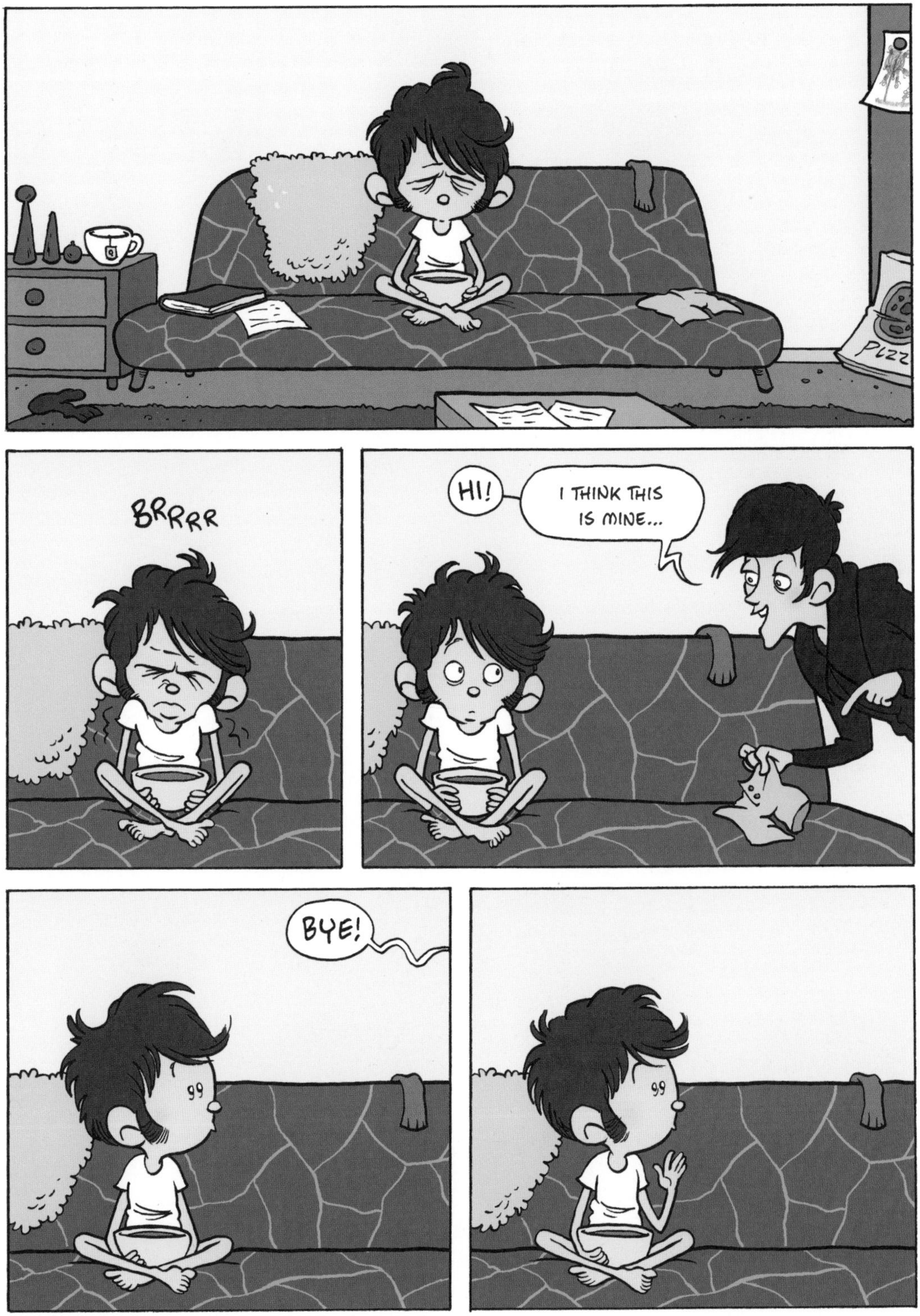
PIZZ
BRRRR
HI!
I THINK THIS IS MINE...
BYE!

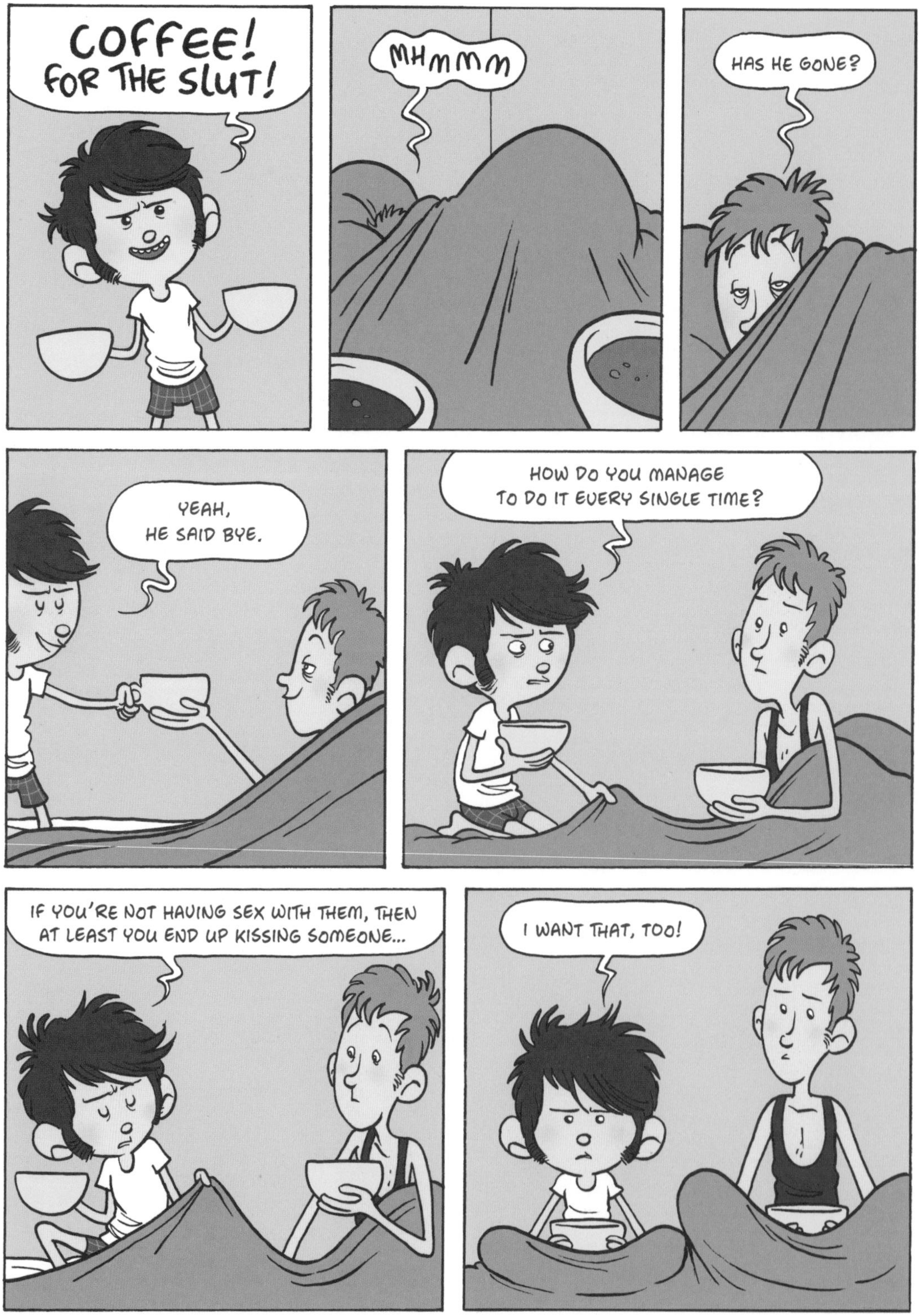
COFFEE! FOR THE SLUT!
MHMMM
HAS HE GONE?
YEAH, HE SAID BYE.
HOW DO YOU MANAGE TO DO IT EVERY SINGLE TIME?
IF YOU'RE NOT HAVING SEX WITH THEM, THEN AT LEAST YOU END UP KISSING SOMEONE...
I WANT THAT, TOO!

YOU'RE JUST TOO TIMID.
IF YOU WANT TO KISS SOMEONE, YOU SHOULD JUST GO FOR IT!
HAHA... JUST CHILL OUT, MAN.
YOU'VE GOT BAS!
THERE WAS A COCKROACH IN MY BED, BY THE WAY.
SO WATCH OUT.

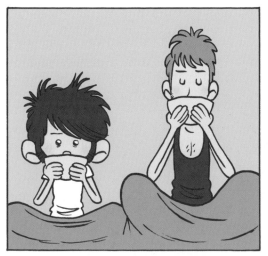

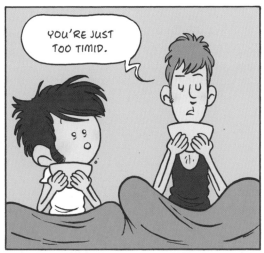

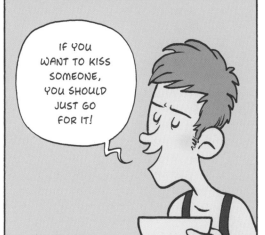

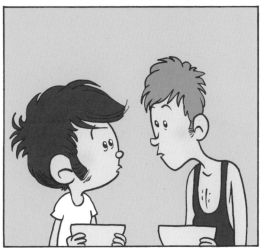

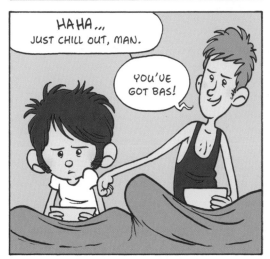

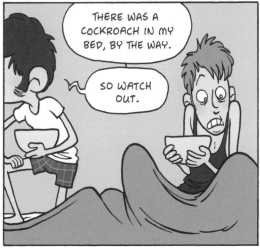

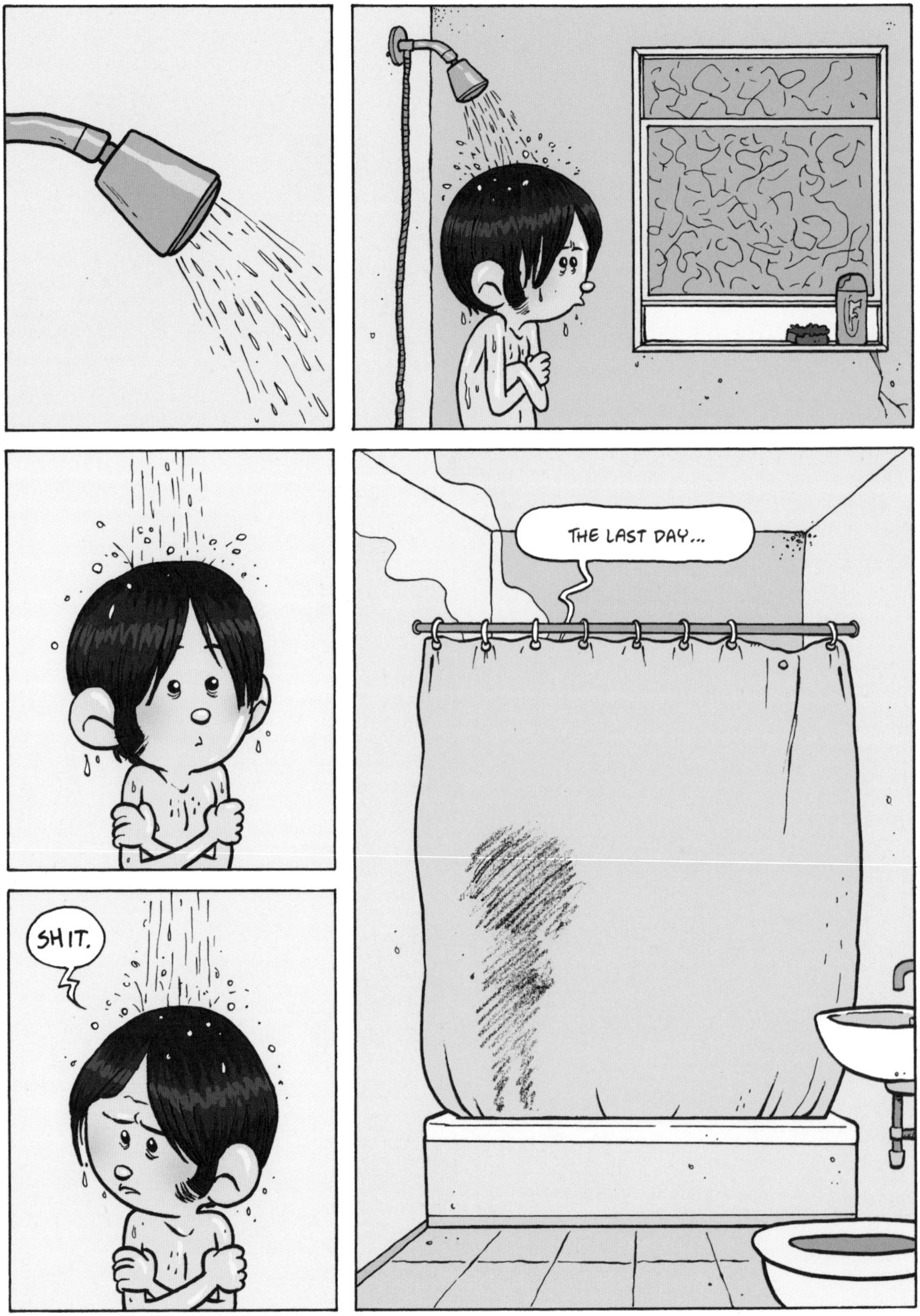
THE LAST DAY...
SHIT.

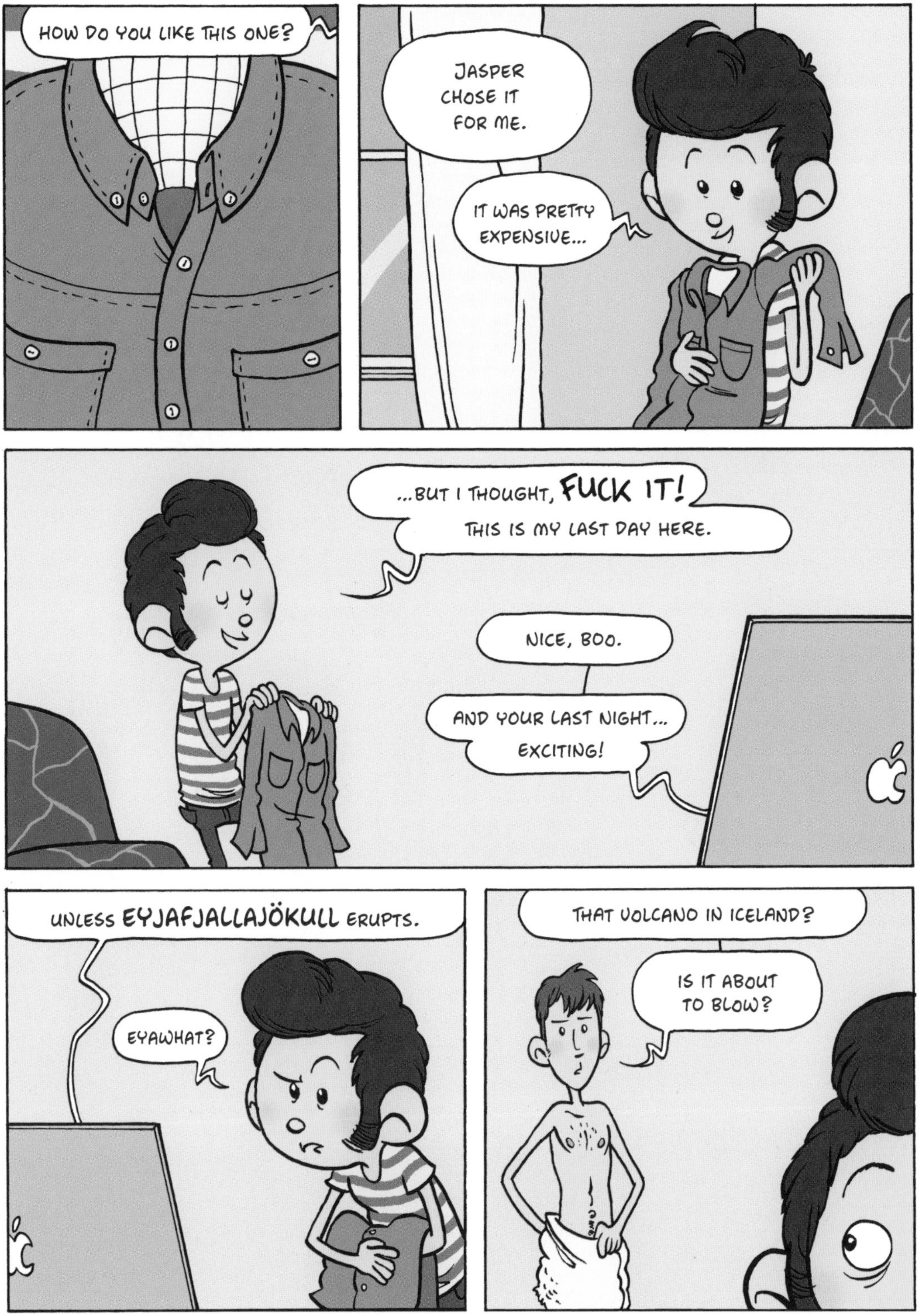
HOW DO YOU LIKE THIS ONE?
JASPER CHOSE IT FOR ME.
IT WAS PRETTY EXPENSIVE...
...BUT I THOUGHT, FUCK IT! THIS IS MY LAST DAY HERE.
NICE, BOO.
AND YOUR LAST NIGHT... EXCITING!
UNLESS EYJAFJALLAJÖKULL ERUPTS.
EYAWHAT?
THAT VOLCANO IN ICELAND?
IS IT ABOUT TO BLOW?

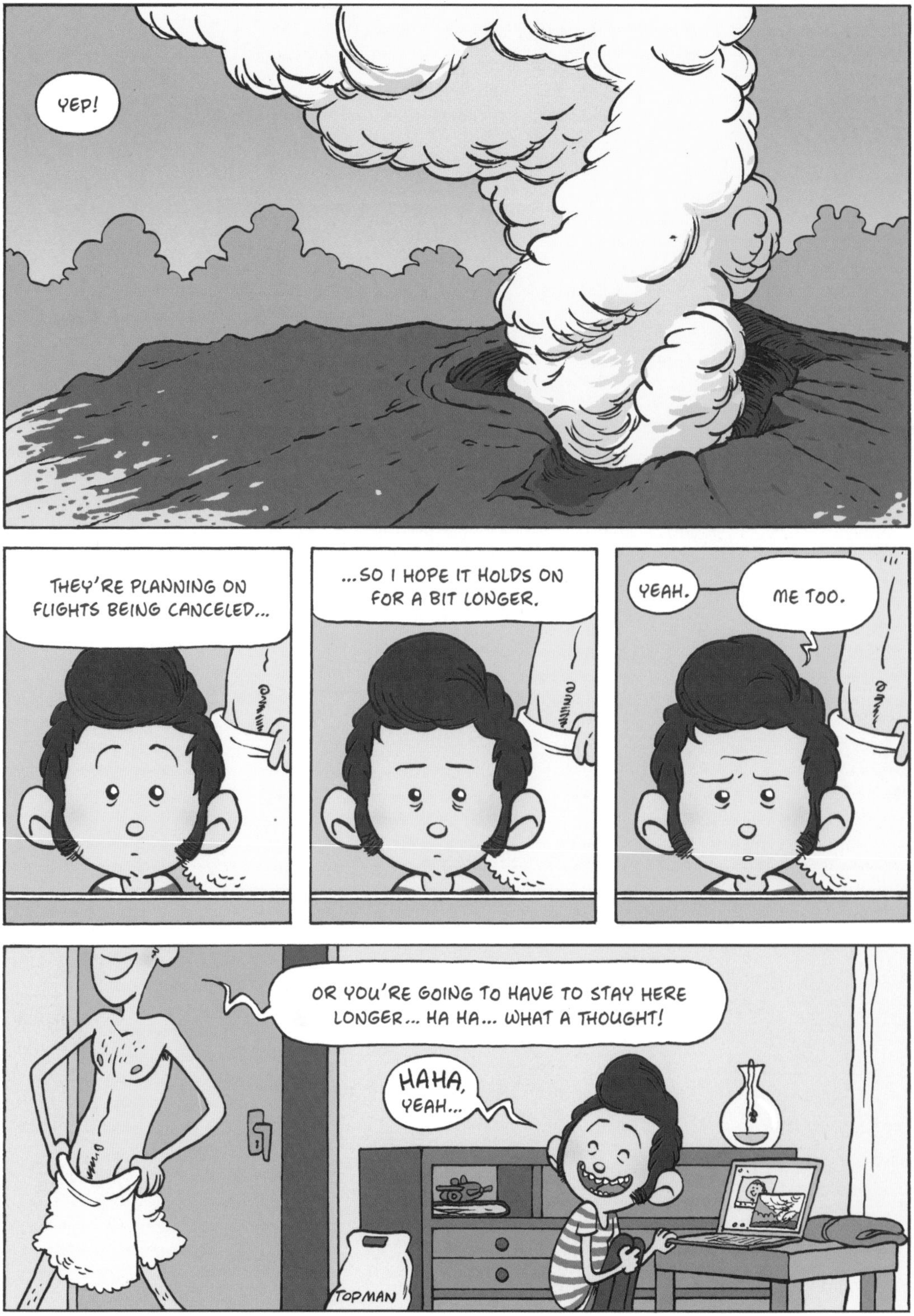
YEP!
THEY'RE PLANNING ON FLIGHTS BEING CANCELED...
...SO I HOPE IT HOLDS ON FOR A BIT LONGER.
YEAH.
ME TOO.
OR YOU'RE GOING TO HAVE TO STAY HERE LONGER... HA HA... WHAT A THOUGHT!
HAHA, YEAH...
TOPMAN

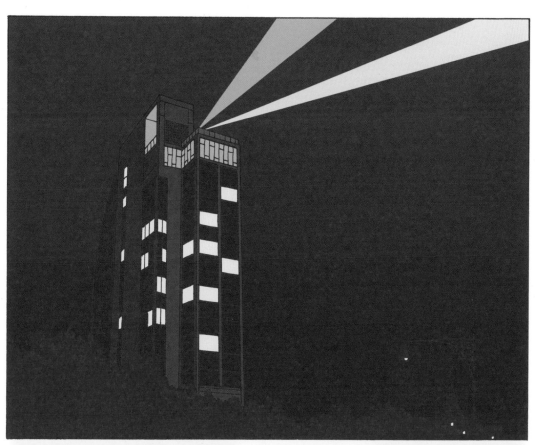

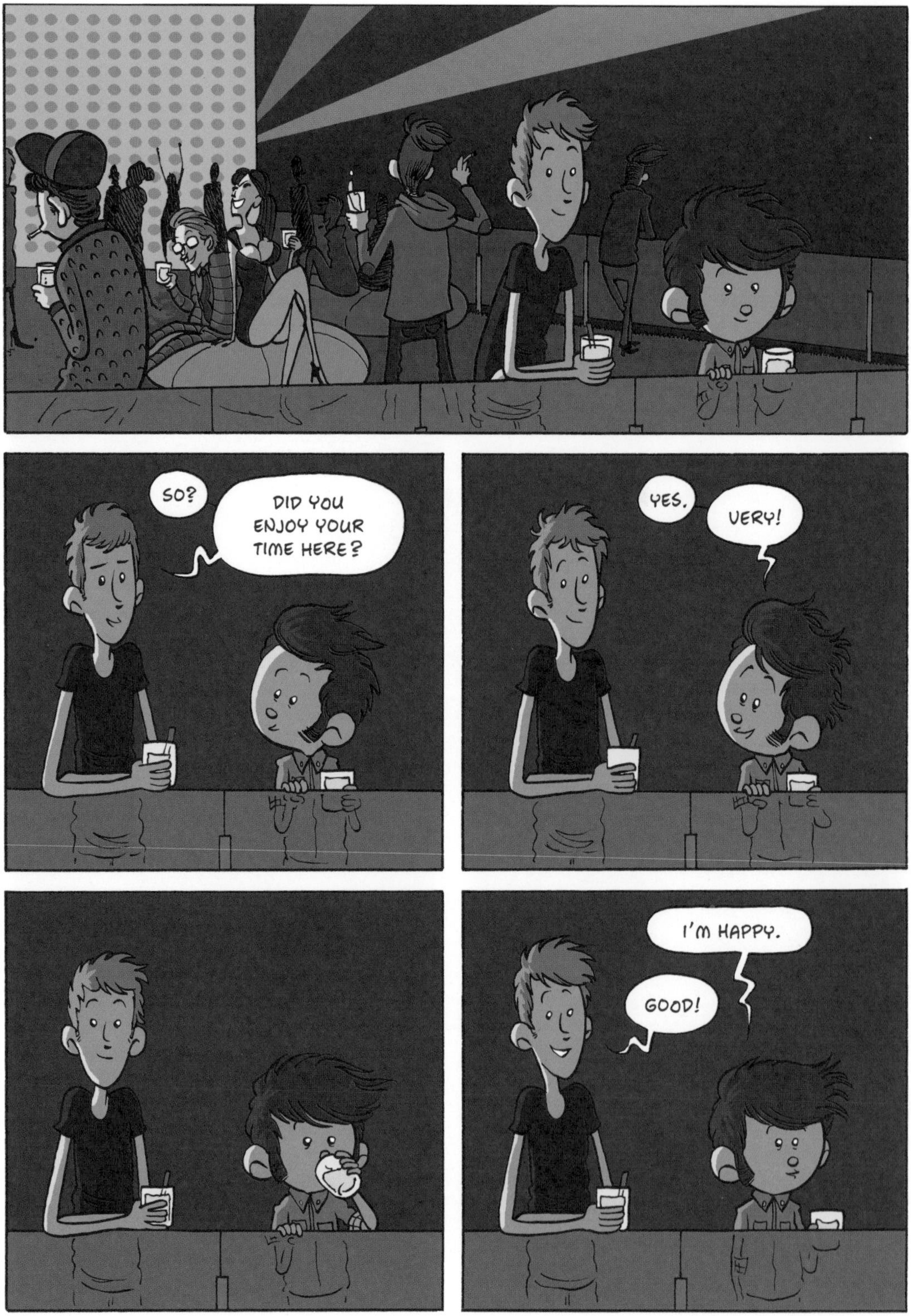
SO?
DID YOU ENJOY YOUR TIME HERE?
YES.
VERY!
I'M HAPPY.
GOOD!

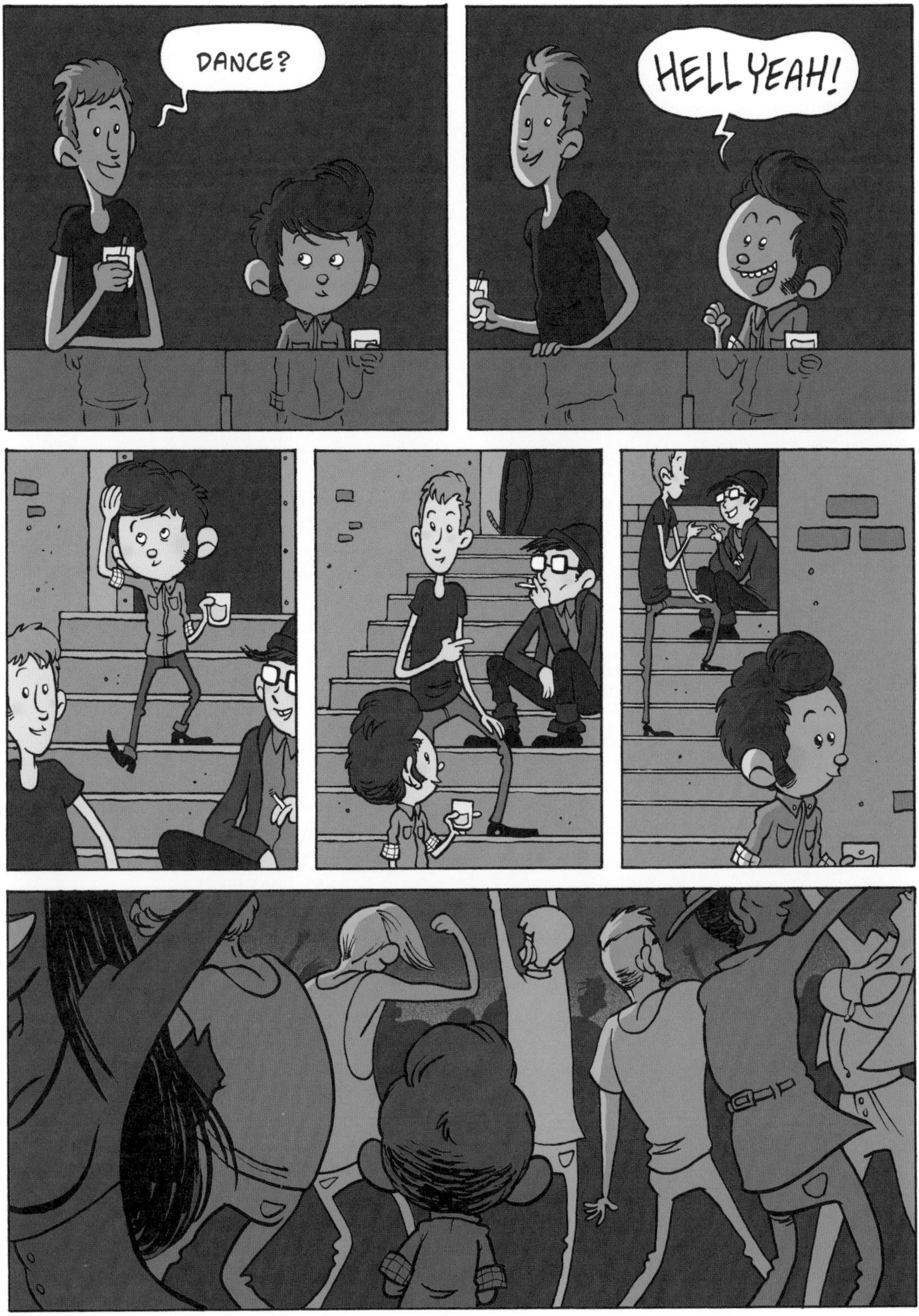
DANCE?
HELL YEAH!

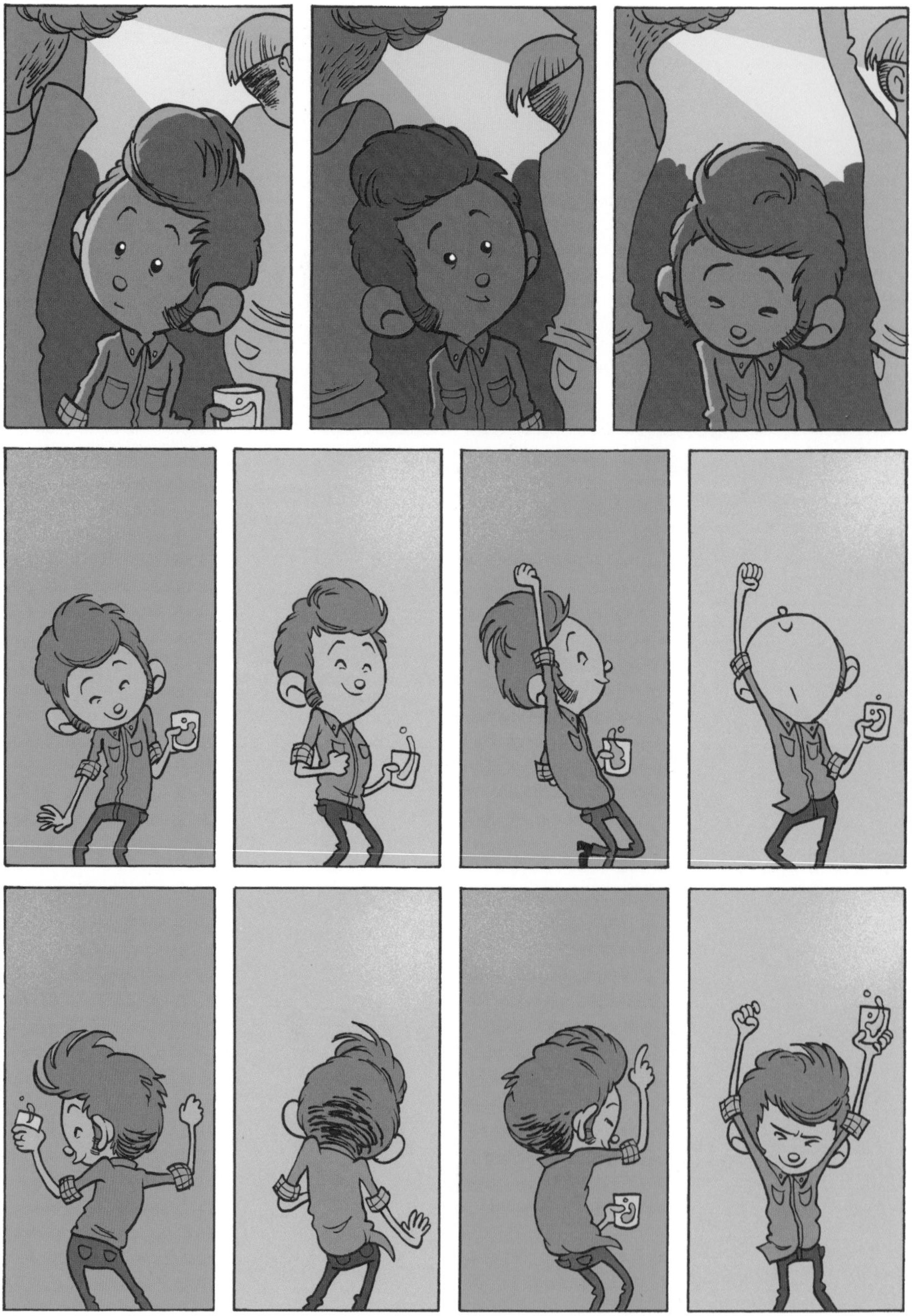

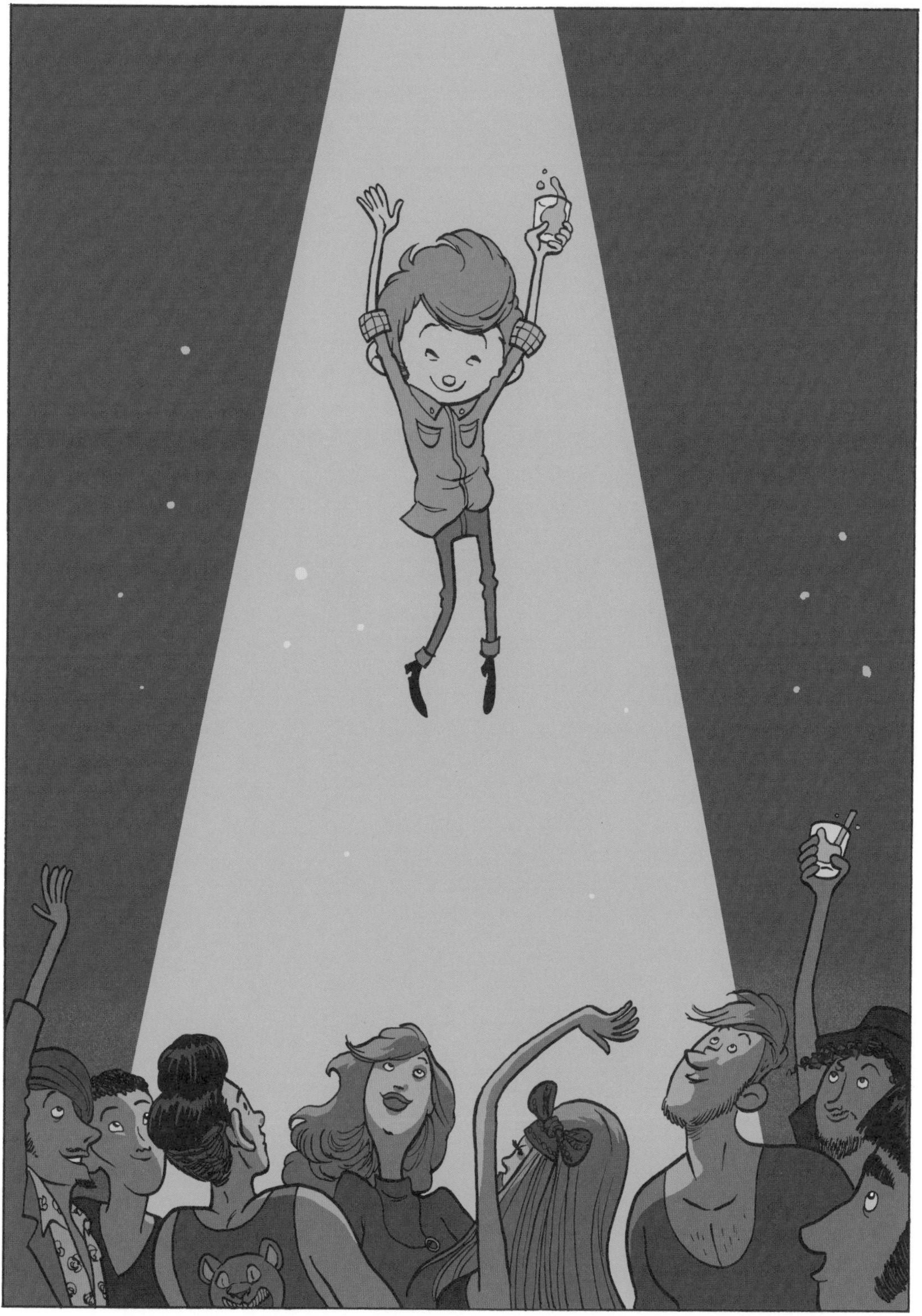

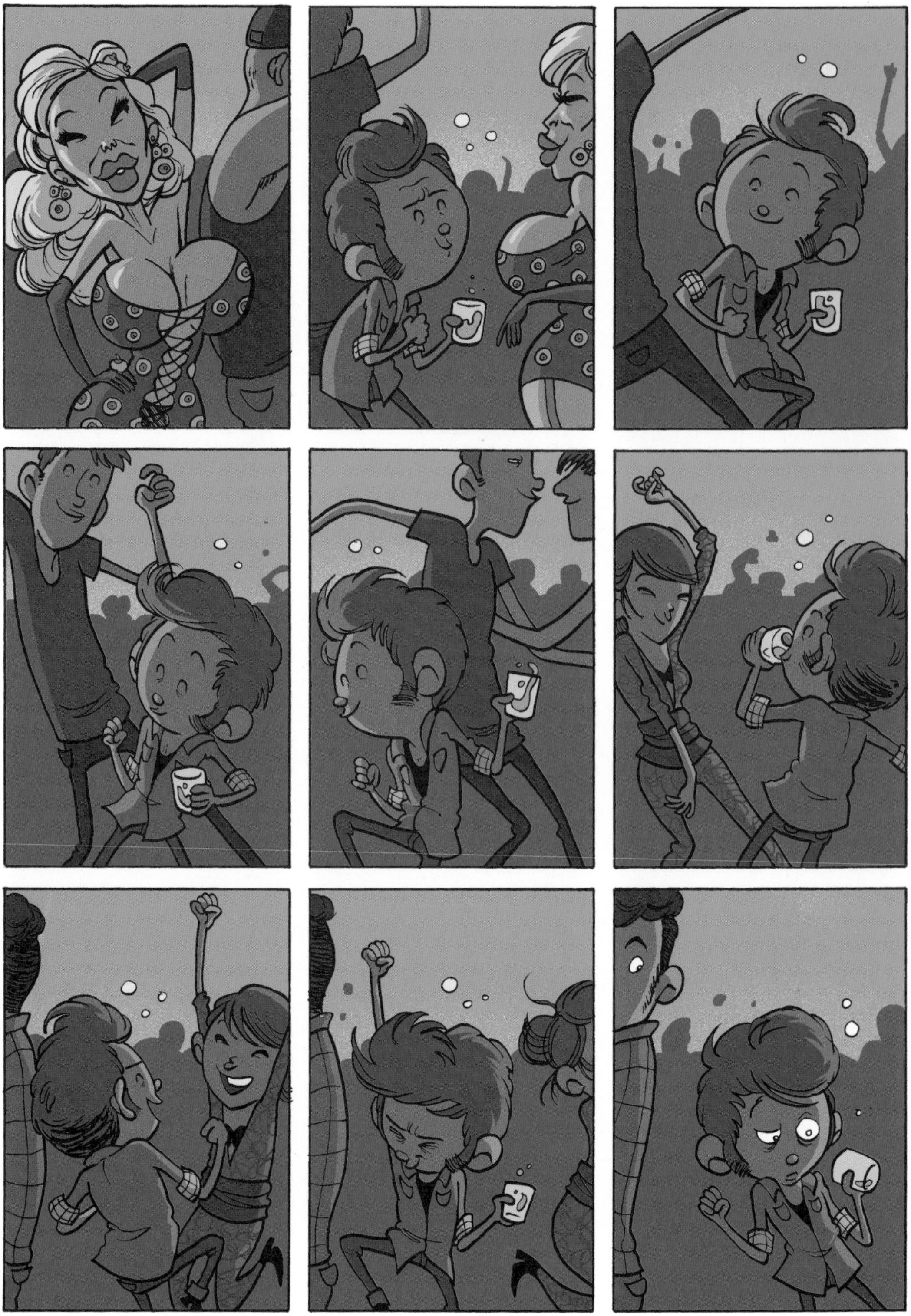

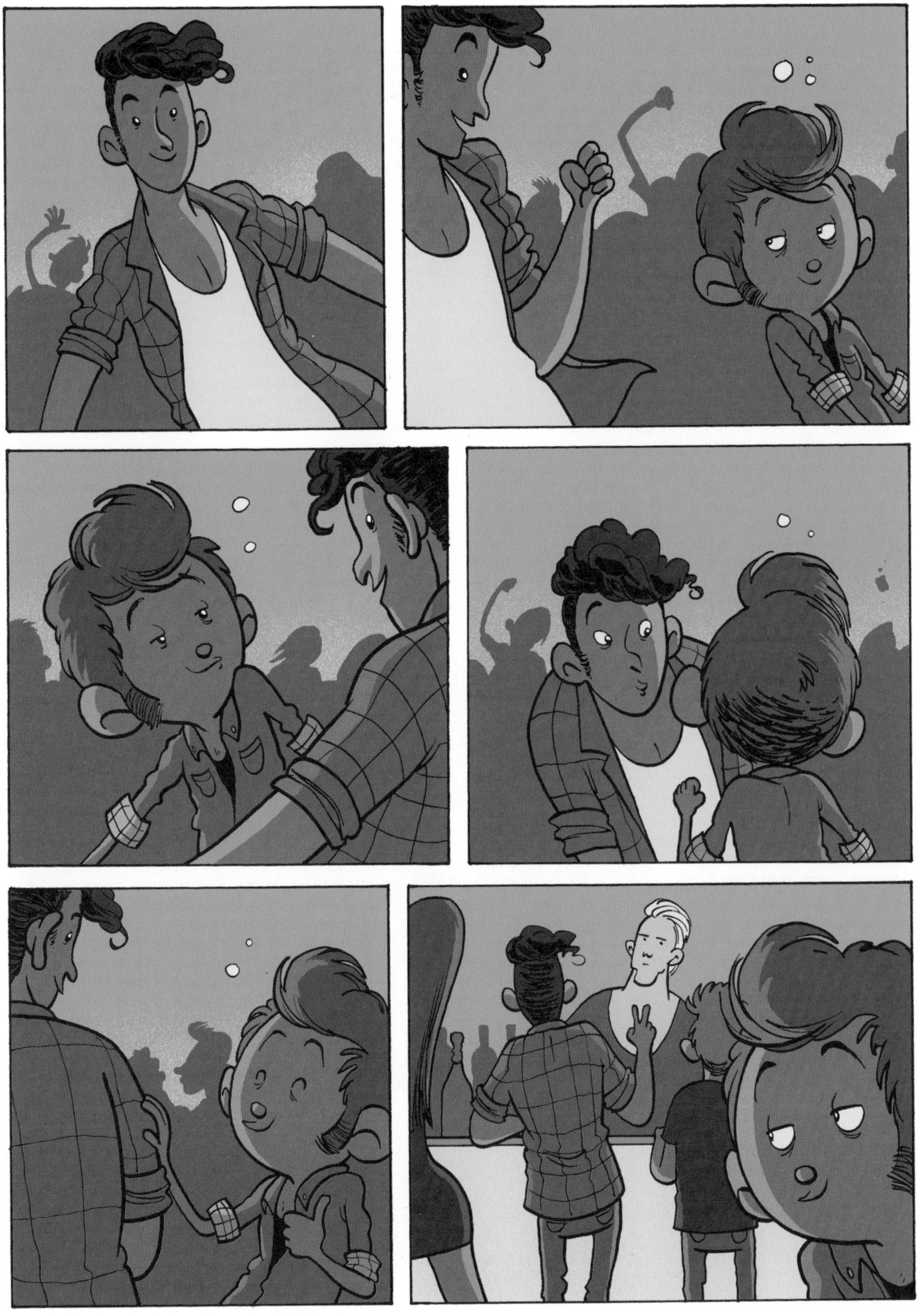

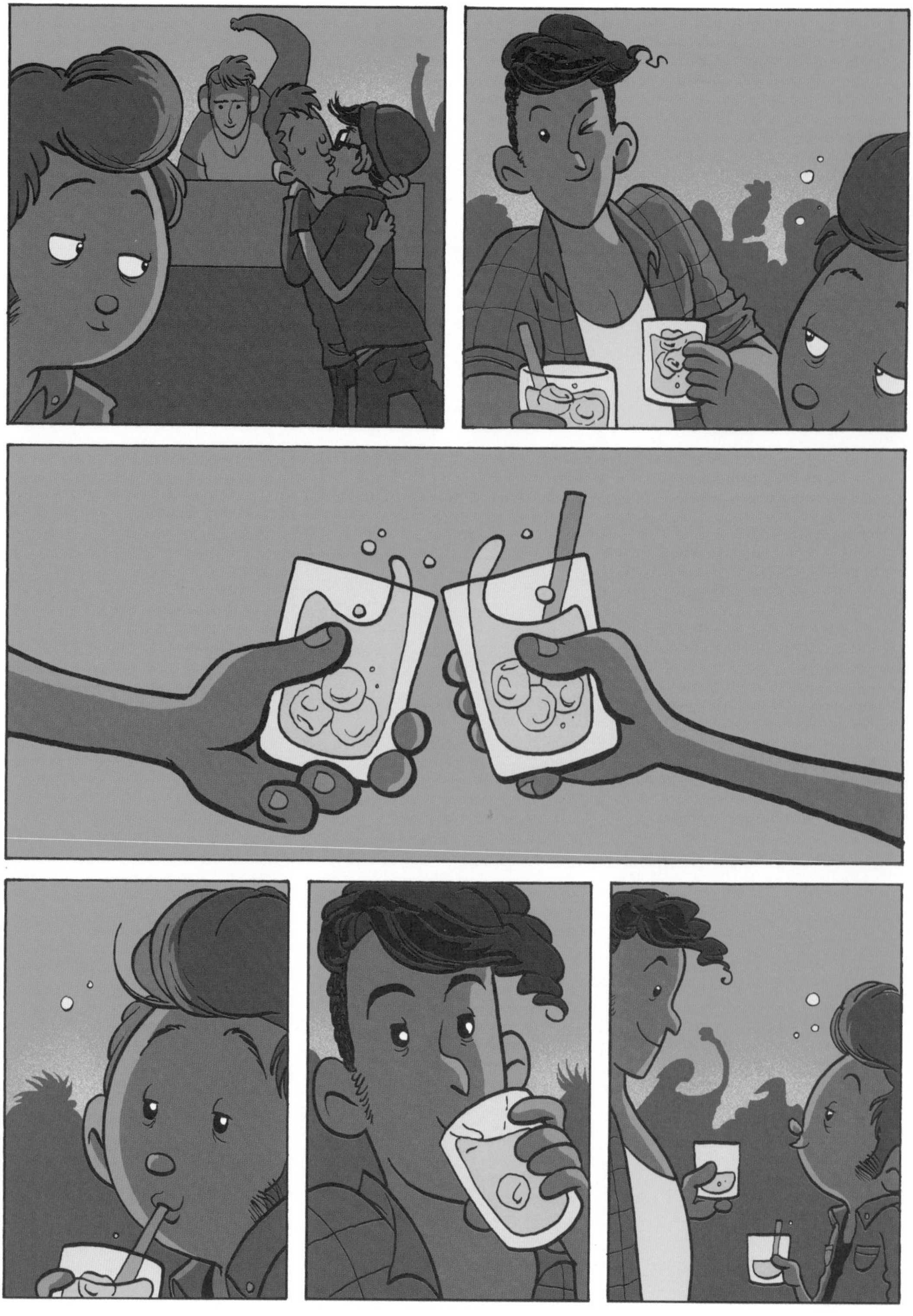

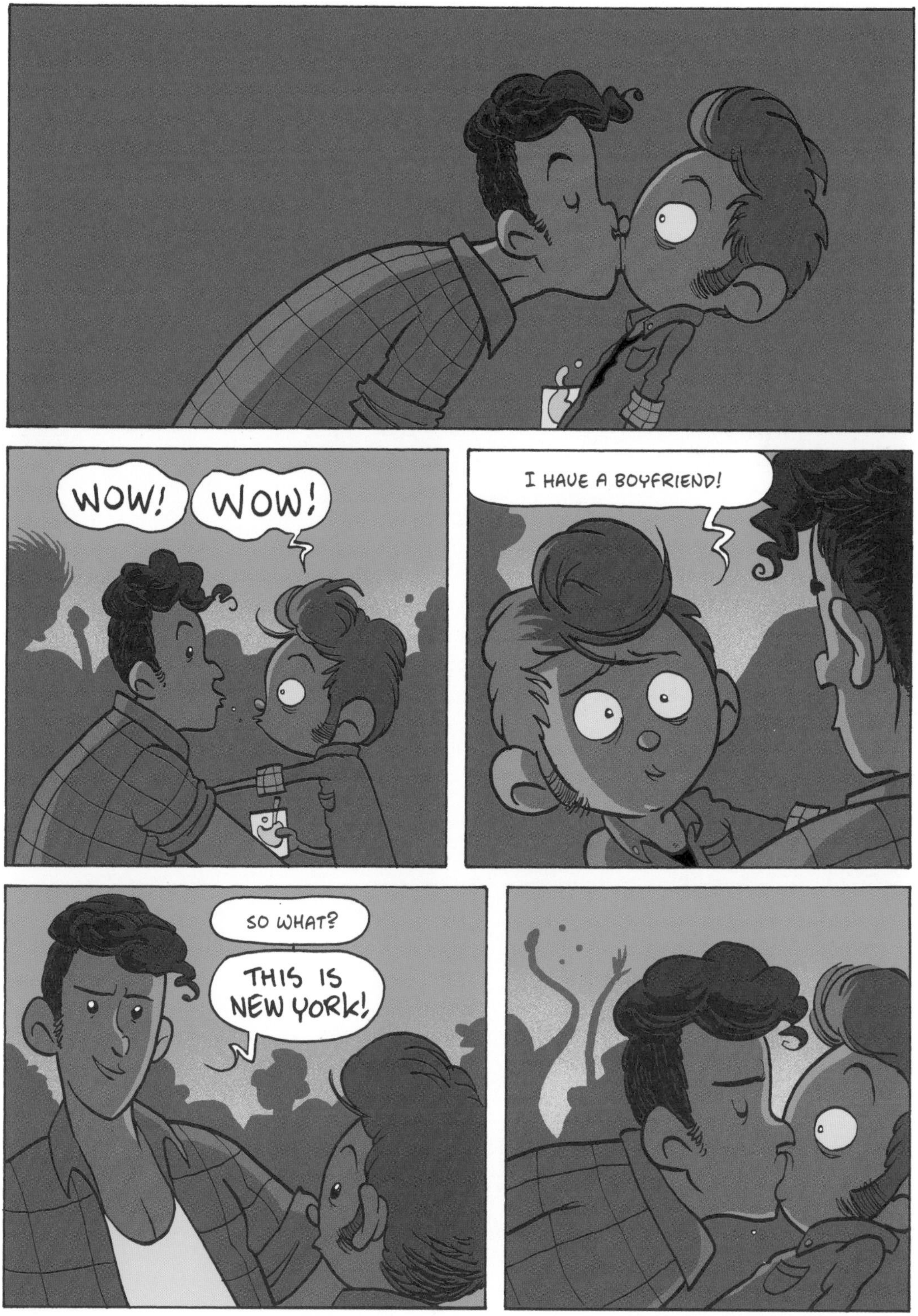
WOW!
WOW!
I HAVE A BOYFRIEND!
SO WHAT?
THIS IS NEW YORK!

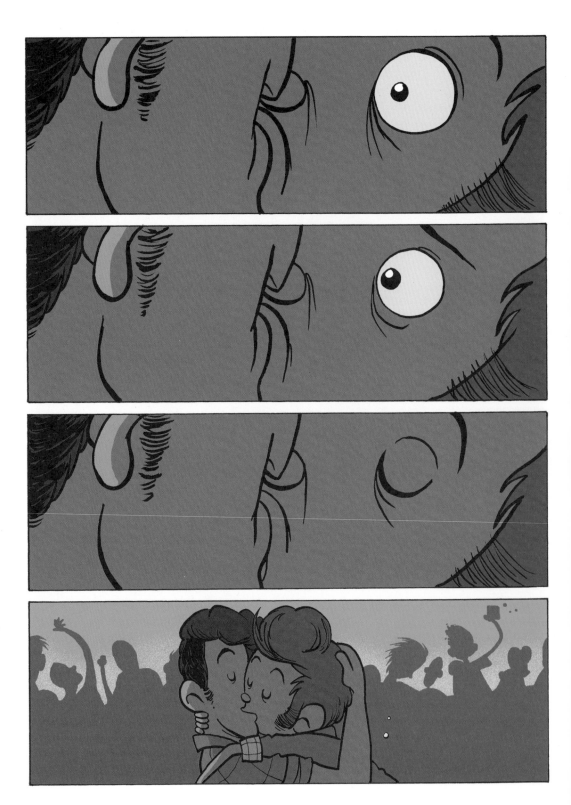

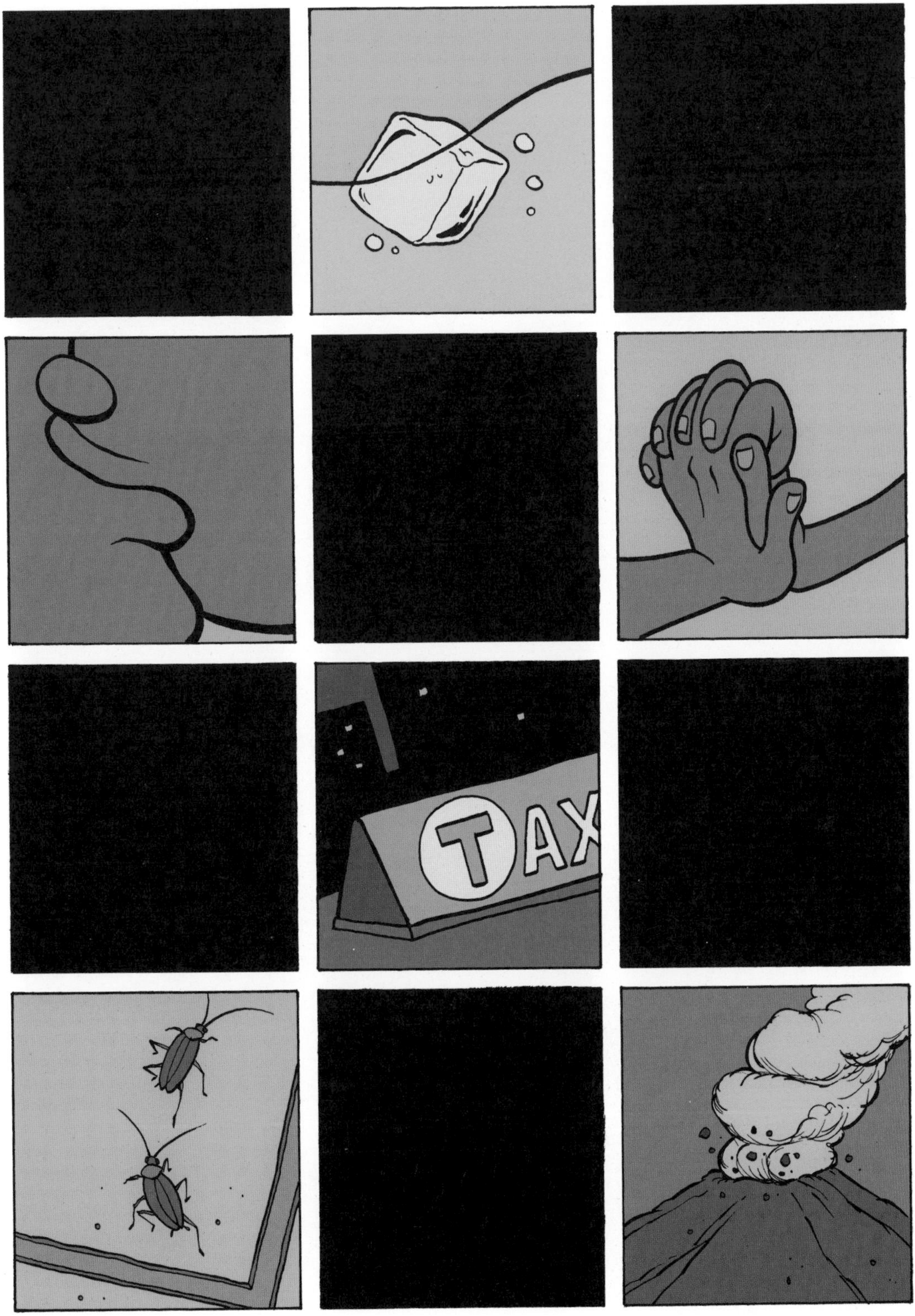
TAX

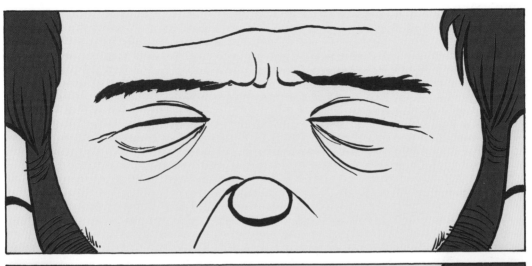

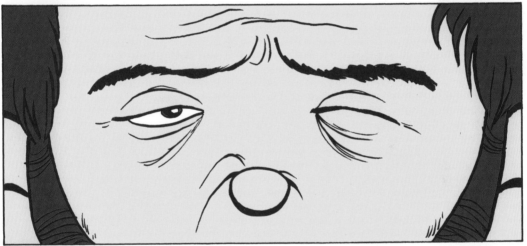

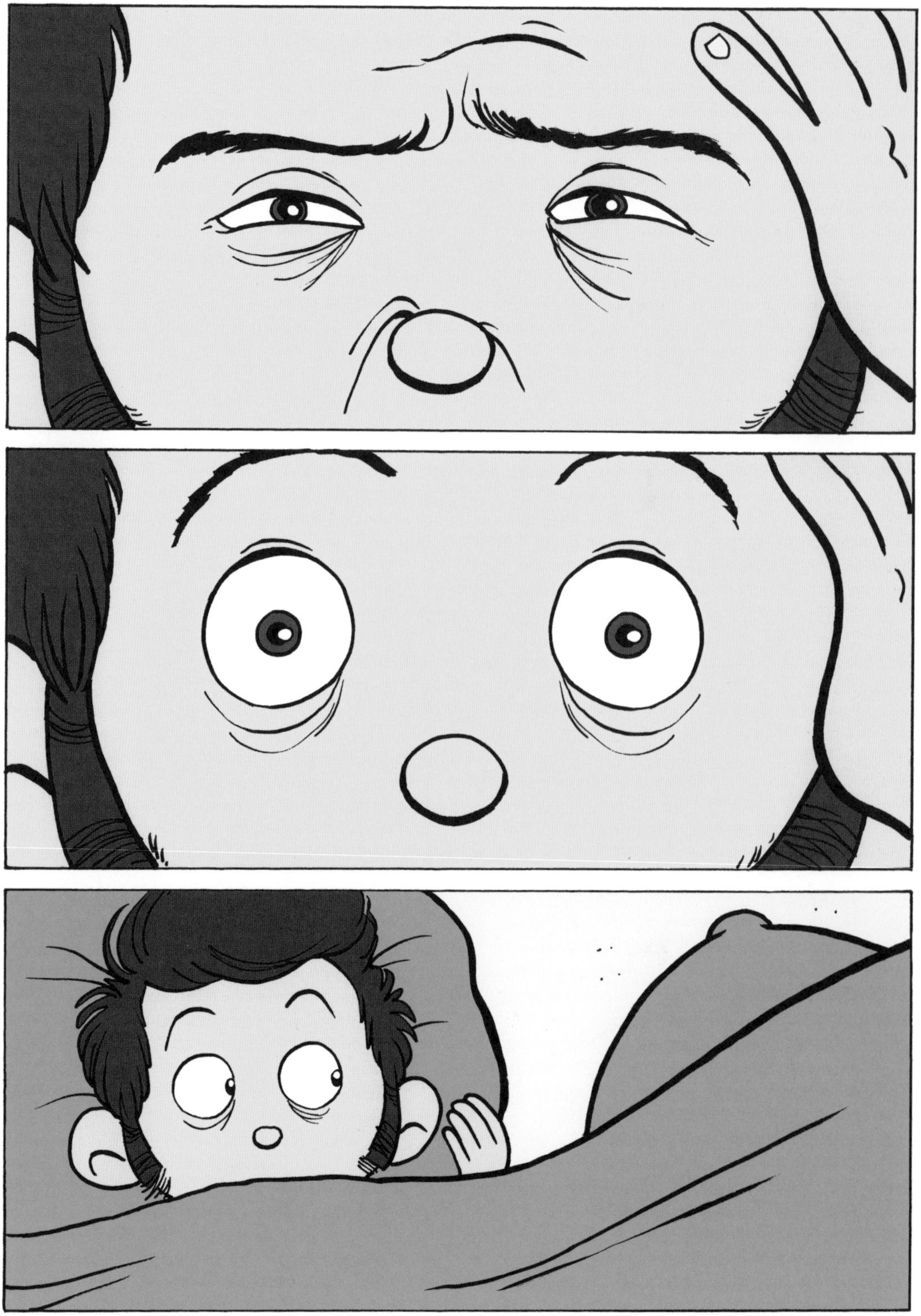

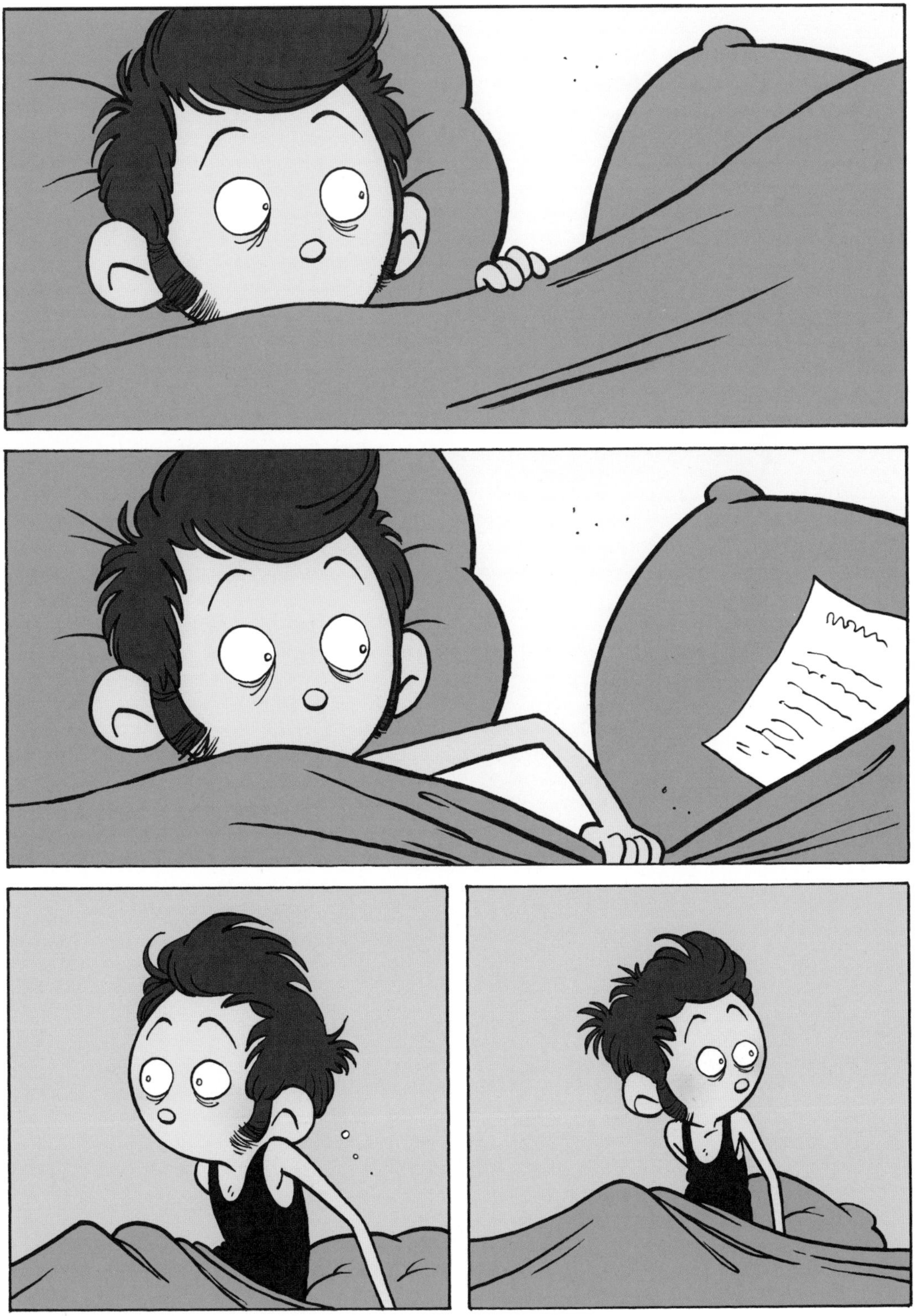

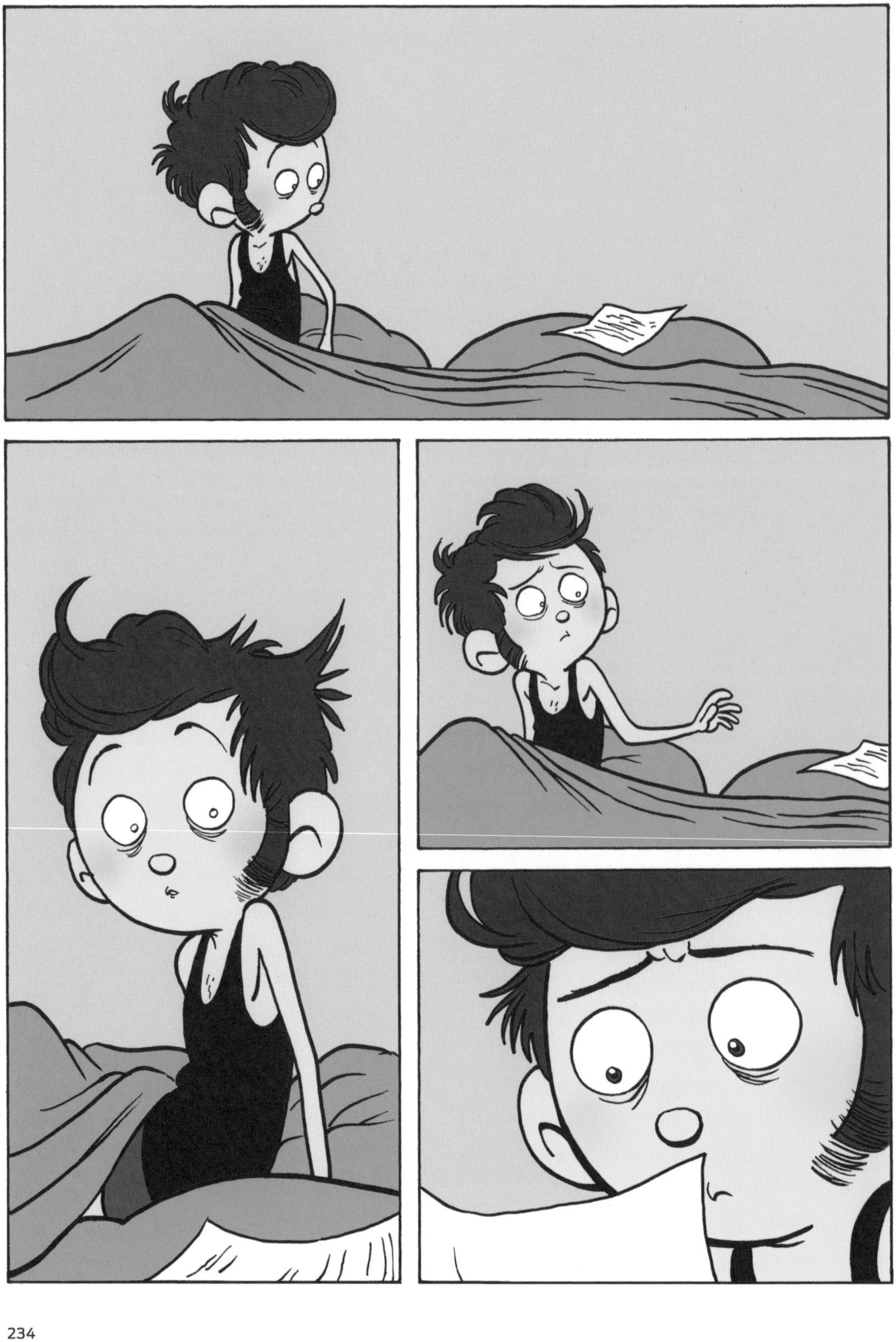

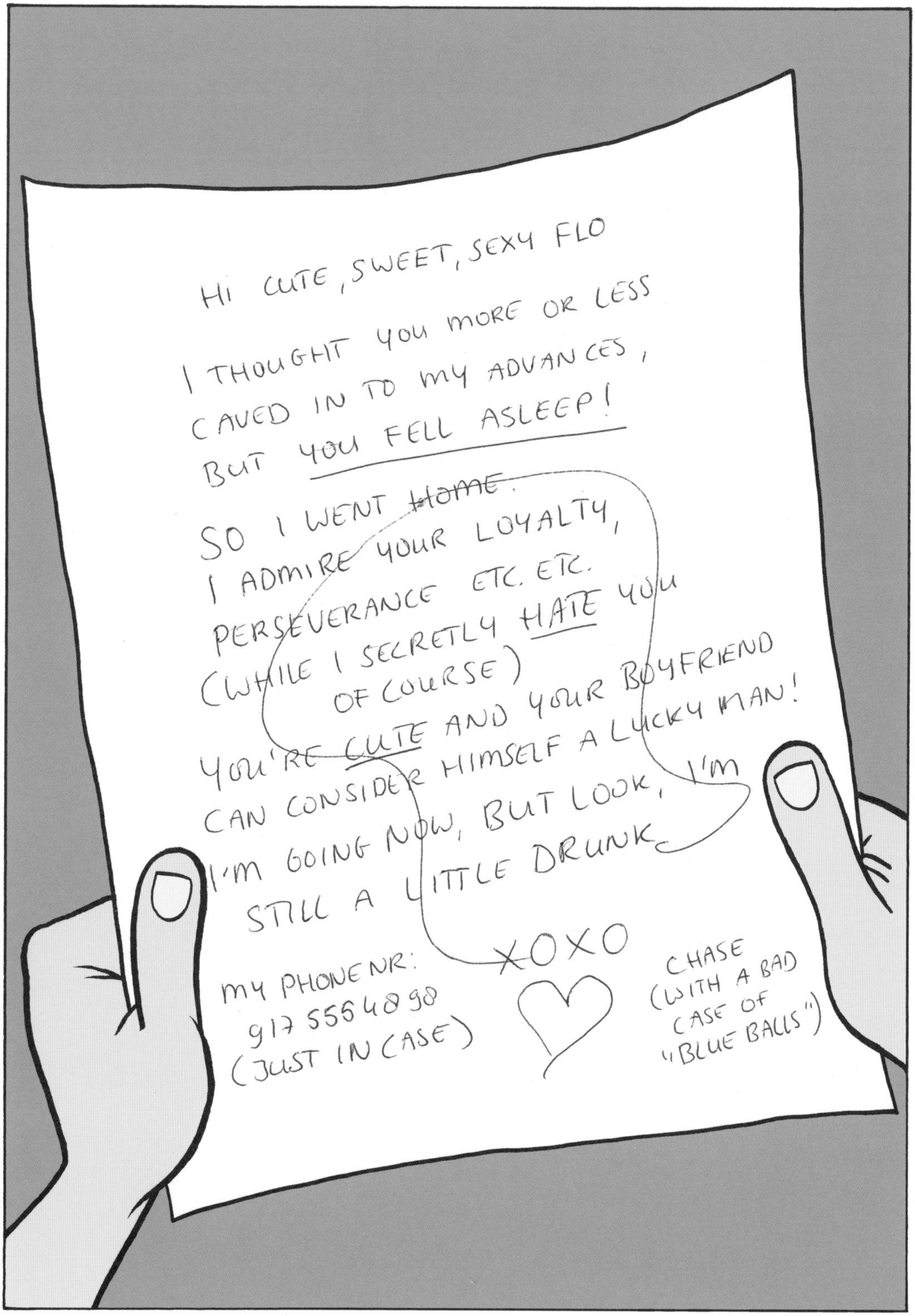
HI CUTE, SWEET, SEXY FLO
I THOUGHT YOU MORE OR LESS CAVED IN TO MY ADVANCES, BUT YOU FELL ASLEEP!
SO I WENT ~~HOME~~.
I ADMIRE YOUR LOYALTY, PERSEVERANCE ETC. ETC. (WHILE I SECRETLY HATE YOU OF COURSE)
YOU'RE CUTE AND YOUR BOYFRIEND CAN CONSIDER HIMSELF A LUCKY MAN!
I'M GOING NOW, BUT LOOK, I'M STILL A LITTLE DRUNK
XOXO
MY PHONE NR: 917 555 4898 (JUST IN CASE)
CHASE (WITH A BAD CASE OF "BLUE BALLS")

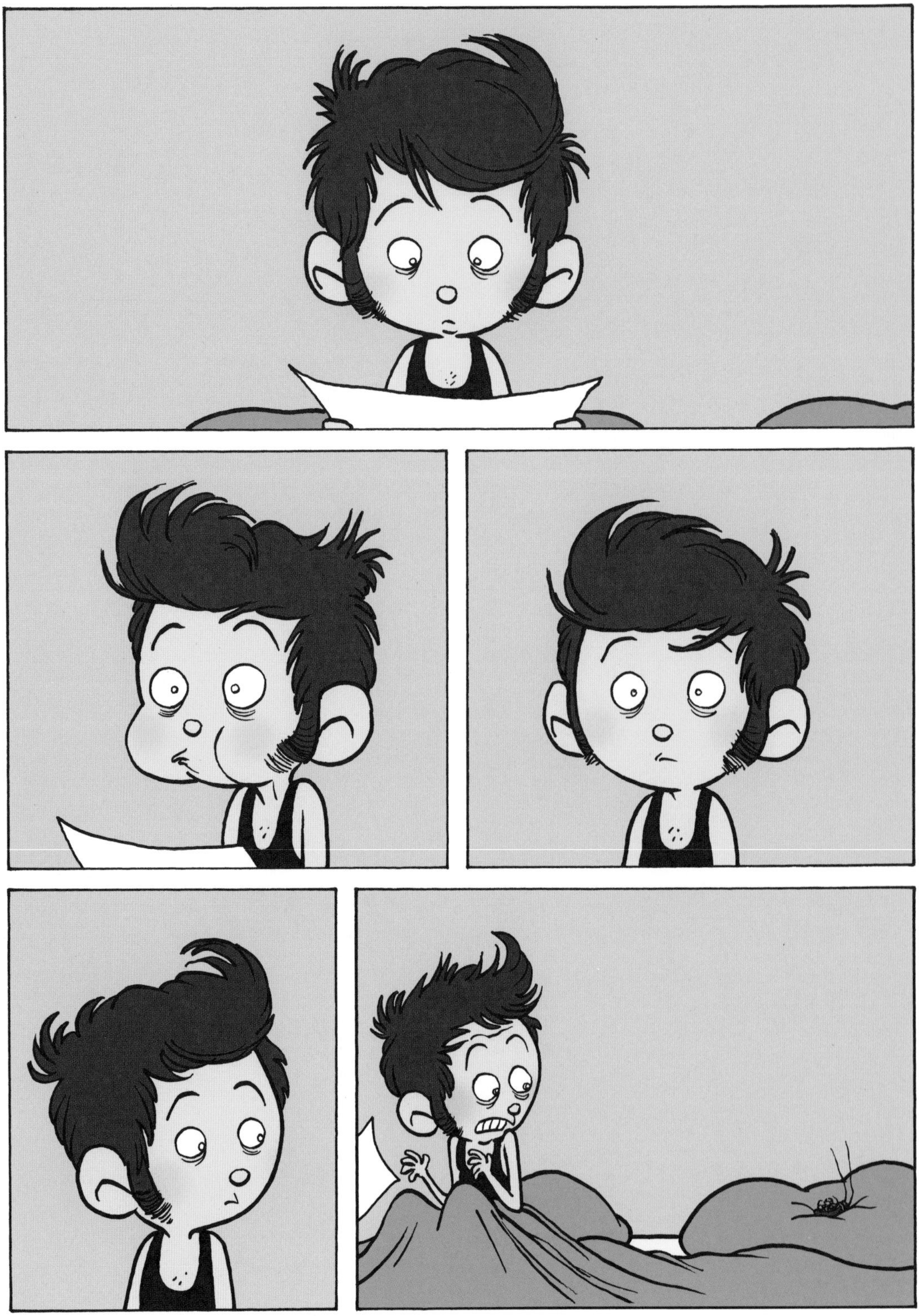

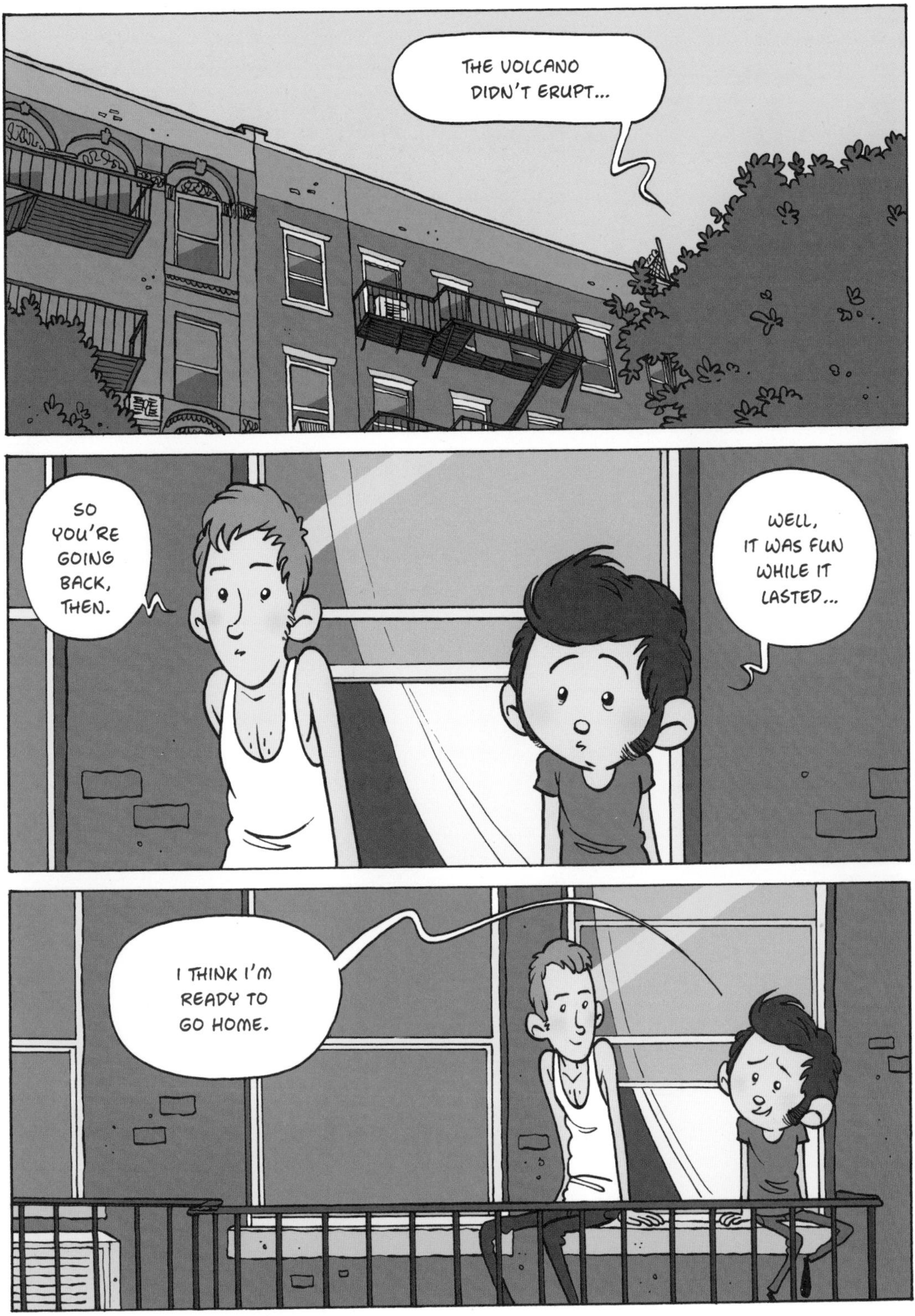
THE VOLCANO DIDN'T ERUPT...
SO YOU'RE GOING BACK, THEN.
WELL, IT WAS FUN WHILE IT LASTED...
I THINK I'M READY TO GO HOME.

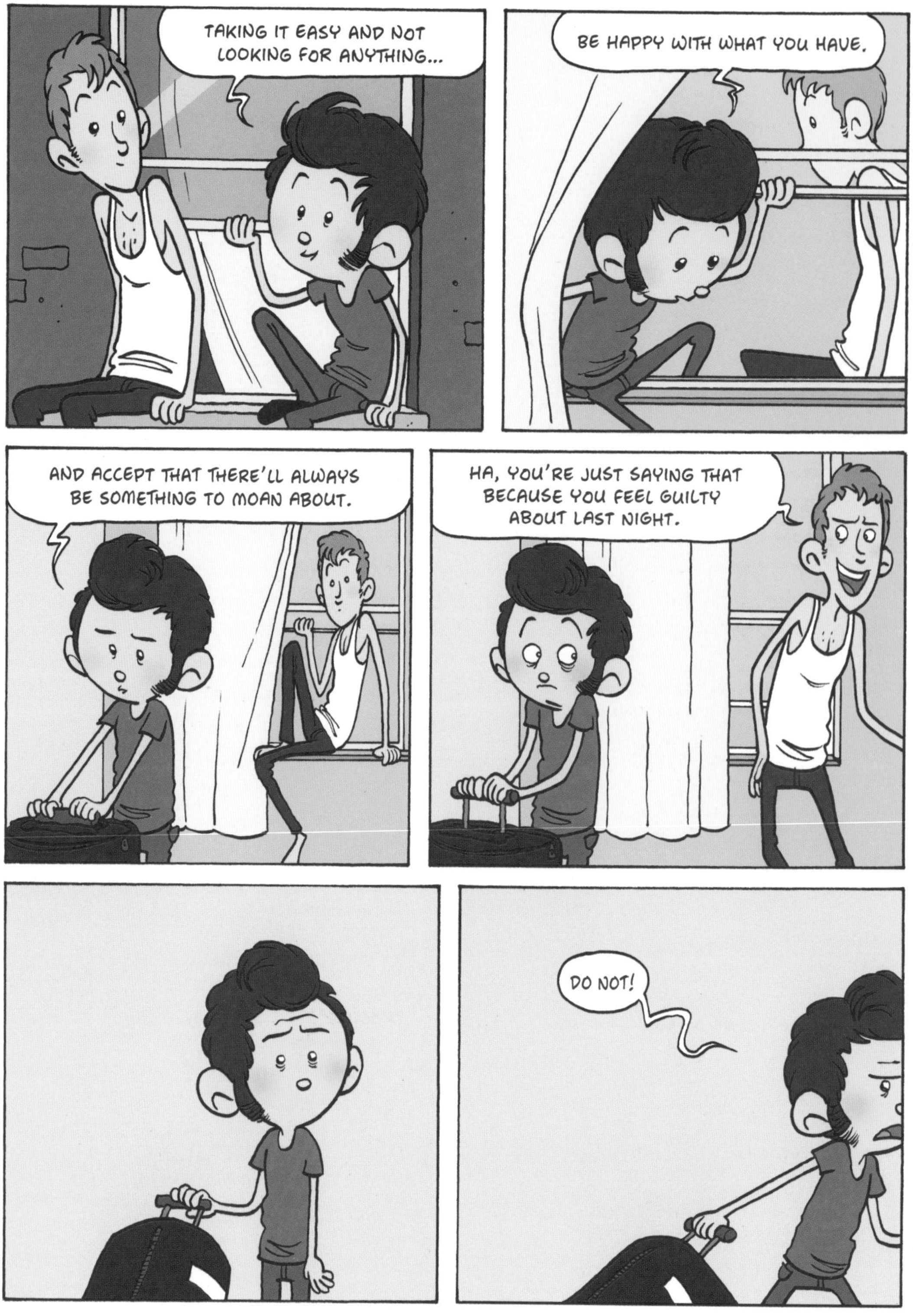
TAKING IT EASY AND NOT LOOKING FOR ANYTHING...
BE HAPPY WITH WHAT YOU HAVE.
AND ACCEPT THAT THERE'LL ALWAYS BE SOMETHING TO MOAN ABOUT.
HA, YOU'RE JUST SAYING THAT BECAUSE YOU FEEL GUILTY ABOUT LAST NIGHT.
DO NOT!

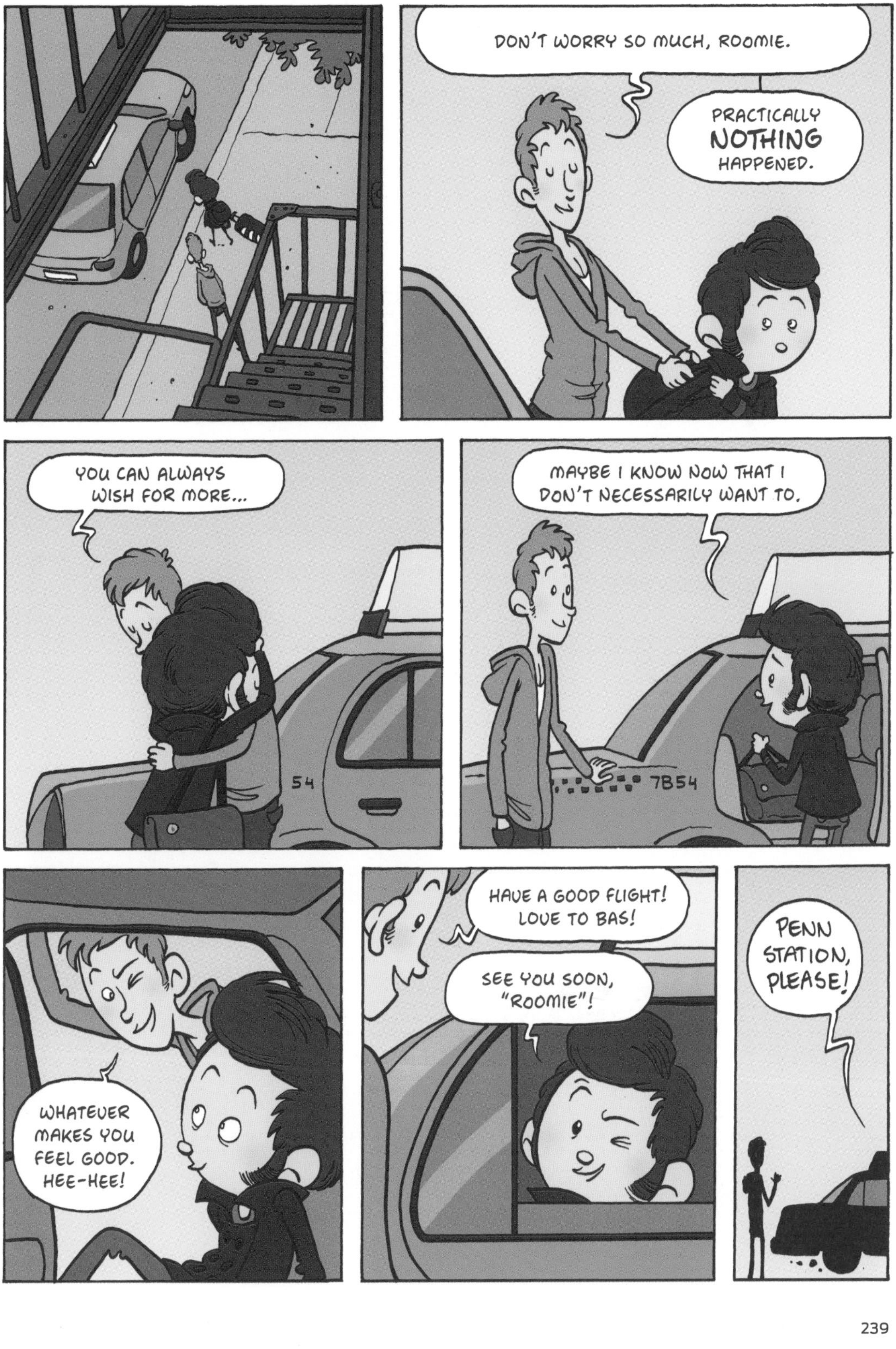
DON'T WORRY SO MUCH, ROOMIE.
PRACTICALLY NOTHING HAPPENED.
YOU CAN ALWAYS WISH FOR MORE...
MAYBE I KNOW NOW THAT I DON'T NECESSARILY WANT TO.
54
7B54
WHATEVER MAKES YOU FEEL GOOD. HEE-HEE!
HAVE A GOOD FLIGHT! LOVE TO BAS!
SEE YOU SOON, "ROOMIE"!
PENN STATION, PLEASE!

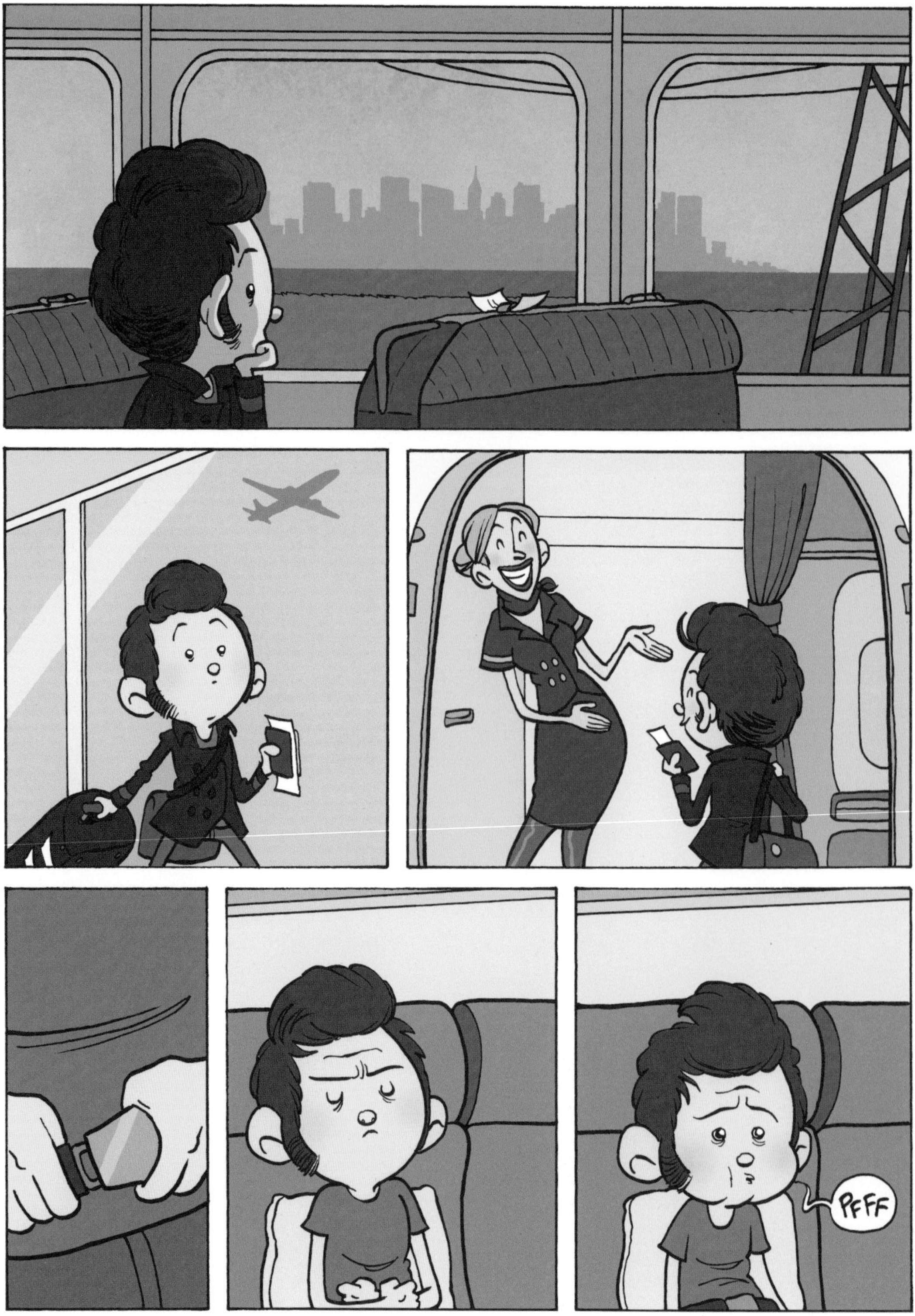
PFFF

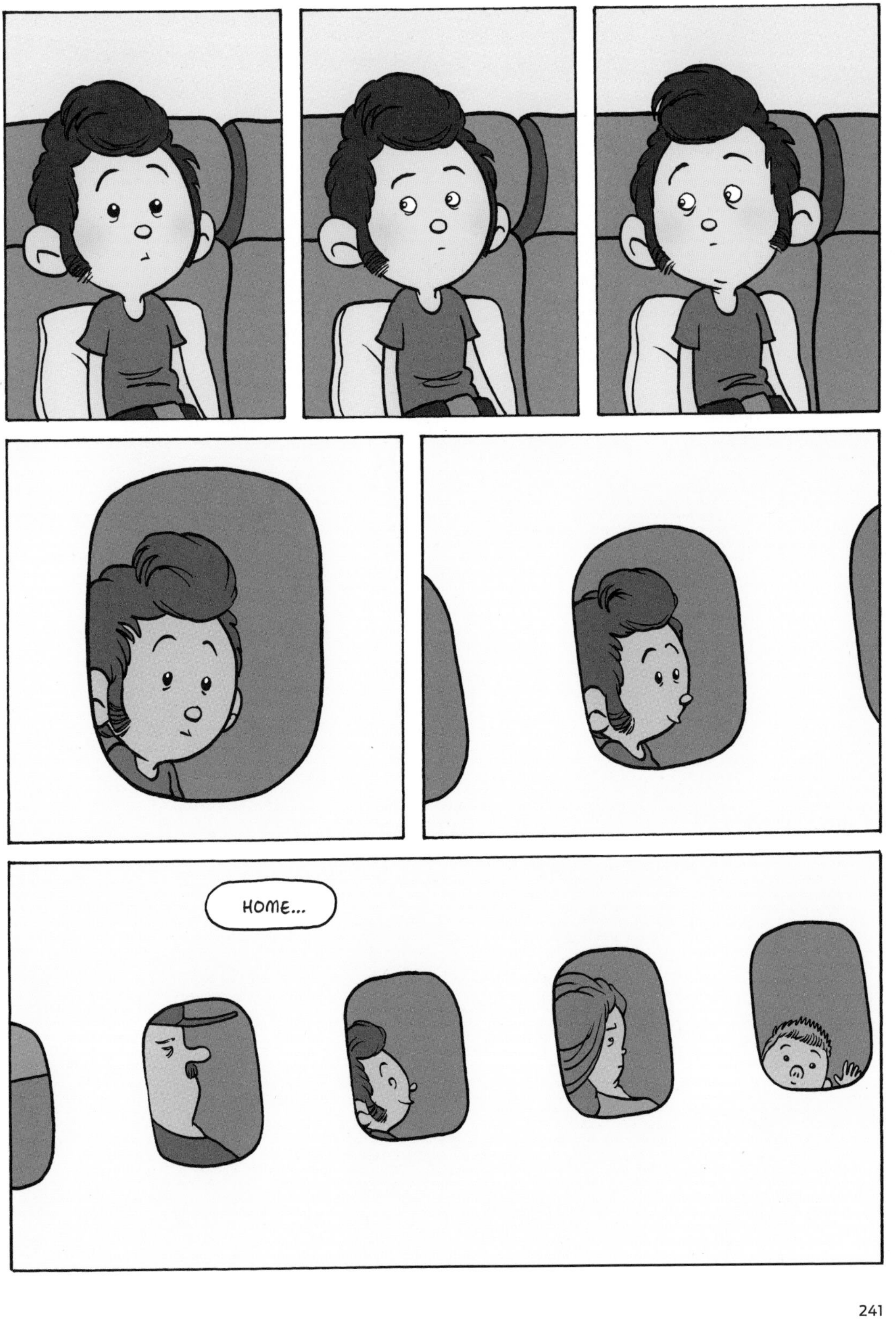
HOME...

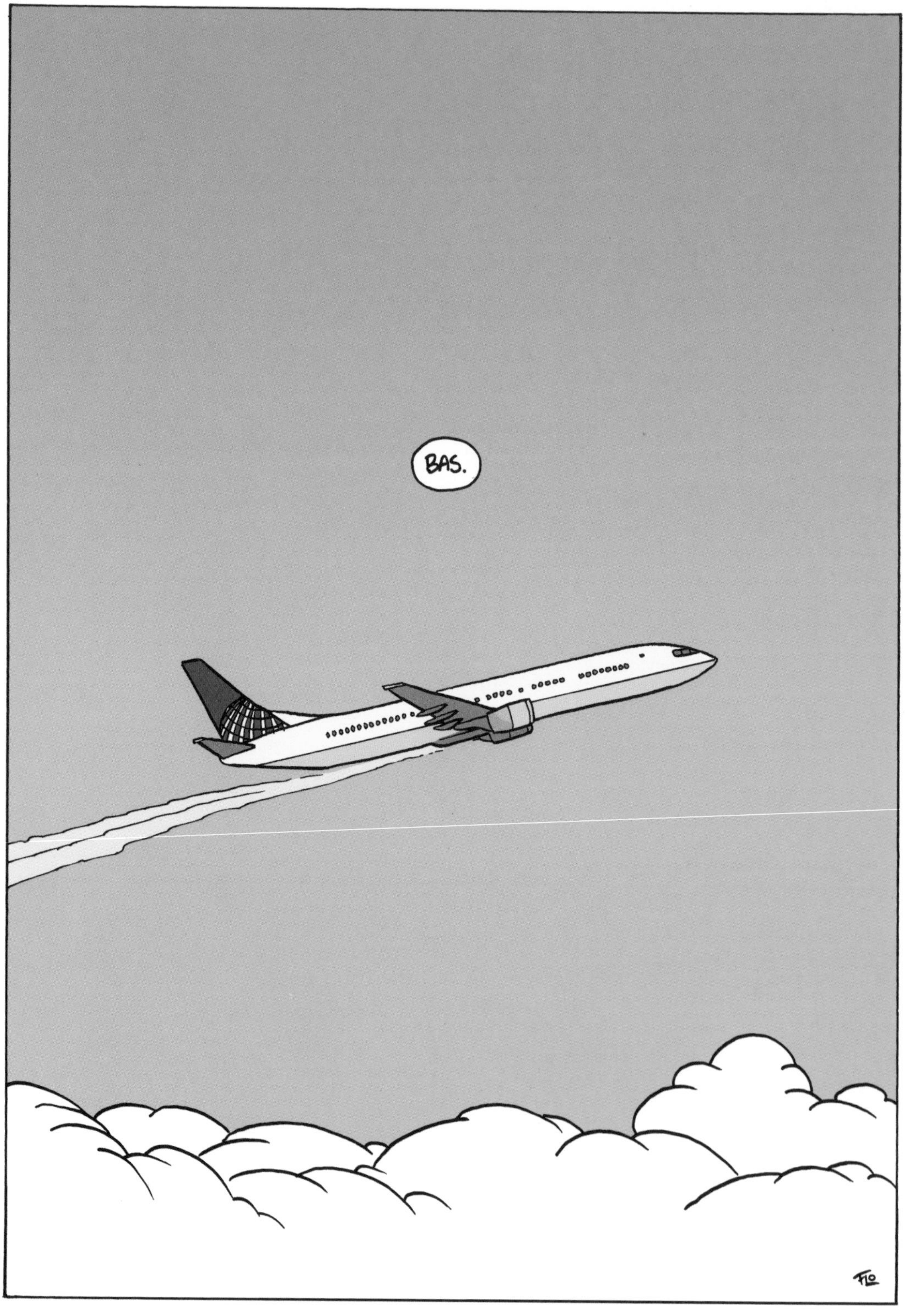
BAS.
FLO

EPILOGUE

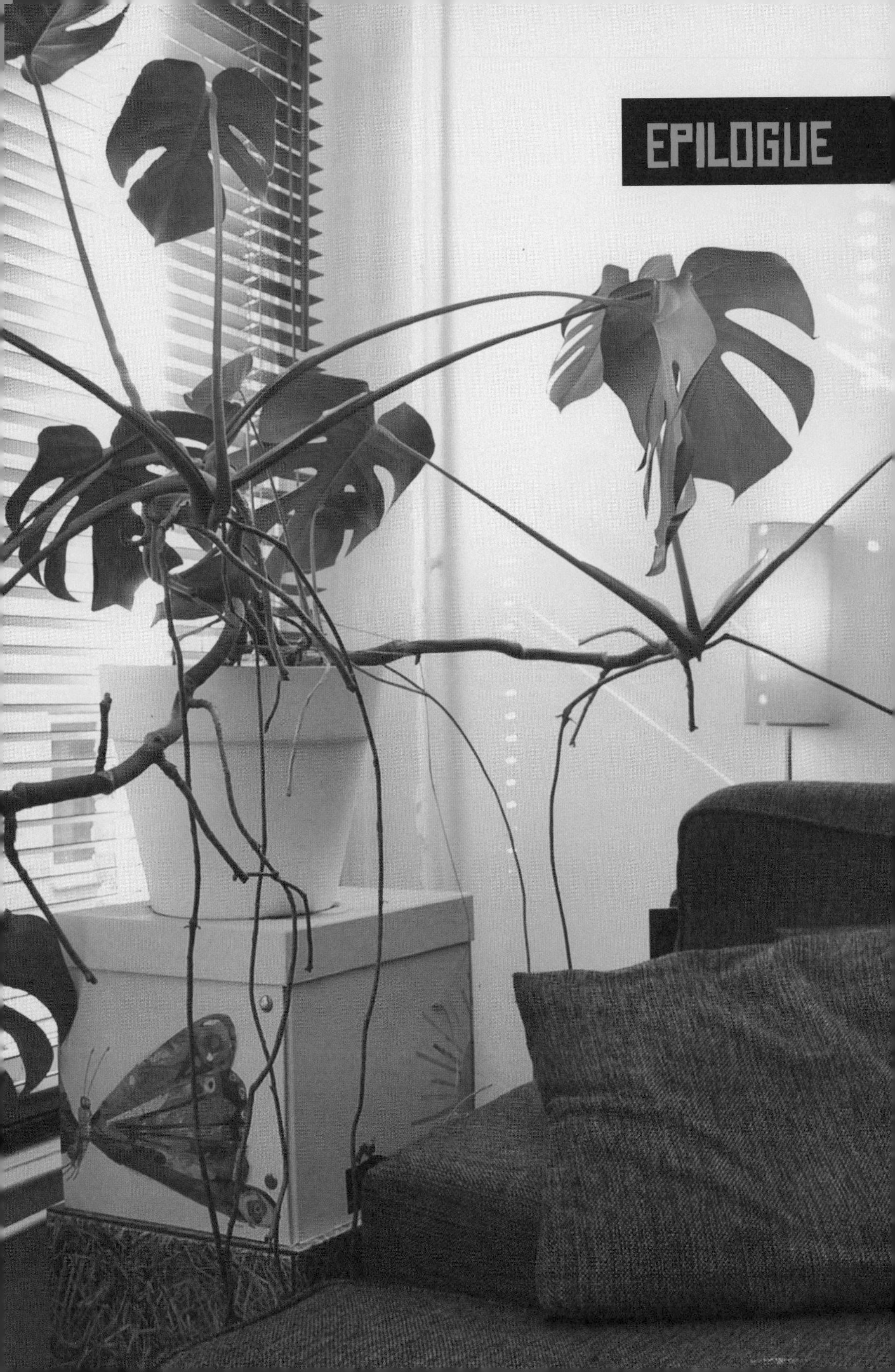

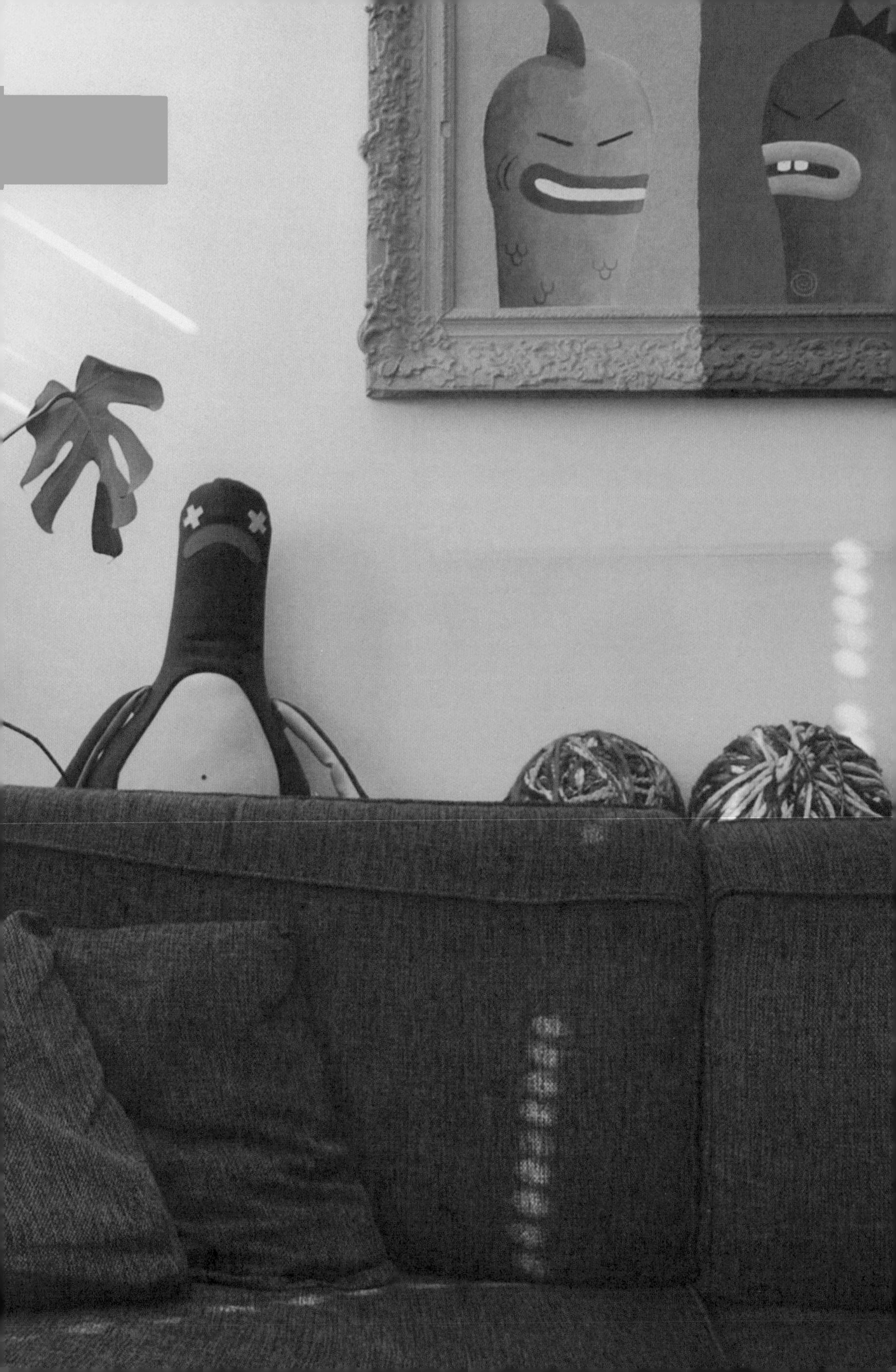

RRRRR
RRRRR

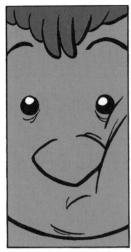

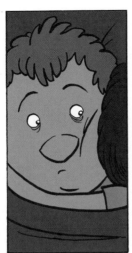

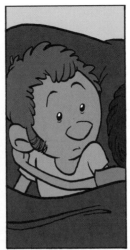

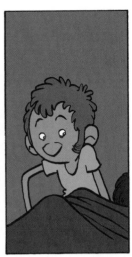

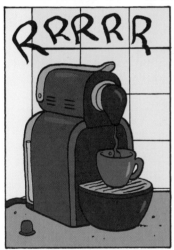

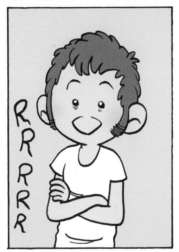

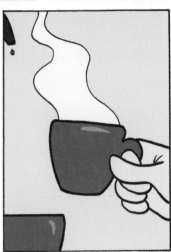

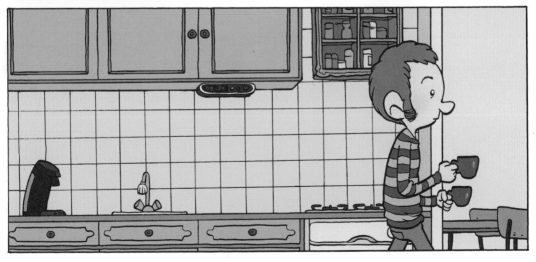

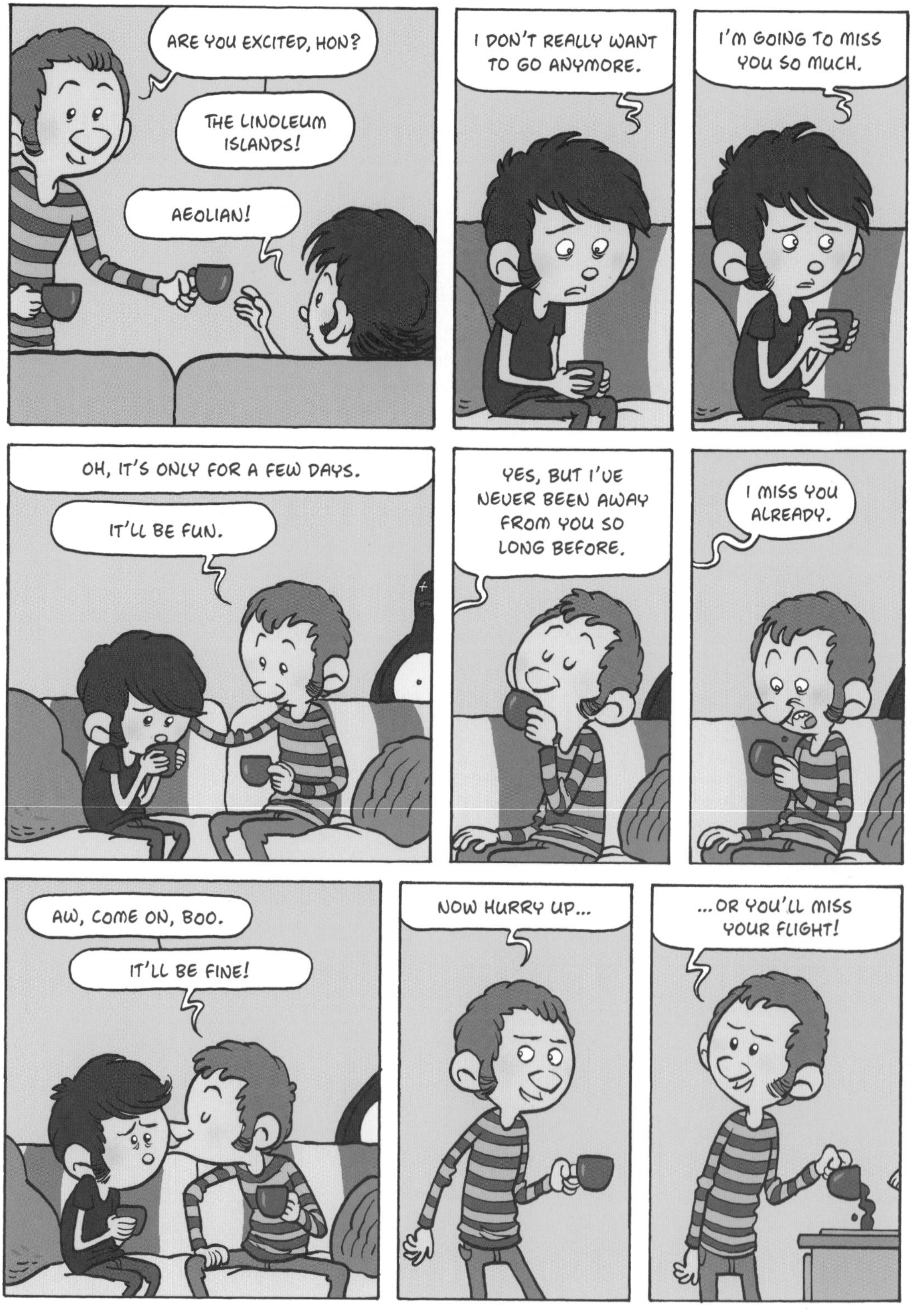

ARE YOU EXCITED, HON?
THE LINOLEUM ISLANDS!
AEOLIAN!
I DON'T REALLY WANT TO GO ANYMORE.
I'M GOING TO MISS YOU SO MUCH.
OH, IT'S ONLY FOR A FEW DAYS.
IT'LL BE FUN.
YES, BUT I'VE NEVER BEEN AWAY FROM YOU SO LONG BEFORE.
I MISS YOU ALREADY.
AW, COME ON, BOO.
IT'LL BE FINE!
NOW HURRY UP...
...OR YOU'LL MISS YOUR FLIGHT!

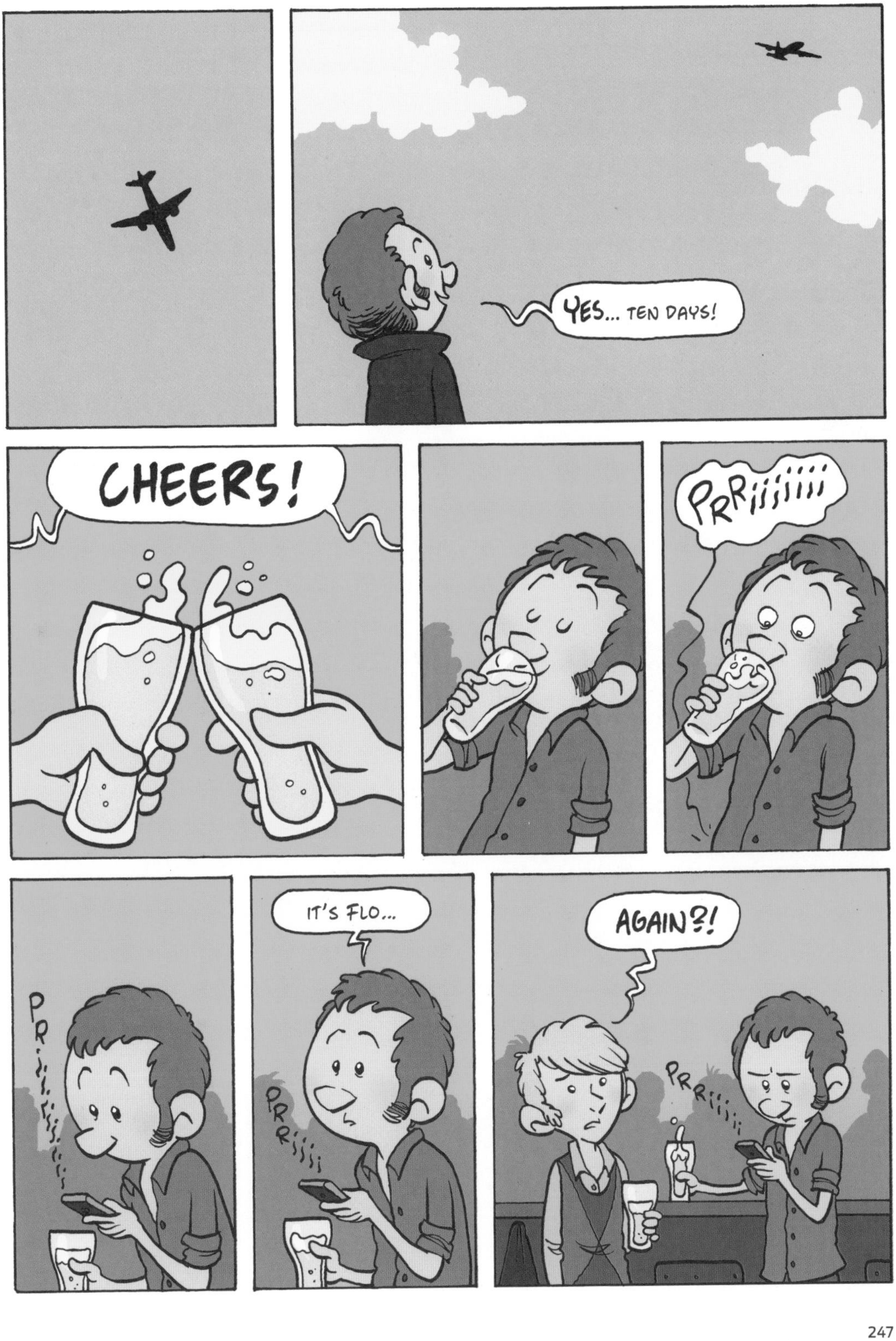
YES... TEN DAYS!
CHEERS!
PRRiiiiiii
IT'S FLO...
AGAIN?!

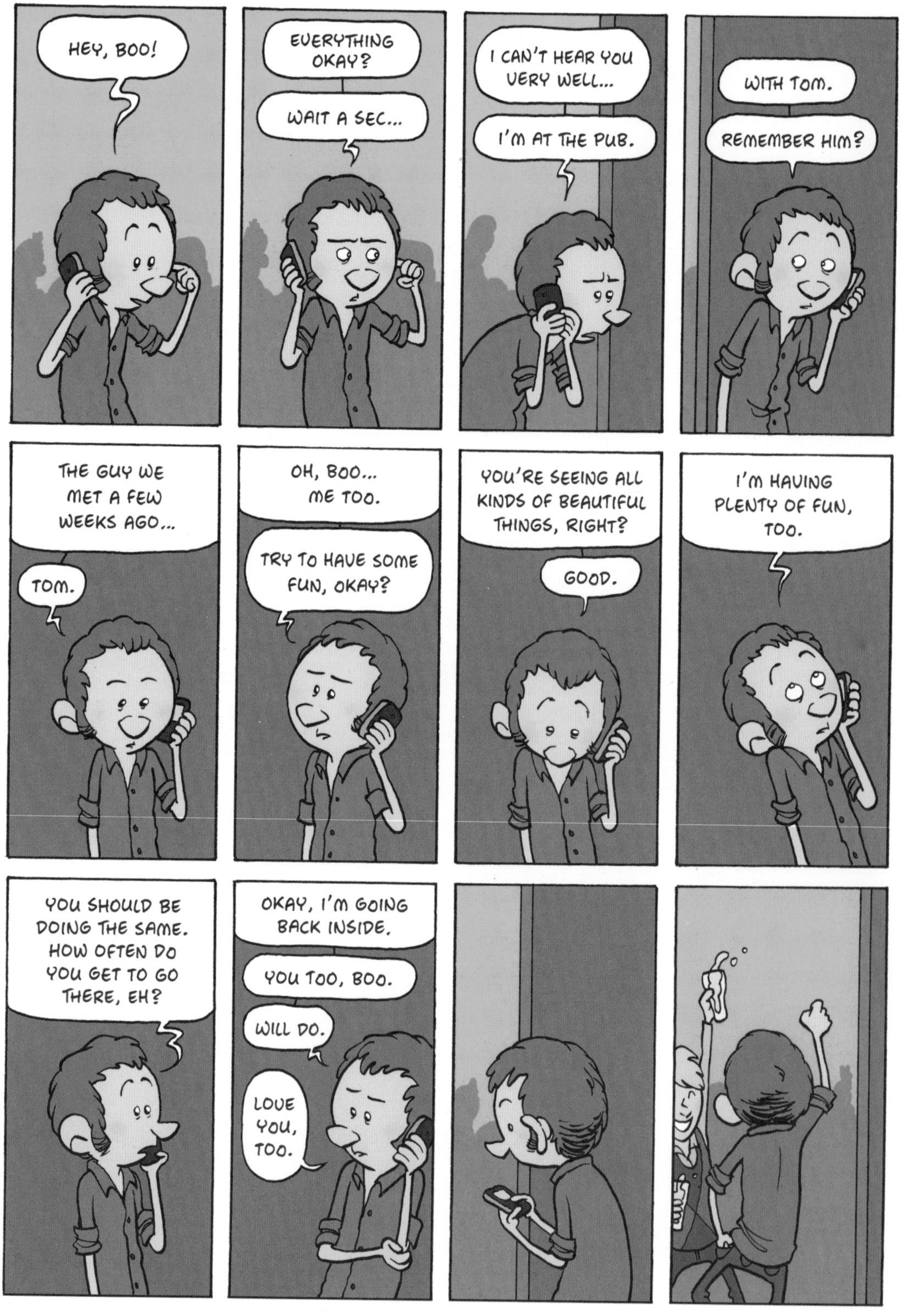
HEY, BOO!
EVERYTHING OKAY?
WAIT A SEC...
I CAN'T HEAR YOU VERY WELL...
I'M AT THE PUB.
WITH TOM.
REMEMBER HIM?
THE GUY WE MET A FEW WEEKS AGO...
TOM.
OH, BOO... ME TOO.
TRY TO HAVE SOME FUN, OKAY?
YOU'RE SEEING ALL KINDS OF BEAUTIFUL THINGS, RIGHT?
GOOD.
I'M HAVING PLENTY OF FUN, TOO.
YOU SHOULD BE DOING THE SAME. HOW OFTEN DO YOU GET TO GO THERE, EH?
OKAY, I'M GOING BACK INSIDE.
YOU TOO, BOO.
WILL DO.
LOVE YOU, TOO.

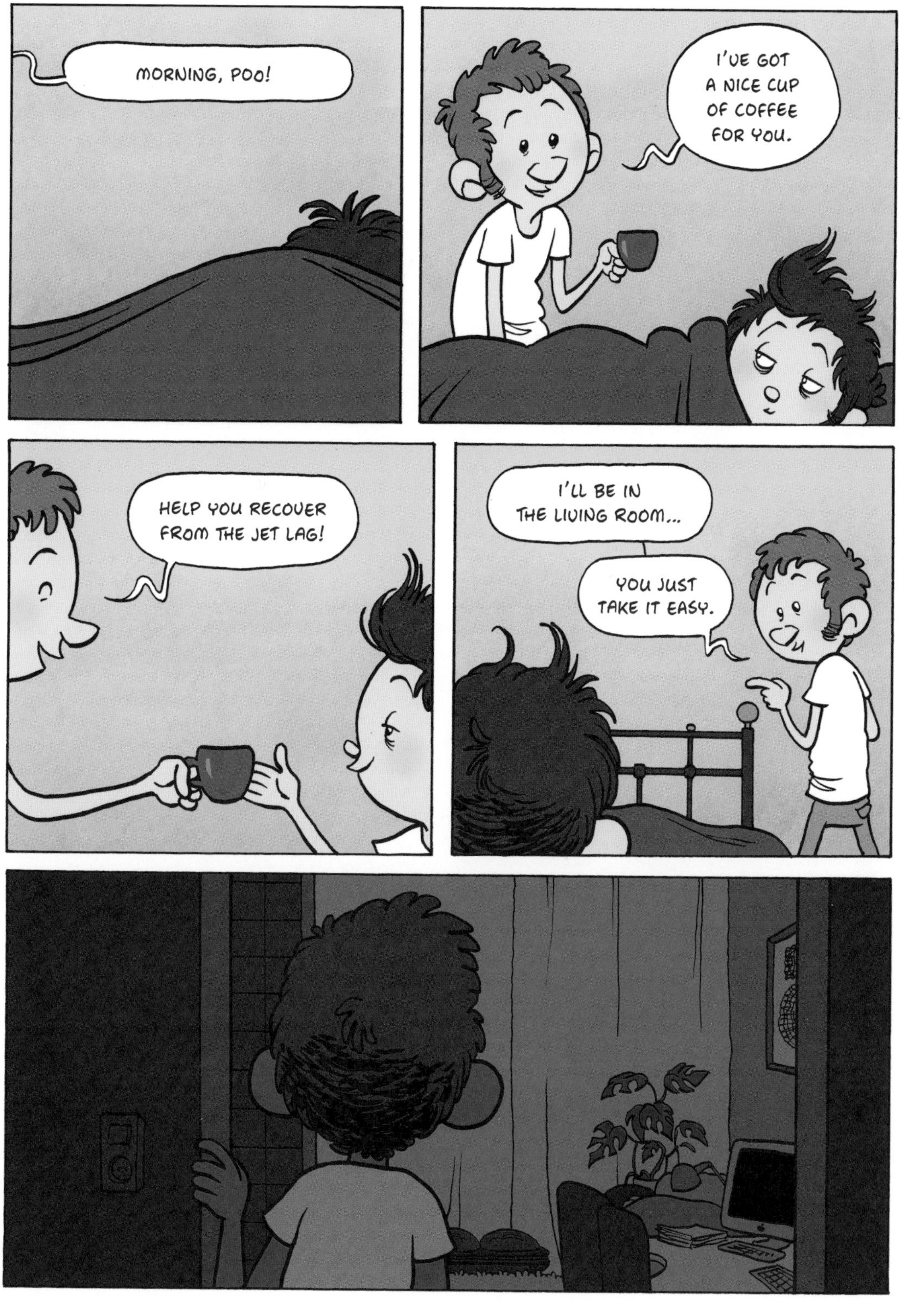
MORNING, POO!
I'VE GOT A NICE CUP OF COFFEE FOR YOU.
HELP YOU RECOVER FROM THE JET LAG!
I'LL BE IN THE LIVING ROOM...
YOU JUST TAKE IT EASY.

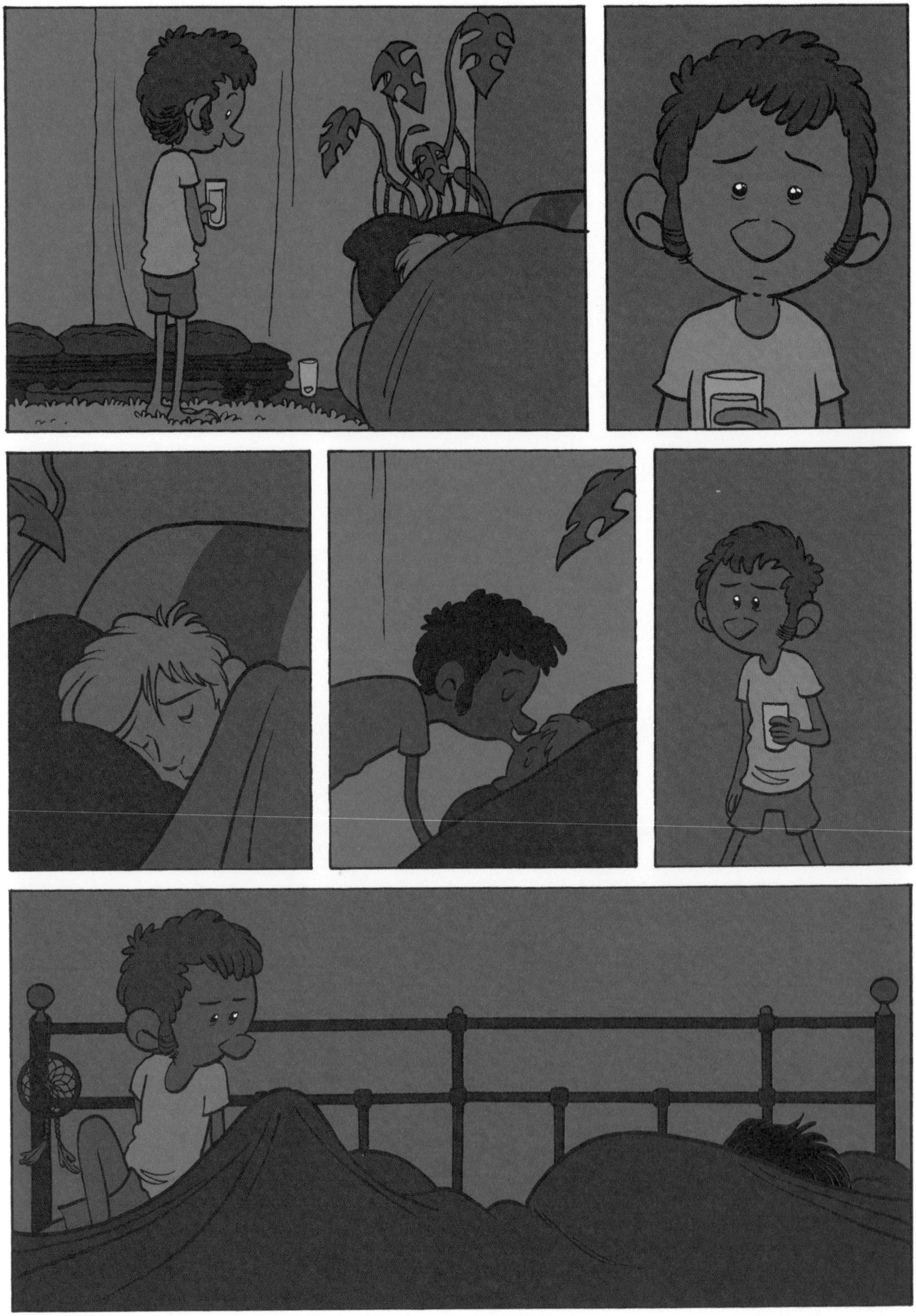

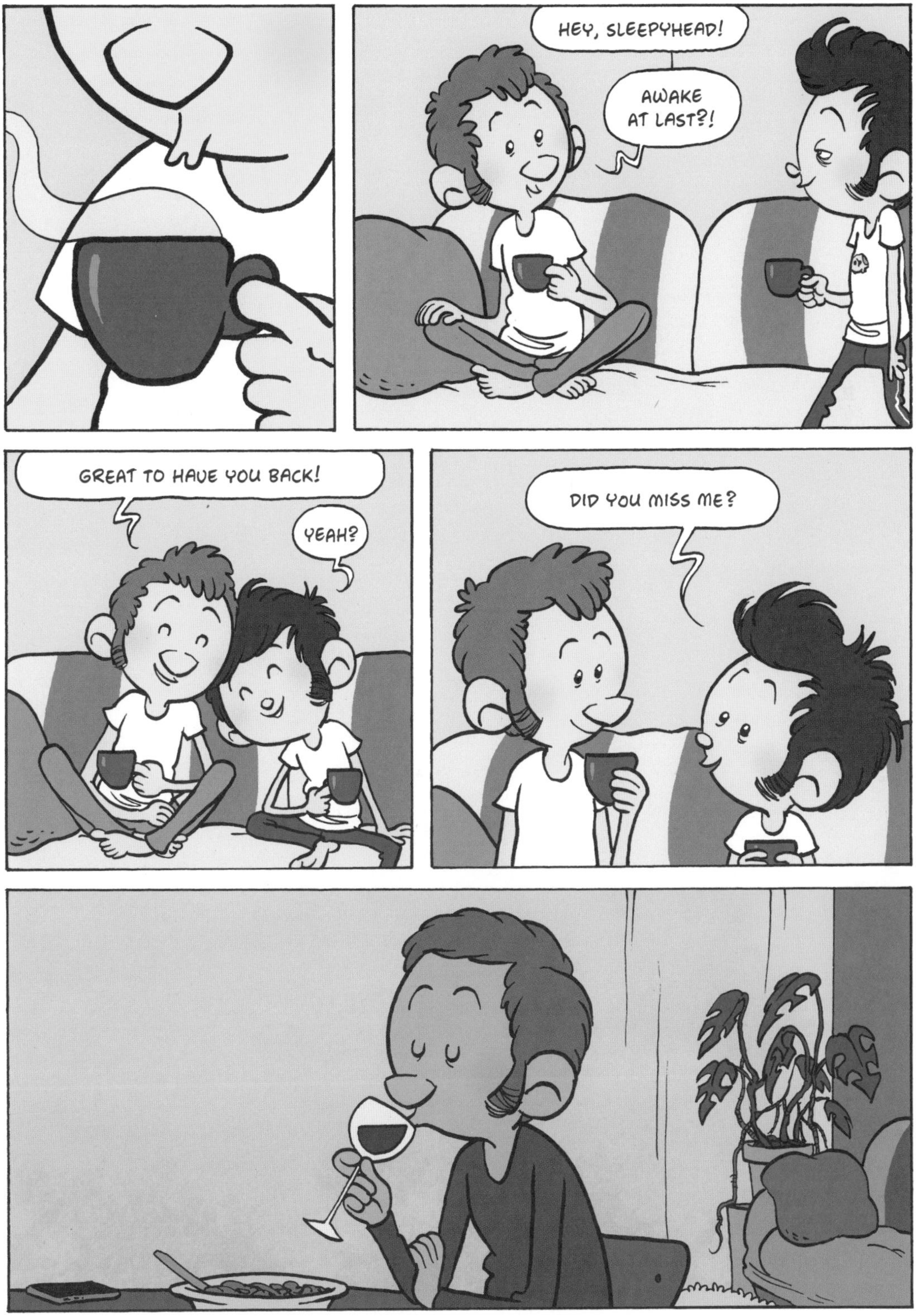
HEY, SLEEPYHEAD!
AWAKE AT LAST?!
GREAT TO HAVE YOU BACK!
YEAH?
DID YOU MISS ME?

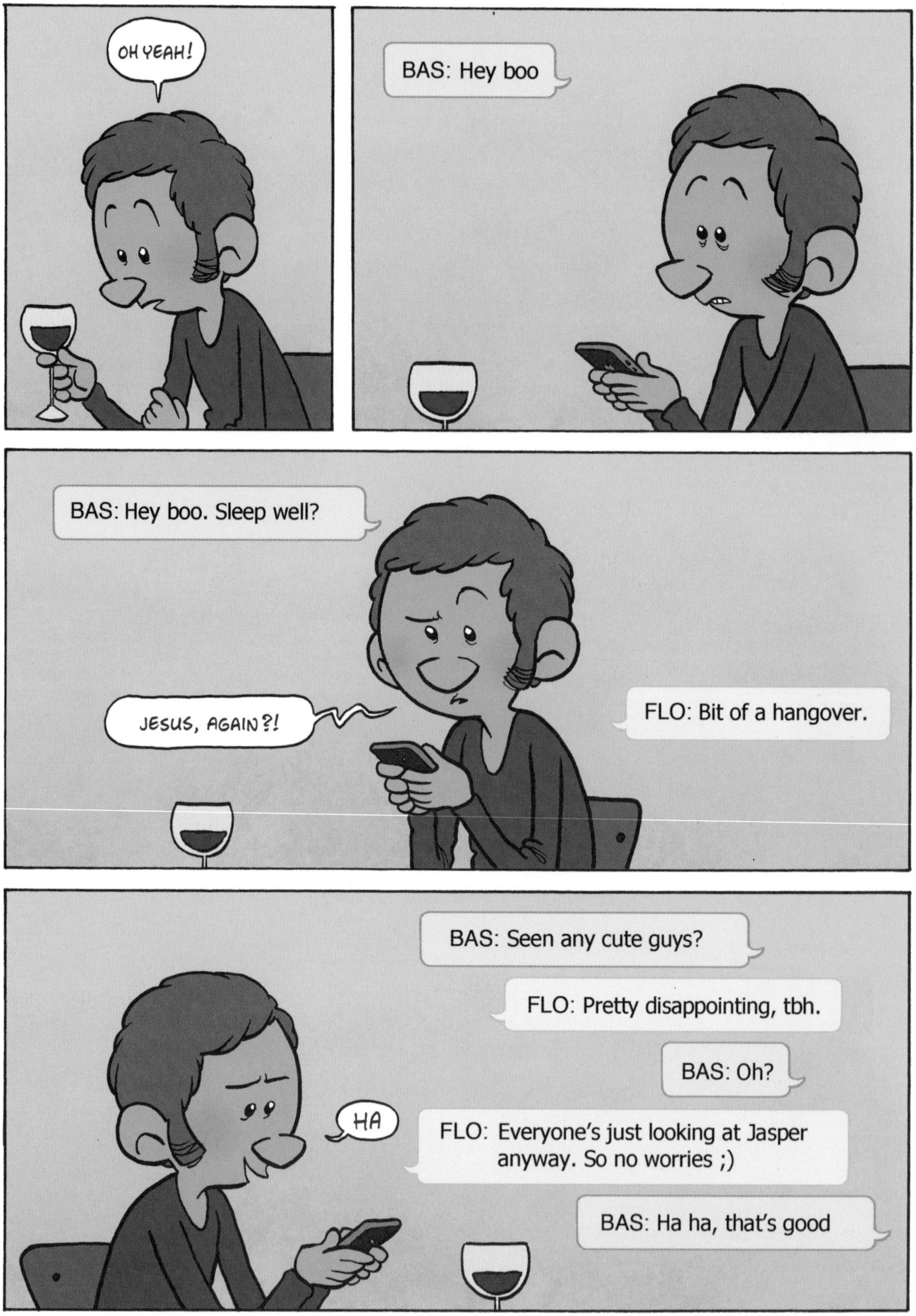
OH YEAH!
BAS: Hey boo
BAS: Hey boo. Sleep well?
JESUS, AGAIN?!
FLO: Bit of a hangover.
BAS: Seen any cute guys?
FLO: Pretty disappointing, tbh.
BAS: Oh?
HA
FLO: Everyone's just looking at Jasper anyway. So no worries ;)
BAS: Ha ha, that's good

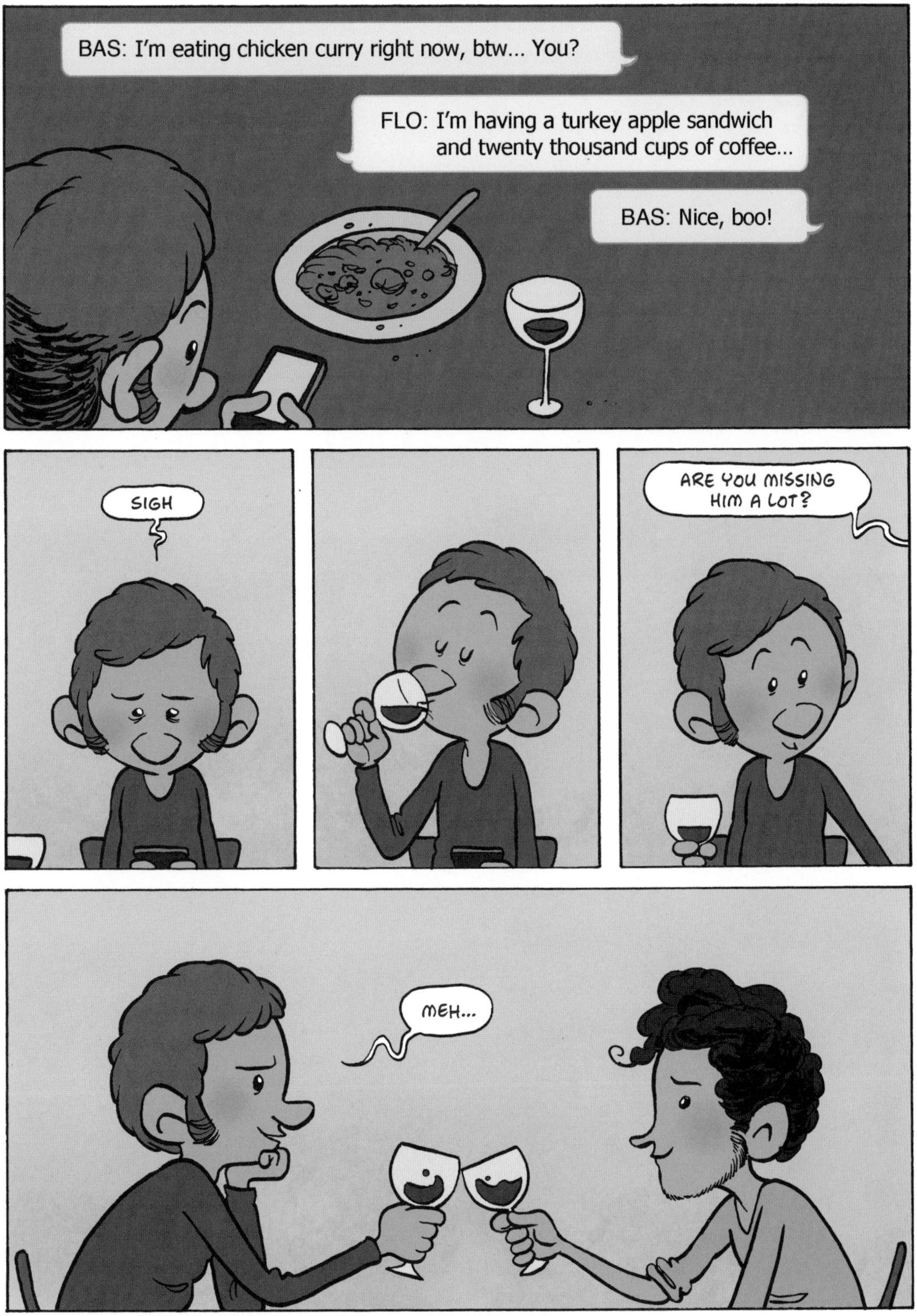
BAS: I'm eating chicken curry right now, btw... You?
FLO: I'm having a turkey apple sandwich and twenty thousand cups of coffee...
BAS: Nice, boo!
SIGH
ARE YOU MISSING HIM A LOT?
MEH...

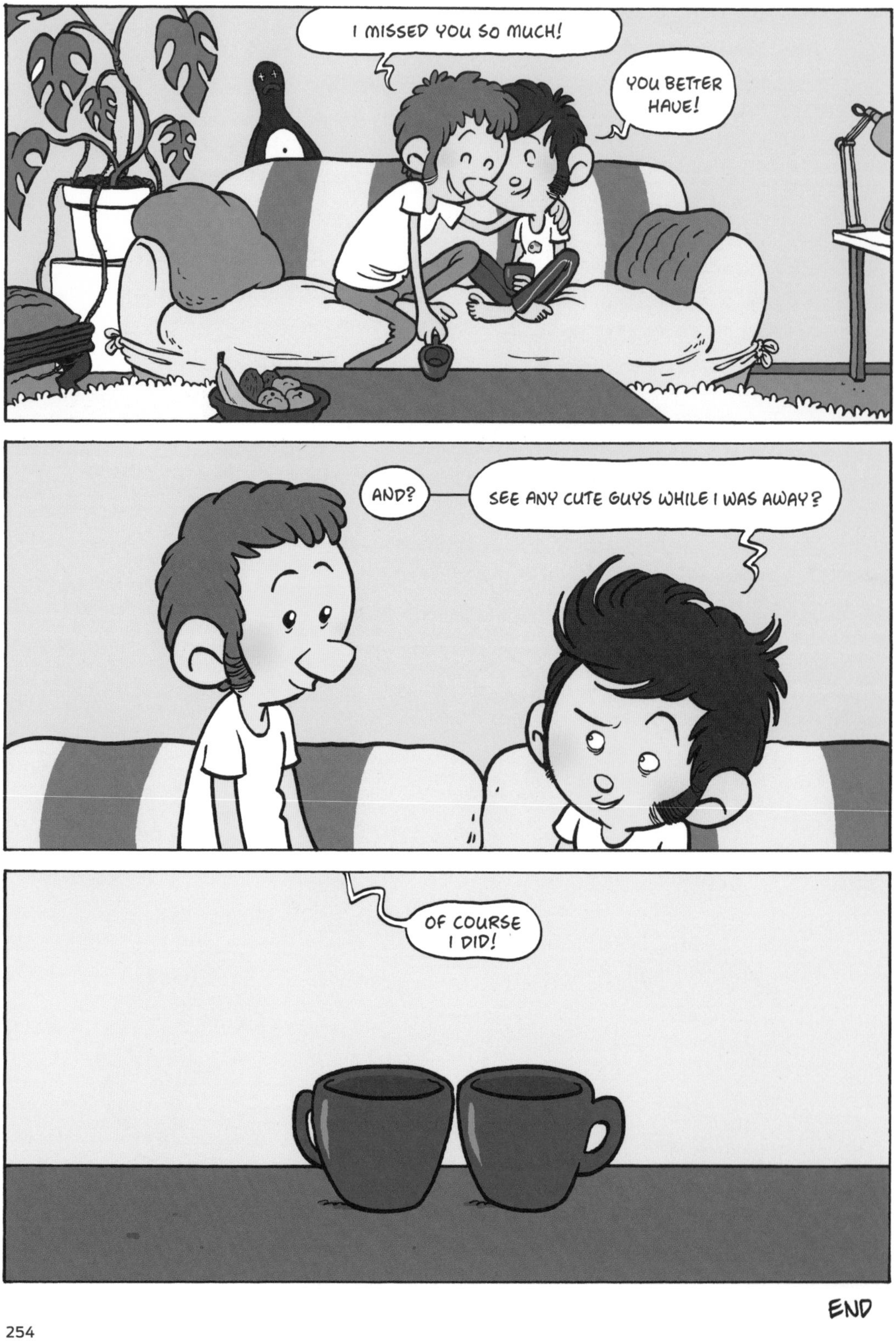
I MISSED YOU SO MUCH!
YOU BETTER HAVE!
AND?
SEE ANY CUTE GUYS WHILE I WAS AWAY?
OF COURSE I DID!

END

BIO

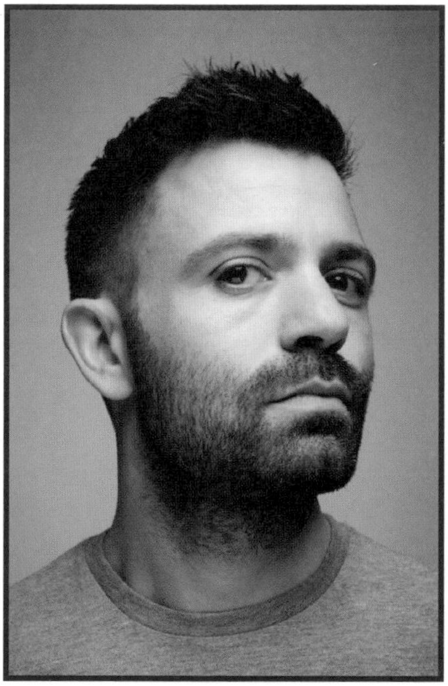

FLOOR DE GOEDE is a Dutch comic artist and children's book illustrator born and raised in Amsterdam. In 2004, he started his autobiographical comic, *Flo*, and gained a loyal fan base with his stories about his life, relationships, and the world around him. *Dancing on the Volcano* is his first work to be published in the US. Follow (most of) his life and work on Instagram @flodego.

Photo by Diederick Bulstra

SPECIAL THANKS

Flo would like to thank Mara, Borinka, Maaike, Diederik, Hanco, Edward, Joris, Jean-Marc, Jasper, Sander, Thom, and the biggest inspiration of all, Bas.

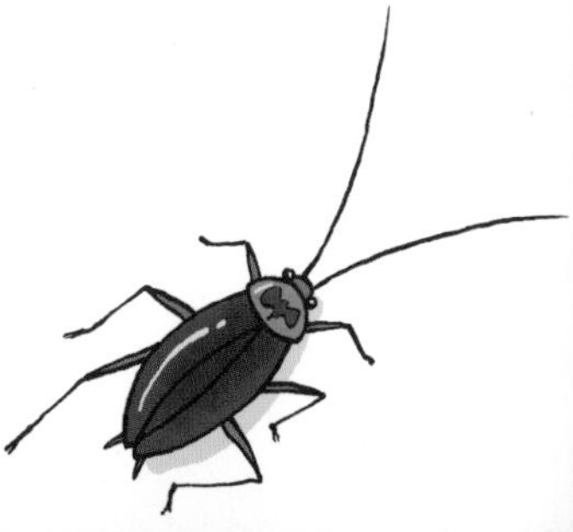

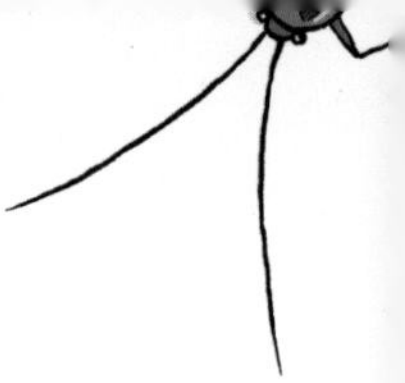

Mirror Mind

Mirror Mind

Tory Woollcott

tory.woollcott@maybemumkin.com
www.maybemumkin.com

This book was made possible with the generous support of The Ontario Branch of the International Dyslexia Association (ONBIDA)
info@idaontario.com
www.idaontario.com
416-716-9296

Library and Archives Canada Cataloguing in Publication
Woollcott, Victoria.
Mirror Mind/Victoria (Tory) Woollcott.
ISBN 978-0-9812766-0-1

You
gave me
words.

Pearl Levey

Eve Crawford

Mrs. Marseille

Foreword

Sometimes children can teach adults a great deal. Parents, and even teachers, can learn many lessons from them.

In the case of dyslexia, seeing it from a child's point of view is eye-opening and helps us to understand it better. Because while academic deficits associated with dyslexia can largely be remediated and accommodated, the pain connected to it can linger throughout an individual's life. That's why MirrorMind is so illuminating, and so vital.

Teachers are often unaware of the power of their words, both the positive and the negative. I am often struck in my work with adults with dyslexia by how they recall in vivid detail the actual harsh, dismissive words that their teachers directed at them. These words are replayed over and over again in their minds and in some cases these words are internalized and the individual believes in his or her lack of worth and limited intellect. In other cases, children do not buy into the negative messages but rather are driven to prove that they are capable of so much more. They are motivated to pursue higher education and confront new challenges.

In this book Tory conveys the pain of being misunderstood, the callousness and lack of sensitivity of her teacher, the rejection by her classmates, and the long uphill battle to be successful. The importance of early diagnosis is highlighted as well. It is only after a diagnosis of dyslexia that appropriate intervention can take place and Tory can move forward, shine, and realize her true potential.

Although Tory's childhood experiences took place many years ago, it is still true today that children with dyslexia are missed in our classrooms. Diagnosis does not always happen early enough and appropriate intervention which we now know so much more about, is unnecessarily delayed. We still have Tory's in our classrooms, suffering in silence and being dismissed by teachers and peers alike.

Aside from highlighting the deficits intrinsic to dyslexia, Tory's powerful book provides insights into the other side of dyslexia: the intelligence, the humour, the talent, the creativity, the resourcefulness and the courage. This book provides inspiration for all children, parents, and teachers whose lives are touched by dyslexia.

Pearl Levey, Ph.D.

Learning Disability Specialist

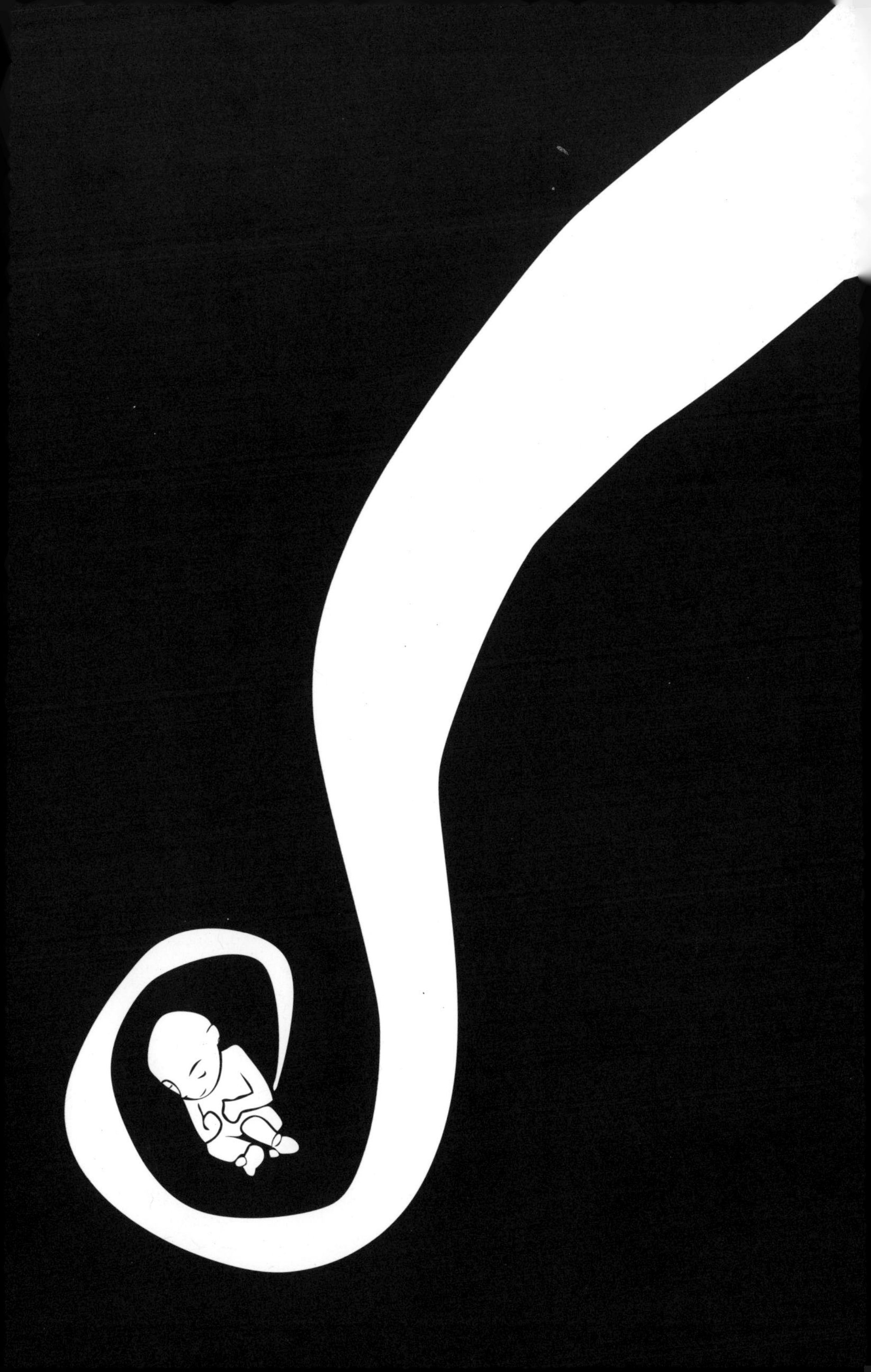

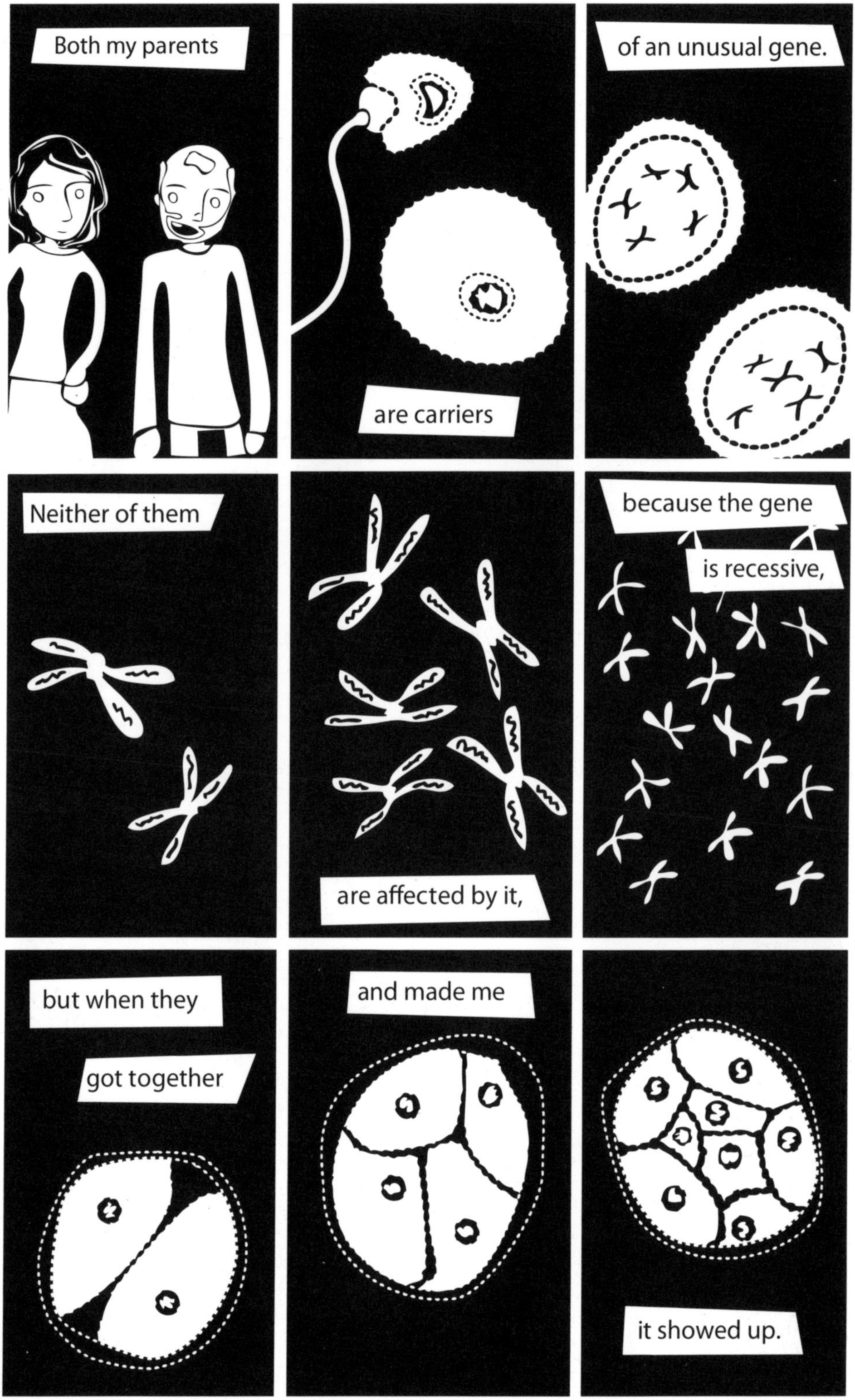
Both my parents
are carriers
of an unusual gene.
Neither of them
are affected by it,
because the gene
is recessive,
but when they
got together
and made me
it showed up.

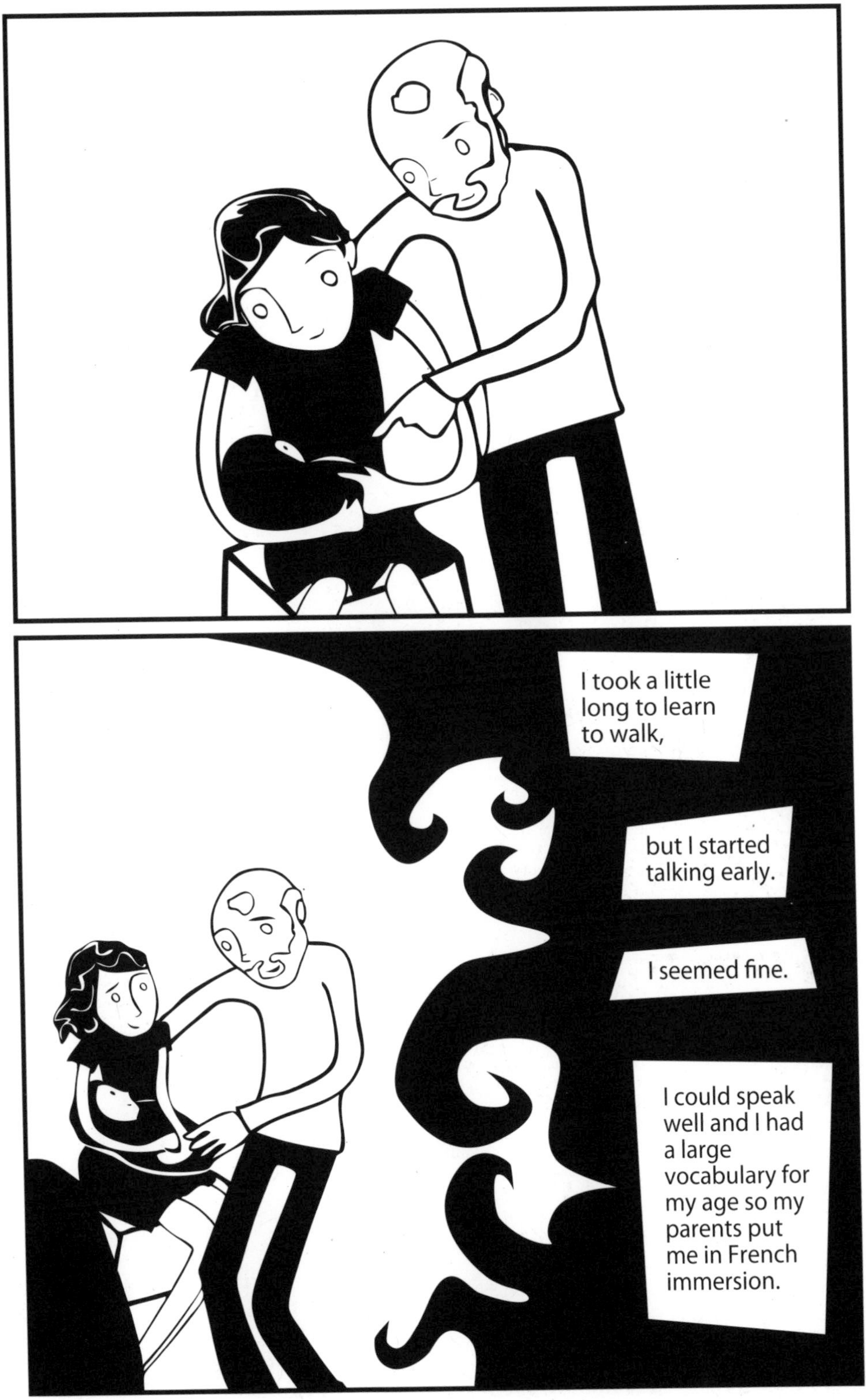
I took a little long to learn to walk,
but I started talking early.
I seemed fine.
I could speak well and I had a large vocabulary for my age so my parents put me in French immersion.

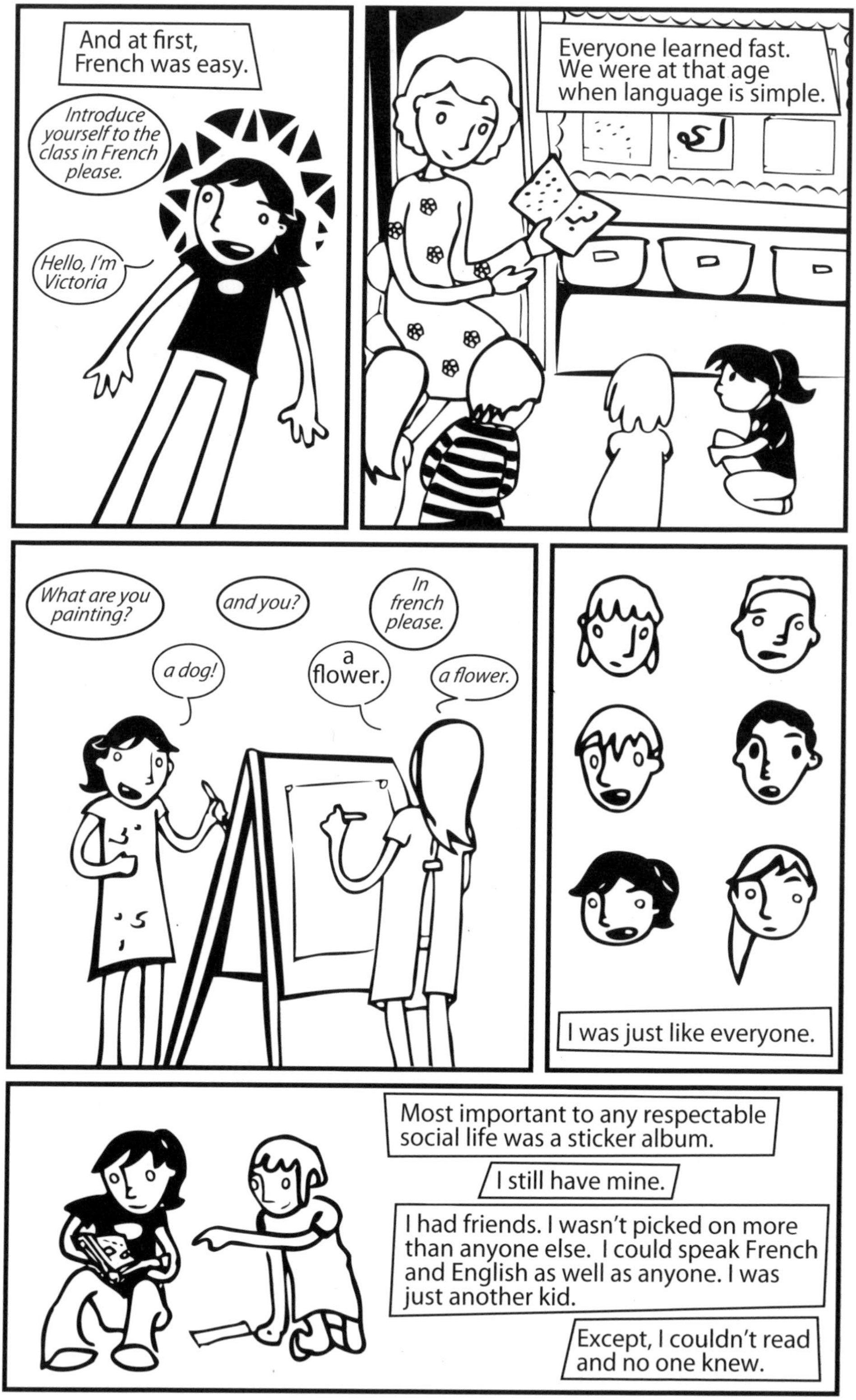
And at first, French was easy.
Introduce yourself to the class in French please.
Hello, I'm Victoria
Everyone learned fast. We were at that age when language is simple.
What are you painting?
a dog!
and you?
a flower.
In french please.
a flower.
I was just like everyone.
Most important to any respectable social life was a sticker album.
I still have mine.
I had friends. I wasn't picked on more than anyone else. I could speak French and English as well as anyone. I was just another kid.
Except, I couldn't read and no one knew.

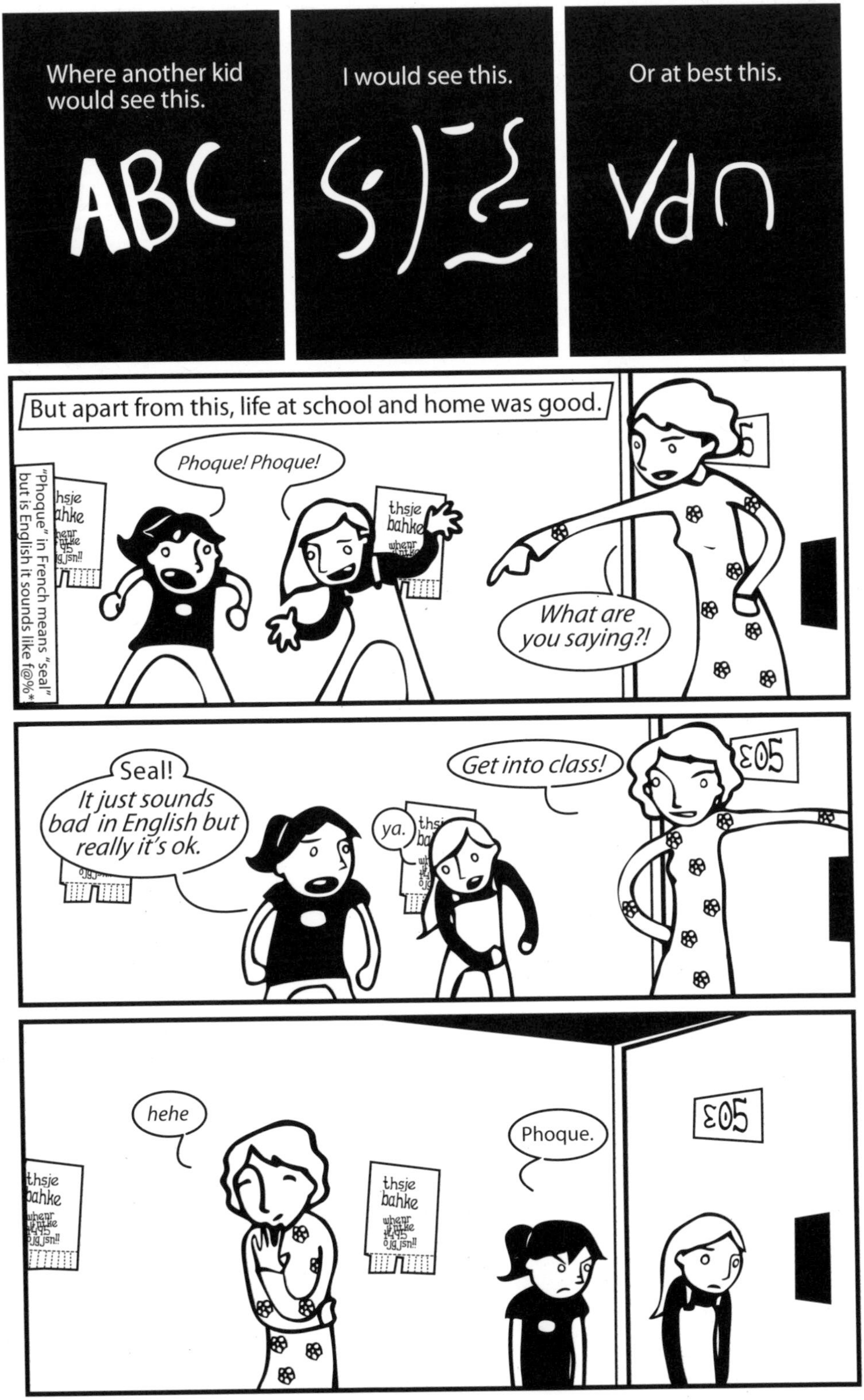
Where another kid would see this.
ABC
I would see this.
Or at best this.
But apart from this, life at school and home was good.
Phoque! Phoque!
"Phoque" in French means "seal" but is English it sounds like f@%*
What are you saying?!
Seal! It just sounds bad in English but really it's ok.
ya.
Get into class!
hehe
Phoque.

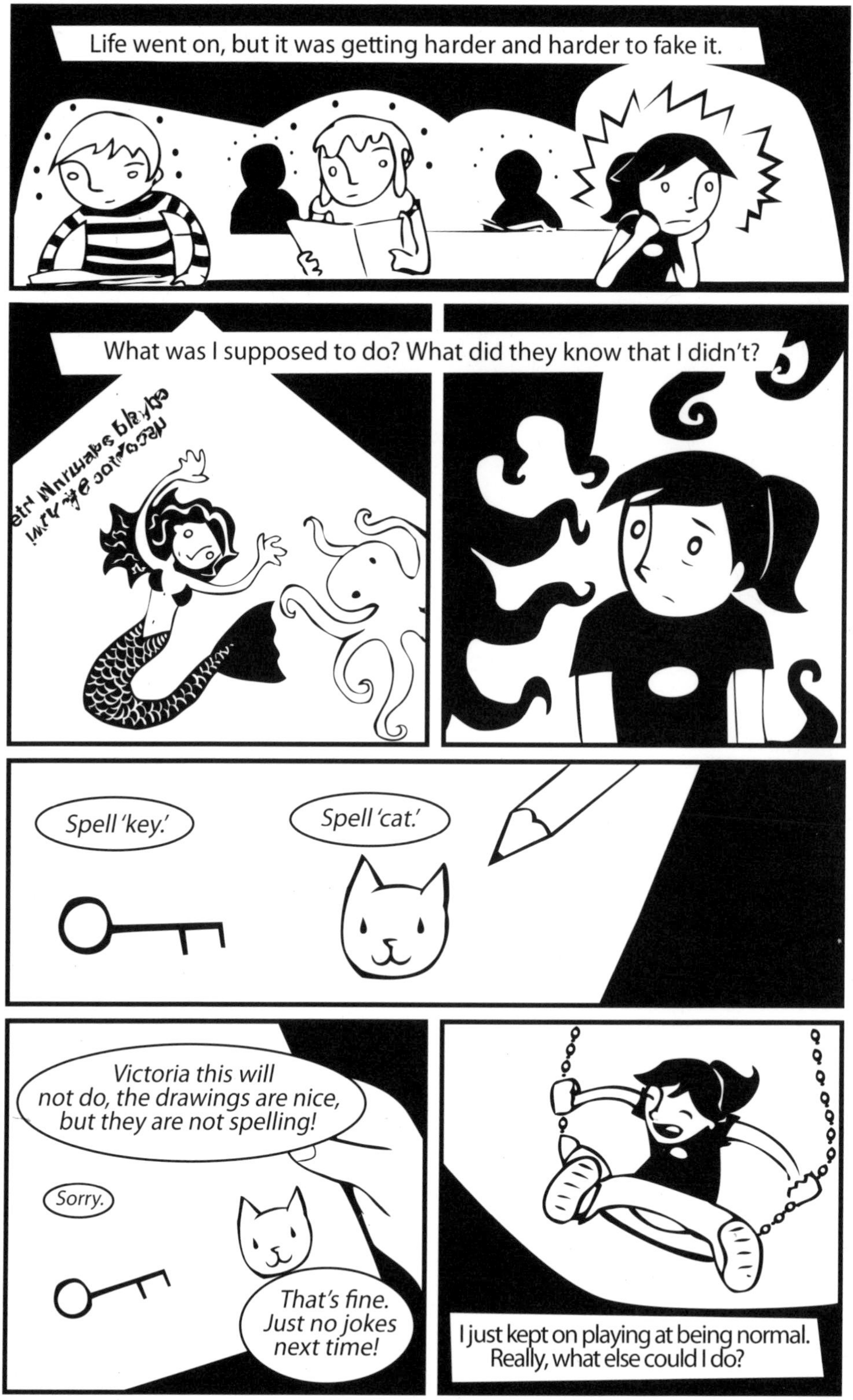
Life went on, but it was getting harder and harder to fake it.
What was I supposed to do? What did they know that I didn't?
Spell 'key.'
Spell 'cat.'
Victoria this will not do, the drawings are nice, but they are not spelling!
Sorry.
That's fine. Just no jokes next time!
I just kept on playing at being normal. Really, what else could I do?

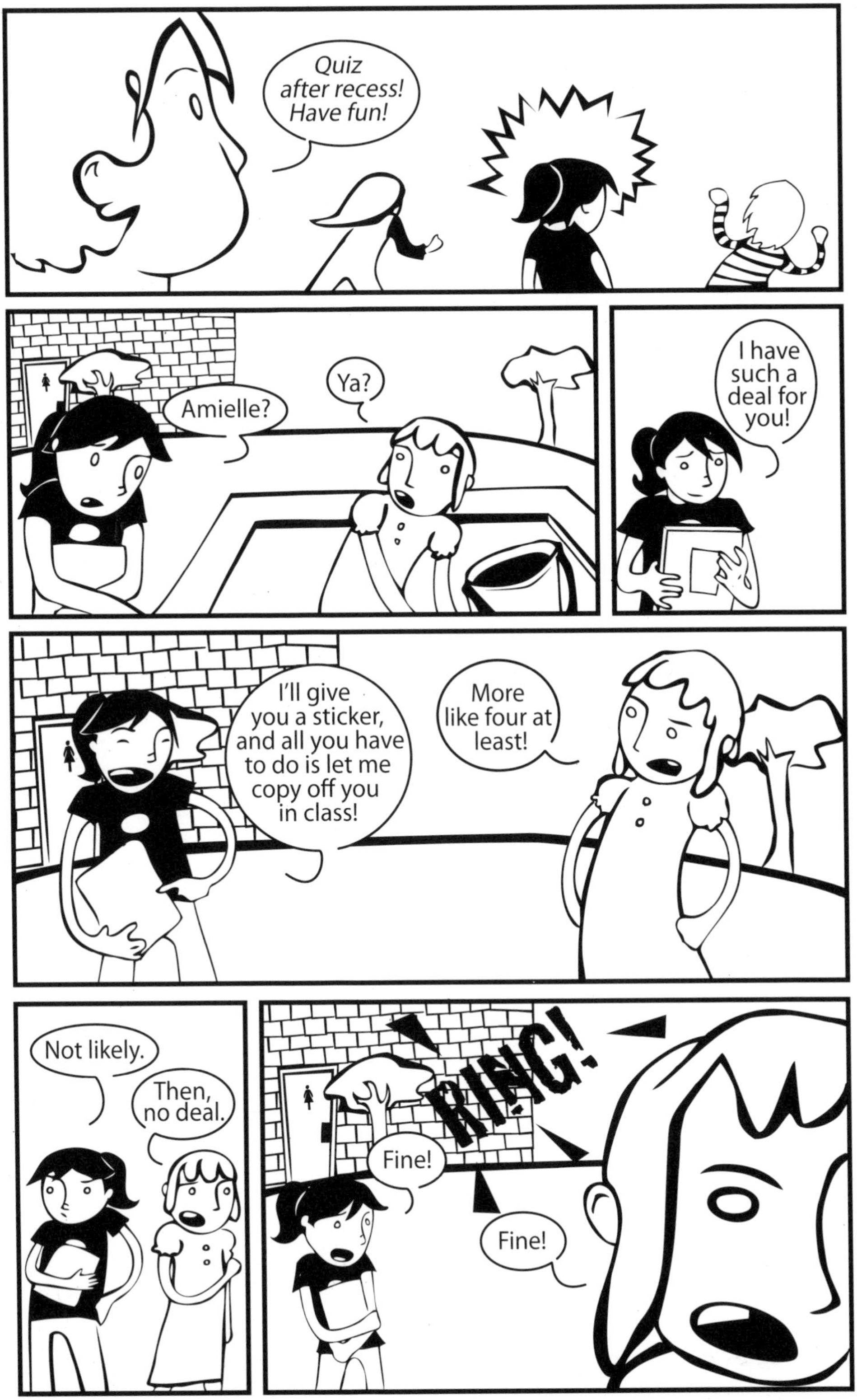
Quiz after recess! Have fun!
Amielle?
Ya?
I have such a deal for you!
I'll give you a sticker, and all you have to do is let me copy off you in class!
More like four at least!
Not likely.
Then, no deal.
RING!
Fine!
Fine!

walk
walk
walk
boy
boe
doe
blue
blue
blug
name: Amielle
walk
boe
blue
mouse
bote
walk
doe
blug
mouse
dote

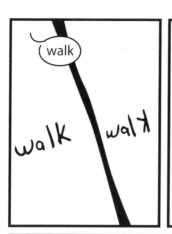

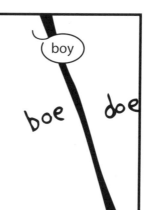

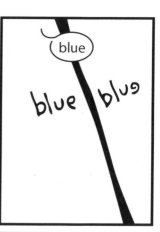

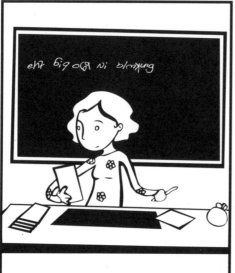

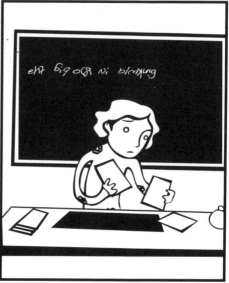

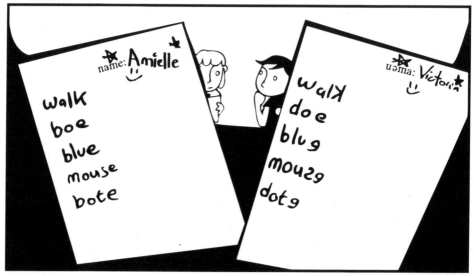

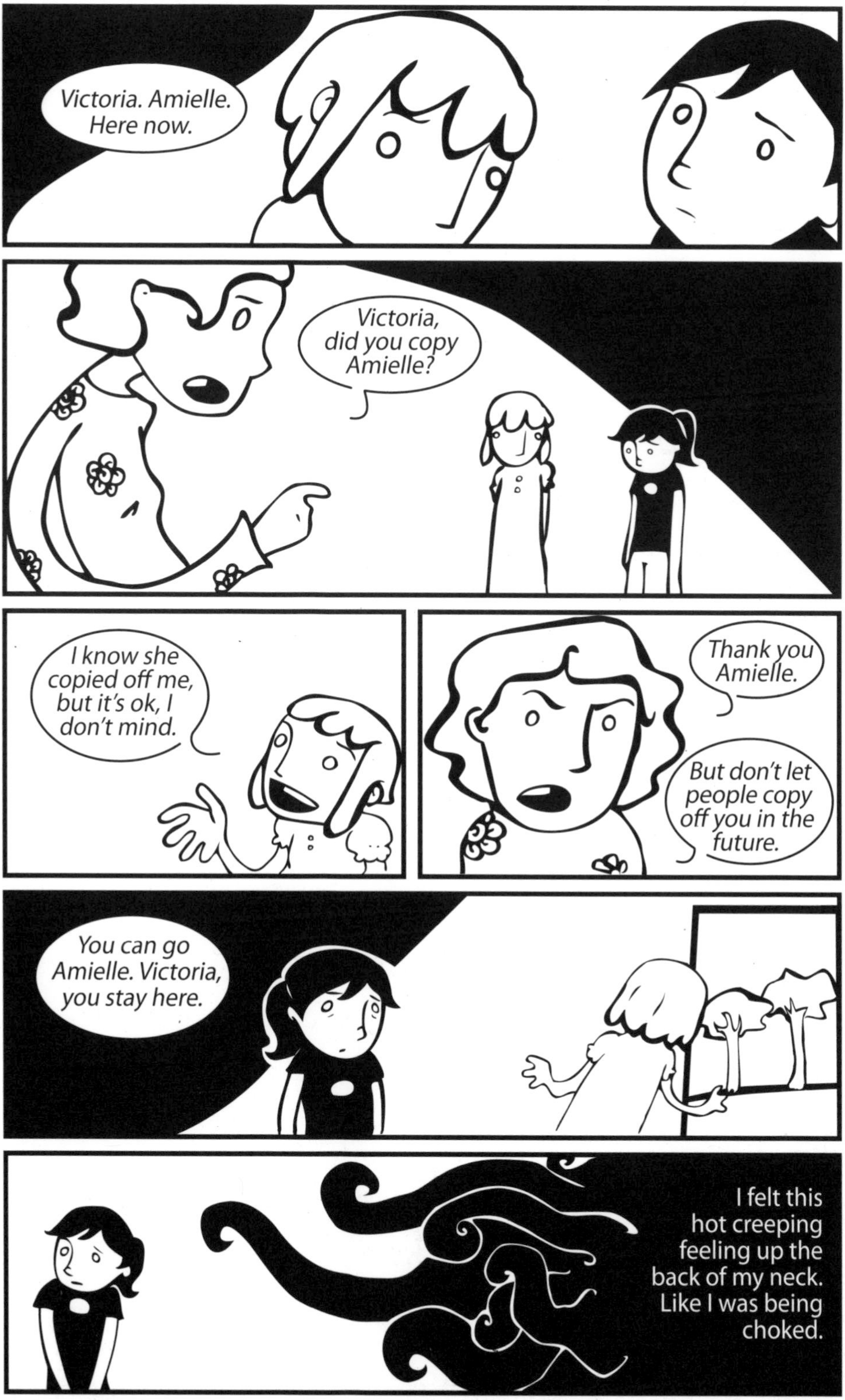
Victoria. Amielle. Here now.
Victoria, did you copy Amielle?
I know she copied off me, but it's ok, I don't mind.
Thank you Amielle.
But don't let people copy off you in the future.
You can go Amielle. Victoria, you stay here.
I felt this hot creeping feeling up the back of my neck. Like I was being choked.

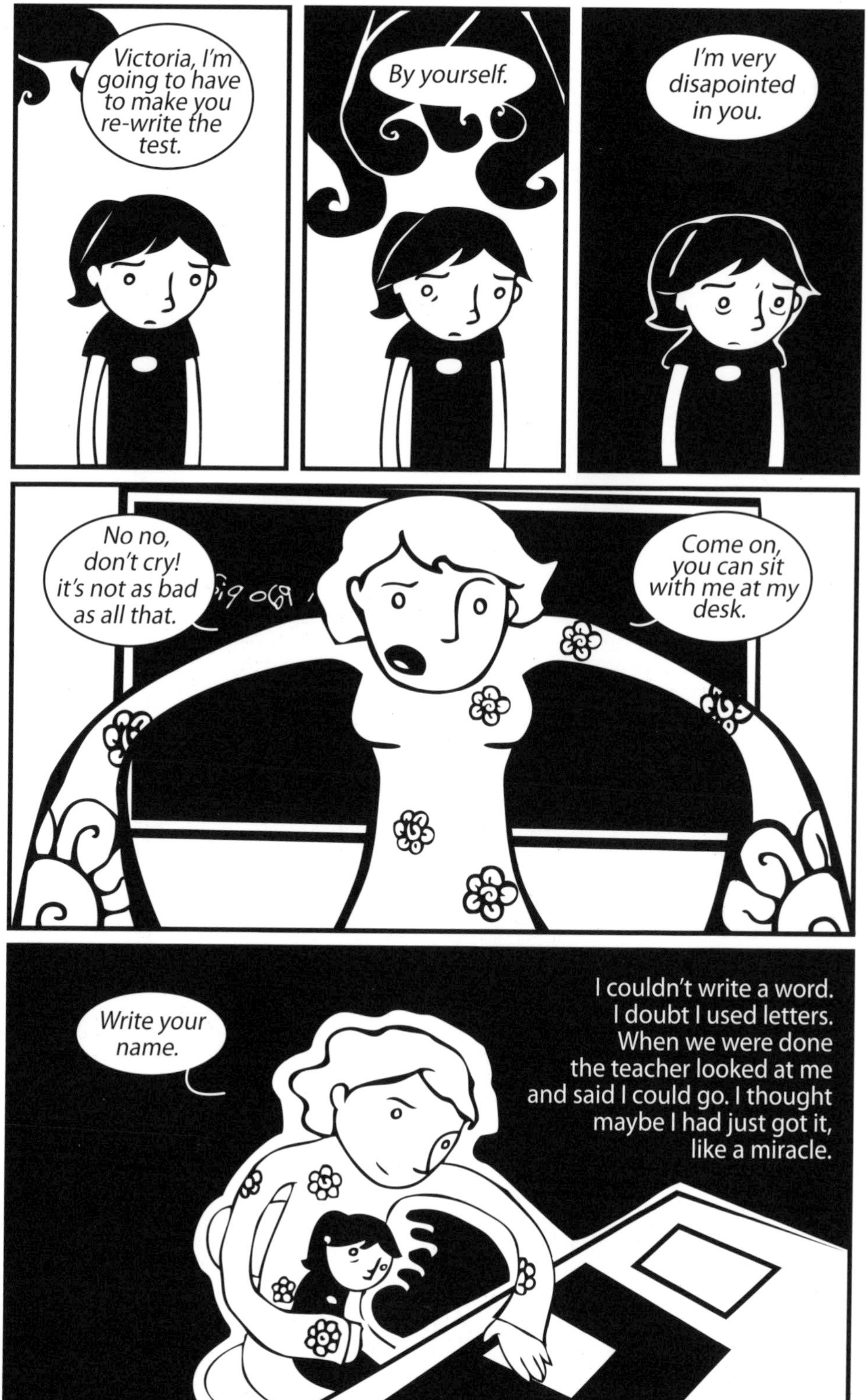
Victoria, I'm going to have to make you re-write the test.
By yourself.
I'm very disapointed in you.
No no, don't cry! it's not as bad as all that.
Come on, you can sit with me at my desk.
Write your name.
I couldn't write a word. I doubt I used letters. When we were done the teacher looked at me and said I could go. I thought maybe I had just got it, like a miracle.

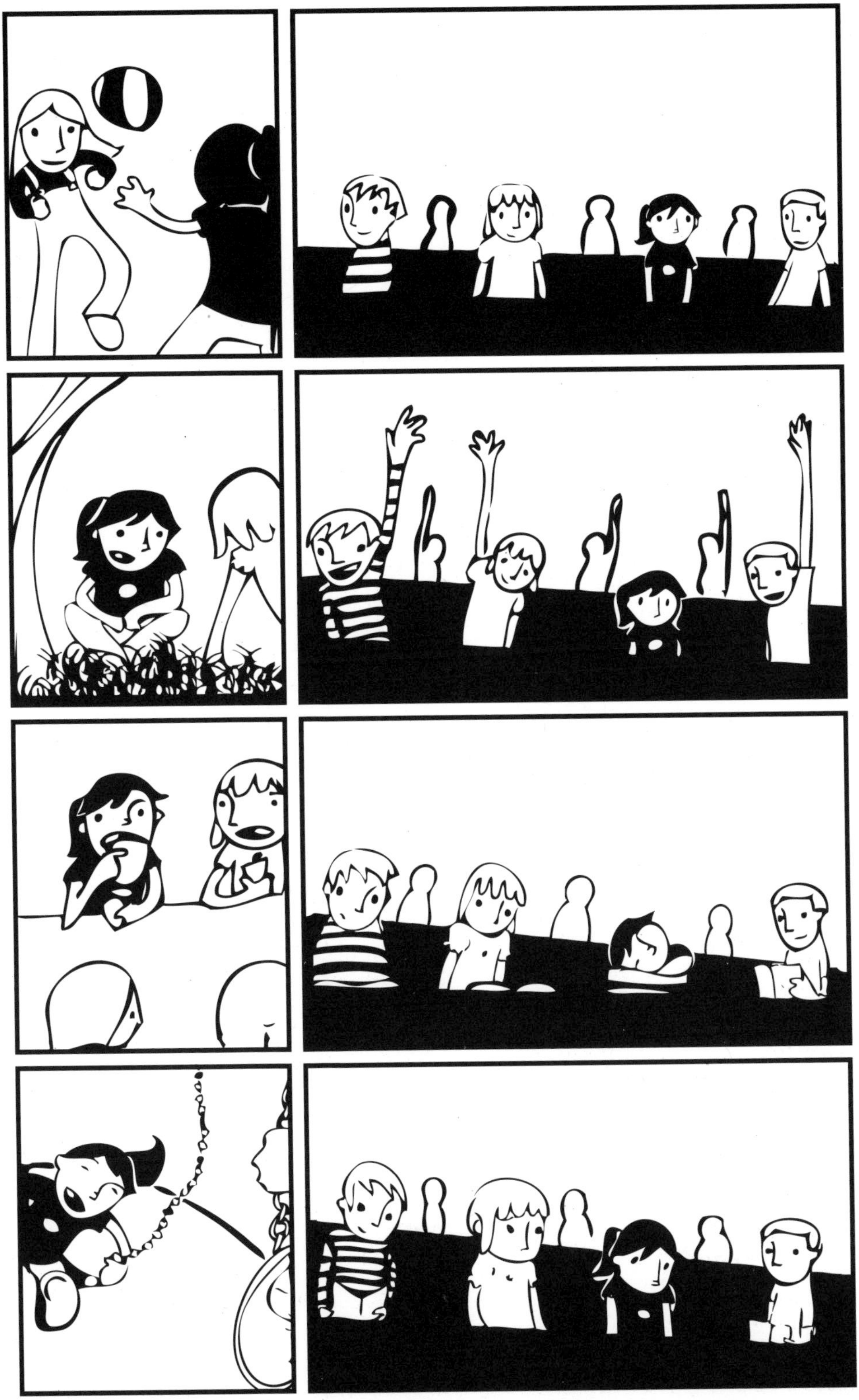

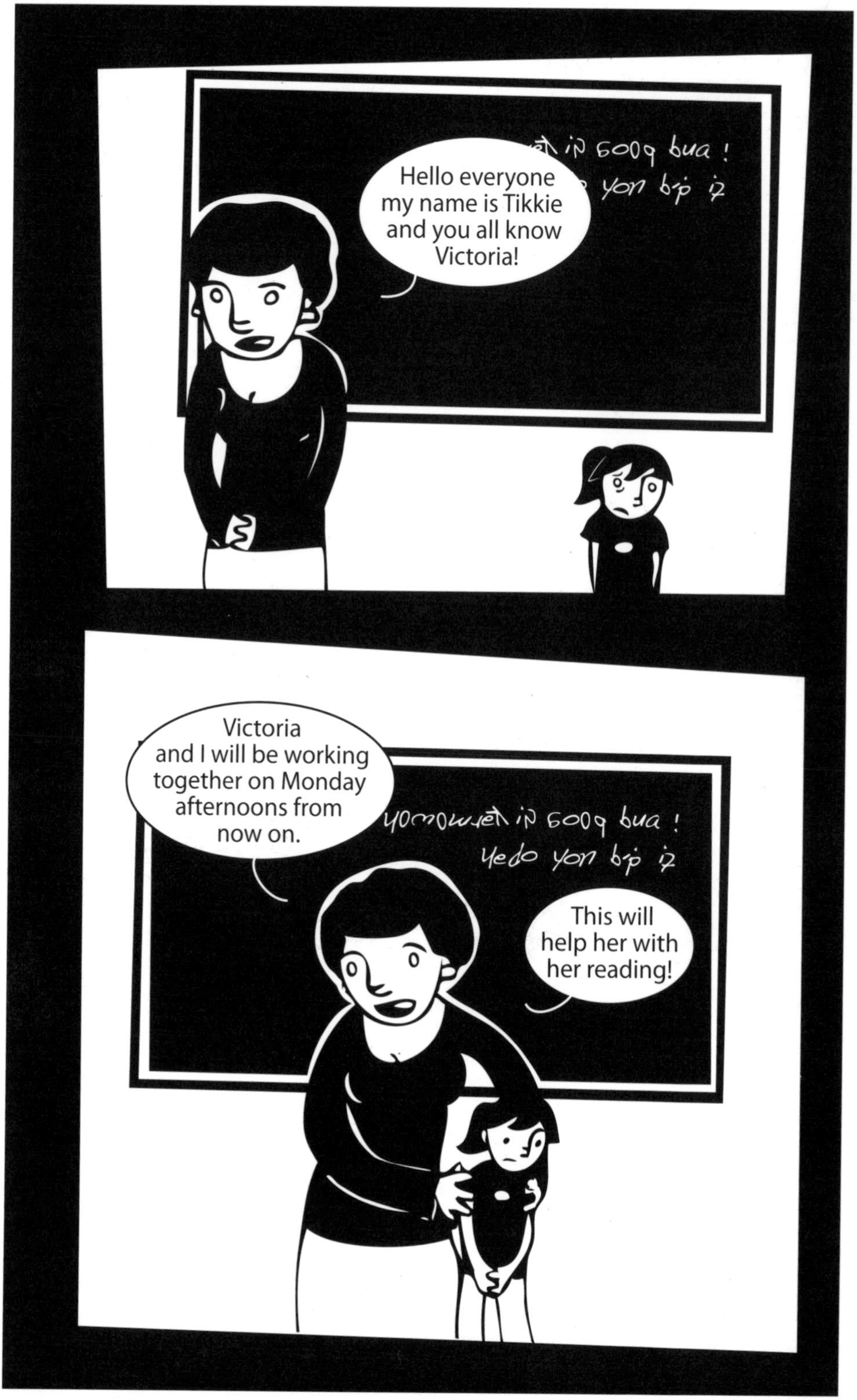
Hello everyone my name is Tikkie and you all know Victoria!
Victoria and I will be working together on Monday afternoons from now on.
This will help her with her reading!

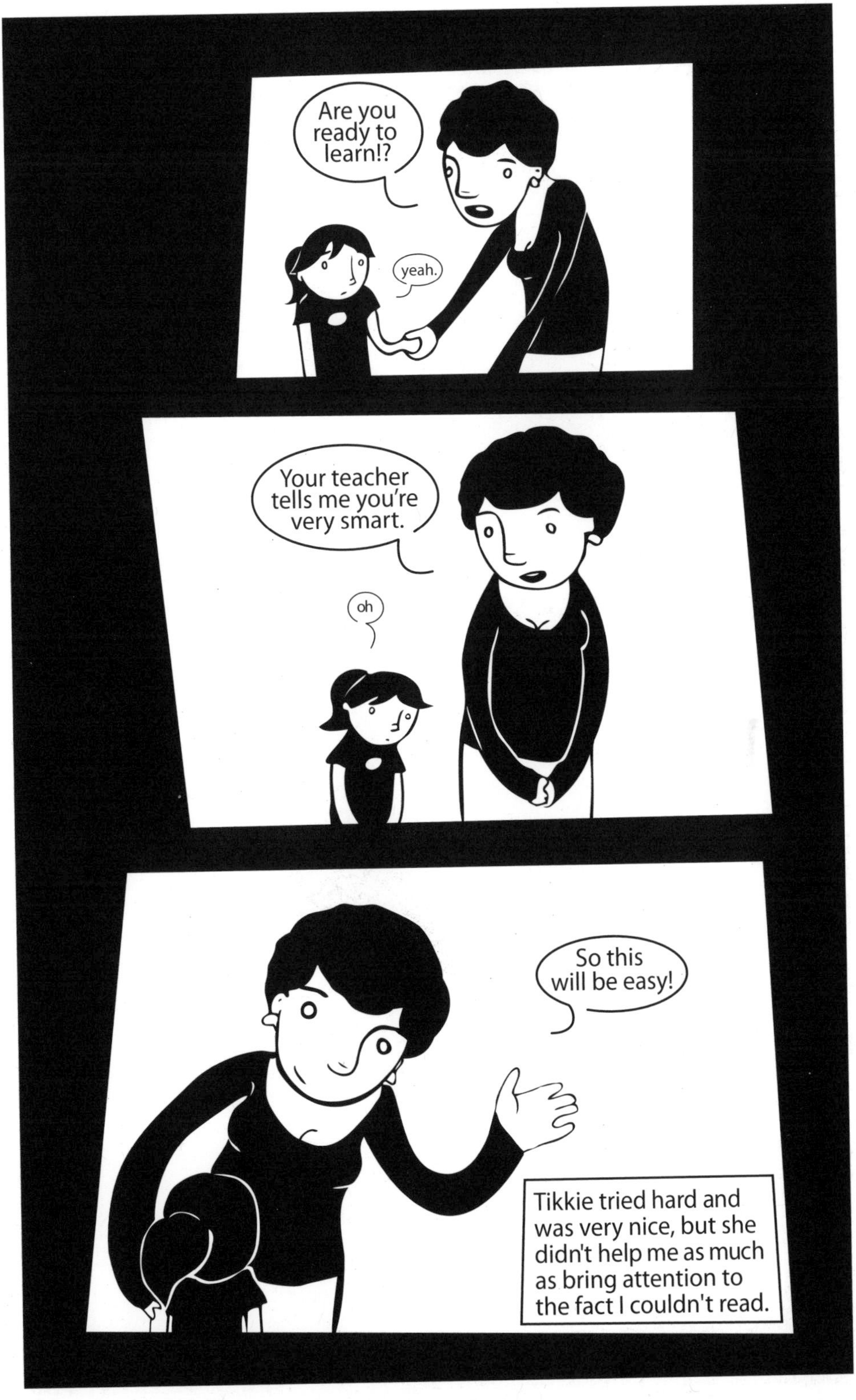
Are you ready to learn!?
yeah.
Your teacher tells me you're very smart.
oh
So this will be easy!
Tikkie tried hard and was very nice, but she didn't help me as much as bring attention to the fact I couldn't read.

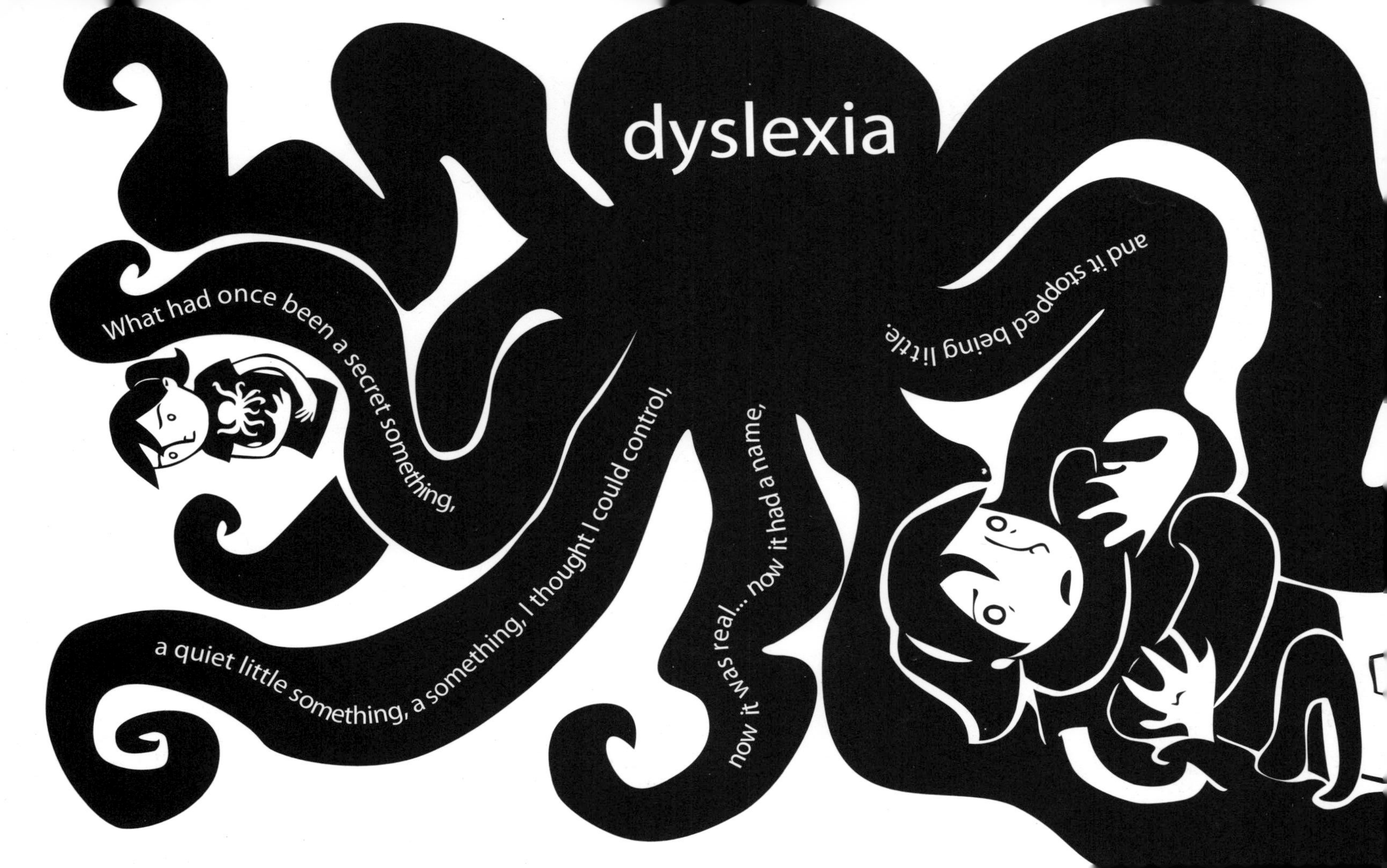
dyslexia
What had once been a secret something,
a quiet little something, a something, I thought I could control,
now it was real... now it had a name,
and it stopped being little.

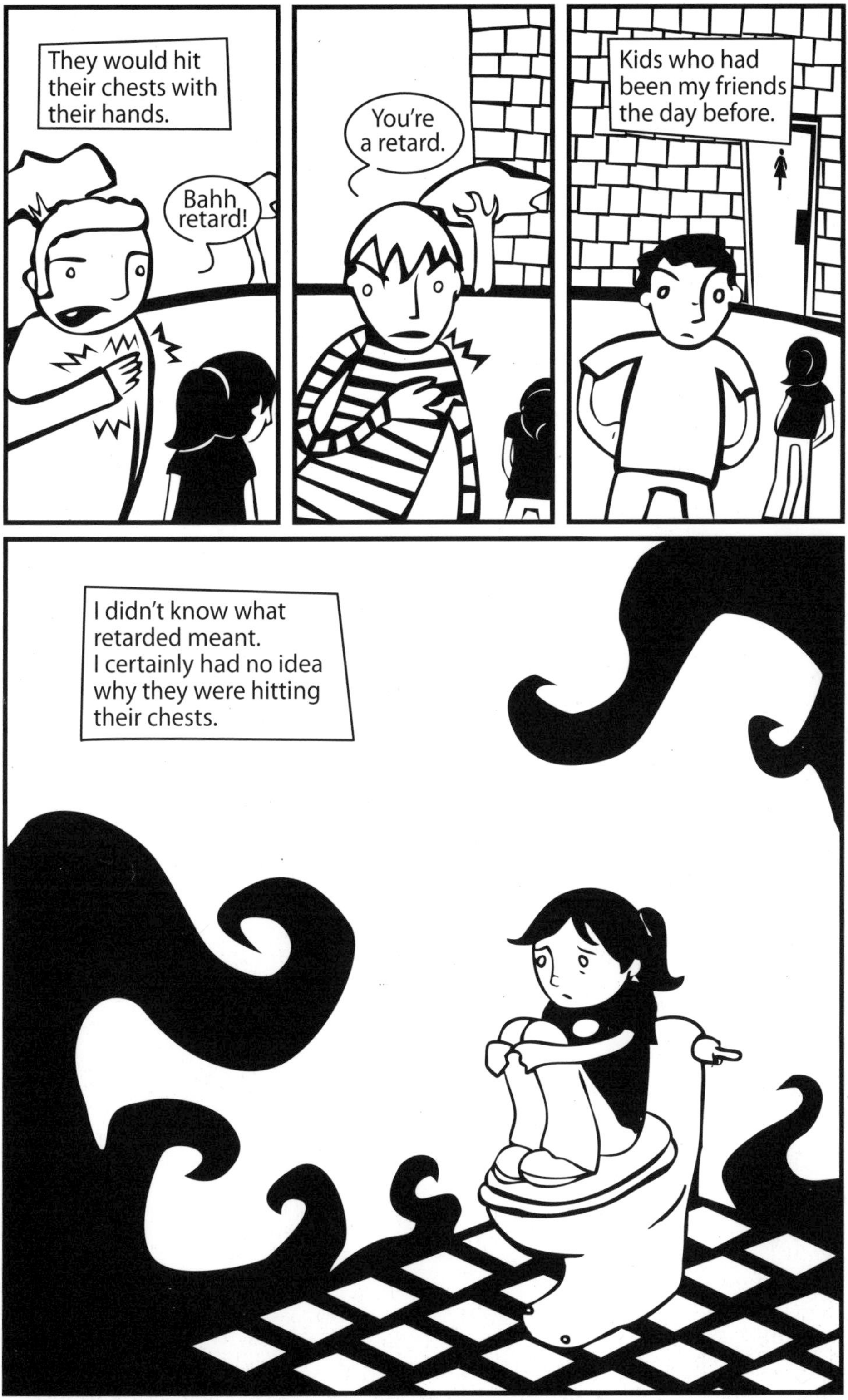
They would hit their chests with their hands.
Bahh retard!
You're a retard.
Kids who had been my friends the day before.
I didn't know what retarded meant. I certainly had no idea why they were hitting their chests.

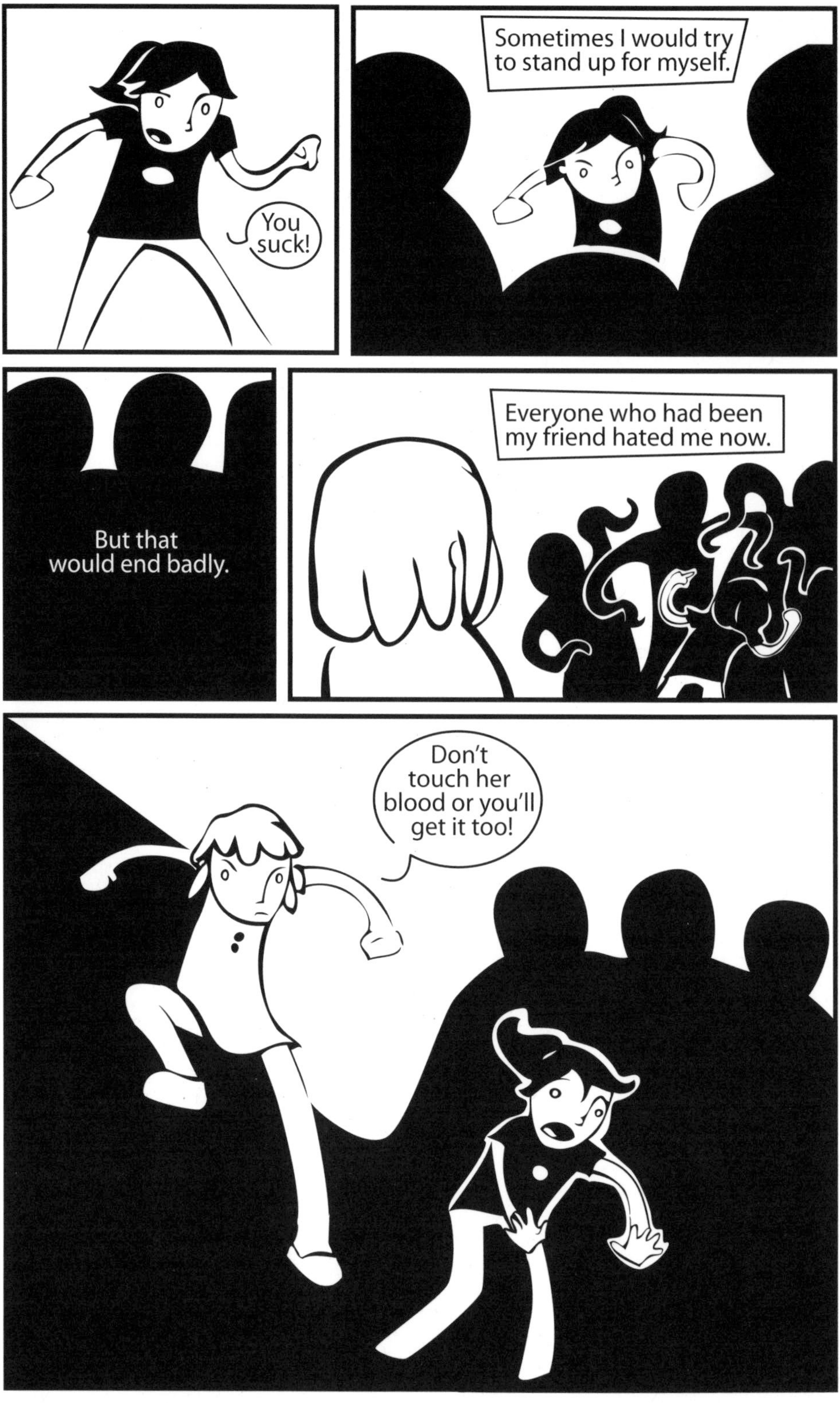
You suck!
Sometimes I would try to stand up for myself.
But that would end badly.
Everyone who had been my friend hated me now.
Don't touch her blood or you'll get it too!

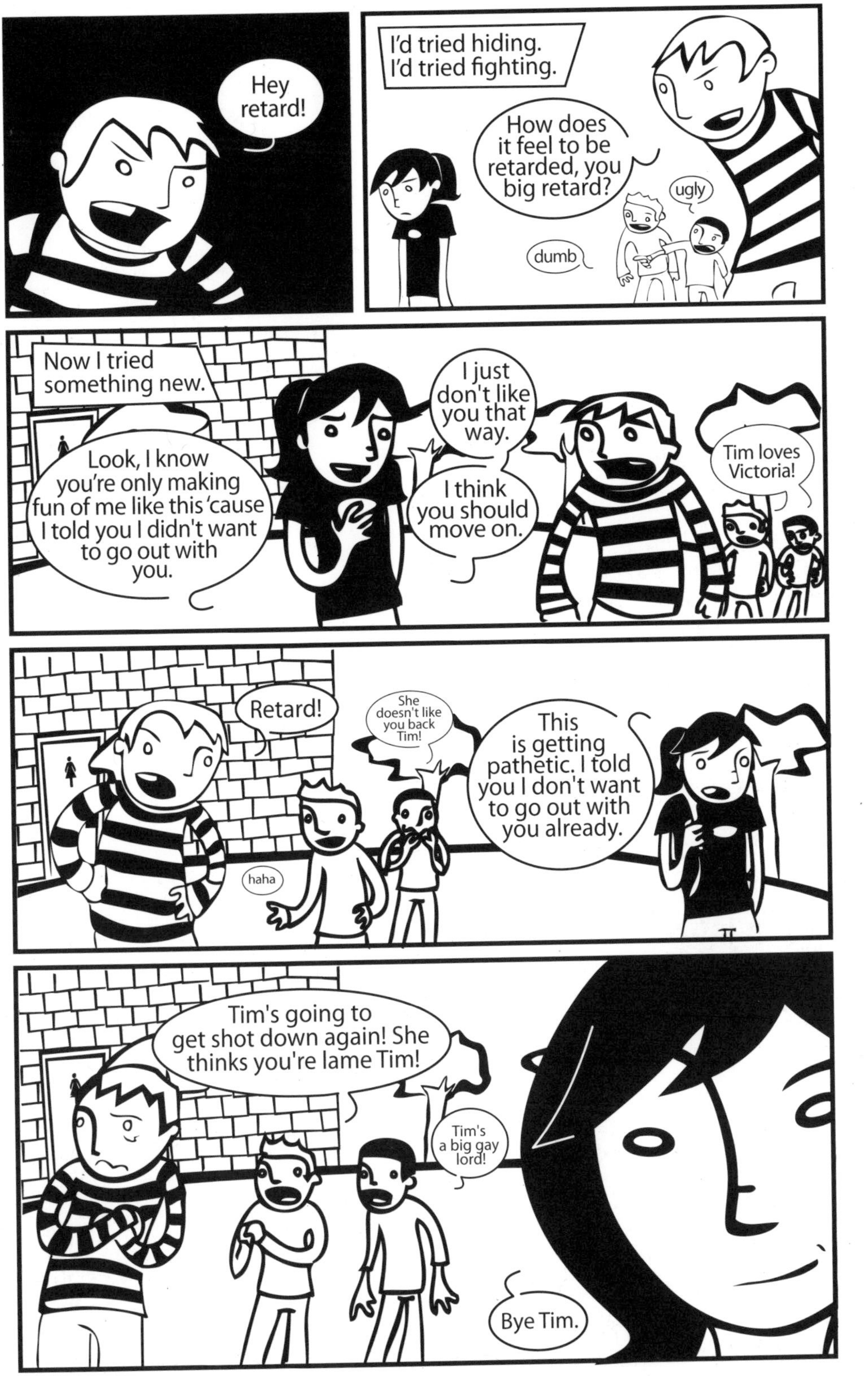
Hey retard!
I'd tried hiding. I'd tried fighting.
How does it feel to be retarded, you big retard?
ugly
dumb
Now I tried something new.
Look, I know you're only making fun of me like this 'cause I told you I didn't want to go out with you.
I just don't like you that way.
I think you should move on.
Tim loves Victoria!
Retard!
She doesn't like you back Tim!
haha
This is getting pathetic. I told you I don't want to go out with you already.
Tim's going to get shot down again! She thinks you're lame Tim!
Tim's a big gay lord!
Bye Tim.

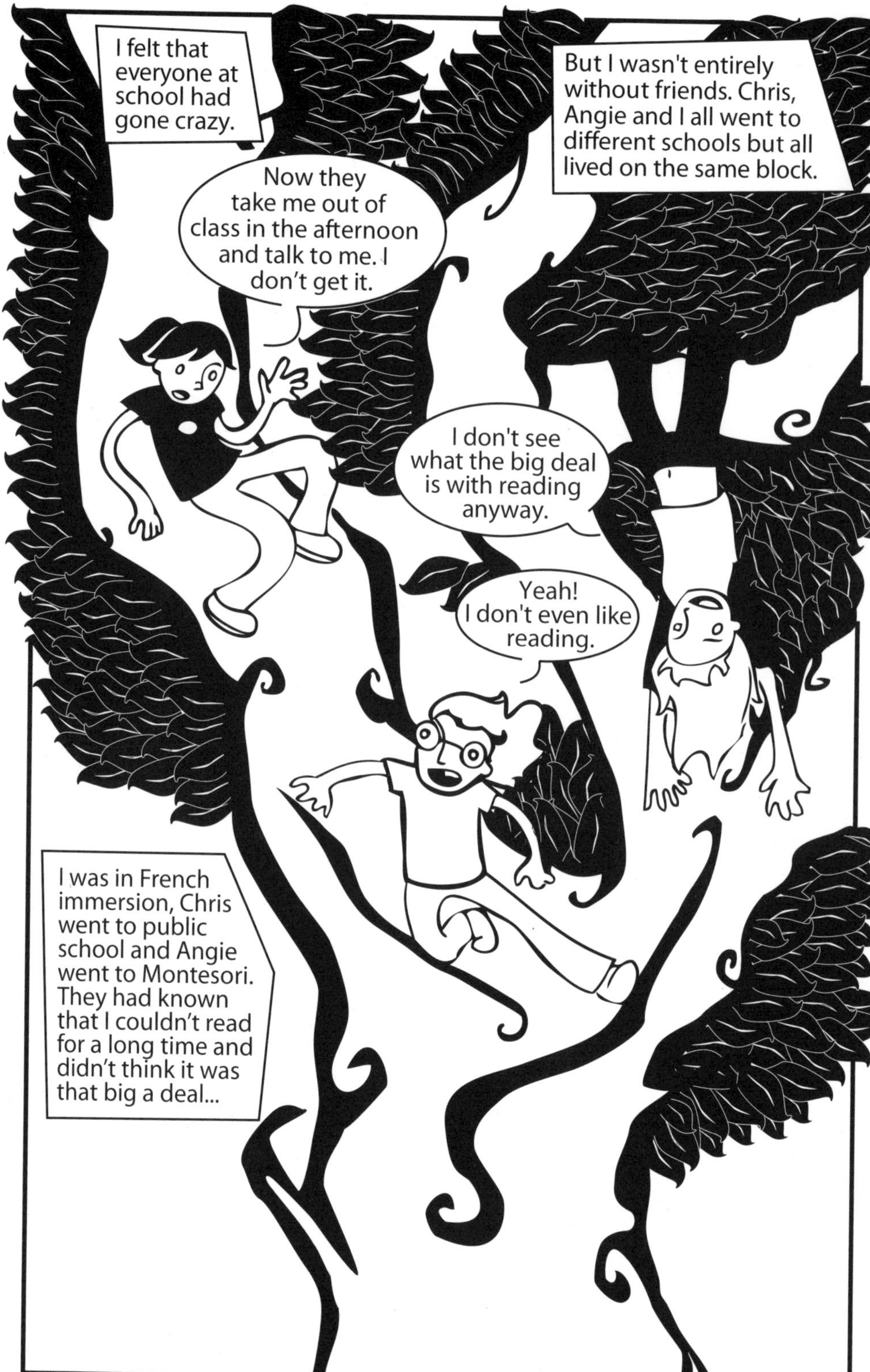
I felt that everyone at school had gone crazy.
Now they take me out of class in the afternoon and talk to me. I don't get it.
But I wasn't entirely without friends. Chris, Angie and I all went to different schools but all lived on the same block.
I don't see what the big deal is with reading anyway.
Yeah! I don't even like reading.
I was in French immersion, Chris went to public school and Angie went to Montesori. They had known that I couldn't read for a long time and didn't think it was that big a deal...

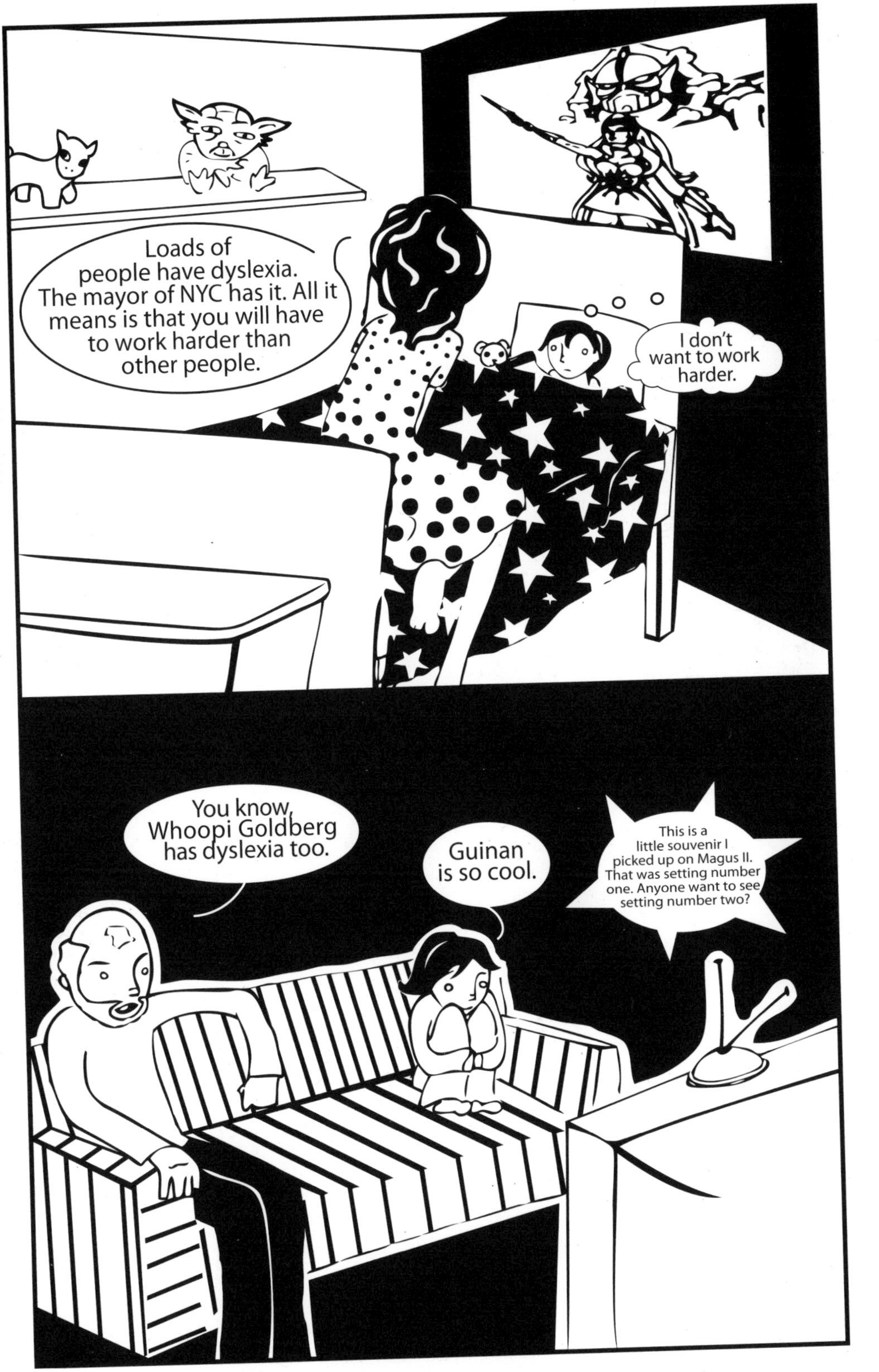
Loads of people have dyslexia. The mayor of NYC has it. All it means is that you will have to work harder than other people.
I don't want to work harder.
You know, Whoopi Goldberg has dyslexia too.
Guinan is so cool.
This is a little souvenir I picked up on Magus II. That was setting number one. Anyone want to see setting number two?

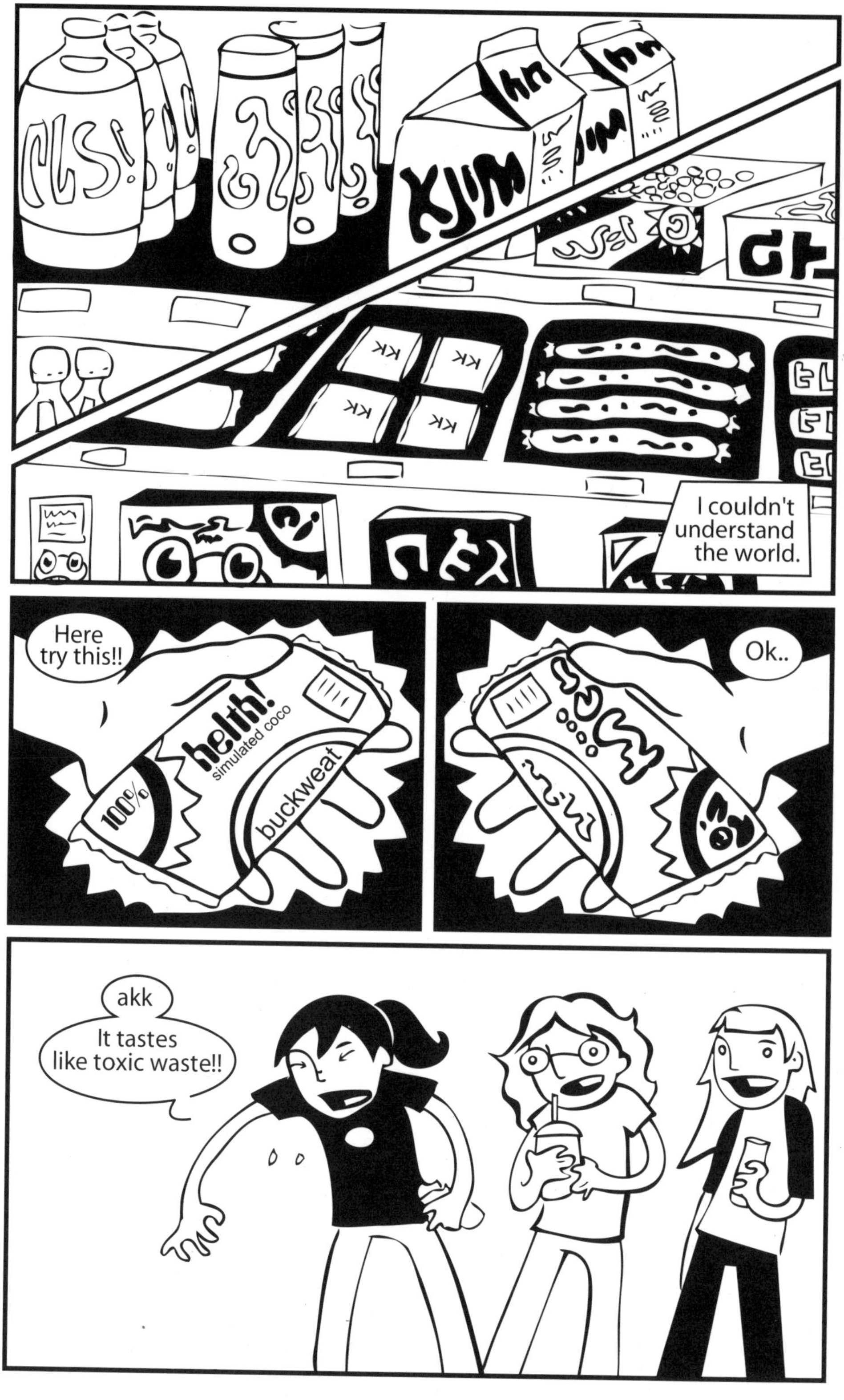

I couldn't understand the world.
Here try this!!
helth!
simulated coco
100%
buckweat
Ok..
akk
It tastes like toxic waste!!

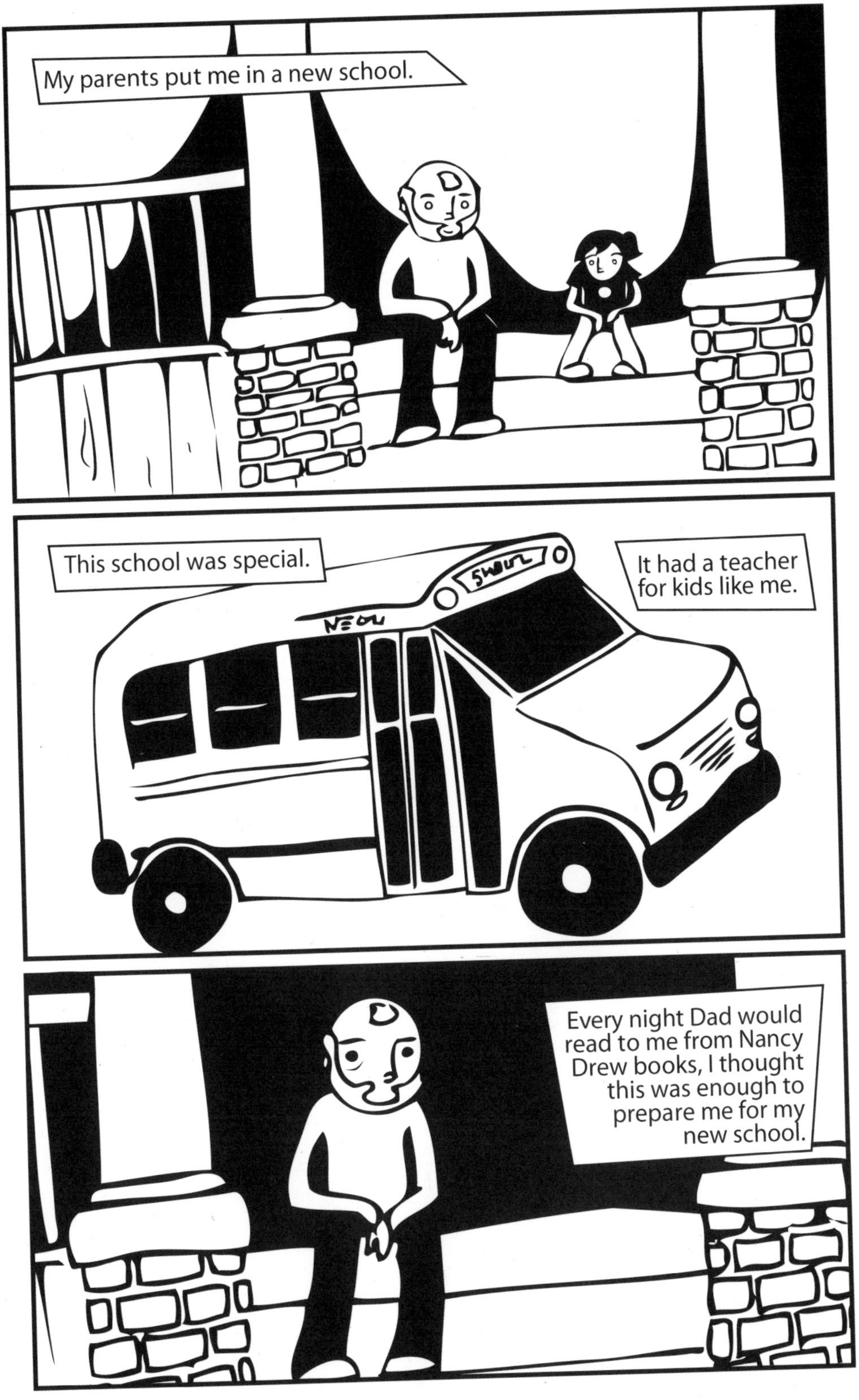
My parents put me in a new school.
This school was special.
It had a teacher for kids like me.
Every night Dad would read to me from Nancy Drew books, I thought this was enough to prepare me for my new school.

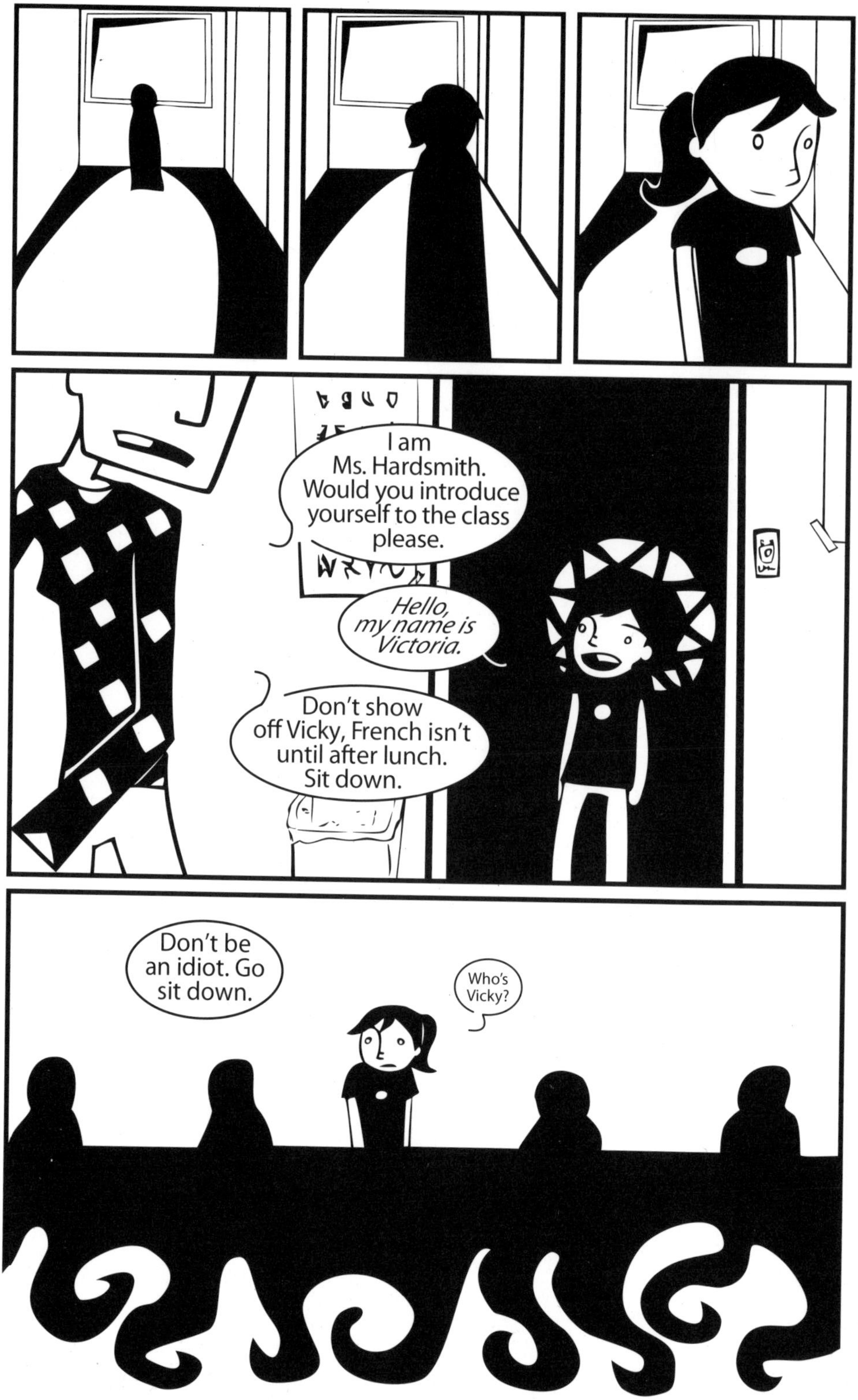
I am Ms. Hardsmith. Would you introduce yourself to the class please.
Hello, my name is Victoria.
Don't show off Vicky, French isn't until after lunch. Sit down.
Don't be an idiot. Go sit down.
Who's Vicky?

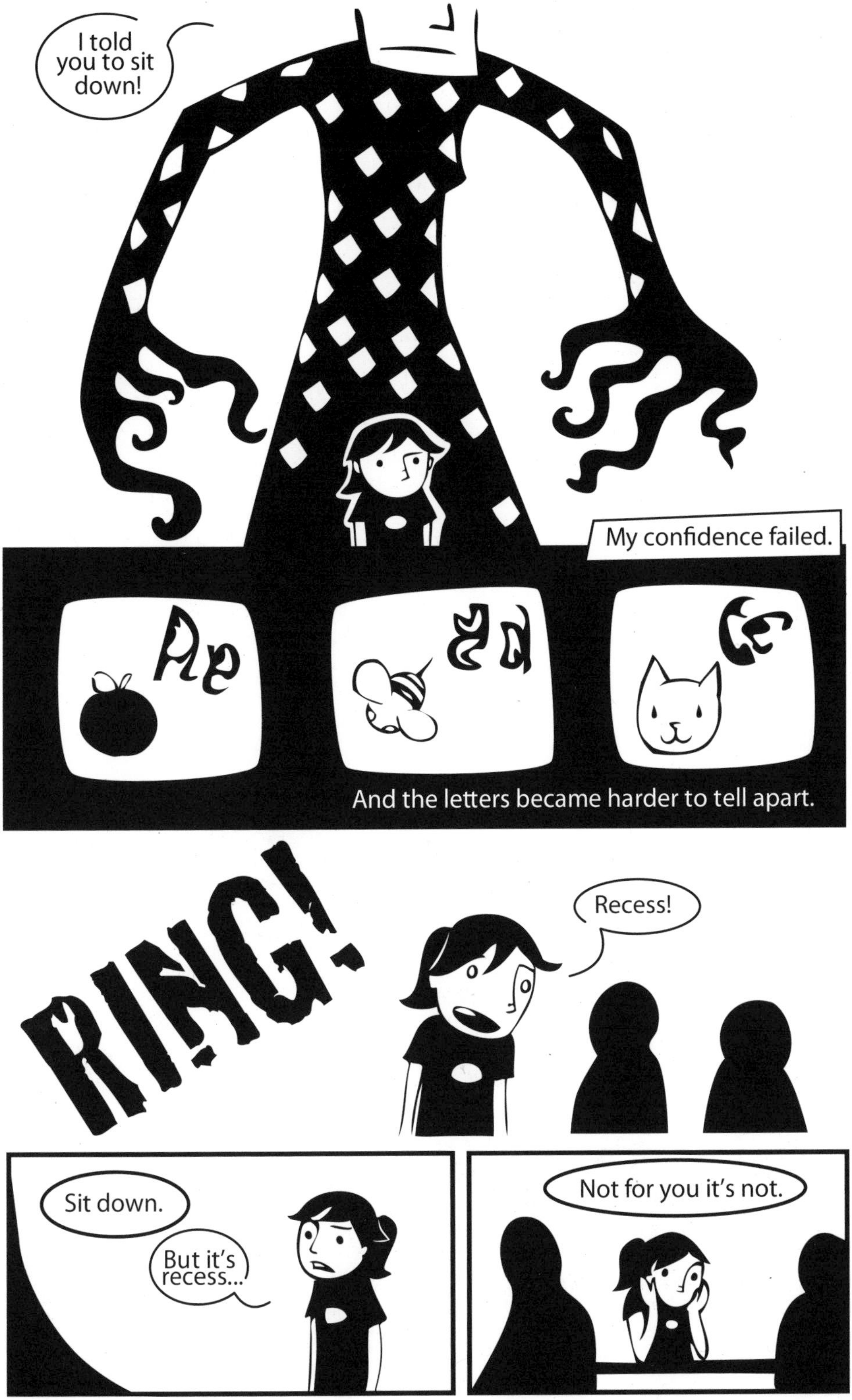
I told you to sit down!
My confidence failed.
And the letters became harder to tell apart.
RING!
Recess!
Sit down.
But it's recess...
Not for you it's not.

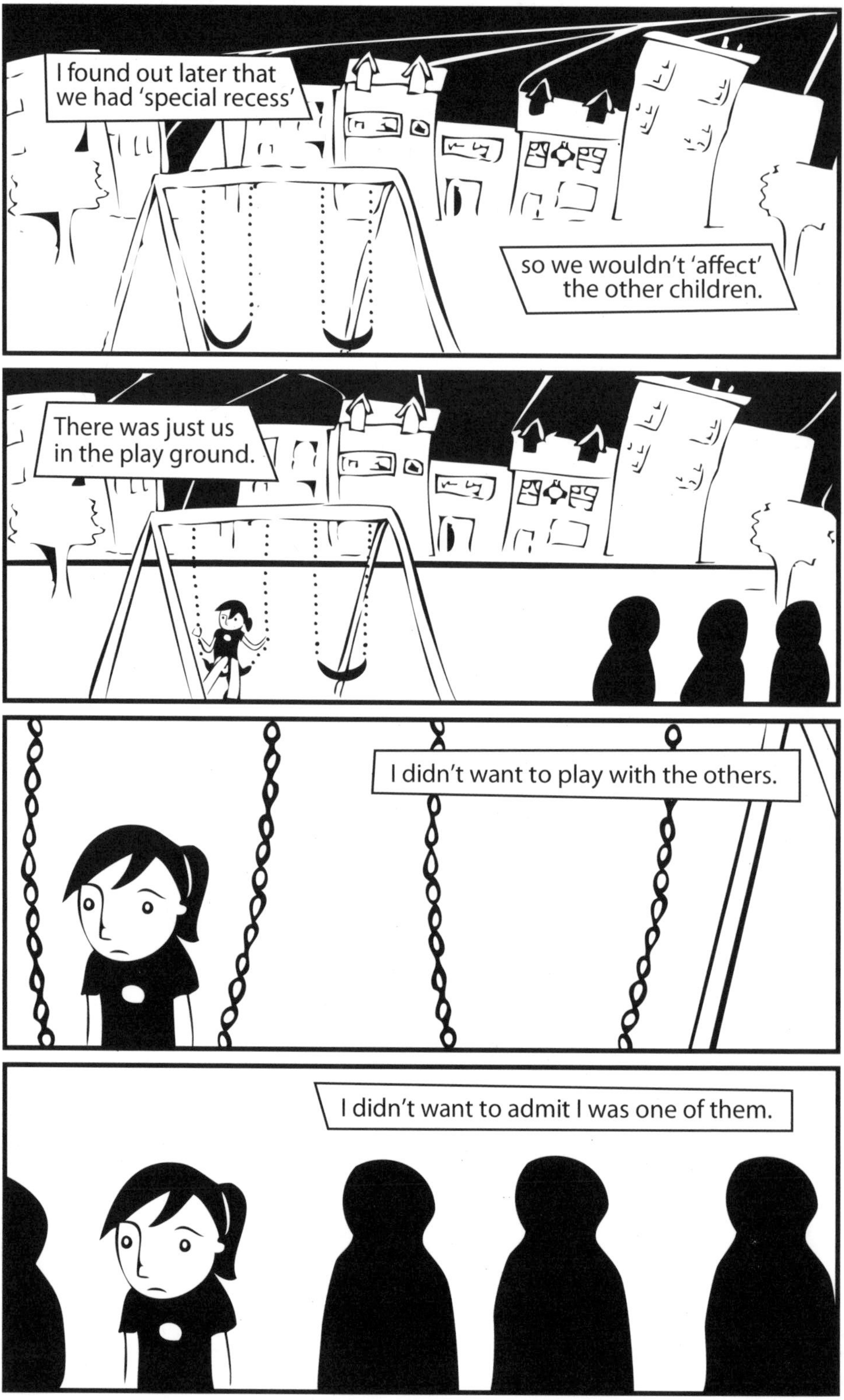
I found out later that we had 'special recess'
so we wouldn't 'affect' the other children.
There was just us in the play ground.
I didn't want to play with the others.
I didn't want to admit I was one of them.

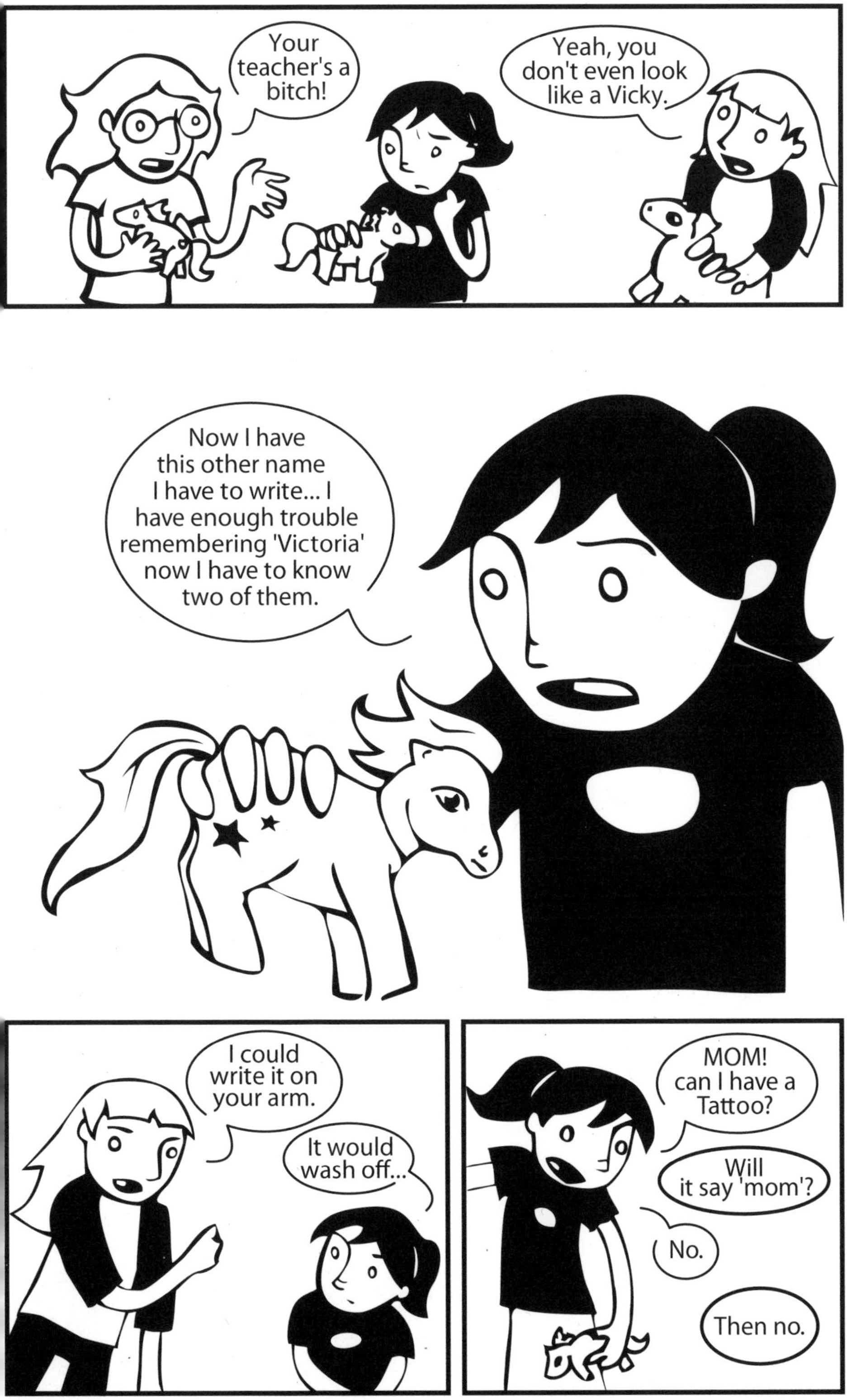
Your teacher's a bitch!
Yeah, you don't even look like a Vicky.
Now I have this other name I have to write... I have enough trouble remembering 'Victoria' now I have to know two of them.
I could write it on your arm.
It would wash off...
MOM! can I have a Tattoo?
Will it say 'mom'?
No.
Then no.

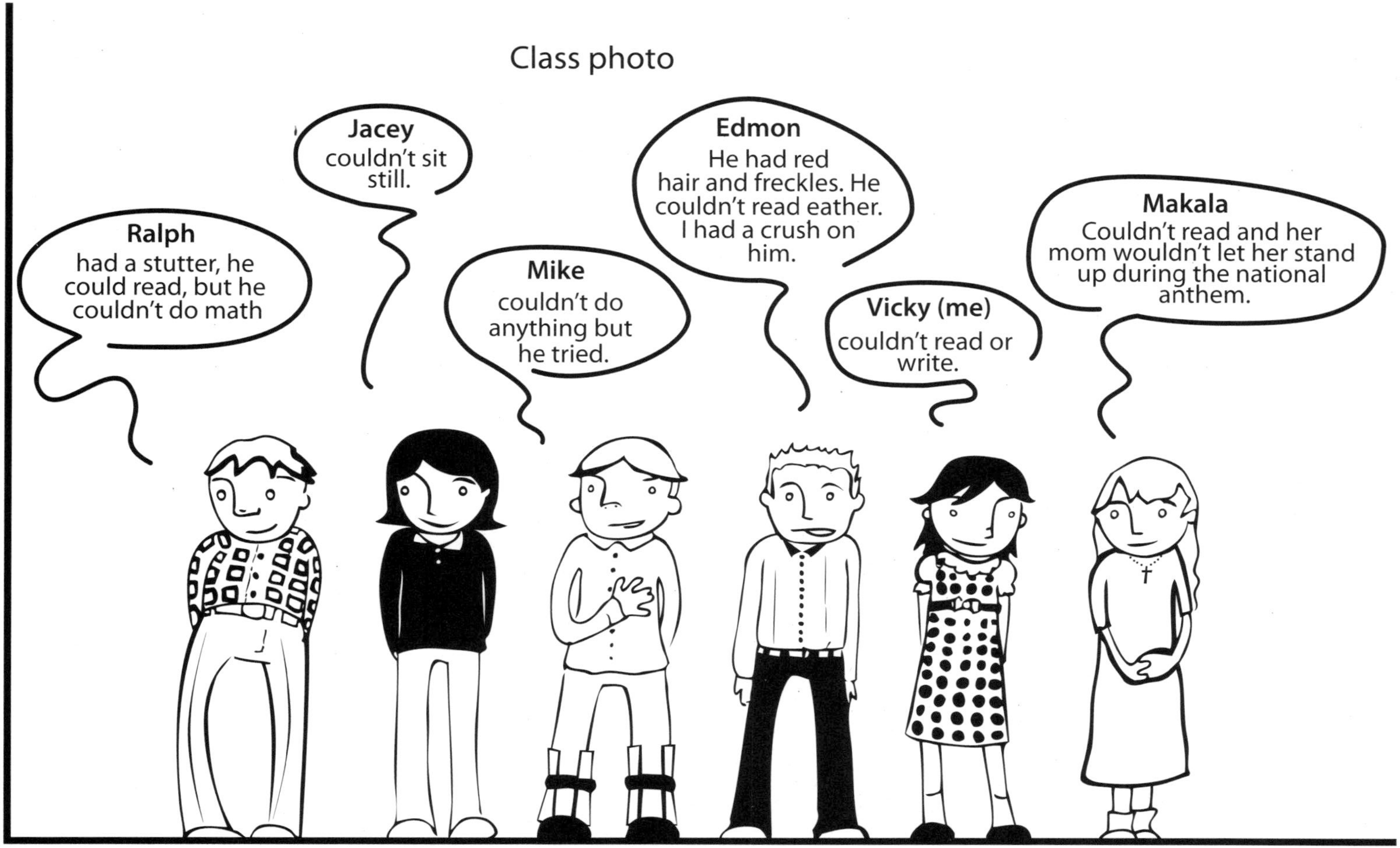
Class photo
Ralph had a stutter, he could read, but he couldn't do math
Jacey couldn't sit still.
Mike couldn't do anything but he tried.
Edmon He had red hair and freckles. He couldn't read eather. I had a crush on him.
Vicky (me) couldn't read or write.
Makala Couldn't read and her mom wouldn't let her stand up during the national anthem.

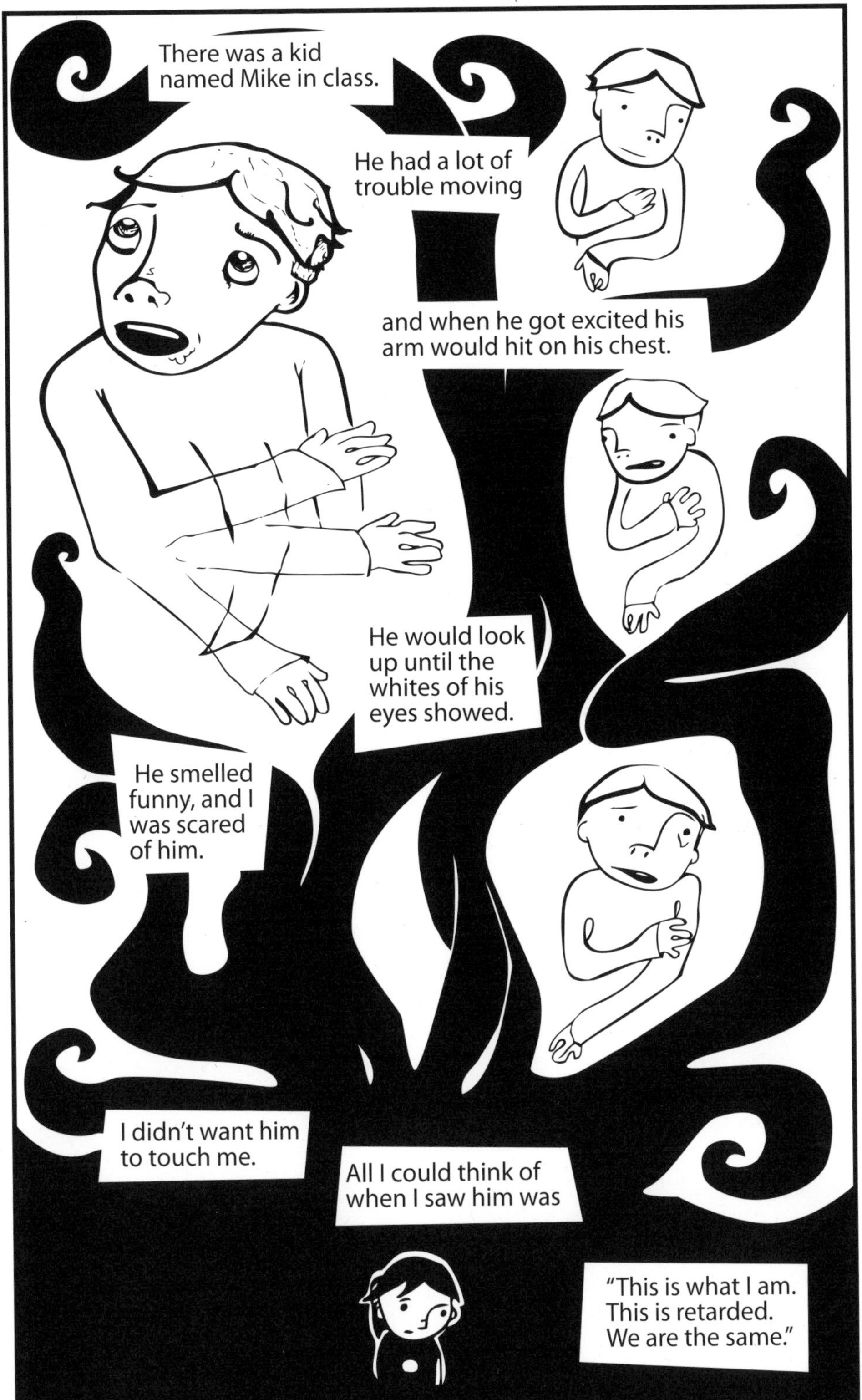
There was a kid named Mike in class.
He had a lot of trouble moving
and when he got excited his arm would hit on his chest.
He would look up until the whites of his eyes showed.
He smelled funny, and I was scared of him.
I didn't want him to touch me.
All I could think of when I saw him was
"This is what I am. This is retarded. We are the same."

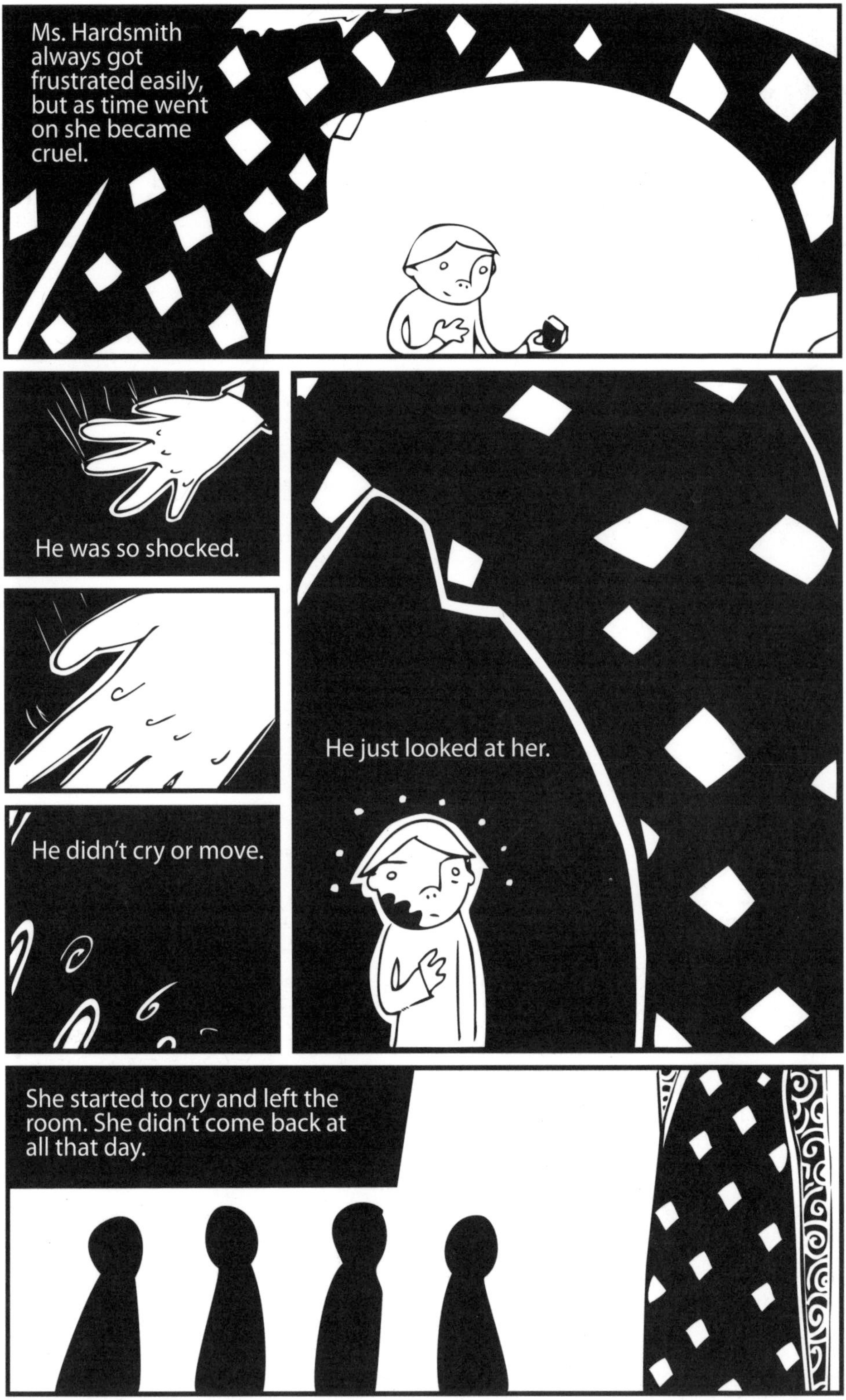
Ms. Hardsmith always got frustrated easily, but as time went on she became cruel.
He was so shocked.
He didn't cry or move.
He just looked at her.
She started to cry and left the room. She didn't come back at all that day.

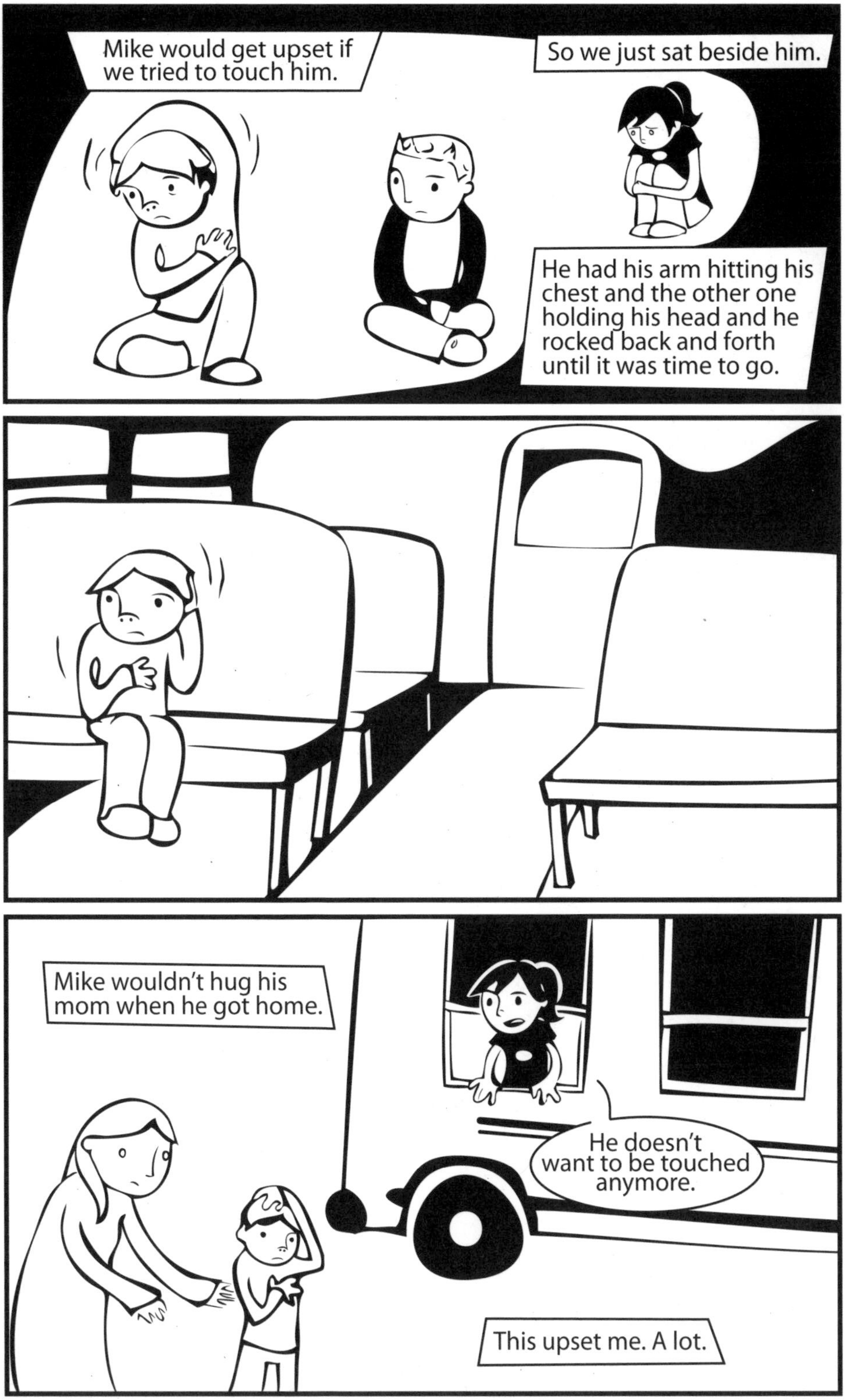
Mike would get upset if we tried to touch him.
So we just sat beside him.
He had his arm hitting his chest and the other one holding his head and he rocked back and forth until it was time to go.
Mike wouldn't hug his mom when he got home.
He doesn't want to be touched anymore.
This upset me. A lot.

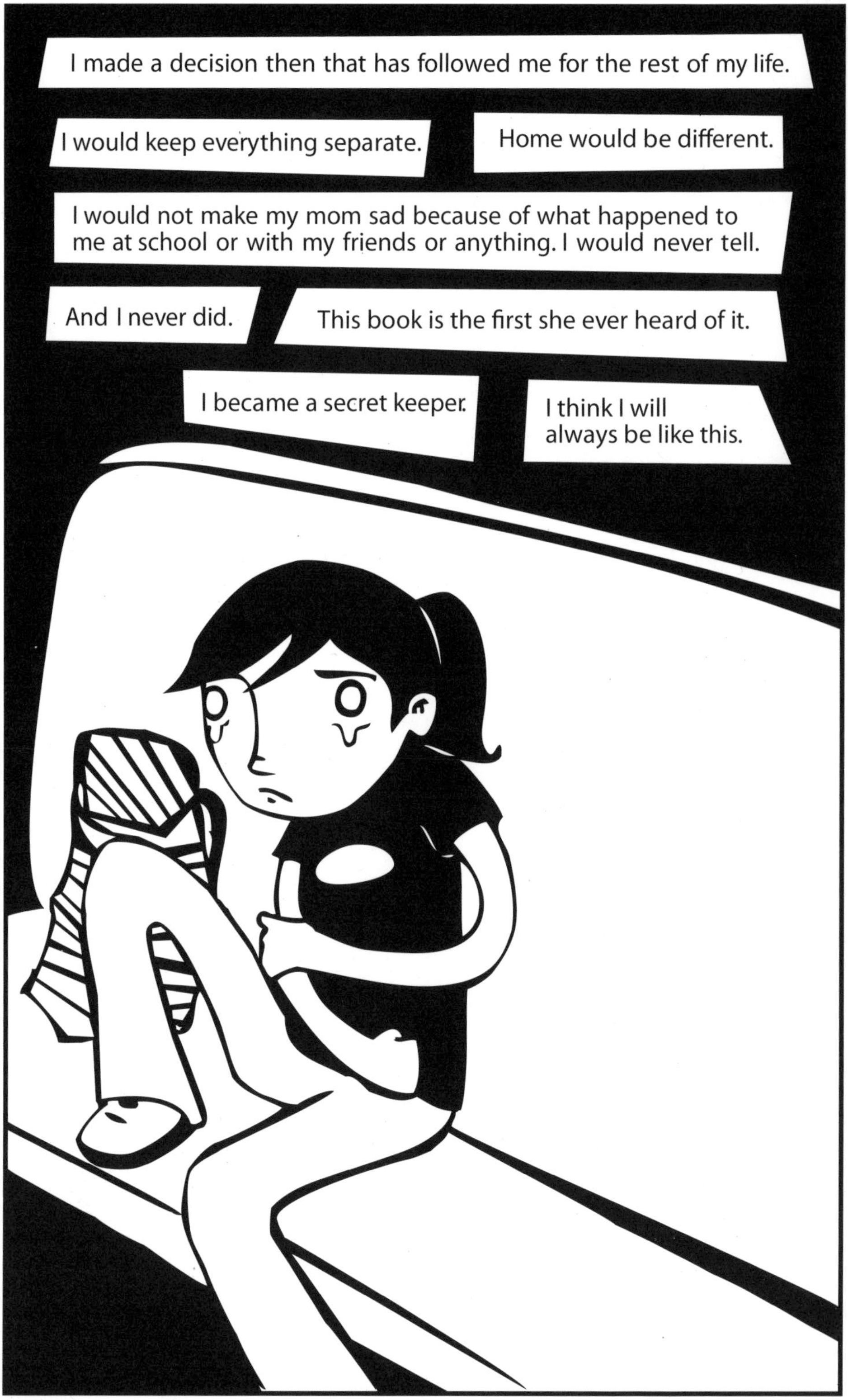
I made a decision then that has followed me for the rest of my life.
I would keep everything separate.
Home would be different.
I would not make my mom sad because of what happened to me at school or with my friends or anything. I would never tell.
And I never did.
This book is the first she ever heard of it.
I became a secret keeper.
I think I will always be like this.

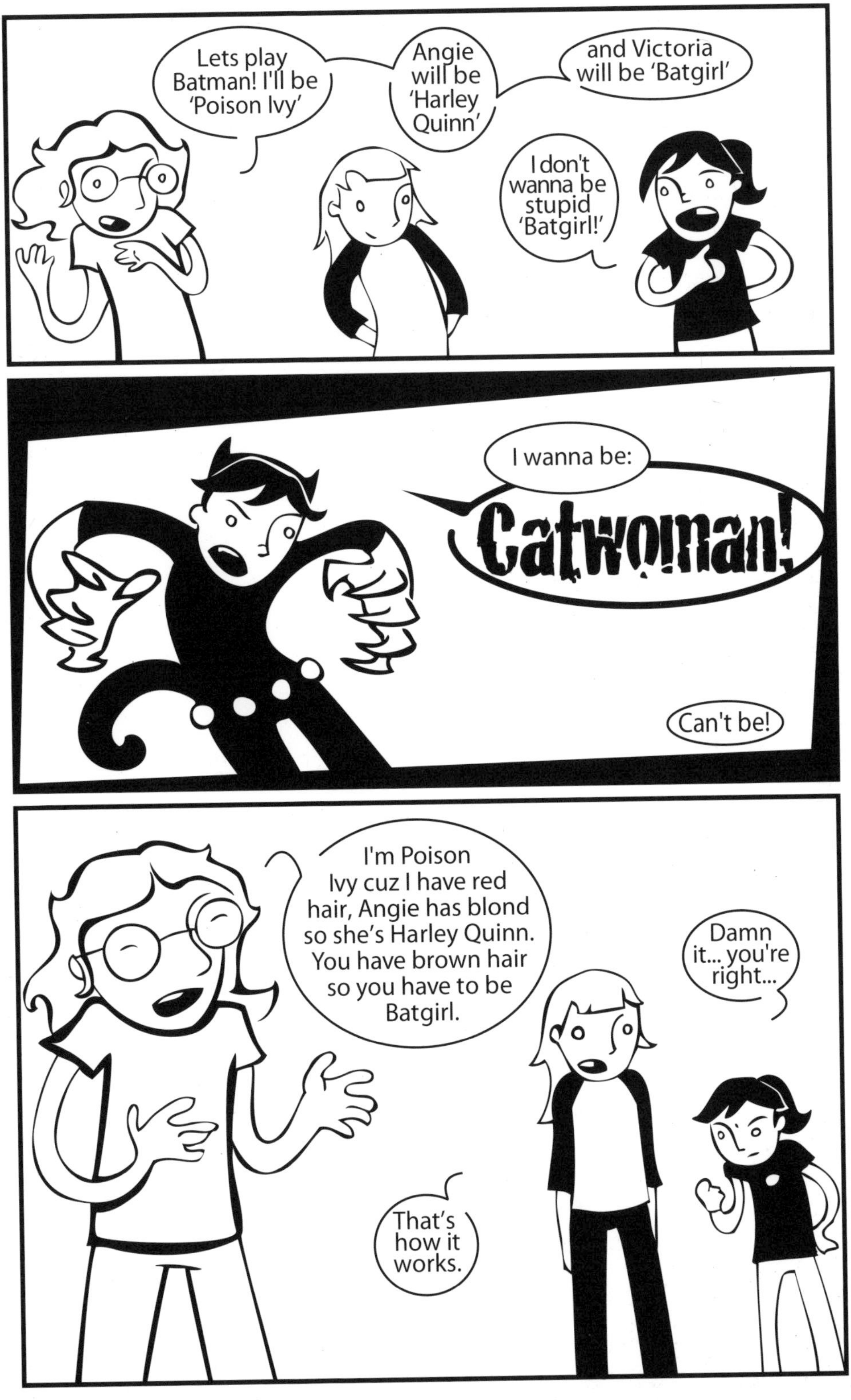
Lets play Batman! I'll be 'Poison Ivy'
Angie will be 'Harley Quinn'
and Victoria will be 'Batgirl'
I don't wanna be stupid 'Batgirl!'
I wanna be:
Catwoman!
Can't be!
I'm Poison Ivy cuz I have red hair, Angie has blond so she's Harley Quinn. You have brown hair so you have to be Batgirl.
That's how it works.
Damn it... you're right...

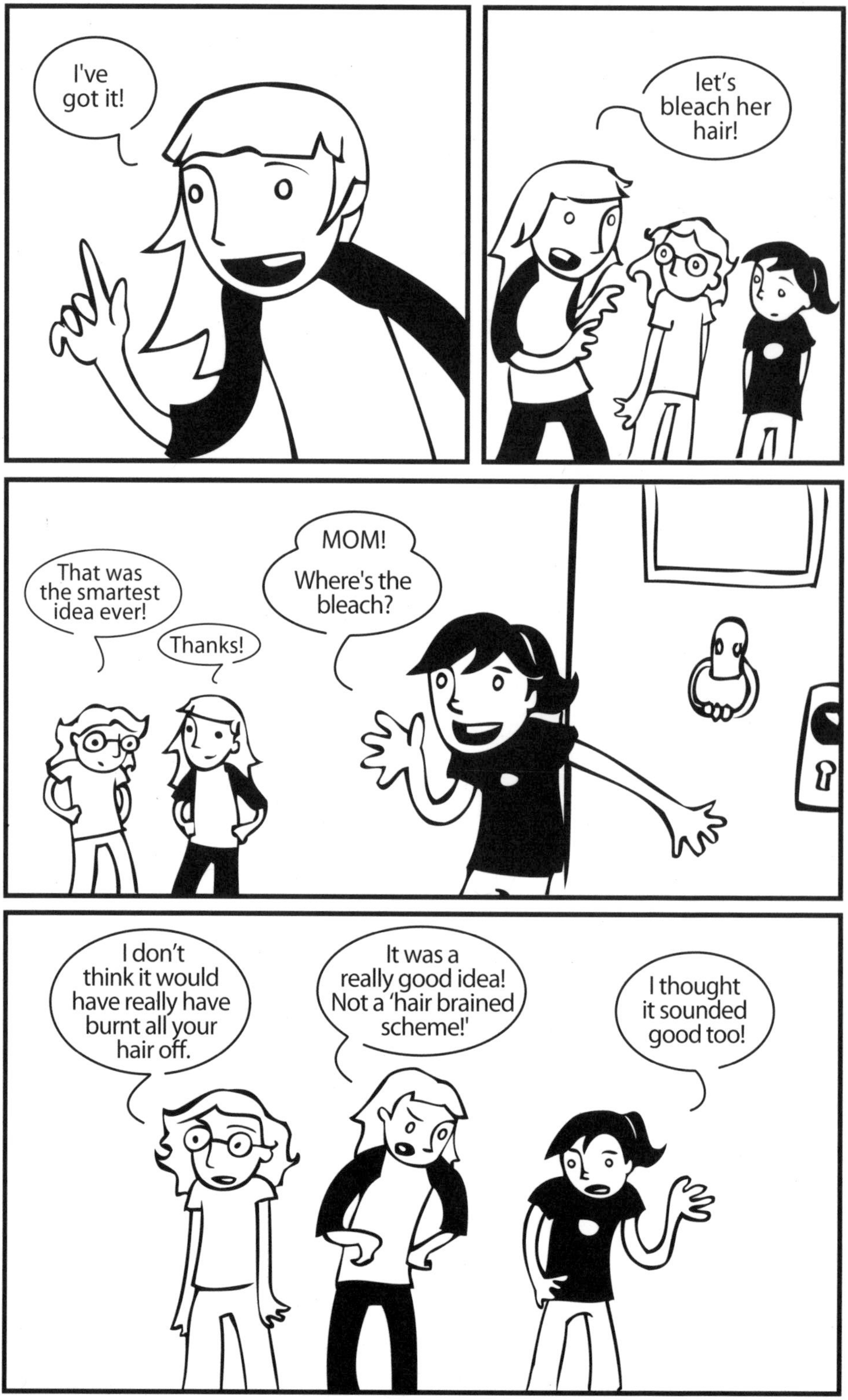
I've got it!
let's bleach her hair!
That was the smartest idea ever!
Thanks!
MOM! Where's the bleach?
I don't think it would have really have burnt all your hair off.
It was a really good idea! Not a 'hair brained scheme!'
I thought it sounded good too!

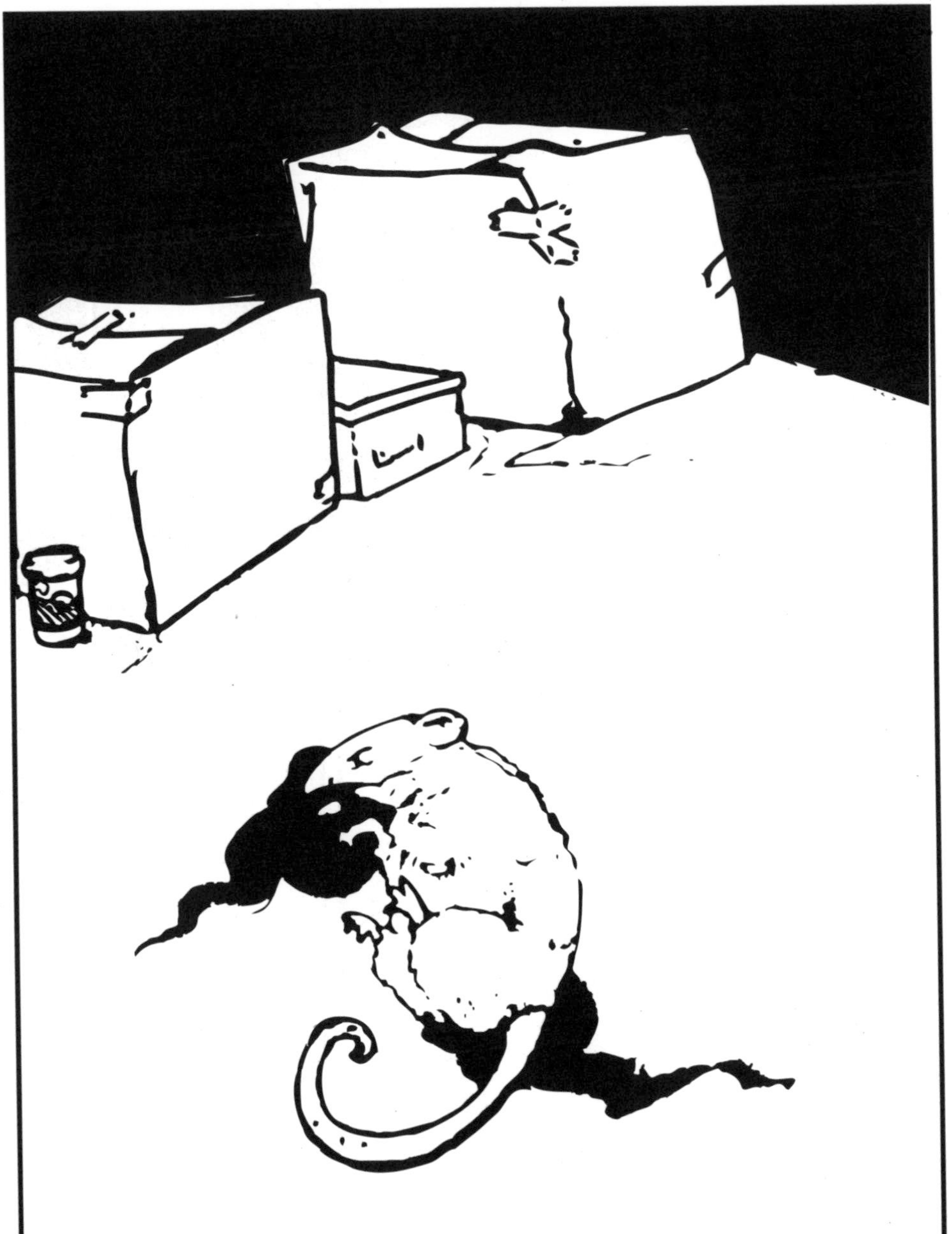

One day at school we found a dead mouse in the closet. We all became terrified of the closet. So she started putting us in there.

Jacey was put in there the most.

Then Eamon.

Ralph too.

Ralph would start stuttering when she would ask him a question.

Ralph, read for us.

the boy -wwwwwwwas thhhhhhhe boy www wwww-assss sae oifi knoooo-knooo he didnnn't know he was sad scared

If you don't read Ralph, you know what I'll have to do.

I KNOW YOU'RE FAKING IT!

He was scared, and I did nothing to help him.

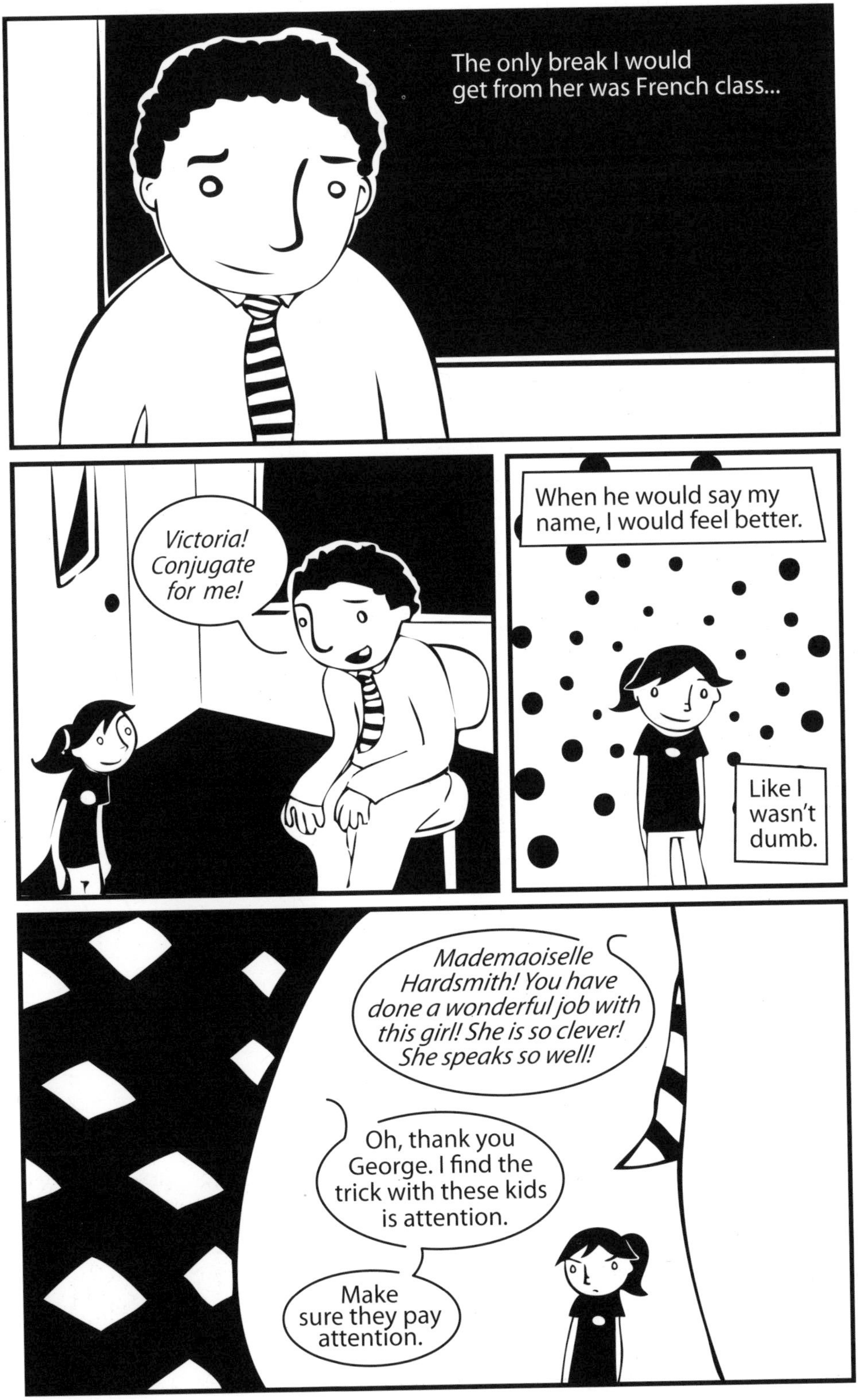

The only break I would get from her was French class...
Victoria! Conjugate for me!
When he would say my name, I would feel better.
Like I wasn't dumb.
Mademaoiselle Hardsmith! You have done a wonderful job with this girl! She is so clever! She speaks so well!
Oh, thank you George. I find the trick with these kids is attention.
Make sure they pay attention.

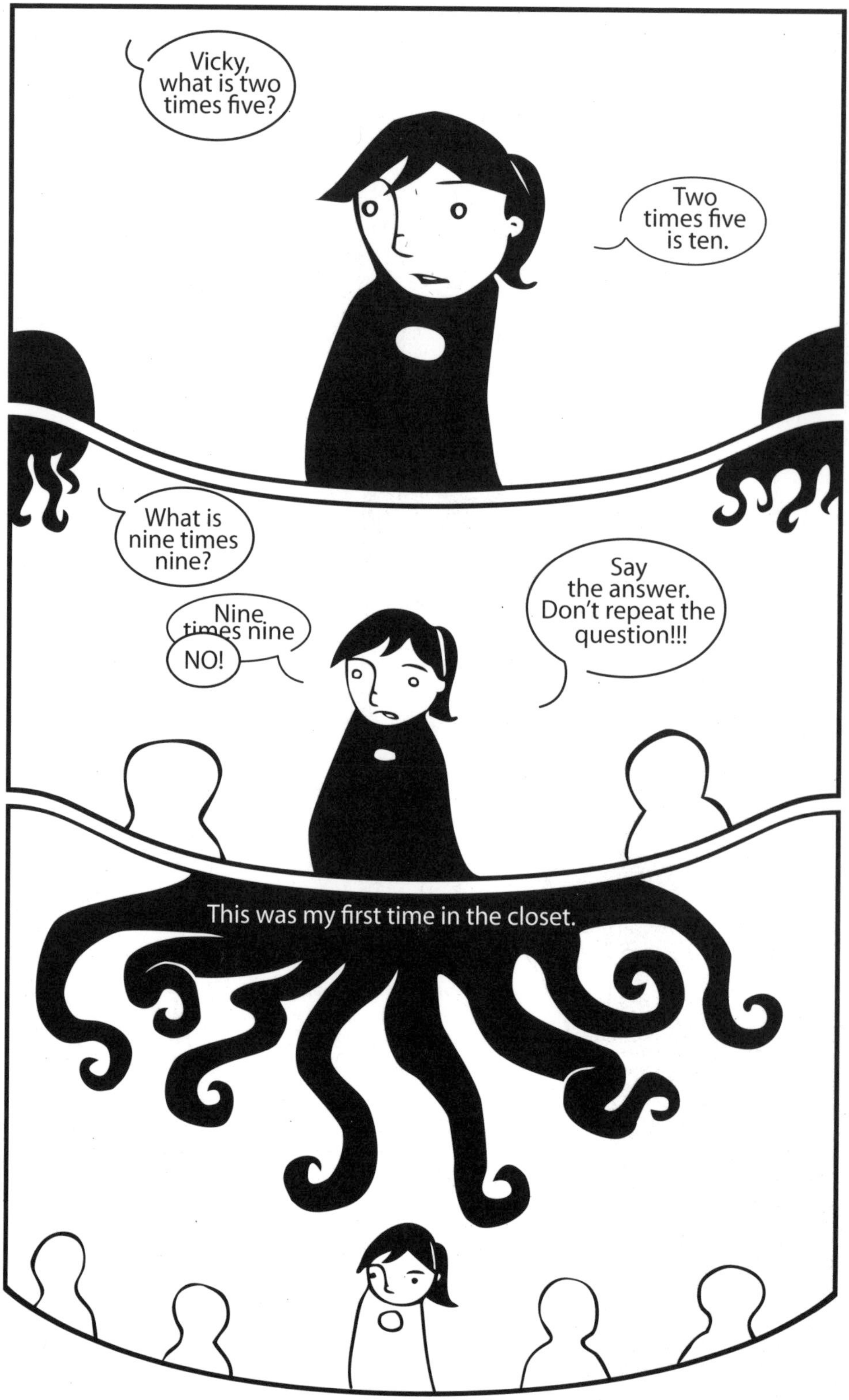
Vicky, what is two times five?
Two times five is ten.
What is nine times nine?
Nine times nine
NO!
Say the answer. Don't repeat the question!!!
This was my first time in the closet.

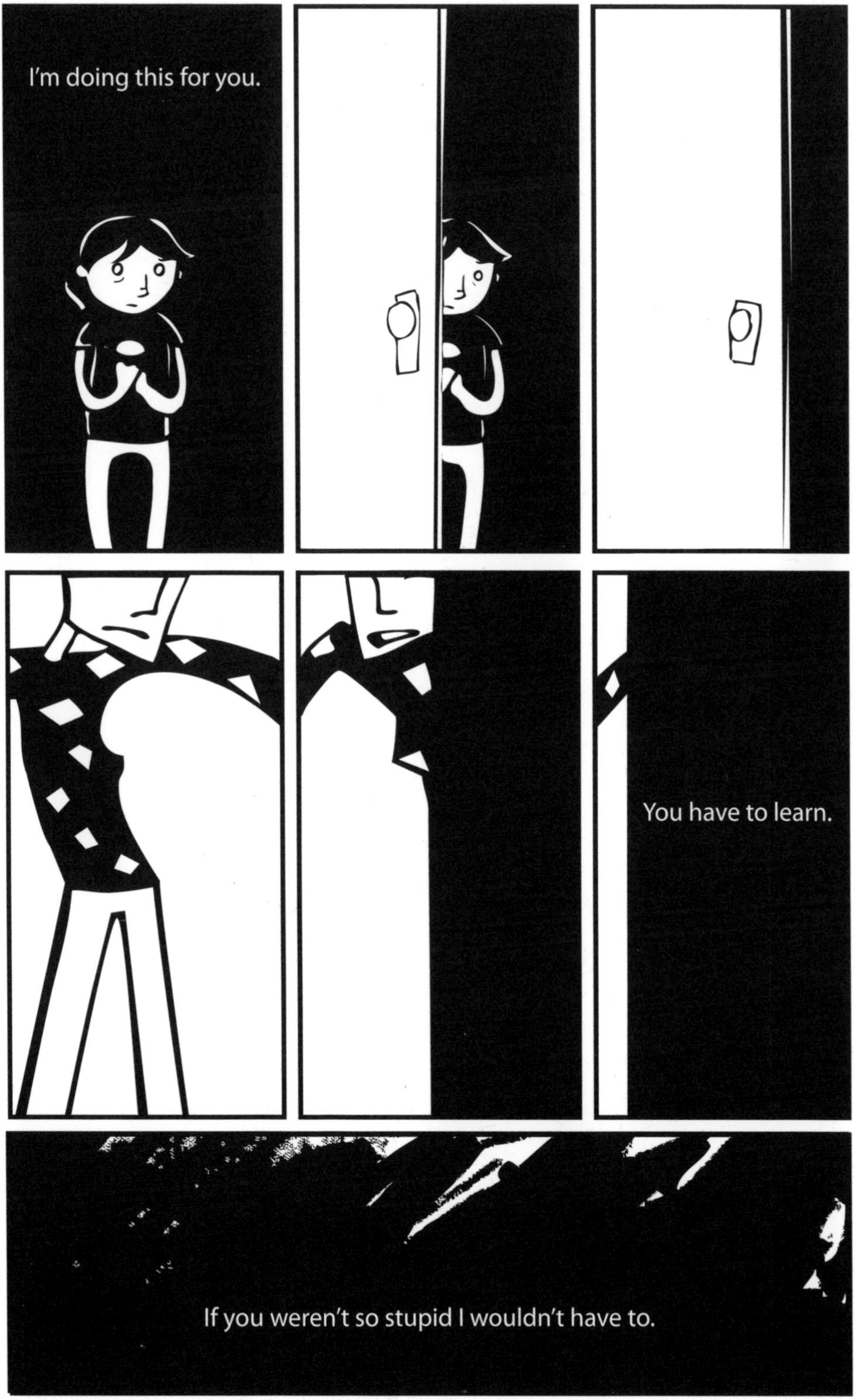
I'm doing this for you.
You have to learn.
If you weren't so stupid I wouldn't have to.

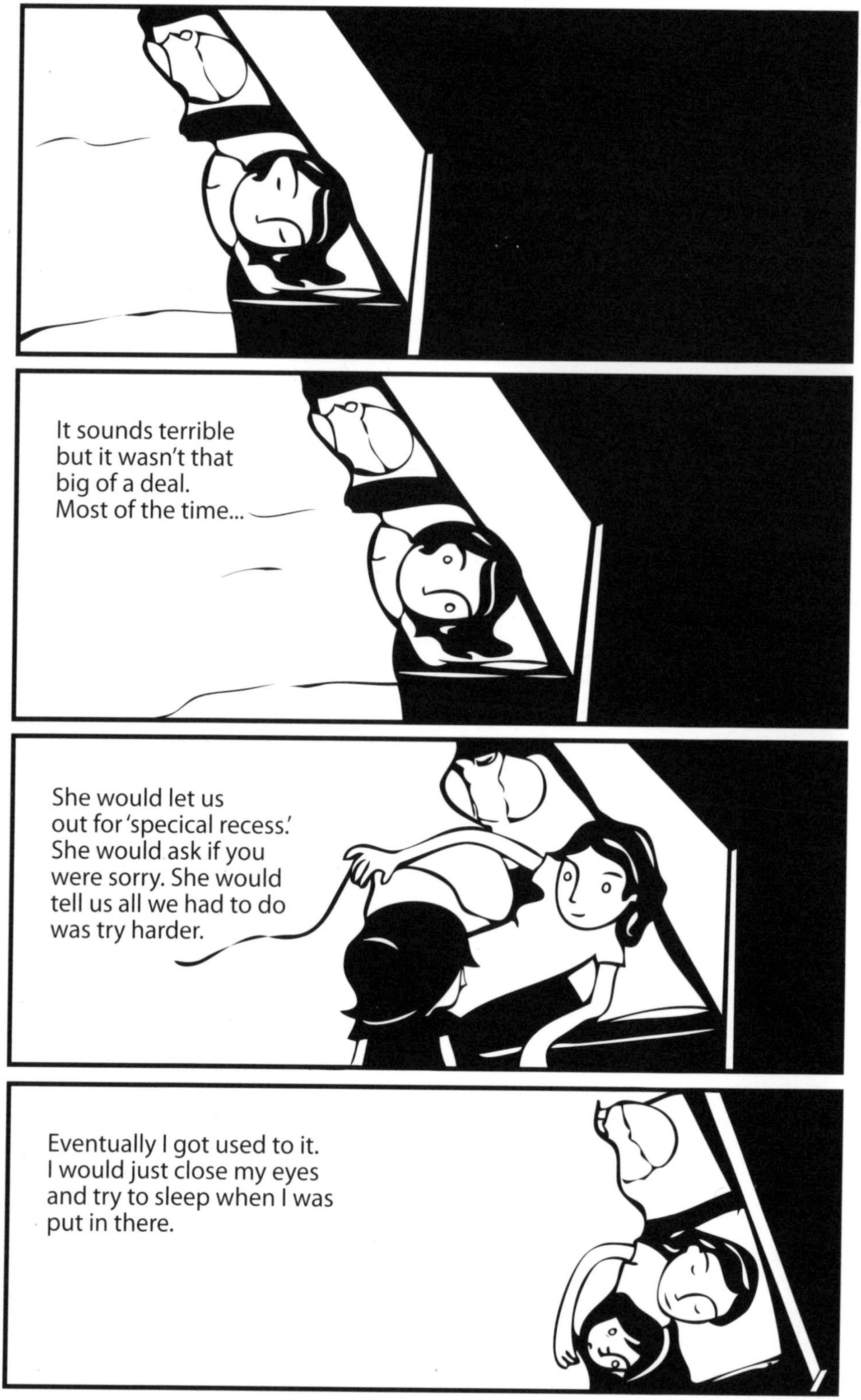
It sounds terrible but it wasn't that big of a deal. Most of the time...
She would let us out for 'specical recess.' She would ask if you were sorry. She would tell us all we had to do was try harder.
Eventually I got used to it. I would just close my eyes and try to sleep when I was put in there.

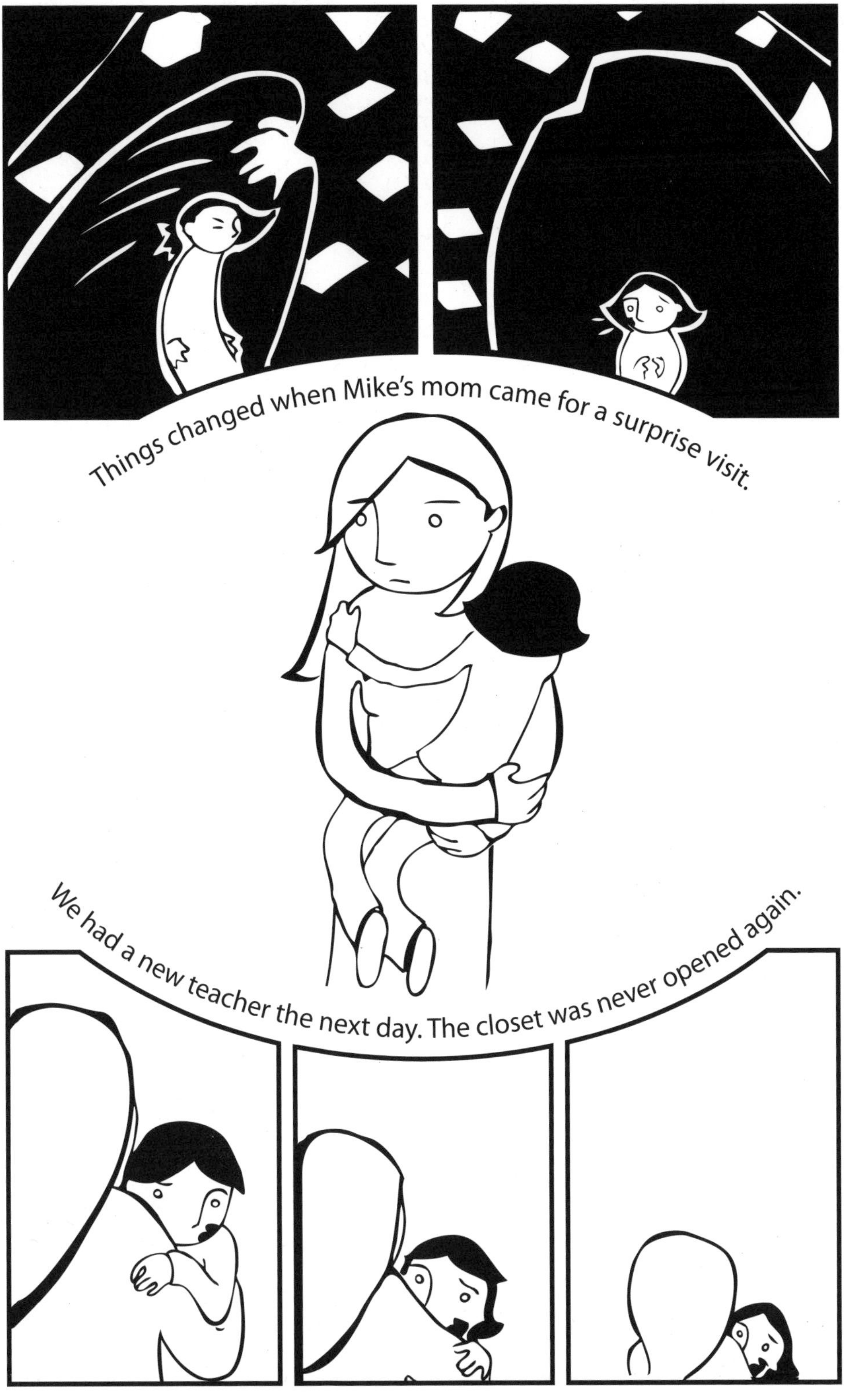
Things changed when Mike's mom came for a surprise visit.
We had a new teacher the next day. The closet was never opened again.

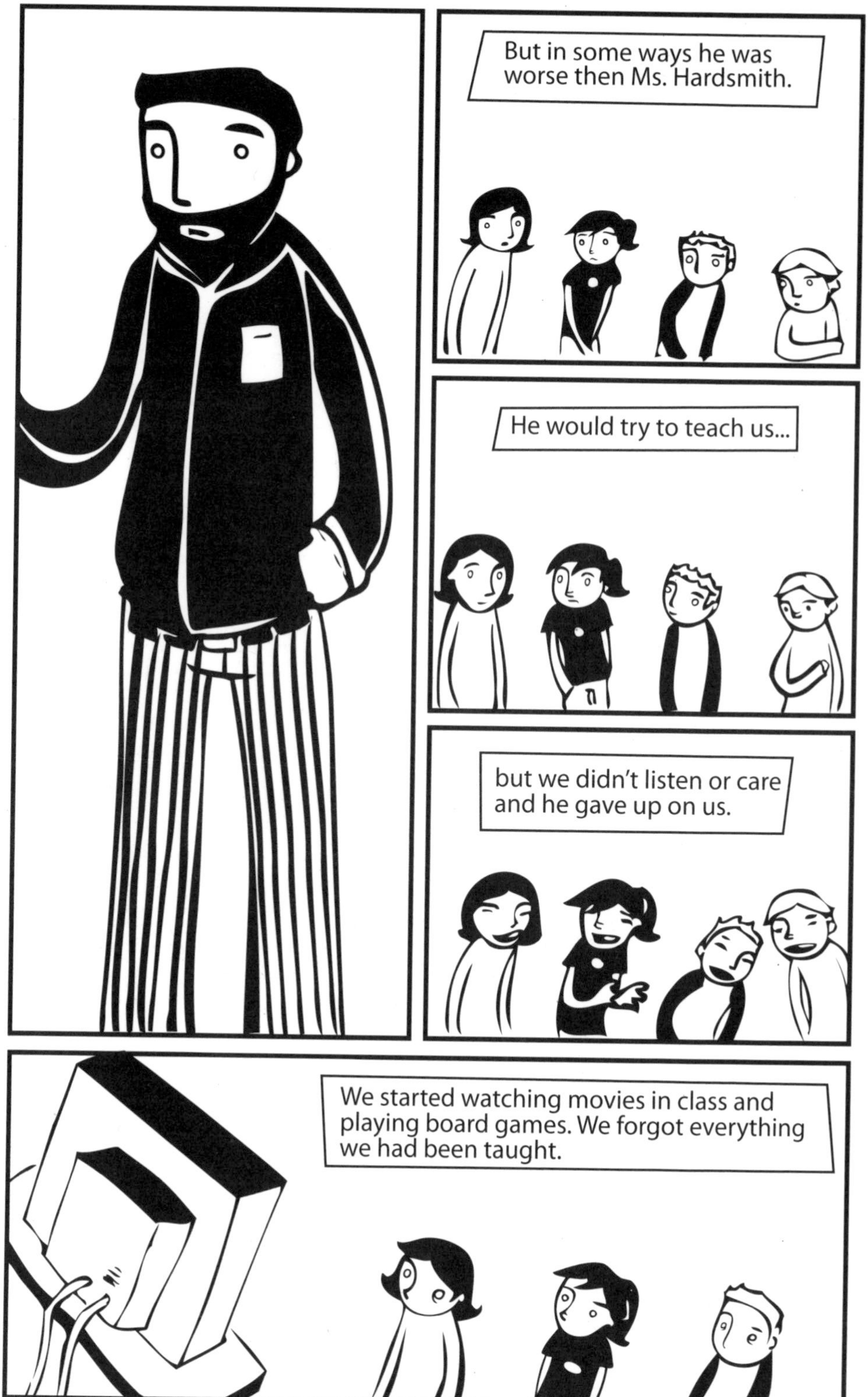
But in some ways he was worse then Ms. Hardsmith.
He would try to teach us...
but we didn't listen or care and he gave up on us.
We started watching movies in class and playing board games. We forgot everything we had been taught.

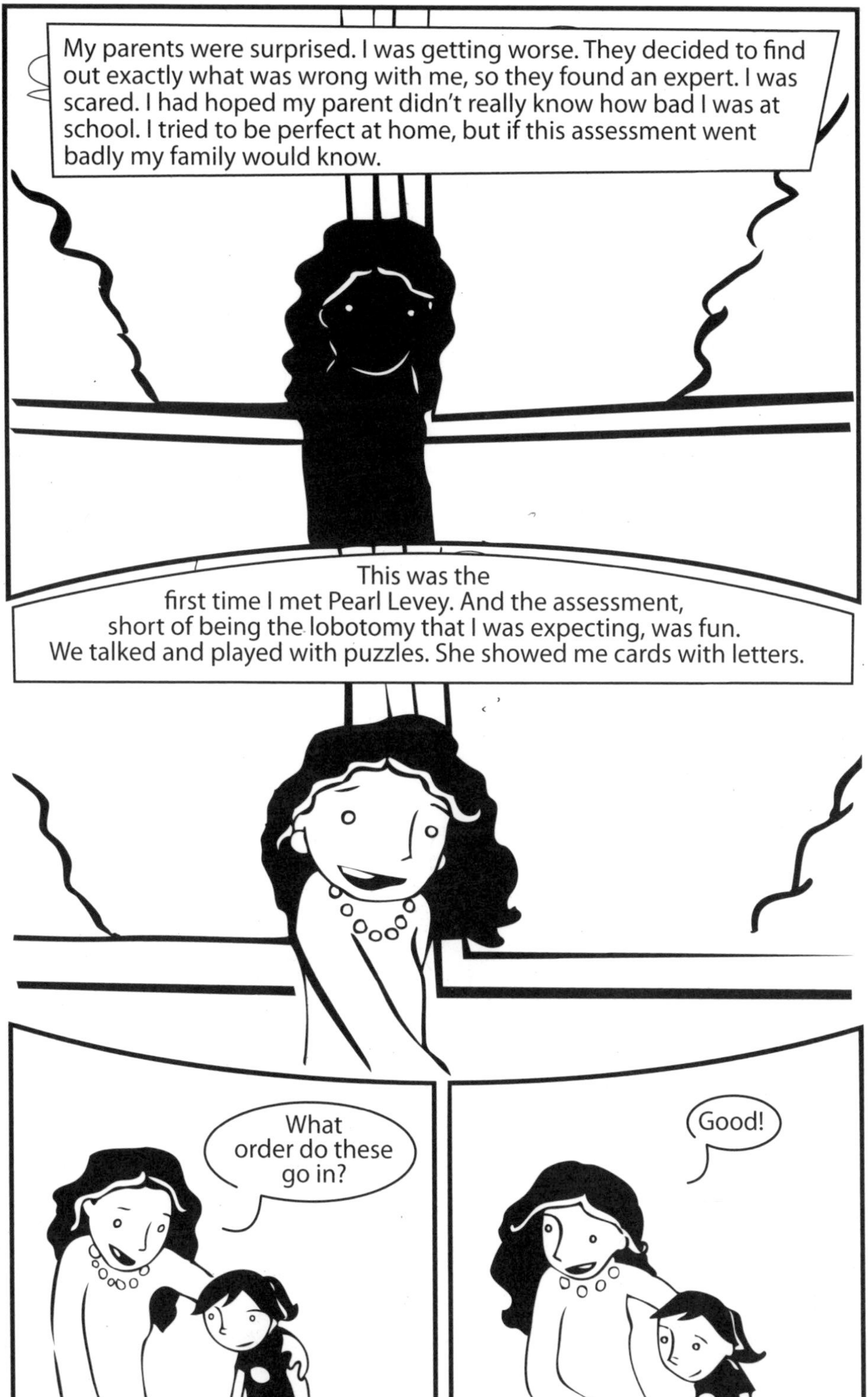
My parents were surprised. I was getting worse. They decided to find out exactly what was wrong with me, so they found an expert. I was scared. I had hoped my parent didn't really know how bad I was at school. I tried to be perfect at home, but if this assessment went badly my family would know.
This was the first time I met Pearl Levey. And the assessment, short of being the lobotomy that I was expecting, was fun. We talked and played with puzzles. She showed me cards with letters.
What order do these go in?
Good!

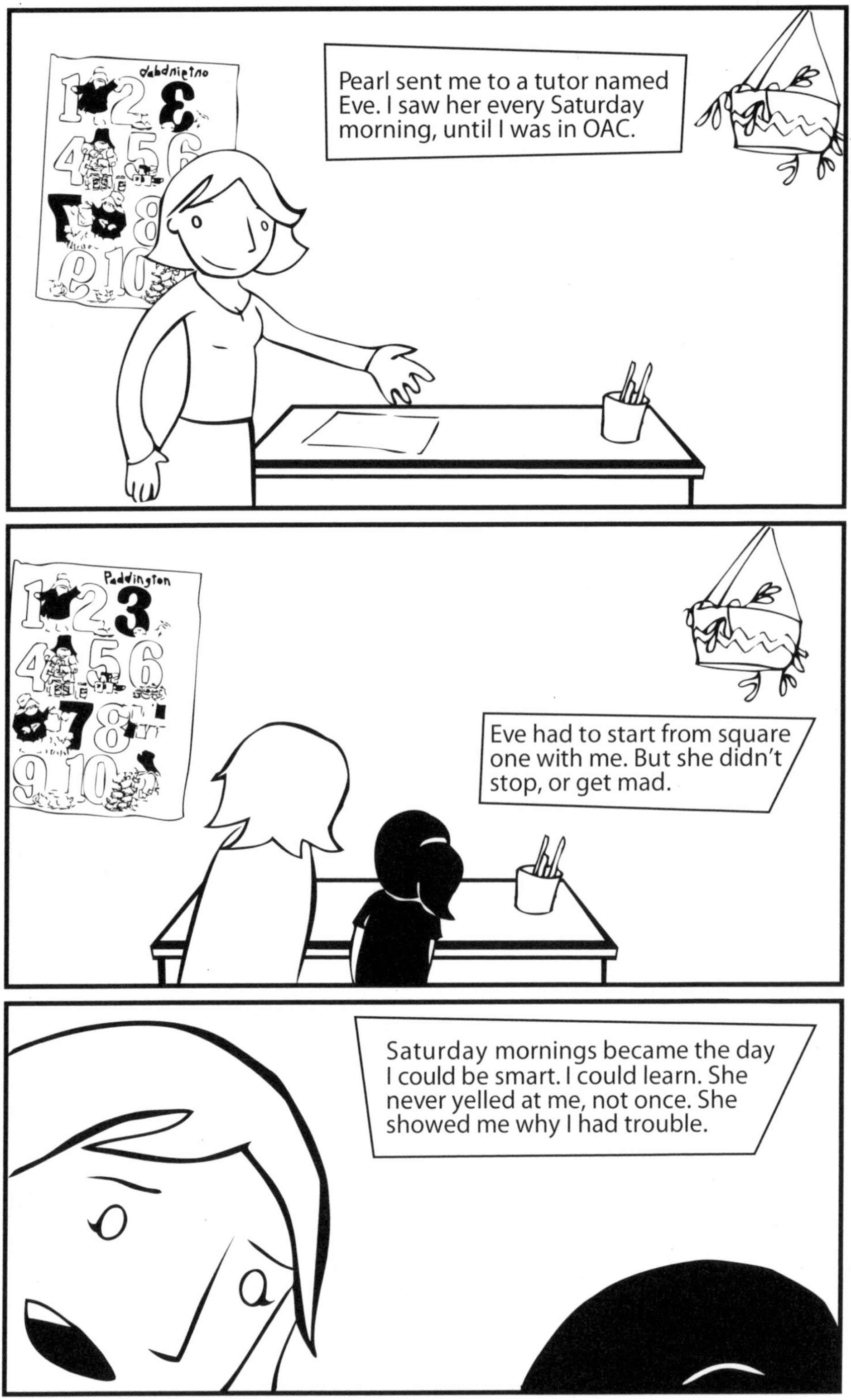
Pearl sent me to a tutor named Eve. I saw her every Saturday morning, until I was in OAC.
Paddington
Eve had to start from square one with me. But she didn't stop, or get mad.
Saturday mornings became the day I could be smart. I could learn. She never yelled at me, not once. She showed me why I had trouble.

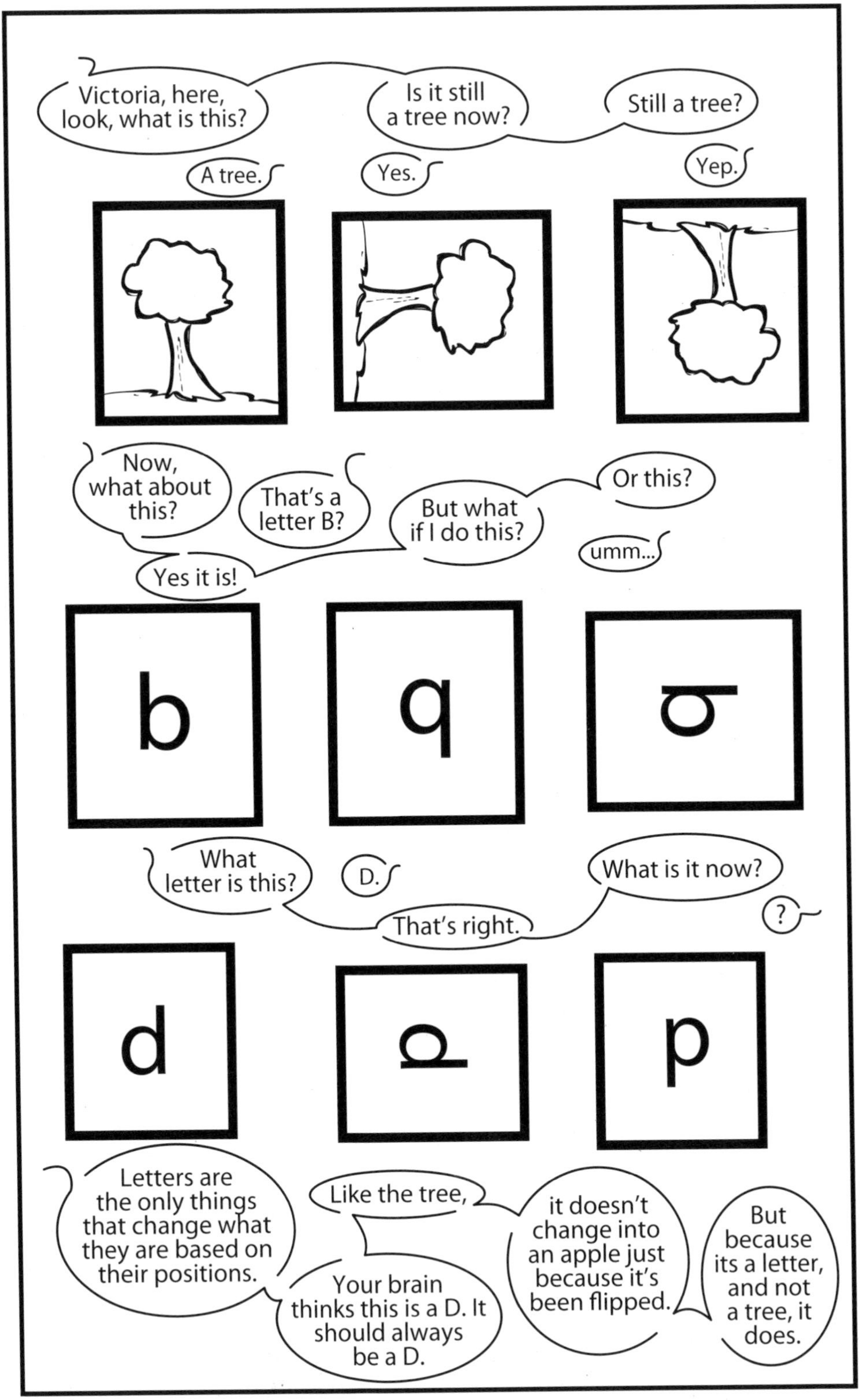

Victoria, here, look, what is this?
A tree.
Is it still a tree now?
Yes.
Still a tree?
Yep.
Now, what about this?
That's a letter B?
Yes it is!
But what if I do this?
Or this?
umm...
b
q
What letter is this?
D.
That's right.
What is it now?
?
d
p
Letters are the only things that change what they are based on their positions.
Like the tree,
it doesn't change into an apple just because it's been flipped.
But because its a letter, and not a tree, it does.
Your brain thinks this is a D. It should always be a D.

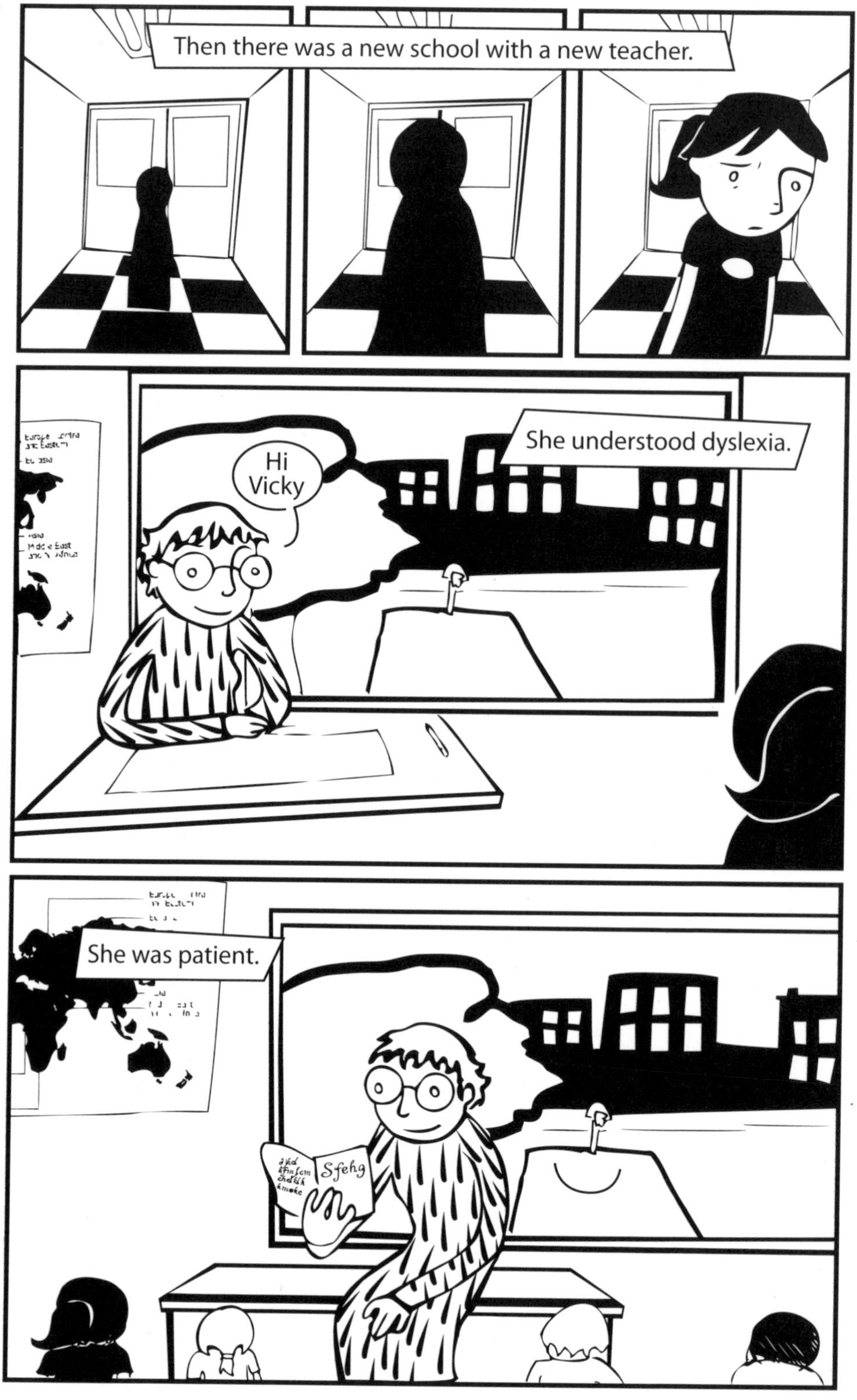
Then there was a new school with a new teacher.
Hi Vicky
She understood dyslexia.
She was patient.

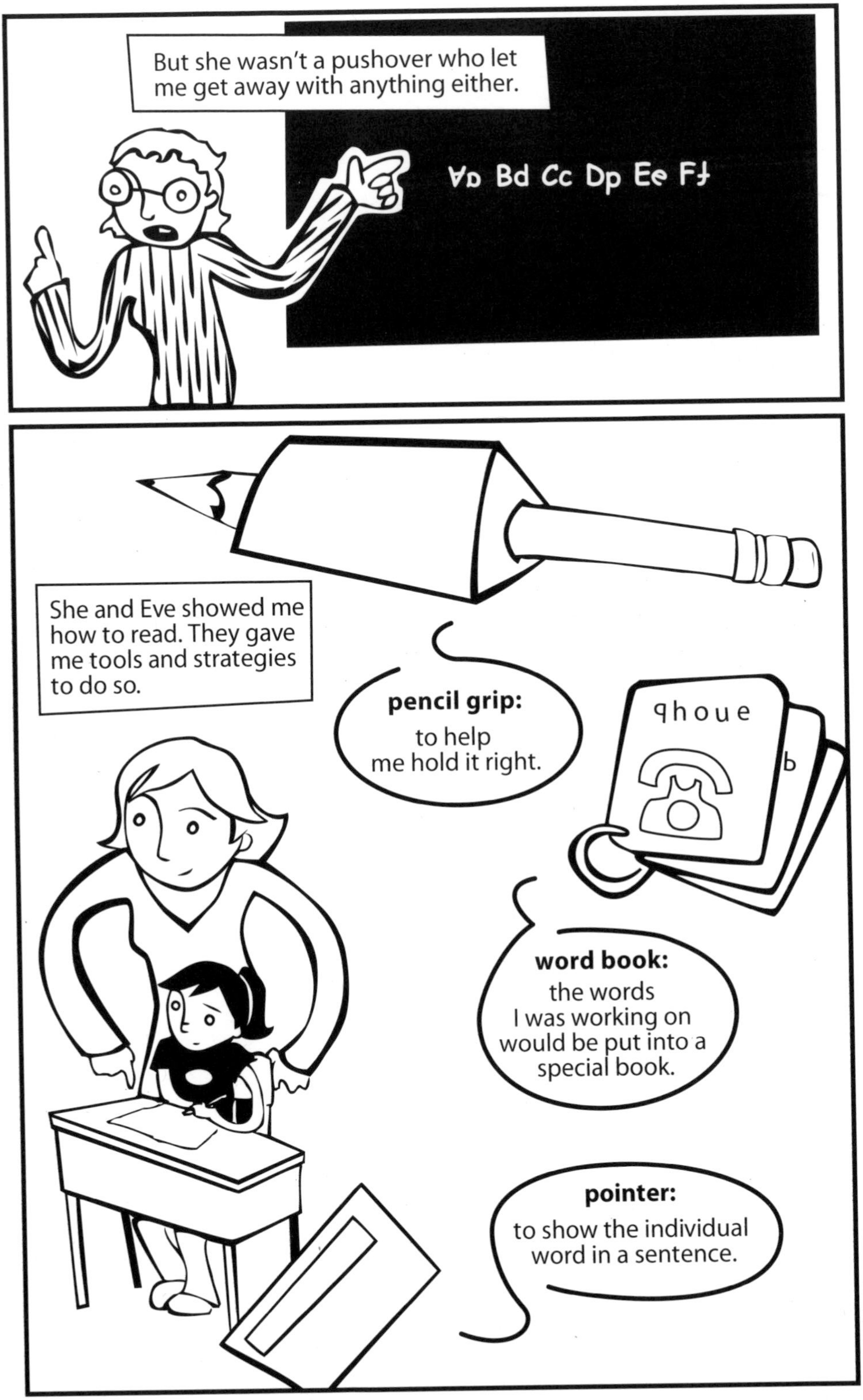

But she wasn't a pushover who let me get away with anything either.
She and Eve showed me how to read. They gave me tools and strategies to do so.
pencil grip: to help me hold it right.
qhoue
word book: the words I was working on would be put into a special book.
pointer: to show the individual word in a sentence.

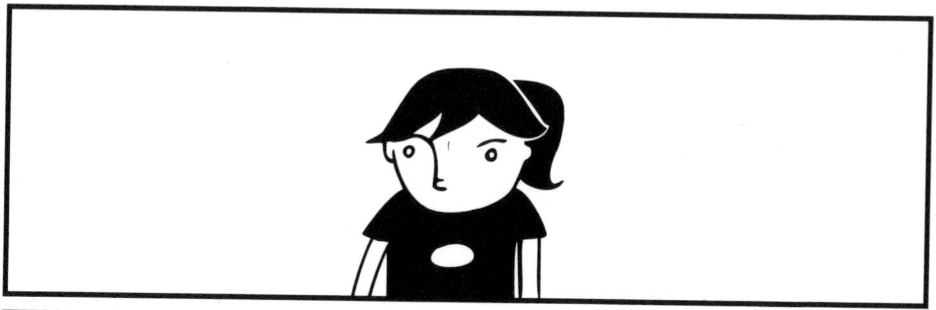

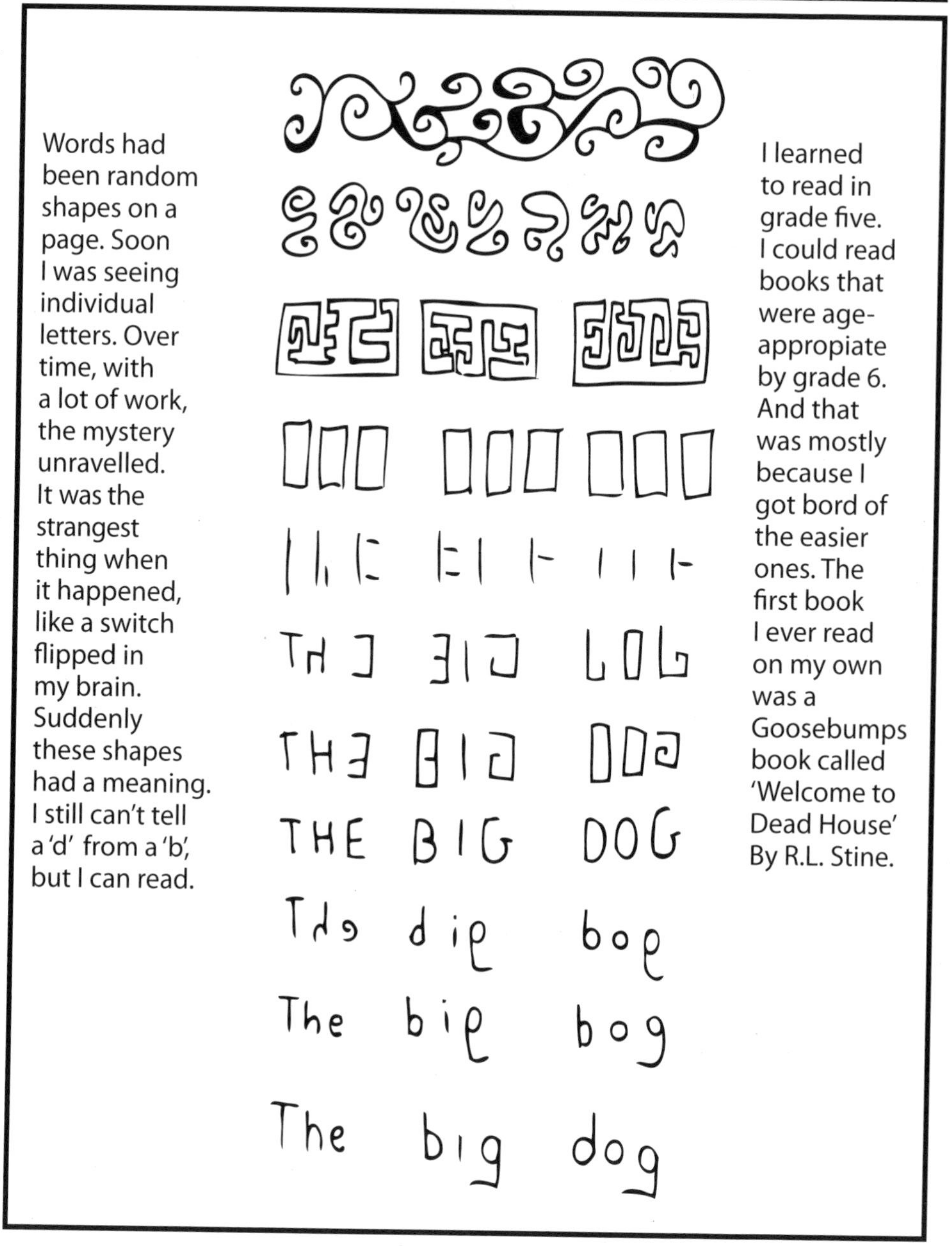

Words had been random shapes on a page. Soon I was seeing individual letters. Over time, with a lot of work, the mystery unravelled. It was the strangest thing when it happened, like a switch flipped in my brain. Suddenly these shapes had a meaning. I still can't tell a 'd' from a 'b', but I can read.
THE BIG DOG
The bie bog
The big dog
I learned to read in grade five. I could read books that were age-appropiate by grade 6. And that was mostly because I got bord of the easier ones. The first book I ever read on my own was a Goosebumps book called 'Welcome to Dead House' By R.L. Stine.

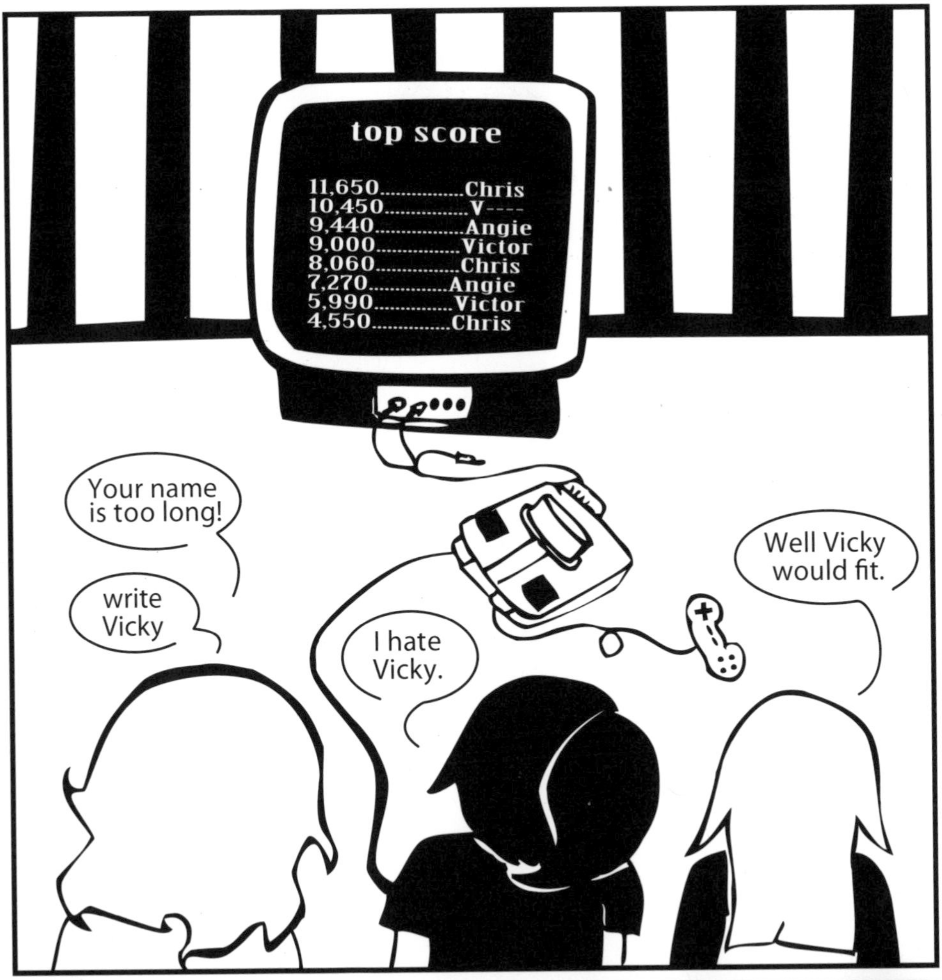
top score
11,650..............Chris
10,450..............V----
9,440..............Angie
9,000..............Victor
8,060..............Chris
7,270..............Angie
5,990..............Victor
4,550..............Chris
Your name is too long!
write Vicky
I hate Vicky.
Well Vicky would fit.

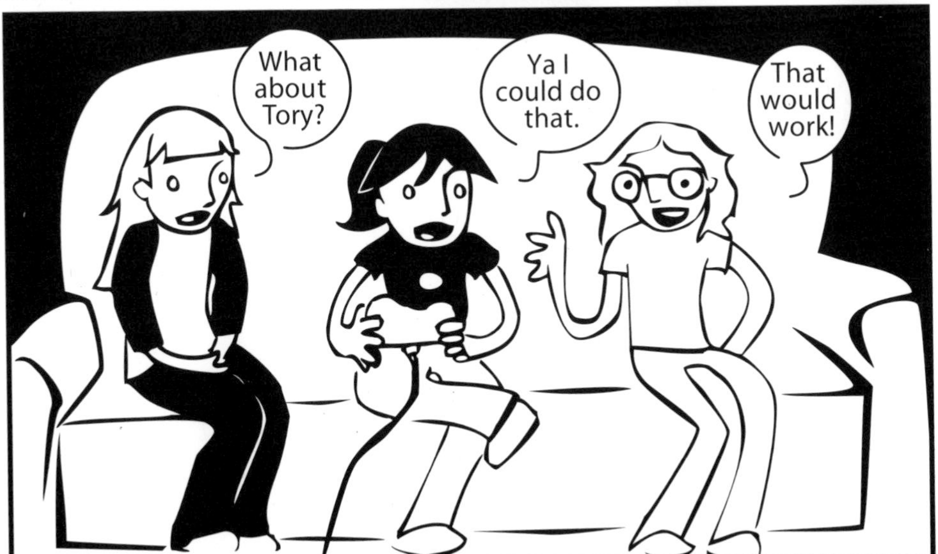
What about Tory?
Ya I could do that.
That would work!

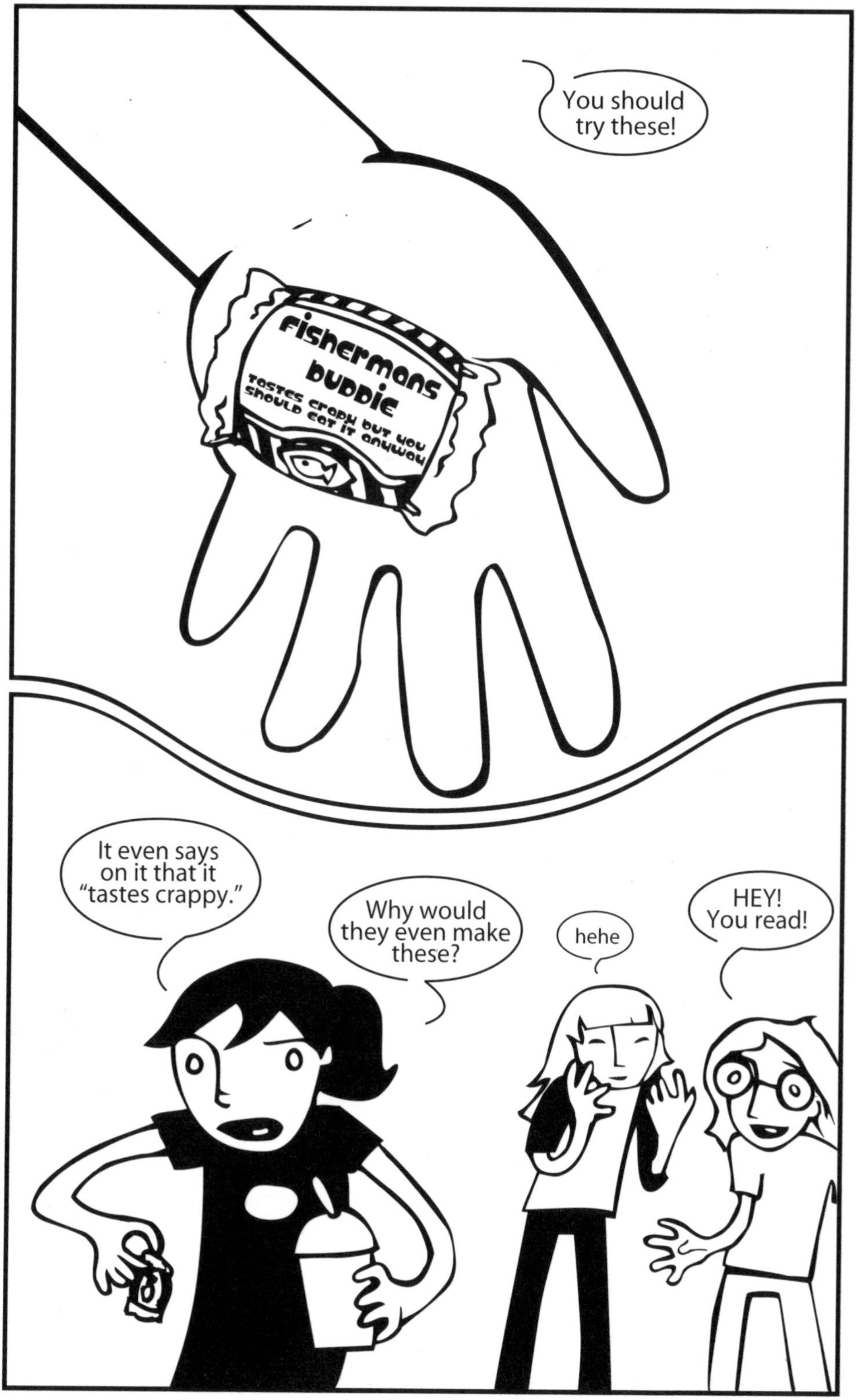
You should try these!
fishermans buddie
tastes crapy but you should eat it anyway
It even says on it that it "tastes crappy."
Why would they even make these?
hehe
HEY! You read!

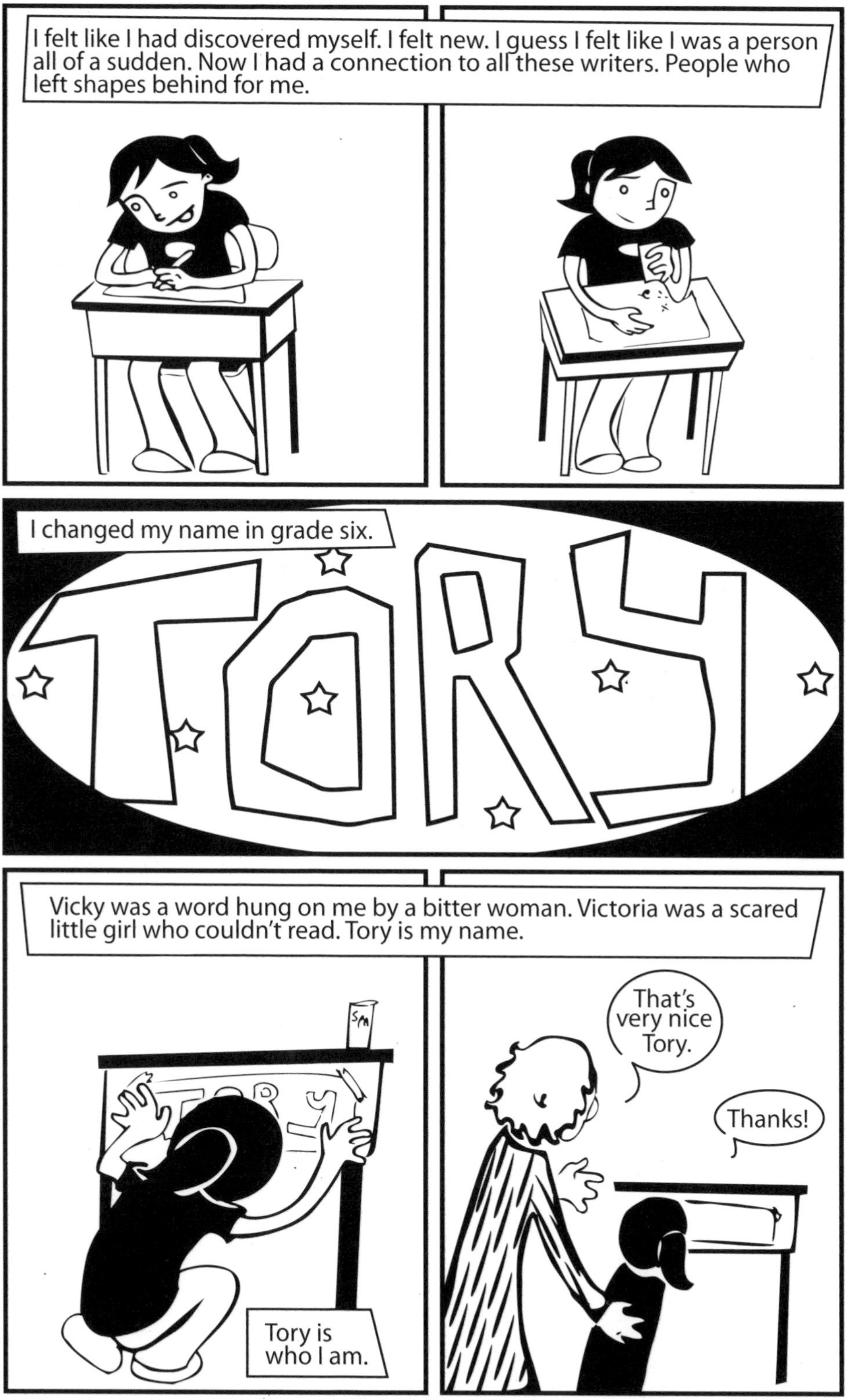
I felt like I had discovered myself. I felt new. I guess I felt like I was a person all of a sudden. Now I had a connection to all these writers. People who left shapes behind for me.
I changed my name in grade six.
TORY
Vicky was a word hung on me by a bitter woman. Victoria was a scared little girl who couldn't read. Tory is my name.
Tory is who I am.
That's very nice Tory.
Thanks!

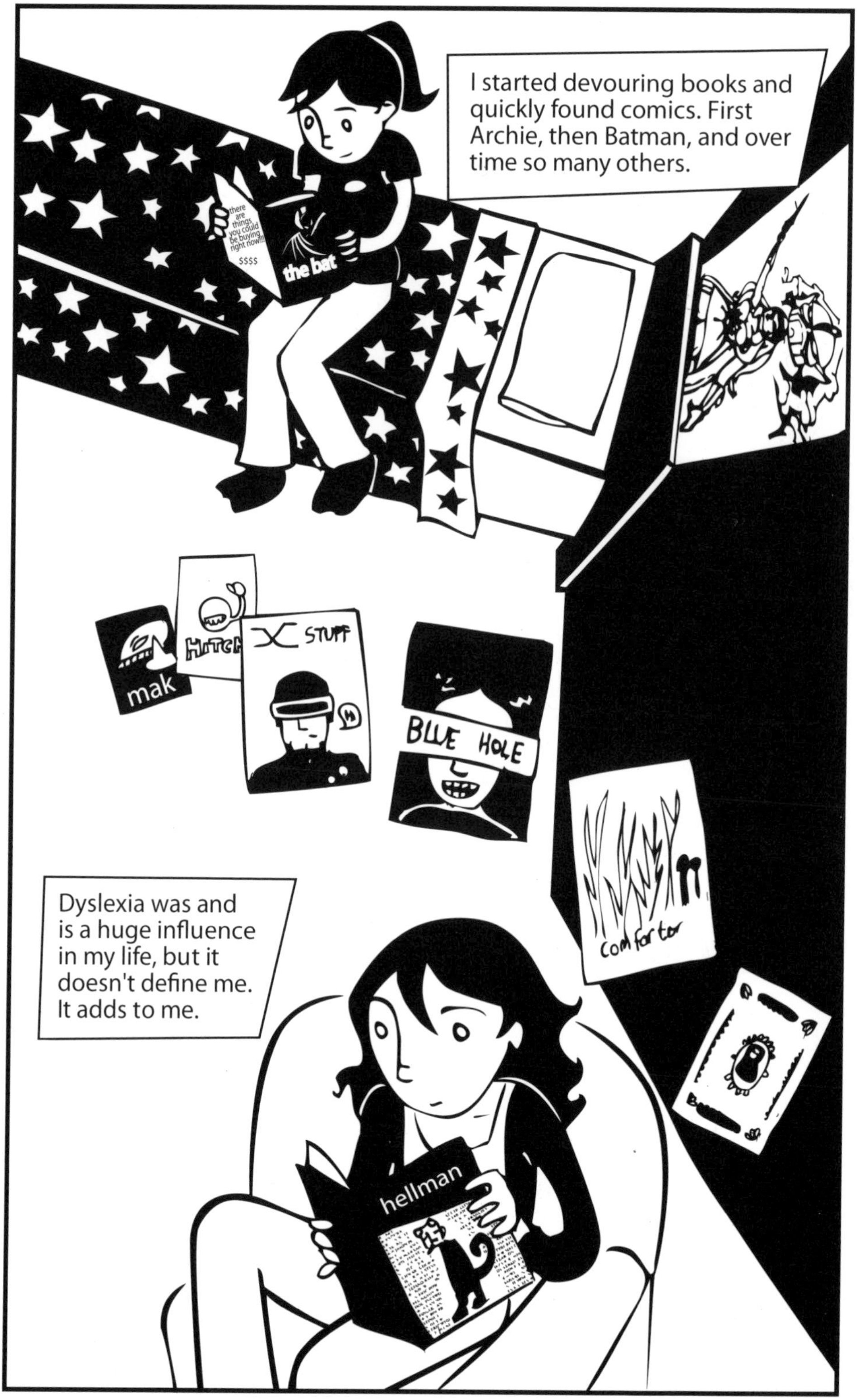
I started devouring books and quickly found comics. First Archie, then Batman, and over time so many others.
there are things you could be buying right now!!!
$$$$
the bat
mak
HITCH
STUFF
BLUE HOLE
comforter
Dyslexia was and is a huge influence in my life, but it doesn't define me. It adds to me.
hellman

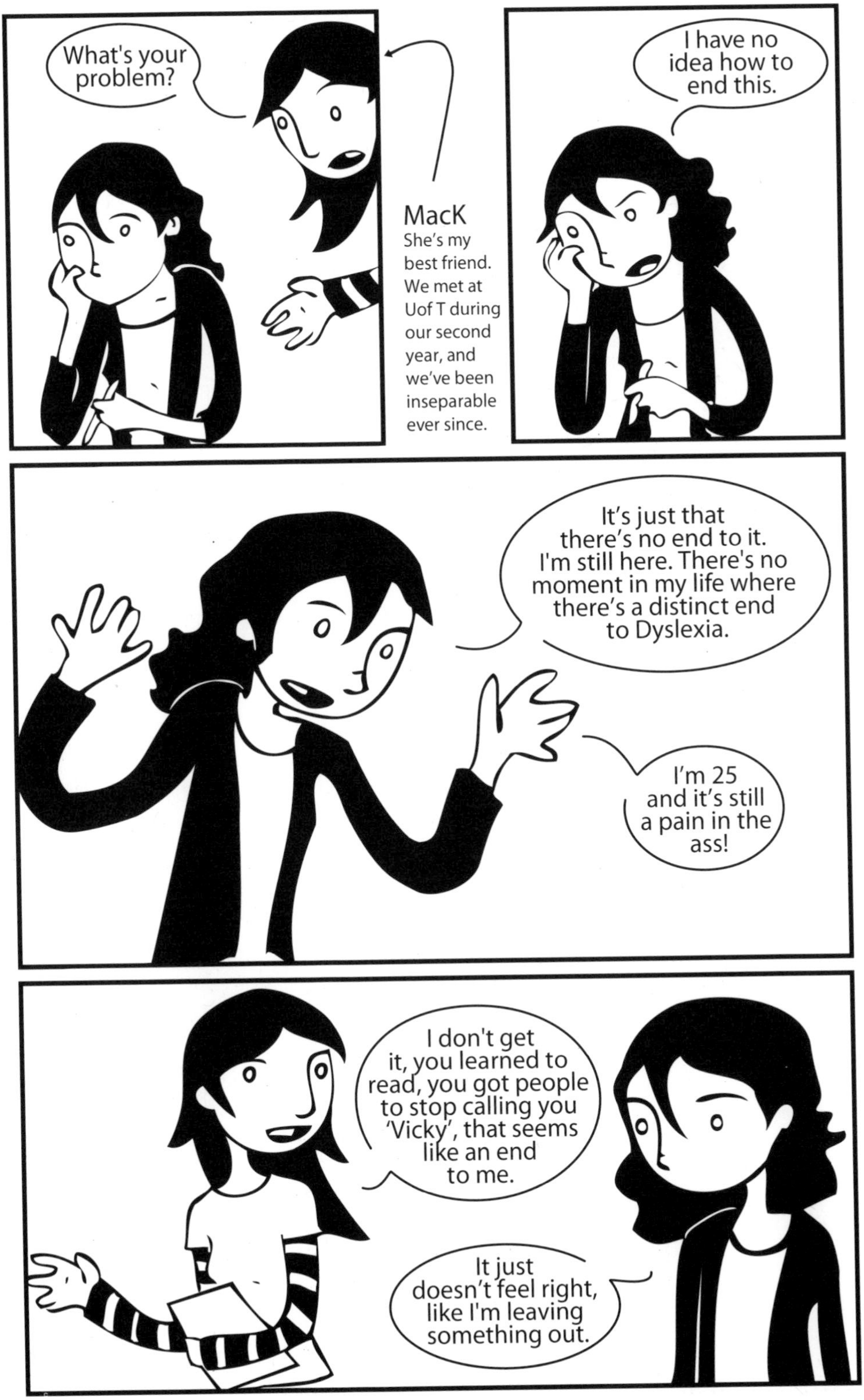
What's your problem?
MacK
She's my best friend. We met at Uof T during our second year, and we've been inseparable ever since.
I have no idea how to end this.
It's just that there's no end to it. I'm still here. There's no moment in my life where there's a distinct end to Dyslexia.
I'm 25 and it's still a pain in the ass!
I don't get it, you learned to read, you got people to stop calling you 'Vicky', that seems like an end to me.
It just doesn't feel right, like I'm leaving something out.

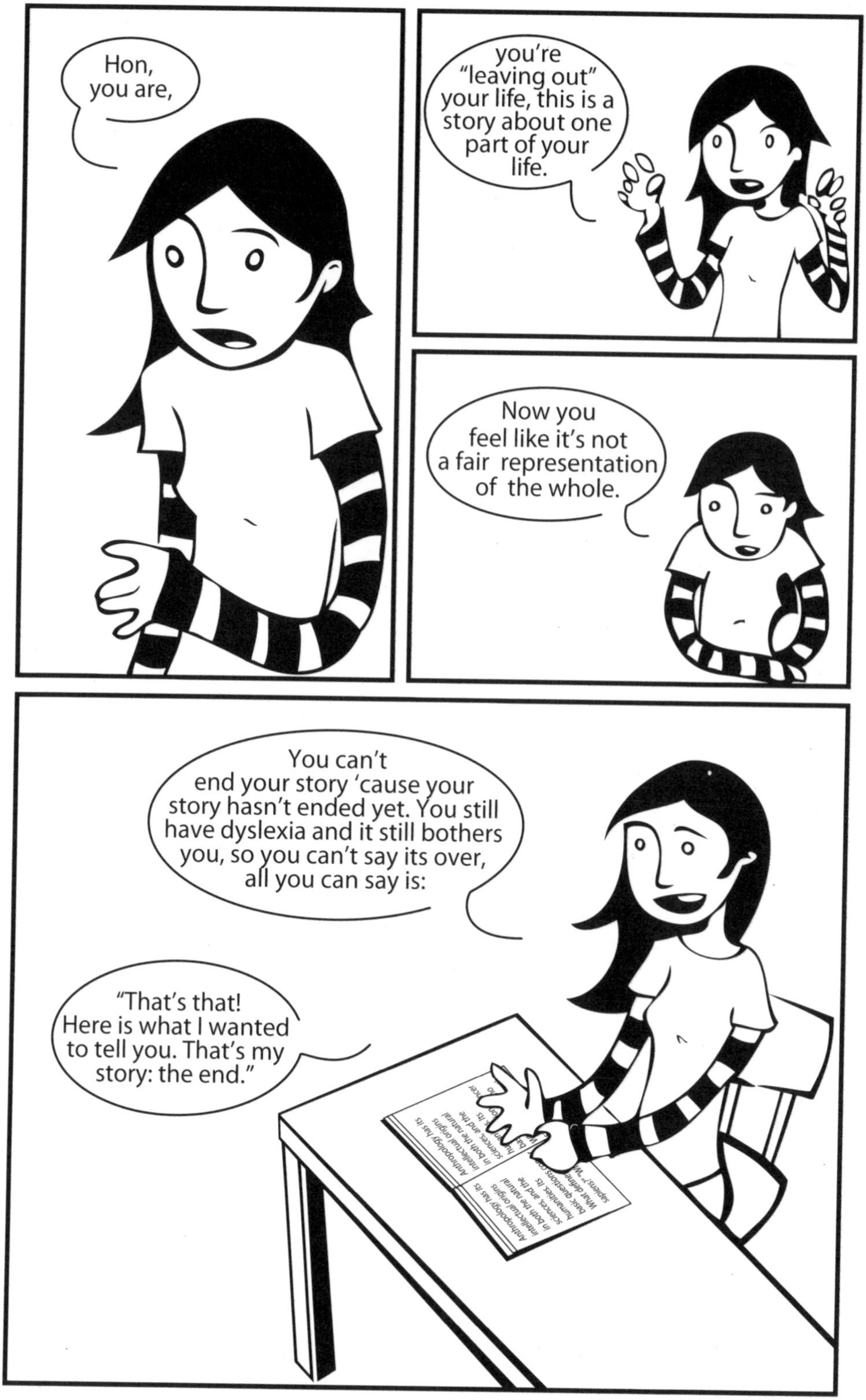
Hon, you are,
you're "leaving out" your life, this is a story about one part of your life.
Now you feel like it's not a fair representation of the whole.
You can't end your story 'cause your story hasn't ended yet. You still have dyslexia and it still bothers you, so you can't say its over, all you can say is:
"That's that! Here is what I wanted to tell you. That's my story: the end."

The end.

According to the World Federation of Neurology: "Specific developmental dyslexia is a disorder manifested by difficulty l earning to read despite conventional instruction, adequate intelligence, and adequate sociocultural opportunity. It is dependent upon fundamental cognitive disabilities that are frequently of constitutional origin."

Dyslexia is a learning disability that affects about 10% of the population. Dyslexia has nothing to do with intelligence, eyesight, hearing, inadequate teaching or inattentive parents. Dyslexia is a difference in the way the brain is formed, just a small difference that changes the way you learn. On a more personal note, Dyslexia is an inconvenience, but there is so much more to it then that, it isn't a curse. Dyslexia lets you see the world in a way that most people can't. And now I'm going to offer some advice, to parents teachers and kids who are experiencing Dyslexia.

Read aloud, just the two or three of you, and when you are alone reading out loud never hurt anyone, and it is fun once you do it a few times.

Get books on tape, you can get a lot on line for free, (see 'tools'). Read along with the book and sometimes just listen and have fun with the story.

Make the letters, use clay or cookie dough, shaving cream in the bath tub! Mud! Anything! This will help the shapes make sense - make them more solid.

Read with a pointer, a ruler or piece of paper under each line and word.

Always be creative. Dyslexia gives you an amazing gift, something most people don't realize, it makes you more creative, you look at the world differently. Because of this you can see things other people can't.

And most of all. Read comic books! Read all the comic books you can get your hands on! These books are important. The pictures give you a clue to what the words say and help you decode the letters. It helps you read alone, all by yourself. Also, they're really good fun!

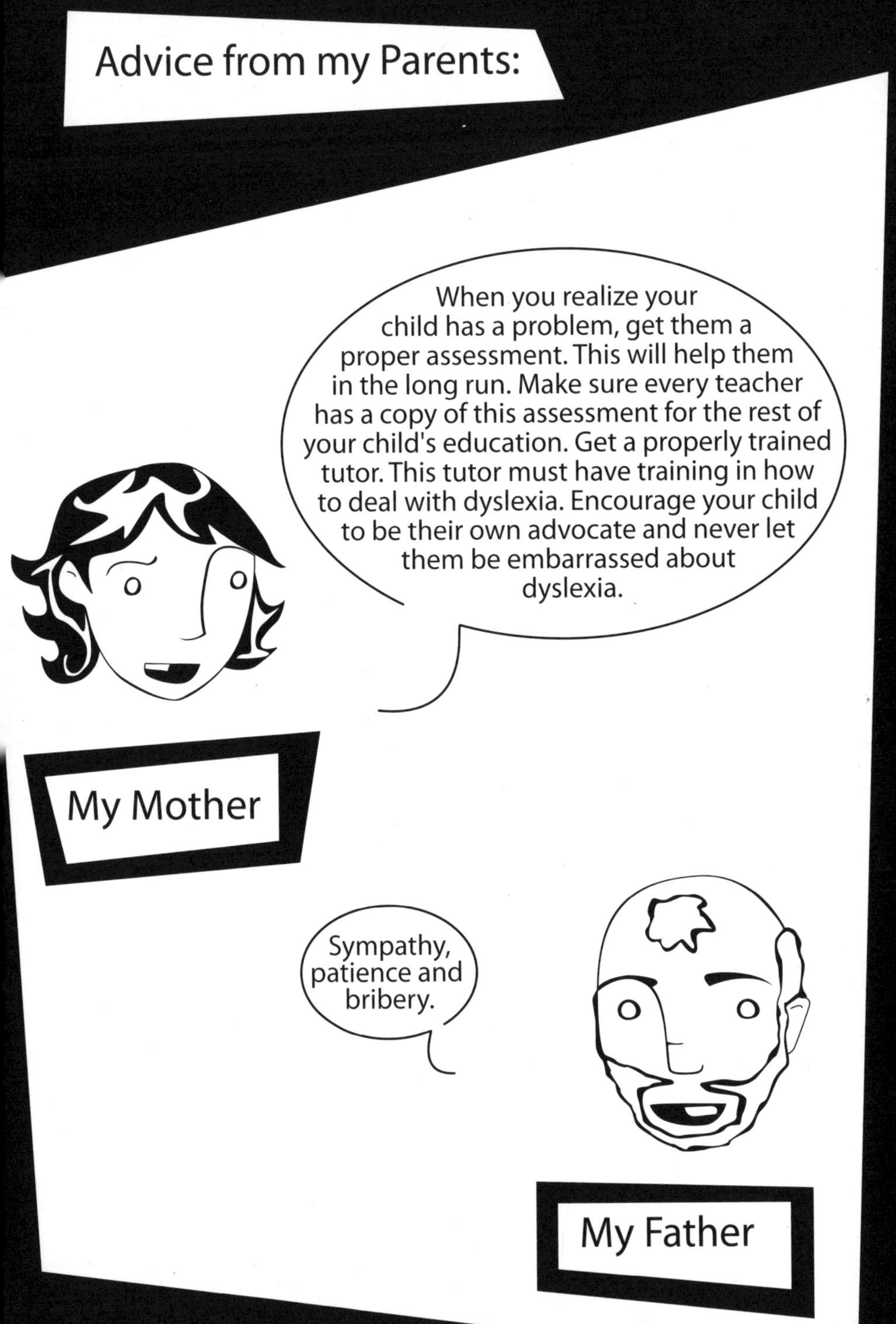
Advice from my Parents:
When you realize your child has a problem, get them a proper assessment. This will help them in the long run. Make sure every teacher has a copy of this assessment for the rest of your child's education. Get a properly trained tutor. This tutor must have training in how to deal with dyslexia. Encourage your child to be their own advocate and never let them be embarrassed about dyslexia.
My Mother
Sympathy, patience and bribery.
My Father

resources

Tools

Adaptive Technology Resource Centre
http://atrc.utoronto.ca/index.php
J.P. Robarts Library, First Floor
University of Toronto
130 St. George St.
Toronto, Ontario, Canada
M5S 1A5
Telephone: 416-978-4360
Fax: 416-971-2629
Email: general.atrc@utoronto.ca

Audio Books

http://www.rfbd.org/
http://librivox.org/

Students

National Educational Association of Disabled
Rm. 426, Unicentre
1125 Colonel By Drive
Carleton University
Ottawa, Ontario, K1S 5B6 Canada
Telephone: 613-380-8065
Toll-Free: 1-877-670-1256
Fax: 613-369-4391
E-mail: info@neads.ca
http://www.neads.ca

Youth 2 youth
http://www.youth2youth.ca/
1877 238 5332

resources

World
The International Dyslexia Association
http://www.interdys.org
40 York Rd., 4th Floor
Baltimore, MD 21204
Phone: 1-410-296-0232 Fax: 410-321-5069

Canada
Canadian Dyslexia Association
http://www.dyslexiaassociation.ca/
57, rue du Couvent
Gatineau, Québec
J9H 3C8
Phone: 613-853-6539 Fax: 819-682-8444
E-mail: info@dyslexiaassociation.ca

The Learning Disabilities Association of Canada
http://www.ldac-taac.ca/index-e.asp
250 City Centre Avenue,
Suite 616, Ottawa,
Ontario K1R 6K7
Phone: 613-238-5721 Fax: 613-235-5391
Toll-Free: 1-877-238-5322
Email: info@ldac-taac.ca

The Council of Ministers of Education, Canada (CMEC)
95 St. Clair Avenue West, Suite 1106
Toronto, Ontario, Canada   M4V 1N6
Telephone: 416-962-8100 Fax: 416-962-2800
E-mail: Information@cmec.ca

USA
National Center for Learning Disabilities
381 Park Avenue South, Suite 1401
New York, NY 10016
Ph: 212-545-7510 Fax: 212-545-9665
Toll-free: 888-575-7373
web: http://www.ncld.org

Learning Disabilities Association of America
http://www.ldanatl.org/
4156 Library Road
Pittsburgh, PA 15234-1349
Phone: 412-341-1515 Fax : 412-344-0224

resources

UK
British Dyslexia Association (BDA)
http://www.bdadyslexia.org.uk/
Unit 8 Bracknell Beeches,
Old Bracknell Lane,
Bracknell, RG12 7BW.
Phone: 0845 251 9002   Fax: 0845 251 9005.
Email: helpline@bdadyslexia.org.uk

Dyslexia Action
http://www.dyslexiaaction.org.uk/
Park House, Wick Road
Egham
Surrey TW20 0HH
Phone: 01784 222300   Fax: 01784 222333
Email: info@dyslexiaaction.org.uk

Northern Ireland Dyslexia Association
17a upper newtownards road
Belfast BT4 3HT
Phone: 028 9065 9212
http://www.nida.org.uk/index.html

Books
Dyslexia: Surviving and Succeeding at College
Sylvia Moody

Overcoming Dyslexia: A New and Complete Science
Sally Shaywitz M.D.